THE REPUBLIC OF LETTERS

The Correspondence between Thomas Jefferson and James Madison 1776–1826

EDITED BY

James Morton Smith

VOLUME TWO

1790–1804

W · W · Norton & Company · New York · London

Copyright © 1995 by James Morton Smith. *All rights reserved*. Printed in the United States of America.

THE TEXT OF THIS BOOK *is composed in Galliard with Janson Alternate and Avanta. The display type is set in Garamond and Naomi Script. Composition and manufacturing by The Haddon Craftsmen. Book design by Marjorie J. Flock.*

Library of Congress Cataloging-in-Publication Data

Jefferson, Thomas, 1743-1826.
    The republic of letters: the correspondence between Thomas Jefferson and James Madison, 1776-1826.
       p.   cm.
    Includes bibliographical references (v.3, p.   ) and index.
    Contents: v.1. 1776-1790 — v.2. 1790-1804 — v.3. 1804-1836
    1. Jefferson, Thomas, 1743-1826 — Correspondence.   2. Madison, James, 1751-1836 — Correspondence.   3. Presidents — United States — Correspondence.   I. Madison, James, 1751-1836.   II. Smith, James Morton.   III. Title.
E332.88.M33   1995
973.4'092'2 – dc20   94-22924

ISBN 0-393-03691-X
(for the set of three volumes)

W. W. Norton & Company, Inc.
500 Fifth Avenue, New York, N.Y. 10110
www.wwnorton.com

W. W. Norton & Company Ltd.
Castle House, 75/76 Wells Street, London W1T 3QT

*To
Scott David and Carolyn Ann Thompson,
the "busy bees,"
who, as John Adams observed to Thomas Jefferson
about Grandchildren,
have "been cheering to have . . . hovering about Us,"
and to the memory of my brother,
Vergil Earl Smith, Jr.*

Contents

VOLUME TWO
1790–1804

Abbreviations	ix
15. The Battle with Hamilton, 1790–1791	662
16. Party Conflicts, 1791–1792	708
17. The French Connection and American Neutrality, 1793	744
18. "Pinching British Commerce," 1793–1794	821
19. Dolley, Domesticity, and the Whiskey Rebellion, 1794–1795	847
20. The Jay Treaty, 1795–1796	881
21. The Election of 1796	940
22. The Vice President and the Farmer: The Partners Trade Places Again, 1797	966
23. Crisis in Freedom: The XYZ Affair and the Alien and Sedition Acts, 1798	995
24. The Kentucky and Virginia Resolutions and American Civil Liberties, 1798–1799	1063
25. The Resolutions Renewed, 1799	1108
26. The Election of 1800 and the Crisis of Succession	1137
27. The Revolution of 1800	1164
28. An Interlude of Peace, 1801–1802	1206
29. "This Affair of Louisiana," 1803	1253
30. "The Empire for Liberty," 1803–1804	1287

The Index appears in Volume Three

ABBREVIATIONS

AHA American Historical Association.
AHR *American Historical Review.*
Amer. Phil. Soc. American Philosophical Society.
ASP Walter Lowrie and Matthew St. Clair Clarke, eds., *American State Papers: Documents, Legislative and Executive*, 38 vols. (Washington, 1832–61): *FR* (Foreign Relations); *M* (Miscellaneous).
Brant Irving Brant, *The Life of James Madison*, 6 vols. (Indianapolis, 1941–61): I, *James Madison: The Virginia Revolutionist* (1941); II, *James Madison: The Nationalist* (1948); III, *James Madison: Father of the Constitution* (1950); IV, *James Madison: Secretary of State* (1953); V, *James Madison: The President* (1956); VI, *James Madison: Commander in Chief* (1961).
Cappon Lester J. Cappon, ed., *The Adams-Jefferson Letters: The Complete Correspondence between Thomas Jefferson and Abigail and John Adams*, 2 vols. (Chapel Hill, 1959).
Fitzpatrick John C. Fitzpatrick, ed., *The Writings of George Washington . . . , 1745–1799*, 39 vols. (Washington, 1931–44).
Ford Paul Leicester Ford, ed., *The Writings of Thomas Jefferson*, 10 vols. (New York, 1892–99).
Hamilton, *Writings of Monroe* Stanislaus Murray Hamilton, ed., *The Writings of James Monroe . . .* , 7 vols. (New York, 1898–1903).
Hening William Waller Hening, ed., *The Statutes at Large; Being a Collection of All the Laws of Virginia, from the First Session of the Legislature, in the Year 1619*, 13 vols. (Richmond and Philadelphia, 1819–23).
Hunt Gaillard Hunt, ed., *The Writings of James Madison*, 9 vols. (New York, 1900–10).
JAH *Journal of American History.*
JER *Journal of the Early Republic.*
JM James Madison.
J. So. Hist. *Journal of Southern History.*
Ketcham Ralph Ketcham, *James Madison: A Biography* (New York, 1971).
L. and B. A. A. Lipscomb and A. E. Bergh, eds., *The Writings of Thomas Jefferson*, 20 vols. (New York, 1903).
Malone Dumas Malone, *Jefferson and His Time*, 6 vols. (Boston, 1948–81): I, *Jefferson the Virginian* (1948); II, *Jefferson and the Rights of Man* (1951); III, *Jefferson and the Ordeal of Liberty* (1962); IV, *Jefferson the President: First Term, 1801–1805* (1970); V, *Jefferson the President: Second Term, 1805–1809* (1974): VI, *The Sage of Monticello* (1981).
MVHR *Mississippi Valley Historical Review.*
Peterson Merrill D. Peterson, *Thomas Jefferson and the New Nation: A Biography* (New York, 1970).
PJM William T. Hutchinson, William M. E. Rachal, Robert A. Rutland, J. C. A. Stagg, *et al.*, eds., *The Papers of James Madison*, 22 vols. to date (Chicago and Charlottesville, 1962–93): **(SS ser.)** is Secretary of State series; **(Pres. ser.)** is Presidential series.
PMHB *Pennsylvania Magazine of History and Biography.*
PTJ Julian P. Boyd, Charles Cullen, John Catanzariti, *et al.*, eds., *The Papers of Thomas Jefferson*, 28 vols. to date (Princeton, 1950–92).
Richardson James D. Richardson, ed., *A Compilation of the Messages and Papers of the Presidents, 1789–1897*, 10 vols. (Washington, 1907).
Syrett Harold C. Syrett and Jacob E. Cooke, eds., *The Papers of Alexander Hamilton*, 26 vols. (New York, 1961–79).
TJ Thomas Jefferson.
VMHB *Virginia Magazine of History and Biography.*
WMQ *William and Mary Quarterly.*

The Republic of Letters

THE BATTLE WITH HAMILTON, 1790–1791

AFTER CONGRESS ADJOURNED in August 1790, the secretary of state joined President Washington on a short trip to Rhode Island to welcome the state into the federal Union after its belated ratification of the Constitution. Madison remained in New York to prepare a memorandum on the residence act and to box up books to be shipped from New York to Philadelphia, where Congress would convene for the next ten years. Both he and Jefferson recommended the appointment of commissioners to lay out the federal district where the permanent seat of government would move to in 1800 and to fix the site for public buildings.[1]

On September 1, Madison and Jefferson left New York on a leisurely trip to Virginia in Jefferson's phaeton. In Philadelphia, they stopped off for a week at Mrs. House's boarding establishment, where Madison had stayed while serving in the Confederation Congress. He reengaged his room for the next session of Congress, which was to move during the autumn from New York. Jefferson rented a house about three blocks away, where he planned to install his elegant furniture and accessories from France.[2]

To take advantage of the late summer weather, the two friends traveled down the Eastern Shore of Maryland, crossing Chesapeake Bay to Annapolis. While waiting for a boat to ferry them across the bay, they were joined by

1. See *PJM*, XIII, pp. 286–89, 294–96; *PTJ*, XVII, pp. 460–61, and XIX, pp. 27–29, 58–60. For the appointments, see William C. Di Giacomantonio, "All the President's Men: George Washington's Federal City Commissioners," *Washington History* 3 (1991): 52–75.

2. For TJ's French furniture, see Julian P. Boyd, "Jefferson's French Baggage, Crated and Uncrated," *Proceedings* (Massachusetts Historical Society) 83 (1971): 16–27; Marie Kimball, "Thomas Jefferson's French Furniture," *Antiques* 15 (1929): 123–28; F. J. B. Watson, "American and French Eighteenth-Century Furniture in the Age of Jefferson," in *Jefferson and the Arts: An Extended View*, ed. William Howard Adams (Washington, 1976), pp. 271–93; James A. Bear, Jr., "Thomas Jefferson's Silver," *Antiques* 74 (1958): 233–36; and James A. Bear, Jr., "The Furniture and Furnishings of Monticello," *Antiques* 102 (1972): 113–23.

Thomas Lee Shippen of Philadelphia, whose tour of Europe two years earlier had introduced him to Jefferson.[3] The young man was delighted to have the excellent company of his "two valuable friends" on their trip to Georgetown. "I never knew two men more agreeable than they were," he told his father, who had been chief administrator of the army hospitals during the Revolution. The trio spent most of the first day in the village of Rock Hall waiting for the ferry. "We talked and dined, and strolled, and rowed ourselves in boats, and feasted on delicious crabs." Once across the bay, they spent three hours on top of the State House in Annapolis, "from which place you descry the finest prospect in the world, if extent, variety Wood and Water in all their happiest forms can make one so."

After a night at Mann's Inn, one of the "most excellent in the world," according to Shippen, they stopped on September 11 at Queen Anne's, "a dirty village 13 miles from Annapolis," where they were greeted by "a most perfect contrast to Mann's—Musquitos, gnats, flees and bugs contended with each other for preference, and we had nothing decent to eat or drink. You can imagine how much we slept from the company we were in."[4]

In Georgetown, Jefferson and Madison turned to business. Washington had stopped there two days earlier to scout the area designated for the permanent residence of the national capital on the Potomac. But he left negotiations with local property owners to Jefferson, who "traversed the whole country," "joined by the different gentlemen who lived upon the confines," ending up with "a cavalcade of thirteen."[5]

Two days later, Jefferson and Madison visited Washington at Mt. Vernon, where the secretary of state presented a summary of his preliminary negotiations.[6] At the president's request, Jefferson and Madison then stopped overnight at Gunston Hall to get George Mason's views on the site of the nation's future capital. He preferred Georgetown to Alexandria, and the emissaries quickly informed the president, enclosing "Sketches for the Conveyance of the Lands whereon the Federal Seat is to be fixed."[7]

From Gunston Hall, the traveling companions headed home, reaching Madison's plantation on September 18. It was Jefferson's first visit to the house that Madison later called Montpellier, even though Monticello was less than 25 miles away. After an overnight visit, Jefferson left on the last leg of his journey with borrowed horses, one of which he later purchased from Madison. But he was reluctant to have Madison fix the price, fearing that Madison

---

3. Thomas Lee Shippen was the son of Dr. William Shippen, Jr., of Philadelphia and Alice Lee Shippen of Virginia, sister of Richard Henry Lee. For his visit with TJ in Europe, see Malone, II, p. 145.
4. Thomas Lee Shippen to William Shippen, Sept. 15, 1790, in *PTJ*, XVII, pp. 464-65.
5. For TJ's role in the location of the federal city, see *Thomas Jefferson and the National Capital, 1783–1818*, ed. Saul K. Padover (New York, 1946).
6. For TJ's report, see *PTJ*, XVII pp. 461-63.
7. TJ and JM to George Washington, Sept. 17, 1790, below.

would undervalue the animal: "I know nobody with whom it is so difficult to settle a price, and with whom I should be so likely to differ. Witness the money disputes on our journey." He suggested that an impartial judge of horseflesh be brought in to do Madison justice.[8]

While Jefferson was waiting for Madison to fix a price, the horse dropped dead, "presumptive evidence," according to Madison, "that he was not sound at the time of sending him." He, therefore, wanted to assume some responsibility for selling faulty merchandise or to submit the matter to arbitration.[9] Jefferson flatly refused: "the horse . . . was fairly sold, and fairly bought . . . so as to exonerate you . . . from all responsibility." In his eagerness to settle that debt and a loan that Madison had advanced to cover their traveling expenses for the return trip to Philadelphia, Jefferson overpaid his bill by $23.26, which Madison promptly refunded.[10]

The reaction of Jefferson and Madison to the horse deal and its aftermath did not cause a ripple in their relations.[11] At Jefferson's invitation, Madison spent several days at Monticello in October 1790, where they planned their return trip to Philadelphia, the temporary location of the national capital.[12] Jefferson left Monticello on November 8 and stopped overnight with Madison. Together they traveled by way of Mt. Vernon, spending two days with President and Mrs. Washington before going to Philadelphia by way of Baltimore, Head of Elk, and Chester, arriving on November 20. Until his furniture arrived from France, Jefferson took a room at Mrs. House's boarding house, where Madison lodged. For six weeks or so they dined together at Mrs. House's with the other residents.[13]

Once Jefferson was settled in his large house, he invited Madison to leave his room at Mrs. House's and "come and take a bed and plate with me." He could choose from four rooms, Jefferson wrote, "and it may lessen your repugnance to be assured it will not increase my expences an atom." Such a move would relieve him "from a solitude of which I have too much," and Madison would find the large library "a convenience in being close at hand." Whatever his friend's decision might be on this invitation, Jefferson also offered a smaller one: "What say you to taking a wade into the country at noon . . . the party to finish by dining here."[14]

Madison quickly accepted the latter invitation—the congressional session had ended a week earlier—and was tempted by the larger one, which would

8. TJ to JM, Sept 20, 1790, below, and Sept. 23, 1790, below.

9. JM to TJ, Jan. 11, 1791, below.

10. TJ to JM, Jan. 10, 1791, below, and Jan. 12, 1791, below; JM to TJ, Jan. 11, 1791, below; *PJM,* XIII, p. 355.

11. Brant, III, p. 322, suggests that "their reaction to that grim stroke could mold the political destiny of the United States."

12. TJ to JM, Sept. 23, 1790, below, and JM to TJ, Sept. 24, 1790, below.

13. Malone, II, p. 322.

14. TJ to JM, Mar. 13, 1791, below.

put him "in a situation where your society would make a part of my hourly enjoyments." But he had just undertaken a "little task"—probably a comparison of his notes on the debates in the federal convention with the manuscript journal of the proceedings[15]—and his "papers and books are all assorted around me." Even though he could not accept Jefferson's generous offer, he promised himself the pleasure of "seeing you more and using oftener one of your plates. Being never more happy than in partaking that hour of unbent conversation."[16]

Congress met from December 1790 until March 1791, and Hamilton again took command by submitting two reports on further measures for establishing public credit. The first recommended additional duties on imported liquor and an excise tax on domestic spirits in order to pay off the state debts assumed at the previous session of Congress. Although Madison had opposed assumption, he favored Hamilton's measures to discharge the debt.[17]

Hamilton's second report called for the incorporation of a national bank modeled on the Bank of England. Its capital would consist largely of public securities, which could be converted into bank stock. The government would furnish one-fifth of the $10 million capitalization, the rest coming from public creditors and private investors; one-fifth of the board of directors would be appointed by the government, the remainder by the investors. Combining public convenience with private advantage, the Bank of the United States would serve as the leading depository of federal funds and the fiscal agent of the treasury in both domestic and foreign transactions. It could also issue bank notes payable in gold and silver and receivable for all payments due to the federal government, thus increasing the circulating medium in the United States.[18]

Although Madison had opposed the first phase of Hamilton's program, his objections to funding and assumption had been based on details rather than principle. But the bill to incorporate the Bank of the United States seemed to him, ordinarily a broad constructionist of the Constitution—indeed, he had originated the doctrine of implied powers in the Confederation Congress—to overleap the limits of delegated power, and he flatly denied its constitutionality. From which of the enumerated powers did the supposed authority come, he asked? The federal convention had rejected a motion to grant charters of incorporation (he did not mention that the motion had been his).[19] Nor did he deny the doctrine of implied powers, although he noted that it "is always a tender one." Hamilton's proposal, however, stretched the doctrine beyond acceptable limits:

15. See *PTJ*, XX, pp. 544-45; *PJM*, XIII, p. 406.
16. JM to TJ, Mar. 13, 1791, below.
17. Brant, III, p. 326.
18. John C. Miller, *The Federalist Era, 1789-1801* (New York, 1960), pp. 55-63.
19. For JM's proposal, see *The Records of the Federal Convention of 1787*, ed. Max Farrand, 4 vols. (New Haven, 1911), II, pp. 325, 615-16.

Mark the reasoning on which the validity of the bill depends. To borrow money is made the *end* and the accumulation of capitals, *implied* as the *means*. The accumulation of capitals is then the *end,* and a bank *implied* as the *means*. The bank is then the *end,* and a charter of incorporation, a monopoly, capital punishments [for counterfeiting], etc. *implied* as the *means.*

If implications, thus remote and thus multiplied, can be linked together, a chain may be formed that will reach every object of legislation, every object within the whole compass of political economy.[20]

The House rejected Madison's objections by a 2-to-1 margin, sending the bill to the president. Washington then called for opinions from his cabinet members on Congress's power to charter corporations. Jefferson and Attorney General Edmund Randolph submitted opinions that agreed with Madison's, and Jefferson apparently enclosed a copy of Madison's speech attacking the constitutionality of the bank bill.[21] A federally incorporated bank might be a public convenience, Jefferson conceded, but it was not "necessary and proper" within the meaning of the Constitution. Unless the president thought the measure clearly unconstitutional, however, Jefferson suggested that "a just respect for the wisdom of the legislature would naturally decide the balance in favor of their opinion."[22]

Washington gave Hamilton the dissenting opinions of Jefferson and Randolph at the same time that he asked Madison to draft a veto message, should the president decide against the bill's constitutionality.[23] Hamilton's bold and persuasive argument laid down the principle of broad construction of the Constitution. He made two essential points, one about governmental power, the other about the "necessary and proper" means to implement it. He defined the latter as meaning "needful, useful, or conducive to." He blended this definition with his fundamental proposition about power to get an expansive interpretation of implied power: "That every power vested in a government is in its nature *sovereign,* and includes, by *force* of the *term,* a right to employ all *means* requisite and fairly applicable to the attainment of the *ends* of such power, and which are not precluded by restrictions and exceptions specified in the Constitution, or not immoral, or not contrary to the *essential ends* of political society." Under this definition a bank was necessary for the collection of taxes, regulation of trade, and governmental efficiency.[24]

Laying aside Madison's draft of a veto message, Washington gave the benefit of the doubt to the legislature, signing the bank bill on the last day allowed under the Constitution. Although Hamilton's partisans in the Senate, where the bank bill originated, had stalled consideration of a bill to expedite

20. For JM's "Remarks in Congress on the Bank Bill," see *PJM,* XIII, pp. 373–81.

21. Both *PTJ,* XIX, p. 280, and *PJM,* XIII, p. 382, make this point.

22. For TJ's opinion on the bank, Feb. 15, 1791, see *Thomas Jefferson: Writings,* ed. Merrill D. Peterson (New York, 1984), pp. 416–21.

23. For JM's draft veto of the bank bill, see *PJM,* XIII, p. 395.

24. Syrett, VIII, pp. 62–134.

the removal of the capital to the Potomac to put pressure on the president, it seems doubtful that this tactic had anything to do with Washington's approval of the bill.[25] But Madison later learned that the president, by withholding his immediate signature to the bill, had become the target of harsh and, Madison thought, indecent criticism by New York speculators: "I have reason to believe that the licentiousness of the tongues of speculators and Tories far exceeded any thing that was conceived," he told Jefferson. "The meanest motives were charged on him, and the most insolent menaces held over him, if not in the open streets, under circumstances not less marking the character of the party."[26]

Madison's use of the phrase "partizans" of the bank bill foreshadowed his use of the term "party" later in the year and highlighted the hardening of political lines in 1791. "You know we have two parties with us," Hamilton had said even before he proposed the bank bill.[27] The bank charter, which dovetailed with the Hamiltonian system of funding and assumption, seemed to Madison and Jefferson to perpetuate debt, speculation, and fraud. Jefferson condemned the speculative scramble for the stock of the Bank of the United States: "It is impossible to say where the appetite for gambling will stop."[28] Madison, who had gone to New York after Congress adjourned, agreed that the subscriptions for bank stock there were "a mere scramble for so much public plunder." "Of all the shameful circumstances of this business," he told Jefferson, "it is among the greatest to see the members of the Legislature who were most active in pushing this Jobb, openly grasping its emoluments."[29] Commenting on "the daring depravity of the times," he feared that "the stock-jobbers will become the pretorian band of the Government, at once its tool and its tyrant; bribed by its largesses, and overawing it, by clamours and combinations."[30]

Madison's hostility to the bank quickly made him the publicly recognized leader of the opposition to Hamilton.[31] Jefferson's views within the cabinet had been expressed in opinions requested by President Washington, which were not made public. But Jefferson's private attitude towards "the political heresies which had of late sprung up among us" soon became public with the publication of his unintended endorsement of *The Rights of Man* by Thomas Paine. The volume, which was a reply to Edmund Burke's conservative *Reflec-*

---

25. Kenneth R. Bowling, "The Bank Bill, the Capital City, and President Washington," *Capitol Studies* 1 (1972): 59–71, explores this issue.

26. JM to TJ, May 1, 1791, below.

27. Conversation of Nov. 10, 1790, with George Beckwith, a British army officer who was acting as agent of Lord Dorchester, governor-general of Canada; see *PTJ*, XIX, p. 88.

28. TJ to James Monroe, July 10, 1791, *ibid.*, XX, p. 298.

29. JM to TJ, July 10, 1791, below.

30. JM to TJ, Aug. 8, 1791, below.

31. Noble E. Cunningham, Jr., *The Jeffersonian Republicans: The Formation of Party Organization, 1789–1801* (Chapel Hill, 1957), p. 9.

tions on the Revolution in France, featured a preface by the secretary of state, a private letter printed without his permission, which set forth his republican views, the antithesis of John Adams's theories and Hamilton's system. "The contest of Burke and Paine, as reviv'd in America,"[32] pitted the former's defense of hereditary monarchy and denunciation of "tyrannical democracy" against the latter's advocacy of the American and French Revolutions. Madison had borrowed Paine's pamphlet from John Beckley, clerk of the House of Representatives, and loaned it to Jefferson. Before the secretary had finished reading it, Beckley asked him to send it to the printer. "To take off a little of the dryness of the note" of transmittal, Jefferson hastily scribbled that he was "pleased to find it was to be reprinted here."[33]

The secretary of state was astonished to see his note printed as the preface to Paine's pamphlet since he "certainly never meant to step into a public newspaper" with his condemnation of "political heresies." To Madison, he admitted that he had in view Vice President John Adams's "doctrines of Davila," a series of essays that Adams had written several months earlier. To the president, Jefferson explained that "Mr. Adams will unquestionably take to himself the charge of political heresy, as conscious of his own views of drawing the present government to the form of the English constitution, and I fear will consider me as meaning to injure him in the public eye. . . . I certainly never made a secret of my being anti-monarchical, and anti-aristocratical: but I am sincerely mortified to be thus brought forward on the public stage, where to remain, to advance or to retire, will be equally against my love of silence and quiet, and my abhorrence of dispute."[34]

Adams was distressed by Jefferson's charge, and Hamilton was "open mouthed" against his cabinet colleague, accusing him of "opposition to the government." Jefferson labeled Hamilton's shaft an inversion of his views, an attempt "to turn on the government itself those censures I meant for the enemies of the government to wit those who want to change it into a monarchy."[35] The incident was the first public manifestation of the differences between Jefferson and Hamilton and brought Jefferson to center stage with Madison as a defender of republicanism and an opponent of the Hamiltonian system.

Both Hamilton and Major George Beckwith, the unofficial British representative in Philadelphia, argued that Jefferson's statements would offend the British court. Madison brushed aside this accusation as the criticism of "British partisans"; it was "truly ridiculous," he added. As for Adams, Madison tried to reassure his friend by repeating his jaundiced view of the vice president: "Mr. Adams can least of all complain. Under a mock defence of the Republican

32. James Monroe used this phrase in his letter to TJ, July 25, 1791, in *PTJ,* XX, p. 304.
33. TJ to JM, May 9, 1791, below.
34. TJ to George Washington, May 8, 1791, in *PTJ,* XX, pp. 291–92.
35. TJ to JM, May 9, 1791, below.

Constitutions of this Country, he attacked them with all the force he possessed, and this in a book with his name to it whilst he was the Representative of his Country at a foreign Court. Since he has been the 2d. Magistrate in the new Republic, his pen has constantly been at work in the same cause; and tho' his name has not been prefixed to his antirepublican discourses, the author has been as well known as if that formality had been observed. Surely if it be innocent and decent in one servant of the public thus to write attacks agst its Government, it can not be very criminal or indecent in another to patronize a written defence of the principles on which that Govt. is founded."[36]

The controversy between Jefferson and Adams brought the ideological clash between Paine and Burke—between revolutionary democracy and reactionary toryism—to the forefront of American politics. Jefferson appeared as a champion of the French Revolution and a critic of aristocracy and monarchy. "I consider the establishment and success of their government," he told George Mason, "as necessary to stay up our own and to prevent it from falling back to that kind of Halfway-house, the English constitution."[37] Adams viewed Jefferson as Paine's godfather, who had written "the Preface to Paine's Nonsense."[38] Although he denied that he had ever advocated monarchy as a form of government for the United States,[39] Adams's "Discourses on Davila" seemed to some to be an attack on the French Revolution and American "maxims, principles, and example."[40] "Amidst all their exultations," Adams wrote, "Americans and Frenchmen should remember that the perfectibility of man is only human and terrestrial perfectibility." The truth is, he argued, that man in society is a creature of "passions, appetites, and propensities, as well as a variety of faculties," and none of these is more "remarkable, than the *passion for distinction*." The purpose of government—its principal end—is "to regulate this passion"; "it is the only adequate instrument of order and subordination in society." In the Roman republic, distinctions of "rank, station, and importance in the state" offered the "consistent method of preserving order, or procuring submission to the laws." Indeed, Adams proclaimed this theme as "the true spirit of republics," which was "universally true."[41]

Adams argued that a system of checks and balances—"the checks of emulation and the balances of rivalry in the orders of society"—was necessary to protect liberty and order. Instead of democratic equality, he recommended deference; "it becomes the more indispensable that every man should know his place, and be made to keep it." In discussing the French republic, he advocated

---

36. JM to TJ, May 12, 1791, below.
37. TJ to George Mason, Feb. 4, 1791, in *PTJ*, XIX, p. 241.
38. John Adams to Henry Knox, June 19, 1791, cited *ibid.*, XX, p. 278.
39. John Adams to Benjamin Rush, Apr. 18, 1791, cited *ibid.*, p. 280.
40. The discourses are printed in John Adams, *The Works of John Adams*, ed. Charles Francis Adams, 10 vol. (Boston, 1850-56), VI, pp. 223-399.
41. *Ibid.*, pp. 279, 232, 234, 243-44.

"an equal, independent mixture" of "monarchy, aristocracy, and democracy" in the constitution, and some interpreted this comment to apply to America, given his earlier statement about what was universally true of republics.[42] Adams later conceded that his "Discourses," which he labeled "a dull, heavy volume," "powerfully operated to destroy his popularity" since it was interpreted—or misinterpreted—to portray him as "an advocate for monarchy, and laboring to introduce a hereditary president in America."[43]

Just as the controversy over Paine's pamphlet erupted—"what a dust . . . [it] has kicked up here," the vice president wrote[44]—Jefferson and Madison took off on a northern excursion, with "health recreation and curiosity" as their objects.[45] Jefferson welcomed the trip as an opportunity to shake a persistent headache "by giving more exercise to the body and less to the mind."[46] He met Madison in New York, and together they headed up the Hudson River valley to Lake George and Lake Champlain before crossing into Vermont, then dropping down the Connecticut River valley to Long Island. Each kept a brief journal of the trip, and Jefferson wrote colorful letters to his daughters on the bark of a birch tree while sailing on the lakes. He described Lake George as "the most beautiful water I ever saw," but he found Lake Champlain "a far less pleasant water." The Virginia tourists also visited several historic sites of the Revolution, including Saratoga, Stillwater, and Bennington, "the principal scenes of Burgoyne's misfortunes," as well as Ticonderoga and Crown Point, "which have been scenes of blood from a very early part of our history."

But they were more pleased with "the botanical objects which continually presented themselves"—a fragrant azalea, "the richest shrub I have seen," Jefferson wrote; wild honeysuckle, gooseberries, cherries, and strawberries; and forests of balsam, birch, hemlock, and white pine. Jefferson also took systematic notes on the Hessian fly and commented on everything from "musketoes and gnats" to loons, ducks, and rattlesnakes. On the economic front, Madison observed that "tobacco, French brandy, [and] tropical fruits are smuggled from the U. S." into Canada.[47]

Hamilton and his friends viewed Madison and Jefferson's trip as a politically motivated journey, an attempt by the southern leaders to forge an alliance with New Yorkers and New Englanders in opposition to Hamilton's system. A New York friend informed the secretary of the treasury that "there was every appearance of a passionate courtship between the Chancellor [Livingston], Burr, Jefferson and Madison when the two latter were in town."[48] Although

---

42. *Ibid.*, pp. 276, 272.
43. Adams made these comments about the "Discourses" in 1812; see *ibid.*, p. 227.
44. TJ to James Monroe, July 10, 1791, in *PTJ*, XX, p. 297.
45. JM to TJ, May 12, 1791, below.
46. TJ to George Washington, May 15, 1791, *PTJ*, XX, p. 417.
47. JM's journal is in *PJM*, XIV, pp. 25-30; TJ's journal and letters are in *PTJ*, XX, pp. 453-73.
48. Robert Troup to Alexander Hamilton, June 15, 1791, in Syrett, VIII. 478-79.

the Virginians no doubt took the pulse of the people along their route—they were entertained in Albany by Hamilton's father-in-law, an ardent Federalist, and in Bennington by Governor Moses Robinson, an ardent republican—they forged no political alliances on their vacation junket.[49]

Madison later recalled, however, that "the scenes and subjects which had occurred during the session of Congress which had just terminated at our departure from New York, entered of course into our itinerary conversations." One scene he recollected with particular delight since it showed his friend in a "characteristic" light. At "a dinner party at which we were both present," the conversation turned to "the new Constitution of the U. States" and "forms of Government," then "the uppermost topics every where, more especially at a convivial board."

The question being started as to the best mode of providing the Executive chief, it was among other opinions, boldly advanced that a hereditary designation was preferable to any elective process that could be devised. At the close of an eloquent effusion against the agitations and animosities of a popular choice and in behalf of birth, as on the whole, affording even a better chance of a suitable head of the Government, Mr. Jefferson, with a smile remarked that he had heard of a university somewhere in which the Professorship of Mathematics was hereditary. The reply, received with acclamation, was a coup de grace to the Anti-Republican Heretic.[50]

The northern excursion reminded Jefferson of his travels in Europe, and he entertained Madison with an account of his trips through France and Italy. When he returned to Philadelphia, he dug out the journal of his travels and sent it to Madison, who had remained in New York. Reminding Madison of his invitation to visit him in France, Jefferson noted facetiously that "you might be willing to acquire of that country a knowlege at second hand which you refuse[d] to acquire at the first. It is written in the way you seemed to approve on our journey."[51] Madison enjoyed the journal but said that he needed a map of France to make it more fully pleasurable.[52] Jefferson promptly sent "the map belonging to my journal, being the one I had in my pocket during the journey."[53]

While they were in New York at the beginning of their excursion, the congressman and the secretary of state did transact one important piece of political business. They tried to persuade Philip Freneau, the poet of the

---

49. For interpretations suggesting political motivation for the trip, see Wilford E. Binkley, *American Political Parties: Their Natural History* (New York, 1962), p. 78; Alfred F. Young, *The Democratic Republicans of New York: The Origins, 1763–1797* (Chapel Hill, 1967), pp. 196–98; and Forrest McDonald, *The Presidency of George Washington* (Lawrence, Kans., 1974), pp. 80–81. For those rejecting such an interpretation, see Peterson, pp. 439–40; Malone, II, pp. 359–63; Brant, III, pp. 336–40; Cunningham, pp. 11–12; *PTJ,* XX, pp. 434–53; and *PJM,* XIV, p. 25.
50. JM to Margaret Bayard Smith, Sept. 1830, in Hunt, IX, pp. 405–6.
51. TJ to JM, July 27, 1791, below.
52. JM to TJ, July 31, 1791, below.
53. TJ to JM, Aug. 3, 1791, below.

American Revolution, to move to Philadelphia and establish a national newspaper for the republican cause. Madison, a classmate of Freneau's at Princeton, had earlier recommended him to Jefferson for a part-time position as translator in the State Department, a position that would not interfere "with any other calling the person may chuse." Freneau had declined this "generous unsollicted proposal," but Madison decided to try to reverse his decision. Before Jefferson arrived in New York, Madison met with Freneau, who was contemplating the establishment of a newspaper in New Jersey. "The more I learn of his character talents and principles," he wrote Jefferson, "the more I should regret his burying himself in the obscurity he had chosen in N. Jersey. It is certain that there is not to be found in the whole catalogue of American Printers, a single name that can approach towards a rivalship."[54]

After Jefferson joined Madison in New York in May, they had breakfast with Freneau but failed to persuade him to move to Philadelphia. When Madison stopped off in New York after his northern excursion, he finally convinced Freneau to come to Philadelphia, only to have him change his mind at the last minute.[55] Jefferson was disappointed, observing that Freneau's genius was clearly "superior to that of his competitors."[56] To his son-in-law, he explained that "we have been trying to get another weekly or half weekly paper set up . . . , so that it might go through the states, and furnish a whig vehicle of intelligence. We had hoped at one time to have persuaded Freneau to set up here, but failed."[57] Nevertheless, the persistent Madison finally persuaded Freneau and happily informed Jefferson that "in the conduct and title of the paper, it will be altogether his own."[58] A month later, Jefferson appointed Freneau as translator, and in the fall the first issue of the *National Gazette* appeared as a "Periodical Miscellany of News, Politics, History, and Polite Literature."[59]

Freneau's paper quickly became an antidote for John Fenno's *Gazette of the United States*, which Jefferson denounced as "a paper of pure Toryism, disseminating the doctrines of monarchy, aristocracy, and the exclusion of the influence of the people."[60] Although the *National Gazette* was not established as a party paper, it provided a national vehicle for the emerging "republican interest." As the conflict in Congress and the cabinet increased, the paper dramatized the divisions, contributing to the rise of the Republican party and the recognition of Madison and Jefferson as its political leaders.[61]

54. JM to TJ, May 1, 1791, below. See also TJ to Philip Freneau, Feb. 28, 1791, in *PTJ*, XIX, p. 351, and Philip Freneau to TJ, Mar. 5, 1791, *ibid.*, pp. 416–17.
55. JM to TJ, July 10, 1791, below.
56. TJ to JM, July 21, 1791, below.
57. TJ to Thomas Mann Randolph, May 15, 1791, in *PTJ*, XX, p. 416.
58. JM to TJ, July 24, 1791, below.
59. Philip Freneau to TJ, Aug. 4, 1791, in *PTJ*, XX, p. 754, and TJ to Philip Freneau, Aug. 16, 1791, *ibid.*, p. 756; Malone, II, pp. 423–28.
60. TJ to Thomas Mann Randolph, May 15, 1791, in *PTJ*, XX, p. 416.
61. Cunningham, pp. 13–19.

THE LETTERS

Jefferson and Madison to George Washington

Fredericksburg Sept. 17, 1790

SIR

In the course of the visit we made the day we left Mount Vernon, we drew our host into conversation on the subject of the federal seat.[1] He came into it with a shyness not usual in him. Whether this proceeded from his delicacy as having property adjoining Georgetown, or from what other motive I cannot say. He quitted the subject always as soon as he could. He said enough however to shew his decided preference of George-town. He mentioned shortly, in it's favor, these circumstances. 1. It's being at the junction of the upper and lower navigation where the commodities must be transferred into other vessels: (and here he was confident that no vessel could be contrived which could pass the upper shoals and live in the wide waters below his island.) 2. The depth of water which would admit any vessels that could come to Alexandria. 3. The narrowness of the river and consequent safeness of the harbour. 4. It's being clear of ice as early at least as the canal and river above would be clear. 5. It's neighborhood to the Eastern branch, whither any vessels might conveniently withdraw which should be detained through the winter. 6. It's defensibility, as derived from the high and commanding hills around it. 7. It's actual possession of the commerce, and the start it already has.

He spoke of Georgetown always in comparison with Alexandria. When led to mention the Eastern branch he spoke of it as an admirable position, superior in all respects to Alexandria.

I have committed to writing a Memorandum for Mr. Carroll of the kind of conveyance I suggested to him, and which I had not the opportunity then to put on paper. I inclose it open for your perusal, and take the liberty of asking you to put a wafer into it, when you are done with it, and forward it to Mr. Carroll.[2] I have the honor to be with the greatest respect and attachment, Sir, Your most obedient and most humble servt.,

TH. JEFFERSON

---

1. After visiting with Washington, TJ and JM stopped at Gunston Hall to consult with George Mason.

2. For TJ's negotiations with Daniel Carroll and other landowners in what became the District of Columbia, see the editorial note "Fixing the Seat of Government on the Potomac," in *PTJ*, XVII, pp. 452–71.

ENCLOSURE
[Jefferson to Daniel Carroll]

[Fredericksburg Sept. 17, 1790]

T.J. has the honor to present his Compliments to Mr. C—— and to send him a memorandum of the substance of the conveyance he suggested to him as best calculated to remove the difficulties which were the subject of conversation between them. He had not the residence act under his eye at the time of writing the memorandum, not being able to get a copy of it: which must account for its deviations from that act, if any should be found. As far as his memory serves him he has adhered to the letter of the Act.

ENCLOSURE
Sketches for the Conveyance of the Lands whereon the Federal Seat is to be fixed

The Conveyance to be executed, according to the forms of the laws of Maryland, by the Proprietors of the land designated by the President for the federal seat.

The preamble to recite the substance of that part of the residence act which authorises the President to receive grants of *lands* and *money* for the use of the United States and to declare that the object of the conveyance is to furnish both *land* and *money* for their use.

The body of the Deed to convey the lands designated for the Seat (suppose 1500 acres) to A and B and their heirs in trust for the following purposes.

1. To reconvey to the Commissioners their heirs and successors to be named by the President, such portions of the said lands, as the President shall designate for the scite of the public buildings, public walks streets etc. to remain for the use of the U.S.

2. To reconvey the residue in such lots, to such persons, and in such conditions as the Commissioners shall direct, for the purpose of raising money, and the money when received to be granted to the President for the use of the U.S. according to the residence act.

The effect of this last clause will be such that the President (without any further legislative authority from Congress) may proceed to lay out the town immediately into: 1. public lots: 2. public walks or gardens: 3. private lots for sale: 4. streets—The 1. 2. and 4th. articles to be reconveyed to the Commissioners, and the 3d. to private purchasers as above proposed.

It is understood that this conveyance will have been preceeded by Articles of Agreement signed by all the Proprietors of the lands in and about those several spots which have such obvious advantages as render it presumeable to every one that some one of them will attract the President's notice and choice.

Jefferson to Madison

Monticello Sept. 20, 1790

DEAR SIR

Your servant now returns with many thanks for the aid of him and your horses. I was disappointed of meeting my family here: however I am told they will arrive today. I wished to have seen Mr. Randolph, before the departure of your servant to know if he had found a horse for me; because if he has not I should determine to accept the offer of yours. I drove him about eight miles in the Phaeton, and he did as well as the awkwardness of so new a situation to him gave me right to expect. If Mr. Randolph should not have been successful in his enquiries, I will send to you for the horse immediately. Notwithstanding your observing 'we should not differ about the price,' I know nobody with whom it is so difficult to settle a price, and with whom I should be so likely to differ. Witness the money disputes on our journey. As I would not chuse to trust to your setting a price therefore, I should propose your getting a Capt. Wood or some such good judge to do you justice. But of this more if I send for the horse. Adieu, my dear Sir. Your's affectionately,

TH: JEFFERSON

Jefferson to Madison

Monticello Sept. 23, 1790

DEAR SIR

Mr. Randolph arrived last night without having been able to get me a horse, or even to hear of one which he could approve of. Presuming you had made up your mind as to parting with yours, I take the liberty of sending for him. I should not hesitate to take him at your own price but that I apprehend you think him of less than his real value, and therefore propose that you should have him valued. If there be no urgency, I should propose to pay you the money not till our return to Philada., perhaps not till the receipt of our December quarter, as the arrival of my furniture from Paris, and commencing housekeeping will perhaps call for my previous resources. But this need make no difficulty.

We shall count on seeing you here about our next court[3] and hope you will make some stay. The time and plan of our return may be then arranged. Adieu. Your's affectionately

TH: JEFFERSON

Madison to Jefferson

[Orange] Sept. 24, 1790

DEAR SIR

I recd. yours of the 23 inst: by the bearer who now returns with the Horse. I will consult with some persons who are acquainted with him and let

---

3. The next session of the Albemarle court was on Oct. 14, 1790; see *PJM,* XIII, p. 299.

you know the price I set on him. The time and place of payment which you propose would suit me as well as immediate payment here: but I consider this credit as a necessary set off agst. advances which you will have made for me in France. If no obstacles not at present in view stand in the way, I shall have the pleasure of seeing Monticello a day or so before your next Court. My father sends the promised seed of the Mountain Cresses. Yours Mo: Affectly.

        Js. MADISON JR.

Jefferson to Madison

[Philadelphia] Dec. 15, 1790

FOR MR. MADISON FROM TH: J.

Extract from a letter of the house of Van Staphorsts.

'So far from Mr. Dohrman having made us any remittance for our friend Mr. Mazzei, that gentleman is greatly in our debt, and we fear will not be able to stand the return of a large amount of bills he drew on Europe on speculations of corn, but which did not arrive. What funds he had in the hands of his London correspondents are attached by his brother Dohrman and Garron of Lisbon. We send out our power of attorney to Leroy and Bayard to recover our demand and would recommend Mr. Mazzei to send his to his friend Madison or any other person he may chuse there.'

Mazzei in his letter to Th: J. goes on. 'My *power of attorney* is already in existence, wherefore it would be superfluous for me to send another. The only thing lacking is to confirm my claims against this fellow Dohrman. My friend Madison in his letter of 10 Dec. 1788 said to me 'he has at my request concurred in an instrument which pledges his Western grant of land as an eventual security for the debt.' I place my hope therefore in your well-known friendship for me, in case he should not be able to be paid, at least to insure that my interests will not be prejudiced by the other creditors. But you would need to be good enough to take my well-being really to heart, and not rely at all on Dohrman's promises. He made a draft in Europe on account of cargoes of grain which he later sold in America, and without even giving notice of this. Such conduct casts grave doubts on his character. Certainly, prudence cannot counsel putting any faith in him.'[4]

4. The portion of this paragraph in quotation marks, except for the interior quotation from JM's letter of Dec. 10, 1788, was written in Italian and translated by Archibald T. MacAllister in *PTJ*, XVIII, p. 218; the letter is not in *PJM*, XIII.

Jefferson to Madison

[Philadelphia] Saturday morning [Jan. 1, 1791]

I intended to have called last night and left with you the inclosed draught of a letter to Otto⁵ but it was so cold I could not give up my hack. I recieved yours soon after I came home.⁶ Of the two constructions I observe you lean more to the 2d. and I more to the 1st. on account of the consequences to which the 2d. may be pursued. My first idea was to write this letter to Otto and previously communicate it to the President, and he perhaps to the Senate. But I have concluded to throw it into the form of a report to the President, to be submitted to the Senate.⁷ This will permit me to speak without reserve, to admit the force of the 2d. construction, and to enforce the proposition I suggest in the close, by shewing what valuable branches of our commerce hang on the will of the French nation. I shall see you at dinner, and be glad to exchange further thoughts on the subject which is an important one.

Jefferson to Madison

[Philadelphia] Jan. 10, 1791

TH: J. TO J. M.

Will you be so good as to let me know how much I am in your debt for travelling expences and the horse. My monstrous bill of freight rendered the question useless till now. I send you a moment's amusement at my expence in the Connecticut paper. I suppose it is from some schoolmaster who does not like that the mysteries of his art should become useless.⁸

Madison to Jefferson

[Philadelphia Jan. 11, 1791]

T: J. TO J. M.

		Dr.
To advances for him on the road to Philada.		£14..5..6
To Horse		
Credit By 50 dollars	£18..15–	
Balance to T. J.		£ 4..9..6. Pa. Curry.

---

5. Otto, the French chargé d'affaires, had protested against the U.S. tonnage acts, which, he claimed, violated the treaty of amity and commerce with France by not excepting French ships from the tonnage duties levied on foreign vessels.

6. JM's letter of Dec. 31, 1790, is missing.

7. For TJ's analysis of the "two constructions" of the Franco-American treaty of amity and commerce, see TJ to George Washington, Jan. 18, 1791, in *PTJ*, XVIII, pp. 516-17.

8. The "schoolmaster" was Noah Webster, whose piece ridiculed TJ's "Report on Weights and Measures"; see *ibid.*, pp. 480-82.

If the intended charge of £25. for the Horse is not cancelled by the presumptive evidence that he was not sound at the time of sending him, the balance will lie on the other side.⁹ The scruples of J. M. on this point are not affected, and are enforced by his having discovered after the death of the Horse from the servant who accompanied Mr. J. that on his return the Horse was taken very sick and drenched, and from the symptoms mentioned it can scarcely be doubted that the malady must have been the prelude of that which proved fatal. To get rid of all embarrassment on either side, J. M. thinks it essential that a common friend shd. hear and decide the case, and for that purpose insists that it be stated to such an one by both, on the first convenient occasion. Mr. Hawkins occurs as an eligible umpire. The map and 1st. chapter of the Magazine seem to contain Pond's western discoveries and excur[s]ions.¹⁰

Jefferson to Madison

[Philadelphia] Jan. 12, 1791

MY DEAR SIR

It being impossible to entertain a doubt that the horse I bought of you was fairly sold, and fairly bought, that his disorder was of the instant, and might have happened years after as well as when it did, so as to exonerate you as is justly established, from all responsibility, I should as soon think of filching the sum from your pocket, as of permitting the loss to be yours. I therefore send you a check on the bank for 95.26 Dollars including the two balances.¹¹ Yours affectionately

TH: J.

Madison to Jefferson

[Philadelphia ca. Jan. 31, 1791]¹²

Memorandum "made for Mr. Jefferson,
when preparing his report [on fisheries] for Congress"¹³

9. TJ paid for the horse. For his calculations, see *PJM,* XIII, p. 352.

10. Peter Pond, fur trader and explorer in the Upper Mississippi Valley, gave information about the Lake Superior country to a writer whose description was published in the *New-York Magazine* in Dec. 1790; see *ibid.*

11. TJ overpaid JM because TJ added, rather than subtracted, the balance due JM in JM's letter of Jan. 11, 1791; see *ibid.,* p. 355.

12. For the dating, see *PJM,* XIII, p. 364. TJ utilized JM's memorandum in his "Report on the American Fisheries" as Appendix No. 18; see *PTJ,* XIX, p. 236.

13. This table was based on Great Britain's wars in Europe.

	[Years] At war			*At Peace*		
G. Britain from May	1689 to Sepr. 1697 = 8y. 4.m.		to May	1702 = 4y. 8.m.		
	May 1702 to Aug. 1712 = 10. 3.		to Decr.	1718 = 6. 4.		
	Decr. 1718 to June 1721 = 2. 6		to Mar.	1727 = 5. 8		
	Mar. 1727 to May 1727 = 0. 2		to Octr.	1739 = 12. 4		
	Octr. 1739 to May 1748 = 8. 7		to June	1755 = 7. 0		
	June 1755 to Novr. 1762 = 7. 5	14	to June	1778 = 15. 7		
	June 1778 to Mar. 1783 = 4. 9		to May	1789 = 6. 2		

3. lost in broken months

42. War   58. peace

Altho' these estimates are from an Underwriter it may be well to consult Mr. T. C^{15} or others, on them.

During war Insurance between U. S. & G. B. may be rated from 12 to 20 PerCt.
     do.   U. S. & W. Inds.   from 12 to 20 do.
During peace   U. S. & G. B   about 2½   do.
                      U. S. & W. Inds.   abt. 2½   do.
During war increase of freight beyond that of peace from 30 to 50 PerCt.
*The annual value of exports from U. S. to G. B. in British Bottoms = Dollars[16]
       Freight of do. from do. in do. to Europe   = do.[17]
       do. of do. from do. in do. to W. Inds   = do.[18]
Annual value of Imports in Brit: Bottoms (see Champion p. 51)   = do.[19]
(See Report of Impost & the 10 PerCt. discount in favr. of Amer. Botts.)[20]

*Champion p. 140.

From these data result the expence of Insurance and freight taxed by Brit: wars on the trade or rather agriculture of U. S. during their present dependence on British Bottoms[21]

From the same may be inferred the loss which war with Spain wd. have cost the U. S. During the prospect of it insurance in some instances rose to near double the peace rate.

14. Neither JM, who prepared this report, nor TJ, who put it in his report, included the first three years of the American Revolution in their calculations, since the tables were based on war or peace in Europe; see *ibid.*, p. 200.

15. Tench Coxe, assistant secretary of the treasury. For an excellent biography, see Jacob E. Cooke, *Tench Coxe and the Early Republic* (Chapel Hill, 1978).

16. TJ filled in this blank with $10,000,000 in Appendix 18 of his "Report on the American Fisheries"; see *PTJ*, XIX, p. 236.

17. TJ filled in this blank with $2,250,000; see *ibid.*

18. TJ did not include this calculation in Appendix 18; see *ibid.*

19. Richard Champion, *Considerations on the Present Situation of Great Britain and the United States of America* . . . , 2d ed. (London, 1784), lists prewar imports at £2,943,000; see *PJM*, XIII, p. 364. A Bristol china manufacturer who settled in Camden, South Carolina, in 1784, Champion wrote his pamphlet in reply to Lord Sheffield [John Baker Holroyd], *Observations on the Commerce of the American States* . . . (London, 1783); see *PJM*, VII, pp. 295-96, XIII, pp. 203, 211.

20. This refers to calculations included in Hamilton's report of Jan. 7, 1791, on import duties from Aug. 1, 1789, to Sept. 1, 1790; see *PJM*, XIII, p. 364.

21. TJ calculated the annual charge at $1,392,857. He listed annual peacetime charges for freight and insurance at 22.5 percent of export value, or $2,250,000, and 55 percent for wartime, or $5,500,000, resulting in an annual difference of $3,250,000. "Of the last 100 years," he wrote in Appendix 18, "Great Britain has had 42 years of War and 58 of peace, which is 3 of War to every 4 of Peace nearly. In every term of 7 years then we pay 3 times 3,250,000 dollars, or 9,750,000 which averaged on the years of peace and War, are annually and constantly 1,392,857 more than we should pay, if we could raise our Shipping to be competent to the carriage of all our productions"; see *PTJ*, XIX, p. 236.

To the wars of the above Period, France was with little exception a party. So was Holland, excluding the war preceding the last. So in fact were the maritime nations in Genl.

Perhaps it may be easiest to make the calculation for all our trade in Foreign Bottoms, than for that in British alone: or expedient to superadd the former to the latter calculation.

Jefferson to Madison

[Philadelphia] Mar. 13, 1791

TH: J. TO J. M.

What say you to taking a wade into the country at noon? It will be pleasant above head at least. The party to finish by dining here. Information that Colo. Beckwith[22] is coming to be an inmate with you, and I presume not a desireable one, encourages me to make a proposition, which I did not venture as long as you had your agreeable Congressional society about you, that is, to come and take a bed and plate with me. I have 4. rooms of which any one is at your service. Three of them are up two pair of stairs, the other on the ground floor, and can be in readiness to recieve you in 24 hours. Let me intreat you, my dear Sir, to do it, if it be not disagreeable to you. To me it will be a relief from a solitude of which I have too much: and it may lessen your repugnance to be assured it will not increase my expences an atom. When I get my library open you will often find a convenience in being close at hand to it. The approaching season will render this situation more agreeable than 5th. street, and even in the winter you will find it not disagreeable.[23] Let me have I beseech you a favorable answer to both propositions.

Madison to Jefferson

[Philadelphia Mar. 13, 1791]

MY DEAR SIR

Your first proposition having been arranged, I have only in answer to your last to acknowledge that I feel all the inducements you suggest and many more to be in a situation where your society would make a part of my hourly enjoyments. In making the sacrifice therefore you will be assured that the

---

22. George Beckwith was in Philadelphia as confidential agent of Sir Guy Carleton, now Lord Dorchester, governor-general of Canada; see *ibid.*, XVII, pp. 35–39.

23. TJ's new quarters were on Market Street near Eighth, about three blocks from JM's room at Mrs. House's.

circumstances which determine me are unaffected. My stay here is so uncertain and limited that a removal would scarcely be justified by it. I am just settled in my harness for compleating the little task I have allotted myself.[24] My papers and books are all assorted around me. A change of position would necessarily give some interruption—and some trouble on my side whatever it might do on yours. Add that my leaving the house at the moment it is entered by the new member might appear more pointed than may be necessary or proper. As the weather grows better I shall however avail myself of it, to make some amends to myself for what I lose by yielding to these circumstances by seeing you more and using oftener one of your plates. Being never more happy than in partaking that hour of unbent conversation and never more sincere than in assuring you of the affection with which I am Yrs

J. MADISON JR

Madison to Jefferson

Philadelphia [ca. Apr. 18, 1791]

Substance of a Conversation held by Js. Madison Jr with Col: Beckwith, at the desire of Mr. Jefferson—[25]

Last evening offered the first opportunity of breaking to Col B—— the subject for which he has been thought a proper channel to the Governour of Canada. It was explicitly made known to him, that besides its being generally understood that the N. W. Indians were supplied with the means of war from their intercourse with Detroit etc. the President had received information, which he considered as certain, that ample supplies of that sort had, about the commencement of last campaign, been received by the hostile tribes from places at present in British hands. It was observed to him at the same time, that as the U. S. had no other object in the present war, but to effect and establish peace on their frontier, it was obvious in what light such a circumstance must be viewed by them. And as a further consideration heightening the colour of the fact, he was reminded that the Indians in question, were without an exception, inhabitants of the acknowledged territory of the U. S. and consequently stood in a certain relation to them, well understood by the nations possessing territories on this continent.

The sum of his answer was that as a fact so stated, however unaccountable

---

24. JM was probably collating his notes on the debates at the Constitutional Convention with the unpublished journal of the convention, which he had copied in 1789; see *PJM,* X, pp. 7-9, XIII, p. 406, and *PTJ,* XIX, p. 552.

25. JM met with Beckwith at TJ's request and probably enclosed this memorandum in his letter to TJ of Apr. 18, 1791, now missing. TJ informed Washington of the conversation; see TJ's letters of Apr. 17, 1791, and Apr. 24, 1791, in Ford, V, pp. 321-24.

it might be, was not to be contradicted, he could only undertake to affirm that it was impossible it could have proceeded directly or indirectly from the British Government, or even have had the sanction or countenance of the authority on the spot. He multiplied assurances that the whole spirit and policy of their Government was opposed to Indian hostilities; and that the sentiments views and orders of Lord Dorchester discouraged them as much as possible. This he knew to be the case. He asked whether there were any particulars of time place or persons contained in the information to the President; whether there was any evidence that the articles supplied were in greater quantities than were usual for other purposes than war; intimating that if there were just ground of complaint, a regular statement and communication of it in *any mode*[26] that might be thought not improper would be most correspondent with the customary proceedings in such cases. For himself he should be very ready on receiving any such statements or communications, to transmit them. He was here however not in any formal character—on the contrary in an informal one; a very informal one to be sure; and he entered into this conversation as between one private gentleman and another. He had indeed been a good while at N. York before, as well as here since the removal of the Government. He hoped his further stay wd. be rendered short by the arrival of some more authentic character. He was at N. York before Mr. Jefferson came into the office he now holds, and he believed it was known on what footing he was. Yet he had not in any respect been turned over to Mr. Jefferson, nor had any thing passed that could give him any pretensions to be in any communication with the Secretary of State. Such a communication was no doubt thought improper by the Secretary of State with so informal a character, though in a way ever so informal. He did not undertake to suppose it was not right; especially as different forms of Govts have different modes of proceedings etc.

The turn given to the conversation shewing pretty clearly a desire to make the occasion subservient to some further and direct intercourse with the Govt. it was thought proper, for that reason as well as for avoiding the necessity of another conversation to reply at once that it was not probable the information received by the President would be made known to him in any way more authentic than on the present; which it was true, as he had observed, was merely a conversation between two private gentlemen; but if the fact, that the President had received the information as stated, was made sufficiently credible, the proper effect of the communication need not depend on the mode of it. If the dispositions of Lord Dorchester were such as were described, and of which his reputation for humanity and prudence left no room to doubt, any evidence amounting to probability only would ensure all the interference that might depend on him. The conduct of Govts. towards formal and informal characters was certainly not within the compass of this conversation. It was probable however that no distinction was made by the Government here,

26. JM's italics.

which was not made by all Governments; the difference between those characters seeming to lie not in the circumstance of the former being possessed of written and the latter of verbal authority; but in the greater publicity and formality of the written credentials produced from the proper source by the former. The evident impropriety of the military supplies afforded to the Indians required no doubt that the countenance of the British Government or even the sanction of the officer on the spot ought not to be presumed as long as the fact could be otherwise explained; but as the effect of such aids was the same whether furnished by public authority or by vindictive or avaritious individuals, it was in every case to be expected that the abuse would be corrected: And the circumstance of the Indians in question being within the acknowledged limits of the U. S. and receiving the means of war agst. them from a foreign source was again brought into view as heightening the color of the affair. With respect to the particulars of the fact, they did not seem to be material. In what degree the President was possessed of them could not be said. It might be difficult to ascertain the particulars and yet the general fact be sufficiently established. As the Indians at war traded with British subjects only, their being able to carry on hostilities was of itself sufficient evidence in the case. It might be difficult also to mark precisely the line between supplies for war and for hunting; but it was probable that not only the difference of quantity demanded, but other indications, must leave little doubt of the purpose for which they were intended. . . .[27]

Col. B. professed the strongest disposition to do any thing in his power having been actuated by this disposition in all his communications to Canada, but repeatd. his wish for more exact information on the subject. The intelligence was itself so vague, and was communicated to him under such reserve, that he was really at a loss how to represent it. "May I sir mention your name in the case?" He was answered, that from the nature of the conversation he cd. be under no restraint from mentiong any circumstance relating to it he pleased. "May I Sir say that I have your permission to use your name?" Ansr. The permission being a part of the conversation, he must be equally free to mention it if he thought fit; tho' it was not perceived to be a circumstance very material. "Will you be so good Sir as to repeat the information you mentioned to have been recd. by the Presidt.?["] This request being complied with, he sd. he should certainly look out for the first opportu[nit]y of making the matter known to Lord D. and if Mr. M. shd. be here on the rect. of an answer he should be made acquainted with it, repeating his declarations that it was impossible the British Govt. cd. in any respect have countenancd or approved any supplies to the Indians as an aid or encouragement to their hostilities. *(Copy)*

J. M.

---

27. A portion of the page is missing here, "as presumably are several lines of JM's account"; see *PJM,* XIV, pp. 9-10.

Madison to Jefferson

New York May 1, 1791

DEAR SIR

Finding on my arrival at Princeton that both Docr. Witherspoon and Smith had made excursions in the Vacation, I had no motive to detain me there; and accordingly pursuing my journey I arrived here the day after I left Philada. My first object was to see Dorhman.[28] He continues to wear the face of honesty, and to profess much anxiety to discharge the claims of Mazzei; but acknowledges that all his moveable property has been brought under such fetters by late misfortunes that no part of it can be applied to that use. His cheif resource consisted of Money in London which has been attached, improperly as he says, by his brother. This calamity brought on him a protest of his bills, and this a necessity of making a compromise founded on a hypothecation of his effects. His present reliance is on an arrangement which appeals to the friendship of his brother and which he supposes his brother will not decline when recovered from the misapprehensions which led him to lay his hands on the property in London. A favorable turn of fortune may perhaps open a prospect of immediate aid to Mazzei, but as far as I can penetrate, he ought to count but little on any other resource than the ultimate security of the Western township. I expect to have further explanations however from Dorhman, and may then be better able to judge. I have seen Freneau also and given him a line to you.[29] He sets out for Philada. today or tomorrow, though it is not improbable that he may halt in N. Jersey. He is in the habit I find of translating the Leyden Gazette and consequently must be fully equal to the task you had allotted for him. He had supposed that besides this degree of skill, it might be expected that he should be able to translate with equal propriety into French: and under this idea, his delicacy had taken an insuperable objection to the undertaking. Being now set right as to this particular, and being made sensible of the advantages of Philada. over N. Jersey for his private undertaking, his mind is taking another turn; and if the scantiness of his capital should not be a bar, I think he will establish himself in the former. At all events he will give his friends there an opportunity of aiding his decision by their information and counsel. The more I learn of his character talents and principles, the more I should regret his burying himself in the obscurity he had chosen in N. Jersey. It is certain that there is not to be found in the whole catalogue of American Printers, a single name that can approach towards a rivalship.

I send you herewith a Copy of Priestley's answer to Burke which has been reprinted here. You will see by a note page 56 how your idea of limiting the right to bind posterity is germinating under the extravagant doctrines of Burke

---

28. Philip Mazzei had asked JM to press Arnold Henry Dohrman to settle his account with him.

29. Philip Freneau was considering a proposition from JM and TJ to establish an opposition newspaper in Philadelphia.

on that subject.[30] Paines answer has not yet been recd. here. The moment it can be got Freneau tells me it will be published in Child's paper. It is said that the pamphlet has been suppressed in England, and that the author withdrew to France before or immediately after its appearance. This may account for his not sending copies to his friends in this Country.[31]

From conversations which I have casually heard, it appears that among the enormities produced by the spirit of speculation and fraud, a practice is spreading, of taking out administration on the effects of deceased soldiers and other claimants leaving no representatives. By this knavery if not prevented a prodigious sum will be unsaved by the public, and reward the worst of its Citizens. A number of adventurers are already engaged in the pursuit, and as they easily get security as Administrators and as easily get a Commission on the usual suggestion of being creditors, they desire nothing more than to ascertain the name of the party deceased or missing, trusting to the improbability of their being detected or prosecuted by the public. It cannot but have happened and is indeed a fact well-understood that the unclaimed dues from the U. S. are of very great amount. What a door is here open, for collusion also if any of the Clerks in the Acct. Offices are not proof agst. the temptation!

We understood in Philada. that during the suspension of the Bank Bill in the hands of the President, its partizans here indulged themselves in reflections not very decent. I have reason to believe that the licentiousness of the tongues of speculators and Tories far exceeded any thing that was conceived. The meanest motives were charged on him, and the most insolent menaces held over him, if not in the open streets, under circumstances not less marking the character of the party.

In returning a visit to Mr. King yesterday, our conversation fell on the Conduct of G. B. towards the U. S, which he evidently laments as much as he disapproves. He took occasion to let me understand, that altho' he had been averse to the appearance of precipitancy in our measures, he should readily concur in those after all probability should be over, of voluntary relaxations in the measures of the other party; and that the next session of Congs. would present such a crisis if nothing to prevent it should intervene. He mentioned also that a young gentleman here (a son of W. Smith now Ch: Justice of Canada) gives out, as information from his friends in England that no Minister will be sent to this Country, until one shall have previously arrived there. What credit may be due to this person or his informers I do not know. It shews at least that the conversation and expectations which lately prevailed are dying away.

A thought has occurred on the subject of your mechanism for the table, which in my idle situation will supply me with another paragraph, if of no

---

30. In his reply to Edmund Burke's *Reflections on the Revolution in France,* Joseph Priestley asked, "Would it not be reasonable to fix some time, beyond which it should not be deemed right to bind posterity?"; see *PJM,* XIV, p. 18.

31. JM refers to Thomas Paine's *The Rights of Man.*

other use. The great difficulty incident to your contrivance seemed to be that of supporting the weight of the Castor without embarrassing the shortning and lengthening of the moveable radius.³² Might not this be avoided by suspending the Castor by a chain or chord on a radius above, and requiring nothing more of yours than to move the swinging apparatus: thus, A. B moveable on a shoulder at A. would be a necessary brace, and must allow C. D.

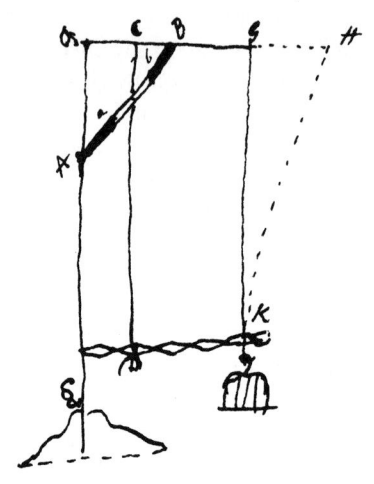

to pass thro' it and play from a. to b. as the tongs are shortned or lengthened. The use of C. D. would be to connect F. G. and the tongs, so as to make them move together on the common perpendicular axis. As the distance from C to D must vary with the protraction of the tongs, the connecting bar ought to be long accordingly, and pass through witht. being fixed to the tongs. Its office would in that state be sufficiently performed. The objections to this plan are 1. the height of the perpendicular axis necessary to render the motion of the Castor easy, and to diminish the degree in which it wd. mount up at the end of the table. Perhaps this objection may be fatal. 2. The nicety of adjusting the friction of the tongs so as not to be inconvenient to the hand, and be sufficient to stop and hold the castor at any part of the table. In this point of view perhaps a slide on a spring would be better than the tongs. In that case C. D. might be fixed, and not moveable in the brace. By projecting F. G. to H. the castor might be made to swing perpendicularly not at the part of the table least distant, but at the mean distance from the Center, and the difference between its greatest and least elevation and pressure diminished. But inconveniences of another sort might be increased by this expedient. If the tongs or slide were to be placed not horizontally, but inclining so as to lessen the effect of the pressure of the Castor without being less moveable by the hand, the 2d objection might be lessened. It wd. in that case be of less conse-

32. TJ was interested in designing a "castor" or coaster so that he could pass a tray of wine bottles around his table; see *PJM,* XIV, p. 18.

quence to project the upper radius as proposed. I am afraid you will hardly understand what I have attempted to describe, and I have not time if the thing deserved it, to write the letter over again for the present mail.

Jefferson to Madison

Philadelphia May 9, 1791

DEAR SIR

Your favor of the 1st. came to hand on the 3d. Mr. Freneau has not followed it: I suppose therefore he has changed his mind back again, for which I am really sorry. I have now before me a huge bundle of letters, the only business between me and my departure. I think I can be through them by the end of the week, in which case I will be with you by Tuesday or Wednesday, if nothing new comes in to delay me. Rittenhouse will probably not go. He says he cannot find a good horse. I shall propose to you when we tack about from the extremity of our journey, instead of coming back the same way, to cross over through Vermont to Connecticut river and down that to New-haven, then through Long-island to N. Y. and so to Philada. Be this however as you will. Our news from Virginia is principally of deaths, to wit, Colo. B. Harrison of Barclay, Turner Southall, Dixon the printer, Colo. Overton of Hanover, Walker Gilmer son of the Doctor. A Peter Randolph of Chatsworth has had a fit of madness, which he has recovered from. Wheat has suffered by drought: yet it is tolerably good, the fruit not entirely killed. At this place little new. F. Hopkinson lies at extremities with regular epileptic fits, from which they think he cannot recover. Colo. Hamilton set out to-day for Bethlehem. Have you seen the Philadelphia edn. of Paine's pamphlet?[33] You know you left Beckley's copy in my hands. He called on me for it, before I had quite finished it, and desired me when done to send it to J. B. Smith whose brother was to reprint it. When I was proceeding to send it, I found it necessary to write a note to Mr. Smith to explain why I, a perfect stranger to him, sent him the pamphlet. I mentioned it to be by the desire of Mr. Beckley, and to take off a little of the dryness of the note, added, currente calamo, that I was pleased to find it was to be reprinted here, that something was at length to be publicly said against the political heresies which had of late sprung up among us, not doubting but that our citizens would rally again round the standard of Common sense. I

---

33. Thomas Paine's *The Rights of Man.*

thought no more of this and heard no more till the pamphlet appeared to my astonishment with my note at the head of it. I never saw J. B. Smith or the printer either before or since. I had in view certainly the doctrines of Davila.[34] I tell the writer freely that he is a heretic, but certainly never meant to step into a public newspaper with that in my mouth. I have just reason therefore to think he will be displeased. Colo. Hamilton and Colo. Beckwith are open mouthed against me, taking it in another view, as likely to give offence to the court of London. H. adds further that it marks my opposition to the government. Thus endeavoring to turn on the government itself those censures I meant for the enemies of the government to wit those who want to change it into a monarchy. I have reason to think he has been unreserved in uttering these sentiments. I send you some letters recieved for you. Adieu. Your's affectionately

TH: JEFFERSON

P. S. F. Hopkinson is dead. Rittenhouse has agreed this afternoon to go with me as far as New York.

Madison to Jefferson

New York May 12, 1791

DEAR SIR

Your favor of the 9th. was recd. last evening. To my thanks for the several inclosures I must add a request that the letter to Baynton[35] which came in one of them may be handed to him by one of your servants. The directory will point out his habitation.

I had seen Payne's pamphlet with the preface of the Philada. Editor. It immediately occurred that you were brought into the Frontispiece in the manner you explain. But I had not foreseen the particular use made of it by the British partizans. Mr. Adams can least of all complain. Under a mock defence of the Republican Constitutions of this Country, he attacked them with all the force he possessed, and this in a book with his name to it whilst he was the Representative of his Country at a foreign Court.[36] Since he has been the 2d. Magistrate in the new Republic, his pen has constantly been at work in the same cause; and tho' his name has not been prefixed to his antirepublican discourses, the author has been as well known as if that formality had been observed. Surely if it be innocent and decent in one servant of the public thus to write attacks agst its Government, it can not be very criminal or indecent in

---

34. Vice President John Adams had published his "Discourses on Davila" in the Philadelphia *Gazette of the United States*.

35. Peter Baynton was a Philadelphia merchant.

36. JM had been critical of John Adams's *A Defence of the Constitutions of Government of the United States of America* since it appeared in 1787, while Adams was American minister to Great Britian.

another to patronize a written defence of the principles on which that Govt. is founded. The sensibility of H. and B.[37] to the indignity to the Brit: Court is truly ridiculous. If offence cd. be justly taken in that quarter, what would France have a right to say to Burke's pamphlet and the Countenance given to it and its author, particularly by the King himself? What in fact might not the U. S. say, whose revolution and democratic Governments come in for a large share of the scurrility lavished on those of France.

I do not foresee any objection to the route you propose. I had conversed with Beckley on a trip to Boston etc. and still have that in view; but the time in view for starting from this place, will leave room for the previous excursion. Health recreation and curiosity being my objects, I can never be out of my way.

Not a word of news here. My letters from Virginia say little more than those you had recd. Carrington says the returns have come in pretty thickly of late and warrant the estimate founded on the Counties named to me some time ago. As well as I recollect, these averaged upwards of 8000 souls, and were considered by him as under the general average. Yrs. Affecly.

Js. MADISON JR.

Jefferson to Madison

Philadelphia June 21, 1791

DEAR SIR

I arrived here on Sunday evening.[38] Yesterday I sent your note to Lieper who immediately called and paid the 200 Dollars, which I have exchanged for a post note and now inclose. I mentioned to the Atty. Gen. that I had a note on him, and afterwards sent it to him, saying nothing as to time. I inclose you also a post note for 35. Dollars to make up my deficit of expences (25.94 D.) to pay Mr. Elsworth and the smith, and also to get me from Rivington's Hamilton More's practical navigator, if his be the 6th. edn., as I believe it is.[39] This is the last edn. revised and printed under the author's eye. The later edns. are so incorrect as to be worth nothing.

The President will leave Mt. Vernon on the 27th. He will be stayed a little at Georgetown. Colo. H. Lee is here. He gives a very different account from Carrington's of the disposition of the upper country of Virginia towards the Excise law. He thinks resistance possible. I am sorry we did not bring with us

---

37. Alexander Hamilton and George Beckwith.

38. TJ and JM had just completed their tour of New York and New England, leaving on May 20 and returning to New York on June 16.

39. John Hamilton Moore, *The Practical Navigator and Seaman's New Daily Assistant,* 6th ed. (London, 1781).

some leaves of the different plants which struck our attention, as it is the leaf which principally decides *specific*[40] differences. You may still have it in your power to repair the omission in some degree. The Balsam tree at Govr. Robinson's[41] is the Balsam poplar, Populus balsamifera of Linnæus. The Azalea I can only suspect to be the Viscosa, because I find but two kinds the nudiflora Vizscosa acknoleged to grow with us, and I am sure it is not the nudiflora. The White pine is the Pinus Strobus. I will thank you if in your journey Northward you will continue the enquiries relative to the Hessian fly, and note them.[42] The post is almost on it's departure so Adieu. Your's affectionately

TH: JEFFERSON

Madison to Jefferson

New York June 23, 1791

DEAR SIR

I received your favor of the 21st. yesterday, inclosing post notes for 235 dollars. I shall obtain the bills of Mrs. Elsworth[43] and the Smith this afternoon and will let you know the amount of them. There is a bill also from the Taylor amounting to £6–7. which I shall pay. The articles for which it is due are in my hands and will be forwarded by the first opportunity. If a good one should fall within your notice, it may be well for you to double the chance of a conveyance by giving a commission for the purpose. I have applied to Rivington for the Book but the only copies in Town seem to be of the *8th. Edition*. This however is advertised as "enlarged etc. by the Author," who I am told by Berry & Rogers is now living and a correspondent of theirs. It is not improbable therefore that your reason for preferring the 6th. Ed: may be stronger in favor of this. Let me know your pleasure on the subject and it shall be obeyed.

I am at a loss what to decide as to my trip to the Eastward. My inclination has not changed, but a journey without a companion, and in the stage which besides other inconveniences travels too rapidly for my purpose, makes me consider whether the next fall may not present a better prospect. My horse is more likely to recover than at the time of your departure. By purchasing another, in case he should get well, I might avoid the Stage, but at an expence not altogether convenient.

You have no doubt seen the French Regulations on the subject of Tobo.

40. TJ's italics.
41. Moses Robinson was governor of Vermont.
42. TJ was chairman of the American Philosophical Society's committee on "the natural history of the Hessian fly"; see *PJM,* XIV, p. 35.
43. Dorothy Ellsworth (Mrs. Verdine Ellsworth) ran the boardinghouse in New York where TJ and JM stayed before leaving on their tour of upstate New York and New England; see *ibid.,* pp. 34–36.

which commence hostilities agst. the British Navigation-Act.[44] Mr. King tells me an attack on Payne has appeared in a Boston paper under the name of Publicola, and has an affinity in the stile as well as sentiments to the discourses on Davila.[45] I observed in a late paper here an extract from a Philada. Pamphlet on the Bank. If the publication has attracted or deserves notice, I should be glad of a copy from you. I will write again in a few days; In the mean time remaining Yrs. mo: affecly.

Js. Madison Jr

Madison to Jefferson

New York June 27, 1791

Dear Sir

By a Capt: Simms who setts off this afternoon in the Stage for Philadelphia I forward the Bundle of Cloaths from the Taylor. His bill is inclosed with that of Mrs. Elsworth including the payment to the Smith.

I have seen Col: Smith more than once. He would have opened his budget fully to me, but I declined giving him the trouble. He has written to the President a state of all his conversations with the British Ministry, which will get into your hands of course. He mentioned to me his wish to have put them there in the first instance and your situation on his arrival as an apology for not doing it. From the complexion of the little anecdotes and observations which dropped from him in our interviews I suspect that report has as usual far overrated the importance of what has been confided to him. General professions which mean nothing, and the sending a Minister which can be suspended at pleasure, or which if executed may produce nothing, are the amount of my present guesses.[46]

Mr. Adams seems to be getting faster and faster into difficulties.[47] His attack on Payne which I have not seen, will draw the public attention to his obnoxious principles, more than every thing he has published. Besides this, I observe in McLean's paper here, a long extract from a sensible letter republished from Poughkeepsie, which gives a very unpopular form to his antirepublican doctrines, and presents a strong contrast of them with a quotation from his letter to Mr. Wythe in 1776.

---

44. The protectionist legislation passed by the French National Assembly canceled the trade concessions negotiated by TJ, reestablished the tobacco monopoly, and levied discriminatory duties on U.S. vessels carrying tobacco; see *ibid.* p. 36.
45. "Publicola" was John Adams's son, John Quincy Adams.
46. William Stephens Smith, son-in-law of John and Abigail Adams, was appointed excise supervisor for the district of New York early in 1791 shortly after he returned from a trip to England; see *PJM*, XIV, p. 37.
47. JM at first thought that "Publicola" was John Adams.

I am still resting on my oars with respect to Boston. My Horse has had a relapse which made his recovery very improbable. Another favorable turn has taken place, and his present appeara[n]ce promises tolerably well. But it will be some time before he can be sound, if he should suffer no other check. Adieu. Yrs.

Js. MADISON JR.

Jefferson to Madison

Philadelphia June 28, 1791

DEAR SIR

Yours of the 23d. has been duly recieved. The parcel from the taylor will probably come safely by the stage. With respect to the edition of Hamilton More's book I took pains to satisfy myself of the best edition when I was in a better situation than I now am, to do it with success. The result was that the 6th. edn. was the last published under the examination of the author, and that the subsequent editions, in order to cheapen them, had been so carelessly supervised as to be full of typographical errors in the tables. I therefore prefer waiting till I can get the 6th. I learned further that after the 6th. edn. the author abandoned all attention to the work himself. I inclose you the pamphlet on the bank, and must trouble you to procure a pamphlet for me which is only in a private hand in N. York. This is a Description of the Genisee country, but more particularly of Mr. Morris's purchase of Goreham and Phelps, in 4to. with a map.[48] It was printed in London under the agency of W. T. Franklin to captivate purchasers. There is no name to it. Colo. Smith brought in 6. copies. If one of them can be drawn from him I should be very glad of it. Will you also be so good as to ask of him whether he can give me any information of the progress of the map of S. America, which he, at my request, put into the hands of an engraver.[49] The French proceedings against our tobo. and ships are very eccentric and unwise. With respect to the former however, which you consider as a *commencement*[50] of hostilities against the Brit. navign. act, it is only a continuation of the decision of the council of Berni,[51] since which the importn. of tobo. into France in any but American or French bottoms has been

---

48. See Orasmus Turner, *History of the Pioneer Settlement of Phelps and Gorham's Purchase and Morris' Reserve* (Rochester, N.Y., 1851); Paul D. Evans, *The Holland Land Company* (Buffalo, 1924); and *PJM*, XIV, p. 38. For maps, see Lester J. Cappon, Barbara B. Petchenik, and John H. Long, eds., *Atlas of Early American History: The Revolutionary Era, 1760–1790* (Princeton, 1976), p. 61.

49. E. Millicent Sowerby, *Catalogue of the Library of Thomas Jefferson*, 5 vols. (Washington, 1952–59), IV, pp. 105–6, traces TJ's efforts to get Juan de la Cruz Cano y Olmedilla's map of South America published.

50. TJ's italics.

51. Bernis was the estate of the French comptroller general of finances, Calonne; see *PJM*, XIV, p. 39.

prohibited. The Spanish as well as English proceedings against our commerce are also serious. Nobody doubts here who is the author of Publicola, any more than of Davila.[52] He is very indecently attacked in Brown's and Bache's papers. From my European letters I am inclined to think peace will take place between the Porte and Russia. The article which separates them is so minute that it will probably be got over, and the war is so unpopular in England that the ministers will probably make that an excuse to the K. of Prussia for not going all lengths with him. His only object is Thorn and Dantzic, and he has secretly intimated at Petersbg. that if he could be accomodated with this he would not be tenacious against their keeping Oczakoff. This has leaked out, and is working duly in Poland. I think the President will contrive to be on the road out of the reach of ceremony till after the 4th. of July. Adieu my dear Sir. Your's affectionately

TH: JEFFERSON

Madison to Jefferson

New York July 1, 1791

DEAR SIR

I recd. yesterday your's of the 28th. and this morning called on Col: Smith from whom I obtained the pamphlet and map, herewith inclosed. The former you are to keep. The latter being the last copy is to be sent back to him after satisfying yourself with it. With respect to the Map of S. America he says that it was obtained from the Engraver by Pitt and Grenville during the squabble with Spain, and remained in their hands for that period as the best geographical information to be had; that it has since been returned to him according to promise, is about ⅔ engraved, and will probably be out this fall.

Inclosed also is a letter from Havre containing an account of the price of Tobo. which perhaps you may not have seen and which it may not be amiss for Leiper to see.

I have been somewhat indisposed for several days with a fever attended with pretty decided symptoms of bile. It has confined me to the House tho' not to my room. I find myself better today, particularly in being relieved from a nausea and irritation in the stomach which were the more disagreeable as they threatened a more serious attack. I now hope though I have still a slight fever and loss of appetite that the cause is a fugitive one, and that the effects are going off. My horse seems to have got out of danger, but has much flesh to regain. I send a little of the true guinea Corn from Jamaica where it forms a great proportion of the food of the Slaves. It grows on the top of the Stalk like broom Corn, and in a figure not unlike a bunch of Sumac berries. This is the

---

52. Like JM, TJ at first thought that "Publicola" was John Adams, not John Quincy Adams.

first time I have seen the grain, tho' it may be familiar to you. The small-eared corn which I have seen in Virginia under the same name is a very different thing. Yrs. mo: affecly.

Js. Madison Jr.

Jefferson to Madison

Philadelphia July 6, 1791

Dear Sir

I have duly recieved your favours of June 27. and July 1. The last came only this morning. I now return Colo. Smith's map with my acknolegements for the pamphlet and sight of the map. I inclose you a 60. Dollar bill, and beg the favor of you to remit 30. Dollars with the inclosed letter to Prince,[53] also, as I see maple sugar, *grained,*[54] advertised for sale at New York in boxes of 400 lb. each, if they can be induced to sell 100 lb only and to pack and send it to Richmond, I will thank you to get it done for me. The box to be directed to me 'to the care of James Brown, mercht. Richmd. to be forwarded to Monticello.' You see I presume on your having got over your indisposition; if not, I beg you to let all this matter rest till you are. Colo. Harry Lee thinks of going on tomorrow, to accompany you to Portsmouth, but he was not quite decided when I saw him last. The President arrived about 10. minutes ago, but I have not yet seen him. I recieved safely the packet by capt Sims. The Guinea corn is new to me, and shall be taken care of. My African upland rice is flourishing. I inclose you a paper estimating the shares of the bank as far as was known three days before it opened. When it opened 24,600 subscriptions were offered, being 4,600 more than could be recieved, and many persons left in the lurch, among these Robt. Morris and Fitzsimmons. They accuse the Directors of a misdeal, and the former proposes to sue them, the latter to haul them up before Congress. Every 25 dollars actually deposited, sold yesterday for from 40. to 50. dollars with the future rights and burthens annexed to the deposit. We have no authentic news from Europe since the last packet. Adieu my dear Sir, take care of yourself and let me hear soon that you are quite re-established. Your's affectionately

Th: Jefferson

P. S. If you leave N. York, will you leave directions with Mr. Elsworth to forward to me the two parcels of Maple seed, and that of the Birch bark respectively as they arrive. The last I think had better come by water.

---

53. TJ visited William Prince's nursery at Flushing, New York, in June and ordered sixty sugar maple trees. For his additional order of July 6 and Prince's shipment of trees, roses, and rhodedendra, see Edwin Morris Betts, ed., *Thomas Jefferson's Garden Book, 1766–1824,* . . . (Philadelphia, 1944), pp. 166–69.

54. TJ's italics.

ENCLOSURE
The capital stock of the bank, ten millions of dollars, divided into 25,000 shares.

	shares
to be subscribed by the President	5,000
already subscribed, Boston	4,000
" New York	6,400
will be subscribed by Philada.	5,000
already subscribed, Baltimore	2,400
" Charleston	700
	23,500
remains to be subscribed	1,500
	25,000

Madison to Jefferson

New York July 10, 1791

DEAR SIR

Your favor of the 6th. came to hand on friday. I went yesterday to the person who advertised the Maple Sugar for the purpose of executing your commission on that subject. He tells me that the cargo is not yet arrived from Albany, but is every hour expected; that it will not be sold in parcels of less than 15 or 16 hundred lb. and only at Auction, but that the purchasers will of course deal it out in smaller quantities; that a part is grained and part not; and that the price of the former will probably be regulated by that of good Muscavado which sells at about £5. N. Y. Currency, a Ct. I shall probably be at Flushing in two or three days and have an opportunity of executing your other Commission on the spot. In case of disappointment, I shall send the Letter and money to Prince by the best conveyance to be had. The Maple seed is not arrived. The Birch-Bark has been in my hands some days and will be forwarded as you suggest.

The Bank-Shares have risen as much in the Market here as at Philadelphia. It seems admitted on all hands now that the plan of the institution gives a moral certainty of gain to the Subscribers with scarce a physical possibility of loss. The subscriptions are consequently a mere scramble for so much public plunder which will be engrossed by those already loaded with the spoils of indi[vi]duals. The event shews what would have been the operation of the plan, if, *as originally proposed,* [55] subscriptions had been limited to the 1st. of april and to the favorite species of stock which the Bank-Jobbers had monopo-

---

55. JM's italics.

lized. It pretty clearly appears also in what proportions the public debt lies in the Country—What sort of hands hold it, and by whom the people of the U. S. are to be governed. Of all the shameful circumstances of this business, it is among the greatest to see the members of the Legislature who were most active in pushing this Jobb, openly grasping its emoluments. Schuyler is to be put at the Head of the Directors, if the weight of the N. Y. subscribers can effect it.[56] Nothing new is talked of here. In fact stockjobbing drowns every other subject. The Coffee House is in an eternal buzz with the gamblers.

I have just understood that Freneau is now here and has abandoned his Philada. project. From what cause I am wholly unable to divine: unless those who know his talents and hate his political principles should have practised some artifice for the purpose.

I have given up for this season my trip Eastward. My bilious situation absolutely forbade it. Several lesser considerations also conspired with that objection. I am at present free from a fever, but have sufficient evidence, in other shapes, that I must adhere to my defensive precautions.

The pamphlet on Weights etc. was put into my hands by Docr. Kemp[57] with a view to be forwarded after perusal to you. As I understand it is a duplicate and to be kept by you. Always and mo: affecly. Yrs.

Js. Madison Jr.

Jefferson to Madison

Philadelphia July 10, 1791

My dear Sir

Your indisposition at the date of your last, and hearing nothing from you since, make me fear it has continued. The object of the present is merely to know how you do, and from another hand, if you are not well enough. We have little new but what you will see in the public papers. You see there the swarm of anti-publicolas. The disavowal by a Printer only does not appear to satisfy. We have no news yet of the event of Scott's expedition.[58] The Marquis Fayette has certainly resumed his command and on a ground which must strengthen him and also the public cause. The subscriptions to the bank from Virginia were almost none. Pickett, Mclurg, and Dr. Lee are the only names I have heard mentioned. This gives so much uneasiness to Colo. H. that he

---

56. Philip Schuyler, Hamilton's father-in-law, was a U.S. senator from New York.

57. John Kemp, professor of mathematics at Columbia College, had helped TJ when the latter wrote his "Report on Weights and Measures"; see *PTJ*, XVI, pp. 607, 614.

58. Brigadier General Charles Scott led an expedition from Kentucky against the Indians on the Wabash River; see Paul Prucha, *The Sword of the Republic: The United States Army on the Frontier, 1783–1846* (New York, 1969), p. 24, and Harry M. Ward, *Charles Scott and the "Spirit of 1776"* (Charlottesville, 1988), pp. 108–14.

thinks to propose to the President to sell some of the public shares to subscribers from Virga. and N. Carolina, if any more should offer. This partiality would offend the other states without pleasing those two: for I presume they would rather the capitals of their citizens should be employed in commerce than be locked up in a strong box here: nor can sober thinkers prefer a paper medium at 13 per cent interest to gold and silver for nothing. Adieu my dear friend. Yours affectionately

TH: JEFFERSON

P. S. Osgood is resigning the Postmaster's place. I shall press Paine for it.

Madison to Jefferson

New York July 13, 1791

DEAR SIR

I received last evening your kind enquiries after my health. My last will have informed you of the state of it then. I continue to be incommoded by several different shapes taken by the bile; but not in a degree that can now be called serious. If the present excessive heat should not augment the energy of the cause, I consider myself as in a good way to get rid soon of its effects.

Beckley has just got back from his Eastern trip. He says that the partizans of Mr. Adam's heresies in that quarter are perfectly insignificant in point of number—that particularly in Boston he is become distinguished for his unpopularity—that Publicola is probably the manufacture of his son out of materials furnished by himself—and that the publication is generally as obnoxious in New England as it appears to be in Pennsylvania. If young Adams be capable of giving the dress in which publicola presents himself, it is very probable he may have been made the Editor of his Father's doctrines. I hardly think the Printer would so directly disavow the fact if Mr. Adams was himself the writer. There is more of method also in the arguments, and much less of clumsiness and heaviness in the stile, than characterize his writings. I mentioned to you some time ago an extract from a piece in the Poughkepsie paper, as a sensible comment on Mr. Adams' doctrines. The whole has since been republished here, and is evidently from a better pen, than any of the Anti-publicolas I have seen. In Greenleafs paper of today is a second letter from the same quarter, which confirms the character I have given of the author.

We understand here that 800 shares in the Bank committed by this City to Mr. Constable,[59] have been excluded by the manner in which the business was conducted—that a considerable number from Boston met with the same fate—and that Baltimore has been kept out in toto. It is all charged on the

---

59. William Constable was a land speculator who tried to sell his lands abroad, especially in France; see A. M. Sakolski, *The Great American Land Bubble* (New York, 1932), pp. 63–68.

manœuvers of Philada. which is said to have secured a majority of the whole to herself. The disappointed individuals are clamorous of course, and the language of the place marks a general indignation on the subject. If it should turn out that the cards were packed, for the purpose of securing the game to Philada. or even that more than half the Institution and of course the whole direction of it have fallen into the hands of that City some who have been loudest in their plaudits whilst they expected to share in the plunder, will be equally so in sounding the injustice of the monopoly, and the danger of undue influence on the Government.

The Packet is not yet arrived. By a vessel arived yesterday newspapers are recd. from London which are said to be later than any yet come to hand. I do not find that any particular facts of moment are handed out. The miscellaneous articles come to me thro' Childs' paper, which you get sooner than I could rehearse to you. It has been said here by the Anglicans that the President's Message to Congs. on the subject of the commercial disposition of G. B. has been asserted openly by Mr. Pitt to be misrepresentation—and as it would naturally be traced to Govr. Morris it has been suggested that he fell into the hands of the Chevr. Luzerne who had the dexterity to play off his negociations for French purposes.[60] I have reason to believe that B—ck—th[61] —has had a hand in throwing these things into circulation. I wish you success with all my heart in your efforts for Payne. Besides the advantage to him which he deserves, an appointment for him, at this moment would do public good in various ways. Always and truly yours

Js. Madison Jr.

Jefferson to Madison

Philadelphia July 21, 1791

My dear Sir

Your favors of July 10. and 13. have been duly recieved and I now return the pamphlet inclosed in the latter, with thanks for the perusal. The author has the appearance of knowing better what has past in England than in America. As to the latter to be sure he has been ignorant enough. I am sincerely sorry that Freneau has declined coming here. Tho' the printing business be sufficiently full here, yet I think he would have set out on such advantageous ground as to have been sure of success. His own genius in the first place is so superior to that of his competitors. I should have given him the perusal of all

---

60. Gouverneur Morris, who was a business partner of William Constable, had recently gone from France to London, where the chevalier de la Luzerne was French ambassador; see *PJM,* XIV, p. 47.

61. At a later time, JM wrote out "Beckwith."

my letters of foreign intelligence and all foreign newspapers; the publication of all proclamations and other public notices within my department, and the printing of the laws, which added to his salary would have been a considerable aid. Besides this, Fenno's being the only weekly or half weekly paper, and under general condemnation for it's toryism and it's incessant efforts to overturn the government, Freneau would have found that ground as good as unoccupied. P——e[62] will not be appointed to the place I had recommended him for. I have a letter from Mazzei asking informn. of his affairs. I must therefore ask from you the letter you were to write me as to Dohrman. He desires to be affectionately remembered to you. He is declared, with the consent of the Diet, Chargé des affaires of the king and nation.[63] No news yet from Genl Scott. Mr. Randolph writes me that our harvest is safely in in general, that the quantity will be half as much again as the acre usually yeilds, and the quality of first rate.[64] The price offered is 5/6 at Richmd. Tobo. there is still 18/ to 20/. I have European letters and papers to the 8th. of May. The Empress has notified the English factory in Russia, that the peace between her and Gr. Britain is likely to be broken, but knowing their good conduct they shall be welcome to remain in her domns., she pays a compliment to the British nation, and says she considers it only as a war with their ministers. Denmark has made a warm offer of mediating alone. Prussia has notified the Porte that they are free to conclude a peace with Russia without any mediation, and that it will not be disagreeable to him. But the Porte has refused to relinquish the mediation of Prussia and England, and has also declined accepting that offered by Spain. France is going on steadily with it's work. On the 7th. of May a report of a commee. was given in to the assembly, confirming their former plan as to the mode of settling the constn. of their colonies, adding further that the Colonies should have the initiative (exclusively) as to the condition of the people of colour, and that each colony should send deputies to the French part of St. Martins to a Congress which should propose a general form of constitution. This was ordered to be printed and taken up at a future day, and there was some symptom of a disposition in the Assembly to over-rule the report so far as it related to the *condition*[65] of the people of colour. Comparing the date of this with the news said by the gazettes to have arrived at St. Domingo July 1. I cannot help suspending my belief of the latter.

I hope your health is better established. Your friends here anxiously enquire after it. Your letters now therefore are doubly interesting, and very feelingly so to Dear Sir your affectionate friend and servt.

Th: Jefferson

62. Thomas Paine.
63. Mazzei had been appointed chargé d'affaires in Paris by King Stanisław II of Poland.
64. Thomas Mann Randolph was TJ's son-in-law.
65. TJ's italics.

Madison to Jefferson

New York July 24, 1791

DEAR SIR

Your favor of the 21st. came to hand last evening. It was meant that you should keep the pamphlet inclosed in it. I have seen Freneau, and, as well as Col: H. Lee, have pressed the establishment of himself in Philada. where alone his talents can do the good or reap the profit of which they are capable. Though leaning strongly agst. the measure, under the influence of little objections which his modesty magnified into important ones, he was less decided on the subject than I had understood. We are to have a further conversation, in which I shall renew my efforts, and do not despair, though I am not sanguine, of success. If he yeilds to the reasoning of his friends, it is probable that he will at least commence his plan in alliance with Childs as to the emoluments. In the conduct and title of the paper, it will be altogether his own. I am not much disappointed tho' I much regret the rejection of P――e in the late appointment. Another opportunity of doing him some justice may not occur, and at the present moment it was to be wished for a thousand reasons that he might have received from this Country such a token of its affection and respect. I must see Dorhman again before I can enable you to answer Mazzei. I will endeavor to do it tomorrow and will write you without delay.

You will recollect that the Pretensions of T. C.[66] to the place now filled by Wolcot,[67] went thro' your hands and with my knowledge. Would you believe that this circumstance has got into circulation in the shape of an attempt in you and myself to intermeddle with the Treasury department, to frustrate the known wishes of the head of it, and to keep back the lineal successor, from a Southern antipathy to his Eastern descent! Col: Lee got hold of the Report and finding that it had made some impression on Hamilton, asked of me an explanation of the matter. As far as I could call to mind, what had left so faint an impression, I enabled him to contradict the misrepresentation. Last evening a favorable opportunity offering, I touched on the subject to Col: Hamilton, who had certainly viewed it thro' a very wrong medium, but seemed disposed to admit the right one. I believe he is now satisfied that misrepresentations had been made to him, that our agency, if to be so called was the effect of complaisance rather than of solicitude for or agst. the candidates—and particularly that it was impossible from the very nature of the case, it could have involved the idea of thwarting his purposes in his own department. This is not the only instance I find in which the most uncandid and unfounded things of a like tendency have been thrown into circulation.

66. Tench Coxe.
67. Oliver Wolcott, Jr., had recently been appointed comptroller of the treasury.

I promised a gentleman who lately sailed for Halifax on his way to England, to send him a copy of the Remarks on Shuffields Book.[68] May I trouble you to send to Cary's or wherever may be proper for a Copy, and let me have it in the course of the week, the earlier the better. I shall endeavor to convey it by the hands of some passenger in the Packet which sails early next week. Will you be so good also as just to let the inclosed letter on the subject of Mr. N. Pendleton be handed to Mr. Lear as from me. He will of course let the President see the pretensions of that gentleman, and I shall then have sufficiently discharged the trust consigned to me by his Unkle.[69] This is the mode in which I have generally conveyed applications to the President.

My health is much improved by the precautions I have observed. From the state of my appetite I hope I have got pretty much rid of my bile. My horse is also nearly well. He has had a third relapse, and there are still remains of the tumor as well as of his leanness. I have already asked when you think of setting out for Virginia. I mean to join you whenever you are ready, and shall be in Philada. in due time for the purpose. Always and mo: affecty. Yours

Js. Madison Jr

Jefferson to Madison

Philadelphia July 24, 1791

My dear Sir

Yours of the 21st. came to hand yesterday. I will keep my eye on the advertisements for Halifax. The time of my journey to Virginia is rendered doubtful by the incertainty whether the President goes there or not. It is rather thought he will not. If so, I shall go later and stay a shorter time. I presume I may set out about the beginning of September, and shall hope your company going and coming. The President is indisposed with the same blind tumour, and in the same place, which he had the year before last in New York. As yet it does not promise either to suppurate or be discussed.[70] He is obliged to lye constantly on his side, and has at times a little fever. The young grandson has had a long and dangerous fever.[71] He is thought better to-day. No news yet from Genl Scott: nor any thing from Europe worth repeating. Several merchants from Richmond (Scotch, English etc.) were here lately. I suspect it

---

68. Tench Coxe, *A Brief Examination of Lord Sheffield's Observations on the Commerce of the United States of America*, was first published in the *American Museum* magazine between Apr. and July 1791 before being issued as a pamphlet. For a penetrating analysis, see Cooke, pp. 201–10.
69. Edmund Pendleton to JM, July 13, 1791, recommended Nathaniel Pendleton, Jr., of Georgia for an appointment to the U.S. Supreme Court; see *PJM*, XIV, p. 48.
70. This archaic usage of "discussed" means "to dissipate, dispel, or disperse"; see *ibid.*, p. 56.
71. George Washington Parke Custis.

was to dabble in federal filth. Let me hear of your health. Adieu my dear Sir. Yours affectionately

TH: JEFFERSON

P. S. The inclosed are for yourself, being duplicates.

Madison to Jefferson

New York July 26, 1791

DEAR SIR

I am just in possession of your favor of the 24 inst: and thank you for the pamphlet which I shall look over without delay. Mr. Dorhman has this moment handed me a letter to Mazzei which will give him the change of prospect as to the balance of the debt. I really believe D's misfortune to have been great and real. Mazzei must rest contented with his ultimate security in the land which I consider as satisfactory. It probably could not at this moment be converted into money at all; and certainly not without an absolute sacrifice of D's interest. The maple sugar was principally bought by the manufacturers to be refined. After some research I have found a parcel from which you can be supplied. But the quality is so far below the standard formd by my imagination, that I inclose a sample in order to have your own decision on the case. The price is £3-8. N. Y. Currency. Nothing New. Yrs. Mo: Affy.

JS. MADISON JR

Jefferson to Madison

Philadelphia July 27, 1791

MY DEAR SIR

I inclose you the pamphlet desired in your's of July 24. Also the one on Weights and measures recieved through you, of which having another copy, be pleased to keep it. In turning over some papers I came across my journal through France, and Italy, and fancied you might be willing to acquire of that country a knowlege at second hand which you refuse to acquire at the first. It is written in the way you seemed to approve on our journey. I gave E. P's letter to Mr. Lear. I write to Mazzei by a vessel which sails on Monday; so shall hope to hear from you by that time. Nobody could know of T. C's application but himself, H. you and myself. Which of the four was most likely to give it out at all, and especially in such a form? Which of the four would feel an inclination to excite an opinion that you and myself were hostile to every thing not Southern? The President is much better. An incision has been made, and a kind suppuration is brought on. If Colo. Lee be with you present my respects to him. Adieu. Yours affectionately

TH: JEFFERSON

P. S. Dispatches from Genl Scott confirm the newspaper accts of his success, except that he was not wounded.

Jefferson to Madison

Philadelphia July 28, 1791

MY DEAR SIR

I this moment recieve yours of the 26th. The sugar of which you inclose a sample would by no means answer my purpose, which was to send it to Monticello, in order, by a proof of it's quality, to recommend attention to the tree to my neighbors. In my letter of yesterday I forgot to tell you there is a brig here to sail for Halif[a]x in 10. days. She is under repair, and therefore may possibly protract her departure. Adieu. Your's affectionately

TH: JEFFERSON

Madison to Jefferson

New York Friday [July 29, 1791]

DEAR SIR

I have this instant recd. yours of the 27th. in which you refer to as inclosed the pamphlet desired by me—to wit T. Coxes answer to Sheffield: As it is not inclosed I snatch this sudden oppty. to request you to forward it by Monday's mail. I thank you for the other inclosures and have only time to add that I am Sir,

JS. MADISON JR.

Madison to Jefferson

New York July 31, 1791

MR [sic] DEAR SIR

I recd. yours of the 28th. last evening. Your preceding one covering among other things your memorandums through France was acknowledged by a few lines put into the hands of a young gentleman bound to Philada. in the Stage of yesterday. The purpose of them was to apprize you that you had omitted Coxe's answer to Sheffield and to request the favor of you to send it by Monday's mail. Should the bearer have failed in his trust I take the liberty of repeating the request. I should be glad to have the pamphlet on Tuesday, but if forwarded after the receipt of this it may possibly be in time, especially if one of your young men should light on a passenger for Wednesday's Stage that runs thro' in one day. I do not wish however any trouble to be taken in enquiring for such a conveyance, and am really sorry that so much in so trifling a matter should have been given to yourself.

Col: H. Lee left this a day or two ago. He will probably mention to you the comments circulated as to the affair of the Comptroller. It is a little singular no doubt that so serious a face should have been put on it by —— who ought to have known the circumstances which explained the nature of the interference complained of. He referred in his conversation with me, to another candidate whom he could not properly name, as the channel thro' which he had recd. his wrong impressions.

I am running over your memorandums; but I find that to enjoy the pleasure fully I must repeat them with a Map of France before me, which I cannot at present command. Yrs. Mo: Affecly.

Js. MADISON JR

Jefferson to Madison

Philadelphia Aug. 3, 1791

DEAR SIR

Your favours of July 31. and Aug. 1. are recieved, but not that of the 30th.[72] which was trusted to a private hand. Having discovered on Friday evening only that I had not inclosed Coxe's pamphlet, I sent it off immediately to the post office. However I suppose it did not leave this place till the post of Monday nor get to your hands till Tuesday evening.

Colo. Lee is here still, and gives me hopes of your coming on soon. The President is got well. If he goes to mount Vernon at all it will be about the beginning of October. However I must go a month sooner. One of my carriage horses is dangerously ill, and become in a few days death-poor and broke out full of sores. I fear his situation portends a difficulty. I inclose you the map belonging to my journal, being the one I had in my pocket during the journey. Adieu, my dear Sir. Your's affectly.

TH: JEFFERSON

72. Letter not found.

Madison to Jefferson

New York Aug. 4, 1791

MY DEAR SIR

It being probable that I shall leave this place early in the ensuing week I drop you an intimation of it, that you may keep back any letters that may fall into your hands for me, or that you might intend to favor me with.

The outward bound packet for Halifax and London sailed to day. The one expected for some time past is not yet arrived, and I do not learn that any foreign news is recd. thro' any other channel. Stock and script continue to be the sole domestic subjects of conversation. The former has mounted in the late sales above par, from which a superficial inference would be drawn that the rate of interest had fallen below 6 PerCt. It is a fact however which explains the nature of these speculations, that they are carried on with money borrowed at from 2½ PrCt. a month to 1 PrCt a week. Adieu. Yrs. mo: Affecly.

JS. MADISON JR

Madison to Jefferson

New York Aug. 8, 1791

MY DEAR SIR

I take the liberty of putting the inclosed into your hands that in case Col: Lee should have left Philada. the contents may find their way to Col: Fisher who is most interested in them.[73] And I leave it open for the same purpose. The Attorney will be a fit channel in the event of Col: Lee's departure, for conveying the information.

You will find an allusion to some mysterious cause for a phænomenon in the stocks. It is surmized that the deferred debt is to be taken up at the next session, and some anticipated provision made for it.[74] This may either be an invention of those who wish to sell: or it may be a reality imparted in confidence to the purchasers or smelt out by their sagacity. I have had a hint that something is intended and has dropt from —— —— which has led to this speculation. I am unwilling to credit the fact, untill I have further evidence, which I am in a train of getting if it exists. It is said that packet boats and expresses are again sent from this place to the Southern States, to buy up the paper of all sorts which has risen in the market here. These and other abuses

---

73. Henry Lee's letter enclosed a diagnosis of a urinary ailment suffered by Colonel Daniel Fisher of Greensville County, Virginia, who was then in Philadelphia; see *PJM,* XIV, pp. 63–65, 69.

74. The Funding Act of 1790 deferred one-third of the national debt until 1800, paying interest during the period but promising redemption at face value "whenever provision shall be made by law for that purpose"; see *ibid.,* p. 70.

make it a problem whether the system of the old paper under a bad Government, or of the new under a good one, be chargeable with the greater substantial injustice. The true difference seems to be that by the former the few were the victims to the many; by the latter the many to the few. It seems agreed on all hands now that the bank is a certain and gratuitous augmentation of the capitals subscribed, in a proportion of not less than 40 or 50 PerCt. and if the deferred debt should be immediately provided for in favor of the purchasers of it in the deferred shape, and since the unanimous vote that no change should be made in the funding system,[75] my imagination will not attempt to set bounds to the daring depravity of the times. The stockjobbers will become the pretorian band of the Government, at once its tool and its tyrant; bribed by its largesses, and overawing it, by clamours and combinations.

Nothing new from abroad. I shall not be in Philada. till the close of the Week. Adieu Yrs. Mo: affy.

Js. MADISON JR.

Madison to Jefferson

New York Aug. 16, 1791[76]

DEAR SIR

Since I learnt that you are not to start for Virginia till the beginning of next month, I have been less in a hurry to shift myself to Philada. from this place, which I have reason to believe the more favorable of the two at this season, to my health, as well as the more agreeable in the present state of the weather. I now propose to suspend my departure till Monday next, and have therefore to ask the favor of you if this should get to hand in time, to forward any letters you may have recd. for me by Friday's mail.

You intimated some time ago that one of your horses was ill and might retard the journey to Virga. Mine is now recovered, and can take his place. Matthew, whom I have no desire to carry with me, will remain in Philada. till my return.

I just hear that the British packet is arrived. From the time of her passage, she can bring nothing new, nor is any thing of that sort supplied here from any other quarter. Adieu My dear Sir, yrs. affey,

Js. MADISON JR.

---

75. Although it was not unanimous, Congress had passed a resolution by a vote of 53 to 2 on Feb. 24, 1791, declaring "that it would be inexpedient to alter the system for funding the public debt"; see *ibid*.

76. This letter, which is listed as "not found" in *PJM*, XIV, and *PTJ*, XXII, was called to my attention in 1988 by John Catanzariti, editor of *PTJ*.

Jefferson to Madison

Philadelphia Aug. 18, 1791

MY DEAR SIR

I have just now recieved your favor of the 16th. and tho late at night I scribble a line that it may go by the morning's post. I inclose you two letters which have been awaiting you here several days. Also a copy of the census which I had made out for you. What is in red ink is conjectural, the rest from the real returns. The return of Virginia is come in this day, seven hundred and forty odd thousand, of which 296,000 blacks, both exclusive of Kentucky.

Try to arrive here on Tuesday time enough (say by 4 a clock) to come and dine with E. Randolph, Ross etc. half a dozen in all en petite comité. I have been much pleased with my acquaintance with the last. He is a sensible merchant, an enemy to gambling and all tricks of finance.[77]

My horse will certainly die from all accounts. He is out at pasture to see what fresh air and grass will do. Yours will be a fortunate aid. I have written to Mr. Randolph to look out for one to bring me back. I set out on Monday fortnight at the latest; but will try to be off some days sooner. I shall be obliged to meet the President at the sale at George town Octob. 17.[78] All your acquaintances are perpetually asking if you are arrived. It has been the first question from the President every time I have seen him for this fortnight. If you had arrived before dinner to-day, I had strong charge to carry you there. Come on then and make us all happy. Adieu my dear friend. Yours affectionately,

TH: JEFFERSON

Jefferson to Madison

[Philadelphia] Friday Aug. 26, [1791]

TH: J. TO J. M.

Will you come and sit an hour before dinner to-day? also take soup with me tomorrow?

Since writing the above the President has been here, and left L'Enfant's plan, with a wish that you and I would examine it together immediately, as to certain matters, and let him know the result. As the plan is very large, will you walk up and examine it here?[79]

---

77. John Ross was a successful merchant and shipowner who had emigrated from Scotland in 1767; see *PJM*, V, p. 204.
78. The first sale of lots in the federal district was set for this date.
79. See the detailed study by Kenneth R. Bowling, *The Creation of Washington,, D.C.: The Idea and Location of the American Capital* (Lanham, Md., 1990), for the most recent appraisal of the roles played by Jefferson, Madison, and Washington in this endeavor.

16

PARTY CONFLICTS, 1791–1792

WHEN JEFFERSON AND MADISON completed their trip through New York and New England, Madison was in better health than Jefferson had ever seen him. But the blistering summer of 1791 "brought on some bilious dispositions,"[1] and Madison lingered in New York until late August. Washington, Jefferson, and others in Philadelphia missed him. "All your acquaintances are perpetually asking if you are arrived," Jefferson wrote. "It has been the first question from the President every time I have seen him for this fortnight. If you had arrived before dinner to-day, I had [a] strong charge to carry you there. Come on then and make us all happy."[2]

Madison reached Philadelphia on August 24, in time to join Jefferson for their trip to Virginia. Before they left, however, the president asked them to review Major L'Enfant's plan for the new capital, and Madison walked over to Jefferson's place, accepting his invitation to "come and sit an hour before dinner."[3] Early in September, the Virginians headed home after Jefferson had attached a new odometer to his carriage to measure the miles along the route. They stopped in Georgetown to inspect progress on the capital-city plan, then took the last lap of their journey through Fauquier and Culpeper counties. The rough road—Jefferson called the countryside "hilly, stumpy . . . frog-eaten, stony"—was too much for the odometer, which had already required repairs costing fifty cents.[4]

After a month on his mountaintop in early autumn, Jefferson and his younger daughter Polly picked up Madison for the trip to Mt. Vernon, where they met the president and Mrs. Washington. Together they attended the first sale of lots in the new capital on October 17. Then Polly joined the Washingtons in the presidential carriage, while Jefferson and Madison rode in the

---

1. TJ to James Monroe, July 10, 1791, in *PTJ,* XX, p. 297.
2. TJ to JM, Aug. 18, 1791, above.
3. TJ to JM, Aug. 26, 1791, above.
4. Brant, III, pp. 343–44.

secretary of state's phaeton. After traveling "through five days of a North East storm," they arrived in Philadelphia on October 22, 1791, only two days before Congress convened.[5]

Their return coincided with the establishment of Freneau's *National Gazette*, and Madison immediately began to contribute short, unsigned essays on a variety of political questions. Some were scholarly discussions of political economy on such topics as population and emigration, money, and property rights. The latter was a brief but brilliant analysis of the Lockean principle of property that equated "the rights of property, and the property in [human] rights." He noted that "government is instituted to protect property of every sort; as well that which lies in the various rights of individuals, as that which the term particularly expresses." Thus:

a man has a property in his opinions and the free communication of them.

He has property of peculiar value in his religious opinions, and in the profession and practice dictated by them.

He has a property very dear to him in the safety and liberty of his person.

He has an equal property in the free use of his faculties and free choice of the objects on which to employ them.

In a word, as a man is said to have a right to his property, he may be equally said to have a property in his rights.

Other essays were more pointedly political and partisan. One dealt with the inevitability of parties in every political society, particularly in a republican system. They arose naturally out of "a difference of interests, real or supposed," and could best be utilized "by making one party a check on the other, so far as the existence of parties cannot be prevented, nor their views accommodated." But natural distinctions should not be confounded with artificial distinctions such as those made possible "by pampering the spirit of speculation within and without the government," the promotion of "unnecessary accumulations of debt of the Union," and "arbitrary interpretations and insidious precedents" that perverted "the limited government of the Union into a government of unlimited discretion." Without naming Hamilton, Madison blasted his policies as being based on "principles of monarchy and aristocracy, in opposition to the republican principles of the Union, and the republican spirit of the people."[6]

As party strife heated up in the summer of 1792, Madison's essays took on a sharper tone. In "A Candid State of Parties," he observed that the recent

---

5. *Ibid.*, p. 344; TJ to Thomas Mann Randolph, Oct. 25, 1791, in *PTJ*, XXII, p. 233. For the early development of Washington, see John W. Reps, *Washington on View: The Nation's Capital since 1790* (Chapel Hill, 1991).

6. JM's essays from Nov. 19, 1791, through Dec. 22, 1792, are in *PJM*, XIV, pp. 110–427 *passim*. The essay "Property" is on pp. 266–68, the essay "Parties" on pp. 197–98, and the essay "The Union: Who Are Its Real Friends" on pp. 274–75. For brief discussions, see Brant, III, pp. 346–48, and Ketcham, pp. 327–31. For a fuller discussion, see Colleen A. Sheehan, "Madison's Party Press Essays," *Interpretation: A Journal of Political Philosophy* 3d ser., 17 (1990): 355–77.

differences over administration policies had created a party division, "which being natural to most political societies, is likely to be of some duration in ours." The antirepublican party, he argued, "consists of those, who from particular interest, from natural temper, or from habits of life, are more partial to the opulent than to the other classes of society; and having debauched themselves into a persuasion that mankind are incapable of governing themselves, it follows with them, of course, that government can be carried on only by the pagentry of rank, the influence of money and emoluments, and the terror of military force. Men of these sentiments must naturally wish to point the measures of government less to the interest of the many than of a few, and less to the reason of the many than to their weaknesses; hoping . . . that by giving such a turn to the administration, the government itself may by degrees be narrowed into fewer hands, and approximated to an hereditary form."

Boldly terming the other division "the Republican party," Madison said that it "consists of those who believing in the doctrine that mankind are capable of governing themselves, and hating hereditary power as an insult to the reason and an outrage to the rights of man, are naturally offended at every public measure that does not appeal to the understanding and to the general interest of the community, or that is not strictly conformable to the principles, and conducive to the preservation of republican government."[7]

Just as Madison's partisanship hardened in 1792, so, too, did the animosities between Jefferson and Hamilton, when President Washington first brought his department heads together collectively as his cabinet.[8] There, the rivalry between Jefferson and Hamilton often flared as they faced each other "like cocks in a pit," as Jefferson later phrased it. One of the basic conflicts between the secretaries turned on the conduct of foreign affairs. Shortly after Jefferson became secretary of state, Hamilton had formed an adverse opinion of him, deploring his "womanish attachment to France and a womanish resentment against Great Britain."[9] Knowing that his financial system gravitated around custom duties flowing from trade with Great Britain, Hamilton feared any measures that threatened to upset British-American relations. As early as the spring of 1790, he had warned Major George Beckwith, the unaccredited representative of the British in New York, against the Francophilism of the secretary of state and urged Beckwith to keep him posted on any discussions with Jefferson. If the secretary of state raised difficulties, Hamilton suggested that Beckwith let him "know them in order that I may be sure they are clearly understood and candidly examined."[10] Hamilton believed that the very exis-

---

7. See *PJM*, XIV, pp. 370-72. See also Marshall Smelser, "The Jacobin Phrenzy: The Menace of Monarchy, Plutocracy, and Anglophilia, 1789-1798," *Review of Politics* 21 (1959): 239-58.

8. Prior to 1791, President Washington consulted his department heads individually. But the smashing defeat of federal troops under General Arthur St. Clair by Indians in the Northwest Territory in Nov. 1791 created a crisis that led Washington to convene his cabinet.

9. John C. Miller, *Alexander Hamilton: Portrait in Paradox* (New York, 1959), pp. 366-67.

10. Hamilton's biographer, John C. Miller, noted that "Hamilton was proposing to aid the representative of a foreign power in counteracting the policies of the Secretary of State. Thus

tence of the republic depended on his financial system and that this, in turn, depended on continued trade with Great Britain. Jefferson and Madison thought the new government and the expanding national economy strong enough to oppose British trade practices, which seemed to them to confine the United States to a position of quasi-colonial dependence. From the beginning of their association under the federal government, they had collaborated on attempts to place commercial relations with Great Britain "on principles of reciprocal advantage,"[11] with Madison's efforts serving as the legislative counterpart of Jefferson's administrative strategy to relieve the United States from any injurious dependence on the navigation of other nations. They favored a greater degree of economic independence, while Hamilton and his supporters sought closer ties with England.[12]

The differences between Jefferson and Hamilton emerged quickly when Great Britain's first accredited minister to the United States, George Hammond, presented his credentials in November 1791. Much to Jefferson's disappointment, Hammond had no instructions relating to commerce, a topic on which the secretary was preparing a report requested by Congress. Instead, Hammond's instructions and subsequent negotiations dealt with unresolved issues growing out of the peace treaty of 1783: the retention of northwest posts by the British, the status of slaves carried off by the British after hostilities ceased, American debts to British creditors, and confiscation of Loyalist property by Americans during the war.

After Hammond arrived, Hamilton connived with him as he had earlier done with Beckwith. When Jefferson informed Hammond that the United States might take retaliatory steps if Hammond's instructions did not authorize him to conclude a commercial treaty, Hamilton kept the minister informed about cabinet discussions. After Jefferson announced at a cabinet meeting that his report on commerce would recommend retaliation against Great Britain, Hamilton "opposed it violently," arguing that such a move might complicate negotiations over British removal from western posts. "It was more important to us," Jefferson reported Hamilton as saying, "to have the posts than to commence a commercial war."

In a conciliatory move, Jefferson agreed to postpone his report recommending retaliation while he negotiated with Hammond. But when Hammond stalled, Jefferson came to suspect that the British minister was being

---

Hamilton helped to establish the conviction in the minds of British officials that Jefferson was their enemy and that the State Department ought to be by-passed when negotiations were undertaken with the United States"; see *ibid.*, p. 368.

11. Washington used this phrase in his message to the Senate and House of Representatives, Feb. 14, 1791; see Richardson, *Messages,* I, p. 96.

12. In 1791, the British government informed its first accredited minister to the United States that in Congress, especially in the Senate, "a party is already formed in favor of a connection with Great Britain"; see Bernard Mayo, ed., "Instructions to the British Ministers to the United States, 1791–1812," in *AHA Annual Report for the Year 1936* (Washington, 1941), pp. 5–6, cited in *PTJ,* XVIII, p. 271.

coached by Hamilton. "It was observable," he confided to a file memorandum written at the time, "that whenever, at any of our consultatns, anything was proposed as to Gr. Br. Hamilton had constantly ready something which Mr. Hammond had communicated to him, which suited the subject, and proved the intimacy of their communication: insomuch that I believe he communicated to Hammond all our views, and knew from him in return the views of the British court."[13] Indeed, Hammond informed Lord Grenville that Hamilton had assured him that Jefferson had abandoned his intention to make any report to Congress on retaliatory measures.[14]

The official negotiations with Hammond opened in March 1792, when the British minister listed ninety-four American infractions of the peace treaty, concentrating on the clauses that specified that British creditors should meet no lawful impediment to the recovery of debts contracted before the war, that Congress would recommend to the states that confiscated property be restored to its owners, and that no future confiscations would be made after the treaty was signed. Jefferson's response, which he referred to Madison, Hamilton, and Attorney General Edmund Randolph as well as to President Washington, has been labeled by diplomatic historian Samuel Flagg Bemis as his greatest state paper while he was secretary of state.[15] Hamilton agreed that "much *strong* ground has been taken and *strongly* maintained,"[16] and Madison congratulated his friend on getting his answer "triumphantly through the ordeal" of cabinet approval, calling its main points unanswerably vindicated.[17]

Hammond argued that American violations of the treaty had triggered England's decision to retain the western posts. Jefferson rehearsed evidence from state and federal records to deny this charge and concluded that "the treaty was violated *in England* before it was known in America; and, *in America,* as soon as it was known." But the king's government had mistakenly cited acts by the states as the reason for its transgressions, thus "inverting the natural order of cause and effect," Jefferson contended, when, in fact, the British infractions had been "committed months and years before" the states' proceedings.[18]

After this acrimonious exchange, Jefferson invited Hammond to his home for a "solo dinner" on June 3 to discuss the next diplomatic steps. Their conversation was "full, unreserved and of a nature to inspire mutual confidence," Jefferson informed Madison. "The result was that he acknoleged ex-

---

13. TJ's memorandum of Mar. 11, 1792, in Ford, I, pp. 186-87.

14. George Hammond to William Lord Grenville, Jan. 9, 1792, in Syrett, X, pp. 493-96. TJ did not submit his report to Congress until Dec. 1793.

15. Samuel Flagg Bemis, ed., *The American Secretaries of State and Their Diplomacy,* 10 vols. (New York, 1927), II, pp. 44-45.

16. Alexander Hamilton to TJ, [May 20-27, 1792], in Syrett, XI, p. 409.

17. JM to TJ, June 12, 1792, below. JM had also read an earlier draft before leaving Philadelphia for Virginia; see TJ to George Washington, May 16, 1792, in Ford, V, pp. 514-15.

18. The letters exchanged by George Hammond and TJ are printed in *ASP, FR,* I, pp. 193-237.

plicitly that his court had hitherto heard one side of the question only, and that from prejudiced persons, that it was now for the first time discussed, that it was placed on entire new ground, his court having no idea of a charge of first infraction on them, and a justification on that ground of what had been done by our states, that this made it quite a new case to which no instructions he had could apply." Nonetheless, Jefferson concluded that the British would not deliver the western posts since they considered their retention "a very imperfect compensation for the losses their subjects had sustained." He also learned from his discussion with Hammond that the British now hoped to rectify an alleged "mistake of the negotiators" of the peace treaty in order to obtain "a slice of our Northwestern territory," which would "admit them to the navigable part of the Missisipi." At the end of their meeting, Hammond promised to seek new instructions and assured Jefferson that he expected to have them by the next meeting of Congress in November 1792.[19]

Unfortunately, Hamilton nullified his colleague's presentation, meeting with Hammond in "the strictest confidence" and denying that Jefferson's "intemperate violence" had his approval or that it represented "a faithful exposition of the sentiments of this government." "The President had not had an opportunity of perusing this representation," Hamilton claimed, and had relied instead on Jefferson's verbal assurance "that it was conformable to the opinions of the other members of the executive government." After Hamilton's confidential review of Jefferson's "extraordinary performance," Hammond discounted the secretary of state's arguments in his report to Lord Grenville, blasting them for containing much irrelevant material, unjustifiable insinuations, and acrimonious style.[20]

Not only did Hamilton subvert his colleague, he also falsified the record. Although he had offered several suggestions to Jefferson's presentation, some of which Jefferson accepted and some of which he referred to the president, Hamilton had approved most of the foreign-policy paper.[21] Indeed, Jefferson sent Madison a copy of Hamilton's suggestions, noting that he had submitted them to the president, "shewing where I agreed, [and] where I did not." After reviewing Jefferson's presentation and Hamilton's suggestions, Washington "approved of the letter's remaining as it was, particularly on the article of Debts, which he thought a subject of justificn. and not merely of extenuation."[22]

Although Jefferson was suspicious of Hamilton, neither he, the president, nor anyone else in official circles learned of the secretary of the treasury's undercover conduct in this instance. But Hammond, acting on Hamilton's

---

19. TJ to JM, June 4, 1792, below.
20. George Hammond to William Lord Grenville, June 8, 1792, in Syrett, XI, pp. 454–55.
21. Alexander Hamilton to TJ, [May 20–27, 1792], in Syrett, XI, pp. 409–14, documents TJ's comments on Hamilton's suggestions.
22. TJ to JM, June 1, 1792, below.

candid advice, failed to deliver his response that fall, as promised; indeed, the British ministry never thought it necessary to reply to Jefferson's powerful presentation while he served as secretary of state.

The growing hostility between Jefferson and Hamilton finally burst into public view in the summer of 1792. Less than a month after his "solo dinner" with Hammond, Jefferson sent Madison a Philadelphia newspaper carrying an anonymous squib—from "Hamilton's pen," according to Jefferson, "daring to call the republican party *a faction*."[23] In a private letter written a month earlier, Hamilton had argued *"that Mr. Madison cooperating with Mr. Jefferson is at the head of a faction decidedly hostile to me and my administration, and actuated by views in my judgment subversive of the principles of good government and dangerous to the union, peace and happiness of the Country."* In Congress, the faction "acted under Mr. Madison's banner," and the Virginian consistently and "boldly led his troops" in attacks on Hamiltonian measures.[24] One month later, after Jefferson had left Philadelphia for Monticello, Hamilton went public with his charges, hitting first at Jefferson, then at Madison for their association with Freneau, editor of the *National Gazette*. Calling attention to the fact that Freneau received a salary from the government, Hamilton asked "whether this salary is paid for *translations;* or for *publications,* the design of which is to vilify those to whom the voice of the people has committed the administration of our public affairs—to oppose the measures of government, and, by false insinuations, to disturb the public peace?"[25]

A week later, Hamilton returned to the attack, naming Jefferson as the party leader who pensioned Freneau with public money. The editor was a front for faction, "the faithful and devoted servant of the head of a party," and "the whole complexion of his paper is an exact copy of the politics of his employer foreign and domestic." While he was in France, Hamilton charged, Jefferson had opposed the Constitution, going "so far as to discountenance its adoption" at first but ultimately recommending it "on the ground of expediency." Writing as "An American," Hamilton suggested that there was something un-American about the secretary of state, who in the cabinet had become "the declared opponent of almost all the important measures which have been devised by the Government; more especially the provision which has been made for the public Debt, the institution of the Bank of the United States, and such other measures as relate to the Public Credit and the Finances of the U States." Indeed, Jefferson's political tenets tended towards "National disunion, National insignificance, Public disorder and discredit."[26] When Freneau denied that Jefferson was responsible for his decision to edit the *National*

---

23. TJ to JM, June 29, 1792, below. Syrett, XI, p. 582, could find no additional evidence to confirm TJ's allegation that Hamilton wrote this article in the *Gazette of the United States* (June 27, 1792).

24. Hamilton's italics; see Alexander Hamilton to Edward Carrington, May 26, 1792, in Syrett, XI, pp. 426–45.

25. Alexander Hamilton, "T. L. No. I," July 25, 1792, *ibid.,* XII, p. 107.

26. Alexander Hamilton, "An American No. I," Aug. 4, 1792, *ibid.,* pp. 157–64.

Gazette, Hamilton conceded that the secretary of state may not have opened negotiations but suggested, without naming Madison, that they had been conducted "by a very *powerful, influential* and *confidential* friend and associate of that Gentleman."[27]

Hamilton's slashing attack spurred Jefferson's friends to rush to his defense. Typically, he remained off the field of battle, while Madison, Monroe, and Attorney General Randolph coordinated their journalistic response. Labeling Hamilton's attack an "extraordinary manœuver of Calum[n]y," Madison made a hurried "excurtion into Albemarle," where he reversed his initial impulse to send "a note to the printer with my name subscribed."[28] Instead, he and James Monroe reviewed his correspondence with Jefferson relating to the Constitution and prepared a joint but anonymous reply that Monroe sent to the press.[29]

The newspaper controversy continued into autumn, when President Washington, anxious to retire at the end of his first term, pressed both secretaries to cool down their heated quarrels. The internecine conflict was "harrowing and tearing our vitals," he warned, and he counseled "that instead of wounding suspicions, and irritable charges, there may be liberal allowances, mutual forbearances, and temporising yieldings on *all sides*."[30]

Jefferson had written Washington before leaving Philadelphia for the summer, urging him to accept a second term: "North and South will hang together, if they have you to hang on." But Jefferson had also gone to great lengths to set forth his views—and those of "the public mind"—on what had caused the sectional differences, penning an indictment of Hamilton's fiscal system that did not name the secretary of the treasury. Nor did he mention Hamilton's interference in foreign affairs.[31]

In a second letter to the president, however, Jefferson pointed out that he had never meddled in legislation, the one exception being the assumption/residence deal when he was "duped" by Hamilton; nor had he intrigued with legislators to defeat Hamiltonian measures. But he candidly admitted that he had privately disapproved of Hamilton's system, which seemed to him to flow "from principles adverse to liberty, and was calculated to undermine and demolish the republic, by creating an influence of his department over the members of the legislature."[32] On his return trip to Philadelphia, Jefferson stopped

---

27. Alexander Hamilton, "An American No. II," Aug. 11, 1792, *ibid.,* p. 192. Hamilton had named JM in "An American No. I," *ibid.,* p. 158.

28. JM to Edmund Randolph, Sept. 13, 1792, in *PJM,* XIV, pp. 364–65.

29. It appeared in *Dunlap's American Daily Advertiser* on Sept. 22, 1792, and is reprinted in *PJM,* XIV, pp. 368–70. See James Monroe to JM, Sept. 18, 1792, *ibid.,* p. 367. Extracts came from TJ's letters to JM of Dec. 20, 1787, above; Feb. 6, May 3, July 31, and Nov. 18, 1788, above; and Mar. 15 and Aug. 28, 1789, above.

30. George Washington to TJ, Aug. 23, 1792, in Fitzpatrick, XXXII, pp. 128–31. Washington wrote a similar letter to Hamilton on Aug. 26; see *ibid.,* pp. 132–34.

31. TJ to George Washington, May 23, 1792, in *PTJ,* XXIII, pp. 535–40.

32. TJ to George Washington, Sept. 9, 1792, *ibid.,* XXIV, pp. 351–59.

at Mt. Vernon, where he tried again to persuade Washington to run for a second term. "He declares himself quite undecided about retiring," he told Madison, "desirous to do so, yet not decided if strong motives against it exist."[33] Ultimately, Jefferson, Madison, Hamilton, and others persuaded the reluctant president to accept another term, and he, in turn, persuaded the secretary of state and the secretary of the treasury to continue in the cabinet in an uneasy truce.

But the antagonism between Jefferson and Hamilton remained. The more Jefferson thought about the expansion of the national banking system into the South with the establishment of a branch in Richmond, the more volatile he got. When he first heard that "the Tresorio-bankites" proposed to do so, he suggested that "a counter-bank be set up to befriend the Agricultural man." "Would not such a bank enlist the legislature in it's favor, and against the Treasury bank?" he asked Madison in midsummer.[34] But Hamilton's summer-long newspaper attack forced Jefferson to reconsider the question, and he concluded that the expansion of the Bank of the United States might change the political contours of the country fundamentally, converting it into the "United States of the Bank."[35] He, therefore, denounced any plan to counter the federal bank with a state one, calling such a move "a milk and water measure."

According to the secretary of state, there was only one means of opposition worthy of a state acting against a "foreign legislature" such as Congress. The state legislature, he told Madison, should start from the basic proposition that the federal government did not legally have the power of erecting banks and corporations, which only the state could do. "For any person to recognise a foreign legislature in a case belonging to the state itself, is an act of *treason* against the state," he wrote at white heat, "and whosoever shall do any act under colour of the authority of a foreign legislature whether by signing notes, issuing or passing them, acting as director, cashier or in any other office relating to it shall be adjudged guilty of high treason and suffer death accordingly, by the judgment of the state courts. . . . I really wish that this or nothing should be done," he concluded, in an effort to protect "the counter-rights of the states."[36]

To this dangerous and doctrinaire proposal, the most radical ever made by Jefferson, Madison meekly subscribed: "Your objections to it [the branch bank] seem unanswerable."[37]

---

33. TJ to JM, Oct. 1, 1792, below.

34. TJ to JM, July 3, 1792, below.

35. Miller, p. 311, credits John Taylor of Caroline with this phrase.

36. TJ to JM, Oct. 1, 1792, below. The Virginia legislature passed laws establishing banks in Alexandria and Richmond; see *PJM,* XIV, pp. 417–18.

37. JM to TJ, Oct. 9, 1792, below. Forrest McDonald, *Alexander Hamilton: A Biography* (New York, 1979), pp. 256–57, is one of the few biographers of Hamilton, TJ, or JM to cite this exchange of letters.

---------------- THE LETTERS ----------------

Jefferson to Madison

[Philadelphia] Nov. 11, 1791

In my report on How's case, where I state that it should go to the President, it will become a question with the house Whether they shall refer it to the President themselves, or give it back to the Petitioner, and let him so address it, as he ought to have done at first.[1] I think the latter proper, 1. because it is a case belonging purely to the Executive. 2. the Legislature should never shew itself in a matter with a foreign nation, but where the case is very serious and they mean to commit the nation on it's issue. 3. because if they indulge individuals in handing through the legislature their applications to the executive, all applicants will be glad to avail themselves of the weight of so powerful a sollicitor. Similar attempts have been repeatedly made by individuals to get the president to hand in their petitions to the legislature, which he has constantly refused. It seems proper that every person should address himself directly to the department to which the constitution has allotted his case; and that the proper answer to such from any other department is, that 'it is not to us that the constitution has assigned the transaction of this business.'

I suggest these things to you, that if they appear to you to be right, this kind of business may in the first instance be turned into it's proper channel.

Jefferson to Madison

[Philadelphia] Thursday morning. [Jan. 12, 1792]

TH: J. TO J. M.

I received the inclosed late last night, and it is not in my power to see Mr. H.[2] this morning. If you can with satisfaction to yourself broach to him what Monroe proposes, well. If not, it must take it's chance.

1. William Howe, a resident of Massachusetts, had submitted a petition to the House of Representatives, alleging that a British court in Nova Scotia, contrary to existing treaties, had ruled against his claim of a debt due him there. TJ believed the request involved executive authority and, therefore, opposed legislative interference with the president's conduct of foreign policy. When TJ's report was read in the House, JM made a motion that Howe have leave to withdraw his petition; see *PJM,* XIV, p. 105. TJ's report on Howe's petition is in *PTJ,* XXII, pp. 295–96.

2. JM wrote "Hawkins" for Senator Benjamin Hawkins of North Carolina.

ENCLOSURE
[James Monroe to Jefferson]

Dear Sir   Thursday 9-oclock. Jan. [11,] 1792

You will have heard that upon the discussion of G. M.'s[3] merits, the foreign business was postponed untill tomorrow, nothing having been done respecting the Hague. The order of proceeding required that a similar question shod. have been taken respecting that court that had been as to the others. But owing I presume to the friends of the gentn. in nomination for it, being in opposition to the system, it was impossible it shod. proceed from them—and the friends of the others being gratified in opening the door for them, were regardless of any other object. Tis important for Mr. S.[4] that the question shod. be previously taken, and I can devise no means of accomplishing it, so effecatious as your communicating it to Mr. Hawkins, either personally or thro Mr. Madison and as soon as possible.

The communication respecting the missisippi, after adjournment, led to a conversation, introduced by Mr. Izard countenanced by my colleague[5] and supported by Cabot, wherein the policy of opening it was strongly reprehended. The arguments in its favor were those of a quondam party; but the ill-success of the military operations have given them new force. As I presume you have heard what passed in the other business and shall omit any thing farther at present. Yrs. affectionately

Jas. Monroe

Jefferson to Madison

[Philadelphia ca. Jan. 12, 1792][6]

Notes on the Alloy of the Dollar

The Spanish dollar, till 1728, had 11 dwt—4 grs. of pure metal to every 12 dwt of mixed

	from 1728 to 1772	10 dwt—21 grs.
	since 1772	10 dwt—17 grs.

The above is from the Encyclopedie
The 1st. dollar gives this proportion

	grs mixed	*grs alloy*	*grs mixed*	*grs alloy*
[1st]	288	: 16	:: 416	: 23.11
the 2d.	288	: 27	:: 416	: 39
the 3d.	288	: 31	:: 416	: 44.77

3. Gouverneur Morris. For the date, see *PJM*, XIV, p. 187.

4. William Short. When Washington nominated Gouverneur Morris as minister plenipotentiary to France and Thomas Pinckney to Great Britain, he proposed Short as minister resident to The Hague. Senator Hawkins headed a group opposing permanent foreign establishments; see TJ to William Short, Jan. 3, 1792, in Ford, V, pp. 417-18.

5. Monroe and Richard Henry Lee were senators from Virginia.

6. JM endorsed these notes, which are in his hand, as received from TJ. The date assigned is based on the Senate's passage of the mint bill on Jan. 12, 1792. The House passed it on Mar. 24, and President Washington signed it on Apr. 2, 1792; see *PJM*, XIV, p. 188.

The vote in the Senate for reducing the dollar from 375.64 grs. pure metal to 371.25 is a presage of what may be expected in the other house. If an opposition to that reduction is desperate, and it's motives liable to be mistaken, would it not be better to let it pass, and to try whether the quantum of alloy may not be usefully changed thus?

The dollar proposed in the bill is to contain 371.25 grs. pure metal.
Instead of 44.75 alloy, add only 38.92 alloy

It will make the Dollar of 410.17 mixed metal which is exactly the Unit proposed in the Report on Measures, weights and coins, viz the Ounce or cubic inch of rain water.

That Avarice which attaches itself to the *pure metal* will see some saving also in the reduction of the *alloy,* both in the alloy saved, and the greater worth of what remains because the more base metal you add, the less is the worth of the mass.

It will preserve this link of the general system, and the possibility of establishing it.

It will try the dispositions of the Representatives towards that system.

It will give us a coin, which instead of 25.8 dwt. of alloy in the pound of mixed (which is that proposed in the bill and taken exactly from the base dollar of 1772) will give us one of 22.75 dwt of alloy only in the pound, which is extremely near to that of the Dollar of 1728–1772, to wit 22.5 dwt in the pound (because 288grs. mixed :27 grs. alloy ::240 dwt :22.5 dwt) and coming nearer to the alloy of our gold, of 20 dwt in the pound, may render more probable some future attempt to raise the pure metal so as to bring the alloy in both coins to the same measure, when the effect on the public debt shall be out of the question.

Madison to Jefferson

[Philadelphia] Feb. 20, [1792]

J. M. returns Mr. J. his note endorsed for negociation at the Bank, but recommends in preference a use of about 300 dollars of J. M. which will not be wanted till the time proposed for the redemption of the note. A Check for 150 dollars is inclosed. As much or a little more can be added as soon as an order from the Speaker can be got which will be tomorrow or next day. J. M. insists that Mr. J. concur in this substitute, assuring him that it is *perfectly*[7] convenient, and moreover that if any contingency should subject J. M to a pecuniary demand before the last of next month, he will resort witht. scruple to the expedient proposed to be waved.

He is also in doubt whether the Bank discounts for more than 40 days.

7. JM's italics.

Madison to Jefferson

[Philadelphia ca. Mar. 1, 1792][8]

Memorandum on New Orleans

Information of Phil. Barbour, who resided long in West Florida

After N. Orleans fell into the hands of Spain her Govr. forbade all British vessels navigating under the Treaty of Paris to fasten to the Shore, and caused such as did so to be cut loose. In consequence of this proceeding a British frigate went up near the Town, fastened to the shore and set out guards with orders to fire on such as might attempt to cut her loose. The Govr after trying in vain by menaces to remove the frigate acquiesced, after which British Vessels were indiscriminately admitted to use the shore; and even the residence of British Merchants in the town of N. O. trading clandestinely with Spaniards as well as openly with their own people, connived at. The Treaty of 1763 stipulated to British subjects, (as well as is recollected) no more than the right of navigating the river. If the right of using the shore was admitted under that stipulation this right must have been admitted to be involved in the right of navigating the river, as incident to the beneficial enjoyment of it.

Madison to Jefferson

[Philadelphia] March 5, [1792]

The inclosed papers which I have got from Mr. Beckleys office furnishes an answer to your letter. There is a Bill depending in favor of claims barred by the limitation of time—which if it passes will provide for those of Owen and Woods as I understand the tenor of the Bill and the nature of their claims.[9] As soon as the fate of the Bill is decided I shall write to the parties.

J. M.

---

8. For the date, see *PJM,* XIV, p. 242. On Mar. 7, 1792, TJ submitted his report to President Washington on negotiations with the Spanish commissioners about navigation rights on the Mississippi; see Malone, II, pp. 407–11.

9. Enclosures not found. John Beckley was clerk of the House of Representatives; see Edmund Berkeley and Dorothy Smith Berkeley, *John Beckley: Zealous Partisan in a Nation Divided* (Philadelphia, 1973). David Owings and David Woods had written to JM on Dec. 12, 1791, about their claims as soldiers in the Revolution. Each received certificates of registered debt in the amount of $14.36 from the Treasury Department on July 25, 1792; see *PJM,* XIV, p. 148.

Jefferson to Madison

[Philadelphia] Mar. 16, 1792

TH: J. TO J. M.

I inclose you my thoughts on a subject extremely difficult, and on which I would thank you for any observations.[10] The exchange of criminals is so difficult between a free and an arbitrary government, that England never would consent to make a convention with any state on the subject. It has accordingly been hitherto the asylum of all fugitives from the oppressions of other governments. The subject is forced on us by the importunities of Govr. Pinkney, and in a day or two I must report on it to the President.

I will call for you a little before 4. to-day.

Jefferson to Madison

[Philadelphia] May 13, 1792

I send you my ideas of what might be said on the distinction between bonds and simple contracts, if any thing should be said. But my office being to vindicate the opinions of the courts, and none of the courts having made any distinction between these two cases, I ought to tread in their footsteps only: and the rather as Mr. Hammond has not raised any such distinction on his part. It would be quite time enough for me to answer any objection founded in that difference, when the objection shall be made. It probably will never be made. To enter into it voluntarily may be to move a peice into prise which there is no occasion to move at all.[11]

ENCLOSURE
Notes on Bonds

[ca. May 13, 1792]

It is certainly unnecessary here to shew that there is no distinction to be taken between debt due on bond with a condition expressed to pay principal and interest, and debts due on simple account or otherwise, whereon it was the usage to pay an interest, because there exists not in reason any difference between the two cases: for obligation results from the *act of contracting*, not from the *evidence of the act*. The condition of a bond is an *evidence in writing* that the debtor had contracted to pay interest. Where usage has established (as in the case of   Douglas   ) that a merchant in a

---

10. The enclosure probably related to TJ's report on a convention with Spain, which would have dealt with extradition of fugitives; see TJ to George Washington, Mar. 22, 1792, in Ford, V, pp. 481–85.

11. In preparing the American position for his negotiations with the British minister George Hammond on the implementation of the Treaty of Paris of 1783, TJ solicited opinions from JM as well as from his colleagues in the cabinet Hamilton and Randolph. The distinction between bonds and contracts related to the right of British creditors to collect debts owed by Americans; see Malone, II, pp. 412–14.

particular line of commerce, purchasing goods from a tradesman, shall pay interest after 15. months, tho' not a word be said about it at the moment of contracting, yet it is in the contemplation of both parties, and is as much a part of the contract as if expressly mentioned; as much so as that the principal shall be paid, tho not a word be said of that when the merchant takes the goods. The mind of each party has assented to the contract for interest equally in the case of the bond and the purchase on account, and the contract is equally real, the only difference being that the one is evidenced by writing, the other by the act of taking the goods under knolege of the custom that interest is to be paid after 15. months. The interest then is as much *contracted* for in the one case as in the other. In both cases too both parties have known at the time of the contract, that circumstances unforeseen might by possibility arise which would, in law, suppress the right to interest, tho it was contracted for. Such circumstances, unforeseen at the time of contracting the debt, whether by bond or account, have in fact happened: they suppress in both cases then the interest contracted for, as well that of the *written* as the *tacit* contract. That a stipulation, because committed to writing, is not therefore to controul all events, is well settled. It is the daily practice for the courts to relieve against either penalties or conditions *where a compensation can be made:* as in the case of Eastwoode v. Vinke. 2 P.W. ca. 192. the condition of a bond relieved against. In 1. Ca. Ch. 51. & Freem. Ch. Rep. 182. conditions against reason may be relieved, so where the breach proceeds from the act of the obligee. And if the courts will relieve, *where a compensation can be made,* so also where circumstances supervene *which suppress the right to compensation.* Accordingly in none of the courts or states has any distinction been taken between the cases of bonds and simple contracts. The allowance or disallowance of interest has never respected that circumstance; you have very properly taken no notice of any such distinction; and I note it merely to exclude the presumption of it's being overlooked.

Madison to Jefferson

[Philadelphia ca. May 16, 1792]

Notes on Jefferson's Letter to George Hammond[12]

p. 1. (a)   Was the evidence of none produced?
p. 1. (b)   What meant by "its different administrations"—and whatever its meaning is it a circumstance sufficiently marked to enforce the appeal?[13]

12. Hoping to reopen negotiations between the United States and Great Britain on violations of the Treaty of Paris, TJ wrote Hammond on May 29, 1792, defending American infractions since 1783 as justifiable responses to Britain's refusal to relinquish western posts in American territory and to restore American slaves evacuated from New York in 1783; see *PTJ,* XXIII, pp. 551–602. Samuel Flagg Bemis describes the letter as TJ's "greatest diplomatic note" (Bemis, II, p. 32), but Charles R. Ritcheson, *Aftermath of Revolution: British Policy toward the United States, 1783–1795* (Dallas, 1969), is more critical.

The +, −, and × marks were inserted by TJ.

13. TJ accepted JM's suggestion and wrote "different forms of administration," meaning that the United States, under both the Articles of Confederation and the Constitution, had desired "to be on the best terms" with Great Britain; see *PTJ,* XXIII, pp. 551, 609.

p. 2. (a) Is not *"foreign"* likely to be criticized as not applicable in its ordinary and strongest sense. Distant Country—unknown judges or some equivalent epithet might be free from the objection if a real one.

+ p. 3. (a) Might not a more apt word be substituted for *perpetual* chains which is not literally just—nor congruous with the idea of becoming murderers etc.

+ p. 5. (a) Wd. it be superfluous to guard the universality of these terms so as to correspond with "the *apud hostes inventas*" and *"apud nos reperta"* of Bynk. In their unqualified sense they extend to hostile property found with neutral nations.—Quer. also whether a *State of war*, as now understood, *permits* the seizure of property in the broad sense of Bynkershook. If there be ground for this doubt, some such words as "in its rigor" might be thrown in.[14]

+ p. 5. (b) Will not this be called drawing up the curtain just dropped on the tragedy of the war? The expression might, if requisite, receive a less harsh form without weakening the inference.[15]

+ p. 7. (a) May not the word "idle" give offence, as Hammond has rejected or disregarded the difference stated.[16]

+ p. 9. (b) Mr. T. Pitt and Mr. Wilberforce seem to have very obscure ideas of the powers of Congs. and the obligation taken on them by the word *recommend*. Lord Hawkes seems not to understand the difference between *recommending*, and the constitutional power of *making requisitions*.

May not these proofs be repelled, if Mr. H. chooses, by alledging want of accuracy and authenticity in the publication—and wd. it be amiss to admit both sub modo—without relinquishing the sufficiency of the general scope and complexion of the debate which could not well be mistaken.[17]

x

+ p. 17. (a) Is this consistent with the journals and reports of the Comissrs., which shew that they opposed and that the British negociators urged the admission of the people in question, to citizenship in this Country.[18]

---

14. TJ accepted JM's suggestion relating to the right of a country at war to seize the property of its enemies "wherever found"; see *ibid.*, pp. 553, 611.

15. TJ accepted JM's suggestion, differentiating between an ordinary war—as the United States viewed the American Revolution—and a rebellion—as Great Britain viewed the conflict; see *ibid.*, pp. 554, 611.

16. TJ accepted JM's suggestion in part by softening an expression relating to "persons whose native language is that of this Treaty"; see *ibid.*, pp. 555, 611.

17. TJ accepted JM's suggestion, inserting "we presume" in order to subdue his discussion of the difference between recommending measures and enacting laws under the Constitution; see *ibid*.

18. TJ accepted JM's suggestion, dropping a sarcastic remark about Great Britain not altering its refusal to recognize the right of expatriation; see *ibid.*, pp. 561, 611.

− p. 15. (b)		Why invert the geographical order of the States—if in compliance with Mr. H. a little explanatory amendment is suggested in loco.
− x p. 15. (a)		Is it so clear, as to need no proof or remark, that *confiscation* is compleat by the Law, without the subsequent process for carrying the law into effect? Perhaps Mr. H.'s Memorial may admit what is assumed and In that case the quere is superseded.
+ p. 28. (a)		Are not these acts of Jany. that is prior to Apl. 11. 1783 thrown out of the question by the distinction with which the review sets out.
+ p. 28. (b)		"will excuse my answering"—Is this phrase correct. Sd. it not be excuse my not answering or excuse me from answering?[19]
− p. 30. (a)		See x p. 15 (a)
− p. 31. (a)		See p. 17 (a).
+ p. 31. (b)		Quer. whether so much here and on p. 32. as animadverts on the Refugees etc. be necessary. And if not whether it be expedient.
+ p. 36. (a)		May not this be viewed as unnecessarily pointed![20]
+ p. 36. (b)		From accts. given of the Furr trade it is doubtful whether so great a proportion of it ever passed thro' the present U.S. as to place it among the *most valuable branches* of their commerce."[21]
+ p. 37. (a)		Is it clear that a nation can rightly make *general war* in the first instance, for a breach of *any* treaty—or even a Treaty of peace?[22]
+ p. 41. (a)		Quer. whether so *dishonorable* an object can be prudently inferred from regulations which ostensibly were not at all, and perhaps really very little considered in that relation.[23]
+ p. 42. (a)		As the laws of all the States as well as of G.B. subject the body to restraint for debt, wd. it not be as well to omit this general

---

19. TJ accepted JM's suggestion, inserting "not" before "answering"; see *ibid.*, pp. 565, 611.

20. TJ accepted JM's suggestion, deleting a sarcastic reference to the British failure to withdraw garrisons from every post within the United States "with all convenient speed" after the end of the Revolutionary war; see *ibid.*, pp. 570, 611.

21. TJ accepted JM's suggestion, calling the fur trade "of great importance" as a branch of American commerce; see *ibid.*, pp. 571, 611.

22. TJ accepted JM's suggestion, deleting war as a reprisal for a breach of an article in a treaty and substituting a dissolution of the treaty, or withholding execution of equivalent articles, or waiving notice of the breach; see *ibid*.

23. TJ accepted JM's suggestion, altering the phrasing, but not the substance, of his appraisal of the relationship between British retention of American posts and British commercial regulations, which he thought the reason for some delay in American payment of debts owed to British creditors; this, in turn, "furnished colour for the detention of our posts"; see *ibid.*, pp. 575, 612.

	denunciation of the practice as agst. reason?²⁴
+ p. 42. (b)	Is not this pre-eminence to the civil law liable to misconstruction?
+ p. 44. (a)	The unwillingness to infringe the Treaty, seems here to be stated as the chief, if not sole motive agst. paper money.²⁵
+ p. 44. (b)	Is not the *value of* paper emissions too strongly expressed. The depreciation was considerable in all and great in some [cases?]. It is also a tender in N. Jersey yet in certain (Quer.) unless superseded by the Constitution.²⁶
+ p. 58. (a)	See p. 31. (b) As it is admitted that modifications in the recovery of the debts existed in some States, is not the position too broad that our Courts have been as open as theirs?²⁷
p. 62. (a)	Quer. whether this reasoning is applicable to the case of positive and express stipulations between two Countries. In ordinary cases the individual foreigner claims under the law and the tribunals for expounding it, and his sovereign can not interfere unless for palpable and culpable wrong. In the former case, an *innocent* error of the Judge which might defeat the stipulation, might be ground of complaint and satisfaction.²⁸
− p. 63. (a)	To this it may be said, that the law being known, justice could not claim interest, and of course no national complaint wd. be warranted.
− p. 65. (a)	Does not this suppose that if America had been conquered, not only forfeitures wd. have taken place, but without payt. of the debts of the traitors, a thing not presumable.²⁹
− p. 66. (a)	Will not the forced exile of some form an exception here? It wd. seem also that the departure of an *alien* creditor in all cases results of necessity on the event of a war, yet it is not the Modern practice to abate interest during war.

24. TJ accepted JM's suggestion, modifying, but not removing, the paragraph on imprisonment or bodily restraint for debt; see *ibid.*

25. TJ accepted JM's suggestion, defending the issuance of paper money by four states as a temporary measure brought on by economic necessity and deleting a slap at Great Britain, which, he said, "had not scrupled to contravene [the treaty] from it's signature"; see *ibid.*, pp. 577, 612.

26. TJ accepted JM's suggestion, dropping his argument that paper money was "for the most part equal in value to gold and silver" and substituting a statement that there was "not great depreciation of value"; see *ibid.*

27. TJ accepted JM's suggestion, stating that the courts of the United States, "whenever the Creditors would chuse that resource, and would press, if necessary, to the highest tribunals, would be found" as open to lawsuits, "as theirs to ours"; see *ibid.*, pp. 587, 613.

28. TJ did not alter his discussion in Section 53 of the administration of justice by the judiciary.

29. TJ did not alter his discussion in Sections 54 and 55 on the payment of interest on prewar debts, but his statement that the "great mass of Suits" in Virginia were "uniformly sustained to judgment and execution" has been disproven by Emory G. Evans, "Private Indebtedness and the Revolution in Virginia, 1776-1796," *WMQ* 28 (1971): 349-74.

Jefferson to Madison

Friday [Philadelphia May 18, 1792]

I have just received a *Northern hare,* and have got from the market a common one. It may be worth your while to come half an hour before we go to E.R's to examine their difference, as they must be skinned soon.[30]

Jefferson to Madison

Philadelphia June 1, 1792

MY DEAR SIR

I sent you last week some of Fenno's papers in which you will have seen it asserted impudently and boldly that the suggestions against members of Congress were mere falshoods. I now inclose his Wednesday's paper.[31] I send you also a copy of Hamilton's notes.[32] Finding that the letter would not be ready to be delivered before the Pr's return, I made notes corresponding with his, shewing where I agreed, where I did not, and I put his and mine into the Pr's hands, to be perused at his leisure. The result was that he approved of the letter's remaining as it was, particularly on the article of Debts, which he thought a subject of justificn. and not merely of extenuation. He never received my letter of the 23d. till yesterday.[33] He mentioned it to me in a moment when nothing more could be said than that he would take an occasion of conversing with me on the subject. I have letters from France censuring the appointment there in the severest terms.[34] Adieu my dear Sir. Your's affectionately

TH: JEFFERSON

Jefferson to Madison

Philadelphia June 4, 1792

No. 2

DEAR SIR

I wrote you the 1st. inst. which I will call No. 1, and number my letters in future that you may know when any are missing. Mr. Hammond has given me

30. For the date, see *PJM,* XIV, p. 310. TJ later presented a white hare, perhaps this one, to Peale's museum; see *ibid.*

31. TJ referred to articles critical of speculators in Congress.

32. Hamilton commented on TJ's proposed reply to British charges against U.S. compliance with the Treaty of Paris.

33. TJ referred to his letter urging Washington not to retire at the end of his first term.

34. Gouverneur Morris's appointment as minister to France.

an answer in writing, saying that he must send my letter to his court and wait their instructions. On this I desired a personal interview that we might consider the matter together in a familiar way. He came accordingly yesterday and took a solo dinner with me, during which our conversation was full, unreserved and of a nature to inspire mutual confidence. The result was that he acknoleged explicitly that his court had hitherto heard one side of the question only, and that from prejudiced persons, that it was now for the first time discussed, that it was placed on entire new ground, his court having no idea of a charge of first infraction on them, and a justification on that ground of what had been done by our states, that this made it quite a new case to which no instructions he had could apply. He found from my expressions that I had entertained an idea of his being able to give an order to the governor of Canada to deliver up the posts, and smiled at the idea; and it was evident from his conversation that it had not at all entered into the expectations of his court that they were to deliver us the posts. He did not say so expressly, but he said that they considered the retaining of the posts as a very imperfect compensation for the losses their subjects had sustained: under the cover of the clause of the treaty which admits them to the navigation of the Missisipi and the evident mistake of the negotiators in supposing that a line due West from the lake of the Woods would strike the Missisipi, he supposed an explanatory convention necessary, and shewed a desire that such a slice of our Northwestern territory might be cut off for them as would admit them to the navigable part of the Missisipi: etc. etc. etc. He expects he can have his final instructions by the meeting of Congress. I have not yet had the conversation mentioned in my last. Do you remember that you were to leave me a list of names? Pray send them to me. My only view is that, if the P. asks me for a list of particulars, I may enumerate names to him, without naming my authority, and shew him that I had not been speaking merely at random.[35] If we do not have our conversation before I can make a comparative table of the debts and numbers of all modern nations, I will shew him how high we stand indebted by the poll in that table. I omitted Hammond's admission that the debt from the Patowmac North might be considered as liquidated, that that of Virginia was now the only great object, and cause of anxiety, amounting to two millions sterling. Adieu. Your's affectionately

Th: Jefferson

---

35. In his letter urging the president not to retire, TJ argued that the national debt "furnished effectual means of corrupting . . . a portion of the legislature"; see TJ to George Washington, May 23, 1792, in Ford, VI, p. 3.

Jefferson to Madison

Philadelphia June 10, 1792

No. 3
DEAR SIR

The poll of the N. Y. election stood the day before yesterday thus.

	Clinton	Jay
Suffolk	481	228.
Queen's cty.	532	288
King's cty.	244	92
city and county of N. Y.	603	739
Orange	551.	80.
Dutchess	751.	945
Westchester	347	824
Richmond	106	4
Ulster.	947	654
Columbia	1303	717
Renslaer	404	717
Washington	758	471
Saratoga.	405	461
	7432	6220

General Schuyler says there will be about 16,000 voters and offers to bet 3. to 1. as far as 500. guineas that Jay will still be elected. However he seems to be alone here in that expectation. We dined together at the P's on Thursday, and happening to set next one another, we got, towards the close of the afternoon, into a little contest whether hereditary descent or election was most likely to bring *wise* and *honest* men into public councils. He for the former, Pinkney and myself for the latter. I was not displeased to find the P. attended to the conversation as it will be a corroboration of the design imputed to that party in my letter.[36] At a dinner of Jay-ites yesterday R. M. mentioned to the company that Clinton was to be vice-president, that the Antis intended to set him up. Bingham joined in attesting the project, which appeared new to the rest of the company. I paid Genl. Irvin *50* D. for Mr. Moore, the receipt he had, vouching it. Adieu. Your's affectionately

---

[36]. TJ referred to his letter to Washington in which he asserted that "the ultimate object" of the Hamiltonian funding system was "to prepare the way for a change, from the present republican form of government, to that of a monarchy, of which the English constitution is to be the model"; see *ibid*. Schuyler was Hamilton's father-in-law.

Madison to Jefferson

Orange June 12, 1792

No. 1

MY DEAR SIR

Since I got to the end of my journey I have been without an opportunity of dropping you a line; and this is written merely to be ready for the first casual conveyance to Fredericksburg. I received yesterday your two favors No. 1 and 2. The gazettes under a preceding cover had come to hand some days before. Your answer to Hammond has on the whole got triumphantly through the ordeal.[37] It is certainly not materially injured, though perhaps a little defaced by some of the criticisms to which you have yielded. The points on which you did not relax appear to me to be fully vindicated; the main ones unanswerably so. The doctrine which would make the States the contracting parties, could have been as little expected from that quarter, as it is irreconcileable with the tenor of their confederation.[38] The expectation of Hammond, if sincere, of final instructions by the meeting of Congress throws light I think on the errand of Bond. He can scarcely calculate on the result of his court's reconsideration of the subject within the short time allowed, by five months after deducting the double voyage.

I have letters from Kentucky down to the 8th. May. Little depredations from the Savages continue to be complained of. The people however are chiefly occupied with the approaching distribution of the new offices. Nothing is said as to their probable Govr. Congress and the Judiciary are thought of more importance to the State. Brown can be what he pleases. Some are disposed to fix him on the Bench. None will object to his going into the Senate if that should be his choice. Campbell and Muter are the other names in conversation for the Senate: and Brackenridge and Greenup for the House of Reps. I have this information from a Mr. Taylor a pretty intelligent man engaged in their public affairs. George Nicholas specifies no names, observing that it is impossible to conjecture those that will succeed in the competitions. Among the contents of the inclosed letter is a printed copy of the Constitution of Kentucky as finally agreed to. You can take out that or any thing else for perusal as you please; after which you will be good eno' to have the letter handed in such way as you may judge best. I would not have thrown the trouble on you, if any other channel had occurred.

The unpopularity of the excise has evidently increased in this quarter, owing partly to the effect of Sidney[39] who has found his way here, and partly to the unavoidable vexations it carries into the family distilleries.

---

37. At a later time, JM added a marginal note: "in the Cabinet."

38. Hamilton had objected to TJ's assertion that the states, "as members of a federal league" that had signed the Treaty of Paris, were "bound by the treaty itself from the time of its conclusion."

39. At a later time, JM added a marginal note: "writer in the [National] Gazette."

The tax on newspapers is another article of grievance. It is not very well understood, but if it were it would not be satisfactory first because too high, secondly because suspected of being an insidious forerunner of something worse. I am afraid the subscriptions will soon begin to be withdrawn from the Philada. papers, unless some step be speedily taken to prevent it. The best that occurs seems to be to advertise that the papers will not be put into the mail, *but sent as heretofore* to all who shall not direct them to be put into the mail. Will you hint this to Freneau? His subscribers in this quarter seem pretty well satisfied with the degree of regularity and safety with which they get the papers, and highly pleased with the paper itself.

I found this Country labouring under a most severe drought. There had been no rain whatever since the 18 or 20 of April. The flax and oats generally destroyed; The corn dying in the hills, no tobacco planted, and the wheat in weak land suffering; in the strong, not injured materially; in the very strong perhaps benefited. 8 days ago there was a very local shower here. A day or two after a better, but still very local. Neither of them from appearances extended as far South as Albemarle. For several days past it has rained almost constantly and is still raining with the wind from North East; with every appearance of a general rain: so that the only danger now is of too much wet for the wheat, which I am happy to find has effectually supplanted Tobacco in the conversation and anxieties of our crop mongers, and is rapidly doing so in their fields.

I met the P. on the road. I had no conversation with him; but he handed me a letter which he had written to me at home. Its contents are very interesting but do not absolutely decide the problem[40] which dictated yours to him.

Monroe and his lady left us on wednesday on their way home. He is to meet the revisors at Richmond about the 15th.[41] I understood Mrs. M. was to be added to the family at Monticello during his absence.

Will you be so good as to cover under your next, a copy of Mease's inaugural oration on the Hydrophobia.[42] Rush sent me a copy which had just been printed, the morning I set out for Docr. Jones. I wished to have got one for another friend, but had not time. If the bulk will permit, send two and I will send one for the amusement of Gilmer, who I hear, though thro' imperfect channels, is still in a critical situation. Always and Affectly Yours

Js. Madison Jr

The promised list of names is inclosed. When your Tableau of Natl. dbts and polls is made out may I ask a copy?

---

40. At a later time, JM added a marginal note: "declining a re-election."

41. Monroe had been appointed to the committee for the revision of the laws of Virginia, succeeding Edmund Pendleton; see *PJM,* XIV, pp. 318–19.

42. James Mease, *An Inaugural Dissertation on the Disease Produced by the Bite of a Mad Dog* (Philadelphia, 1792), cited *ibid.,* p. 319.

Jefferson to Madison

[Philadelphia June 18, 1792]

Nothing new.

TH: J.

P. S. Opening Freneau's paper this moment I see a peice against the [new?] impost duties and it mentions the insufficiency of the revenue cutters for their object. This suggests a Quere. How comes an armed force to be in existence, and under the revenue department, and not the department of war? Would it not be well to call for a separate statement of the expence of these cutters, and either put them down, or turn them over to the war-office?

Jefferson to Madison

Philadelphia June 21, 1792

No. 4

DEAR SIR

Your No. 1. came to hand two days ago. When I inclosed you the papers of the last week I was too much hurried to write. I now therefore write earlier, and inclose only one of Fenno's papers. The residue of the New York election was as follows

	Clinton	Jay
Albany	444.	1178
Montgomy.	306.	424
Herkimer.	247.	401
Ontario.	28.	92
Total.	8,457.	8,315
difference		142

The Otsego votes were rejected, about 1000. in number, of which Jay had about 850. say a majority of 700. so that he was really governor by a majority of 500. votes, according to his friends.[43] The Clintonians again tell strange tales about these votes of Otsego. I inclose you two New York papers which will put you fully in possession of the whole affair (take care of them if you please, as they make part of a collection). It does not seem possible to defend Clinton as a just or disinterested man if he does not decline the office, of which there is no

---

43. Although John Jay received a majority of votes for governor, a joint committee of the legislature disqualified the returns from three frontier counties for "a number of irregularities," thus giving the post to George Clinton by a margin of 108 votes; see Alfred F. Young, *The Democratic Republicans of New York: The Origins, 1763–1797* (Chapel Hill, 1967), p. 301.

symptom; and I really apprehend that the cause of republicanism will suffer, and it's votaries be thrown into schism by embarking it in support of this man, and for what? To draw over the Antifederalists, who are not numerous enough to be worth drawing over. I have lately seen a letter from —— to —— on receiving his appointment.[44] He pleads guilty to the charge of indiscretion hitherto, and promises for the future the most measured circumspection, and in terms which mark him properly and gratefully impressed with the counsel which had been given him pretty strongly as you know. I have made out my table; but instead of settling the proportion of the debt of each country to it's population, I have done it to it's revenue. It is as follows.

Date	Country	Public debt	Annual revenue	Proportion of debt to revenue	Authority
	U.S. of Amer.				
1786.	Gr. Britain	£ sterl. 239,154,879	£ sterl. 15,000,000	16:1	Zimmerm. 224.[45]
1785.	France	livres 3,400,000,000	livres 430,000,000	8:1	265.
1772.	Sweden	silver dollrs. 60,000,000	11,089,122	5.4:1	59.
	Austria.	florins. 200,000,000	florins 95,000,000	2.1:1	157
1765.	Russia.	rubles 40,000,000	rubles 20,000,000	2:1	40
1774.	Portugal	£. sterl. 3,675,381	£ sterl. 1,800,000	2:1	336
1785.	Spain	piastres 152,000,000	piastres 100,000,000	1.5:1	317
1769	Denmark	dollars 1,400,000	dollars 6,272,000	0.22:1	79.
	Prussia.	*	dollars. 21,000,000		143.

I have not yet examined into the debt of the U. S. but I suppose it to be about 20. years revenue, and consequently that tho the youngest nation in the world we are the most indebted nation also. I did not go into the debts and revenues of the United Netherlands, because they are so jumbled between General and provincial, and because a great deal of their debt, is made by borrowing at low interest and lending it at high, and consequently not only this part is to be struck off from the amount of their debt, but so much of the residue of it also as has it's interest paid by this means. Brandt, the famous Indian is arrived

---

44. From Gouverneur Morris to President Washington; see *PJM,* XIV, p. 326.

45. Eberhard A. W. von Zimmerman, *A Political Survey of the Present State of Europe* (London, 1787).

here; he dined with the P. yesterday, will dine with Knox to-day, Hammond on Sunday, the Presidt. on Monday etc. Adieu my dear Sir. Your's affectionately

TH: JEFFERSON

Madison to Jefferson

Orange June 24, 1792

DEAR SIR

Since my last I have had the pleasure of your two letters of the 10. and 17. inst.[46] The latter has but just come to hand, and I can not say any thing as to the legal arrangement of the Cutters.

We have had very seasonable weather of late in this quarter. I understand it has been less so farther South. How Albemarle and Bedford have fared I can not tell. Notwithstanding the good weather the very latter wheat is injured, in some instances very much, by the rust. Below, the injury is much complained of. In general in our region the harvest will be great.

Shelby is Govr. of Kentucky. The Senate does credit to the mode of choice. The elite of the Country compose it. A *partial* list of the House of Delegates also looks pretty well. The appointments to Congs. had not taken place, nor is any further aid given to conjectures.

The error in the sum left for Irwine proceeded either from myself or the young gentleman at Carlisle, I can not say which. I thank you for correcting it. If Leiper shd. lodge money in your hands as I left word, you will replace the 10 dollars advanced. I write in a hurry to catch a very safe conveyance to Fredg. Yrs. always and affly.

JS. MADISON JR.

Madison to Jefferson

[Orange] June 25, [1792]

No. 3

I wrote last evening by a conveyance that hast[i]ly occurred to Fredg. This, an idea occurred which I have executed in the inclosed;[47] and shall carry with me to Orange Ct. today whence I expect to find another to the post office. Yrs. affy.

J. M.

---

46. JM meant TJ's undated letter that was franked on June 18.

47. Enclosure not found, but JM's list of letters to TJ indicates that it discussed TJ's answer to Hammond; see *PJM,* XIV, p. 328.

Madison to Jefferson

Orange June 29, 1792

No. 4

DEAR SIR

Your favor of June 21. No. 4. came to hand yesterday. I shall take due care of the N. Y. gazettes and return them by some safe conveyance to the post office. I have given a hasty perusal to the controversial papers on the election. The spirit of party sufficiently appears in all of them. Whether Clinton ought to wave the advantage of forms may depend I think on the question of substance involved in the conduct of the Otsego election. If it be clear that a majority of *legal* honest votes was given agst. him, he ought certainly not to force himself on the people. On a contrary supposition, he cannot be under such an obligation, and would be restrained by respect for his party if not by a love of power. It is curious eno' to see Schuyler who is supposed to have made millions by jobbing in paper, under his own measures, accusing and abusing Clinton in the face of the world for jobbing in land under the same aggravation. Should Clinton's character suffer in any way by the transaction, the consequence you have always apprehended, will be made certain and worse; but from the attachment of a number of respectable and weighty individuals, a reconsideration is not much to be looked for; unless the aspect of the man shd. be greatly varied in their eyes by this or some other occurrence. Our harvest goes on well. The weather has been hot, but otherwise favorable. The crop will be great in this neighbourhood. A little farther South the rust is said to have been hurtful. The Thermometer for several days has been remarkably high. Yesterday at 2 oC. it was at 92. During the early part of the month, distinguished by such extremes of cold and heat, I find by Philada. papers, that the heat there was two degrees greater than here, and the cold here two degrees less than there, a fact much in favor of our climate.

In Crantz's History of Greenland[48] I find a curious phenomenon of Looming, which, to supply the want of the Book if not at hand, or the trouble of searching it, if at hand and not of the same edition, I will transcribe "Vol. 1. p. 49—But nothing more surprized me, or entertained my fancy more, than when on a fine, warm, serene summer's day, the Kookoernen, or the islands that lie four leagues west of Good-Hope, presented a quite different form than what they have naturally. We not only saw them far greater, as thro' a magnifying perspective glass, and plainly descried all the Stones, and the furrows filled with ice, as if we stood close by, but when that had lasted a while, they all looked as if they were but one contiguous land, and represented a wood or tall cut hedge. Then the Scene shifts, and shews the appearance of all sorts of curious figures as ships with sails, streamers and flags, antique elevated castles,

---

48. David Cranz, *The History of Greenland*, trans. John Gombold (London, 1767); see *PJM*, XIV, p. 333.

with decayed turrets, stork's nests, and a hundred such things, which at length retire aloft or distant and then vanish. At such times the air is quite serene and clear, but yet compressed with subtle vapours, as it is in very hot weather, and according to my opinion, when these vapours are ranged at a proper distance between the eye and the islands, the object appears much larger, as it would thro' a convex glass; and commonly a couple of hours afterwards a gentle west wind and a visible mist follows, which puts an end to this lusus naturæ." To this paragraph the following note is subjoined from Gmelin's journey P. III vol. 129.[49] "I have observed something like this at Bern and Neufchatel, of the Glaetshers, lying towards the South. When these mountains appear nearer, plainer and larger than usual, the country man looks for rain to follow, which commonly makes good his expectation the next day. And the Tartars at the Mouth of the river Jenisei in Siberia, look upon a magnified appearance of the Islands as the presage of a storm." Adieu. Yrs. Affy.

Js. Madison Jr

Jefferson to Madison

Philadelphia June 29, 1792

No. 5

Dear Sir

I wrote you last on the 21st. The present will cover Fenno of the 23d. and 27th. In the last you will discover Hamilton's pen in defence of the bank, and daring to call the republican party *a faction.*[50]

I learn that he has expressed the strongest desire that Marshall should come into Congress from Richmond, declaring there is no man in Virginia whom he wishes so much to see there, and I am told that Marshall has expressed half a mind to come. Hence I conclude that Hamilton has plyed him well with flattery and sollicitation, and I think nothing better could be done than to make him a judge.

I have reason to believe that a regular attack, in phalanx, is to be made on the Residence act at the next session, with a determination to repeal it if the further assumption is not agreed to. I think this also comes from Hamilton tho' it is thro' two hands, if not more, before it comes to me.

Brandt went off yesterday, apparently in the best dispositions, and with some hopes of effecting peace. A letter received yesterday from Mr. Short gives the most flattering result of conversations he had had with Claviere and

---

49. Johann Georg Gmelin, *Reise durch Sibirien, von dem Jahr 1733 bis 1740*, 4 vols. (Göttingen, 1751–52), III, p. 129; see *PJM*, XIV, p. 333.

50. TJ's italics. The editors of *The Papers of Alexander Hamilton* conclude that, except for TJ's attribution, there was "no additional evidence that H. was the author of this article"; see Syrett, XI, p. 582.

Dumourier[51] with respect to us. Claviere declared he had nothing so much at heart as to encourage our navigation, and the freest system of commerce with us. Agreed they ought immediately to repeal their late proceedings with respect to tobo. and ships, and recieve our salted provisions favorably, and to proceed to treat with us on broad ground. Dumourier expressed the same sentiments. Mr. Short had then recieved notice that G. M. would be there in a few days, and therefore told the ministers that this was only a preliminary conversation on what Mr. Morris would undertake regularly. This ministry, which is of the Jacobin party, cannot but be favorable to us, as that whole party must be. Indeed notwithstanding the very general abuse of the Jacobins, I begin to consider them as representing the true revolution-spirit of the whole nation, and as carrying the nation with them. The only things wanting with them is more experience in business, and a little more conformity to the established style of communication with foreign powers. The latter want will I fear bring enemies into the feild, who would have remained at home; the former leads them to domineer over their executive so as render it unequal to it's proper objects. I sincerely wish our new minister may not spoil our chance of extracting good from the present situation of things.

The President leaves this about the middle of July. I shall set out some days later, and have the pleasure of seeing you in Orange. Adieu my dear Sir. Your's affectionately

Th: Jefferson

Jefferson to Madison

Philadelphia July 3, 1792

No. 6

Dear Sir

Since my last of June 29. I have received your Nos. 2. and 3. of June 24. and 25. The following particulars occur. Vining has declined offering at the next election. It is said we are to have in his room a Mr. Roach, formerly of the army, an anti-cincinnatus, and good agricultural man. Smith of S. C. declines also. He has bought a fine house in Charleston for 5000. £ and had determined not even to come to the next session. But his friends it is said have made him promise to come. One gentleman from S. Carolina says he could not be re-elected. Another says there could be no doubt of his re-election. Commodore Gillon is talked of as his successor. Izard gives out that it is all false that Mr. Smith is so rich as has been pretended, that he is in fact poor, cannot afford to live here, and therefore has retired to Charleston. Some add that he has entered again at the bar. The truth seems to be that they are alarmed, and

---

51. Étienne Clavière was finance minister and Charles-François du Périer Dumouriez the foreign minister in the short-lived Girondist cabinet in France in 1792; see *PJM,* XIV, p. 334.

he driven out of the feild, by the story of the modern Colchis.[52] His furniture is gone off from hence.[53] So is Mr. Adams's. Some say he declines offering at the next election. This is probably a mere conjecture founded on the removal of his furniture. The most likely account is that Mrs. Adams does not intend to come again, and that he will take private lodgings. It seems nearly settled with the Tresorio-bankites that a branch shall be established at Richmond. Could not a counter-bank be set up to befriend the Agricultural man by letting him have money on a deposit of tobo. notes, or even wheat, for *a short time,* [54] and would not such a bank enlist the legislature in it's favor, and against the Treasury bank? The President has fixed on Thursday the 12th. for his departure, and I on Saturday the 14th. for mine. According to the stages I have marked out I shall lodge at Strode's on Friday the 20th. and come the next morning, if my horses face Adams's mill hills boldly, to breakfast at Orange C. H. and after breakfast will join you. I have written to Mr. Randolph to have horses sent for me on that day to John Jones's about 12 miles from your house, which will enable me to breakfast the next day (Sunday) at Monticello. All this however may be disjointed by unexpected delays here, or on the road. I have written to Dr. Stewart and Ellicot to procure me *renseignements* on the direct road from Georgetown to Elkrun church which ought to save me 20. or 30. miles. Adieu my dear Sir. Your's affectionately

TH: JEFFERSON

P. S. I shall write you again a day or two before I leave this.

Madison to Jefferson

Orange July 5, 1792

No. 5

DEAR SIR

My last acknowledged the last of yours that has come to hand. From the date of that I shall probably have the pleasure of another as soon as an oppor-

---

52. In Greek mythology, Colchis was the country that lost the Golden Fleece to Jason and the Argonauts; see *ibid.,* p. 337. TJ's use of this allusion suggests that he referred to the financial panic on Wall Street (the Stock Exchange was established in 1792) created by the failure of William Duer, who had tried to corner the market in government bonds. See Miller, pp. 303–7; see also Robert F. Jones, *"The King of the Alley": William Duer, Politician, Entrepreneur, and Speculator,* vol. 202 of *Memoirs* (Am. Phil. Soc., 1992), and Cathy Matson, "Public Vices, Private Benefit: William Duer and His Circle, 1776–1792," in *New York and the Rise of American Capitalism,* ed. Conrad Wright and William Pencak (Charlottesville, 1989), pp. 72–123.

53. William Loughton Smith speculated heavily in government securities, suffered heavy losses, and considered retiring from politics. After the death of his wife in the fall, however, he reconsidered and remained in the House until 1797, when he was appointed minister to Portugal; see George C. Rogers, junior, *Evolution of a Federalist: William Loughton Smith of South Carolina, 1758–1812* (Columbia, S.C., 1962), pp. 236–37.

54. TJ's italics.

tunity from Fredericksbg. happens. I write at present merely for the sake of one thither which has just fallen in my way. The most remarkable occurrence of late date here, was the excessive heat on sunday the first instant. At two OClock the Thermometer in its ordinary position was at 99°. At four it had got up to 103°. On being taken into the passage the coolest part of the House it stood at the former hour at 97°, and at the latter at 98°. On applying the heat of the body it fell to 96°. The wind blew very briskly from West from morning till abt. 5 OC. and during the hottest part of the time was so sensibly above the annual heat, that it was more disagreeable to be in its current than out of it. The day following the heat about 2 OC approached very near, but not equal that of the first. Our harvest is now closing and will all be got in well in this quarter. The wheat is fine and the quantity equal to every reasonable calculation. There have been several fine showers during the harvest which have aided the Corn, without injuring the Wheat. Yrs. Always and Affy.

Js. MADISON JR

The Thermr. this morning as low as 58°.

Jefferson to Madison

Philadelphia July 11, 1792

DEAR SIR

I wrote you my No. 6. on the 3d inst. Since that I have received your No. 4. of June 29. The President sets out this afternoon, which being a day sooner than was expected, will enable me to set out a day sooner, to wit on Friday afternoon. This however will produce no other effect than to enable me to rest a day at George town and thereby ensure my being with you as I had mentioned on Saturday morning the 21st, or at the most on Friday evening, and to rest with you a day. I shall be with you so soon after this letter that I add nothing more. Your's affectionately

TH: JEFFERSON

Jefferson to Madison

Philadelphia July 13, 1792

DEAR SIR

I wrote you two days ago but by a bungle of the servant it did not get to the post office in time. This serves to cover another paper. I set out this afternoon. Adieu. Your's affectionately

TH: JEFFERSON

Madison to Jefferson

[Orange] July 27, 1792

Dr Sir

I recd. yesterday your letters containing the papers inclosed. I recd. at the same time a letter from Mr. Maury of Liverpool in which was the little note which I also inclose.

Brown and a Col Edwards[55] are the Senators for Kentucky. The latter sd. to be a good man and not likely to differ from the politics of his colleague. A distant kinsman of Mine Hubbard Taylor is likely to be one of the Reps. The other altogether uncertain. Muter is appd. a Judge and out of the question. I am this moment setting out for Frederick and only add in haste that I am Yrs. always and Affly.

Js. Madison Jr

Be so good as to let Col. Monroe have the Kentucky paper after you have done with it.

Jefferson to Madison

Monticello Sept. 17, 1792

My dear Sir

I thank you for the perusal of the two letters which are now inclosed. I would also have inclosed Fenno's two last papers but that Mr. Randolph, who has them, has rode out. If he returns in time they shall be sent you by the bearer. They contain nothing material but the Secretary's progress in paying the national debt, and attacks and defences relating to it. The simple question appears to me to be What did the Public owe, principal and interest, when the Secretary's taxes began to run? and what does it owe now, Principal and interest? If less, it must have been paid. But if he was paying old debts with one hand and creating new ones with the other, it is such a game as Mr. Pitt is playing. My granddaughter has been at death's door.[56] The Doctor left us only this morning. She is now we think out of danger. While we sent for him for one patient, two others were prepared for him, to wit, my daughter[57] and a grandson[58] which she produced. All are now doing well. Yet I think I shall not be able to leave her till about Tuesday, and even then it will depend on the little accidents to which her present situation leaves her liable. Adieu my dear Sir. Your's affectionately

Th: Jefferson

---

55. John Edwards moved from Stafford County, Virginia, to Kentucky in 1780 and became a leader in the movement that brought statehood in 1792; see *PJM,* XIV, p. 341.
56. Anne Cary Randolph.
57. Martha "Patsy" Jefferson Randolph.
58. Thomas Jefferson Randolph was born on Sept. 11, 1792.

Jefferson to Madison

Georgetown Oct. 1, 1792

MY DEAR SIR

I called at Gunston hall. The proprietor just recovering from a dreadful attack of the cholic. He was perfectly communicative, but I could not, in discretion let him talk as much as he was disposed.[59] I proceeded to M. Vernon and had a full, free, and confidential conversation with the President. The particulars shall be communicated when I see you. He declares himself quite undecided about retiring, desirous to do so, yet not decided if strong motives against it exist. He thinks if he declares a month before the day of election it will be sufficient: consequently that he may make his declaration even after the meeting of Congress. Bishop Madison whom I met here is just stepping into the stage, therefore I can only add assurances of my sincere affection

TH: JEFFERSON

Jefferson to Madison

Bladensburg Oct. 1, 1792

MY DEAR SIR

In the line I scribbled to you from Georgetown to-day I omitted to inform you that I had unfortunately dropped your letter with some papers of my own in the road between Mount Vernon and Alexandria. Proper measures are taken to recover them.

I have reflected on Govr. Lee's plan of opposing the Federal bank by setting up a state one, and find it not only inadequate, but objectionable highly, and unworthy of the Virginia assembly. I think they should not adopt such a milk and water measure, which rather recognises than prevents the planting among them a source of poison and corruption to sap their catholicism, and to annihilate that power, which is now one, by dividing it into two which shall counterbalance each other. The assembly should reason thus. The power of erecting banks and corporations was not given to the general government it remains then with the state itself. For any person to recognise a foreign legislature in a case belonging to the state itself, is an act of *treason*[60] against the state, and whosoever shall do any act under colour of the authority of a foreign legislature whether by signing notes, issuing or passing them, acting as director, cashier or in any other office relating to it shall be adjudged guilty of high treason and suffer death accordingly, by the judgment of the state courts. This is the only opposition worthy of our state, and the only kind which can be

---

59. In less than a week, George Mason died.

60. TJ's italics. This letter shows TJ at his most doctrinare against the Hamiltonian system.

effectual. If N. Carolina could be brought into a like measure, it would bring the General government to respect the counter-rights of the states. The example would probably be followed by some other states. I really wish that this or nothing should be done. A bark [bank] of opposition, while it is a recognition of the one opposed, will absolutely fail in Virginia. Adieu. Yours affectionately.

Jefferson to Madison

Baltimore Oct. 2, 1792

TH: J. TO J. M.

I wrote you twice yesterday. This is chiefly to cover the inclosed. On a sum of the poll last night at Annapolis and Baltimore (the only places of polling in Mercer's district) he was ahead of Thomas only about 25. votes in upwards of 400. The election was then to continue 3. days more. From every thing I can hear it is so doubtful that I would take up 100. to 99 either way. Thomas is a quaker, unaffected to our cause during the war, now a farmer and also factor for British merchants in the shipping business, of the purest character, and a man of letters, that is to say, a poet. Here is also a great contest between Smith[61] and Ridgeley. The Baltimorians say Smith will carry it, but they wish it. The other is the man of the landed interest.[62] Three days more will decide. Adieu.

The result of the poll here and in the county for to-day is this moment brought me. Out of 1500 polled, Smith has a majority of 450. and they pronounce that of the whole poll which it is thought will be about 3000, Smith will have 2000.

Madison to Jefferson

[Orange] Oct. 9, 1792

MY DEAR SIR

Your 3 favors from G. Town, Bladg. and Balte: have come safe to hand. The accident mentioned in the 2d. has caused no small anxiety; which wd. be much greater were it not hoped from your not waiting to repair it, that a *safe*[63] train had been laid for the purpose, and particularly that the article had been

---

61. For Samuel Smith, who served as congressman or senator from 1793 until 1833, see Frank Cassell, *Merchant Congressman in the Young Republic: Samuel Smith of Maryland, 1752–1839* (Madison, 1971), and John S. Pancake, *Samuel Smith and the Politics of Business, 1752–1839* (University, Ala., 1972).

62. There were two Charles Ridgely's in Baltimore, both of whom served in the Maryland assembly; see *PJM,* XIV, p. 376.

63. JM's italics.

put under seal. The possibility of its falling into base hands at the present crisis cannot be too carefully guarded agst. I beg you to let me know its fate the moment it is in your power. Was my letter for Carroll and that for Beckley in your lost packet? I hear nothing more on the project of Govr. Lee. Your objections to it seem unanswerable. I see no probability however that the politics of the Session, will be saved from the random course to which they are exposed. Monroe left me the day before yesterday. He calculates on setting out from Fredg. abt. the 20 or 21. Adieu

Jefferson to Madison

Philadelphia Oct. 17, 1792

DEAR SIR

I recd yesterday yours of the 9th. and perceive that the hurry in which I wrote from Bladensbg. has exposed you to an anxiety against which I ought to have guarded by being more explicit. The morning I was at mount Vernon, I took out of my phaeton box (wherein all my papers were) your letter to Mr. Carrol (because I was to see him that day) and five letters from individuals to me which I wished to shew to the President. These not being returned to me till my carriage was prepared for the journey, I put them in my pocket. A neighbor of his going to Alexa. that day picked up your letter to Mr. Carrol and two of mine abovementd. The former he put into the post-office and it was delivd to Mr. Carrol even at the moment I wrote from Bladsbg. tho' I did not know it, the latter he carried to the Presidt.

The other three letters I have not yet recd. but the whole five were so unimportant that I had not a moment's uneasiness about *them*.[64]

You will have heard of the reelection of Mercer, and of the death of Colo. Mason. This last is a great loss, and especially at a moment when our state seems ripening for a constitution. Beckley has got a house for Monroe, in Arch street between 6th and 7th. Adieu à revoir. Your's affectionately

TH: JEFFERSON

Madison to Jefferson

Fredericksburg Oct. 23, 1792

MY DEAR SIR

I got here a few days ago, and shall set out in company with Col: Monroe tomorrow. Parker Giles and Venable[65] are here also on their way to Philada.

64. TJ's italics.
65. Josiah Parker, William Branch Giles, and Abraham B. Venable were Republican members of the Virginia congressional delegation.

The information they give of the temper of the Assembly is in all respects favorable. The vacancy produced by R. H. Lee's resignation is filled with Col: J. Taylor.⁶⁶ He had 90 odd votes, A. Lee, 39. and Corbin 33. Great efforts were made for A. L. among others it is said by the *Supervisor.* ⁶⁷ My brother writes me that the vote for vice P. is most likely to be unanimous in favor of the republican Candidate, that the excise is generally reprobated; but the public temper as to direct taxes not yet ascertained. I have discovered that my inference from the expression in your letter at Bladensbg. was erroneous; which has relieved me from some inquietude. Adieu Yrs. Affy.

Js. MADISON JR.

66. For Taylor, who succeeded Richard Henry Lee as U.S. senator from Virginia, see Robert E. Shalhope, *John Taylor of Caroline: Pastoral Republican* (Columbia, S.C., 1980).

67. The "Supervisor" was Edward Carrington, federal collector of revenue in Virginia.

17

THE FRENCH CONNECTION AND AMERICAN NEUTRALITY, 1793

*I*N THE FALL OF 1792, George Washington gave in to the urgings of Madison, Jefferson, Hamilton, and others, consenting to serve a second term as president. Although he was above party considerations, the congressional contests emerged as a "struggle between the Treasury department and the republican Interest."[1] Hamilton admitted that his differences with Madison over discrimination between original holders and subsequent purchasers of government securities had "laid the foundation of the great schism which has since prevailed."[2] Madison agreed that Hamilton's system had encouraged "the spirit of speculation within and without the government," disgusting "the best friends of the Union" and forcing a choice "between the loss of the Union, and the loss of what the union was meant to secure."[3]

From the beginning, Madison had assumed the leadership of the congressional opposition to the Hamiltonian system. By 1792, congressmen spoke of "Mr. Madison's party," and William L. Smith, a South Carolina supporter of Hamilton, labeled Madison as the "General" and Jefferson as the "Generalissimo" of the Republican party, which raised a "pretended outcry against Monarchy and Aristocracy."[4] One of the targets of Republican animosity was Vice President John Adams, whom they hoped to replace with a candidate of more republican leanings. Madison and Monroe cooperated with New York Republicans in coordinating a campaign on behalf of Governor George Clinton of

1. John Beckley to JM, Sept. 2, 1792, in Noble E. Cunningham, Jr., *The Jeffersonian Republicans: The Formation of Party Organization, 1789–1801* (Chapel Hill, 1957), p. 29.
2. John C. Miller, *Alexander Hamilton: Portrait in Paradox* (New York, 1959), p. 241.
3. JM, "The Union: Who Are Its Real Friends?" Mar. 31, 1792, in *PJM,* XIV, pp. 274–75.
4. Cunningham, pp. 28–29; John C. Miller, *The Federalist Era: 1789–1801* (New York, 1960), pp. 102–3.

New York, who received the unanimous vote of New York, Virginia, North Carolina, and Georgia.[5]

The results of the congressional elections of 1792 pleased both Madison and Jefferson since it produced "a decided majority in favor of the republican interest."[6] But the new Congress would not convene until December 1793. In the meantime, the lame-duck Congress met in the fall of 1792, and Jefferson thought "the less they do, and the more they leave to their successors, the better."[7] When a bankruptcy bill was introduced in the House, he drafted his "extempore thoughts and doubts" in a memorandum to Madison, his only letter to his friend during that session. But they must have gotten together regularly since his covering note said, "I dine at home and alone to-day and Saturday of the present week," a standing invitation for Madison to drop by.[8]

One thing that they discussed in person was Jefferson's overwhelming desire to retire with the outgoing Congress. "It is probable," Madison informed a friend, "that Mr. Jefferson will not remain very long in his public station; but it is certain that his retirement is not to be ascribed to the Newspaper calumnies which may have had that in view."[9] Three days later, Jefferson informed his landlord that he would terminate his lease in March 1793.[10]

But a month before he was to leave, Jefferson decided to stay on, "perhaps till summer, perhaps autumn."[11] One reason for his reversal was a congressional attempt to discredit Hamilton, a move that Jefferson secretly joined despite his personal standards of official propriety. In January 1793, William B. Giles, a congressman from Virginia, called for a report by Hamilton on his handling of public funds. The secretary's response, according to Madison, showed "that there has been at least a very blameable irregularity and secrecy in some particulars of it, and many appearances, which at least require explanation."[12] Jefferson went further, drafting a set of resolutions that declared Hamilton unworthy of office. Giles watered these down, indicting Hamilton for a technical violation of an appropriation law, an unwarranted failure to inform Congress of his management of federal funds, and "indecorum" in his

5. Of the 55 anti-Adams votes in the electoral college, 50 went to Clinton; Adams received 77. See Cunningham, pp. 45–49.

6. TJ to Thomas Pinckney, Dec. 3, 1792, in *PTJ,* XXIV, p. 696, and JM to Edmund Pendleton, Dec. 6, 1792, in *PJM,* XIV, p. 421.

7. TJ to Thomas Mann Randolph, Nov. 2, 1792, in *PTJ,* XXIV, p. 556.

8. TJ to JM, [ca. Dec. 12, 1792], below. See also Charles Warren, *Bankruptcy in United States History* (Cambridge, Mass., 1935), pp. 6–22.

9. JM to Edmund Pendleton, Dec. 6, 1792, in *PJM,* XIV, p. 421.

10. Malone, II, p. 485.

11. TJ, "Notes of a conversation with Washington," Feb. 7, 1793, "The Anas, 1791–1806," in *Thomas Jefferson: Writings,* ed. Merrill D. Peterson, (New York, 1984), p. 683.

12. JM to Edmund Pendleton, Feb. 23, 1793, in *PJM,* XIV, p. 452. For TJ's first attempt to discredit Hamilton, see TJ to JM, "Notes on Mal-Administration of Treasury," [Philadelphia ca. Jan. 18, 1793], below.

responses to congressional calls for information. When Congress voted on the charges, the Republicans were defeated on every count, and Hamilton was virtually vindicated as Washington's first term closed.[13]

Despite this "negative of palpable truth" by the lame-duck Congress, Jefferson thought that the inquiry would show the public "the extent of their danger, and a full representation at the ensuing session will doubtless find occasion to revise the decision."[14] An uneasy truce prevailed between the two secretaries, with neither yielding to the other in cabinet discussions, each convinced that the other's principles tended to subvert the government—Hamilton fearful of anarchy, Jefferson of monarchy.

Explosive events in Europe heightened these fears in 1793. The French Revolution quickly became the central issue in national politics following the execution of Louis XVI, the proclamation of the French Republic, and France's declaration of war on England as part of the "war of all peoples against all Kings." By its abolition of the monarchy, France duplicated America's rejection of King George; by establishing a republican system, it followed America's lead in political organization; by declaring war against Great Britain, it raised the issue of American aid under its treaty of alliance made during the American Revolution; and with the dramatic arrival of Edmond-Charles-Édouard Genet, the French Republic's minister to the United States, it created a crisis in Franco-American affairs.[15]

This catastrophic cluster of events in Europe brought mixed reactions in America, varying from "the warmest Jacobinism" of some Republicans "to the most heartfelt aristocracy" of some Monocrats, a label that Jefferson used increasingly for Federalists. Dormant hostility for revolutionary democracy erupted in Federalist circles. The ladies of Philadelphia, Jefferson observed, "are all open-mouthed against the murderers of a sovereign, and they generally speak those sentiments which the more cautious husband smothers."[16] Fisher Ames, Madison's leading opponent in Congress, thought that "France is madder than Bedlam, and will be ruined," and Vice President Adams worried that so many Americans were "so blind . . . and enthusiastic of everything that has been done by that light, airy, and transported people."[17]

But the vast mass of Americans supported France, identifying the revolution there as an imitation of the American Revolution. From his post in the nation's capital, Jefferson watched the buildup of Republican strength based

---

13. For TJ's role in the effort to censure Hamilton, see TJ to JM, "Draft of Giles's Treasury Resolutions Censuring Hamilton," [Philadelphia ca. Feb. 21-27, 1793], below; *PTJ*, XXV, p. 292, dates it "before 27 Feb. 1993." For the fullest analysis of TJ's role in the attack on Alexander Hamilton, see the brilliant detective work by Eugene R. Sheridan, "Thomas Jefferson and the Giles Resolutions," *WMQ* 49 (1992): 589-608. See also Malone, III, pp. 21-33; Peterson, pp. 477-80; and Cunningham, pp. 50-54.

14. TJ to Thomas Mann Randolph, Mar. 3, 1793, in Malone, III, p. 27.

15. See Patrice Higonnet, *Sister Republics: The Origins of French and American Republicanism* (Cambridge, Mass., 1989), for a comparative view.

16. TJ to JM, Mar. 25, 1793, below.

17. Cited in Ketcham, p. 338.

on public reaction to the war and revolutionary frenzy abroad. "The war between France and England," he told Madison, who was spending the summer in Virginia, "has brought forward the Republicans and Monocrats in every state so openly, that their relative numbers are perfectly visible. It appears that the latter are as nothing."[18] As he saw the political divisions, "the line is now drawing so clearly as to shew, on one side, 1. the fashionable circles of Phila., N. York, Boston and Charleston (natural aristocrats), 2. merchants trading on British capitals. 3. paper men, (all the old tories are found in some one of these three descriptions) [.] on the other side are 1. merchants trading on their own capitals. 2. Irish merchants. 3. tradesmen, mechanics, farmers and every other possible description of our citizens."[19]

None of the Republicans was more committed to the concept of the revolution in France as an extension of the one in America than was Madison. Shortly after the arrest of the king in August 1792, the National Assembly conferred French citizenship on seventeen foreigners, including Washington, Hamilton, and Madison, citing them as "friends of liberty and universal brotherhood" whose writings and actions had not only proclaimed the rights of man but had also smoothed the way for a nation made free by their enlightenment.[20] Although Washington and Hamilton let their elections go unnoticed, Madison warmly embraced his, applauding America's "public connection with France" and citing "their mutual liberty." In his letter of acceptance, he also expressed his hope that the French nation would complete "the triumphs of Liberty, by a victory over the minds of all its adversaries."[21]

Between the arrest and imprisonment of Louis XVI and the calling of the National Convention in 1792, the United States suspended payments on the American debt to France until a legitimate government was established. Jefferson and Hamilton disagreed on what constituted a legitimate government, the secretary of state thinking in terms of people and the secretary of the treasury in terms of rulers. When the National Convention assembled after the fall of the monarchy, Jefferson argued persuasively that "it accords with our principles to acknolege any government to be rightful which is formed by the will of the nation substantially declared."[22] The National Convention, therefore, should be recognized as the legitimate government. Although Hamilton disagreed, Washington sided with Jefferson. The principle, said the author of the Declaration of Independence, was a new but enduring one established by

---

18. TJ to JM, June 29, 1793, below.

19. TJ to JM, May 13, 1793, below.

20. The French decree is printed in Syrett, XII, pp. 545-46; an abstract is in *PJM,* XIV, p. 381. The French edition of *The Federalist* was published in Paris in 1792 and identified Hamilton, Madison, and Jay as authors; see R. R. Palmer, *The Age of the Democratic Revolution: A Political History of Europe and America, 1760–1800,* 2 vols. (Princeton, 1959–64), II, p. 55, and Brant, III, pp. 372–74.

21. JM to the minister of the interior of the French Republic, Apr. 1793, enclosure, JM to TJ, May 29, 1793, below.

22. TJ to Gouverneur Morris, Nov. 7, 1792, in *PTJ,* XXIV, pp. 592–94.

the American Revolution. "We certainly cannot deny to other nations that principle whereon our government is founded, that every nation has a right to govern itself internally under what forms it pleases, and to change these forms at its own will: and externally to transact business with other nations thro' whatever organ it chuses, whether that be a king, convention, assembly, committee, president, or whatever it be. The only thing essential is the will of the nation."[23] Accordingly, Washington decided to receive France's new minister, Edmond Genet, and to resume payments of the American debt to France.

Before Genet arrived in the United States, however, war had erupted between France and England. Both Jefferson and Hamilton kept the president informed at Mt. Vernon, with the former favoring "every justifiable measure for preserving our neutrality, and at the same time to provide [to the warring nations] those necessities for war which must be brought across the Atlantic."[24] Hamilton also favored neutrality, but he and Jefferson disagreed on the method and the timing for declaring it. On method, Jefferson at first thought that a decision on neutrality, like a decision on war, should be made by Congress, not the president. On the day that Madison reached Montpellier after Congress had adjourned, Jefferson fired off a letter saying that Congress might be recalled immediately. "As the Executive cannot decide the question of war on the affirmative side," he wrote, "neither ought it to do so on the negative side, by preventing the competent body from deliberating on the question." If Congress formulated national policy, he hoped that it would set "another precious example to the world, by shewing that nations may be brought to do justice by appeals to their interests as well as by appeals to arms."[25] On timing, he wanted to avoid quick action, preferring instead to use a declaration of neutrality as a bargaining weapon in negotiations with the belligerent powers, forcing them to bid for it in exchange for "the *broadest privileges* of neutral nations."[26] Indeed, he suspected that the British minister "might have been instructed to have asked it, and to offer *the broadest neutral privileges,* as the price, which was exactly the price I wanted that we should contend for."[27]

In response to urgent letters from Jefferson and Hamilton, Washington returned to Philadelphia in mid-April to preside over cabinet discussions of ways to maintain neutrality. Hamilton favored a proclamation by the president without delay and tried to reverse the earlier decision to recognize Genet as the representative of a legitimate government. At first, he argued that the treaties with France were void since the republic had not been "finally *established* and secured," but he modified that stance and concluded that they should be declared "temporarily and provisionally suspended," citing a passage, Jefferson

---

23. TJ to Thomas Pinckney, Dec. 30, 1792, *ibid.,* p. 803.
24. TJ to George Washington, Apr. 7, 1793, in Ford, VI, p. 212.
25. TJ to JM, Mar. 25, 1793, below.
26. TJ to JM, June 23, 1793, below.
27. TJ to JM, June 29, 1793, below.

said, from an "ill-understood scrap" by Vattel.[28] If Washington received Genet, the president would not only recognize the French Republic, he would also recognize the Franco-American treaties, which Hamilton thought were incompatible with neutrality.[29]

In making his decision, Washington sided with Jefferson on recognizing Genet and the treaties with France and with Hamilton on the authority to issue a proclamation and the timing of its release. The president's proclamation, which was drafted by Attorney General Edmund Randolph and issued on April 22, omitted the word "neutrality" out of deference to Jefferson's views.[30] Despite that fact, it has ever since been universally denominated the Proclamation of Neutrality. Calling for conduct "friendly and impartial towards the belligerent powers," it warned Americans against "aiding or abetting hostilities" or committing acts in violation of "the modern usage of nations."

Jefferson, who equated the cause of France with the cause of liberty, confessed to Madison that "a fair neutrality will prove a disagreeable pill to our friends," but he thought it "necessary to keep us out of the calamities of a war."[31] Madison conceded that "the bitter pills ... must be administered" in order to preserve peace, but he doubted "whether the term *impartial* in the Proclamation is not stronger than was necessary." He reserved his most severe criticism, however, for Hamilton's "attempt to shuffle off the Treaty altogether by quibbling on Vattel," labeling it "equally contemptible for the meanness and folly of it. If a change of Govt. is an absolution from public engagements, why not from those of a domestic as well as of a foreign nature; and what then becomes of public debts etc. etc. In fact, the doctrine would perpetuate every existing Despotism, by involving in a reform of the Govt. a destruction of the Social pact, an annihilation of property, and a compleat establishment of the State of Nature. What most surprises me is that such a proposition *shd. have been discussed*."[32]

To Jefferson, a "fair neutrality" was one compatible with the treaties with France and with the rights of neutral nations, which defined contraband narrowly and blockade realistically. He preferred "a manly neutrality, claiming the liberal rights ascribed to that condition," but he feared the proclamation would be interpreted by the cabinet as "a mere English neutrality." The cabinet, he informed Madison, met almost daily on questions of neutrality, with Hamilton, Attorney General Randolph, and Secretary of War Henry Knox on one side and himself on the other. "In short, my dear Sir, it is impossible for you to concieve what is passing in our conclave: and it is evident that one or two at least, under pretence of avoiding war on the one side have no great antipathy to run foul of it on the other, and to make a part in the confederacy

---

28. TJ to JM, Apr. 28, 1793, below.
29. Miller, *Federalist Era,* pp. 128–29.
30. TJ to JM, June 23, 1793, below.

31. TJ to JM, Apr. 28, 1793, below.
32. JM to TJ, May 8, 1793, below.

of princes against human liberty." The only things preventing such a policy were the president, whose penchant "is not that way, and above all, the ardent spirit of our constituents."³³

The more Madison learned about the proclamation, the less he liked "the anglified complexion charged on the Executive politics."³⁴ He had written his letter accepting honorary French citizenship before learning of the Proclamation of Neutrality. Once he heard of it, he stewed for a month before finally deciding to enclose his acceptance in a letter to Jefferson that endorsed "the affection to France in her struggles for liberty."³⁵ Although he was clearly worried about the propriety of sending an answer after the Proclamation of Neutrality had been promulgated, he was more concerned about the reception it would receive in France than about "any comments which the publication attending all such things, may produce here."³⁶ Nor was Jefferson any more concerned. "I found every syllable of it strictly proper," he wrote, and he, therefore, delivered it to Genet to be forwarded to France's new minister of the interior.³⁷

Nonetheless, the increasing hostility to the excesses of the French Revolution and the stresses and strains of organizing an opposition party forced Madison and Jefferson to be more circumspect about letters that they put into the public mail, a precaution dictated in part because the Federalists controlled the post offices. Both ceased signing most of their letters to each other in April, confining signed correspondence to letters carried by trusted couriers. By August, they resorted to their 1785 cipher for encoding sensitive passages.³⁸

Isolated on his farm in Virginia, Madison read the Republican newspapers, full of criticism of the president's proclamation, and took a doctrinaire line on its constitutionality—or unconstitutionality. He was surprised that Washington "should have declared the U. S. to be neutral in the unqualified terms used, when we were so notoriously and unequivocally under *eventual engagements* to defend the American possessions of F[rance]." He was especially worried that "an assumption of prerogatives not clearly found in the Constitution and having the appearance of being copied from a Monarchical model, will beget animadversion equally mortifying to him, and disadvantageous to the Government."³⁹

One week later, Madison concluded that "the proclamation was in truth a

---

33. TJ to JM, May 13, 1793, below, and May 19, 1793, below.
34. JM to TJ, June 19, 1793, below.
35. JM to TJ, May 29, 1793, below.
36. JM to TJ, June 13, 1793, below.
37. TJ to JM, June 9, 1793, below.
38. See *PJM,* XV, p. xx.
39. JM to TJ, June 13, 1793, below.

most unfortunate error. It wounds the National honor, by seeming to disregard the stipulated duties to France. It wounds the popular feelings by a seeming indifference to the cause of liberty. And it seems to violate the forms and spirit of the Constitution, by making the executive Magistrate the organ of the disposition[,] the duty and the interest of the Nation in relation to war and peace, subjects appropriated to other departments of the Government. It is mortifying to the real friends of the P[resident]," he continued, "that his fame and his influence should have been unnecessarily made to depend in any degree on political events in a foreign quarter of the Globe: and particularly so that he should have any thing to apprehend from the success of liberty in another country, since he owes his pre-eminence to the success of it in his own."[40]

As Madison's animosity mounted, Jefferson became more critical of "the pusillanimity of the proclamation," calling it "officious and improper," "milk and water," and impolitic, though not illegal or unconstitutional.[41] It had been "badly drawn" by Attorney General Randolph, Jefferson lamented, but he confessed that when he hastily reviewed it, he had "only run an eye over it to see that it was not made a declaration of neutrality, and gave it back again, without, I believe, changing a tittle."[42]

Both Jefferson and Madison expected the popular reception of Genet to offset "the cold caution of their government" and reveal "the real affections of the people" for France and republicanism.[43] The war between France and England, Jefferson enthused, was rekindling "all the old spirit of 1776."[44] Although the proclamation betrayed no affection for France, "our constituents . . . are coming forward to express it themselves."

Genet had landed at Charleston on April 8 and made a leisurely trip north with the soft southern spring, arriving in Philadelphia on May 16, where he received a tumultuous welcome from "a vast concourse of the people," according to the secretary of state. When the new French minister presented his credentials two days later, he endorsed neutrality: " 'We know that under present circumstances we have a right to call upon you for the guarantee of our islands. But we do not desire it.' " What France wanted were American products and supplies, and Genet brought a decree opening " 'our country and it's colonies to you for every purpose of utility, without your participating [in] the burthens of maintaining and defending them.' " He was also authorized to negotiate a more liberal treaty of commerce. "In short," Jefferson told Madison, "he offers every thing and asks nothing." "It is impossible for any thing to

---

40. JM to TJ, June 19, 1793, below.
41. See TJ's letters to JM of May 19, June 29, and Aug. 11, 1793, below.
42. TJ to JM, Aug. 11, 1793, below.
43. TJ to JM, Apr. 28, 1793, below, and JM to TJ, May 8, 1793, below.
44. TJ to James Monroe, May 5, 1793, enclosure, TJ to JM, May 5, 1793, below.

be more affectionate," he added, or "more magnanimous than the purport of his mission."[45]

Drawing the line of neutrality until it "be fairly understood by ourselves, and the belligerent parties" was not an easy assignment, as Jefferson in Philadelphia explained to Madison in Virginia.[46] Neutrality—"manly neutrality," as Jefferson defined it—leaned towards the French connection, treaty ties, and widespread public sympathy for the republican cause abroad. Neutrality as interpreted by Hamilton leaned towards the British connection, existing commercial ties, and revulsion with the Reign of Terror in France. President Washington tried to balance these two views of neutrality, leaning to Jefferson's stance until Genet's effrontery and audacious behavior pushed him towards Hamilton's position.

The insolence of Genet was compounded by the vehemence and vituperation of Freneau and the Republican press in their attacks on Washington. Jefferson was sincerely sorry to see these attacks on the president, who was "extremely affected" by them. "I think," he told Madison, "he feels those things more than any person I ever yet met with." And he added, "it is the more unfortunate that this attack is planted on popular ground, on the love of the people to France and it's cause, which is universal."[47]

Although Jefferson sympathized with the president, he became increasingly critical of his kinsman and former protégé Attorney General Edmund Randolph. Accustomed to counting on his vote to offset Hamilton and Knox in a 2-to-2 tie in cabinet deliberations, Jefferson was chagrined when Randolph took his lead from the president, creating a vote of 3 to 1 or 4 to 1. "Every thing my dear Sir," he complained to Madison in May, "now hangs on the opinion of a single person, and that the most indecisive one I ever had to do business with. He always contrives to agree in principle with one, but in conclusion with the other."[48] By midsummer, he labeled Randolph "the poorest Cameleon I ever saw. . . . When he is with me he is a whig, when with H[amilton] he is a tory, when with the P[resident] he is what he thinks will please him. The last is his strongest hue, tho' the 2d. tinges him very strongly."[49] Abandoned by Randolph, the beleagured Jefferson moaned—a bit melodramatically—that he was committed single-handedly "in desperate and eternal contest against a host who are systematically undermining the public liberty and prosperity."[50]

Jefferson's loneliness in the cabinet was compounded by Genet's impetuosity, and the secretary of state's letters soon contained a litany of complaints against the French minister's warlike actions that violated American

45. TJ to JM, May 19, 1793, below.
46. TJ to JM, Apr. 28, 1793, below.
47. TJ to JM, June 9, 1793, below.
48. TJ to JM, May 13, 1793, below.
49. TJ to JM, Aug. 11, 1793, below.
50. TJ to JM, June 9, 1793, below.

neutrality. "A French frigate is now bringing here . . . prizes which left this [city] but 2. or 3. days before," Jefferson wrote Madison even before Genet arrived in Philadelphia. "Shall we permit her to sell them? The treaty does not say we shall, and it says we shall not permit the like to England? Shall we permit France to fit out privateers here? The treaty does not stipulate that we shall, tho' it says we shall not permit the English to do it."[51]

The honeymoon with Genet was soon over. The French minister made a mockery of the president's proclamation by issuing military commissions to American citizens and letters of marque to armed merchantmen. By July, Jefferson had given up on him. "Never . . . was so calamitous an appointment made," he confided to Madison. "Hotheaded, all imagination, no judgment, passionate, disrespectful and even indecent towards the P[resident] in his written as well as verbal communications, talking of appeals from him to Congress, from them to the people, urging the most unreasonable and groundless propositions, and in the most dictatorial style etc. etc. etc." Yet he wished to avoid a break if possible, so Jefferson continued "to advise him freely, and he respects it. But," he added, "he breaks out again on the very first occasion, so as to shew that he is incapable of correcting himself." Indeed, Jefferson concluded, "he renders my position immensely difficult,"[52] so much so that the secretary of state began again to think of resigning his post.

As difficult as Jefferson's position was, Madison urged him to postpone his retirement. "I feel for your situation," he wrote sympathetically, "but you must bear it. . . . You must not make your final exit from public life till it will be marked with justifying circumstances which all good citizens will respect, and to which your friends can appeal. At the present crisis, what would the former think, what could the latter say?"[53]

Jefferson's sharp reply showed how raw his nerves had been rubbed by the daily combat in the cabinet. "The motion of my blood no longer keeps time with the tumult of the world," he wrote. His tour of public duty now spanned twenty-four years, and he had, therefore, discharged his responsibility for such service: "I am pledged by no act which gives any tribunal a call upon me before I withdraw. Even my enemies do not pretend this. . . . My friends I have not committed. . . . If the public then has no claim on me," he concluded testily, "and my friends nothing to justify, the decision will rest on my own feelings alone."[54] Accordingly, he notified the president that he would retire at the end of September.

By the end of June, the worst of the crisis generated by Genet seemed over. Washington welcomed a summer break at Mt. Vernon, Hamilton adjourned to the country, and Jefferson thought contentedly of Monticello,

51. TJ to JM, Apr. 28, 1793, below.
52. TJ to JM, July 7, 1793, below.
53. JM to TJ, May 27, 1793, below.
54. TJ to JM, June 9, 1793, below.

farming, and crop rotation.⁵⁵ As soon as the president was out of town, however, Hamilton, writing as "Pacificus," launched a series of newspaper articles based on his interpretation of the Proclamation of Neutrality, reading into that document what Washington had left out. He defended the constitutionality of the executive prerogative to issue the proclamation, argued that the treaty with France was suspended, denigrated the idea of gratitude towards France, denounced the French Revolution, and deplored the possibility of entering the war on the side of France.⁵⁶

Jefferson instantly recognized the pen of "Pacificus" "because it is an amplification only of the topics urged [in the cabinet] in discussing the question when first proposed. The right of the *Executive* to declare that we are *not bound to execute the guarantee* was then advanced by him and denied by me. No other opinion [was] expressed on it. In this paper he repeats it, and even considers the proclamation as such a declaration. But if any body intended it as such (except himself) they did not then say so. The passage beginning with the words 'the answer to this is etc.['] is precisely the answer he gave at the time to my objection that the Executive had no authority to issue a declaration of neutrality, nor to do more than declare the actual state of things to be that of peace. 'For until the new government is acknoleged the treaties etc. are of course suspended.' This also is the sum of his arguments the same day on the great question which followed that of the Proclamn., to wit Whether the Executive might not, and ought not to declare the treaties suspended?"⁵⁷

Jefferson lamented that Hamilton's "heresies" might pass unchallenged or that "mere bunglers and brawlers" might give ineffective answers. Without a powerful and prudent response, he argued, Hamilton's "doctrine will therefore be taken for confessed. For god's sake, my dear Sir," he urged Madison, "take up your pen, select the most striking heresies, and cut him to peices in the face of the public. There is nobody else who can and will enter the lists with him."⁵⁸

Despite his surprise and indignation with Hamilton's essays, Madison was reluctant to take on the assignment since he lacked "some material facts and many important lights."⁵⁹ Some of these Jefferson tried to supply, but he did not feel at liberty to reveal some details of confidential cabinet discussions. To Madison's questions, he replied:

1. What concessions have been made on particular points behind the curtain [in the cabinet]. I think it is better you should not know them. 2. How far *the president* considers himself as committed with respect to some doctrines. He is certainly uneasy

---

55. TJ to JM, June 29, 1793, below.
56. Hamilton's first "Pacificus" essay is printed in Syrett, XV, pp. 33–43.
57. TJ to JM, June 29, 1793, below.
58. TJ to JM, July 7, 1793, below.
59. JM to TJ, July 18, 1793, below.

at those grasped at by *Pacificus* and as *the author* is universally known and I believe indeed denied not even by himself, it is foreseen that the vulnerable points, well struck, stab the party vitally. 3. Lights from the law of nations on the constructions of treaties. Vattel has been most generally the guide. Bynkerschoeck ofter quoted, Wolf sometimes. 4. No call was made by any *power* previous to the *proclamation*. . . . [5]. The question whether the war between France and Gr. Br. is offensive or defensive *has not been particularly discussed*. *Hamilton* has insisted it was offensive by the former. I will send you the French collection of papers on that subject.[60]

Even before Madison received this information, he agreed to take on Hamilton in a series of newspaper essays. "I have forced myself into the task of a reply," he reported reluctantly. "I can truly say I find it the most grating one I ever experienced; and the more so as I feel at every step I take the want of counsel on some points of delicacy as well as of information as to sundry matters of fact."[61] Writing as "Helvidius," he drafted five articles on the constitutional issues, basing them on his and Jefferson's views and denying Hamilton's sweeping claims of executive prerogative, which seemed to him imitative of "*royal prerogatives* in the *British government*." Although he thought that "none but intelligent readers will enter into such a controversy," he tried to avoid leading his readers into "the wilderness of Books"; so he asked Jefferson to review his essays for readability before sending them to the press.[62]

In his essays, Madison had to walk a political tightrope, forcefully questioning the constitutionality of declaring neutrality by executive proclamation while affirming loyalty to the popular president and prudently avoiding any discussion of the merits of neutrality. At the same time, he had to reject Genet's shenanigans while pressing for American support of the French Revolution. While Madison labored to neutralize Hamilton and his followers, Genet "played into their hands." "He is so evidently in the wrong," Jefferson confessed, "that those are pressing for an appeal to the people, who never looked towards that tribunal before." What he feared was that "an open rupture will take place between the Fr[ench] min[ister] and us," thus arraying "each nation with it's own agents . . . against one another," consequently putting the United States on the side of England.[63]

Two weeks later, the president and his cabinet agreed unanimously to demand Genet's recall, and Jefferson warned Madison that "*he will sink the republican* interest if they do not *abandon him*."[64] In a confidential conveyance

60. For JM's queries, see JM to TJ, July 22, 1793, below; for TJ's responses, see TJ to JM, Aug. 3, 1793, below.
61. JM to TJ, July 30, 1793, below.
62. JM to TJ, July 22, 1793, below, July 30, 1793, below, and Aug. 12, 1793, below. The "Helvidius" essays are printed in *PJM,* XV, pp. 64–120 *passim.* JM's remarks about *"royal prerogatives"* are taken from the first number, *ibid.,* p. 72. The complete essays have been reprinted, with an excellent introduction, by Richard Loss, ed., *The Letters of Pacificus and Helvidius* . . . (Delmar, N.Y., 1976).
63. TJ to JM, July 14, 1793, below.
64. TJ to JM, Aug. 3, 1793, below.

a week later, he described his dilemma in dealing with the French minister. "I adhered to him as long as I could have a hope of getting him right, because I knew what weight we should derive to our scale by keeping in it the love of the people for the French cause and nation, and how important it was to ward off from that cause and nation any just grounds of alienation. Finding at length that the man was absolutely incorrigible, I saw the necessity of quitting a wreck which could not but sink all who should cling to it."[65]

How could he now help keep the Republican party afloat? It was time, Jefferson thought, for a major change in Republican strategy, a time to quit criticizing the president and to quit quibbling about the propriety of the Proclamation of Neutrality:

With respect to the Proclamation, as the facts it declared were true, and the desire of neutrality is universal, it would place the republicans in a very unfavble. point of view with the people to be cavilling about small points of propriety; and would betray a wish to find fault with the President in an instance where he will be approved by the great body of the people who consider the substance of the measure only, and not the smaller criticisms to which it is liable. The conduct of Genet too is transpiring and exciting the indignation it is calculated to excite. The towns are beginning generally to make known their disapprobation of any such opposition to their govmt. by a foreigner, are declaring their firm adherence to their President, and the Proclamation is made the groundwork of these declarations. In N. York, while Genet was there, the vote of a full meeting of all classes was 9. out of 10. against him, i.e. for the Proclamation. We are told that the cortege which was collected to recieve him (except the committee) consisted only of boys and negroes. All the towns Northwardly are about to express their adherence to the proclamation and chiefly with a view to manifest their disapprobation of G[enet]'s conduct. Philadelphia, so enthusiastic for him, before his proceedings were known, is going over from him entirely, and if it's popular leaders have not the good sense to go over with them, they will go without them, and be thus transferred to the other party.

To the acknowledged leader of the Republicans in Congress, he concluded:

So in Congress, I believe that it will be true wisdom in the Republican party to approve unequivocally of a state of neutrality, to avoid little cavils about who should declare it, to abandon G[enet] entirely, with expressions of strong friendship and adherence to his nation and confidence that he has acted against their sense. In this way we shall keep the people on our side by keeping ourselves in the right.[66]

Jefferson was goaded into this letter on party strategy by Hamilton and Knox's proposal to press an appeal to the people identifying the recently established Democratic Society of Philadelphia, "which they considered as the *antifederal and discontented faction*," as a creation of Genet that would "draw the

---

65. TJ to JM, Aug. 11, 1793, below.
66. *Ibid.* See Cunningham, pp. 54–62, for a discussion of the leadership of Jefferson, Madison, and Monroe in the emerging Republican party.

mass of the people, by dint of misinformation, into their vortex and overset the governmt. The Pres.," he told Madison, "was strongly impressed by this picture, drawn by H[amilton] in three speeches of ¾ of an hour length each. I opposed it totally, told the President plainly in their presence, that the intention was to dismount him from being the head of the nation, and make him the head of a party: that this would be the effect of making him in an appeal to the people declare war against the Republican party." Washington agreed to put off such an appeal indefinitely. "If the demonstrations of popular adherence to him become as general and warm as I believe they will," Jefferson concluded, "I think he will never again bring on the question." If, on the other hand, "there is any appearance of their supporting Genet, he will probably make the appeal."[67]

Less than a week after this explosive cabinet meeting, the president visited Jefferson at the country quarters he had taken after shipping most of his furnishings to Virginia as a prelude to retirement. Washington was worried about finding a successor as secretary of state. His first choice, he said, would be Madison, but "he could not expect he would undertake it." Other candidates were discussed, but no agreement was reached. Before asking Jefferson to stay on a while longer, the president dropped a bombshell: Hamilton also planned to retire at the end of the next session of Congress. If the two resignations coincided, the president "might consult both the particular talents and geographical situation of our successors." He hoped that Jefferson would agree to stay at least until the end of the year; "it would get us through the difficulties of this year, and he was satisfied that the affairs of Europe would be settled with this campaign, for that either France would be overwhelmed by it, or the confederacy [of England and her allies] would give up the contest." Jefferson consented reluctantly, moving his retirement date from September 30 to December 31.[68]

Jefferson kept Madison informed about the proposed recall of Genet, sending Madison copies of his letter of August 7 to the French minister and of August 16 to Gouverneur Morris, American minister to France, requesting Genet's recall. These were temperate but strong, but they did not suspend Genet's functions. Instead, they urged the French government to withdraw the discredited representative for the sake of continuing Franco-American friendship. In his overwhelming indictment of the envoy, Jefferson stressed Genet's attempt "to put himself within the country on a line with its government, to act as co-sovereign of the territory." But he drew a clear line between Genet and the French government, for he wanted to avoid a clash between the two republics, which would amount to " 'the war of liberty on herself,' " as he phrased it. Hamilton, who denied that the cause of France was the cause of

67. TJ to JM, Aug. 11, 1793, below.
68. TJ, "Record of Conversation with President Washington, on Subject of Retirement," Aug. 6, 1793, enclosed in TJ to JM, Aug. 11, 1793, below.

liberty, objected, as did Knox and Randolph; and even though the president agreed with Jefferson, he bowed to the majority and struck out the "liberty" clause.[69]

As for the envoy, Robespierre and the new Jacobin government, which had overthrown Genet's faction, instructed his successor to return him to France under arrest. But the American authorities intervened, and Genet, instead of facing the guillotine, lost his head to the daughter of Governor Clinton, married her, and lived the rest of his life as an upstate New York farmer.[70] Until his successor arrived, however, he remained a thorn in the American side, issuing commissions to citizens "to cruize and commit hostilities against nations at peace with us" and authorizing the use of armed force to thwart federal marshals in their efforts to preserve neutrality. "Was there ever an instance before," an exasperated Jefferson asked Madison, "of a diplomatic man overawing and obstructing the course of the law in a country by an armed force?"[71]

Jefferson learned from local leaders that "Genet has totally overturned the Republican interest in Philadelphia," giving room "for the enemies of liberty and of France to come forward in a stile of acrimony against that nation which they never would have dared to have done. The disapprobation of the agent mingles with the reprehension of his nation and gives a toleration to that which it never had before."[72] Madison, still puzzled by Genet's "unaccountable" behavior, reported from Virginia that "the Anglican party is busy as you may suppose in making the worst of every thing, and in turning the public feelings against France, and thence, in favor of England. The only antidote for their poison," he thought, "is to distinguish between the nation and its Agent, between principles and events; and to impress the well mea[n]ing with the fact that the enemies of France and of Liberty are at work to lead them from their honorable connection with these, into the arms and ultimately into the Government of G. B."[73]

As soon as he completed his "Helvidius" essays in August, Madison dashed to Senator James Monroe's place near Charlottesville, where they spent a fortnight planning "an early and well digested effort for calling out the real sense of the people." Although Madison confessed the difficulty of offsetting the Federalist gains, he thought that "something ought to be attempted on that head." Together, the Republican leaders of the House and Senate drafted a series of general resolutions to be adopted at rallies as "expressions of

---

69. TJ to JM, Aug. 18, 1793, below.

70. Malone, III, pp. 124–31, and Peterson, pp. 503–7. TJ mentions Genet's engagement in his letter to JM of Nov. 2, 1793, below.

71. TJ to JM, Aug. 11, 1793, below, Sept. 1, 1793, below, and Sept. 8, 1793, below.

72. TJ to JM, Sept. 1, 1793, below.

73. JM to TJ, Sept. 2, 1793, below.

the public mind in important Counties, and under the auspices of respectable names."[74] While advocating solidarity with republicanism and revolution in France, the resolutions affirmed loyalty to the president for "his distinguished agency in promoting" peace, liberty, and safety, and carefully avoided any direct discussion of the Proclamation of Neutrality.[75]

Throughout the summer, Jefferson, even though he was preoccupied with foreign affairs, continued his campaign against Hamiltonian fiscal measures. Hamilton's forthcoming retirement, he wrote Madison, "would be the moment for dividing the Treasury between two equal chiefs of the Customs, and Internal taxes, if the Senate were not so unsound." Even so, one House would be sufficient to declare "the true sense of the Constn. on the question of the bank," and thus "divorce that from the government."[76]

On the same day that Jefferson made this suggestion, Madison told him that he had received a manuscript from Senator John Taylor of Caroline County written against Hamilton's "fiscal system, particularly the Bank." "It really has merit," Madison thought, "always for its ingenuity, generally for its solidity, and is enriched with many fine strokes of imagination, and a continued vein of pleasantry and keen satire, that will sting deeply."[77] Taylor proposed to have it printed as a pamphlet and asked Madison to consult Jefferson.[78]

Jefferson was "charmed" when he first saw Taylor's piece, and he was filled "with enchantment" when he reviewed it more carefully, praising its "profound arguments presented in the simplest point of view." What he particularly liked was that there was not a sentence to reveal which section of the country it came from, until "a whole page of Virginia flashed on me." In a discussion of political parties, Taylor had entered an apology for slavery in the Old Dominion. "However this circumstance may be justly palliated," he told Madison, "it had nothing to do with the state of parties, [or] with the bank [and] encumbered a good cause with a questionable argument; many readers who would have gone heart and hand with the author so far would have flown off in a tangent from that paragraph. I struck it out."[79]

Jefferson had no doubt that Taylor's pamphlet would "produce great effect," but its appearance "should be timed to the best advantage." With Congress not in session, "it might as well be thrown into a church yard, as come out now." Instead, it should appear two weeks before Congress met in

---

74. JM to TJ, Aug. 27, 1793, below, and Sept. 2, 1793, below.
75. JM's "Resolutions on Franco-American Relations," [ca. Aug. 27, 1793], is in *PJM,* XV, pp. 76–80.
76. TJ to JM, Aug. 11, 1793, below.
77. JM to TJ, Aug. 11, 1793, below.
78. John Taylor to JM, June 20, 1793, in *PJM,* XV, pp. 34–36.
79. TJ to JM, Sept. 1, 1793, below, and Sept. 8, 1793, below.

December in order to "prevent suspicions of it's coming with them." In that way, it would "be a new thing when they arrive, ready to get into their hands while yet unoccupied."[80]

Amid all the serious and critical thinking about foreign policy and the Hamiltonian financial system, one humorous aside peeped out of one of John Taylor's letters to Madison. "Having but a moment," he wrote, "I will employ it in an Ejaculation—Be Happy!"[81]

But there was little happiness in Philadelphia in 1793. As the hot and hectic summer wound down, the greatest plague of yellow fever struck the nation's capital. "Every body, who can, is flying from the city," Jefferson wrote on September 1. A week later, he reported that the disease was increasing. On the twelfth, he sent a cryptic note to Madison saying that it "spreads faster. Deaths are now about 30. a day. It is in every square of the city. All flying who can. Most of the offices are shut or shutting. The banks shut up this day. All my clerks have left me but one: so that I cannot go on with business. I shall therefore set out in 3. or 4. days and perhaps see you before you get this."[82]

THE LETTERS

Jefferson to Madison

[Philadelphia ca. Dec. 12, 1792]

TH: J. TO J. M.

I dine at home and alone to-day and Saturday of the present week. I inclose some loose thoughts on the bankrupt bill.[1]

ENCLOSURE
Extempore thoughts and doubts on very superficially running over the bkrpt. bill.

The British statute excepts expressly *farmers, graziers, drovers,* as such, tho they buy to sell again. This bill has no such exception.

The British adjudications exempt the buyers and sellers of bank stock, governmt paper etc. What feelings guided the draughtsman in adhering to his original in this case and departing from it in the other?

---

80. TJ to JM, Sept. 1, 1793, below, and "P.S." of Sept. 2, 1793, below. The publishing history of Taylor's pamphlet *An Enquiry into the Principles and Tendency of Certain Public Measures* is discussed in Robert E. Shalhope, *John Taylor of Caroline: Pastoral Republican* (Columbia, S.C., 1980).

81. John Taylor to JM, Aug. 5, 1793, in *PJM,* XV, p. 52.

82. TJ to JM, Sept. 1, 1793, below, Sept. 8, 1793, below, and Sept. 12, 1793, below. The best account is J. H. Powell, *Bring Out Your Dead: The Great Plague of Yellow Fever in Philadelphia in 1793* (Philadelphia, 1949).

1. A bankruptcy bill was introduced in the House on Dec. 10, 1792, but died in committee; see *PJM,* XIV, p. 423; the italics in the enclosure are TJ's.

The British courts adjudge that artists may be bankrupts if the materials of their art are bought, such as shoemakers, blacksmiths, carpenters, etc. Will the body of our artists desire to be brought within the vortex of this law?

It will follow as a consequence that the master who has an artist of this kind in his family, whether hired, indentured, or a slave, to serve the purposes of his farm or family, but who may at leisure times do something for his neighbors also, may be a bankrupt.

The British law makes a departure from the *realm* i.e. out of the jurisdiction of British law, an act of bkrptcy. This bill makes a departure from the *state wherein he resides,* (tho' into a neighboring one where the laws of the U. S. run equally) an act of bankruptcy.

The Commrs. may enter houses, break open doors, chests, etc. Are we really ripe for this? Is that spirit of independance and sovereignty which a man feels in his own house, and which Englishmen felt when they denominated their houses their castles, to be absolutely subdued, and is it expedient that it should be subdued?

The lands of the bankrupt are to be taken, sold etc. Is not this a fundamental question between the general and state legislatures?

Is Commerce so much the basis of the existence of the U. S. as to call for a bankrupt law? On the contrary are we not almost merely agricultural? Should not all laws be made with a view essentially to the husbandmen? When laws are wanting for particular descriptions of other callings, should not the husbandman be carefully excepted from their operation, and preserved under that of the general system only, which general system is fitted to the condition of the husbandman?

Jefferson to Madison

[Philadelphia ca. Jan. 18, 1793][2]

Notes on Mal-Administration of Treasury

The most prominent suspicion excited by the Report of the S. of the T. of Jan. 3. 1793. is that the funds raised in Europe and which ought to have been applied to the paiment of our debts there, in order to stop interest, have been drawn over to this country and lodged in the bank, to extend the speculations and increase the profits of that institution.

To come at the truth of this, it becomes necessary to arrange the articles of this Report into two accounts. viz.

1. An account of the funds provided *in Europe,* for which the treasury is to be debited: while it is to be credited for the application of these funds to such disbursements as they were by law appropriated to. The balance remaining on hand there, must still belong to the same purposes.

2. Ford, VI, p. 168, gives the date of Feb. 7, 1793; *PTJ,* XXV, p. 20, dates it "after 4 Jan. 1793." For TJ's role in the Republican effort to oust Hamilton from President Washington's cabinet, see Sheridan, 589–608; Lance Banning, *The Jeffersonian Persuasion: Evolution of a Party Ideology* (Ithaca, 1978), pp. 126–78; and *PTJ,* XXV, pp. 280–96.

2. An account of the funds provided *in America* for the objects which are entered in this report, or may be brought forward to support it; which are to be Debited to the Treasury, while it is Credited for the applications of them to the purposes to which they have been appropriated by law. The two following Accounts are raised on these principles.

	The Treasury, for Receipts and Disbursements in Europe, *in account*	Dr.		with the U.S. of America		Cr.	
pa. 2.)	To nett amount of monies borrowed in Amstdm. and Antwerp. florins *f* D 18,678,000 (@ 99 = 40)	D 7,545,912		By disbursements for the purposes to which the loans were appropriated by law. vz (bank law §.11.) To the bank for the subscription of the U.S.		D 2,000,000	
Note.	We have here admitted that the whole 2,000,000 D subscribed to the bank might have been paid out of the funds in Europe. Whereas in truth their subscription being on the 1st Jan. 1792. there should have been paid on that day the first instalment only of 500,000 D. and before any other instalment became due, there was the loan of 2,000,000 D. from the bank, on the same day, which might have been applied, so as to spare the European fund. There would then have remained 1,500,000 D. more in Europe to pay off the French debt and stop it's interest, instead of lying dead in the bank. But wave this, because it admits some cavil.			(pa. 2.) To France (pa. 3.) for other foreign loans Commission etc. postage, and advertizing interest to foreign officers To Spain balance stated to be in hands of the Commissioners 407,287–7–8 = 164,544 = Deficit not found in their hands 282,447.24	*f s* 10,083,116–9 1,733,189–2–8 19,172. 613–8–8 105,000 680,000 12,621,091 = 446,991.24	 5,098,920.76 7,545,912	
	To Deficit in the *European* fund as per contra To loan from the bank To Surplusses of revenues approprd to Purchase of Public debt. (suppose)	282,447.24 2,000,000 967,821.65	 3,250,268.89	(pa. 5.) By Departmt. of state for Barbary and foreign transactions [acts 90. July 1, c.22. 92. May 8. c.41.] By paid to France for St. Domingo By paid in purchase of Public debt [see Report of Commrs. of Nov 17. 92. pa. 4.] Balance remaining in bank ought to be 1,708,416.74. but if to avoid cavil, we admit the 191,316.90 D rightly drawn from Europe into the hands of the bank to pay *certain foreign officers* in Europe as by contract, then we must credit that sum the Balance in bank will then be 1,517,099.84	D 128,766.67 445,263.83 967,821.65 191,316.90	 1,541,852.15 1,517,099.84 3,250,268.89	
				The only possible deduction which could be made from this balance further would be so much of the 967,821.65 D paid in purchase of the public debt as exceeds the Surplusses of Revenue applicable to that purchase. If there has been no surplus at all then from we must deduct the whole which would leave a balance in the bank still of		1,517,099.84 967,821.65 549,278.19	

There being certainly then a balance of 549,278.19 D. and probably much more in the bank, there must have been a balance of 39,278.19 D. before the last draughts for 510,000 D. were made in it's favor. Why then were they made? But to put these matters out of question two further statements are requisite. viz

1. The account of the U.S. with the bank, from which we may see whether the state of the account was such as to require this paiment?
2. a statement of the surplusses of revenue which actually arose, and might have been applied to the purchase of the publick debt. The amount of these surplusses are to be added to our balance against the bank.

Jefferson to Madison

[Philadelphia ca. Feb. 21–27, 1793]

[Draft of Giles's Treasury Resolutions Censuring Hamilton]

1. *Resolved*, That it is essential to the due administration of the Government of the United States, that laws making specific appropriations of money should be strictly observed by the Secretary of the Treasury thereof.

2. *Resolved*, That a violation of a law making appropriations of money is a violation of that section of the Constitution of the United States which requires that no money shall be drawn from the Treasury but in consequence of appropriations made by law.

3. *Resolved*, That the Secretary of the Treasury, in drawing to this country and lodging in the bank the funds raised in Europe, which ought to have been applied to the paiments of our debts there in order to stop interest, has violated the instructions of the President of the United States for the benefit of speculators and to increase the profits of that institution.

4. *Resolved*, That the Secretary of the Treasury has deviated from the instructions given by the President of the United States, in exceeding the authorities for making loans under the acts of the 4th and 12th of August, 1790.

5. *Resolved*, That the Secretary of the Treasury has omitted to discharge an essential duty of his office, in failing to give Congress official information in due time, of the moneys drawn by him from Europe into the United States; which drawing commenced December, 1790, and continued till January, 1793; and of the causes of making such drafts.

6. *Resolved*, That the Secretary of the Treasury has, without the instruction of the President of the United States, drawn more moneys borrowed in Holland into the United States than the President of the United States was authorized to draw, under the act of the 12th of August, 1790; which act appropriated two millions of dollars only, when borrowed, to the purchase of the Public Debt: And that he has omitted to discharge an essential duty of his office, in failing to give official information to the Commissioners for purchasing the Public Debt, of the various sums drawn from time to time, suggested by him to have been intended for the purchase of the Public Debt.

7. *Resolved*, That the Secretary of the Treasury did not consult the public

interest in negotiating a Loan with the Bank of the United States, and drawing therefrom four hundred thousand dollars, at five per cent. per annum, when a greater sum of public money was deposited in various banks at the respective periods of making the respective drafts.

8. *Resolved*, That the Secretary of the Treasury has been guilty of an indecorum to this House, in undertaking to judge of its motives in calling for information which was demandable of him, from the constitution of his office; and in failing to give all the necessary information within his knowledge, relatively to the subjects of the reference made to him of the 19th January, 1792, and of the 22d November, 1792, during the present session.

9. *Resolved*, That at the next meeting of Congress, the act of Sep 2d, 1789, establishing a Department of Treasury should be so amended as to constitute the office of the Treasurer of the United States a separate department, independent of the Secretary of the Treasury.

10. *Resolved*, That the Secretary of the Treasury has been guilty of maladministration in the duties of his office, and should, in the opinion of Congress, be removed from his office by the President of the United States.

Jefferson, Madison, and Randolph to Washington

[Philadelphia] Mar. 11, 1793

Qu. 1? What sacrifice may be made to retain Mr Johnson in the office of Commissioner for the federal territory?[3]

Answ. For such an object it is worth while to give up the plan of an allowance per diem, to give, instead of that, a sum in gross, and to extend that sum to 500. Dollars per annum, and expences; the latter to be rendered in account.

If Mr. Johnson persists in resigning, as it is evident Dr. Stewart will not continue even for the above allowance; and Mr. Carrol does not appear to make any conditions, the President will be free as to Mr. Carrol and two new associates to adhere to the allowance per diem already proposed, or to substitute a sum in gross.

Qu. 2? May new commissioners be chosen in the town?

Answ. It is strongly desireable that the Commissioners should not be of the town, nor interested in it; and this objection is thought a counterpoise for a sensible difference in talents. But if persons of adequate talents and qualifica-

---

3. Two days earlier, Washington relayed to TJ letters from Thomas Johnson, Daniel Carroll, and David Stuart, commissioners for the federal district, concerning their compensation and asked him to consult with JM and Attorney General Edmund Randolph; see *PJM,* XIV, p. 471.

tions cannot be found in the country, it will be better to take them from the town, than to appoint men of inadequate talents from the country.

Qu. 3. How compensate them?

Answ. If they come from the country, the per diem allowance is thought best. If from the town, a sum in gross will be best, and this might be as far as 300. D. a year, and no allowance for expenses: if partly from the town and partly from the country, then 300. Dol. a year to the former, and the same with an allowance of expences to the latter.

Mr. Madison, Mr. Randolph and Th: Jefferson having consulted together on the preceding questions, with some shades of difference of opinion in the beginning, concurred ultimately and unanimously in the above answers.

TH: JEFFERSON

Madison to Jefferson

Alexandria Mar. 24, 1793

DEAR SIR

I wrote at Baltimore, but the letter being too late for the mail, I have suppressed it. It contained nothing of consequence. We arrived here to day (2 OC) and shall proceed to Colchester tonight.[4] Our journey has been successful; tho' laborious for the horses. The roads bad generally from Head of Elk; on the North of Baltimore, and thence to George Town, excessively so. I am just told by Mr. R. B. Lee here, that Rutherford is elected, so is Griffin, Nicholas, and New.[5] The other elections are unknown here. Yrs. always and affey.

JS. MADISON JR

Jefferson to Madison

[Philadelphia Mar. 25, 1793][6]

TH: JEFFERSON TO J. MADISON.

The idea seems to gain credit that the naval powers combining against France will prohibit supplies even of provisions to that country. Should this be formally notified I should suppose Congress would be called, because it is a

---

4. JM was traveling with James Monroe.

5. Robert Rutherford, John Nicholas, and Anthony New were Republicans; Samuel Griffin was a Federalist.

6. Although undated, the letter was postmarked "25 MR"; see *PJM*, XV, p. 2.

justifiable cause of war, and as the Executive cannot decide the question of war on the affirmative side, neither ought it to do so on the negative side, by preventing the competent body from deliberating on the question. But I should hope that war would not be their choice. I think it will furnish us a happy opportunity of setting another precious example to the world, by shewing that nations may be brought to do justice by appeals to their interests as well as by appeals to arms. I should hope that Congress instead of a denunciation [declaration?] of war, would instantly exclude from our ports all the manufactures, produce, vessels and subjects of the nations committing this aggression, during the continuance of the aggression and till full satisfaction [be] made for it. This would work well in many ways, safely in all, and introduce between nations another umpire than arms. It would relieve us too from the risks and the horrors of cutting throats. The death of the king of France has not produced as open condemnations from the Monocrats as I expected. I dined the other day in a company where the subject was discussed. I will name the company in the order in which they manifested their partialities, beginning with the warmest Jacobinism and proceeding by shades to the most heartfelt aristocracy. Smith (N. Y.) Coxe. Stewart. T. Shippen. Bingham. Peters. Breck. Meredith. Wolcott.[7] It is certain that the ladies of this city, of the first circle are all open-mouthed against the murderers of a sovereign, and they generally speak those sentiments which the more cautious husband smothers.

I believe it is pretty certain that Smith (S. C.) and miss A. are not to come together. Ternant has at length openly hoisted the flag of monarchy by going into deep mourning for his prince.[8] I suspect he thinks a cessation of his visits to me a necessary accompaniment to this pious duty. A connection between him and Hamilton seems to be springing up. On observing that Duer was secretary to the old board of treasury, I suspect him to have been the person who suggested to Hamilton the letter of mine to that board which he so tortured in his Catullus.[9] Dunlap has refused to print the peice which we had heard of before your departure, and it has been several days in Bache's hands, without any notice of it.[10]

The President will leave this about the 27th. inst. and return about the 20th. of April. Adieu.

7. The dinner guests included William Stephens Smith, Tench Coxe, Walter Stewart, Thomas Lee Shippen, William Bingham, Richard Peters, Samuel Breck, Samuel Meredith, and Oliver Wolcott, Jr.

8. Jean Baptiste de Ternant was succeeded by Edmond-Charles-Édouard Genet as French minister to the United States in May.

9. For Hamilton's newspaper attacks on TJ, see Miller, *Hamilton,* pp. 345–49, especially his use of a letter TJ had written in 1786 suggesting the transfer of the American debt from France to Dutch bankers.

10. John Beckley's anonymous pamphlet attacking Hamilton's program was not submitted to Bache's paper; see TJ to JM, Mar. 31, 1793, below. Instead, it was soon published in Richmond as *An Examination of the Late Proceedings in Congress, Respecting the Official Conduct of the Secretary of the Treasury;* see *PJM,* XV, p. 2.

Jefferson to Madison

Philadelphia Mar. 31, 1793

TH: J. TO J. MADISON.

Nothing remarkeable this week. What was mentioned in my last respecting Bache's paper was on misinformation, there having been no proposition there. Yours of the 24th. from Alexandria is received. I inclose you the rough draught of a letter I wrote on a particular subject on which the person to whom it is addressed desired me to make a statement according to my view of it.[11] He told me his object was perhaps to shew it to some friends whom he wished to satisfy as to the original destination of the 3. mill. of florins, and that he meant to revive this subject. I presume however he will not find my letter to answer his purpose.

The President set out on the 24th. I have got off about one half my superfluous furniture already and shall get off the other half within two or three days to be shipped to Virginia: and shall in the course of the week get on the banks of the Schuylkill.[12] Ham. has given up his house in Market Street and taken a large one in Arch. Street near 6th.

Jefferson to Madison

Philadelphia Apr. 7, 1793

TH: J. TO J. MADISON.

We may now I believe give full credit to the accounts that war is declared between France and England. The latter having ordered Chauvelin[13] to retire within eight days, the former seemed to consider it as too unquestionable an evidence of an intention to go to war, to let the advantage slip of her own readiness, and the unreadiness of England. Hence I presume the first declaration from France.[14] A British packet is arrived. But as yet we learn nothing more than that she confirms the accounts of war being declared. Genest not yet arrived.

An impeachment is ordered here against Nicholson their Comptroller general, by a vote almost unanimous of the house of Representatives. There is little doubt I am told but that much mala fides will appear: but E. R. thinks he

---

11. TJ enclosed his letter to Alexander Hamilton of Mar. 27, 1793 (Syrett, XIV, pp. 255–56), which explained the Dutch loan negotiated by him and John Adams and subsequently administered by the Treasury Department. The administration of that loan was one of the subjects raised in Giles's resolution censuring Hamilton's official conduct.

12. TJ planned to resign later in the year and, therefore, rented temporary quarters near Grays Ferry.

13. The marquis de François Bernard Chauvelin was French ambassador to Great Britain.

14. France had declared war against Great Britain on Feb. 1, 1793.

has barricaded himself within the fences of the law.[15] There is a good deal of connection between his manœuvres and the *accomodating*[16] spirit of the Treasury deptmt. of the US. so as to interest the impeachors not to spare the latter. Duer now threatens that, if he is not relieved by certain persons, he will lay open to the world such a scene of villainy as will strike it with astonishment.[17]

The papers I *occasionally* inclose you, be so good as to return, as they belong to my office. I move into the country tomorrow or next day. Adieu your's affectionately.

Madison to Jefferson

Orange April 12, 1793

DEAR SIR

Your favor of the 31. Ult: and the preceding one without date have been received. The refusal of Dunlap in the case you mention confirms the idea of a combined influence against the freedom of the Press. If symtoms of a dangerous success in the experiment should shew themselves, it will be necessary before it be too late to convey to the public through the channels that remain open, an explicit statement of the fact and a proper warning of its tendency. In the mean time it is perhaps best to avoid any premature denunciations that might fix wavering or timid presses on the wrong side. You say that the subject of the 3 Mil. flos. is to be revived. Have you discovered in what mode; whether through the next Congs. or thro' the press; and if the latter, whether avowedly or anonymously. I suspect that the P. may not be satisfied with the aspect under which that and other parts of the fiscal administration have been left.

As far as I can learn, the people of this country continue to be united and firm in the political sentiments expressed by their Reps. The re-election of all who were most decided in those sentiments is among the proofs of the fact. The only individual discontinued, is the one who dissented most from his colleagues. The vote at the election stood thus—for R. 886—S. 403—W. 276.[18] *It is said*[19] that the singular vote on assuming the [state] balances, gave the coup de grace to his popularity. We were told at Alexa. that if the member for that district had been opposed, his election wd. have failed;[20] and at Fredg.

---

15. John Nicholson, comptroller general of Pennsylvania, was impeached but acquitted; see *PJM*, XV, p. 5.

16. The italicized word here and that below are TJ's.

17. William Duer, former assistant secretary of the the treasury, was in debtor's prison following the collapse of his speculative ventures.

18. Robert Rutherford, John Smith, and Alexander White.

19. JM's italics.

20. Richard Bland Lee. In the Compromise of 1790 on federal assumption of state debts and the location of the national capital, he and White were the only Virginia congressmen to vote for assumption; see ch. 14, above.

that a notice of G's vote on the resolutions of censure had nearly turned the scale agst. him.[21] I have seen and conversed with Mr. F. Walker.[22] I think it impossible he can go otherwise than right. He tells me that I. Cole, and not Clay as in the Newspaper is elected for the Halifax District. Hancock, is the new member from the district adjoining Moore; and Preston for that beyond him.[23] I fell in with Mr. Brackenridge on his way to Kentucky. He had adverted to Greenup's late vote[24] with indignation and dropped threats of its effect on his future pretensions.

The sympathy with the fate of Louis has found its way pretty generally into the mass of our Citizens; but relating merely to the man and not to the Monarch, and being derived from the spurious accts. in the papers of his innocence and the bloodthirstyness of his enemies, I have not found a single instance in which a fair statement of the case, has not new modelled the sentiment. "If he was a Traytor, he ought to be punished as well as another man." This has been the language of so many plain men to me, that I am persuaded it will be found to express the universal sentiment whenever the truth shall be made known.

Our fields continue to anticipate a luxuriant harvest. The greatest danger is apprehended from too rapid a vegetation under the present warm and moist weather. The night before last it received a small check from a smart frost. The thermometer was down at 37° and we were alarmed for the fruit. It appears however that no harm was done. We have at present the most plentiful prospect of every kind of it.

Will you be so good, in case an oppy. shd. offer to enquire of Docr. Logan as to the plows he was to have made and sent to Mrs. House's;[25] and to repay there what may have been advanced for those and two or three other articles that were to be forwarded to Fredg. by water. I forgot to make the proper arrangements before I left Philada. Adieu Yrs. Affy.

Jefferson to Madison

Philadelphia Apr. 28, 1793

DEAR SIR

Yours of the 12th. inst. is received, and I will duly attend to your commission relative to the ploughs. We have had such constant deluges of rain and

---

21. Samuel Griffin was a federalist.
22. Francis Walker was the congressman from TJ's district.
23. Isaac Coles defeated Matthew Clay. George Hancock, Andrew Moore, and Francis Preston represented counties in the Blue Ridge area or beyond; see *PJM,* XV, p. 8.
24. John Breckinridge, who served briefly as JM's colleague in TJ's cabinet in 1805, moved from Albemarle County to Kentucky in 1793; see the excellent article by Lowell H. Harrison, "A Virginian Moves to Kentucky, 1793," *WMQ* 15 (1958): 201–13. Christopher Greenup, congressman from Kentucky, voted against the Giles resolutions censuring Hamilton.
25. George Logan of Philadelphia.

bad weather for some time past that I have not yet been able to go to Dr. Logan's to make the enquiries you desire, but I will do it soon. We expect Mr. Genest here within a few days.[26] It seems as if his arrival would furnish occasion for the *people*[27] to testify their affections without respect to the cold caution of their government. Would you suppose it possible that it should have been seriously proposed to declare our treaties with France void on the authority of an ill-understood scrap in Vattel 2.§.197. ('toutefois si ce changement &c—gouvernement') and that it should be necessary to discuss it?[28]

Cases are now arising which will embarras us a little till the line of neutrality be fairly understood by ourselves, and the belligerent parties. A French frigate is now bringing here, as we are told, prizes which left this but 2. or 3. days before. Shall we permit her to sell them? The treaty does not say we shall, and it says we shall not permit the like to England? Shall we permit France to fit out privateers here? The treaty does not stipulate that we shall, tho' it says we shall not permit the English to do it. I fear that a fair neutrality will prove a disagreeable pill to our friends, tho' necessary to keep us out of the calamities of a war. Adieu, my dear Sir. Your's affectionately

TH: JEFFERSON

Jefferson to Madison

[Philadelphia] May 5, 1793

TH: J. TO J. MADISON.

No letter from you since that of Apr. 12.

I received one from Mr. Pinckney yesterday informing me he expected to send me by the next ship a model of the threshing mill.[29] He had been to see one work, which with 2. horses got out 8. bushels of *wheat* an hour. But he was assured that the mill from which my model was taken gets out 8 quarters (i.e 64 bushels) of *oats* an hour with 4. horses.

I have seen Dr. Logan. Your ploughs will be done in a week and shall be attended to.

Seal and forward Monroe's letter after reading it.[30] Adieu. Your's affectly.

26. Genet landed at Charleston on Apr. 8 and arrived in Philadelphia on May 16; see Harry Ammon, *The Genet Mission* (New York, 1973), pp. 44, 54–55.

27. TJ's italics.

28. Hamilton contended that the change of government from a monarchy to a republic had created chaos in France and urged a policy of nonrecognition of Genet and suspension of Franco-American treaties until a stable government was established; see Miller, *Hamilton*, pp. 368–69, and Malone, III, pp. 73–79.

29. Thomas Pinckney, minister to Great Britain, had the model built at TJ's request; see Edwin M. Betts, ed., *Thomas Jefferson's Farm Book* . . . (Princeton, 1953), pp. 68–76.

30. In his letter to Monroe, May 5, 1793, TJ wrote that "the war between France and England seems to be producing an effect not contemplated. All the old spirit of 1776. is rekindling"; see enclosure, TJ to Monroe, May 5, 1793, below.

P. S. I inclose a Boston paper as a proof of what I mention to Monroe of the spirit which is rising. The old tories have their names now raked up again; and I believe if the author of 'Plain truth' was now to be charged with that pamphlet, this put along side of his present Anglomany would decide the voice of the yeomanry of the country on his subject.[31]

ENCLOSURE
[Jefferson to Monroe]

Dear Sir.   Philadelphia May 5, 1793

The expectation that you are always from home prevents my writing to you with regularity; a matter of little consequence to you, as you probably receive Freneau's paper regularly, and consequently all the news of any importance.

The fiscal party having tricked the house of representatives out of the negative vote they obtained, seem determined not to lose the ground they gained by entering the lists again on matters of fact and reason. They therefore preserve a triumphant silence notwithstanding the attacks of the pamphlet entitled "an examination etc." and of Timon. They shew their wisdom in this if not their honesty. The war between France and England seems to be producing an effect not contemplated. All the old spirit of 1776. is rekindling. The newspapers from Boston to Charleston prove this; and even the Monocrat papers are obliged to publish the most furious Philippics against England. A French frigate took a British prize off the capes of Delaware the other day, and sent her up here. Upon her coming into sight thousands and thousands of the *yeomanry* of the city crowded and covered the wharves. Never before was such a crowd seen there, and when the British colours were seen *reversed,* and the French flying above them they burst into peals of exultation. I wish we may be able to repress the spirit of the people within the limits of a fair neutrality.

In the meantime H. is panic-struck if we refuse our breach to every kick which Gr Brit. may chuse to give it. He is for proclaiming at once the most abject principles, such as would invite and merit habitual insults. And indeed every inch of ground must be fought in our councils to desperation in order to hold up the face of even a sneaking neutrality, for our votes are generally $2\frac{1}{2}$ against $1\frac{1}{2}$. Some propositions have come from him which would astonish Mr. Pitt himself with their boldness. If we preserve even a sneaking neutrality, we shall be indebted for it to the President, and not to his counsellors.

Immense bankruptcies have taken place in England. The last advices made them amount to 11. millions sterling, and still going on. Of the houses connected with America they have fallen only on those who had dealt in American paper. The beginning of the business was from the alarm occasioned by the war, which induced cautious people to withdraw their money from the country banks. This induced the bank of England to stop discounting, which brought on a general crash, which was still going on. It is said that 2. millions of manufacturers etc. would be put out of employ by these failures. This is probably exaggerated.

The stocks are very low here now, and an immense mass of paper is expected to be returned immediately from England, so that they will be still lower. Notwithstanding this, the sinking fund is idle, not having had a shilling to lay out (except the interest of the part sunk).

31. TJ mistakenly attributed *Plain Truth,* an attack on Thomas Paine, to Hamilton; see *PJM,* XV, p. 12.

You will see in Freneau's next paper a most advantageous decree of the French National assembly in our favor. They have lately sustained some severe checks. The papers will confuse you on the subject. The truth is that in a combination of three operations Clairfayt killed and wounded 1400, took 600. Saxe Cobourg killed and wounded 4000, and took 1600. Brunswick killed and wounded 1300, and took 700. This is the sum. Their defeats are as sensibly felt at Philadelphia as at Paris, and I foresee we are to have a trying campaign of it. Great Br has as yet not condescended to notice us in any way. No wish expressed of our neutrality, no answer of any kind to a single complaint for the daily violations committed on our sailors and ships. Indeed we promise beforehand so fast that she has not time to ask anything.

We expect Genest daily. When Ternant received certain account of his appointment thinking he had nothing further to hope from the Jacobins, he that very day found out something to be offended at in me (in which I had been made *ex officio* the ostensible agent in what came from another quarter, and he has never been undeceived) attached himself intimately to Hamilton, put on mourning for the king, and became a perfect Counter-revolutioner. A few days ago he received a letter from Genest giving him a hope that they will employ him in the army. On this he tacked about again, became a Jacobin, and refused to present the Viscount Noailles and some French aristocrats arrived here. However he will hardly have the impudence to speak to me again. From what I learn from Noailles, la Fayette has been more imprudent than I expected, but certainly innocent. Present my best affections to Mrs. Monroe and accept them for yourself also. Yours sincerely.

Madison to Jefferson

Orange May 8, 1793

Dear Sir

Your last recd. was of the 28 Apl. The rect. of all the preceeding is verified by the uninterrupted dates of the Gazettes inclosed. I anxiously wish that the reception of Genest may testify what I believe to be the real affections of the people. It is the more desireable as a seasonable plum after the bitter pills which it seems must be administered. Having neither the Treaty nor Law of Nations at hand I form no opinion as to the stipulations of the former, or the precise neutrality defined by the latter. I had always supposed that the terms of the Treaty made some sort of difference, at least as far as would consist with the Law of Nations, between France and Nations not in Treaty, particularly G. Britain. I should still doubt whether the term *impartial*[32] in the Proclamation is not stronger than was necessary, if not than was proper. Peace is no doubt to be preserved at any price that honor and good faith will permit. But it is no less to be considered that the least departure from these will not only be most likely to end in the loss of peace, but is pregnant with every other evil that could happen to us. In explaining our engagements under the Treaty with France, it would be honorable as well as just to adhere to the sense that would at the time have been put on them. The attempt to shuffle off the Treaty altogether by

---

32. JM's italics here and at the end of this paragraph.

quibbling on Vattel is equally contemptible for the meanness and folly of it. If a change of Govt. is an absolution from public engagements, why not from those of a domestic as well as of a foreign nature; and what then becomes of public debts etc. etc. In fact, the doctrine would perpetuate every existing Despotism, by involving in a reform of the Govt. a destruction of the Social pact, an annihilation of property, and a compleat establishment of the State of Nature. What most surprizes me is that such a proposition *shd. have been discussed*.

Our weather has not been favorable of late, owing more to want of sun, than excess of rain. Vegetation of all sorts even the wheat, nevertheless continues to flourish; and the fruit having no longer any thing to fear from frost, we are sure of good crops of that agreeable article. Yrs. Always and Affy.[33]

Js. MADISON JR.

Will you send me a copy of the little pamphlet advertised under the title of an Examination of the proceedings in the case of the Secy. of the Treasy?

Jefferson to Madison

[Philadelphia May 13, 1793]

TH: J. TO J. MAD.

I wrote you on the 5th. covering an open letter to Colo. Monroe. Since that I have received yours of Apr. 29. We are going on here in the same spirit still. The Anglophobia[34] has seised violently on three members of our council. This sets almost every day on questions of neutrality. H. produced the other day the draught of a letter from himself to the Collectors of the customs, giving them in charge to watch over all proceedings in their districts contrary to the laws of neutrality or tending to infract our peace with the belligerent powers, and particularly to observe if vessels pierced for guns should be built, and to inform *him*[35] of it. This was objected to 1. as setting up a system of espionage, destructive of the peace of society. 2. transferring to the Treasury departmt. the conservation of the laws of neutrality and our peace with foreign nations. 3. it was rather proposed to intimate to the judges that the laws respecting neutrality being now come into activity, they should charge the grand juries with the observance of them; these being constitutional and public informers, and the persons accused *knowing* of what they should do, and having an opportunity of justifying themselves. E. R. found out a hair to split, which, as always happens, became the decision. H. is to write to the collectors of the customs, who are to convey their information to the Attornies of the districts, to whom E. R. is to write to receive their information and proceed by

---

33. Although he makes no reference to it, JM apparently enclosed a "plan of a house," which TJ acknowledged in his letter of May 19, 1793, below.
34. TJ meant those favoring England.
35. TJ's italics here and below. For Hamilton's proposal, see Syrett, XIV, pp. 412–14.

indictment.³⁶ The clause respecting the building vessels pierced for guns was omitted. For tho' 3. against 1. thought it would be a breach of neutrality, yet they thought we might defer giving a public opinion on it as yet. Every thing my dear Sir, now hangs on the opinion of a single person, and that the most indecisive one I ever had to do business with. He always contrives to agree in principle with one, but in conclusion with the other. Anglophobia, secret Antigallomany, a federalisme outrée, and a present ease in his circumstances not natural, have decided the complexion of our dispositions, and our proceedings towards the Conspirators against human liberty and the Assertors of it, which is unjustifiable in principle, in interest, and in respect to the wishes of our constituents. A manly neutrality, claiming the liberal rights ascribed to that condition by the very powers at war, was the part we should have taken, and would I believe have given satisfaction to our allies. If any thing prevents it's being a mere English neutrality, it will be that the penchant of the P. is not that way, and above all, the ardent spirit of our constituents. The line is now drawing so clearly as to shew, on one side, 1. the fashionable circles of Phila., N. York, Boston and Charleston (natural aristocrats), 2. merchants trading on British capitals. 3. paper men, (all the old tories are found in some one of these three descriptions) on the other side are 1. merchants trading on their own capitals. 2. Irish merchants. 3. tradesmen, mechanics, farmers and every other possible description of our citizens. Genest is not yet arrived tho' hourly expected. I have just heard that the workmen I had desired from Europe were engaged and about to embark. Another strong motive for making me uneasy here.³⁷ Adieu my dear Sir.

Jefferson to Madison

Philadelphia May 19, 1793

TH: J. TO J. MAD.

I wrote you last on the 13th. Since that I have received yours of the 8th. I have scribbled on a separate paper some general notes on the plan of a house you inclosed.³⁸ I have done more. I have endeavored to throw the same area, the same extent of walls, the same number of rooms, and of the same sizes, into another form so as to offer a choice to the builder. Indeed I varied my plan by shewing what it would be with alcove bedrooms, to which I am much attached. I dare say you will have judged from the pusillanimity of the procla-

---

36. Hamilton instructed the customs collectors to inform both the U.S. attorneys and the state governors of violations of the Neutrality Proclamation; see *ibid.*, XV, pp. 178–81.

37. TJ planned to remodel Monticello after he retired as secretary of state.

38. The home of William Madison, JM's brother, is located on the campus of Woodberry Forest School in Orange County; see Conover Hunt-Jones, *Dolley and the "Great Little Madison"* (Washington, 1977), pp. 63, 131.

mation, from whose pen it came.³⁹ A fear lest any affection should be discovered is distinguishable enough. This base fear will produce the very evil they wish to avoid: for our constituents seeing that the government does not express their mind, perhaps rather leans the other way, are coming forward to express it themselves. It was suspected that there was not a clear mind in the P's consellors to receive Genet. The citizens however determined to recieve him. Arrangements were taken for meeting him at Gray's ferry in a great body. He escaped that by arriving in town with the letters which brought information that he was on the road. The merchants i.e. Fitzsimmons and co. were to present an address to *the P.*⁴⁰ on the neutrality proclaimed. It contained much wisdom but no affection. You will see it in the papers inclosed. The citizens determined to address *Genet.* Rittenhouse, Hutcheson, Dallas, Sargeant etc. were at the head of it.⁴¹ Tho a select body of only 30. was appointed to present it, yet a vast concourse of the people attended them. I have not seen it: but it is understood to be the counteraddress. Ternant's hopes of employment in the French army turn out to be without grounds. He is told by the minister of war expressly that the places of Marechal de camp are all full. He thinks it more prudent therefore to remain in America. He delivered yesterday his letters of recall, and Mr. Genet presented his of credence. It is impossible for any thing to be more affectionate, more magnanimous than the purport of his mission. 'We know that under present circumstances we have a right to call upon you for the guarantee of our islands. But we do not desire it. We wish you to do nothing but what is for your own good, and we will do all in our power to promote it. Cherish your own peace and prosperity. You have expressed a willingness to enter into a more liberal treaty of commerce with us; I bring full powers (and he produced them) to form such a treaty, and a preliminary decree of the National convention to lay open our country and it's colonies to you for every purpose of utility, without your participating the burthens of maintaining and defending them. We see in you the only persons on earth who can love us sincerely and merit to be so loved.' In short he offers every thing and asks nothing. Yet I know the offers will be opposed, and suspect they will not be accepted. In short, my dear Sir, it is impossible for you to concieve what is passing in our conclave: and it is evident that one or two at least, under pretence of avoiding war on the one side have no great antipathy to run foul of it on the other, and to make a part in the confederacy of princes against human liberty. The people in the Western parts of this state have been to the excise officer and threatened to burn his house etc. They were blacked and otherwise disguised so as to be unknown. He has resigned, and H. says there is no possibility of getting the law executed there, and that probably the evil will spread. A proclamation is to be issued, and another instance of my

39. Attorney General Edmund Randolph drafted the Neutrality Proclamation.
40. TJ's italics here and below.
41. For the welcoming address presented by David Rittenhouse, James Hutchinson, Alexander J. Dallas, and Jonathan Dickinson Sergeant, see Malone, III, pp. 93–94.

being forced to appear to approve what I have condemned uniformly from it's first conception. I expect every day to receive from Mr. Pinckney the model of the Scotch threshing machine. It was to have come in a ship which arrived 3. weeks ago, but the workman had not quite finished it. Mr. P. writes me word that the machine from which my model is taken threshes 8. quarters (64. bushels) of oats *an hour,* with 4. horses and 4. men. I hope to get it in time to have one erected at Monticello to clean out the present crop. I inclose you the pamphlet you desired. Adieu.

Jefferson to Madison

[Philadelphia] May 27, 1793

I wrote you last on the 19th. The doubts I then entertained that the offers from the Fr. rep. would be declined, will pretty certainly be realized. One person represents them as a snare into which he hopes we shall not fall. His second of the same sentiment of course. He whose vote for the most part, or say always, is casting, has by two or three private conversations or rather disputes with me, shewn his opinion to be against doing what would be a mark of predilection to one of the parties, tho not a breach of neutrality in form. And an opinion of still more importance is still in the same way. I do not know what line will be adopted: but probably a procrastination, which will be immediately seen through. You will see in the papers two blind stories, the one that DuMourier is gone over to the Austrians; the other that he has cut to peices 10,000 Prussians, and among them the K. of Prussia and D. of Brunswick. The latter has come through another channel placing Custiné instead of DuMourier, and sayg nothing of the K. and Duke. But no attention is paid to either story. We want an intelligent prudent native, who will go to reside at N. Orleans as a secret correspondent, for 1000. D. a year. He might do a little business, merely to cover his real office. Do point out such a one. Virginia ought to offer more loungers equal to this and ready for it, than any other state. Adieu. Yours affectionately.

Madison to Jefferson

[Orange] May 27, 1793

DEAR SIR

I have recd. your letter with the unsealed one for Monroe and have forwarded the latter. Your subsequent one, which I calculate to have been written on the 12th. inst: came to hand two days ago.[42] I feel for your situa-

42. TJ's undated letter was written on May 13; see TJ to JM, May 19, 1793, above.

tion but you must bear it. Every consideration private as well as public require a further sacrifice of your longings for the repose of Monticello. You must not make your final exit from public life till it will be marked with justifying circumstances which all good citizens will respect, and to which your friends can appeal. At the present crisis, what would the former think, what could the latter say? The real motives, whatever they might be would either not be admitted or could not be explained; and if they should be viewed as satisfactory at a future day, the intermediate effects would not be lessened and could not be compensated. I am anxious to see what reception Genest will find in Philada. I hear that the fiscal party in Alexa. was an overmatch for those who wished to testify the American sentiment. George Town it is said repaired the omission. A public dinner was intended for him at Fredericksburg, but he passed with such rapidity that the compliment miscarried. It would not be amiss, if a knowledge of this could be in a proper mode got to him. I think it certain that he will be misled if he takes either the fashionable cant of the Cities or the cold caution of the Govt. for the sense of the public; and I am equally persuaded that nothing but the habit of implicit respect will save the Executive from blame if thro' the mask of Neutrality, a secret Anglomany should betray itself. I forgot when I requested your attention to my plows to ask the favor of you to pay for them, and to let me know the amount of your several advances. Yours always and affy.

Js. Madison Jr

The plows are to be consigned to the care of Mr. Jno. Anderson Mercht: Fredg. Billy at Mrs. Houses was charged to look out for the first Vessel that offers.[43] If the Newspapers shd. present one to your eye be so good as to let him have notice that he put them on board.

Madison to Jefferson

Orange May 29, 1793

Dear Sir

I wrote you two or three days ago with an inclosure of Newspapers etc. since which I have been favored with yours of the 19th. I thank you for the plans and observations which far exceeded the trouble I meant to give you. The sentiments expressed by Genest would be of infinite service at this crisis. As a regular publication of them cannot be expected till the meeting of Congress, if then, it were to be wished they could in some other mode make their way to the press. If he expressed the substance of them in his verbal answer to the address, or announces them in open conversation, the Printers might surely hand them to the public. The affection to France in her struggles for liberty would not only be increased by a knowledge that she does not wish us

---

43. Billey was the former slave whom JM had manumitted in Philadelphia in 1783. He became William Gardner, a merchant's agent in Philadelphia; see Brant, III, p. 380, and Ketcham, p. 374.

to go to war; but prudence would give its sanction to a bolder enunciation of the popular sentiment. I inclose a letter to the French Minister of the Interior which has been written some time. I pray you to look it over with an eye to every proper consideration, and if you find a particle in it wrong or doubtful not to seal and forward it, till I have an opportunity of makg. the requisite variations. I hope your model of the Threshing Machine is by this time arrived and answerable to expectation. You will have much use for it if your harvest should turn out according to the promises of our fields in this quarter. Wheat was never known to be more uniformly excellent. Adieu. Yrs. always and affy.

Js. Madison Jr

ENCLOSURE
To the Minister of the Interior of the French Republic

Sir   Virginia April 1793[44]

I have recd. your letter of the 10th. of Octr. accompanying the decree of the National assembly of the 26. of Augst. last; which confers the title of French Citizen on several foreigners among whom I have the honor to be named.

In the catalogue of sublime truths and precious sentiments recorded in the revolution of France, none is more to be admired, than the renunciation of those prejudices which have perverted the artificial boundaries of nations into exclusions of the philanthropy which ought to cement the whole into one great family. The recitals of the Act which you communicate, contain the best comment on this great principle of humanity: and in proportion, as they speak the magnanimity of the French Nation, must claim the gratitude and affection of the Individuals so honorably adopted into her citizenship. For myself I feel these sentiments with all the force which that reflection can inspire; and I present them with peculiar satisfaction as a Citizen of the U. S. which have borne so signal a part towards banishing prejudices from the World and reclaiming the lost rights of Mankind; and whose public connection with France is endeared by the affinities of their mutual liberty, and the sensibility testified by the Citizens of each Country to every event interesting to the fortunes of the other.

To this tribute of respectful affection, I beg leave to add my anxious wishes for all the prosperity and glory to the French Nation which can accrue from an example corresponding with the dignified maxims they have established, and compleating the triumphs of Liberty, by a victory over the minds of all its adversaries.

Be pleased, Sir, to accept acknowledgts. due to the sentiments you have personally expressed in transmittg. the public act with which you were charged.

J. M.

Jefferson to Madison

[Philadelphia] June 2, 1793

I wrote you on the 27th. Ult. You have seen in the papers that some privateers have been fitted out in Charleston by French citizens, with their

---

44. This is the draft of the original that was delivered to Genet; see TJ to JM, June 9, 1793, below.

own money, manned by themselves, and regularly commissioned by their nation. They have taken several prizes and brought them into our ports. Some native citizens had joined them. These are arrested and under prosecution, and orders are sent to all the ports to prevent the equipping privateers by any persons foreign or native. So far is right. But the vessels so equipped at Charleston are ordered to leave the ports of the US. This I think was not right. Hammond demanded further a surrender of the prizes they had taken. This is refused, on the principle that by the laws of war the property is transferred to the captors. You will see, in a paper I inclose, DuMourier's address to his nation, and also Saxe Cobourg's. I am glad to see a probability that the constitution of 1791. would be the term at which the combined powers would stop.[45] Consequently that the reestablishment of that is the worst the French have to fear. I am also glad to see that the combiners adopt the slow process of nibbling at the strong posts on the frontiers. This will give to France a great deal of time. The thing which gives me uneasiness is their internal combustion. This may by famine be rendered extreme.[46] E. R. sets out, the day after tomorrow, for Virginia. I have no doubt he is charged to bring back a faithful statement of the disposition of that state. I wish therefore he may fall into hands which will not deceive him. Have you time and the means of impressing Wilson Nicholas, (who will be much with E. R.) with the necessity of giving him a strong and perfect understanding of the public mind?[47] Considering that this journey may strengthen his nerves, and dispose him more favorably to the proposition of a treaty between the two republics, knowing that in this moment the division on that question is 4. to 1. and that the last news has no tendency to proselyte any of the majority, I have myself proposed to refer [defer?] taking up the question till his return. There is too at this time a lowering disposition perceivable both in England and Spain. The former keeps herself aloof and in a state of incommunication with us, except in the way of demand. The latter has not begun auspiciously with C. and S. at Madrid,[48] and has lately sent 1500. men to N. Orleans, and greatly strengthened her upper posts on the Missisipi. I think it more probable than otherwise that Congress will be convened before the constitutional day. About the last of July this may be known. I should myself wish to keep their meeting off to the beginng of October, if affairs will permit it. The invasion of the Creeks is what will most likely occasion it's convocation. You will see Mrs. House's death mentioned in the papers. She extinguished almost like a candle. I have not

---

45. Dumouriez, commander of the French army, had checked the invasion of France at Valmy in Sept. 1792 but was defeated by an Austro-Prussian force under Saxe-Coburg in the spring of 1793. Dumouriez then defected to the Austrians, and both Dumouriez and Saxe-Coburg pledged to restore the French constitution of 1791; see *PJM,* XV, p. 25.

46. The Jacobins shortly thereafter established the revolutionary government, since named the Terror; see François Furet and Mona Ozouf, eds., *A Critical Dictionary of the French Revolution* (Cambridge, Mass., 1989), pp. 137–50, 704–15.

47. Edmund Randolph had married Elizabeth Nicholas, Wilson Cary Nicholas's sister, in 1776.

48. William Carmichael and William Short were attempting to negotiate a treaty with Spain.

seen Mrs. Trist since, but I am told she means to give up the house immediately, and that she has suffered great loss in her own fortune by exertions hitherto to support it. Browse is not returned, nor has been heard of for some time.[49] Bartram is extremely anxious to get a large supply of seeds of the Kentucky coffee tree.[50] I told him I would use all my interest with you to obtain it, as I think I heard you say that some neighbor of yours had a large number of the trees. Be so good as to take measures for bringing a good quantity if possible to Bartram when you come to Congress. Adieu. Yours affectionately.

Jefferson to Madison

[Philadelphia] June 9, 1793

I have to acknolege the receipt of your two favors of May 27. and 29. since the date of my last which was of the 2nd inst. In that of the 27th. you say 'you must not make your final exit from public life till it will be marked with justifying circumstances which all good citizens will respect, and to which your friends can appeal.' To my fellow-citizens the debt of service has been fully and faithfully paid. I acknolege that such a debt exists: that a tour of duty, in whatever line he can be most useful to his country, is due from every individual. It is not easy perhaps to say of what length exactly this tour should be. But we may safely say of what length it should not be. Not of our whole life, for instance, for that would be to be born a slave. Not even of a very large portion of it. I have now been in the public service four and twenty years; one half of which has been spent in total occupation with their affairs, and absence from my own. I have served my tour then. No positive engagement, by word or deed, binds me to their further service. No commitment of their interests in any enterprize by me requires that I should see them through it. I am pledged by no act which gives any tribunal a call upon me before I withdraw. Even my enemies do not pretend this. I stand clear then of public right in all points. My friends I have not committed. No circumstances have attended my passage from office to office, which could lead them, and others through them, into deception as to the time I might remain; and particularly they and all have known with what reluctance I engaged and have continued in the present one, and of my uniform determination to retire from it at an early day. If the public

---

49. Browse Trist was Mrs. Mary House's grandson.
50. William Bartram and his brother John Bartram, Jr., ran a botanical garden and nursery south of Philadelphia across the Schuykill River from TJ's rental house at Grays Ferry; see Brooke Hindle, *The Pursuit of Science in Revolutionary America, 1735–1789* (Chapel Hill, 1956), pp. 308–9. Bartram's Garden, one of the first botanical gardens in America, and the Bartram House have recently been restored and are open to the public at Fifty-fourth Street and Lindbergh Boulevard in Philadelphia.

then has no claim on me, and my friends nothing to justify, the decision will rest on my own feelings alone. There has been a time when these were very different from what they are now: when perhaps the esteem of the world was of higher value in my eye than every thing in it. But age, experience and reflection, preserving to that only it's due value, have set a higher on tranquility. The motion of my blood no longer keeps time with the tumult of the world. It leads me to seek for happiness in the lap and love of my family, in the society of my neighbors and my books, in the wholesome occupations of my farm and my affairs, in an interest or affection in every bud that opens, in every breath that blows around me, in an entire freedom of rest or motion, of thought or incogitancy, owing account to myself alone of my hours and actions. What must be the principle of that calculation which should balance against these the circumstances of my present existence! Worn down with labours from morning till night, and day to day; knowing them as fruitless to others as they are vexatious to myself, committed singly in desperate and eternal contest against a host who are systematically undermining the public liberty and prosperity, even the rare hours of relaxation sacrificed to the society of persons in the same intentions, of whose hatred I am conscious even in those moments of conviviality when the heart wishes most to open itself to the effusions of friendship and confidence, cut off from my family and friends, my affairs abandoned to chaos and derangement, in short giving every thing I love, in exchange for every thing I hate, and all this without a single gratification in possession or prospect, in present enjoyment or future wish. Indeed my dear friend, duty being out of the question, inclination cuts off[f] all argument, and so never let there be more between you and me, on this subject.

I inclose you some papers which have passed on the subject of a new loan.[51] You will see by them that the paper-Coryphæus is either undaunted, or desperate. I believe that the statement inclosed has secured a decision against his proposition. I dined yesterday in a company where Morris and Bingham were, and happened to set between them. In the course of a conversation after a dinner Morris made one of his warm declarations that, after the expiration of his present Senatorial term, nothing on earth should ever engage him to serve again in any public capacity. He did this with such solemnity as renders it impossible he should not be in earnest. The President is not well. Little lingering fevers have been hanging about him for a week or ten days, and have affected his looks most remarkably. He is also extremely affected by the attacks made and kept up on him in the public papers. I think he feels those things more than any person I ever yet met with. I am sincerely sorry to see them. I remember an observation of yours, made when I first went to New York, that the satellites and sycophants which surrounded him had wound up the ceremonials of the government to a pitch of stateliness which nothing but his personal character could have supported, and which no character after him

51. The enclosure was probably TJ's opinion of June 5, 1793, on Hamilton's proposal for a new Dutch loan; see Ford, VI, pp. 283–85, and Syrett, XIV, pp. 516, 521–22.

could ever maintain. It appears now that even his will be insufficient to justify them in the appeal of the times to common sense as the arbiter of every thing. Naked he would have been sanctimoniously reverenced. But inveloped in the rags of royalty, they can hardly be torn off without laceration. It is the more unfortunate that this attack is planted on popular ground, on the love of the people to France and it's cause, which is universal. Genet mentions freely enough in conversation that France does not wish to involve us in the war by our guarantee. The information from St. Domingo and Martinique is that those two islands are disposed and able to resist any attack which Great Britain can make on them by land. A blockade would be dangerous, could it be maintained in that climate for any length of time. I delivered to Genet your letter to Roland. As the latter is out of office, he will direct it to the Minister of the Interior. I found every syllable of it strictly proper. Your ploughs shall be duly attended to. Have you ever taken notice of Tull's horse-houghing plough?[52] I am persuaded that that, where you wish your work to be very exact, and our great plough where a less degree will suffice, leave us nothing to wish for from other countries as to ploughs, under our circumstances. I have not yet received my threshing machine. I fear the late long and heavy rains must have extended to us, and affected our wheat. Adieu. Your's affectionately.

Madison to Jefferson

Orange June 13, 1793

MY DEAR SIR

My last was of the 27 [29] May. It inclosed among other things a letter to the French Ministre de l'Interieur, in answer to one inclosing a Decree of the Nat: Assemb. On the propriety of the answer I wished your freest judgment; and as the sending one at all may be rendered by events improper, I must request the favor of you not to forward the letter, if intelligence should confirm such to be the State of things that it would be totally mal-apropos *there*. Provided it be proper there, and consequently proper in itself, I shall not trouble myself about any comments which the publication attending all such things, may produce here. The letter preceding my last as well as the last, contained some other papers which I wish to know have been recd.

Your two last favors were of May 27. and June 2. The latter confirms the apostacy of Dumourier, but relieves us from the more alarming account of his being supported in it by the army. Still however much is to be dreaded from the general posture of things. Should they take a turn decidedly wrong, I fear

---

52. Jethro Tull, an English agricultural reformer, wrote *Horse-Hoeing Husbandry,* 4th ed. (London, 1762); see *PJM,* XV, p. 28.

little regard will be paid to the limited object avowed by the Austrian General in his first proclamation. In fact if the plan of Dumourier had succeeded, it is probable that under the clause of the Proclamation relating to an amendment of imperfections in the Constitution of 1791 the form of the national sanction would have been obtained, as in the Restoration of Charles II, to whatever establishment military despotism might please to dictate. The only hope of France, next to the success of her own efforts, seems to lie in the number of discordant views of her combined enemies.

I observe that the Newspapers continue to criticise the President's proclamation; and I find that some of the criticisms excite the attention of dispassionate and judicious individuals here. I have heard it remarked by such with some surprise that the P. should have declared the U. S. to be neutral in the unqualified terms used, when we were so notoriously and unequivocally under *eventual engagements*[53] to defend the American possessions of F. I have heard it remarked also that the impartiality enjoined on the people was as little reconciliable with their moral obligations, as the unconditional neutrality proclaimed by the Government is with the express articles of the Treaty. It has been asked also whether the Authority of the Executive extended by any part of the Constitution to a declaration of the *Disposition* of the U. S. on the subject of war and peace? I have been mortified that on these points I could offer no bona fide explanations that ought to be satisfactory. On the last point I must own my surprise that such a prerogative should have been exercised. Perhaps I may have not attended to some part of the Constitution with sufficient care, or may have misapprehended its meaning: But, as I have always supposed and still conceive, a proclamation on the subject could not properly go beyond a declaration of the fact that the U. S. were at war or peace, and an enjunction of a suitable conduct on the Citizens. The right to decide the question whether the duty and interest of the U. S. require war or peace under any given circumstances, and whether their disposition be towards the one or the other seems to be essentially and exclusively involved in the right vested in the Legislature, of declaring war in time of peace; and in the P. and S. of making peace in time of war. Did no such view of the subject present itself in the discussions of the Cabinet? I am extremely afraid that the P. may not be sufficiently aware of the snares that may be laid for his good intentions by men whose politics at bottom are very different from his own. An assumption of prerogatives not clearly found in the Constitution and having the appearance of being copied from a Monarchical model, will beget animadversion equally mortifying to him, and disadvantageous to the Government. Whilst animadversions of this sort can be plausibly ascribed to the spirit of party, the force of them may not be felt. But all his real friends will be anxious that his public conduct may bear the strictest scrutiny of future times as well as of the present day: and all such friends of the Constitution will be doubly pained at infrac-

---

53. JM's italics here and below.

tions of it under auspices that may consecrate the evil till it be incurable.

It will not be in my power to take the step with the Friend of our Friend,[54] which you recommend. It is probable too that it would be either unnecessary or without effect. If the complexion of the former be such as is presumed, he will fairly state the truth and that alone is wanted. If, as I deem not impossible, his complexion be a little different from the general belief, there would be more harm than good in the attempt. The great danger of misconstruing the sentiment of Virginia with regard to Liberty and France is from the heretical tone of conversation in the Towns on the post-road. The voice of the Country is universally and warmly right. If the popular disposition could be collected and carried into effect, a most important use might be made of it in obtaining contributions of the necessaries called for by the danger of famine in France. Unfortunately the disaffection of the Towns which alone could give effect to a plan for the purpose, locks up the public gratitude and beneficence.

Our fine prospects in the wheat fields have been severely injured by the weather for some time past. A warm and moist spring had pushed the wheat into rather a luxuriant state. It had got safe into the head however, and with tolerable weather would have ripened into a most exuberant crop. Just as the grain was in a milky state, the weather became wetter than ever, and has continued raining or cloudy almost constantly since. This has brought on a little of the rust, and pretty universally in this quarter a decay of the ear called the Rot. Should the weather be ever so favorable henceforward, a considerable proportion will be lost: And if unfavorable, the loss may be almost entire. We are at this moment both excessively wet and hot. The forwardest wheat is turning fast and may be nearly safe. The generality is not sufficiently advanced to be out of danger of future or beyond the effect of past causes.

The (Kentucky) Coffee Trees in this Neighbourhood are all too young to bear for some years. I will do all I can to get the seed for Bartram from Kentucky as soon as possible. Adieu.

Madison to Jefferson

Orange June 17, 1793

MY DEAR SIR

Your favor of the 9th. I recd. late last night by a messenger from the neighbourhood of Fredg. who returns early this morning. I have therefore not had time to read the papers inclosed in it and even the letter itself but hastily. Its silence as to France is a cordial to the fears we have been kept in by the newspapers and reports here, of hearing every moment of her final catastro-

---

54. Wilson Cary Nicholas and Edmund Randolph.

phe. If the army had stood by Dumourier's treason,[55] as was the uncontradicted idea for a time, scarce a possibility seemed to remain of any other result. I fell in two days ago with French Strother who was returning circuitously from Richmond. He had seen W.[56] Nicholas on his way, and spoke of him as among the decided friends of the French cause. In general I discovered that his testimony and conviction corroborated the fact that the people of this country, where you can not trace the causes of particular exceptions, are unanimous and explicit in their sympathy with the Revolution. He was in Richmond during the session of the Court of the U. S. and heard the opinions of the Judges on the subject of the British debts. Jay's he says was that the depreciated paymts. into the Treasury discharged the debtor, but leave the State liable to the Creditor. It would be a hard tax on those who have suffered themselves by the depreciation to bear such a burden. It would be severely felt by those who put money into the Treasury on loan and have received certificates by the scale, and those again further reduced by the modifications of the assumption.[57] I asked S. who told me he was under the same roof with Jay and a good deal in his Society, what language he held on French topics. He never opened his lips, was the answer. In Fredg. on his way to Richmond, he was less reserved. I understood that in a conversation there with M. Page who was full of zeal, on the side of France, his enmity broke out in a very decided tone.

We have had no rain since my last which was of the 13th. The wheat however has continued to suffer, partly by the rust, but cheifly by the rot. In the lower country the damage is said to be very great. In this quarter I think very saving crops will be made; perhaps as much as would be called a good crop in ordinary years. Several fields I examined yesterday, will I am confident not lose as much by the late bad weather, as they had gained beyond the medium fecundity by the previous influence of the season. I have not heard from Albemarle, but have no reason to doubt that it has as good fare as its neighbour county. The harvest will commence in two or three days here.

My imagination has hunted thro' the whole State without being able to find a single character fitted for the mission to N. O. Young Marshal seems to possess some of the qualifications, but there would be objections of several sorts to him. In general the men of understanding in this Country are either preoccupied or too little acquainted with the world in the sense necessary for such functions. As a mercantile mask would be politic, the difficulty of providing a man here is the greater.

My plows I find have been finished and forwarded. They are not meant so much as innovations here, as models of a proper execution. One of them is the common barr share, the other a plow preferred in the practice of Dr. Logan. I

---

55. After his defeat by Saxe-Coburg, Dumouriez had defected to the Austrians.
56. At a later time, JM added "C" for Wilson Cary Nicholas.
57. See Charles F. Hobson, "The Recovery of British Debts in the Federal Circuit Court of Virginia, 1790 to 1797," *VMHB* 92 (1984): 176–200.

have Tull and have noticed superficially that [what] you allude to. We are not yet ripe for such nice work. In a former letter I asked the favor of you to see to the re-payment of the price, and must still rely on your goodness for that purpose. The price will be made known by Billey. Yrs. always and affy.

J. M. Jr.

Madison to Jefferson

Orange June 19, 1793

Dear Sir

The date of my last was the 17th. It acknowledged yours of the 9th. instant. Our harvest commenced today. It will turn out I think far beyond expectation. On one of two little farms I own, which I have just surveyed, the crop is not sensibly injured by either the rot or the rust, and will yield 30 or 40 perCt. more than would be a good crop in ordinary years. This farm is on the Mountain Soil. The other is on a vein of limestone and will be less productive, having suffered a little both from the rot and the rust. My father's and brother's crops will not be inferior to mine. From these samples, and those of the neighbourhood generally as far as I am informed, the alarm which has of late prevailed is greater than the calamity. I have not heard from the neighbourhood of Monticello, but can not doubt that its situation ensures it an equal fortune with the similar one here. The weather at present is extremely favorable for the harvest, being dry. It is the reverse however for the laborers, being excessively hot. The Thermometer at this moment (4 OC. P. M.) is up at 96°.

Every Gazette I see (except that of the U. S.) exhibits a spirit of criticism on the anglified complexion charged on the Executive politics. I regret extremely the position into which the P. has been thrown. The unpopular cause of Anglomany is openly laying claim to him. His enemies masking themselves under the popular cause of France are playing off the most tremendous batteries on him. The proclamation was in truth a most unfortunate error. It wounds the National honor, by seeming to disregard the stipulated duties to France. It wounds the popular feelings by a seeming indifference to the cause of liberty. And it seems to violate the forms and spirit of the Constitution, by making the executive Magistrate the organ of the disposition the duty and the interest of the Nation in relation to war and peace, subjects appropriated to other departments of the Government. It is mortifying to the real friends of the P. that his fame and his influence should have been unnecessarily made to depend in any degree on political events in a foreign quarter of the Globe: and particularly so that he should have any thing to apprehend from the success of liberty in another country, since he owes his pre-eminence to the success of it in his own. If France triumphs the ill-fated proclamation will be a millstone, which would sink any other character, and will force a struggle even on his.

Your plan is much approved and will be adopted by my brother. I find I was misunderstood in my enquiry as to the proper width of the Portico: I did not mean the proportion it ought to bear to the side of the House to which it is attached: but the interval between the columns and the side of the House; or the distance which the Pediment ought to project. If there be any fixt rule on this subject, I will thank you to intimate it in your next. Yrs. always and affey.

Jefferson to Madison

[Philadelphia] June 23, 1793

DEAR SIR

My last was of the 17th. if I may reckon a single line any thing.[58] Yours of the 13th. came to hand yesterday. The proclmn. as first proposed was to have been a declaration of neutrality. It was opposed on these grounds 1. that a declaration of neutrality was a declaration there should be no war, to which the Executive was not competent. 2. that it would be better to hold back the declaration of neutrality, as a thing worth something to the powers at war, that they would bid for it, and we might reasonably ask as a price, the *broadest privileges* of neutral nations. The 1st. objection was so far respected as to avoid inserting the term *neutrality,* and the drawing the instrument was left to E. R. That there should be a proclamn. was passed unanimously with the approbation or the acquiescence of all parties. Indeed it was not expedient to oppose it altogether, lest it should prejudice what was the next question, the boldest and greatest that ever was hazarded, and which would have called for extremities, had it prevailed. Spain is unquestionably picking a quarrel with us. A series of letters from her commissioners here prove it. We are sending a courier to Madrid. The inevitableness of war with the Creeks, and the probability, I might say the certainty of it with Spain (for there is not one of us who doubts it,) will certainly occasion your convocation. At what time I cannot exactly say. But you should be prepared for this important change in the state of things. The President is got pretty well again. He sets off this day to Mount Vernon, and will be absent a fortnight. The death of his manager, hourly expected, of a consumption, is the call. He will consequently be absent on the 4th. of July. He travels in a Phaeton and pair. Doctr. Logan sends you the inclosed pamphlet.[59] Adieu. Your's affectionately.

58. Letter not found. TJ's italics below.

59. TJ may have enclosed Logan's anonymous pamphlet on confining the public revenue to a fixed proportion of the net produce of the land; see *PJM,* XV, p. 38.

Madison to Jefferson

[Orange] June 29, 1793

MY DEAR SIR

Your last was of the 17th. inst: and covered *one*[60] paper of the 12th. The weather has been very unfavorable for saving our crops of wheat. It has been from the commencement of the harvest either rainy, cloudy, or hot and damp. I still hope however our crops will be respectable. I have not been able to learn how Albemarle has fared. I have no reason to apprehend that you have more to complain of than we have. The present appearance of the weather is rather favorable. A few days more will put the wheat out of its reach.

My last was of the 19th. I have since seen several of the Natl. Gazettes which continue to teem with animadversions on the Proclamn. My opinion of it was expressed in my last. I foresee that a communication of it will make a part of the Speech to the next Congs. and that it will bring on some embarrassments. Much will depend on events in Europe; and it is to be regretted that the popularity of the President, or the policy of our Government should ever be staked on such contingencies. I observe that our vessels are frequently and insolently seized and searched for French goods. Is not this complained of by our own people as a breach of the *Modern* law of nations; and whilst British goods are protected by the Neutrality of our bottoms, will not remonstrances come from France on the subject? The present conveyance to Fredg. being made known at this instant only, I am obliged to conclude in haste with assurances of the affection with which I remain Dear Sir Yrs. sincerely

J. M. JR

Jefferson to Madison

[Philadelphia] June 29 and 30, 1793

I wrote you on the 23d. and yesterday I received yours of the 17th. which was the more welcome as it acknoleged mine of the 9th. about the safety of which I was anxious. I now risk some other papers, the sequel of those conveyed in that. The result I know not. We are sending a courier to Madrid to make a last effort for the preservation of honorable peace. The affairs of France are recovering their solidity: and from the steadiness of the people on the defection of so popular and capital a commander as Dumourier, we have a proof that nothing can shake their republicanism. Hunger is to be excepted; but the silence of the late papers on that head and the near approach of harvest

---

60. JM's italics here and below.

makes us hope they will weather that rock. I do not find that there has been serious insurrection but in Brittany, and there, the noblesse having been as numerous as the people, and indeed being almost the people, the counterrevolutionary spirit has been known always to have existed since the night in which titles were suppressed. The English are trying to stop the torrent of bankruptcies by an emission of 5. millions of Exchequer bills, to be loaned on the pawn-broking plan: consequently much inferior to the assignats of France. But that paper will sink to an immediate level with their other public paper, and consequently can only complete the ruin of those who take it from government at par, and on a pledge of pins, buckles etc. of double value, which will not sell so as to pay storage in a country where there is no specie, and now we may say no paper of confidence. Every letter which comes expresses a firm belief that the whole paper system will now vanish into that nothing on which it is bottomed. For even the public faith is nothing, as the mass of paper bottomed on it is known to be beyond it's possible redemption. I hope this will be a wholsome lesson to our future legislature. The war between France and England has brought forward the Republicans and Monocrats in every state so openly, that their relative numbers are perfectly visible. It appears that the latter are as nothing. H. is endeavoring to engage a house in town for the next year. He is in the country for the summer.

As I must ere long put my general plan of farming into the hands of my Elkton manager,[61] I have lately endeavored to establish a proper succession of crops for a farm of red highland of about 500. acres of open land fit for culture. In all successions of crops, the feilds must be supposed equal, each feild to go through the same succession, and each year's crop be the same. On these data, the laws of combination pronounce that the number of feilds and number of years constituting a compleat rotation, must be always equal. If you cultivate three equal feilds only, your rotation will be of 3. years, 5. feilds, 5 years etc. I propose 8. feilds of 60. acres each, and of course an 8. years rotation, in the following succession. 1st. year, wheat and fall fallow. 2d peas with Indn. corn thinly planted. 3d. wheat and fall fallow. 4th. potatoes with Indn. corn thinly planted. 5th. rye or barley and fall fallow. 6th. 7th. and 8th. red clover. The following diagram will shew the system better; the initials of every article only being written in each square or feild, to wit

cl.	for clover
co.	corn
f.	fallow
pe.	peas
po.	potatoes
r.	rye
w.	wheat.

---

61. TJ hired Samuel Biddle of Elkton, Maryland, as overseer of Monticello beginning in Oct. 1793; see Edwin M. Betts, ed., *Thomas Jefferson's Garden Book, 1766–1824*, . . . (Philadelphia, 1944), pp. 182–84.

	1st year	2d	3d	4th	5th	6th	7th	8th
A	wf	pe. co.	wf	po. co.	rf	cl.	cl.	cl.
B	pe. co.	wf.	po. co.	rf.	cl.	cl.	cl.	wf.
C	wf	po. co.	rf.	cl.	cl.	cl.	wf.	pe. co.
D	po. co.	rf.	cl.	cl.	cl.	wf.	pe. co.	wf.
E.	rf.	cl.	cl.	cl.	wf.	pe. co.	wf.	po. co.
F	cl.	cl.	cl.	wf.	pe. co.	wf.	po. co.	rf.
G	cl.	cl.	wf.	pe. co.	wf.	po. co.	rf.	cl.
H.	cl.	wf	pe. co.	wf	po. co.	rf.	cl.	cl.

This gives 2. feilds of wheat   120. acres
         1.   of rye or barly   60
         1.   of peas and corn   60
         1.   of potatoes and corn   60.
         1. of the 1st. year's clover   60
         1.   2d.   do   60
         1.   3d.   do   60
                                             ―――
                                              480.

Also 2. eighths of your farm are cleansing ⎫
     3. eighths   fallowing ⎬ every year.
     3. eighths   resting   ⎭
    ―――
     8.

Bye articles as follow.
Oats and flax, a few acres only wanting. To be with the new sown clover.
Hemp, turneps, pumpkins, in the new clearings.
Artichokes in a perpetual feild.
Orchard grass in the hill sides too steep for the plough. Qu?
Lucerne, St. foin, cotton, in appropriate feilds.
Buckwheat to be ploughed into the washed lands.
When a 9th. feild shall be added by new clearings, add it to the rotation as a feild at absolute rest or spring fallowed.
So of a 10th. etc.

As you are now immersed in farming and among farming people, pray consider this plan for me, well, and give me your observations fully and freely as soon as you can. I mean to ask the same from the President, and also from my son in law. Cattle to be raised in proportion to the provision made for them. Also what number of labourers and horses will be necessary? Errors are so much more easy to avoid than to correct afterwards, that I am anxious to be well advised before I begin. Adieu, Yours affectionately.

P. S. June 30. Since writing the above yours of June 19, is received. A Portico may be from 5. to 10. diameters of the column deep, or projected from the building. If of more than 5. diameters there must be a column in the middle of each flank, since it must never be more than 5. diameters from center to center of column. The portico of the Maison quarrée is 3 intercolonnations deep. I never saw as much to a private house. The Commissioners (Irvine etc.) yesterday delivered in their books and accounts, so that that business is closed.[62] The result not yet known. In Fenno's paper of yesterday you will see a peice signed pacificus in defence of the proclmn. You will readily know the pen. I know it the more readily because it is an amplification only of the topics urged in discussing the question when first proposed. The right of the *Executive*[63] to declare that we are *not bound to execute the guarantee* was then advanced by him and denied by me. No other opinion expressed on it. In this paper he repeats it, and even considers the proclamation as such a declaration. But if any body intended it as such (except himself) they did not then say so. The passage beginning with the words 'the answer to this is etc.['] is precisely the answer he gave at the time to my objection that the Executive had no authority to issue a declaration of neutrality, nor to do more than declare the actual state of things to be that of peace. 'For until the new government is acknoleged the treaties etc. are of course suspended.' This also is the sum of his arguments the same day on the great question which followed that of the Proclamn., to wit Whether the Executive might not, and ought not to declare the treaties suspended? The real—milk and water—views of the Proclamn. appeared to me to have been truly given in a piece published in the papers soon after, and which I knew to be E. R's from it's exact coincidence with what he had expressed.[64] Upon the whole, my objections to the competence of the Executive to declare neutrality (that being understood to respect the future) were supposed to be got over by avoiding the use of that term. The declaration of the *disposition* of the US. can hardly be called illegal, tho' it was certainly officious and improper. The truth of the fact lent it some cover. My objections to the impolicy of a premature declaration were answered by such arguments as timid-

---

62. For the report of the commissioners on the balances due to and from the states, see E. James Ferguson, *The Power of the Purse: A History of American Public Finance, 1776–1790* (Chapel Hill, 1961), pp. 203–19, 306–25.

63. TJ's italics here and below. Hamilton's essay is in Syrett, XV, pp. 33–43.

64. The editors of *PJM*, XV, p. 43, found no evidence to confirm TJ's suggestion that Edmund Randolph wrote such a piece in 1793.

ity would readily suggest. I now think it extremely possible that Hammond might have been instructed to have asked it, and to offer *the broadest neutral privileges,* as the price, which was exactly the price I wanted that we should contend for. But is it not a miserable thing that the three heresies I have above quoted from this paper, should pass unnoticed and unanswered, as they certainly will? For none but mere bunglers and brawlers have for some time past taken the trouble to answer any thing. The Probationary odes (written by S. G. T. in Virga.) are saddled on poor Freneau,[65] who is bloodily attacked about them.

Jefferson to Madison

[Philadelphia] July 7, 1793

DEAR SIR

I wrote you on the 30th. ult. and shall be uneasy till I have heard you have received it. I have no letter from you this week. You will perceive by the inclosed papers that they are to be discontinued in their present form and a daily paper published in their stead, *if subscribers enough can be obtained.*[66] I fear they cannot, for nobody here scarcely has ever taken his paper. You will see in these Colo. H's 2d. and 3d. pacificus. Nobody answers him, and his doctrine will therefore be taken for confessed. For god's sake, my dear Sir, take up your pen, select the most striking heresies, and cut him to peices in the face of the public. There is nobody else who can and will enter the lists with him. Never in my opinion, was so calamitous an appointment made, as that of the present minister of F. here. Hotheaded, all imagination, no judgment, passionate, disrespectful and even indecent towards the P. in his written as well as verbal communications, talking of appeals from him to Congress, from them to the people, urging the most unreasonable and groundless propositions, and in the most dictatorial style etc. etc. etc. If ever it should be necessary to lay his communications before Congress or the public, they will excite universal indignation. He renders my position immensely difficult. He does me justice personally, and, giving him time to vent himself and then cool, I am on a footing to advise him freely, and he respects it. But he breaks out again on the very first occasion, so as to shew that he is incapable of correcting himself. To complete our misfortune we have no channel of our own through which we can correct the irritating representations he may make. Adieu. Yours affectionately.

65. St. George Tucker's "The Probationary Odes of Jonathan Pindar" appeared in the *National Gazette* in thirteen installments; see *ibid.*
66. TJ's italics.

Jefferson to Madison

[Philadelphia] July 14, 1793

I wrote you on the 7th. since which yours of the 29th. of June is received acknoledging mine to the 17th. of June. I am anxious to know as early as possible the *safe*[67] delivery of my letters to you. I am not able to say any thing more about the convening of Congress at an earlier day than the regular one. I have lately suspected some disinclination to it. But the grounds are slight. I must see you and be with you some days before it meets. Whether here or at Monticello must depend on the time of it's meeting. But we shall have warning enough to arrange the particulars. I am excessively afraid that an open rupture will take place between the Fr. min. and us. I think there has been something to blame on both sides, but much more on his. He is so evidently in the wrong that those are pressing for an appeal to the people, who never looked towards that tribunal before. They know too well that the whole game is played into their hands, and that there is right enough on both sides to marshal each nation with it's own agents, and consequently against one another, and consequently also us with England. I have written a long letter to-day to Munroe, and must therefore be shorter with you. Adieu. Your's affectionately.

Madison to Jefferson

[Orange] July 18, 1793

DEAR SIR

The season of harvest havg. suspended all intercourse with Fredg. your favor of the 7th. inst: has but just been recd. That of the 29th. Ult: came to hand at the same time. The preceding one of the 23d. would have been acknowledged before but for the cause above mentioned. The present is the first opportunity and like several others leaves me but a moment to prepare for it.

I have read over the subject which you recommend to my attention. It excites equally surprise and indignation, and ought certainly to be taken notice of by some one who can do it justice. In my present disposition which is perfectly alienated from such things, and in my present situation which deprives me of some material facts and many important lights, the task would be in bad hands if I were otherwise better qualified for it. I am in hopes of finding that some one else has undertaken it. In the meantime I will feel my own pulse, and if nothing appears, may possibly try to supply the omission. Return my

---

67. TJ's italics.

thanks to Docr. Logan for the pamphlet and also for the plows arrived at Fredg, tho' by a singular succession of errors and accidents lie still on the road between this and that. Your acct. of G——[68] is dreadful. He must be brought right if possible. His folly will otherwise do mischief which no wisdom can repair. Is there no one thro' whom he can be *effectually*[69] counselled. D. L. F:[70] is said to be able, and if himself rightly disposed as I have understood him to be, might perhaps be of great use. The result of the Harvest is perhaps less favorable than I once supposed. I hope however the crop of wheat as to quantity at least will be tolerable. Of the quality I have great apprehensions. The season for getting it in was as bad as was possible. Every other article of our cultivation is prosperous, and will help to make amends, if the rest of the year be favorable. The corn is particularly luxurient in all quarters. Yrs. always and affy

Jefferson to Madison

[Philadelphia] July 21, 1793

I wrote you on the 14th. since which I have no letter from you. It appears that two considerable engagements took place between France and the combined armies on the 1st. and 8th. of May. In the former the French have had rather the worst of it, as may be concluded by their loss of cannon and loss of ground. In the latter they have had rather the best: as is proved by their remaining on the ground, and their throwing relief into Condé which had been the object of both battles. The French attacked in both. They have sent commissioners to England to sound for peace. Genl. Felix Wimpfen is one. There is a strong belief that the bankruptcies and demolition of manufactures through the three kingdoms, will induce the English to accede to peace. E. R. is returned. The affair of the loan has been kept suspended, and is now submitted to him. He brings very flattering information of the loyalty of the people of Virginia to the general government, and thinks the whole indisposition there is directed against the Secretary of the Treasury *personally,*[71] not against his measures. On the whole he has quieted uneasiness here. I have never been able to get a sight of Billy till yesterday. He has promised to bring me the bill of your ploughs which shall be paid. Adieu. Your's affectionately.

68. At a later time, JM filled in the rest of Genet's name.
69. JM's italics.
70. At a later time, JM filled in "De La Forest," French consul general for New York, New Jersey, Pennsylvania, and Delaware; see *PJM,* XV, p. 45.
71. TJ's italics.

Madison to Jefferson

[Orange] July 22, 1793

DEAR SIR

My last was on the 18th. and acknowledged yours of the 30th. ult: and 7th. inst. I had not then time to mention that W. N.[72] passd. an evening with me on his way home from his brother's where he had met E. R.[73] on his return to Pha. From his conversation, his sentiments are right and firm on the French Revoln. and in other respects I discovered no symptoms of heresy. He spoke particularly and emphatically of the unquestionable unanimity of the Country in favor of the cause of F. I have no doubt that he held this language to every one, and consequently that the impressions depending on him have been rightly made. I could not but infer from all that he said with regard to E. R. that he considered the sentiments of him on French affairs as similar to his own, and to such as were expressed by myself. Some allowance however in all such conversations must be made for the politeness or policy of respecting the known sentiments of the party to which they are addressed or communicated. He had seen the first part of H's publication and spoke of it as from that quarter.[74] He expressed some surprise at the doctrines and cabinet efforts of the Author as he had learnt them from E. R. and seemed unable to account for some things without suspecting H. of a secret design to commit and sacrifice the Pt. His ideas on this subject must have grown out of the language of E. R. if not actually copied from it. I have read over with some attention the *printed*[75] papers you inclosed, and have made notes towards a discussion of the subject.[76] I find myself however under some difficulties first from my not knowing how far concessions have been made on particular points behind the curtain, 2dly. from my not knowing how far the P. considers himself as actually committed with respect to some doctrines, 3dly. from the want of some lights from the Law of Nations as applicable to the construction of the Treaty, 4th. from my ignorance of some material facts—such as whether any call was made by G. B, or any other Belligerent power for the intentions of the U. S. prior to the Proclamation—whether F. was heard on the subject of her constructions and pretensions under the Treaty—whether the Ex. had before them any authentic documents or entered into any discussions, on the question whether the war between F. and G. B is offensive or defensive etc.: I do not mean that all such information ought to be brought into the controversy, tho' some of it is necessary and some more might be used to advantage. But all or most of it seems proper in order to avoid vulnerable assertions or supposi-

---

72. At a later time, JM added "W. C. Nicholas."
73. At a later time, JM added "Edmund Randolph."
74. At a later time, JM added "Pacificus."
75. JM's italics.
76. JM's notes were used in his "Helvidius" essays.

tions which might give occasion to tr[i]umphant replies. If an answer to the publication be undertaken, it ought to be both a solid, and a prudent one. None but intelligent readers will enter into such a controversy, and to their minds it ought principally to be accomodated. If you can lay your hands on the Explanatory publication of the real object of the Proclamn. referred to in your last, or the preceding one, send it to me. The one I had is no longer in my hands. I expect to day to receive your letter next in date to the 7th.

Jefferson to Madison

[Philadelphia] July 28, 1793

Your last was of June 29. acknoledging mine of the 17th. Since that I wrote you June 23. 29. July 1.[77] 7. 14 and 22 [21]. I have only time to mention the death of Roger Sherman. Adieu.

Jefferson to Madison

July 28, 1793

Your last received was of June 29. which acknoleged a scrip of mine of June 17. Consequently my subsequent letters of June. 23. 29. July 1. 7. 14. and 22. are unacknoleged, and give me so much anxiety lest some infidelity should be practised on the road, that I am afraid to do any thing more than warn you of it, if it should be so. I will send this through Mr. Maury, and the newspaper as usual through Mr. Blair.[78] If there is any thing wrong this may get to you. Roger Sherman is dead. Adieu.

Madison to Jefferson

[Orange] July 30, 1793

DEAR SIR

My last was of the 22d inst. I have since red. yours covering the paper now returned, that covering the report of the Commsrs of Accts between the U. S. and the particular States, and that of the 21st. inst. The intermediate one of the 14th. was left by mistake in a secure place by the person who was to bring it

77. Letter not found.
78. TJ wrote two letters to JM on July 28, enclosing the shorter one with the newspaper sent via James Blair in Fredericksburg and this one going through Fontaine Maury in Fredericksburg.

up from Fredg., and is not yet arrived. The delay has been inconvenient as it deprives me of part of the publication which I wish to see in all its parts before I formed a regular view of any. As I intimated in my last I have forced myself into the task of a reply. I can truly say I find it the most grating one I ever experienced; and the more so as I feel at every step I take the want of counsel on some points of delicacy as well as of information as to sundry matters of fact. I shall be still more sensible of the latter want when I get to the attack on French proceedings, and perhaps to the last topic proposed by the writer, if I ever do get to it. As yet I have but roughly and partially gone over the first; and being obliged to proceed in scraps of time, with a distaste to the subject, and a distressing lassitude from the excessive and continued heat of the season, I can not say when I shall finish even that. One thing that particularly vexes me is that I foreknow from the prolixity and pertinacity of the writer, that the business will not be terminated by a single fire, and of course that I must return to the charge in order to prevent a triumph without a victory.

Do you know what is the idea of France with regard to the defensive quality of the Guarantee;[79] and of the criterion between offensive and defensive war which I find differently defined by different jurists; also what are the ideas of the P. on these points. I could lay my course with more advantage thro' some other parts of the subject if I could also know how far he considers the Procln. as expressing a neutrality in the sense given to that term, or how far he approves the vindication of it on that ground.

I am sorry to find the journey to Virga. from which useful lessons were hoped, ending in a confirmation of errors.[80] I can only account for it by supposing the public sentiment to have been collected from tainted sources wch. ought to have suggested to a cautious and unbiassed mind the danger of confiding in them. The body of the people are unquestionably attached to the Union, and friendly to the Constitution: but that they have no dissatisfaction at the measures and spirit of the Government, I consider as notoriously untrue. I am the more surprised at the misconception of our Friend as the two latest sources consulted, the two brothers I mean, are understood to be both of them, right[l]y disposed as well as correctly informed.[81]

I have got my plows at last. They are fine ones and much admired. Repeat my thanks to Dr. Logan if you have an oppy. and think of it. The *patent plow*[82] is worth your looking at if you should visit his farm. You will see your theory of a mouldboard more nearly realised than in any other instance, and with the advantage of having the iron wing, which in common bar shares or in great lies useless under the wood, turned up into the sweep of the Board and relieving it from the brunt of the friction.[83] By fixing the Colter, which is detached, to the

---

79. JM was concerned about Article 11 of the Franco-American treaty of 1778 by which the United States pledged to defend the French West Indies; see *PJM,* XV, p. 49.
80. JM referred to Edmund Randolph's report to Washington on political sentiments in Virginia.
81. JM meant Congressman John Nicholas and Wilson Cary Nicholas, both strong Republicans.
82. JM's italics.
83. For TJ's "mouldboard of least resistance," see Edwin M. Betts, ed., *Thomas Jefferson's Farm Book . . .* (Princeton, 1953), pp. 47–50.

point of the share, it will I think be nearly compleat. I propose to have one so constructed. The detached form may answer best in old clean ground; but will not stand the shocks of our rough and rooty land, especially in the hands of our ploughmen.

Little wheat having been yet tried in bread I can not say how the quality will turn out. The more I see and hear of it, the more I fear it will be worse than was at first supposed. The Corn suffers now for want of rain, but appearances as to that article are on the whole very flattering. The worst effect of the dry weather, at present felt, is the extreme hardness of the earth which makes plowing, particularly in fallow land, but barely possible. So many heavy rains on ground wet for six months, succeeded by the present hot spell, has almost beat it and baked it into Brick.

Jefferson to Madison

[Philadelphia] Aug. 3, 1793

Yours of July 18. and 22. are received and have relieved my anxi[e]ties about mine of June 27.[84] 30. and July 7. Those of July 14. 21. and 28. I hope soon to have acknoleged. We have decided unanimously to *require* the *recall of Genet.*[85] *He will sink the republican* interest if they do not *abandon him.* *Hamilton pressed eagerly an appeal* to the *people.* It's consequences you will readily seize, but *I hope we shall prevent it* tho the *president is inclined* to it. The *loan* is agreed to the full extent on *E. R.'s advice* splitting off a *few dollars* to give himself the airs of *independence.*

I will send you the little peice written by him on *the proclamation* if I can find it. I will here note your several requisitions in your letter of July 22. 1. What concessions have been made on particular points behind the curtain. I think it is better you should not know them. 2. How far *the president* considers himself as committed with respect to some doctrines. He is certainly uneasy at those grasped at by *Pacificus* and as *the author* is universally known and I believe indeed denied not even by himself, it is foreseen that the vulnerable points, well struck, stab the party vitally. 3. Lights from the law of nations on the constructions of treaties. Vattel has been most generally the guide. Bynkershoeck often quoted, Wolf sometimes. 4. No call was made by any *power* previous to the *proclamation. Genet* has been fully heard on his most unfounded pretensions under *the treaty.* His ignorance of every thing written on the subject is astonishing. I think he has never read a book of any sort in that branch of science. The question whether the war between France and Gr. Br.

---

84. TJ meant his letter of June 23.
85. The italicized words in this sentence and in the rest of the letter were written in code.

is offensive or defensive *has not been particularly discussed*. Hamilton has insisted it was offensive by the former. I will send you the French collection of papers on that subject. A paper inclosed will lead you to inform yourself on questions which may come into discussion perhaps at the next session of Congress. They were prepared *for the judges who however will not agree* I believe *to give opinions.* [86] *I informed the president by letter three* days ago that *I should resign* the last day of *September.* Consequently *I shall see you* the middle of *October.* Adieu.

Madison to Jefferson

[Orange] Aug. 5, 1793

At the date of my last which was on thursday last, yours of the 14. had not arrived. I have since recd. it. That of the 28th. is also just handed me. A review of mine will shew you that all yours from June 23 forward have now been acknowledged. Your acct. of the ticklish situation with respect to Genet in the 14th. is truly distressing. His folly would almost beget suspicions of the worst sort. The consequences you point out in case matters come to an extremity are so certain and obvious that it is hardly conceivable he can be blind to them. Something must be done if possible to get him into a better train. I find by the paper of the 27. that P. has entered and I suppose closed his last topic.[87] I think it a feeble defence of one important point I am striking at: viz, the making a declaration *in his sense of it,* [88] before the arrival of Genet. I argue that the Act does not import a decision agst. the Cas: fed:[89] from the manifest impropriety of doing so on the ground that F was the aggressor in *every* war, without at least waiting for evidence as to the question of fact who made the first attack admitting for the sake of argt. that to be the criterion. A difficulty has occurred which will retard my remarks more than I expected. They must be prepared for the *same Gazette,* consequently copied into another hand. I am laying a plan for havg it done here, but it cannot be done as quickly as I wish. The drouth begins to be severe and alarming for the corn. In a hurry yrs. always

---

86. Washington's cabinet discussed questions relating to American neutrality in July, then decided to consult the Supreme Court for an opinion; see TJ to John Jay, July 18, 1793, in Ford, VI, pp. 351–52. But the Court refused to answer the questions, citing the constitutional separation of powers; see Malone, III, pp. 118–19.

87. Hamilton's "Pacificus" articles concluded on July 27.

88. JM's italics here and below.

89. "Cas: fed:," or *casus foederis,* means the case within the provisions of a treaty: Under what conditions of the Franco-American treaty of 1778 would the United States have to give support to France?

Madison to Jefferson

[Orange] Aug. 11, 1793

DEAR SIR

Yrs. of Aug: 3. has just come to hand. All the precedg. have been ackd. I am extremely mortified in looking for the Key to the Cypher, to find that I left it in Philada. You must therefore repeat any thing that may be of use still to be known, particularly any thing that may relate to the time of your leavg. Phila. which I wish to know as long as possible before it takes place. The task on which you have put me, must be abridged so as not to go beyond that period. You will see that the first topic is not yet compleated. I hope the 2d. and 3. to wit the meang. of the Treaty and the obligations of gratitude will be less essential. The former is particularly delicate; and tho' I think it may be put in a light that wd. reflect ignominy on the author of P. yet I had rather not meddle with the subject if it cd. be avoided. I can not say when I shall be able to take up those two parts of the job. Just as I was embarking in the general subject I recd. from the reputed Author of Franklyn a large pamphlet written by him agst. the fiscal system, particularly the Bank; which I could not but attend to. It is put on a footing that requires me to communicate personally with Monroe, whom I ought to have seen before this, as the publication of the work is to be contrived for the Author. It really has merit; always for its ingenuity, generally for its solidity, and is enriched with many fine strokes of imagination, and a continued vein of pleasantry and keen satire, that will sting deeply. I have recd. a letter from the Author wishing to hear from me.[90] I must therefore take a ride as far as Charlottesville as soon as I make out the next packet for you, and suspend the residue of the business till I return. I shall endeavor in my absence to fulfil a promise to Wilson Nicholas which will lengthen the suspension. I forwd. to F―――[91] a copy of the little thing of Ld. Ch: the last sentence is struck out as not necessary, and which may perhaps wound too indiscriminately certain characters, not at present interested in supporting public corruptions.[92] The drouth has done irreparable injury to the Corn in many parts of the Country. It has been interrupted within a few days past, by a pretty extensive rain. We shared in it here but scantily. I understand that at Charlottesville which had been favd. with several preceding ones, it was plentiful. Be good eno' to contrive an excuse to Mr. R. at Monto: for my not forwding. the Gazettes latterly: if you have not already thought of it. I

---

90. During the winter, John Taylor of Caroline, who used the pseudonym of "Franklin," had published six essays against the banking system. He proposed to publish these in a pamphlet if JM and Monroe agreed; see John Taylor to JM, Aug. 5, 1793, in *PJM*, XV, p. 52.

91. Philip Freneau of the *National Gazette*.

92. Lord Chatham's speech on the Falkland Islands in Nov. 1770 attacked the "monied interest" as "that *bloodsucker,* that *muckworm,* which calls itself *the friend of government*"; see *PJM*, XV, pp. 53–54.

know not how to apologize myself—and shall feel some awkwardness, as I shall not carry them when I go into his neighbourhood.[93]

Jefferson to Madison

[Philadelphia] Aug. 11, 1793

DEAR SIR

I wrote you last on the 3d. inst. Your's of July 30. came to hand yesterday. Besides the present which goes by post, I write you another today to go by Mr. D. Randolph[94] who sets out the day after tomorrow for Monticello, but whether by the direct route or viâ Richmond is not yet decided. I shall desire that letter to be sent to you by express from Monticello. I have not been able to lay my hands on the newspaper which gave a short but true view of the intention of the proclamation. However having occasion to state it in a paper which I am preparing,[95] I have done it in the following terms, and I give you the very words from the paper, because just as I had finished so far, *the president*[96] called on me, I read it to him, he said it presented fairly his view of the matter, he recalled to my mind that I had, at the time, opposed it's being made a declaration of neutrality on the ground that the Executive was not the competent authority for that, and therefore that it was agreed the instrument should be drawn with great care. My statement is in these words. 'On the declaration of war between France and England, the US. being at peace with both, their situation was so new and unexperienced by themselves that their citizens were not, in the first instant, sensible of the new duties resulting therefrom, and of the laws it would impose *even on their dispositions* towards the belligerent powers. Some of them imagined (and chiefly their transient seafaring citizens) that they were free to indulge those dispositions, to take side with either party, and enrich themselves by depredations on the commerce of the other, and were meditating enterprizes of this nature, as was said. In this state of the public mind, and before it should take an erroneous direction difficult to be set right, and dangerous to themselves and their country, the President thought it expedient, by way of Proclamation, to remind our fellow citizens that we were in a state of peace with all the belligerent powers, that in that state it was our duty neither to aid nor injure any, to exhort and warn them against acts which might contravene this duty, and particularly those of positive hostility, for the punishment of which the laws would be appealed to,

93. Fenno's *Gazette of the United States* carried Hamilton's "Pacificus" essays. TJ explained to his son-in-law that the delay in forwarding these papers was his fault, not JM's; see *ibid.*, p. 54.
94. David Meade Randolph.
95. TJ was preparing a letter of instructions to Gouverneur Morris, U.S. minister to France, and quoted from that letter in the passages within quotation marks below; see TJ to Gouverneur Morris, Aug. 16, 1793, in Ford, VI, pp. 376-77.
96. These italicized words and those below were written in code.

and to put them on their guard also as to the risks they would run if they should attempt to carry articles of contraband to any.'

'Very soon afterwards we learnt that he[97] was undertaking to authorize the fitting and arming vessels in that port, enlisting men, foreigners and citizens, and giving them commissions to cruize and commit hostilities against nations at peace with us, that these vessels were taking and bringing prizes into our ports, that the Consuls of France were assuming to hold courts of Admiralty on them, to try, condemn and authorize their sale as legal prize, and all this before Mr. —— had presented himself or his credentials to the President, before he was received by him, without his consent or consultation, and directly in contravention of the state of peace existing and declared to exist in the Pres's proclmn., and which it was incumbent on him to preserve till the constitutional authority should otherwise declare. These proceedings became immediately, as was naturally to be expected, the subject of complaint by the representative here of that power against whom they would chiefly operate etc.' This was the true sense of the proclamn. in the view of the draughtsman and of the two signers, but H. had other views. The instrument was badly drawn, and made the P. go out of his line to declare things which, tho' true, it was not exactly his province to declare. The instrument was communicated to me after it was drawn, but I was busy, and only run an eye over it to see that it was not made a declaration of neutrality, and gave it back again, without, I believe, changing a tittle.

Pacificus has now changed his signature to 'No Jacobin.' Three papers under this signature have been publd. in Dunlap. I suppose they will get into Fenno. They are commentaries on the laws of nations, and on the different parts of our treaty with France. As yet they have presented no very important heresy.[98] Congress will not meet till the legal day. It was referred to a meeting at my office to consider and advise on it. I was for calling them. Kn. against it. H. said his judgment was against it, but he would join any two who should concur so as to make a majority either way. R. was pointedly against it. We agreed to give our opinions separately, and tho' the P. was in his own judgment for calling them, he acquiesced in the majority. I pass on to the other letter: so Adieu. Your's affectionately.

Jefferson to Madison

Philadelphia Aug. 11, 1793

DEAR SIR

I write a second letter to-day, because going by a private conveyance[99] I can venture in it a paper which never could have been hazarded by the

97. Genet.

98. The essays are in Syrett, XV, pp. 145–228.

99. This letter was enclosed in TJ to Thomas Mann Randolph, Jr., Aug. 11, 1793, and both were carried by David Meade Randolph; see *PJM,* XV, p. 59.

post.¹⁰⁰ Timely information of it's contents (which must be sacredly kept to yourself unless you have an opportunity of communicating them to Monroe) may enable you to shape your plan for the state of things which is actually to take place. It would be the moment for dividing the Treasury between two equal chiefs of the Customs, and Internal taxes, if the Senate were not so unsound. A declaration of the true sense of the Constn. on the question of the bank, will suffice to divorce that from the government, tho' made by a single house. Censures on censurable things clearly confessed in the report etc. With respect to the Proclamation, as the facts it declared were true, and the desire of neutrality is universal, it would place the republicans in a very unfavble. point of view with the people to be cavilling about small points of propriety; and would betray a wish to find fault with the President in an instance where he will be approved by the great body of the people who consider the substance of the measure only, and not the smaller criticisms to which it is liable. The conduct of Genet too is transpiring and exciting the indignation it is calculated to excite. The towns are beginning generally to make known their disapprobation of any such opposition to their govmt. by a foreigner, are declaring their firm adherence to their President, and the Proclamation is made the groundwork of these declarations. In N. York, while Genet was there, the vote of a full meeting of all classes was 9. out of 10. against him, i.e. for the Proclamation. We are told that the cortege which was collected to recieve him (except the committee) consisted only of boys and negroes. All the towns Northwardly are about to express their adherence to the proclamation and chiefly with a view to manifest their disapprobation of G's conduct. Philadelphia, so enthusiastic for him, before his proceedings were known, is going over from him entirely, and if it's popular leaders have not the good sense to go over with them, they will go without them, and be thus transferred to the other party. So in Congress, I believe that it will be true wisdom in the Republican party to approve unequivocally of a state of neutrality, to avoid little cavils about who should declare it, to abandon G. entirely, with expressions of strong friendship and adherence to his nation and confidence that he has acted against their sense. In this way we shall keep the people on our side by keeping ourselves in the right. I have been myself under a cruel dilemma with him. I adhered to him as long as I could have a hope of getting him right, because I knew what weight we should derive to our scale by keeping in it the love of the people for the French cause and nation, and how important it was to ward off from that cause and nation any just grounds of alienation. Finding at length that the man was absolutely incorrigible, I saw the necessity of quitting a wreck which could not but sink all who should cling to it. It is determined to insist on his recall, and I am preparing a statement of his conduct to be laid before the Executive council. Hamilton and Knox have pressed an appeal to the people with an eagerness I never before saw in them. They made the establishment of

---

100. TJ enclosed a copy of his "Record of Conversation with President Washington, on Subject of [TJ's] Retirement," Aug. 6, 1793, below.

the democratic society here the ground for sounding an alarm that this society (which they considered as the *antifederal and discontented faction*)[101] was put into motion by Mr. G. and would by their corresponding societies in all the state draw the mass of the people, by dint of misinformation, into their vortex and overset the governmt. The Pres. was strongly impressed by this picture, drawn by H. in three speeches of ¾ of an hour length each. I opposed it totally, told the President plainly in their presence, that the intention was to dismount him from being the head of the nation, and make him the head of a party: that this would be the effect of making him in an appeal to the people declare war against the Republican party. R. according to his half-way system between wrong and right urged the *putting off* the appeal. The Pr. came into his idea; or rather concluded that the question on it might be put off indefinitely to be governed by events. If the demonstrations of popular adherence to him become as general and warm as I believe they will, I think he will never again bring on the question: if there is any appearance of their supporting Genet, he will probably make the appeal. I can by this confidential conveyance speak more freely of R. He is the poorest Cameleon I ever saw having no colour of his own, and reflecting that nearest him. When he is with me he is a whig, when with H. he is a tory, when with the P. he is what he thinks will please him. The last is his strongest hue, tho' the [102]2d. tinges him very strongly. The first is what I think he would prefer in his heart if he were in the woods where he could see nobody, or in a society of *all whigs*. You will remark an expression in the inclosed paper with respect to him. It has in some degree lessened my apprehensions of the estimation in which the Pr. held him. Still it is not the less true that his opinion always makes the majority, and that the President acquiesces *always* in the majority; consequently that the government is now solely directed by him. As he is not yet openly thrown off by the whig party, it gives to the public a false security that fair play is given to the whiggism of the Pr. by an equal division of whig and tory among his counsellors. I have kept on terms of strict friendship with him hitherto, that I might make some good out of him, and because he has really some good private qualities. But he is in a station infinitely too important for his understanding, his firmness, or his circumstances. I mentioned to you that we had convened the judges to consult them on the questions which have arisen on the law of nations. They declined being consulted. In England you know such questions are referred regularly to the judge of Admiralty. I asked E. R. if we could not prepare a bill for Congress to appoint a board or some other body of advice for the Executive on such questions. He said he should propose to annex it to his

---

101. TJ's italics here and below.

102. TJ inserted an asterisk here and added this footnote: "When he is with people whom he thinks he can guide, he says without reserve that the party in opposition to the fiscal system, are antifederal, and endeavoring to overturn the constitution. These people name you as having apostatised from your antient federalism, and myself as having never been of that sentiment. I say *they* name us, because my information is not expressly that R. named us so to them."

office. In plain language this would be to make him the sole arbiter of the line of conduct for the US. towards foreign nations. You ask the sense of France with regard to the defensive quality of the guarantee. I know it no otherwise than from Genet. His doctrine is that without waiting to be called on, without waiting till the islands were attacked the moment France was engaged in war, it was our duty to fly to arms as a nation, and the duty of everyone to do it as an individual. He insisted much on Henfeild's counsel (who were engaged and paid by him) defending Henfeild on this ground.[103] But they had more sense. Adieu. Your's affectionately

TH: JEFFERSON

P. S. The Pres. is extremely anxious to know your sentiments on the Proclamation. He has asked me several times. I tell him you are so absorbed in farming that you write to me always about ploughs, rotations etc.

ENCLOSURE
Record of Conversation with President Washington, on Subject of Retirement.[104]

Aug. 6, 1793

The President calls on me at my house in the country, and introduces my letter of July 31. announcing that I should resign at the close of the next month. He again expressed his repentance at not having resigned himself, and how much it was increased by seeing that he was to be deserted by those on whose aid he had counted; that he did not know where he should look to find characters to fill up the offices, that mere talents did not suffice for the departmt of state, but it required a person conversant in foreign affairs, perhaps acquainted with foreign courts, that without this the best talents would be awkward and at a loss. He told me that Col? Hamilton had 3. or 4. weeks ago written to him, informg him that private as well as public reasons had brought him to the determination to retire, and that he should do it towards the close of the next session. He said he had often before intimated dispositions to resign, but never as decisively before: that he supposed he had fixed on the latter part of the next session to give an opportunity to Congress to examine into his conduct: that our going out at times so different increased his difficulty, for if he had both places to fill at one he might consult both the particular talents and geographical situation of our successors. He expressed great apprehensions at the fermentation which seemed to be working in the minds of the public, that many descriptions of persons actuated by different causes appeared to be writing, what it would end in he knew not, a new Congress was to assemble, more numerous, perhaps of a different spirit; the first expressions of their sentiments would be important: if I would only stay to the end of that it would relieve him considerably.

I expressed to him my excessive repugnance to public life, the particular uneasiness of my situation in this place where the laws of society oblige me to move always exactly

103. Gideon Henfield, an American citizen, enlisted on the French privateer *Citizen Genet* and was arrested when the vessel docked in Philadelphia. He was indicted for violating the Proclamation of Neutrality, which forbade citizens to engage in war, but the jury acquitted him; see Malone, III, pp. 119-21.

104. This memorandum became a part of TJ's "Anas"; see Ford, I, pp. 256-59.

in the circle which I know to bear me peculiar hatred, that is to say the wealthy Aristocrats, the Merchants connected closely with England, the created paper fortunes that thus surrounded, my words were caught, multiplied, misconstrued, and even fabricated and spread abroad to my injury, that he saw also that there was such an opposition of views between myself and another part of the admn as to render it peculiarly unpleasing, and to destroy the necessary harmony. Without knowͽ the views of what is called the Republican party, here, or havͽ any communication with them, I could undertake to assure him from my intimacy with that party in the late Congress, that there was not a view in the Republican party as spread over the US. which went to the frame of the government, that I believed the next Congress would attempt nothing material but to render their own body independant, that that party were firm in their dispositions to support the government: that the maneuvres of Mr Genet might produce some little embarrassment, but that he would be abandoned by the Republicans the moment they knew the nature of his conduct, and on the whole no crisis existed which threatened any thing.

He said he believed the views of the Republican party were perfectly pure, but when men put a machine into motion it is impossible for them to stop it exactly where they would chuse or to say where it will stop. That the constn we have is an excellent one if we can keep it where it is, that it was indeed supposed there was a party disposed to change it into a monarchical form, but that he could conscientiously declare there was not a man in the US. who would set his face more decidedly against it than himself.

Here I interrupted him by saying 'no rational man in the US. suspects you of any other disposn, but there does not pass a week in which we cannot prove decent dropping from the monarchical party that our governmt is good for nothing, it is a milk and water thing which cannot support itself, we must knock it down and set up something of more energy.

He said if that was the case he thought it a proof of their insanity, for that the republican spirit of the Union was so manifest and so solid that it was astonishͽ how any one could expect to move them.

He returned to the difficulty of naming my successor, he said Mr Madison would be his first choice, but he had always expressed to him such a decision against public office that he could not expect he would undertake it. Mr Jay would prefer his present office. He sd that Mr Jay had a great opinion of the talents of Mr King, that there was also Mr Smith of S. Carolā E. Rutledge eqe.: but he observed that name whom he would some objections would be made, some would be called speculators, some one thing, some another, and he asked me to mention any characters occurrͽ to me. I asked him if Govr Johnson of Marlyd had occurred to him? He said he had, that he was a man of great good sense, an honest man, and he believed clear of speculations, but this says he is an instance of what I was observing, with all these qualifications, Govr Johnson, from a want of familiarity with foreign affairs, would be in them like a fish out of water, every thing would be new to him, and he awkward in every thing. I confessed to him that I had considered Johnson rather as fit for the Treasury department. Yes, says he, for that he would be the fittest appointment that could be made; he is a man acquainted with figures, and having as good a knolege of the resources of this country as any man. I asked him if Chancr Livingston had occurred to hims He said yes, but he was from N. York, and to appoint him while Hamilton was in and before it should be known that he was going out, would excite a newspaper conflagration, as the ultimate arrangement would not be known. He said Mclurg had occurred to him as a man of first rate abilities, but it is said that he is a speculator. He asked me what sort of a man Wolcot was. I told him I knew nothing of him myself; I had heard him characterised as a cunning man. I asked him whether some person could not take my office par interim, till he should make an app.^t ment? as M.r Randolph for instance. Yes, says he, but there you would raise the expectation of keeping it, and I do not know that he is fit for it nor what is thought of M.r Randolph. I avoided noticing the last observation, and he put the question to me directly. I then told him that I went into society so little as to be unable to answer it. I knew that the embarrasments in his private affairs had obliged him to use exped.^{ts} which had injured him with the merch.^{ts} and shop-keepers and affected his character of independance; that these embarrasments were serious, and not likely to cease soon. He said if I would only stay in till the end of another quarter (the last of Dec.) it would get us through the difficulties of this year, and he was satisfied that the affairs of Europe would be settled with this campaign, for that either France would be overwhelmed by it, or the confederacy would give up the contest. By that time too Congress will have manifested it's character and views.

I told him that I had set my private affairs in motion in a line which had powerfully called for my presence the last spring, and that they had suffered immensely from my not going home; that I had now calculated them to my return in the fall, and to fail in going then would be the loss of another year, and prejudicial beyond measure. I asked him whether he could not name Govr Johnson to my office, under an express arrangement that at the close of the session he should take that of the treasury. He said that men never chose to descend. that being once in a higher department he would not like to go into a lower one, he asked me[105] and he concluded by desiring that I would take 2. or 3. days to consider whether I could not stay in till the end of another quarter, for that like a man going to the gallows he was willing to put it off as long as he could; but if I persisted, he must then look about him and make up his mind to do the best he could: and so he took leave.

Madison to Jefferson

[Orange Aug. 12, 1793]

The paper for J. F.[106] could not otherwise get to him than with your aid. You must therefore take the trouble of having it handed into the post office whence the penny post will take it, unless you can do it at some shorter hand. I wish you to look over what is sd. critically, and if you think there be any thing of importance wrong, or that may do more harm than good, that you will either erase it, where that will not break the sense, or arrest the whole till I can

---

105. TJ inserted an asterisk here and added this footnote: "He asked me whether I could not arrange my affairs by going home. I told him I did not think the publick business would admit of it, that there was never a day now in which the absence of the Secretary of state would not be inconvenient to the public."

106. John Fenno was editor of the Philadelphia *Gazette of the United States,* which had published Hamilton's "Pacificus" essays. JM enclosed the first two number of his "Helvidius" essays so that TJ could mail them anonymously to Fenno; see *PJM,* XV, p. 60.

make the correction. Delay I know is bad; but vulnerable parts that wd. be siezed for victories and triumphs would be worse. I beg you also to attend particularly to three passages slightly marked with a pencil, the first, the declaration of the principles and sentiments of the author—2d. beginning with "Writers such as Locke & Montesqeue etc.["]—to the pencil mark in the ¶. 3 the quotation from the Federalist. If you think the first had better be omitted it can come out without leavg. the least gap. So can the 2d. My doubts as to that proceed from the danger of turning the controversy too much into the wilderness of Books: I use Montesqeue also from memory, tho I believe witht. inaccuracy. The 3d. can also come out witht. affecting the piece, and I wish you to erase it if you think the most scrupulous delicacy, conjecturing the author, cd. disapprove it. One No. more or 2 short Nos. will close the first topic and supersede the last. They will be sent as soon as finished and copied. These wd. have been sent somewhat sooner, but for the delay caused by the last circumstance.

Jefferson to Madison

[Philadelphia] Aug. 18, 1793

DEAR SIR

My last was of the 11th. since which yours of the 5th. and 11th. are received. I am mortified at your not having your cypher. I now send the key of the numbers in mine of the 3d. This with my letter of the 11th. by post and another of the same date by Davy Randolph who will be at Monticello the last week of this month will put you in possession of the state of things to that date. The paper I now inclose will fill up chinks and needs not a word of explanation. To these I must add that orders are given to drive out of our ports the privateers which have been armed in them before the 5th. of June, by gentler means if it can be done, and if not, by the ultima ratio: and we are seising the prizes brought in since Aug. 7. to restore them to their owners. For those between June 5. and Aug. 7. we engage restitution or compensation. The inclosed paper will explain these distinctions of date, and justify the proceedings.[107] I return you the little thing of Ld. Chath's because, for particular reasons, were it now to appear it would be imputed to me, and because it will have more effect if publd. after the meeting of Congress. I rejoice at the resurrection of Franklin. There was a charming thing from the same pen (I conjecture) on the subject of instrumentality lately publd. by Freneau from the Virga. papers. The addresses in support of the proclmn. are becoming universal, and as universal a rising in support of the President against Genet. Observe

107. For TJ's letter of Aug. 7 to Genet, see Ford, VI, pp. 365-66. For a discussion, see Ammon, pp. 94-110.

that the inclosed paper has been only read in cabinet for the 1st. time as yet.[108] On that reading H. objected to expressions implying a censure on other nations ('the war of liberty on herself etc.').[109] He thought expressions of frdship to France suited the occasion. But R. protested against every expression of friendship to that nation lest they should offend the other party, and intimated that he should move to eradicate them all. It will pretty effectually tear up the instrument if he succeeds. Nous verrons. Adieu.

P. S. You are free to shew the inclosed to Colo. Monroe. If the appeal which I have mentioned to you, should be pushed, I think that by way of compromise, I shall propose that instead of that, the whole correspondence be laid before Congress, merely as a matter of information. What would you think of this?

Madison to Jefferson

[Orange] Aug. 20, 1793

DEAR SIR

Your favor of the 11th. came to hand the day before yesterday. I am just setting off to Monroe's and hope to prevent the trouble of an express from Monticello with the letter referred to in it. I have already acquainted you with the immediate object of this visit. I have just recd. a line from him expressing a particular desire to communicate with me, and reminding me that he sets off the last of this month for the Courts, and of course will be occupied for some days before with preparations. This hurries me: and has forced me to hurry what will be inclosed herewith, particularly the last No. V which required particular care in the execution.[110] I shall be obliged to leave that and the greater part of the other Nos. to be transcd. sealed up and forwarded in my absence. It is certain therefore that many little errors will take place. As I can not let them be detained till I return, I must pray you to make such corrections as will not betray your hand. In pointing and *erasures*[111] not breaking the sense, there will be no difficulty. I have already requested you to make free with the latter. You will find more quotations from the Fedt [*The Federalist*]. Dark them out if you think the most squeamish Critic could object to them. In No. 5. I suggest to your attention a long preliminary remark into which I suffered myself to be led before I was aware of the prolixity. As the piece is full long without it, it had probably better be lopped off. The propriety of the two

---

108. TJ's letter to Gouverneur Morris, Aug. 16, 1793, demanded the recall of Genet; see Ford, VI, pp. 371-93. A copy is in the Madison Papers at the Library of Congress.

109. See Malone's chapter " 'Liberty Warring on Herself': The Downfall of Genet," III, pp. 114-31.

110. JM probably enclosed "Helvidius" Numbers III and IV. TJ did not acknowledge Number V until Sept. 8, below.

111. JM's italics.

last paragraphs claims your particular criticism. I wd. not have hazarded them without the prospect of your revisal, and if proper, your erasure. That which regards Spain etc. may contain unsound reasoning, or be too delicate to be touched in a Newspaper. The propriety of the last, as to the President's answers to addresses, depends on the truth of the fact, of which you can judge. I am not sure that I have seen all the answers. My last was of the 12th. and covered the 2 first Nos. of H——s.[112] I am assured that it was put into the post office on tuesday evening. It ought therefore to have reached you on Saturday last. As an oppy. to Fredg may happen before more than the 3d. No. may be transcribed, it is possible, that this may be accompanied by that alone.

The drouth has been dreadful to the Corn. There has been no rain making any sensible impression for seven weeks, of the hottest weather of the hottest year rem[em]bered: and at the very period critical to that crop. Yesterday afternoon we had a small shower—and more seemed to be passing around us. No weather however can now possibly add 5 perCt. to the prospect. There can not be more than half crops made generally and much less in many places. Yrs. affy

Madison to Jefferson

At Col. M——[113] [ca. Aug. 22, 1793]

DEAR SIR

I left home the day before yesterday which was the date of my last. It was to be accompanied by 2. and perhaps tho' not probably 3 additional Nos. of H—l—vd—s. The last towit No. 5. contained two paragraphs the one relating to the accession of S. and P. to the war against F. the other to the answer's of the P. to the addresses on his proclamation, which I particularly requested you to revise, and if improper, to erase. The whole piece was more hurried than it ought to have been, and these paragraphs penned in the instant of my setting out which had been delayed as late as would leave eno' of the day for the journey. I mention this as the only apology for the gross error of fact committed with respect to the term neutrality, which it is asserted the P. has not used in any of his answers. I find on looking into them here, that he used it in the first of all to the Merchts. of Philada. and in one other out of three which I have examined. I must make my conditional request therefore an absolute one as to that passage. If he should forbear the use of the term in all his answers subsequent to the perversion of it by Pacificus, it will strengthen the argument used; but that must be a future and contingent consideration. Mr. D. R. was not arrived yesterday. The family here well—so also at M. as you will no doubt learn from the Spot itself. Adieu. Yrs. Affy

112. At a later time, JM filled in "Helvidius."
113. JM was at Monroe's home near Monticello.

Jefferson to Madison

[Philadelphia] Aug. 25, 1793

You will percieve by the inclosed papers that Genet has thrown down the gauntlet to the President by the publication of his letter and my answer, and is himself forcing that appeal to the people, and risking that disgust, which I had so much wished should have been avoided.[114] The indications from different parts of the continent are already sufficient to shew that the mass of the republican interest has no hesitation to disapprove of this intermeddling by a foreigner, and the more readily as his object was evidently, contrary to his professions, to force us into the war. I am not certain whether some of the more furious republicans may not schismatise with him.

The following arrangements are established.

Sep. 10. the Pr. sets out for Mt. Vernon, and will be here again the 30th. Oct. 5th. or a little sooner I set out to be absent 6. weeks, by agreement. Consequently I shall be here again about Nov. 17. to remain to Dec. 31. I break up my house the last of Septemb. Shall leave my carriage and horses in Virginia and return in the stage, not to have the embarrassment of ploughing them through the mud in January. I shall take private lodgings on my return. Billy who is just going on a nautical expedition to Charleston, called on me yesterday to desire I would send you the inclosed account which he said was necessary for you to debit those for whom the articles were. Adieu.

Madison to Jefferson

[At Col. Monroe's] Aug. 27, 1793

DEAR SIR

I wrote you a few lines by the last post from this place just to apprize you of my movement to it.[115] I have since seen the Richmond and the Philada. papers containing, the latter the certificate of Jay and King and the publications relating to the subject of it,[116] the former the proceedings at Richmond dictated no doubt by the Cabal at Philada. It is painful to observe the success of the management for putting Wythe at the head of them.[117] I understand

---

114. For Genet's appeal over the head of the president to the "sovereign people" of the United States, see Malone, III, pp. 135–36.

115. JM was still at Monroe's home near Monticello.

116. John Jay and Rufus King had certified that Genet proposed to appeal from the president to the people.

117. George Wythe presided over the Richmond rally denouncing Genet; see Imogene M. Brown, *American Aristides: A Biography of George Wythe* (Rutherford, N.J., 1981), pp. 258–61.

however that a considerable revolution has taken place in his political sentiments under the influence of some disgusts he has recd. from the State Legislature. By what has appeared I discover that a determination has been formed to drag before the public the indiscretions of Genèt; and turn them and the popularity of the P. to the purposes driven at. Some impression will be made here of course. A plan is evidently laid in Richd. to render it extensive. If an early and well digested effort for calling out the real sense of the people be not made, there is room to apprehend they may in many places be misled. This has employed the conversation of —— and myself. We shall endeavor at some means of repelling the danger; particularly by setting on foot expressions of the public mind in important Counties, and under the auspices of respectable names. I have written with this view to Caroline, and have suggested a proper train of ideas, and a wish that Mr. P. would patronise the measure.[118] Such an example would have great effect. Even if it shd. not be followed it would be considered as an authentic specimen of the *Country*[119] temper; and would put other places on their guard agst. the snares that may be laid for them. The want of opportunities, and our ignorance of trust worthy characters will circumscribe our efforts in this way to a very narrow compass. The rains for several days have delayed my trip to the Gentleman named in my last.[120] Unless tomorrow shd. be a favorable day, I shall be obliged to decline it altogether. In two or three days I shall be in a situation to receive and answer your letters as usual. That by Mr. DR. has not yet reached me.

Jefferson to Madison

[Philadelphia] Sept. 1 and 2, 1793

My last was of the 25th. Since that I have received yours of the 20th. and Colo. M's of the 21st.[121] Nothing further has passed with Mr. Genet, but one of his Consuls has committed a pretty serious deed at Boston, by going with an armed force taken from a French frigate in the harbour, and rescuing a vessel out of the hands of the marshal who had arrested her by process from a court of justice. In another instance he kept off the Marshal by an armed force from serving a precept on a vessel. He is ordered consequently to be arrested himself

---

118. Edmund Pendleton presided at a public meeting on Sept. 10; see the editorial note "Resolutions on Franco-American Relations," [Aug. 27, 1793], in *PJM,* XV, pp. 76–79.
119. JM's italics.
120. Wilson Cary Nicholas.
121. JM was at Monroe's home from Aug. 20 until Sept. 1.

prosecuted and punished for the rescue, and his Exequatur will be revoked.[122] You will see in the newspapers the attack made on our commerce by the British king in his *additional instructions*[123] of June 8. Tho' we have only newspaper information of it, *provisional* instructions are going to Mr. Pinckney to require a revocation of them and indemnification for all losses which individuals may sustain by them in the mean time.[124] Of the revocation I have not the least expectation. I shall therefore be for laying the whole business (respecting both nations) before Congress. While I think it impossible they should not approve of what has been done disagreeable to the friendly nation, it will be in their power to soothe them by strong commercial retaliations against the hostile one. Pinching their commerce will be just against themselves, advantageous to us, and conciliatory towards our friends of the hard necessities into which their agent has driven us. His conduct has given room for the enemies of liberty and of France to come forward in a stile of acrimony against that nation which they never would have dared to have done. The disapprobation of the agent mingles with the reprehension of his nation and gives a toleration to that which it never had before. He has still some defenders in Freneau's and Greenleaf's papers. Who they are I know not: for even Hutcheson and Dallas give him up. I inclose you a Boston paper which will give you a specimen of what all the papers are now filled with. You will recognise Mr. A—— under the signature of Camillus. He writes in every week's paper now, and generally under different signatures. This is the first paper in which he has omitted some furious incartade against me.[125] Hutcheson says that Genet has totally overturned the Republican interest in Philadelphia. However, the people going right themselves, if they always see their republican advocates with them, an accidental meeting with the Monocrats will not be a coalescence. You will see much said and gainsaid about G's threat to appeal to the people. I can assure you it is a fact. I received yesterday the M. S. you mentioned to me from F——n.[126] I have only got a dozen pages into it, and never was more charmed with any thing. Profound arguments presented in the simplest point of view entitle him really to his antient signature. In the papers received from you I have seen nothing which ought to be changed, except a part of one sentence, not neces-

---

122. For the revocation of the exequatar of Antoine Charbonnet Duplaine as French vice-consul, see Charles M. Thomas, *American Neutrality in 1793: A Study in Cabinet Government* (New York, 1931), pp. 212–19.

123. TJ's italics here and below.

124. The British order-in-council expanded the definition of contraband of war to include such provisions as corn, flour, and meal. TJ instructed Thomas Pinckney, U.S. minister to Great Britain, to protest the order.

125. The Boston essays by "Camillus" attacked the Republican party and Genet and defended Hamilton. The editors of the *PJM* found no evidence to confirm TJ's attribution of these essays to John Adams but suggested Fisher Ames as a more likely candidate; see *PJM,* XV, p. 91.

126. "Franklin" was John Taylor of Caroline.

sary for it's object, and running foul of something of which you were not apprised.[127]

A malignant fever has been generated in the filth of Water street which gives great alarm. About 70. people had died of it two days ago, and as many more were ill of it. It has now got into most parts of the city and is considerably infectious. At first 3. out of 4. died. Now about 1. out of 3. It comes on with a pain in the head, sick stomach, then a little chill, fever, black vomiting and stools, and death from the 2d. to the 8th. day. Every body, who can, is flying from the city, and the panic of the country people is likely to add famine to disease. Tho becoming less mortal, it is still spreading, and the heat of the weather is very unpropitious. I have withdrawn my daughter from the city, but am obliged to go to it every day myself. My threshing machine is arrived at New York. Mr. Pinckney writes me word that the original from which this model is copied threshes 150 bushels of wheat in 8. hours with 6. horses and 5. men. It may be moved either by water or horses. Fortunately the workman who made it (a millwright) is come in the same vessel to settle in America. I have written to persuade him to go on immediately to Richmd. offering him the use of my model to exhibit, and to give him letters to get him into immediate employ in making them. I expect an answer before I write to you again. I understand that the model is made mostly in brass, and in the simple form in which it was first ordered, to be worked by horses, it was to have cost 5. guineas, but Mr. Pinckney having afterwards directed it to be accomodated to a water movement also, it has made it more complicated, and costs 13. guineas. It will thresh any grain from the Windsor bean down to the smallest. Adieu.

P. S. The market, was the last winter from 25. to 50 percent higher than it was in the winter preceding. It is now got to from 50. to 100. percent higher. I think by the winter it will be generally 100 percent on the prices of 1790. European goods are also much risen. Of course you must expect a rise in the boarding houses compounded of these two. In the mean time the produce of the farmer, say wheat, rice, tobacco has not risen a copper. The redundancy of paper then in the cities is palpably a tax on the distant farmer.

P. S. Sep. 2. I have made great progress into the M. S. and still with the same pleasure. I have no doubt it must produce great effect. But that this may be the greatest possible, it's coming out should be timed to the best advantage. It should come out just so many days before the meeting of Congress as will prevent suspicions of it's coming with them, yet so as to be a new thing when they arrive, ready to get into their hands while yet unoccupied, before the panic of the culprits shall be over, or any measures for defeating it's first effect may be taken. I will direct it to appear a fortnight before their meeting unless you order otherwise. It might as well be thrown into a church yard, as come out now.

---

127. JM's "Helvidius" essays.

Madison to Jefferson

[Orange] Sept. 2, 1793

DEAR SIR

I write this by your servant on his way to George Town with a Horse. He applies to me for his best route. I advise the circuitous one by Fredg. in preference to the shorter one, in which he would probably lose more by mistakes than would be equal to the difference between the two in point of distance. I left Monroe's yesterday. My stay was spun out by waiting for Mr. D. R. who did not arrive at Monto: till Friday evening. Your letter by him was duly recd. On getting home last night I found your subsequent one of the 18th. inst. I have not yet read the paper inclosed in it. I shall write you in the course of the day by another opportunity for the post which will afford me time to say what I could not say now without detaining the Servant.

Madison to Jefferson

[Orange] Sept. 2, 1793

DEAR SIR

I dropped you a few lines this morning by the servant going to George Town with your horse. I had not time, without detaining him to say more than that I had your two favors of the 11th. Ult: by Mr. D. R.[128] and of the 18th. by post. The former was communicated to Monroe, as shall be the latter in case of opportunity. The conduct of Genèt as developed in these, and in his proceedings as exhibited in the newspapers, is as unaccountable as it is distressing. The effect is beginning to be strongly felt here in the surprize and disgust of those who are attached to the French cause, and viewed this minister as the instrument for cementing instead of alienating the two Republics. These sensations are powerfully reinforced by the general and habitual veneration for the President. The Anglican party is busy as you may suppose in making the worst of every thing, and in turning the public feelings against France, and thence, in favor of England. The only antidote for their poison, is to distinguish between the nation and its Agent, between principles and events; and to impress the well mea[n]ing with the fact that the enemies of France and of Liberty are at work to lead them from their honorable connection with these, into the arms and ultimately into the Government of G. B. If the genuine sense of the people could be collected on the several points comprehended in the occasion, the calamity would be greatly alleviated if not absolutely controuled. But this is scarcely possible. The Country is too much uninformed, and too inert to speak for itself; and the language of the towns which are generally directed by

---

128. David Meade Randolph.

an adverse interest will insidiously inflame the evil. It is however of such infinite importance to our own Government as well as to that of France, that the real sentiments of the people here should be understood, that something ought to be attempted on that head. I inclose a copy of a train of ideas sketched on the first rumour of the war between the Ex. and Genet, and particularly suggested by the Richmond Resolutions, as a groundwork for those who might take the lead in county meetings. It was intended that they should be modified in every particular according to the state of information and the particular temper of the place. A copy has been sent to Caroline with a hope that Mr. P. might find it not improper to step forward. Another is gone to the District Court at Staunton in the hands of Monroe, who carried a letter from me on the subject to A. Stuart; and a third will be for consideration at the District Ct. at Charlottesville. If these examples should be set, there may be a chance of like proceedings elsewhere: and in themselves they will be respectable specimens of the principles and sensations of the Agricultural, which is the commanding part of the Society. I am not sanguine however that the effort will succeed. If it does not, the State Legislatures, and the federal also if possible, must be induced to take up the matter in its true point of view. Monroe and myself read with attention your despatch by D. R. and had much conversation on what passed between you and the P. It appd. to both of us that a real anxiety was marked to retain you in office, that over and above other motives, it was felt that your presence and implied sanction might be a necessary shield against certain criticisms from certain quarters; that the departure of the only counsellor possessing the confidence of the Republicans would be a signal for new and perhaps very disagreeable attacks; that in this point of view, the respectful and conciliatory language of the P. is worthy of particular attention; and that it affords a better hope than has existed of your being able to command attention, and to moderate the predominant tone. We agreed in opinion also that whilst this end is pursued, it would be wise to make as few concessions as possible that might embarrass the free pursuit of measures which may be dictated by Repubn. principles and required by the public good. In a word we think you ought to make the most of the value we perceive to be placed on your participation in the Ex: Counsels. I am extremely glad to find that you are to remain another quarter. The season will be more apropos in several respects; and it will prevent any co-operation which a successor might be disposed to make towards a final breach with France. I have little hope that you will have one whose policy will have the same healing tendency with yours. I foresee, I think, that it will be either King, if Johnson is put at the Treasy: or E. Rutlege, if Walcot should be put there. I am glad the President rightly infers my determination from antecedent circumstances, so as to free me from imputations in his mind connected with the present state of things. Monroe is particularly solicitous that you should take the view of your present position and opportunities above suggested. He sees so forcibly the difficulty of keeping the feelings of the people as to Genèt distinct from those due to his Constituents, that he can hardly prevail on himself absolutely, and *openly*, to abandon him. I concur with him that it ought to be done no further than is forced upon us, that in general silence is better than open denunciation and crimination; and that it is not unfair to admit the apologetic influence of the errors in our own Government which may have inflamed the passions which now discolor every object to his eye: such as the refusal in the outset of the Government to favor the commerce of F. more than that of G. B—the unfortunate appt. of G. M.[129] to the former: the language of the proclamation—the attempts of Pacificus to explain away and dissolve the Treaty, the notoriety of the Author, and the appearance of its being an informal manifestation of the views of the Ex. etc.

I paid a short visit to Mr. W. N.[130] as I proposed. He talks like a sound Republican, and sincere friend to the French cause in every respect. I collected from him that E. R. had admitted to him that he drew the Procln., that he had been attacked on it at Chatham by Mr. Jos: Jones, that he reprobated the comment of Pac—f—s—etc. W. N observed that H.[131] had taken the Ex. in by gaining phrases of which he could make the use he has done. The circumstances which derogate from full confidence in W. N. are 1st. his being embarked in a variety of projects which call for money, and keep him in intercourse with the merchts. of Richd. 2d. his communication and intimacy with Marshal of whose *disinterestedness*[132] as well as understanding he has the highest opinion. It is said, that Marshal who is at the head of the great purchase from Fairfax,[133] has lately obtained pecuniary aids from the Bank or people connected with it. I think it certain that he must have felt, in the moment of the purchase an absolute dependence on the monied interest, which will explain him to every one that reflects, in the active character he is assuming. I have been obliged to write this in great haste, the bearer impatiently waiting the whole time.

I hope you have rcd. the five Nos. of Hel—v—d—s. I must resume the task I suppose, in relation to the *Treaty*—and *Gratitude*. I feel however so much awkwardness under the new posture of things, that I shall deliberate whether a considerable postponement at least may not be adviseable. I found also on my return a House full of particular friends who will stay some weeks and receive and return visits from which I can not decently exclude myself. If I sd. perceive it impossible or improper to continue the publication so as to avail myself the channel used to the press, I shall suspend it till I see and talk with you on the whole matter. Adieu.

---

129. At a later time, JM wrote out "Gouverneur Morris."

130. At a later time, JM wrote out "W. C. Nicholas."

131. At a later time, JM wrote out "Hamilton."

132. JM's italics here and below.

133. Albert J. Beveridge, *The Life of John Marshall*, 4 vols. (Boston, 1916-19), II, pp. 203-11, denied that Marshall received money from the Bank of the United States for the Fairfax purchase. The more recent account in John Marshall, *The Papers of John Marshall*, vol. I, ed. Charles T. Cullen and Herbert A. Johnson (Chapel Hill, 1977), pp. 140-56, does not discuss the matter.

Jefferson to Madison

[Philadelphia] Sept. 8, 1793

I have received and am charmed with No. V.[134] I thought the introduction an useful lesson to others as I found it to myself, for I had really, by constantly hearing the sound, been led into a pretty free use of it myself. I struck out the passage you desired in the last page. I struck out also the words 'and neutrality' in the following passage 'taking the proclamation *in it's proper sense*[135] as reminding all concerned that as the US. were at peace, the laws of peace *and neutrality* were still obligatory.' Also a paragraph of 4. lines that a minister from France was hourly expected when the proclamation issued. There was one here at the time—the other did not arrive in 6. weeks. To have waited that time would have given full course to the evil.

I went through Franklin with enchantment; and what peculiarly pleased me was that there was not a sentence from which it could be conjectured whether it came from N.S.E. or West. At last a whole page of Virginia flashed on me. It was in the section on the state of parties, and was an apology for the continuance of slavery among us. However this circumstance may be justly palliated, it had nothing to do with the state of parties, with the bank, encumbered a good cause with a questionable argument; many readers who would have gone heart and hand with the author so far would have flown off in a tangent from that paragraph. I struck it out. Justify this if you please to those concerned, and if it cannot be done say so and it may still be reestablished. I mentioned to you in my last that a Fr. Consul at Boston had rescued a vessel out of the hands of a marshal by military force. Genet has at New York forbidden a marshal to arrest a vessel and given orders to the French squadron to protect her by force. Was there ever an instance before of a diplomatic man overawing and obstructing the course of the law in a country by an armed force? The yellow fever increases. The week before last about 3. a day died. This last week about 11. a day have died; consequently from known data about 33. a day are taken, and there are about 330. patients under it. They are much scattered through the town, and it is the opinion of the physicians that there is no possibility of stopping it. They agree it is a non-descript disease, and no two agree in any one part of their process of cure. The Presidt. goes off the day after tomorrow as he had always intended. Knox then takes flight. Hamilton is ill of the fever as is said. He had two physicians out at his house the night before last. His family think him in danger, and he puts himself so by his excessive alarm. He had been miserable several days before from a firm persuasion he should catch it. A man as timid as he is on the water, as timid on horseback, as timid in sickness, would be a phænomenon if the courage of which he has the

134. JM's fifth installment of his "Helvidius" essays.
135. TJ's italics here and below.

reputation in military occasions were genuine. His friends, who have not seen him, suspect it is only an autumnal fever he has. I would really go away, because I think there is rational danger, but that I had before announced that I should not go till the beginning of October, and I do not like to exhibit the appearance of panic. Besides that I think there might [be] serious ills proceed from there being not a single member of the administration in place. Poor Hutcheson dined with me on Friday was sennight, was taken that night on his return home, and died the day before yesterday. It is difficult to say whether the republican interest has suffered more by his death or Genet's extravagance. I sometimes cannot help seriously believing the latter to be a Dumourier, endeavoring to draw us into the war against France as Dumourier while a minister, drew on her the war of the empire. The Indians have refused to meet our Commissioners unless they would make the Ohio a boundary by preliminary condn. Consequently they are on their return and we may suppose Wayne in movement. Since my last which was of the 1st. your's of the 22d. Aug. and 2d. Sep. are received. Adieu.

Jefferson to Madison

[Philadelphia] Sept. 12, 1793

The fever spreads faster. Deaths are now about 30. a day. It is in every square of the city. All flying who can. Most of the offices are shut or shutting. The banks shut up this day. All my clerks have left me but one: so that I cannot go on with business. I shall therefore set out in 3. or 4. days and perhaps see you before you get this. H had truly the fever, and is on the recovery, and pronounced out of danger.

Jefferson to Madison

Schuylkill Sept. 15, [1793]

I have to acknolege yours of Aug. 27. and Sep. 2. The fever in town is become less mortal, but extends. Dupont the Fr. Counsul is dead of it. So is Wright the painter. His wife also. Lieper is said to be dead, but that is not certain. J. Barclay ill. Ham. and his wife recovered. Willing on the recovery.[136] The banks are not shut up, as I had been falsely informed when I wrote you

136. François Dupont was the French consul in Philadelphia, and Joseph Wright, who had studied with Benjamin West in London, was a designer at the U.S. Mint. Thomas Leiper, formerly TJ's landlord, did not die at this time. John Barclay was president of the Bank of Pennsylvania, and Thomas Willing was president of the Bank of the United States; see *PJM,* XV, p. 112.

last. I have some expectation to set out tomorrow, and shall make it eight days to your house; but it is very possible I may yet be detained here two or three days. The arrangement on which I had consented to remain another quarter was that the President was to be absent three weeks, and after that I was to be absent 6. weeks. This got me rid of 9. weeks of the 13. and the remaining 4. Congress would be setting. My view in this was precisely to avoid being at any more councils as much as possible, that I might not be committed in any thing further. This fever by driving me off sooner, will bring me back sooner, and so far counteract my view. But I need not take the trouble of writing on this subject, as I shall see you as early as you will get this letter. Adieu.

Madison to Jefferson

[Orange Sept. 16, 1793]

The want of oppy. has left me in debt for 3 favors those of Aug. 18. 25. and Sepr. 8th. which I now acknowledge by one which is too precarious for any thing confidential. I have long been uneasy for your health amidst the vapors of the Schuylkil. The new and more alarming danger has made me particularly anxious that you were out of the sphere of it. I cannot altogether condemn your unwillingness to retire from your post under the circumstances you describe; but if your stay be as unessential as I conceive it to be rendered by the absence of the P. and the fever does not abate, I pray you not to sacrifice too much to motives which others do not feel. As I intimated in my last, my time has been *totally* diverted from my object.[137] I have scarcely been able to turn it even in my thoughts. It is probable therefore that you will not hear further from me in relation to it before you leave P. In fact the temper of the present moment and the uncertainty of many things seems to advise a postponement if nothing more. All the liberties you have taken will I am sure be approved. I have neglected hitherto to comply with your request as to a rotation farm. In the main it appears to be judicious and unobjectionable. Of this opinion are those with whom I have conferred. One or two alterations not very material occurred; but as they may be doubtful, and if proper, can be made at any time, I do not now trouble you with them. I have tried the patent plow amended by fixing the Colter in the usual way. It succeeds perfectly, and I think forms the plow best suited to its object. I am happy at the arrival of your Threshing Model. What will be about the cost of the Machine? Will it be removeable from one to another part of an extensive farm? Adieu. Yrs. always and affy.

The other Newspapers in my next.

137. JM's italics. He referred to his "Helvidius" essays.

18

"PINCHING BRITISH COMMERCE," 1793–1794

TRAVELING WITH his daughter Maria, Jefferson left Philadelphia on September 17, 1793, stopping first with President and Mrs. Washington at Mt. Vernon, then with Madison at Montpellier. As early as July, Jefferson had suggested that he and Madison meet during the fall to discuss political matters before Congress convened in December.[1] They now agreed to meet in October with Jefferson's neighbor Senator James Monroe, and the three Republican leaders gathered at Monticello as scheduled to plan party strategy in their efforts to "keep the people on our side by keeping ourselves in the right."[2] They also discussed the publication of John Taylor's pamphlet attacking Hamilton and formulated a reply to President Washington's inquiries about convening Congress at some place other than Philadelphia because of the persistence of the yellow-fever epidemic in the capital city.[3] Finally, they reviewed reports that Great Britain had issued an order-in-council that seemed to Madison a virtual declaration of "war on our commerce, by intercepting uncontraband articles bound to unblockaded ports. . . . This must bring on a crisis with us," he feared, "unless the order be revoked on our demand," but he knew "there is not the least probability" of such a revocation.[4]

After a month at Monticello, Jefferson made what he thought was his

---

1. TJ to JM, July 14, 1793, above.

2. Brant, III, p. 385, mentions the meeting. TJ used this phrase in his letter to JM, Aug. 11, 1793, above.

3. JM was visiting TJ when the latter received a letter from Washington about the meeting place for the congressional session; see TJ to George Washington, Oct. 17, 1793, in Ford, VI, p. 436. Washington sent a similar letter to JM on Oct. 14, 1793, and JM replied on Oct. 24, 1793; see *PJM,* XV, pp. 126–31.

4. JM to James Monroe, Sept. 15, 1793, in *PJM,* XV, p. 111. Although TJ, JM, and Monroe left no record of their joint discussions except for their deliberations about where Congress should convene, these four items were the major issues that they mentioned on the eve of their meeting.

final trip north as a public official. On his usual stop overnight with Madison, the farmer became so delighted with a new variety of corn, "which is forwarder by three weeks than the ordinary sort," that "he took an Ear with him to be brought back on his return."[5] In Baltimore, he overtook President Washington, and they traveled together to Germantown, where they waited for the yellow-fever scourge to subside in Philadelphia. The crowded village "cannot lodge a single person more," Jefferson informed Madison. "As a great favor I have got a bed in the corner of the public room of a tavern: and must so continue till some of the Philadelphians make a vacancy by removing into the city."[6]

Within a week, the first frost came, and the fever had almost disappeared when the refugees began flocking back to Philadelphia, leaving some lodging space for returning congressmen. "I have got good lodgings for Monroe and yourself," the secretary of state informed his coadjutor, "that is to say, a good room with a fire place and two beds, in a pleasant and convenient position, with a quiet family."[7]

In his last two months in office, Jefferson resumed his contest with Hamilton as Washington's cabinet discussed the subject of the president's message to Congress. Over Hamilton's objections, Jefferson won the support of the president in setting forth the administration's views on international affairs. On the problem of Genet, there was agreement that the correspondence between the envoy and the secretary of state should be published. But there was disagreement over publishing the correspondence between the secretary and the British minister about the long-stalled negotiations on the implementation of the peace treaty of 1783 and the more recent grievance against the British order-in-council authorizing the seizure of neutral vessels carrying foodstuffs to France. Hamilton thought that matters relating to the British should be submitted to Congress in a secret communication, but the president ruled that both the French and British documents should go to Congress in a public message.[8]

From the moment that Jefferson learned of the "attack made on our commerce by the British king in his *additional instructions* of June 8," he had favored coupling the British aggressions with Genet's violations and "laying the whole business (respecting both nations) before Congress. While I think it impossible that they should not approve of what has been done disagreeable to the friendly nation, it will be in their power to soothe them by strong commercial retaliations against the hostile one. Pinching their commerce," he advised Madison, "will be just against themselves, advantageous to us, and conciliatory

---

5. JM to James Monroe, Oct. 29, 1793, *ibid.,* p. 132.

6. TJ to JM, Nov. 2, 1793, below.

7. TJ to JM, Nov. 9, 1793, below, and Nov. 17, 1793, below.

8. Malone, III, pp. 147–54, and John C. Miller, *Alexander Hamilton: Portrait in Paradox* (New York, 1959), pp. 384–87.

towards our friends of the hard necessities into which their agent has driven us."⁹

Even Hamilton agreed that British seizure of noncontraband goods bound for unblockaded ports created an international crisis. Corn, grain, and foodstuffs were not contraband commerce; moreover, a blockade to be binding had to be effectively patrolled by ships on station, a requirement that was not met by the so-called British blockade of France. In short, Hamilton said, the order-in-council was a "very harsh and unprecedented measure" aimed specifically at the commerce of the United States.¹⁰

Jefferson promptly protested the British action as contrary to the law of nations and sent provisional instructions to Thomas Pinckney, the American minister in London, "to require a revocation of them and indemnification for all losses which individuals may sustain by them in the mean time."¹¹ Instead of revoking the order, the British soon expanded their system, issuing another order-in-council on November 6, 1793, authorizing British warships to search and seize all neutral ships carrying provisions to the French West Indies or transporting the produce of those islands. The British fleet then swept the Caribbean clear of American ships, the chief carriers of provisions to and produce from the French islands.¹²

Before news of these ravages reached the United States, Congress had convened, and Jefferson had submitted his long-delayed "Report on the Privileges and Restrictions on the Commerce of the United States in Foreign Countries," his last major act as secretary of state. It had been almost three years in the making, originating at the request of the House of Representatives when they sidetracked Madison's Navigation Act in February 1791 and asked Jefferson to prepare such a report along with suggested remedies. With Madison's assistance, Jefferson prepared his report in the summer of 1791; but at Hamilton's request, he postponed submitting it until Hammond answered the American demand for the evacuation of the northwest posts. After updating the report in 1792, Jefferson was ready to submit it in February 1793 but withheld it pending the arrival of Genet, who carried proposals for a new commercial treaty. Then Genet's blunders and the eruption of the war of the French Revolution pushed peacetime commercial issues to one side. So on the eve of his retirement at the end of 1793, Jefferson finally decided to submit his report, which the British depredations had once again made a timely topic.

The secretary of state viewed trade as a weapon of diplomacy, and he proposed to use it to assure "fair and equal access to market . . . our productions" and "our due share in the transportation of them." Ideally, trade should move without restrictions, with each nation "free to exchange with others

---

9. TJ to JM, Sept. 1, 1793, above.
10. Miller, pp. 386–87.
11. TJ to JM, Sept. 1, 1793, above. Also see Malone, III, pp. 150–54.
12. John C. Miller, *The Federalist Era: 1789–1801* (New York, 1960), pp. 140–42.

mutual surplusses for mutual wants" on the basis of reciprocity. But trade was burdened with restrictions which made for closed commercial systems that discriminated in one form or another. Since this was the case, he argued, "free commerce and navigation are not to be given in exchange for restrictions and vexations; nor are they likely to produce a relaxation of them."[13]

Jefferson submitted his report to Congress on December 16 and resigned on December 31, 1793. According to Hamilton, he "threw this firebrand of discord into the midst of the representatives of the states . . . and instantly *decamped* to Monticello."[14] But his departure was not that sudden since he stayed in Philadelphia for a round of farewells, a meeting of the American Philosophical Society early in the new year, and the reintroduction in Congress of Madison's commercial resolutions of 1791, designed to implement his recommendations for commercial retaliation against Great Britain.

On January 3, 1794, Madison introduced proposals recommending discriminatory duties on British ships and manufactures in order to free the American economy from "the caprice, the passions, the mistaken calculations of interest, the bankruptcies, and the wars of a single foreign country."[15] "Mr. Madison's Resolutions" dominated congressional debate in the early months of 1794, and a Massachusetts Republican credited their author with an "Eloquence which baffles every thing I had ever heard." During a marathon performance, Madison's "Elegance Accuracy Method and extensive Information . . . Engaged our Attention for two hours and a half during which time in a full House and thronged with Spectators there was such perfect Silence that you might almost have heard a Pin Fall."[16]

To counter Madison's speeches, Hamilton furnished information to opponents of discriminatory duties and drafted speeches for the leading Federalist spokesman, William Loughton Smith of South Carolina.[17] Jefferson instantly recognized Hamilton's hand in Smith's speech. "Every tittle of it is Hamilton's except the introduction," he told Madison. "There is scarcely any thing there which I have not heard from him in our various private tho' official discussions. The very turn of the arguments is the same, and others will see as well as myself that the style is Hamilton's. The sophistry is too fine, too ingenious even to have been comprehended by Smith, much less devised by him."[18]

The Federalists feared that Madison's commercial propositions might

---

13. See Malone, III, pp. 154–60, and Peterson, pp. 512–16.
14. Miller, *Federalist Era*, p. 143.
15. For a brief review of these proposals, see Brant, III, pp. 389–400, and *PJM*, XV, pp. 147–52.
16. For William Lyman's comments on JM's speech of Jan. 14, 1794, see *PJM*, XV, pp. 148–49.
17. For Hamilton's relations with "his Congressman Friday, William Smith," see Miller, *Hamilton*, pp. 388–91, and Syrett, XIII, p. 407.
18. TJ to JM, Apr. 3, 1794, below.

provoke war with Great Britain and threaten the fiscal system of the United States, which was based on trade revenues from its largest customer. But Madison replied that reciprocity would not lead to war. Instead, he argued, his proposals would stimulate domestic manufacturing and shipping, thus furnishing a home market for agricultural products. Early in February, his arguments won House approval of the first of his seven resolutions, which levied additional duties on manufactures from European nations having no commercial treaty with the United States, a diplomatic way of designating Great Britain. To give his New England supporters time to consult their constituents on this new policy, Madison agreed to a postponement of further consideration of his other proposals until March. He spent the interval writing out his speeches for national circulation in the press. To Jefferson, he complained that he was writing "as fast as I can write," but he found the task both tedious and laborious because of "the extreme length of it, the brevity of my notes, and the time that has run since the observations were delivered."[19]

He also took time out to read public reaction to his proposals, as his first report to Jefferson indicated:

The Interval has produced vast exertions by the British party to mislead the people of the Eastern States. No means have been spared. The most artful and wicked calumnies have been propagated with all the zeal which malice and interest could invent. The blackest of these calumnies, as you may imagine have fallen to the lot of the mover of the Resolutions. The last Boston paper contains a string of charges framed for the purpose of making the Eastern people believe that he has been the counsellor and abettor of Genèt in all his extravagances, and a corrupt tool of France ever since the embassy of Gerard.

Despite these "diabolical manœuvers," however, Republican sentiment seemed on the rise in Boston and New York, he reported. Another reason for postponing action on the resolutions for so long, according to Madison, "was the chance of hearing from England, and the probability that the intelligence would strengthen the arguments for retaliation." Recent information from the American minister in London made it clearer than ever that British policy towards the United States was "unjust and unfriendly."[20]

One week later, the news of British belligerence in the Caribbean burst on the nation's capital—Madison labeled it "a terrible slam in the W. Indies"— and the Federalists joined the Republicans in calling for more vigorous measures than resolutions against "the progress of British outrages." "This new symtom of insolence and enmity in Britain," Madison wrote his friend in retirement, "shews rather that she meditates a formal war as soon as she shall have crippled our marine resources, or that she calculates on the pusilanimity

19. JM to TJ, Mar. 12, 1794, below. For JM's speeches, see *PJM,* XV, pp. 167–71, 182–202, 204, 206–8, 210–43, and 247–48.
20. JM to TJ, Mar. 2, 1794, below.

of this country and the influence of her party, in a degree that will lead her into aggressions which our love of peace can no longer bear." Under these circumstances, Madison conceded, "the commercial propositions are . . . not the precise remedy to be pressed as first in order; but they are in every view and in any event proper to make part of our standing laws till the principle of reciprocity be established by mutual arrangements."[21]

Overtaken by events, Madison's resolutions now did not go far enough. Accordingly, they were pushed aside for more drastic measures of retaliation. "The partizans of England," Madison confided to Jefferson, "considering a war as now probable are endeavoring to take the lead in defensive preparations, and to acquire merit with the people by anticipating their wishes." He noted specifically that "an Embargo, on American vessels—on these and British also—and even on a seisure of British property, are in the mouths of some."[22]

Late in March, Congress adopted a thirty-day embargo, with the support of Republicans and New England Federalists, "whose constituents were growing so clamorous under their losses in the W. Indies, as to alarm their representatives." Federalist Jonathan Dayton proposed to sequester American debts owed to British creditors, suggesting that these be paid into the federal Treasury to be used as a fund for indemnifying citizens for losses inflicted by ships acting under the authority of the British king.[23] By mid-April, Madison summarized for Jefferson the congressional propositions "levelled at G[reat] B[ritain]":

1. to sequester British debts. 2. to establish a lien on British merchandize or the value of it, as it arrives. 3. to suspend imports from G. B. and Ireland till the spoliations be redressed and the Treaty of peace be executed.[24]

By the spring of 1794, the drift towards war seemed so strong that President Washington and his cabinet began to consider sending an envoy extraordinary to Great Britain. After receiving news from London that the obnoxious order-in-council of November 1793 had been withdrawn, Washington decided to dispatch a minister plenipotentiary in an attempt to arrange a settlement of differences. To Madison, this meant the substitution of executive efforts for legislative initiatives, showing a preference for "further negociation to any legislative operation of a coercive nature." Even more distressing, he notified Jefferson, was the rumor that "Hamilton is talked of, is much pressed by those attached to his politics, and will probably be appointed unless overruled by an apprehension from the disgust to Republicanism and to France."[25]

21. JM to TJ, Mar. 9, 1794, below, and Mar. 12, 1794, below.
22. *Ibid.*
23. JM to TJ, Mar. 26, 1794, below, and Mar. 31, 1794, below.
24. JM to TJ, Apr. 14, 1794, below.
25. *Ibid.*

The Republican party strongly opposed Hamilton as a peace envoy. Senator James Monroe and Congressman John Nicholas from Virginia wrote to the president, remonstrating against a special mission in general and Hamilton in particular, but Washington had already "laid aside" the secretary of the treasury, much to "his great mortification," as too controversial. Instead, the president persuaded Chief Justice John Jay to undertake the delicate mission to Great Britain.[26]

Thus, Madison's resolutions, based on Jefferson's commercial report, were sidetracked, and relations with Great Britain moved from legislative retaliation to executive negotiations. Indeed, Jay's appointment came while Congress was debating a nonimportation bill to replace the thirty-day embargo just before it expired. That measure, which passed the House by a bipartisan majority of 59 to 34, would have prohibited the importation of "all articles of British or Irish production after the 1st. [of] Nov. until the claims of the U. S. be adjusted and satisfied." Madison predicted that the bill would probably "miscarry in the Senate." He was correct. But, surprisingly, in view of the fact that the Senate had already confirmed Jay's appointment, it won an equal number of votes in the Federalist-dominated Senate and was defeated only by the tie-breaking vote of Vice President John Adams.[27]

An attempt to extend the embargo also failed in May, and Madison observed that "measures of this sort are not the fashion. To supplicate for peace, and under the uncertainty of success, to prepare for war by taxes and troops is the policy which now triumphs under the patronage of the Executive." Indeed, he concluded, "the influence of the Ex[ecutive] on events, the use made of them, and the public confidence in the P[resident] are an overmatch for all the efforts Republicanism can make. The party of that sentiment in the Senate is compleatly wrecked," he lamented to Jefferson, "and in the H[ouse] of Rep[resentative]s. in a much worse condition than at an earlier period of the Session."[28]

The only comfort for the Republicans was President Washington's appointment of James Monroe as minister to France. After the recall of Genet, France demanded the removal of Gouverneur Morris, who had lost favor with the French government because of his unfriendly views of the revolution. Monroe won confirmation easily, and Madison accompanied the minister and Mrs. Monroe to Baltimore, saw them off to France, then traveled to Virginia in June for the congressional recess.[29]

---

26. JM to TJ, Apr. 28, 1794, below. Also see Miller, *Hamilton,* pp. 393-95. The Republicans preferred to work through Thomas Pinckney, American minister in London, rather than a special envoy; see *PJM,* XV, p. 316.

27. *PJM,* XV, p. 313.

28. JM to TJ, May 25, 1794, below.

29. JM to James Madison, Sr., June 6, 1794, and June 15, 1794, in *PJM,* XV, pp. 344-46.

─────────── THE LETTERS ───────────

Jefferson to Madison

Germantown Nov. 2, 1793

DEAR SIR

I overtook the President at Baltimore, and we arrived here yesterday, myself fleeced of seventy odd dollars to get from Fredericksburg here, the stages running no further than Baltimore. I mention this to put yourself and Monroe on your guard. The fever in Phila. has so much abated as to have almost disappeared. The inhabitants are about returning. It has been determined that the President shall not interfere with the meeting of Congress. R. H. and K.[1] were of opinion he had a right to call them to any place but that the occasion did not call for it. I think the President inclined to the opinion. I proposed a proclamn. notifying that the Executive business would be done here till further notice, which I believe will be agreed. H. R. Lewis, Rawle[2] etc. all concur in the necessity that Congress should meet in Phila. and vote there their own adjournment, if it shall then be necessary to change the place. The question will be between N. York and Lancaster. The Pensylva. members are very anxious for the latter, and will attend punctually to support it as well as to support Muhlenburg and oppose the appointment of Smith (S. C.) speaker, which is intended by the Northern members. According to present appearances, this place cannot lodge a single person more. As a great favor I have got a bed in the corner of the public room of a tavern: and must so continue till some of the Philadelphians make a vacancy by removing into the city. Then we must give from 4. to 6 or 8. dollars a week for cuddies[3] without a bed, and sometimes without a chair or table. There is not a single lodging-house in the place. Ross and Willing are alive, Hancock is dead. Johnson of Maryld has *refused*. Ru. L. and Mcl. in contemplation.[4] The last least. You will have seen Genet's letters to Moultrie and to myself. Of the last I know nothing but from the public papers; and he published Moultrie's letter and his answer the moment he wrote it. You will see that his inveteracy against the President leads him to meditate the embroiling him with Congress.[5] They say he is going to

1. Edmund Randolph, Alexander Hamilton, and Henry Knox.

2. Alexander Hamilton, Edmund Randolph, William Lewis, and William Rawle. Rawle was U.S. attorney for the district of Pennsylvania, having succeeded Lewis; see *PJM,* XV, p. 134.

3. A closet or small room.

4. The last four listed—Thomas Johnson of Maryland, Edward Rutledge of South Carolina, Robert R. Livingston of New York, and James McClurg of Virginia—were candidates for TJ's post when his resignation became effective.

5. Governor William Moultrie of South Carolina asked Genet about reports that the foreign minister would appeal to the people over the president's head against the neutrality policy. Genet

be married to a daughter of Clinton's. If so, he is afraid to return to France.[6] Hamilton is ill, and suspicious he has taken the fever again by returning to his house. He of course could not attend here to-day. But the Pr. had shewed me his letter on the right of calling Congress to another place. Adieu.

Jefferson to Madison

Germantown Nov. 9, 1793

The stages from Philadelphia to Baltimore are to be resumed tomorrow. The fever has almost disappeared. The Physicians say they have no new subjects since the rains. Some old ones are still to recover or die, and it is presumed that will close the tragedy. The inhabitants, refugees, are now flocking back generally; this will give us accomodation here. The Pr. sets out tomorrow for Reading, and perhaps Lancaster to return in a week. He will probably remain here till the meeting of Congress, should Philadelphia become ever so safe, as the members may not be satisfied of that point till they have time to inform themselves. Toulon has surrendered to Engld. and Spain. Grand Anse in St. Domingo to England. The British have received a check before Dunkirk, probably a great one, but the particulars cannot yet be depended on. It happened about the 10th of September. When Monroe and yourself arrive here, come to Bockeus's tavern (sign the K. of Prussia) I will have engaged beds there for you for your temporary accomodation. Adieu.

Jefferson to Madison

Germantown Nov. 17, 1793

I have got good lodgings for Monroe and yourself, that is to say, a good room with a fire place and two beds, in a pleasant and convenient position, with a quiet family. They will breakfast you, but you must mess in a tavern; there is a good one across the street. This is the way in which all must do, and all I think will not be able to get even half beds. The President will remain here

---

denied the reports but denounced Washington's advisers, "whose schemes could only darken his glory." Genet's letter to TJ denied the right of the president to revoke the credentials of the French consul in Boston; see *PJM*, XV, p. 134.

6. Genet married Governor Clinton's daughter a year later.

I believe till the meeting of Congress, merely to form a point of union for them before they can have acquired information and courage. For at present there does not exist a single subject in the disorder, no new infection having taken place since the great rains the 1st. of the month, and those before infected being dead or recovered. There is no doubt you will set in Philadelphia, and therefore I have not given Monroe's letter to Seckel.[7] I do not write to him, because I know not whether he is at present moving by sea or by land, and if by the latter, I presume you can communicate to him. Wayne has had a convoy of 22. waggons of provision and 70. men cut off 15 miles in his rear by the Indians. 6. of the men were found on the spot scalped, the rest supposed taken. He had nearly reached Fort Hamilton.[8] R. has given notice that he means to resign. Genet by more and more denials of powers to the President and ascribing them to Congress, is evidently endeavoring to sow tares between them, and at any event to curry favor with the latter to whom he means to turn his appeal, finding it was not likely to be well received with the people. Accept, both of you, my sincere affections.

Madison to Jefferson

Fredericksburg Nov. 24, 1793

DEAR SIR

I have your 3 letters. The last of the 17th. fell into my hands here when I arrived on friday night. Col. Monroe was a day before me. Accept our thanks for your provision in our behalf at Germanto[w]n. We set off in 5 Minutes in a machine we have procured here, and which we shall keep on with till it fails us, or we can do better. I hope we shall be with you by sunday evening, or monday morning. Giles and Venable being before us, they will give you the intelligence from Richmond. The inclosed paper contains a scrap which may be of later date. If the Senate rejected as we understand, the vote relating to the procln., the answer of the Govr. *jointly* to the Come. of the two houses is a curious one.[9] Yrs. affly.

J. M. JR

---

7. Monroe had leased a house on Eighth Street from David Seckel; see *PJM*, XV, p. 139.

8. For a map showing Wayne's western campaign in 1793–94, see Paul David Nelson, *Anthony Wayne: Soldier of the Early Republic* (Bloomington, Ind., 1985), p. 230.

9. JM's italics. The Virginia House complimented Governor Henry Lee on his support of the Proclamation of Neutrality, but the Senate rejected it on one occasion and was silent on another. Lee, however, thanked both houses for their commendation of his stand; see Norman K. Risjord, *Chesapeake Politics, 1781–1800* (New York, 1978), pp. 431–32.

Jefferson to Madison

Monticello Feb. 15, 1794

DEAR SIR

We are here in a state of great quiet, having no public news to agitate us. I have never seen a Philadelphia paper since I left that place, nor learnt any thing of later date except some successes of the French the account of which seemed to have come by our vessel from Havre. It was said yesterday at our court that Genet was to be recalled: however nobody could tell how the information came. We have been told that Mr. Smith's speech and your's also on your propositions have got into Davis's papers, but none of them have reached us. I could not have supposed, when at Philadelphia, that so little of what was passing there could be known even at Kentuckey, as is the case here. Judging from this of the rest of the Union, it is evident to me that the people are not in a condition either to approve or disapprove of their government, nor consequently to influence it. I have been occupied closely with my own affairs, and have therefore never been from home since my arrival here. I hear nothing yet of the second person whom I had engaged as an overseer from the head of Elk, and the first I fear will prove a poor acquisition. Consequently I am likely to lose a year in the reformation of my plantations. The winter has been remarkeably mild—no demand for produce of any kind, at any market of James river. Tobacco and wheat may be bartered at low prices for goods at high. But neither can be sold for cash. This was the state of things at Richmond when business was stopped by the smallpox. Here we can get tea at $2\frac{1}{2}$ Dollars, white sugar at 38 Cents, coffee @ 25. cents etc. for wheat @ $66\frac{2}{3}$. Accept for yourself, Colo. and Mrs. Monroe[10] my affectionate respects

TH: JEFFERSON

Madison to Jefferson

Philadelphia Mar. 2, 1794

DEAR SIR

Your favor of the 15th. Ult: came to hand two days ago. It was not my intention that my first to you should have been procrastinated to the present date; but several causes have concurred in producing the effect. Among others I was in hopes every week to be able to furnish you with the proceedings on the subject grounded on your Commercial Report;[11] and particularly with such of them as related to yourself. It has so happened that I never could find leisure

---

10. JM lived with the Monroes during the first session of the Third Congress.

11. JM had introduced resolutions for commercial discrimination to implement TJ's farewell report to Congress.

to make out for the press, the share I had in them till very lately. The earlier part of my observations were sent to the Printer several weeks ago, but never made their appearance till thursday evening last.[12] The latter part is following, as you will find, as fast as I can write it out, which from the extreme length of it, the brevity of my notes, and the time that has run since the observations were delivered, is a task equally tedious and laborious. The sequel will be forwarded to you as soon as it gets into print. As you are so little supplied with the current information it may be necessary to apprize you that after the general discussions on the measure proposed by me, had been closed, and the first general resolution agreed to by a majority of 5 or 6, several of the Eastern members friendly to the object insisted on a postponement till the first monday in March. It was necessary to gratify them, and the postponement was carried by a small majority against the efforts of the adverse party, who counted on the votes of the timid members if forced before they could learn the sense of their constituents. The Interval has produced vast exertions by the British party to mislead the people of the Eastern States. No means have been spared. The most artful and wicked calumnies have been propagated with all the zeal which malice and interest could invent. The blackest of these calumnies, as you may imagine have fallen to the lot of the mover of the Resolutions.[13] The last Boston paper contains a string of charges framed for the purpose of making the Eastern people believe that he has been the counsellor and abettor of Genêt in all his extravagances, and a corrupt tool of France ever since the embassy of Gerard. It appears however that in spite of all these diabolical manœuvres, the town of Boston has been so far awakened as to have a Meeting in the town house, and a pretty unanimous vote for a committee to consider the subject and report proper instructions for their members in Congress. The Committee consists of men of weight, and for the most part of men of the right sort. There are some however who will endeavor to give a wrong turn to the business. I see by a paper of last evening that even in N. York a meeting of the people has taken place at the instance of the Republican party, and that a committee is appointed for the like purpose. As far as I know the names, the majority is on the right side. One motive for postponing the question so long was the chance of hearing from England, and the probability that the intelligence would strengthen the arguments for retaliation. Letters from Pinkney have accordingly arrived. As yet they are under the seal of confidence but it is in universal conversation that they mark precisely and *more strongly* than ever the unjust and unfriendly features which have characterized the British policy towards the U. States.[14] Soon after the arrival of the Packet, Mr. Randolph wrote to Hammond desiring to know whether an answer had

12. JM's speeches were reported in the *Philadelphia Gazette;* see *PJM,* XV, p. 271.

13. JM was "the mover of the Resolutions."

14. JM's italics. Washington sent to Congress the recent correspondence between Pinckney and Grenville about British retention of the western posts and "the interruption of our commerce and neutral rights"; see *PJM,* XV, p. 271.

been received to your letter of May 1792.[15] His reply was simply that it had not.

The scheme of Frigates to block up the Mediterranean has been pushed slowly, but successfully to the stage of resolutions on which a Bill is to be reported. The Majority has never exceeded two or three votes. Whether the scheme will finally take effect, is not certain. It probably will, unless accounts from Europe furnish hopes that Spain, or Portugal particularly the latter which is friendly and interested in our trade, may interpose.

Genèt has been superseded by Fauchèt, the Secretary to the Executive Council. The latter has not been here long eno' to develope his temper and character. He has the aspect of moderation. His account of things in France is very favorable on the whole. He takes particular pains to assure all who talk with him of the perseverance of France in her attachment to us, and her anxiety that nothing which may have taken place, may lessen it on our side. In his interview with the President, he held the same language; and I am told by E. R. that the P. not only declared explicitly his affectionate solicitude for the success of the Republic, but after he had done so with great emphasis, desired, in order to be as pointed as possible, that his expressions might be repeated, by E. R. who acted as Interpreter. Fauchet does not speak our language. La Forest comes over with the Minister as Consul General: And Petry, formerly Consul of S. C. as Consul for this place.[16] The political characters of these gentlemen as heretofore understood, give some uneasiness to the Republican party; and the uneasiness has been increased by the homage paid by the leaders of the other party to the new Minister. They may probably aim at practising on him, by abusing the madness of Genèt and representing the Republicans as rather his partisans, than the friends of the French cause. But if he is not an uncommon fool, or a traytor, it is impossible he can play into their hands, because the Anglicism stamped on the aristocratic faction must warn him of its hostility to his objects. Genèt has not taken any decided step in relation to his future movements. He is said to be poor; and by some to meditate a return to France with a view to join the army, by others a settlement in this Country as a farmer. If he is prudent he will not venture to France in her present temper, with all the suspicions and follies with which he is loaded. You must have seen that Brissot and his party have been cut off by the Guillotine.

I am informed by an anonymous letter from N. York, that large purchases are making there, and in the Eastern States, for supplying the British armaments in the W. Indies; and that American Vessels are chartering for the conveyance of them. This is really horrible. Whilst we allow the British to stop our supplies to the French Dominions, we allow our citizens to carry supplies

15. TJ's letter included American charges of British violations of the peace treaty of 1783.
16. In a move designed to prevent the sorts of embarrassments created by the impetuous Genet, the French government appointed the Comte de la Forest, Jean-Baptiste Petry, and Georges-Pierre Le Blanc, secretary of legation, as commissioners to counsel with the new minister, Jean Antoine Joseph Fauchet; see *PJM,* XV, p. 271.

to hers, for the known purpose of aiding her in taking from France the Islands we have guaranteed to her; and transferring these valuable markets from friendly and to unfriendly hands. What can be done. The letter writer suggests an Embargo. Perhaps the best step wd. be to declare that so long as G. B. will not allow the French to be supplied by us, we will not allow our supplies to go to her. It is not clear however that such a measure wd. stand the clamor of the merchts. seconded by the interest of the farmers and ship owners.

Madison to Jefferson

Philadelphia Mar. 9, 1794

DEAR SIR

I send you the continuation promised in my last, which I believe makes up the whole. If there should be any chasm let me know, and I will supply it. I have some little doubt the paper of Tuesday March 4. may have been omitted, and would now add it, but can not get it conveniently in time.

The commercial propositions were postponed for one week longer, on the arrival of the appointed day. Tomorrow they will again come on, unless precluded by debates on other business, or again postponed. You will see by the inclosed in what manner the Meeting at Boston issued, and the course the subject is taking at N. York. There was a large Mercantile Meeting last night in this City, for obtaining a vote of remonstrance agst. the propositions. A paper was accordingly introduced by Fitzimmons, Bingham etc. It was warmly and I am told ably attacked by Swanwick who explained and defended the propositions. He was clapped, and on the question, there were three or four nos for 1 aye to the paper. The minority had the arrogance notwithstanding to sign the paper individually, and will recruit all the names they can to day, among the Quaker's and others not present at the Meeting, in order to deliver in the paper with more effect tomorrow Morning. What the fate of the propositions will be is more uncertain than ever. Some of the friends of them, begin to say that more vigorous measures are rendered necessary by the progress of British outrages. The *additional*[17] instruction of Novr. 6. which you will find in the inclosed papers,[18] is so severely felt by the Merchants that some of them also, without relinquishing their opposition to what is proposed, talk of measures more congenial with the crisis. An Embargo, on American vessels—on these and British also—and even on a seisure of British property, are in the mouths of some of them. The additional instruction is questioned by some as inauthentic; but it is infinitely probable that it is genuine. The doubt is founded on the earliness of its date compared with that of our last intelligence from

17. JM's italics.
18. This British order-in-council authorized the seizure of any ship carrying cargo produced in any French colony or provisions destined for the use of any such colony.

Europe which is silent as to that matter. But it may have been decreed in the Cabinet and not put in force; or given into the hands of officers clandestinely, that the American prey might not escape. Our situation is certainly ripening to a most serious crisis. It does not appear however that in any event the commercial retaliation can be improper; but on the contrary that in every event it will be advantageous.

You will perceive that Fauchét is going on in the conciliatory plan of reversing the errors of his Predecessor.

The project of a squadron of frigates is pursued with unremitting ardor. In the course of the Bill the two 20 gun ships have been turned into 2 of 36 guns. So that the force is to consist of 6 in the whole, 4 of which will be of 40 guns. As the danger of a war has appeared to increase, every consideration rendering them at first unwise, now renders them absurd; yet the vague idea of protecting trade when it most needs it, misleads the interested who are weak, and the weak who are not interested.

I have this moment recd. a note informing me that there are letters from N. Y. containing definitive intelligence concerning Toulon. The British burnt sixteen French Sail of the Line in their escaping out of the Harbour. Many of the Toulonese were drowned in attempting to get on board the British Ships. All the remaining Inhabitants were drawn up in the public Square, and underwent military execution.[19] The information comes by a Vessel from Carthagena. Adieu. Yrs. Affy.

Js. Madison Jr

Madison to Jefferson

[Philadelphia] Mar. 12, 1794

Dear Sir

The Merchants, particularly of N. England have had a terrible slam in the W. Indies. About a hundred vessels have been seized by the British for condemnation, on the pretext of enforcing the laws of the Monarchy with regard to the Colony trade. The partizans of England, considering a war as now probable are endeavoring to take the lead in defensive preparations, and to acquire merit with the people by anticipating their wishes. This new symtom of insolence and enmity in Britain, shews rather that she meditates a formal war as soon as she shall have crippled our marine resources, or that she calculates on the pusilanimity of this country and the influence of her party, in a degree that will lead her into aggressions which our love of peace can no longer bear. The commercial propositions are in this State of things, not the precise remedy to be pressed as first in order; but they are in every view and in

19. For the recapture of Toulon from French royalists and British forces in Dec. 1793, see Georges Lefebvre, *The French Revolution from 1793 to 1799* (New York, 1964), pp. 15–16.

any event proper to make part of our standing laws till the principle of reciprocity be established by mutual arrangements. Adieu

JS. MADISON JR

Madison to Jefferson
Philadelphia Mar. 14, 1794

DEAR SIR

The paper of yesterday inclosed, will give you a clue to the designs of the faction which has used Sedgwick for its organ.[20] His immediate prompter will be seen both in his speech and in his propositions.[21] Whether more be seriously aimed at than to embarrass the others which have been long depending, is by some doubted. Perhaps this may be one of the objects; but you understand the game behind the Curtain too well not to perceive the old trick of turning every contingency into a resource for accumulating force in the Government. It would seem however that less subtlety has prevailed in this than in some other instances. The ostensible reason for the provisional army is not only absurd; but remote from the present sensations of the public; and at the same time disarms the projectors of the cavil and calumny used with most success against the commercial propositions, towit, that they tended to provoke war by an unnecessary alarm and irritation to G. Britain. The commercial propositions were the subject of yesterday and will probably be resumed today. We admit that the change of appearances may require something further, but we contend that they ought to make part of our code, until the end be obtained; and that they will be proper whether we are to be at peace or war. In the former case they will have their intended operation: In the latter they will put our Extive. on the right ground for negocia[tion.]

Madison to Jefferson
[Philadelphia] Mar. 24, 1794

DEAR SIR,

The past week has been spent chiefly on the question of an Embargo. It was negatived on Friday by 48 against 46, the former composed chiefly of Eastern, the latter of Southern members. The former are now for giving the

20. Theodore Sedgwick proposed a provisional army of fifteen regiments of 1,000 men each and authorization of discretionary power for the president to impose an embargo during the congressional recess; see *PJM*, XV, pp. 284–85, and Jerald A. Combs, *The Jay Treaty: Political Battleground of the Founding Fathers* (Berkeley, 1970), pp. 122–23.

21. JM meant Alexander Hamilton.

power to the Executive, even during the session of Congress. In France, everything is in a state of vigor beyond what has been seen there. Fauchèt proceeds with great circumspection and prudence here.

Madison to Jefferson

[Philadelphia] Mar. 26, 1794

DEAR SIR

My last informed you that an embargo had been proposed and negatived. You will see by the inclosed that on a renewal of the proposition yesterday it went thro' the H. of Reps. by a very large majority.[22] The change took place among the Eastern members whose constituents were growing so clamorous under their losses in the W. Indies, as to alarm their representatives. The Senate will have the subject before them today, and will probably concur. It is said that some further measures are to be discussed in that House. The commercial propositions have not yet recd. a vote. The progress of the evils which they were to remedy, having called for more active medicine, it has not been deemed prudent to force them on the attention of the House during more critical discussions. They will however notwithstanding a change of circumstances, cooperate with other measures as an alter[n]ative System and will be pressed to a vote at the first favorable moment. Whether they can be carried into a law at the present Session is doubtful, on acct. of the lateness of the day, and the superior urgency of other questions. The point immediately depending is the discrimination between G. B and other nations as to the proposed duties on manufactures. If this should succeed, the future parts will I think meet with little difficulty. The Enquiry into the Treasury is going on, tho' not very rapidly.[23] I understand that it begins to pinch where we most expected—the authority for drawing the money from Europe into the Bank. H. endeavored to parry the difficulty by contesting the right of the Committee to call for the authority. This failing he talks of constructive written authority from the P. but relies on parol[24] authority, which I think it impossible the P. can support him in.[25] The old question of referring the origination of Taxes comes

---

22. The House voted unanimously to impose a thirty-day embargo on all ships in American ports bound to any foreign destination; see Combs, pp. 120–21.

23. After the failure of the Giles Resolutions against Hamilton in Mar. 1793, Hamilton himself in Dec. requested a fuller investigation to clear his name. The House prepared a report, but it was tabled in May 1794; see *PJM,* XV, p. 296.

24. *Parol* means "by word of mouth."

25. Washington later wrote Hamilton that his approval of foreign loan transactions was made "upon condition, that what was to be done by you, should be agreeable to the Laws." Hamilton was dissatisfied with this qualified endorsement and did not introduce the letter during the investigation; see Syrett, XV, pp. 462–63, XVI, pp. 194–96, 241, 249, and 250–53, and Brant, III, pp. 396–97.

on today; and will in some degree test the present character of the House:[26] I have written abundance of letters of late but fear they are stopped by the small pox at Richmond.

The people of Charlestown are taking a high tone. Their memorial, which is signed by Ramsay—the Gadzdens Young Rutlege and a very great no. of respectable citizens marks the deliberate sense of the people.[27] The more violent has been ex[pres]sed by hanging and burning the effigies of Smith, Ames[,] Arnold, Dumourier and the Devil en groupe.[28]

Madison to Jefferson

Philadelphia Mar. 31, 1794

DEAR SIR

I have written of late by almost every mail, that is, three times a week. From your letter to Monroe I fear the small pox has stopped them at Richmond. I shall continue however to inclose you the newspapers as often as they are worth it. It is impossible to say what will be the issue of the proposition discussed in those of today.[29] I forgot to mention in my last that the question whether the ways and means should be referred to the Secy. of T. as heretofore, or to a Come. lately came on and decided the sense of the House to be degenerated on that point. The fiscal party, perceiving their danger, offered a sort of compromise which took in Mercer and with him sundry others in principle agst. them. Notwithstanding the success of the strategem, the point was carried by 49 agst. 46. If the question had divided the House fairly there would have been a majority of ten or a dozen at least.[30]

26. Later that day, JM was appointed a member of the newly created Committee on Ways and Means, which resulted in moving the initiative on taxation from Secretary of the Treasury Hamilton to a legislative committee, thus altering relations between the executive and the legislative branches in the direction favored by the Republicans: see *PJM,* XV, pp. 150, 208, 299.

27. Two days earlier, Congressman Andrew Pickens had presented a South Carolina petition denouncing British policies and praising JM's resolutions favoring commercial discrimination; see *ibid.,* p. 296.

28. William Loughton Smith of South Carolina and Fisher Ames of Massachusetts led the Federalist forces against JM's resolutions. Dumouriez, the French commander who defected to the Austrians after his defeat, was linked with Benedict Arnold and the devil.

29. Jonathan Dayton, a New Jersey Federalist, introduced a motion to sequester debts owed to British creditors by American citizens, who could discharge their debts by paying the federal Treasury, which, in turn, would use the money to compensate Americans suffering losses by British actions; see Combs, pp. 121–22, and Miller, *Hamilton,* p. 391.

30. For the creation of the House Committee on Ways and Means, see JM to TJ, Mar. 26, 1793, above.

Jefferson to Madison

Monticello Apr. 3, 1794

DEAR SIR

Our post having ceased to ride ever since the inoculation began in Richmond till now, I received three days ago, and all together your friendly favors of Mar. 2. 9. 12. 14. and Colo. Monroe's of Mar. 3. and 16. I have been particularly gratified by the receipt of the papers containing your's and Smith's discussion of your regulating propositions. These debates had not been seen here but in a very short and mutilated form. I am at no loss to ascribe Smith's speech to it's true father. Every tittle of it is Hamilton's except the introduction.[31] There is scarcely any thing there which I have not heard from him in our various private tho' official discussions. The very turn of the arguments is the same, and others will see as well as myself that the style is Hamilton's. The sophistry is too fine, too ingenious even to have been comprehended by Smith, much less devised by him. His reply shews he did not understand his first speech: as it's general inferiority proves it's legitimacy as evidently as it does the bastardy of the original. You know we had understood that Hamilton had prepared a Counter-report, and that some of his humble servants in the Senate were to move a reference to him in order to produce it. But I suppose they thought it would have a better effect if fired off in the H. of Representatives. I find the Report however so fully justified that the anxieties with which I left it are perfectly quieted. In this quarter all espouse your propositions with ardour, and without a dissenting voice. The rumor of a declaration of war has given an opportunity of seeing that the people here, tho' attentive to the loss of value of their produce, in such an event, yet find in it a gratification of some other passions, and particularly of their antient hatred to Gr. Britain. Still I hope it will not come to that: but that the propositions will be carried, and justice be done ourselves in a peaceable way. As to the guarantee of the French islands, whatever doubts may be entertained of the moment at which we ought to interpose yet I have no doubt but that we ought to interpose at a proper time and declare both to England and France that these islands are to rest with France, and that we will make common cause with the latter for that object. As to the naval armament, the land armament, and the Marine fortifications which are in question with you, I have no doubt they will all be carried. Not that the Monocrats and Papermen in Congress want war; but they want armies and debts: and tho' we may hope that the sound part of Congress is now so augmented as to ensure a majority in cases of general interest merely, yet I have always observed that in questions of expence, where members may hope either for offices or jobs for themselves or their friends, some few will be debauched, and that is sufficient to turn the decision where a majority is at most but small.

31. For the Hamilton-Smith speech, see Miller, *Hamilton*, p. 389, and Syrett, XIII, p. 407.

I have never seen a Philadelphia paper since I left it, till those you inclosed me; and I feel myself so thoroughly weened from the interest I took in the proceedings there, while there, that I have never had a wish to see one, and believe that I never shall take another newspaper of any sort. I find my mind totally absorbed in my rural occupations. We are suffering much for want of rain. Tho' now at the 3d. of April, you cannot distinguish the wheat feilds of the neighborhood yet from hence. Fruit is hitherto safe. We have at this time some prospect of rain. Asparagus is just come to table. The Lilac in blossom, and the first Whip-poor-will heard last night. No Martin's yet, I have some hopes Short has sent Cortez's letters for me by Blake.[32] Pray ask E. R. if he has. My best affections to Colo. and Mrs. Monroe. The correspondence with Hammond has never yet come into this quarter. Accept sincere assurances of affection.

Th: Jefferson

Madison to Jefferson

Philadelphia Apr. 14, 1794

Dear Sir

Having recd. one letter only from you, and that of very old date, I conclude that mine which have been numerous do not pass thro' the obstructions thrown in the way of the Mail by the small pox. I continue however to write, hoping that the channel will have been reopened by the time each letter may get to Richmond. I have also written a request to Mr. Dawson to have my letters to you taken out of the post office and forwarded from Richmond by private hands if necessary.

Three propositions levelled at G. B. have latterly occupied the H. of Reps. 1. to sequester British debts. 2. to establish a lien on British merchandize or the value of it, as it arrives. 3. to suspend imports from G. B. and Ireland till the spoliations be redressed and the Treaty of peace be executed. The last has taken the pas[33] in discussion. A majority are apparently in favor. Delay is consequently one of the arts of opposition. It is uncertain therefore when a vote will be obtained. It is probable also that much will depend on the state of foreign intelligence which is hourly changing in some of its circumstances. The Executive is said to meditate an envoy Extraordy. to G. B. as preferring further negociation to any legislative operation of a coercive nature. Hamilton is talked of, is much pressed by those attached to his politics, and will probably be appointed unless overruled by an apprehension from the

---

32. James Blake was a diplomatic courier who carried dispatches between the U.S. government and William Short and William Carmichael in Madrid; see *PJM*, XV, p. 302. TJ referred to Hernando Cortés, *Historia de Nueva-España*, ed. Francisco Antonio Lorenzana y Butron (Mexico City, 1770).

33. *Pas* means "precedence."

disgust to Republicanism and to France.³⁴ His trial is not yet concluded. You will see the issue it will have in the inclosed papers. The letter from the P. is inexpressibly mortifying to his friends,³⁵ and marks his situation to be precisely what you always described it to be. The committee on ways and means was unfortunately composed of a majority infected by the fiscal errors which threaten so ignominious and vexatious a system to our country. A land tax will be reported, but along with its excises on articles imported, and manufactured at home, a stamp tax pervading almost all the transactions of life, and a tax on carriages as an *indirect*³⁶ tax. The embargo will soon be a subject of deliberation again, as its continuance if proper ought to be decided some time before its expiration. Whether this will be the case cannot now be foretold. The French continue to triumph over their Enemies on the Rhine. We learn nothing from the W. Inds. except that Martinique had not surrendered on the 25th. Ult.

I put into the hands of your Cabinet workman here the Editn: of Milton sent you from France. He was packing up things for you which afforded a commodious berth for it. Yrs. always and Affy

Js. MADISON JR.

Fauchet has informally intimated the distaste to Gour. M. whose recall will follow of course.

Madison to Jefferson

Philadelphia Apr. 28, 1794

DEAR SIR

I have recd. yours of the 3d. instant. I have already informed you of my having forwarded you the French Edition of Milton red. from E. R. Cortez's letters are not come to hand. It seems that Blake by whom you expected them is not the person thro' whom the Milton came, and that he is not yet arrived. The correspondence with Hammond has been forwarded in detachments by Col. Monroe.

The non-importation bill has passed the H. of Reps. by 59. agst. 34. It will probably miscarry in the Senate. It prohibits all articles of British or Irish production after the 1st. Novr. until the claims of the U. S. be adjusted and satisfied. The appointment of H. as envoy Extry was likely to produce such a sensation that to his great mortification he was laid aside, and Jay named in his

---

34. On the day that JM wrote this letter, Hamilton withdrew himself from consideration as envoy to Great Britain and recommended Chief Justice John Jay, whom Washington appointed two days later; see Combs, pp. 125–26.
35. See JM to TJ, Mar. 26, 1794, above.
36. JM's italics.

place. The appointment of the latter would have been difficult in the Senate, but for some adventitious causes. There were 10 votes agst. him in one form of the opposition and 8 on the direct question. As a resignation of his Judiciary character might, for any thing known to the Senate, have been intended to follow his acceptance of the Ex. trust, the ground of incompatibility could not support the objections, which, since it has appeared that such a resignation was no part of the arrangement, are beginning to be pressed in the Newspapers. If animadversions are undertaken by skilful hands, there is no measure of the Ex. administration perhaps that will be found more severely vulnerable.

The English prints breathe an unabated zeal for the war agst. France. The Minister carries every thing as usual in Parlt. notwithstanding the miscarriages at Toulon etc., and his force will be much increased by the taking of Martinique and the colouring it will give to the W. India prospects. Nothing further appears as to the views prevailing in relation to us. The latter accts. from the W. Inds. since the new Instruction of Jany. 8 are rather favorable to the Merchants and alleviate their resentments: so that G. B. seems to have derived from the excess of her aggressions a title to commit them in a less degree with impunity. The French arms continue to prosper, tho' no very capital event is brought by the latest arrivals.

Madison to Jefferson

Philadelphia May 11, 1794

DEAR SIR

Col. Monroe wrote you last week, and I refer to his letter for the state of things up to that date. The H. of Reps. has been since employed chiefly on the new taxes. The Report of the Committee which was the work of a subcommittee in understanding with the Fiscal Department, was filled with a variety of items copied as usual from the British Revenue laws. It particularly included, besides stamp duties, excises on tobacco and sugar manufactured in the U. S. and a tax on carriages as an *indirect*[37] tax. The aversion to direct taxes which appeared by a vote of seventy odd for rejecting them will saddle us with all those pernicious innovations, without ultimately avoiding direct taxes in addition to them. All opposition to the new excises, tho' enforced by memorials from the manufacturers was vain. And the tax on carriages succeeded in spite of the Constitution by a majority of twenty, the advocates for the principle being reinforced by the adversaries to luxury. Six of the *N. Carolina* members were in the majority. This is another proof of the facility with which usurpation triumphs where there is a standing corps always on the watch for favorable conjunctures, and directed by the policy of dividing their honest but undiscerning adversaries. It is very possible however that the authors of these precedents may not be the last to lament them. Some of the motives which they

37. JM's italics here and below.

decoyed to their support ought to premonish them of the danger. By breaking down the barriers of the constitution and giving sanction to the idea of sumptuary regulations, wealth may find a precarious defence in the sheild of justice. If luxury, *as such*, is to be taxed, the greatest of all luxuries, says Payne, is a great estate. Even on the present occasion, it has been found prudent to yield to a tax on transfers of stock in the funds, and in the Banks.

The appointment of Jay continues to undergo the animad[v]ersions of the Press. You will see that the Democratic Societies are beginning to open their batteries upon it. The measure however has had the effect of impeding all legislative measures for extorting redress from G. B. The non-importation bill which passed the H. of Reps. by a great majority, was so instantly and peremptorily rejected in the Senate as an interference with the proposed Mission, that no further efforts of the same type have been seriously contemplated. Clarke did indeed move to insert among the new ways and means an additional duty of 10 perCt. on *British* manufactures, but the symptoms of desertion soon induced him to withdraw it. A member from N. Carolina afterwards was incautious eno' to try a discriminating duty on British tonnage and by pushing it to a question with the yeas and nays, placed us in a very feeble minority. Notwithstanding this effect of the Executive measure, there is little serious confidence in its efficacy; and, as involving the appointment of Jay, is the most powerful blow ever suffered by the popularity of the President.

The embargo is Still in force. A member from Connecticut moved a few days ago to abridge its term a few days, as a notification that it would not be continued. A large majority was against taking up the proposition; but how far with a view to adhere to the embargo, I know not. Yesterday a motion was laid on the table by Smith (of S. C) for continuing the embargo to June 25. The motion from that quarter excited surprize: and must be either a fetch at popularity, an insidious thing, or suggested by an idea that the balance of the effects of the embargo is in favor of G. Britain.[38]

There are no late accounts of moment from Europe. Those from the W. Indies, as well with respect to the treatment of our vessels as the effects of the embargo, are so various and contradictory that it is impossible to make any thing of them. Yrs. Affecy.

Js. Madison Jr

Jefferson to Madison

Monticello May 15, 1794

Dear Sir

I wrote you on the 3d. of April, and since that have received yours of Mar. 24. 26. 31. Apr. 14. and 28. and yesterday I received Colo. Monroe's of the 4th. inst. informing me of the failure of the non-importation bill in the Senate.

---

38. JM voted with the majority to defeat Smith's motion; see *PJM,* XV, p. 328.

This body was intended as a check on the will of the Representatives when too hasty. They are not only that but completely so on the will of the people also: and in my opinion are heaping coals of fire not only on their persons, but on their body as a branch of legislature. I have never known a measure more universally desired by the people than the passage of that bill. It is not from my own observation of the wishes of the people that I decide what they are, but from that of the gentlemen of the bar who mix much with them, and by their intercommunications with each other, have under their view a greater portion of the country than any other description of men. It seems that the opinion is fairly launched into public, that they should be placed under the controul of a more frequent recurrence to the will of their constituents. This seems requisite to compleat the experiment whether they do more harm or good? I wrote lately to Mr. Taylor for the pamphlet on the bank. Since that I have seen the 'Definition of parties,' and must pray you to bring it for me.[39] It is one of those things which merits to be preserved. The safe arrival of my books at Richmond, and some of them at home, has relieved me from anxiety, and will not be indifferent to you. It turns out that our fruit has not been as entirely killed as was at first apprehended. Some latter blossoms have yeilded a small supply of this precious refreshment. I was so improvident as never to have examined at Philadelphia whether negro cotton and oznabrigs can be had there. If you do not already possess the information, pray obtain it before you come away. Our spring has on the whole been seasonable, and the wheat as much recovered as it's thinness would permit. But the crop must still be a miserable one. There would not have been seed made but for the extraordinary rains of the last month. Our highest heat as yet has been 83. This was on the 4th. inst. That Blake should not have been arrived at the date of your letter, surprizes me. Pray enquire into the fact before you leave Philadelphia. According to Colo. Monroe's letter this will find you on the point of departure. I hope we shall see you here soon after your return. Remember me affectionately to Colo. and Mrs. Monroe, and accept the sincere esteem of Dear Sir your sincere friend and servt

TH: JEFFERSON

Madison to Jefferson

Philadelphia May 25, 1794

DEAR SIR

Your favr. of the 15th. Inst: came to hand yesterday. I will procure you the "Definition of parties," and one or two other things from the press which merit a place in your archives. Osnabrigs can be had here. Negro Cotton I am

---

39. For the publication of Taylor's pamphlet *An Enquiry into the Principles and Tendency of Certain Public Measures* (Philadelphia, 1794), see Robert E. Shalhope, *John Taylor of Caroline: Pastoral Republican* (Columbia, S.C., 1980), pp. 219, 275–76. Taylor's pamphlet on parties was entitled *A Definition of Parties: or, The Political Effects of the Paper System Considered* (Philadelphia, 1794).

told can also be had; but of this I am not sure. I learn nothing yet of Blake. The inclosed paper[40] will give you the correspondence of E. R. and Hammond on an occurrence particularly interesting. You will be as able to judge as we are of the calculations to be founded on it. The embargo expires today. A proposition some days ago for continuing it was negatived by a vast majority; all parties in the main concurring. The Republican was assured that the Embargo if continued would be considered by France as hostility: The other had probably an opposite motive. It now appears that throug[h]out the Continent the people were anxious for its continuance, and it is probable that its expiration will save the W. Inds. from famine, without affording any sensible aid to France. A motion was put on the table yesterday for re-enacting it. Measures of this sort are not the fashion. To supplicate for peace, and under the uncertainty of success, to prepare for war by taxes and troops is the policy which now triumphs under the patronage of the Executive. Every attack on G. B. thro' her commerce is at once discomfited; and all the taxes, that is to say excises, stamps, etc. are carried by decided majorities. The plan for a large army has failed several times in the H. of Reps. It is now to be sent from the Senate, and being recommended by the Message of the P. accompanying the intelligence from the Miami, will probab[l]y succeed.[41] The influence of the Ex. on events, the use made of them, and the public confidence in the P. are an overmatch for all the efforts Republicanism can make. The party of that sentiment in the Senate is compleatly wrecked; and in the H. of Reps. in a much worse condition that at an earlier period of the Session.

Madison to Jefferson

Philadelphia June 1, 1794

DEAR SIR

The Stamp Act was poisoned by the ingredient of the tax on transfers.[42] The centinels of Stock uniting with the adversaries of the general plan formed a large majority. The carriage tax which only struck at the Constitution, has passed the H. of Reps. and will be a delicious morsel to the Senate. The attempt of this Branch to give the P. power to raise an army of 10,000, if he should please, was strangled more easily in the H. of R. than I had expected. This is the 3d or 4th. effort made in the course of the Session to get a powerful military establishment, under the pretext of public danger and under the aus-

---

40. The *Philadelphia Gazette* of May 24, 1794, published the exchange between the secretary of state and the British minister about the speech of Lord Dorchester, governor-general of Canada, to a delegation of Indians predicting war with the United States; see *PJM,* XV, p. 338.

41. Washington had sent documents to Congress on May 21 about British provocation of Indian attacks on the frontier; see *ibid.*

42. The House Ways and Means Committee had called for a stamp tax, including duties on the transfer of government and bank stock, a move that JM and the House rejected; see *ibid.,* p. 341.

pices of the P.'s popularity. The bill for punishing certain crimes etc. including that of selling prizes has been unexpectedly called up at the last moment of the Session. It is pretended that our Citizens will arm under French Colors if not restrained. You will be at no loss for the real motive, especially as explained by the circumstances of the present crisis.[43] The bill for complying with Fauchet's application for a million of dollars, passed the H. of R. by a large majority. The Senate will certainly reject it. Col. M. is busy in preparing for his embarkation.[44] He is puzzled as to the mode of getting to France. He leans towards an American vessel which is to sail from Baltimore for Amsterdam. A direct passage to F is scarcely to be had, and is incumbered with the risk of being captured and carried into England. It is not certain that Negro Cotton can be had here. German linnens of all sorts can. Nothing of Blake. Tomorrow is the day of adjournment as fixt by the vote of the two Houses; but it will probably not take place till the last of the week. We have had 8 or 10 days of wet weather from the N. E., which seems at length to be breaking up. Yrs. Affy.

Js. MADISON JR

43. Washington had authorized the sale of French prizes. The bill that JM mentioned forbade the sale of prizes captured by foreign warships or privateers, but JM and the majority struck out that provision; see *ibid.*, pp. 343–44, and Brant, III, p. 399.

44. James Monroe had been appointed by George Washington as minister to France.

19

DOLLEY, DOMESTICITY, AND THE WHISKEY REBELLION, 1794–1795

In May 1794, at the very moment that "Mr. Madison's Resolutions" were pushed aside by Chief Justice John Jay's mission to Great Britain, a young Quaker widow, Dolley Payne Todd, wrote a brief but vibrant note to her best friend: "Thou must come to me. Aaron Burr says that the great little Madison has asked to be brought to see me this evening."[1] For the first time since his romance with the teen-aged daughter of a New York congressman in 1783, "the great little Madison" was in love. The wife of Congressman Isaac Coles of Virginia, a long-time friend of Madison's and a cousin of Mrs. Todd, wrote a teasing letter to Dolley about a recent conversation with Madison: "To begin, he thinks so much of you in the day that he has Lost his Tongue, at night he Dreames of you and Starts in his Sleep a Calling on you to relieve his Flame for he Burns to such an excess that he will be shortly consumed and he hopes that your Heart will be calous to every other swain but himself." And she added, "He has Consented to every thing that I have wrote about him with Sparkling Eyes."[2]

After a whirlwind courtship, Dolley accepted Madison's proposal in a letter now missing, and Madison replied "that the confirmation of that welcome event was endeared to me by the style in which it was conveyed." They were married on September 15, 1794, at Harewood, near what is now Charles Town, West Virginia, the home of Dolley's sister Lucy and George Steptoe Washington, nephew of the president.[3]

Although Madison had kept his retired friend at Monticello informed

---

1. Brant, III, p. 406.
2. Catherine Coles to Dolley Payne Todd, June 1, 1794, in *PJM*, XV, p. 342.
3. For the few documents on JM and Dolley Payne Todd's courtship and marriage, see *ibid.*, pp. 341–58. The best accounts are in Brant, III, pp. 401–14; Ketcham, pp. 376–82; Virginia Moore, *The Madisons: A Biography* (New York, 1979), pp. 10–17; and Conover Hunt-Jones, *Dolley and the "Great Little Madison"* (Washington, 1977), pp. 7–15.

about political issues throughout the spring of 1794, he had made no mention of his romantic interest. Nor did the two exchange letters during the summer recess of Congress. But late in August, Madison made a quick visit to Monticello and, among other things, talked about his forthcoming marriage and his desire to retire from Congress. Jefferson was delighted to hear about the wedding—he wished "a thousand respects to Mrs. Madison and joys perpetual to both"—but he was appalled to hear that his friend wanted to emulate his retreat to private life: "I do not see in the minds of those with whom I converse a greater affliction than the fear of your retirement."[4]

For Jefferson, retirement was going well. He portrayed himself as a plain farmer, little interested and less involved in politics, living instead "like an Antediluvian patriarch among my children and grand children, and tilling my soil."[5] He reported proudly that he devoted more attention to crop rotation and the establishment of a nailery than he did to political correspondence. "Instead of writing 10. or 12. letters a day, which I have been in the habit of doing as a thing of course," he told John Adams, "I put off answering my letters now, farmer-like, till a rainy day, and then find it sometimes postponed by other necessary occupations."[6] As for Philadelphia newspapers and their reports of political issues, he thought that he was "so thoroughly weened from the interest I took in the proceedings there . . . that I have never had a wish to see one, and believe that I never shall take another newspaper of any sort. I find my mind totally absorbed in my rural occupations."[7]

In addition to farming and reading, Jefferson began the remodeling of Monticello, a long-time project that transformed the first house into its present form, dominated by the first dome to be erected over an American dwelling, creating "the most imaginative, original home in America."[8]

In a moment of self-analysis, Jefferson observed that "architecture is my delight, and putting up and pulling down one of my favorite amusements."[9] The playful business of rebuilding his home involved some inconvenience, however, as he informed his mentor, George Wythe, during his first year of retirement: "We are now living in a brick-kiln, for my house, in its present state, is nothing better." But after five years in France and four in Washing-

---

4. TJ to JM, Oct. 30, 1794, below, and Dec. 28, 1794, below. See also Brant, III, p. 411, and Malone, III, p. 187.

5. TJ to Edward Rutledge, Nov. 30, 1795, in Ford, VII, p. 39. For a charming look at TJ in retirement, see Donald Jackson, *A Year at Monticello, 1795* (Golden, Col., 1989).

6. TJ to John Adams, Apr. 25, 1794, in Cappon, I, p. 254.

7. TJ to JM, Apr. 3, 1794, above.

8. For a fascinating and perceptive account, see William Howard Adams, *Jefferson's Monticello* (New York, 1983), pp. 87–143; the quotation is from p. 112. For a more extended account of the entire Monticello building project, see Jack McLaughlin, *Jefferson and Monticello: The Biography of a Builder* (New York, 1988); this book was called to my attention by P. L. Harrison.

9. Malone, III, p. 222. For the impact of TJ's remodeling of urban rental housing in Paris, New York, and Philadelphia on his architectural remodeling of Monticello, see Mark R. Wagner, "Thomas Jefferson, Tenant," *Winterthur Portfolio* 26 (1991): 249–65.

ton's cabinet, he was ready to affirm what he later wrote: "I am happy nowhere else and in no other society, and all my wishes end, where I hope my days will end, at Monticello."[10]

During Madison's call on Monticello prior to his wedding, he and Jefferson had visited Monroe's nearby farm to inspect sites for a new house. "The one preferred by us," Madison wrote to his friend in Paris, "is that which we favored originally on the East Side of the road.... All that could be suggested by way of preparation was, that Trees be planted promiscuously and pretty thickly in the field adjoining the wood."[11]

Knowing Jefferson's passion for architecture, Madison sent him inquiries on behalf of his brother and his brother-in-law. In the letter that announced his marriage—"the epoch at which I had the happiness to accomplish the alliance which I intimated to you I had been sometime soliciting," he forwarded a plan for his brother-in-law's house and notified Jefferson that the builder would "visit Monticello not only to profit of examples before his eyes, but to ask the favor of your advice on the plan of the House."[12]

Earlier, Madison had submitted a floor plan for his brother's house, requesting Jefferson's suggestions for improvement. Jefferson took the assignment seriously and first "scribbled on a separate paper some general notes on the plan." But his enthusiasm carried him so far that he drafted a new plan: "I have endeavored to throw the same area, the same extent of walls, the same number of rooms, and of the same sizes, into another form so as to offer a choice to the builder. Indeed I varied my plan by shewing what it would be with alcove bedrooms, to which I am much attached."[13]

When the Monroes left for France, the Madisons rented the house the Monroes had occupied in Philadelphia on North Eighth Street. There they moved in October 1794 for the short winter session of Congress. Early next spring, Madison, after counseling with his bride, asked the Monroes to shop in Paris for secondhand furniture, "which cannot be had here of equal quality, but at a forbidding price," in order to meet "the wants incident to my new situation." After listing carpets, curtains, and china, he suggested other items that the Monroes "may know to be acceptable to a young House-Keeper." He left matters entirely to Monroe's judgment or, he added playfully, to "Mrs. Monroes better one."[14]

Marriage may have mellowed Madison's political outlook, according to some Federalists. Congressman Jonathan Trumbull of Connecticut thought that "the present campaign of politics will be carried on with much more

---

10. TJ to George Wythe, Oct. 24, 1794, quoted *ibid.*, p. 233; TJ to George Gilmer, Aug. 12, 1787, in *PTJ*, XII, p. 26.
11. JM to James Monroe, Dec. 14, 1794, in *PJM*, XV, p. 408.
12. JM to TJ, Oct. 5, 1794, below.
13. For JM's inquiry, see his letters of May 8, 1793, above, and June 19, 1793, above; for TJ's response, see his letter of May 19, 1793, above.
14. JM, "Memorandum to James Monroe," Mar. 26, 1795, in *PJM,* XV, pp. 497–98. For the furnishings purchased by Monroe, see Hunt-Jones, pp. 18–20.

mildness and good humour, than the last. Mr. Madison's late connection it is said has drawn off much of his atrabilious Gall—and indeed he appears with much more complacency and sociability than I have ever yet seen in him."[15]

But the aftermath of the Whiskey Rebellion, which had exploded in July 1794, removed mildness and good humor from politics when the Federalists tried to link the Republicans with the outbreak of armed resistance to excise taxes on whiskey. Although Hamilton had written in *The Federalist* that "the genius of the people will ill brook the inquisitive and peremtory spirit of excise laws," the need for increased revenues after the federal assumption of state debts led him to recommend the enactment of an excise on whiskey in 1791. Many Republicans, including Madison, condemned the principle of excise taxes but acceded to them in order to discharge the national debt.[16] As secretary of state, Jefferson had helped enforce the excise, at first agreeing to forgive arrearages by Kentucky distillers on the promise that they would pay the tax in the future but later refusing to extend the period of forgiveness in 1793.[17] Thus, the law remained unpopular, especially in the West, where residents denounced it as discriminatory because it fell on their most easily exportable product. Until 1794, the resistance, though massive, was largely passive, and Congress responded by amending the law in 1792.[18] Before the new law became effective, however, armed demonstrations had begun in four western counties of Pennsylvania. Federal revenue agents were terrorized; one agent's home was burned to the ground. The U.S. mails were seized; federal judicial proceedings were halted; and a small detachment of federal troops guarding a tax collector was forced to surrender. Early in August 1794, a mass of insurgents held a rally at Braddock's Field as a prelude to an attack on Pittsburgh, but the local militia prevented a confrontation by joining the insurgents, swelling their force to 7,000 as they marched through the frontier town in a demonstration of settler solidarity.[19]

Viewing forcible resistance to federal laws as a threat to the Union, President Washington issued a proclamation ordering the insurgents to disperse and sent federal commissioners to offer amnesty in exchange for pledges to comply with the law. To assure compliance, he also called up 12,950 militiamen from four states and took personal command of the federalized militia in order to dramatize the critical situation in the West. Hamilton accompanied

---

15. Quoted in *PJM,* XV, p. 152.

16. *Ibid.,* p. 399; John C. Miller, *Alexander Hamilton: Portrait in Paradox* (New York, 1959), p. 397.

17. Mary K. Bonsteel Tachau, "A New Look at the Whiskey Rebellion," in *The Whiskey Rebellion: Past and Present Perspectives,* ed. Steven R. Boyd (Westport, Conn., 1985), p. 102.

18. See Alexander Hamilton, "Report on the Difficulties in the Execution of the Act Laying Duties on Distilled Liquors," Mar. 5, 1792, in Syrett, XI, pp. 77-106.

19. Leland D. Baldwin, *Whiskey Rebels: The Story of a Frontier Uprising* (Pittsburgh, 1939), long the standard study, is still useful, but see also the revisionist view in Thomas P. Slaughter, *The Whiskey Rebellion* (New York, 1986).

the general to check on enforcement of the excise and to represent him after he returned to Philadelphia to brief the returning congressmen. Under the command of Governor Henry Lee of Virginia ("Light Horse Harry" Lee of Revolutionary fame), the soldiers marched west to Pittsburgh, rounded up 150 suspects, and marched 20 to Philadelphia in irons. All were charged with treason, but only two were convicted. President Washington pardoned both, characterizing one as a simpleton and the other as insane. By winter, nearly all of the troops were withdrawn and the army disbanded.[20]

Shortly after Madison and his new bride arrived in Philadelphia in the fall, he informed Jefferson that "the Western Scene is closed" but that Hamilton was still with the army. "When I first arrived here," he continued, "the conversation ran high for a standing army to enforce the laws," and he fully expected the Federalists to attempt such an innovation "if circumstances should be favorable." But he thought it improbable that the president would embark on such a measure, and Washington did not.[21]

Nonetheless, Washington, in what Madison called "the greatest error of his political life," lashed out in his address to Congress at the Democratic societies—"certain self-created societies," he labeled them—as subversive organizations that had fomented the armed insurrection in the West by the dissemination of "suspicions, jealousies, and accusations" against the government.

Not wishing to drag Washington into the political maneuvers between Federalists and Republicans, Madison persuaded the House committee preparing the response to the president's message to avoid any reference to "self-created societies" and get on with the substantive business before Congress. The committee, he told Jefferson, consisted of two Federalists, "Sedgwick[,] Scott and myself. The draught was made as strong as possible on all proper points"—it endorsed the president's action "through this delicate and distressing period"—and omitted "the improper one. This succeeded in the Come.; Scott concurring in the *expediency* of silence on that." But over the weekend, Hamilton convinced Representative FitzSimons of Pennsylvania of the need "to *reprobate* the self-created Societies etc. which tho' in strictness not *illegal,* contributed by their proceedings to mislead the weak and ignorant."[22] After the Republicans narrowly defeated the FitzSimons/Hamilton motion, they

---

20. Richard A. Ifft, "Treason in the Early Republic: The Federal Courts, Popular Protest, and Federalism during the Whiskey Insurrection," in *The Whiskey Rebellion: Past and Present Perspectives* pp. 165-82, 192-201, and James T. Flexner, *Washington: The Indispensable Man* (Boston, 1974), pp. 315-23. For his role in commanding the detachment of Virginia troops to suppress the rebellion, Lee was ousted as governor, the Republicans in the House of Delegates claiming that he had violated the statute that prohibited officials from simultaneously holding positions under the state and federal governments; see Norman K. Risjord and Gordon DenBoer, "The Evolution of Political Parties in Virginia, 1782-1800," *JAH* 60 (1974): 978.

21. JM to TJ, Nov. 16, 1794, below.

22. For JM on President Washington's error, see JM to James Monroe, Dec. 4, 1794, in *PJM,* XV, pp. 405-8. JM to TJ, Nov. 30, 1794, below, quotes FitzSimons's motion. For Hamilton's role, which JM does not mention, see Miller, pp. 412-14.

feared "that some evil accomodation would come from the other side and succeed," and they, therefore, substituted, on the motion of the representative from Jefferson's district, the words "combinations of men" for the phrase "self-created Societies."[23]

During the five days of House debates on the president's allegations, the Federalists argued that a failure to endorse his stand would be a renunciation of executive leadership and a blow to the president's prestige at the same time that it allowed the "rekindling [of] the fire-brands of sedition[,] ... unchaining the demon of anarchy."[24] Federalists quickly parroted the president's charge, condemning the publications of the Democratic societies—or Madisonian societies, as Fenno's *Gazette of the United States* called them—as "wicked, false and seditious misrepresentation[s] of public men and public measures" propagated "with the seditious intention of slandering the measures of government and its administrators."[25] According to a Maryland Federalist, the Republican "press is the rack on which they place the government, and it would have expired on the rack had it not been for the patriotism of the citizens" in quelling the Whiskey Rebellion. "This lesson," he argued, "calls the attention of the country to draw a line between the use and abuse of the inestimable right of free opinion."[26]

Madison and the Republicans condemned the Federalist arguments as repressive attempts to suppress opinions offensive to the administration, striking at the root of freedom of speech, press, and assembly. Although Madison said that he took little part in the debate, he argued consistently that "opinions are not the objects of legislation. ... If we advert to the nature of republican government," he said in a classic encapsulation of his political philosophy, "we shall find that the censorial power is in the people over the government, and not in the government over the people."[27]

To Jefferson, Madison observed that "you will easily conceive my situation thro' this whole business. It was obvious that a most dangerous game was playing agst. Republicanism. The insurrection was universally and deservedly odious. The Democratic Societies were presented as in league with it. The Republican part of Congs. were to be drawn into an *ostensible,* patronage of those Societies, and into an ostensible opposition to the President." The blow aimed at the "self-created Societies," he was convinced, was an attack "on the

---

23. See JM's address of the House of Representatives to the president, Nov. 21, 1794, below. For the FitzSimons/Hamilton connection, see Miller, pp. 412–14.

24. John C. Miller, *The Federalist Era: 1789–1801* (New York, 1960), p. 162.

25. This portion of the speech by Congressman Theodore Sedgwick of Massachusetts on Nov. 25, 1794, is not reported in the congressional *Debates,* 3d Cong., 2d sess., 1794, 911–12, but is found in the *Gazette of the United States* (Nov. 27, 1794).

26. This portion of William Vans Murray's speech of Nov. 24 is not reported in the congressional *Debates,* 3d Cong., 2d sess., 1794, 906–7, but is found in the Philadelphia *Aurora* (Nov. 28, 1794).

27. JM, speech of Nov. 27, 1794, in *PJM,* XV, pp. 390–92.

most sacred principle of our Constitution and of Republicanism," since the arguments "in favor of the motion fell with equal weight on the press and every mode of animadverting on public men and measures."[28]

"If the people of America," Madison continued, "are so far degenerated already as not to see or to see with indifference, that the Citadel of their liberties is menaced by the precedent before their eyes, they require abler advocates than they now have, to save them from the consequences." Nothing could be more indefensible in reason or more dangerous in practice, he told Monroe, than the proposition that "the Govt. may stifle all censures whatever on its misdoings; for if it be itself the Judge it will never allow any censures to be just, and if it can suppress censures flowing from one lawful source it may those flowing from any other—from the press and from individuals as well as from Societies, etc."[29]

Jefferson, who a year before had warned Washington that censure of the Democratic societies would be viewed as an attempt calculated "to dismount him from being the head of the nation, and make him the head of a party,"[30] was stunned by the president's denunciation of the societies, calling it "one of the extraordinary acts of boldness of which we have seen so many from the faction of Monocrats. It is wonderful indeed," he wrote Madison, "that the President should have permitted himself to be the organ of such an attack on the freedom of discussion, the freedom of writing, printing and publishing. It must be a matter of rare curiosity to get at the modifications of these rights proposed by them, and to see what line their ingenuity would draw between democratical societies, whose avowed object is the nourishment of the republican principles of our constitution, and the society of the Cincinnati [which was headed by the president], a *self-created* one, carving out for itself hereditary distinctions, lowering over our constitution eternally, meeting together in all parts of the Union periodically, with closed doors, accumulating a capital in their separate treasury, corresponding secretly and regularly, and of which society the very persons denouncing the democrats are themselves the fathers, founders or high officers." Jefferson viewed the debate as a contest between "the friends of general freedom" and "those who wish to confine that freedom to the few," a naked attack and "an inexcusable aggression" on the "natural and constitutional rights" of the people.[31]

Although the Federalist Senate joined the president in denouncing "self-created Societies," the House, under Madison's leadership, refused to sanction the censure of the political clubs for their criticism of governmental measures. Nor, Madison observed, did "the attack made on the essential and constitutional right of the Citizen" silence the clubs. Instead, they began a public

28. JM to TJ, Nov. 30, 1794, below.
29. *Ibid.*; JM to James Monroe, Dec. 4, 1794, in *PJM,* XV, pp. 405-8.
30. See TJ to JM, Aug. 11, 1793, above.
31. TJ to JM, Dec. 28, 1794, below.

campaign to deny responsibility for the Whiskey Rebellion, with the Republican Society of Baltimore setting the example. "In Boston," Madison continued, "the subject is well understood, and handled in the Newspaper on the republican side, with industry and address." In New York, the "invigorated exertions of the Democratic Society" helped Edward Livingston, a member of the society, defeat the Federalist incumbent for a congressional seat.[32]

Although Madison and Jefferson both blasted the Federalist attack on self-created societies, they disagreed over the mopping-up operations that followed the Whiskey Rebellion. Isolated on his mountaintop at Monticello, Jefferson was as critical of Madison's involvement with adminstration policy in western Pennsylvania as Madison had been of the Proclamation of Neutrality when, a year earlier, he had been isolated at Montpellier and Jefferson had been a part of the administration. He was especially put out with Madison's support of a bill authorizing the president to station troops in western Pennsylvania during the winter "to compleat the good work of peace order and tranquility begun by the executive."[33] "With respect to the transactions against the excise-law," Jefferson wrote captiously, "it appears to me that you are all swept away in the torrent of governmental opinions, or," he added as a safety net, "that we do not know what these transactions have been." He had heard of nothing in western Pennsylvania, he protested, that constituted "any thing more than riotous" conduct. He condemned the excise law as "an infernal one," the potential "instrument of dismembering the Union." And he was harshly critical of the president for "arming one part of the society against another, of declaring a civil war the moment before the meeting of that body which has the sole right of declaring war." Comparing Washington's speech to "stuff from Aesop's fables and Tom Thumb," he concluded that "the part of the speech which was to be taken as a justification of the armament reminded me of parson Saunders's demonstration why minus into minus makes plus."[34]

Despite his jaundiced view of the present, Jefferson was optimistic about the future. "The time is coming," he predicted, "when we shall fetch up the lee-way of our vessel. The changes in your house I see are going on for the better, and even the Augean herd over your heads are slowly purging off their impurities. Hold on then, my dear friend, that we may not ship-wreck in the mean while." When the time came for a new captain for the ship of state, Jefferson hoped that Madison would be elevated to that "more splendid and . . . more efficacious post." He would rejoice to see Madison as president, something that he had long wanted to discuss with his friend. "But," he noted, "double delicacies have kept me silent." How could he, secure in his

---

32. JM to TJ, Dec. 21, 1794, below.
33. JM used these words in his speech in Congress, Nov. 27, 1794; see *PJM,* XV, p. 392.
34. TJ to JM, Dec. 28, 1794, below.

retirement at Monticello—a situation that he would not give up "for the empire of the Universe"—wish his best friend, "whose happiness I have as much at heart as yours, to take the front of the battle which is fighting for my security?" His answer would be easy enough to give, he wrote, "but not at the heel of a lengthy epistle." But he did add a parting shot for Dolley: "Pray her to keep you where you are," for he could think of no "greater affliction than the fear of your retirement."[35]

Madison wrote Jefferson three times before taking any notice of his friend's suggestion about the presidency. Instead of a lengthy rebuttal, he said that "reasons of *every* kind, and some of them, of the most *insuperable* as well as *obvious* kind, shut my mind against the admission of any idea such as you seem to glance at. I forbear to say more, because I can have no more to say with respect to myself; and because the great deal that may and ought to be said beyond that restriction will be best reserved for some other occasion, perhaps for the latitude of a free conversation." But he made it clear that he planned to turn the tables and press Jefferson to come out of retirement to run for the presidency: "You ought to be preparing yourself . . . to hear truths, which no inflexibility will be able to withstand."[36]

Even so, Jefferson remained inflexible about his retirement, leaving no "opening for future discussion" and denying that he could "be reasoned out of it." Instead, he repeated his hope that Madison would become president, "the only change of position I ever wished to see you make," and added that "there is not another person in the US. who being placed at the helm of our affairs, my mind would be so completely at rest for the fortune of our political bark." As for his personal plans, he continued, "the subject had been thoroughly weighed and decided on, and my retirement from office had been meant from all office high or low, without exception." Not vanity, but continual insinuations in Federalist newspapers while he was secretary of state, had forced him to consider the idea. All of the suggestions had come from a hostile quarter, he observed, and were designed "to poison the public mind as to my motives, when they were not able to charge me with facts. But the idea being once presented to me, my own quiet required that I should face it and examine it. . . . I decided then on those general grounds which could alone be present to my mind at that time, that is to say, reputation, tranquillity, labor: for as to public duty; it could not be a topic of consideration in my case." His decision then had been "a firm resolution never to permit myself to think of the office or be thought of for it." After more than a year of retirement, new grounds had been added to "still more insuperably bar the door to it": broken health; advancing age; his personal affairs, which could no longer be neglected; his

---

35. *Ibid.*

36. JM to TJ, Mar. 23, 1795, below. For JM's concern that he might have epilepsy, see "Introduction: An Intimate Friendship," above.

delight in the midst of his family; and "the agricultural pursuits in which I am so eagerly engaged."

"The little spice of ambition, which I had in my younger days," he concluded, "has long since evaporated, and I set still less store by a posthumous than present name." For all these reasons—past, present, and future—"the question is for ever closed with me, my sole object is to avail myself of the first opening ever given me from a friendly quarter (and I could not with decency do it before) of preventing any division or loss of votes, which might be fatal to the Southern interest.[37] If that has any chance of prevailing, it must be by avoiding the loss of a single vote, and by concentrating all it's strength on one object. Who this should be is a question I can more freely discuss with any body than yourself."[38]

For Madison and Jefferson in 1795, the one bright spot in the national political picture was the announcement that Hamilton would resign from Washington's cabinet at the end of the year, to be followed by Secretary of War Henry Knox, Madison reported, "as the shadow, follows the substance." But their pleasure over Hamilton's departure was offset by his "arrogant valedictory Report," which recommended the reduction of the public debt over a period of thirty years. Since the means proposed seemed inadequate to discharge the debt, Madison thought that Hamilton's plan would only perpetuate it. He was convinced that the only way to "work down the debt faster than new emergenc[i]es will probably add to it" was by levying direct taxes.[39]

Although Hamilton left the nation's capital before Congress adjourned, his report stung the Republicans to reply. Written anonymously by Madison, the party pamphlet *Political Observations* was "extorted" from him by the entreaties of friends "just at the close of the session, under a surfeit of politics." Although he did not mention Hamilton by name, he placed the blame for party animosity and "discoloured representations of our public affairs" on those who supported "the perpetuity and progression of public debts and taxes" and "a gradual assumption or extension of discretionary powers in the executive departments," seconded by "newspapers of a certain stamp." Without mentioning himself, he denied Federalist charges that "tremendous calamities," such as war with Great Britain, would have followed had Congress passed "certain commercial resolutions moved by a member from Virginia, in the house of Representatives." But after hacking away for nearly a month and a half, Madison cut his pamphlet short, omitting "about half [of] what was sketched and meant for the press." "The nausea of the subject," he confessed to Jefferson, "and other circumstances" forced him to leave the job unfinished. Like most authors, however, he seemed proud of the pamphlet and carried a

---

37. Most documentary sources give this as "Republican" interest. But see the note to TJ's letter to JM, Apr. 27, 1795, below.
38. TJ to JM, Apr. 27, 1795, below.
39. JM to TJ, Dec. 21, 1794, below, and JM to TJ, Feb. 15, 1795, below.

copy of this "fugitive publication" to Jefferson when he and Mrs. Madison visited Monticello in the summer.⁴⁰

––––––––––––––– THE LETTERS –––––––––––––––

Madison to Jefferson

Harewood Oct. 5, 1794

DEAR SIR

On my return to Orange I dropped you a few lines on the subject of the deer. On my way into this part of the Country I passed Col. John Thornton of Culpeper, who has a Park, and will spare you with pleasure two or three, if you can not be otherwise supplied. He thinks he could by advertizing a premium of 10 or 12 dollars a head procure from his neighbors as many fawns to be delivered at Monticello as you would want. If you chuse to make use of his assistance, a line to the care of Mr. Fontaine Maury at Fredg. would soon get to hand.¹

This will be handed to you by Mr. Bond who is to build a large House for Mr. Hite my brother in law. On my suggestion He is to visit Monticello not only to profit of examples before his eyes, but to ask the favor of your advice on the plan of the House. Mr. Hite particularly wishes it in what relates to the Bow-room and the Portico, as Mr. B. will explain to you. In general, any hints which may occur to you for improving the plan will be thankfully accepted.² I beg pardon for being the occasion of this trouble to you, but your goodness has always so readily answered such draughts on it, that I have been tempted to make this additional one.

I write at present from the seat of Mr. G. Washington of Berkeley, where, with a deduction of some visits, I have remained since the 15th. Ult: the epoch at which I had the happiness to accomplish the alliance which I intimated to you I had been sometime soliciting. We propose to set out in 8 or 10 days for Philada. where I shall always receive your commands with pleasure, and shall continue to drop you a line as occasions turn up. In the mean time I remain Yrs. Mo: affecy

JS. MADISON JR

40. JM to TJ, June 14, 1795, below. The pamphlet is printed in *PJM*, XV, pp. 511-33; it is discussed in Robert A. Rutland, *James Madison: The Founding Father* (New York, 1987), pp. 138-39, and Brant, III, pp. 399-400.

1. TJ had planned a deer park as early as 1771 and had "a score of these animals" by 1782; see *Travels in North America in the Years 1780, 1781 and 1782 by the Marquis de Chastellux*, ed. Howard C. Rice, Jr., 2 vols. (Chapel Hill, 1963), II, p. 394.

2. Isaac Hite built Belle Grove near Middletown but did not include a half-octagon bow room; see Frederick D. Nichols, "Belle Grove in the Developing Civilization of the Valley of Virginia," *Historic Preservation* 20 (1968): 18.

Jefferson to Madison

Monticello Oct. 30, 1794

TH: J. TO J. M.

In the moment of the departure of the post it occurs to me that you can, by the return of it, note to me the amount of Mazzei's claim against Dohrman, for the information of the Van Staphorsts. I will put off my answer to them for that purpose. The day you left me I had a violent attack of the Rheumatism which has confined me ever since. Within these few days I have crept out a little on horseback, but am yet far from being well, or likely to be so soon. I wish much to see the speech, and to know how such an armament against people at their ploughs, will be represented, and an appeal to arms justified before that to the law had been tried and *proved* ineffectual, by the *fact,* not by the certified *opinion* of a magistrate paving the way to an embassy.[3] Adieu, a thousand respects to Mrs. Madison and joys perpetual to both.

Jefferson to Madison

Monticello Nov. 6, 1794

TH: J. TO J. MADISON.

A merchant neighbor of mine, sets out to-day for Philadelphia for his fall goods, and will return with them by water himself. This furnishes me a favorable opportunity of gleaning and getting the books I left in Philadelphia. But I must ask your friendly aid. Judge Wilson has Mably sur l'histoire de la France 4. v. 12mo. and Houard's Britton, Fleta, Glanville etc. 4. v. 4to. which he promised to deliver you. Pray press for them in my name. E. R. has several, partly lent here during my absence, partly in Philadelphia. I write to him by this post to ask his lodging them with you. He will probably need being sent to for them. After a very long drought which threatened to be fatal to our small grain, we have had two most abundant rains at an interval of a week, both followed by warm weather. The thermometer in the middle of the day from 55. to 69. It has been once only at the freezing point. Smart white frosts in the neighborhood, but none has extended yet to this place. Fine beef 2d. Corn from the tub 8/, both cash. Wheat 5/ in goods @ 61⅓ per cent on the Philadelphia price, which brings the wheat down to half a dollar at Philadelphia. The Sheriffs, who are now going down with their money, declare that there never was so miserable a collection; men, hitherto the most punctual, having been obliged to ask indulgence, from the scarcity of cash. My best respects to Mrs. Madison. Adieu.

3. TJ's italics. On Aug. 4, James Wilson, an associate justice of the Supreme Court, had certified that combinations too powerful to be suppressed by judicial proceedings had fomented the Whiskey Rebellion; see Richard H. Kohn, "The Washington Administration's Decision to Crush the Whiskey Rebellion," *JAH* 59 (1972): 567–84.

Madison to Jefferson

Philadelphia Nov. 16, 1794

DEAR SIR

I have recd. your two favors of Ocr. 30 and Novr. 6, the former not in time to be answered on Monday last. Mazzei's claim on Dorhman is £2000 N. Y. Currency, with interest at 7 per Ct. from Novr. 1788. It is secured by a Deed of Trust empowering me to sell a tract of land granted to Mr. D. by an Act of Congress of Octr. 1. 1787. (see Journals of that date). Mr. Randolph thinks that a Court of Equity would not interfere with a summary execution of the trust. I hear nothing from Dorhman; nor can even say whether he is still in N. York. I have mentioned to Mr. R. the books and he has promised to let me have them. Judge Wilson is on the Southn. Circuit, and I suppose the volumes in his hands can not be got till he returns. I will however make the trial. The gentleman by whom they are to be sent to you has not yet made his appearance.

The Senate having not yet a Quorum I cannot send you the P.'s Speech. You will have seen by the papers that the Western Scene is closed. H. is still with the army. You will perceive his colouring on all the documents which have been published during his Mentorship to the commander in cheif.[4] When I first arrived here the conversation ran high for a standing army to enforce the laws. It is said the Militia will all return with the same doctrine in their mouths. I have no doubt that such an innovation will be attempted in earnest during the session, if circumstances should be favorable. It is probable however that the P. will not embark in the measure; and that the fear of alarming N. England will be another obstacle.

The elections for the next Congs. are generally over except in Virginia and N. Carola. and N. York. In N. Hampshire the choice is much the same. In Masshts. there has been a violent contest in most of the districts. All that will probably be gained is a spirit of enquiry and competition in that quarter. Ames is re-elected after the most unparall[el]ed exertions and calumnies in his favor, and according to report by the addl. aid of bad votes.[5] Dexter is to run a second heat but will probably succeed. Sedgwick's fate is not known. The chance is said to be in his favor; but it is agreed that he will be well sweated. As he has not yet appeared, he is probably nursing his declining popularity during the crisis. From N. Y. we are promised at least half of the new representatives for the republican scale. N. Jersey has lost old Clarke who will no doubt be replaced by a successor of other sentiments. In this State, the election, not-

---

4. George Washington and Alexander Hamilton left Philadelphia on Sept. 30 for western Pennsylvania, where they met the army dispatched against the Whiskey rebels. Washington stayed until Oct. 19, and Hamilton remained for another month as liaison with the army's commander Governor Henry Lee of Virginia; see Slaughter, p. 216.

5. See Winfred E. A. Bernhard, *Fisher Ames: Federalist and Statesman* (Chapel Hill, 1965), pp. 237-41.

withstanding its inauspicious circumstances, is more republican than the last. Nine at least out of thirteen are counted on the right side; among them Swanwick in the room of Fitzimmons, a stunning change for the aristocracy. Maryland pretty much as heretofore. I shd. have first noted that in Delaware Patten the Republican ex-member, is chosen by a large Majority. The representation of Maryland will vary little from the present. In S. C. Smith has been carryed by the British merchants in Charleston and their d[e]btors in the Country, in spite of the Rutledges and Pinkney's who set up agst. him Jno. Rutlege jur. Tucker was also a candidate. Smith had a majority of all the votes. In general the changes also in that State will be for the worse. The death of Gillon has made way for Barnwell if he chuses to step in. Hunter also is out; but it is said his successor (a Mr. Harper) will be a valuable acquisition, being sound able and eloquent.[6] The prospects for the Senate are—the reelection of Langdon for N. H. The election of Payne, an incognitum, in place of Bradley for Vermont who appears to have been out of favor with both parties—the reelection of King in N. Y. owing to the death of 2 Repubn. members of the State Legislature—the chance of a Republican successor to R Morris, said to be a good one; a like chance in Delaware. In Maryland the Chance is bad, but nothing worse than the present delegation is to [be] apprehended. Potts has resigned, and Henry it is supposed will either withdraw or be rejected. The event in Virga. you will know. The information from N. C. is not decisive, but favorable; the same as to S. C. Izard has relinquished his pretensions. In Georgia the question lies between Gun and Telfair. The former it is thought will be rechosen.

I must refer to Newspapers which I suppose you occasionally see from Richd. for the posture of things in Europe. In general they are extremely favorable to F. and alarming to all the Sovereigns of Europe. England seems still bent notwithstanding, on the war. She is now to subsidize the Emperor as well as the K. of Prussia. Accordg. to the intelligence handed to the public it would seem that the humiliating memorial of Jay inspires less contempt, than the French victories do terror, and that the tone towards this Country will be much changed. It is even intimated that satisfactory arrangements will be made on most, if not all the points in question. Not a line official or private from Monroe. His enthusiastic reception you will have seen.

Prices here are very different from those you mention. Wheat at 12/- Corn 6/6. Beef at 8d. and other things in proportion. House Rent 50 PerCt. higher than last Winter. Mrs. M. offers her best returns to you. Always and affecy. Yours

Js. Madison

---

6. Robert Goodloe Harper became a Federalist leader. For details on the above elections, see *PJM*, XV, pp. 381–82.

Madison to Jefferson

Philadelphia Nov. 30, 1794

DEAR SIR

Mr. Fleming has been here and set out on his return yesterday. I did not however know of his arrival till a very short time before his departure. Contrary to your expectation he returns by land, not with his goods. On this acct. added to the lateness of the Season, and my not being able to get all your books, I concluded it would be best to put off sending what I could get, till the Spring, when they can all be sent together, and perhaps be less exposed to accidents. The books in the hands of Wilson could not be obtained in his absence. And Mr. R. has not been able yet to find the Book on Mineralogy left with him. You will see by the inclosed that you are to receive a sett of Chalmer's Treaties. I send you the letter to me accompanying it, for the sake of the references which if correct may deserve notice; tho' they come from a Quarter not very learned one would suppose on such subjects. You will be so good as to return the letter, as I am yet to answer it.

The attack on the most sacred principle of our Constitution and of Republicanism, thro' the Democratic Societies, has given rise to much discussion in the H. of Reps. and has left us in a critical situation. You will have seen the P.'s Speech. The answer of the Senate was hurried thro', with the most full and emphatic eccho of the denunciation of these Societies. In the mean time the answer of the H. of Reps. tho' prepared and reported without any loss of time, was, contrary to usage, printed for consideration, and put off from Friday, till monday. On the intervening saturday, the Senate presented them, which with the P.'s reply was immediately out in the Newspapers. I refer for both to the Richd. Newspapers which you will probably have seen. The answer of the H. of Reps. both as reported and as agreed to are inclosed. The Come. consisted of Sedgwick Scott and myself. The draught was made as strong as possible on all proper points, in order the better to get it thro', without the improper one. This succeeded in the Come.; Scott concurring in the *expediency*[7] of silence on that; tho' in the House he changed his ground. When the report was taken up on Monday Fitzimmons moved "to *reprobate* the self-created Societies etc. which tho' in strictness not *illegal,* contributed by their proceedings to mislead the weak and ignorant." This opened the debate which you will no doubt have an oppy. of reading in the Virga. papers if you chuse. It so happens that I can not send them by the mail. The argts. in favor of the motion fell with equal weight on the press and every mode of animadverting on public men and measures. After some time the proposition was new modelled, and in a less pointed shape underwent discussion for several days. On the first question wch. tried the sense of the House, the division was 47 agst. 45. for the usurped power. This was in a Committee of the whole. On a

---

7. JM's italics here and below.

renewal of the same question in the House the decision was reversed by 47 in the affirmative and 45 in the negative. A motion was then made to limit the censure to the Societies within the scene of insurrection, which was carried by the casting vote of the Speaker. In this form the whole proposition was abandoned. This was on thursday. On friday, it being foreseen that some evil accomodation would come from the other side and succeed, It was proposed by Mr. Nicholas to insert the sentence which distinguishes the first ¶ of the Answer agreed to, from the Report. An attempt was made to add "and self created Societies," after "combinations," but it had so little prospect of success that it was withdrawn. The Answer was presented on saturday, and rec'd the reply in the inclosed paper, which you will be at no loss to understand. The Republicans were considered by their opponents as rather victorious by the result in the House. The reply of the P. is claimed by the latter as a final triumph on their side; and it is probable that so it will prove.[8] You will easily conceive my situation thro' this whole business. It was obvious that a most dangerous game was playing agst. Republicanism. The insurrection was universally and deservedly odious. The Democratic Societies were presented as in league with it. The Republican part of Congs. were to be drawn into an *ostensible,* patronage of those Societies, and into an ostensible opposition to the President. And by this artifice the delusion of N. Engld. was to be confirmed, and a chance afforded of some new turn in Virga. before the elections in the Spring. What the success of this game will really be, time must decide. If the people of America are so far degenerated already as not to see or to see with indifference, that the Citadel of their liberties is menaced by the precedent before their eyes, they require abler advocates than they now have, to save them from the consequences. Lengthy as the debate was, I took but little part in it; and that little is very erroneously as well as defectively stated in the Newspapers. No private letters from Monroe. An official one of Sepr. 15—speaks of the utmost prosperity at home—of the irresistable discipline and enthusiasm of their armies, and of the most unalterable affection to this Country. All that is given out from Jay's negociation is in favr. of some advantageous result. How is your Rheumatism—and Mr. Randolph's complaint?

ENCLOSURE
[Madison's Address of the House of Representatives to the President]

[Nov. 21, 1794]

The House of Representatives calling to mind the blessings enjoyed by the people of the United States, and especially the happiness of living under Constitutions and laws which rest on their Authority alone, could not learn with other emotions than

---

8. In his reply, President Washington declared that "it is far better that the artful approaches to such a situation of things should be checked by the vigilant and duly admonished patriotism of our fellow-citizens, than that the evil should increase until it becomes necessary to crush it by the strength of their arms"; see *PJM,* XV, p. 398.

those you have expressed, that any part of our fellow Citizens should have shewn themselves capable of an insurrection.[9]

We feel with you the deepest regret at so painful an occurrence in the annals of our country. As men regardful of the tender interests of humanity, we look with grief, at scenes which might have stained our land with civil blood. As lovers of public order, we lament that it has suffered so flagrant a violation: as zealous friends of republican government, we deplore every occasion, which in the hands of its enemies, may be turned into a calumny against it.

This aspect of the crisis, however, is happily not the only one, which it presents. There is another which yields all the consolations which you have drawn from it. It has demonstrated to the candid world, as well as to the American people themselves, that the great body of them, every where, are equally attached to the luminous and vital principle of our constitution, which enjoins that the will of the majority shall prevail: that they understand the indissoluble union between true liberty and regular government; that they feel their duties no less than they are watchful over their rights; that they will [be] as ready, at all times, to crush licentiousness, as they have been to defeat usurpation: in a word, that they are capable of carrying into execution, that noble plan of self government, which they have chosen as the guarantee of their own happiness, and the asylum for that, of all from every clime, who may wish to unite their destiny with ours.

These are the just inferences from the promp[t]itude with which the summons to the standard of the laws has been obeyed; and from sentiments which have been witnessed in every description of citizens, in every quarter of the Union. The spectacle therefore when viewed in its true light may well be affirmed to display in equal lustre, the virtues of the American character, and the value of Republican government. All must particularly acknowledge and applaud the patriotism of that portion of citizens who have freely sacrificed every thing less dear than the love of their country, to the meritorious task of defending its happiness.

In the part which you have yourself borne through this delicate and distressing period, we trace the additional proofs it has afforded of your solicitude for the public good. Your laudable and successful endeavors to render lenity in executing the laws conducive to their real energy, and to convert tumult into order without the effusion of blood, form a particular title to the confidence and praise of your constituents. In all that may be found necessary, on our part to complete this benevolent purpose, and to secure ministers and friends of the laws against the remains of danger, our due co-operation will be afforded.

The other subjects which you have recommended, or communicated, and of which several are peculiarly interesting, will all receive the attention which they demand.[10] We shall on this, as on all occasions, be disposed to adopt every measure

---

9. On Nov. 28, 1794, John Nicholas of Virginia offered the following compromise amendment denouncing "combinations of men" instead of "self-created societies," the term that Washington had used: "And we learn, with the greatest concern, that any misrepresentations whatever, of the Government and its proceedings, either by individuals or combinations of men, should have been made and so far credited, as to foment the flagrant outrage, which has been committed on our laws"; see *ibid.*, p. 388.

10. In the address as finally agreed to, the following amendment was added: "We are deeply impressed with the importance of an effectual organization of the militia. We rejoice at the intelligence of the advance and success of the army under the command of General Wayne;

which may advance the safety and prosperity of our Country. In nothing can we more cordially unite with you, than in imploring the supreme Ruler of Nations to multiply his blessings on these United States: to guard our free and happy Constitution against every machination and danger; and to make it the best source of public happiness, by verifying its character of being the best safeguard of human rights.

Jefferson to Madison

[Monticello] Dec. 9, 1794

TH: J. TO MR. MADISON.

I write this merely as a way bill. The Orange post arrives at Charlottesville on Tuesday morning about 10. oclock and returns in half an hour. The Richmond post arrives in Charlottesville on Tuesday evening and returns on Friday morning. I wish to know the difference this makes in the conveyance of a letter to Philadelphia. I therefore write this by the Orange post, and will write such another by that of Richmond, and pray you to note to me the days on which you recieve both. Your favor of Nov. 16. came to hand the 2d. inst. Our militia are returning it is said, without having been to Detroit. Where then have they been? The explanation of this phænomenon is ardently wished here. Adieu. Yours affectionately.

Jefferson to Madison

[Monticello] Friday morning. Dec. 12, 1794

TH: J. TO J. MADISON

I wrote you a kind of way-bill by the Orange post, which arrived at, and left Charlottesville on Tuesday forenoon. I write this by the Richmond post which leaves Charlottesville on Friday Morning. The object is to know what difference there will be in the arrival of the two letters at Philadelphia.

We have nothing new for you; for it is not new that we have fine weather. It is, and has been delicious, with only two short intervals of cold. In one of them (about the 22d of Nov.) it was extraordinarily cold, the mercury being at 19°. But it was only three mornings below freezing. In the other (Dec. 4.) it was one morning below the freezing point. But it has never once continued so

---

whether we regard it as a proof of the perseverance, prowess and superiority of our troops, or as a happy presage to our military operations against the hostile Indians, and as a probable prelude to the establishment of a lasting peace, upon terms of candor, equity and good neighbourhood. We receive it with the greater pleasure, as it increases the probability of sooner restoring a part of the public resources to the desirable object of reducing the public debt." In his address to Congress, President Washington had praised Major General Anthony Wayne's victory over the Indians at Fallen Timbers on August 20; see *ibid*.

thro the day. We have had fine rains at proper intervals, which is the only interruption our ploughs have had. Corn has sold at 6/6 per barrel, half goods, half cash. It is now at 8/. Purchasers talk of that, sellers of 10/. Wheat 5/ in goods. Adieu. Yours affectionately.

Madison to Jefferson

Philadelphia Dec. 21, 1794

DEAR SIR

Your favor of the 9th. by the Orange post arrived here on the 18th. that of the 12 by the Richmond post, on the 20st. so that it appears the latter was one day less on the way. It is to be remarked however that as the Orange post leaves Charlottesville on tuesday, he might easily be in Fredericksburg on thursday, in time for the mail which passes thro' it on that day to Dumfries. If this despatch is not required of him it ought to be. It would make a difference of two days in the journey. Or at least the post might wait a day in Charlottesville and be in time for the saturday's mail at Fredericksburg.

Our weather here has been as fine as you describe yours. Yesterday there was a change. It was cold, cloudy, and inclined to snow. To day we have a bright day, and not very cold. Prices here are very different from yours. Wheat is at 13 or 14/. and flour in proportion. In general things are 50 PerCt. beyond the prices of last Winter. The phenomenon you wish to have explained is as little understood here as with you; but it would be here quite unfashionable to suppose it needed explanation. It is impossible to give you an idea of the force with which the tide has set in a particular direction. It has been too violent not to be soon followed by a change. In fact I think a change has begun already. The danger will then be of as violent a reflux to the opposite extreme.

The attack made on the essential and constitutional right of the Citizen, in the blow levelled at the "self-created Societies" does not appear to have had the effect intended. It is and must be felt by every man who values liberty, whatever opinion he may have of the use or abuse of it by those institutions. You will see that the appeal is begun to the public sentiment, by the injured parties. The Republican Society of Baltimore set the example.[11] That of Newark has advertised a meeting of its members. It is said that if Edwd. Livingston, as is generally believed, has outvoted Watts, for the H. of Reps. he is indebted for it to the invigorated exertions of the Democratic Society of that place, of which he is himself a member. In Boston the subject is well understood, and handled in the Newspaper on the republican side, with industry and address.

11. The Baltimore Society denied President Washington's allegation that the Democratic societies had stirred up the Whiskey Rebellion; see Philip S. Foner, ed., *The Democratic-Republican Societies, 1790–1800: A Documentary Sourcebook of Constitutions, Declarations, Addresses, Resolutions, and Toasts* (Westport, Conn., 1976), pp. 339–43.

The Elections in Massts. have turned out rather better than was of late expected. The two republican members have stood their ground; in spite of the most unexampled operations agst. them. Ames is said to owe his success to the votes of negroes and British sailors smuggled under a very lax mode of conducting the election there. Sedgwick and Goodhue have *bare*[12] majorities. Dexter is to run another heat, but will succeed; Gerry, his only considerable compet[it]or and who would outvote him, refusing to be elected. There are several changes in the remainder of the Delegation, and some of them greatly for the better. In New York there will be at least half republicans; perhaps more. It has unluckily happened that in a districts two *republicans* set up agst. *one* Anti: The consequence is that a man is re-elected who would not otherwise have taken the field: and there is some danger of a similar consequence in the other district. In N. Jersey, it is said that not more than one of the old members will be returned. The people all over the State are signing with avidity a remonstrance agst. the high salaries of the Govt.

Hamilton is to resign, according to his own notification the last of Feby. His object is not yet unfolded. Knox, as the shadow, follows the substance. Their successors are not yet designated by any circumstance that has escaped.

What think you of a project to disfranchise the insurgent Counties by a bill of exclusion agst. their Reps. in the State Legislature? The object is to pave the way for Bingham or Fitzimmons—as Senator—and to give an example for rejecting Galatine in the H. of Reps. at the next Congress—of which he is a member. The proposition has been laid on the table, and the event is uncertain. There is some probabil[it]y the violence of the measure may defeat it; nor is it certain I am told that if carried thro', it would answer the purpose of its authors.

Jefferson to Madison

Monticello Dec. 28, 1794

DEAR SIR

I have kept Mr. Joy's letter a post or two, with an intention of considering attentively the observations it contains: but I have really now so little stomach for any thing of that kind that I have not resolution enough even to endeavor to understand the observations. I therefore return the letter, not to delay your answer to it, and beg you in answering for yourself, to assure him of my respects and thankful acceptance of Chalmer's treaties, which I do not possess: and if you possess yourself of the scope of his reasoning, make any answer to it you please for me. If it had been on the rotation of my crops, I would have answered myself, lengthily perhaps, but certainly *con gusto*.[13]

12. JM's italics here and below.
13. TJ's italics here and below.

The denunciation of the democratic societies is one of the extraordinary acts of boldness of which we have seen so many from the faction of Monocrats. It is wonderful indeed that the President should have permitted himself to be the organ of such an attack on the freedom of discussion, the freedom of writing, printing and publishing. It must be a matter of rare curiosity to get at the modifications of these rights proposed by them, and to see what line their ingenuity would draw between democratical societies, whose avowed object is the nourishment of the republican principles of our constitution, and the society of the Cincinnati, a *self-created* one, carving out for itself hereditary distinctions, lowering over our constitution eternally, meeting together in all parts of the Union periodically, with closed doors, accumulating a capital in their separate treasury, corresponding secretly and regularly, and of which society the very persons denouncing the democrats are themselves the fathers, founders or high officers. Their sight must be perfectly dazzled by the glittering of crowns and coronets, not to see the extravagance of the proposition to suppress the friends of general freedom, while those who wish to confine that freedom to the few, permitted to go on in their principles and practices. I have put out of sight the persons whose misbehavior has been taken advantage of to slander the friends of popular rights; and I am happy to observe that as far as the circle of my observation and information extends, every body has lost sight of them, and viewed the abstract attempt on their natural and constitutional rights in all it's nakedness. I have never heard, or heard of a single expression or opinion which did not condemn it as an inexcusable aggression. And with respect to the transactions against the excise-law, it appears to me that you are all swept away in the torrent of governmental opinions, or that we do not know what these transactions have been. We know of none which according to the definitions of the law, have been any thing more than riotous. There was indeed a meeting to consult about a separation. But to consult on a question does not amount to a determination of that question in the affirmative, still less to the acting on such a determination: but we shall see I suppose what the court lawyers, and courtly judges and would-be Ambassadors will make of it. The excise-law is an infernal one. The first error was to admit it by the constitution. The 2d. to act on that admission. The 3d. and last will be to make it the instrument of dismembering the Union, and setting us all afloat to chuse which part of it we will adhere to. The information of our militia returned from the Westward is uniform, that tho the people there let them pass quietly, they were objects of their laughter, not of their fear, that 1000 men could have cut off their whole force in a thousand places of the Alleganey, that their detestation of the excise law is universal, and has now associated to it a detestation of the government, and that separation which perhaps was a very distant and problematical event, is now near, and certain and determined in the mind of every man. I expected to have seen some justification of arming one part of the society against another, of declaring a civil war the moment before the meeting of that body which has the sole right of declaring war, of being so patient of the kicks and scoffs of our enemies, and rising at a feather against our friends, of adding a million to the public debt and deriding us with recommendations to pay it if we can, etc. etc. But the part of the speech which was to be taken as a justification of the armament reminded me of parson Saunders's demonstration[14] why minus into minus makes plus. After a parcel of shreds of stuff from Aesop's fables and Tom Thumb, he jumps all at once into his Ergo, minus multiplied into minus makes plus. Just so the 15,000 men enter after the fables in the speech. However the time is coming when we shall fetch up the lee-way of our vessel. The changes in your house I see are going on for the better, and even the Augean herd over your heads are slowly purging off their impurities. Hold on then, my dear friend, that we may not ship-wreck in the mean while. I do not see in the minds of those with whom I converse a greater affliction than the fear of your retirement; but this must not be, unless to a more splendid and a more efficacious post. There I should rejoice to see you: I hope I may say I shall rejoice to see you. I have long had much in my mind to say to you on that subject. But double delicacies have kept me silent. I ought perhaps to say, while I would not give up my own retirement for the empire of the Universe, how I can justify wishing one, whose happiness I have as much at heart as yours, to take the front of the battle which is fighting for my security. This would be easy enough to be done, but not at the heel of a lengthy epistle. Let us quit this, and turn to the fine weather we are basking in. We have had one of our tropical winters. Once only a snow of 3. inches deep, which went off the next day, and never as much ice as would have cooled a bottle of wine. And we have now but a month to go through of winter weather. For February always gives us good samples of the spring of which it is the harbinger. I recollect no small news interesting to you. You will have heard I suppose that Wilson Nicholas has bought Carr's lowground's and Harvey's barracks. I rejoice in the prosperity of a virtuous man, and hope his prosperity will not taint his virtue. Present me respectfully to Mrs. Madison, and pray her to keep you where you are for her own satisfaction and the public good, and accept the cordial affections of us all. Adieu.

Madison to Jefferson

Philadelphia Jan. 11, 1794 [1795]

DEAR SIR

The last subject before the H. of Reps. was a Bill revising the Naturalization law, which from its defects and the progress of things in Europe was exposing us to very serious inconveniences. The Bill requires 1. A probationary residence of 5 instead of 2 years, with a formal declaration on oath of the

---

14. Nicholas Saunderson, *The Elements of Algebra* (London, 1740-41), cited in *PJM,* XV, p. 428.

intention 3 years at least prior to the admission. 2. an oath of *abjuration,* as well as of allegiance. 3. proof of good character, attachment to the principles of our Government, and of being well disposed to the good order and happiness of the U. S. 4. Where the candidate has borne any title or been of any order of Nobility, he is to renounce both on record. This last raised some dust. The Eastern members were weak eno' to oppose it; and Dexter as a setoff moved a correspondent clog on emigrants attached to slave holding. Whether they will [be] able to throw the dust they have raised into the eyes of their Constituents I know not. It will not be easy I think to repair the blunder they have committed if it reaches the people. On the yeas and nays there [were] more thn. 60 for and little more than 30 agst. the clause. The Bill is gone to the Senate. Our revenue from trade is so increased as to supply a fund for commencing the discharge of the public debt. The excises laid at the last Session will probably be left as they stand. The treasury bench have attempted to make them perpetual, and brought about a Report of a Come. to prolong them till the year 1801. Another Come. after conferring with the Sugar Bakers and Snuff Makers have agreed on a Counter Report which will probably defeat the project. The French gain victories faster than we can relate them. In Spain, Sardinia and Holland they are equally sweeping every thing before them. They were not in Amsterdam but expected in a few days. The patriotic party was openly revived, and it was not doubted that the Stadholder would move off to England for his personal safety. The D. of York has been well drubbed again at Nimeguen. It was said to be agitated in the British Cabinet whether he should not with all his troops be withdrawn from the Continent. It is surmised that Prussia has actually treated with France, and that the Emperor is taking the same Course. It is indeed agreed that France can dictate peace to all her enemies, except England; and that she will probably do so in order to have a fair campaign with Engld. alone. Nothing final yet from Jay. It is expected here that he will accomplish much if not all he aims at. It will be scandalous, if we do not under present circumstances, get all that we have a right to demand. Not a word from Monroe. Knox is succeded by Pickering. The successor to H. not fixt, but likely to be Wolcot. He will probably go to N. Y. with the word *poverty* for his label. The Legislature of Pennsylva. have voted out the Western Members. It is said they will suspend important business till the seats can be refilled—but this will make little difference as the City party will still be a majority. Bingham will be the Senator—Unless the Germans can be prevailed on to vote for Tench Coxe. They like neither the one nor the other; not Bingham because an Aristocrat—not Coxe on the old score of his being a Tory in the War.

Madison to Jefferson

Philadelphia Jan. 26, 1795

DEAR SIR

I have recd. your favor of Decr. 28. but [not] till three weeks after the date of it. It was my purpose to have answered it particularly, but I have been robbed of the time reserved for the purpose. I must of consequence limit myself to a few lines and to my promise given to the Fresco Painter to forward you the inclosed letter.[15] Nothing since my last from Jay or Monroe. The Newspapers as usual teem with French victories and rumors of peace. There seem to be very probable indications of a progress made to this event, except in relation to G. B. with whom a Duet Campaign is the cry of France. The Naturalization [bill] has not yet got back from the Senate. I understand however it will suffer no material change. They have the prudence not to touch the Nobility clause. The House of Reps. are on the Military estabt. and the public debt. The difficulty and difference of opinion as to the former, produced a motion to request the P. to cause an estimate of the proper defence etc. It was in its real meaning, saying we do not know how many troops ought to be provided by our legislative duty, and ask your direction. It was opposed as opening the way for dragging in the weight of the Ex. for one scale, on all party questions—as extorting his opinion where he shd. reserve for his negative, and as exposing his unpopular opinions to be extorted at any time by an unfriendly majority. The prerogative men chose to take the subject by the wrong handle, and being joined by the weak men, the resolution passed. I fancied the Cabinet are embarrassed on the subject. On the subject of the Debt, the Treasury faction is spouting on the policy of paying it off as a great evil; and laying hold of two or three little excises passed last session under the pretext of war, are claiming more merit for their zeal than they allow to the opponents of these puny resources. Hamilton has made a long Valedictory Rept. on the subject. It is not yet printed, and I have not read it. It is said to contain a number of improper things. He got it in, by informing the Speaker, he had one ready, predicated on the *actual* revenues, for the House whenever they shd. please to receive.[16] Budinot the ready agent for all sycophantic jobbs, had a motion cut and dry just at the moment of the adjournment, for informing him in the language applied to the P. on such occasions, that the House was ready to receive the Rept. when he pleased, which passed without opposition and almost without notice. H. gives out that he is going to N. Y. and does not mean to return into public life at all. N. Jersey has changed all her members except Dayton whose zeal agst. G. B. saved him. There are not more than 2 or 3 who are really on all points Repubns. Dexter is under another sweat in

---

15. TJ negotiated—unsuccessfully—for three years to have frescoes painted at Monticello; see *ibid.*, p. 455.
16. See Syrett, XVIII, pp. 56–148.

his district, and it is said to be perfectly uncertain whether he or his Repub: competitor will succeed. Adieu Yrs.

Js. M. Jr.

Jefferson to Madison

Monticello Feb. 5, 1795

TH: J. TO J. MADISON.

Congress drawing to a close, I must trouble you with a bundle of little commissions

1. to procure for me a copy of the correspondence between Genet, Hammond and myself at large.
2. a pamphlet entitled 'Sketches on rotations of crops,' to be had I believe at Dobson's. The author in a note pa. 43. mentions some former publication of his, which I should be glad to have also; as I am sure it must be good. Who is the author? Is it Peters? I do not think it is Logan.
3. to procure for me from some of the seedsmen some of the seed of the Winter vetch (it is the Vicia sativa, semine albo of Millar) as it is cheap, you may be governed in the quantity by the convenience of bringing. I think it must be valuable for our fall-fallows.[17]
4. to commission your barber to find for me such a seal as he let you have.
5. to enquire of J. Bringhurst whether Donath is returned from Hamburg, who was to bring me some glass? I know nobody who can give the information but Bringhurst, and I would not trouble you with it could I have got a word from him otherwise. But I have written twice to him, and got no answer, and I have sent twice to Philadelphia by a neighbor of mine, whom he has put off by saying he would write to me. If I could only find out whether Donath is returned, and what is his address in Philadelphia, I could then enquire about my glass of himself by letter.

We have now had about 4. weeks of winter weather, rather hard for our climate—many little snows which did not lay 24. hours, and one 9. I. deep which remained several days. We have had few thawing days during the time. It is generally feared here that your collegue F. Walker will be in great danger of losing his election. His competitor is indefatigable attending courts etc. and wherever he is, there is a general drunkenness observed, tho' we do not know that it proceeds from his purse.[18] Wilson Nicholas is attacked also in his election. The ground on which the attack is made is that he is a speculator. The explanations which this has produced, prove it a serious crime in the eyes of

---

17. For TJ's use of vetch, see Edwin M. Betts, ed., *Thomas Jefferson's Farm Book* . . . (Princeton, 1953), pp. 310-19.

18. Samuel Jordan Cabell defeated his fellow Republican Francis Walker in TJ's district; see *PJM*, XV, p. 468.

the people. But as far as I hear he is only investing the fruits of a first and only speculation. Almost every carriage-owner has been taken in for a double tax: information through the newspapers not being actual, tho legal, in a country where they are little read. This circumstance has made almost every man, so taken in, a personal enemy to the tax. I escaped the penalty only by sending an express over the county to search out the officer the day before the forfeiture would have been incurred. We presume you will return to Orange after the close of the session, and hope the pleasure of seeing Mrs. Madison and yourself here. I have past my winter almost alone, Mr. and Mrs. Randolph being at Varina. Present my best respects to Mrs. Madison, and accept them affectionately yourself. Adieu.

Madison to Jefferson

Philadelphia Feb. 15, 1795

DEAR SIR

Your favor of the 5th. came to hand yesterday. I will attend to your several commissions. Mr. Hawkins tells me, that the seed of the Winter Vetch is not to be got here.

Altho' nearly three months have passed since the signing of the Treaty by Jay, the official account of it has not been received, and the public have no other knowledge of its articles than are to be gleaned from the imperfect scraps of private letters. From these it is inferred that the bargain is much less in our favor than might be expected from the circumstances which co-operated with the justice of our demands. It is even conjectured that on some points, particularly the Western posts, the arrangements will be inadmissible. I find that in N. Y. there are accounts which are credited, that the posts, after the surrender, are to be *thoroughfares,* [19] for the traders and merchandizes of both parties. The operation of this will strike you at once, and the sacrifice is the greater, if it be true as is stated, that the former regulation on this subject, secured to the U. S. the monopoly of the fur trade, it being impossible for the Canadian Traders to get to and from the markets, without using our portages, and our parts of the lakes. It is wrong however to prejudge, but I suspect that Jay has been betrayed by his anxiety to couple us with England, and to avoid returning with his finger in his mouth. It is apparent that those most likely to be in the secret of the affair, do not assume an air of triumph.

The elections in N. York give *six* republicans instead of the former *three.* E. Livingston had in the City 205 votes more than Watts the present member. In Massachts. the elections are in several instances, still to be repeated. Dexter is to run a *third* heat. In the last his rival outvoted him, but was disappointed by a few scattering votes, which prevented his having a majority of the whole.

---

19. JM's italics here and below.

It is said that if nothing new turns up, Varnum will be sure to succeed on the next trial. The choice of Senators continues to run on the wrong side. In Delaware, where we were promised of late, a republican, it was contrived by a certain disposition of offices as some tell us, or according to others, occasioned by particular sicknesses, that Latimer of the H. of Reps. lately dropped by the people, has been appointed by the Legislature. N. Carolina has appointed Bloodworth whom you may recollect. His country men here do not augur favorably of his political course. Clinton has declined a re-election to the Govt. of N. Y. His party set up Yates and Floyd agst. Jay and Van-Ranslaer. Hamilton does not interfere with Jay. It is pompously announced in the Newspapers, that poverty drives him back to the Bar for a livelihood.

The Session has produced as yet, but few acts of Consequence. Several important ones are depending on the subjects of the Militia, of the military Establishment, and the discharge of the public debt. On the first little more will probably be done than to digest some regulations which will be left for public consideration till the next session. On the second, the present military Establishment will be continued and compleated; notwithstanding the late treaty with the Six Nations, the success of Wayne agst. the other tribes, and the disappearance of ominous symtoms in the aspect of G. Britain. I am extremely sorry to remark a growing apathy to the evil and danger of standing armies. And a vote passed two days ago, which is not only an evidence of that, but if not the effect of unpardonable inattention, indicates a temper still more alarming. In the Military Acts now in force, there are words, limiting the use of the army to the protection of the Frontiers. The Bill lately brought in revised the whole subject, and omitted this limitation. It was proposed to re-instate the words. This was rejected by a large majority. It was then proposed to substitute another phrase free from the little criticisms urged agst. the first proposition. The debate brought out an avowal that the Executive ought to be free to use the regular troops, as well as the Militia in support of the laws against our own Citizens. Notwithstanding this the amendment was lost by 8 votes. The House was very thin, and it is supposed, that the majority would have been in favor of the amendment, if all the members had been present. The mischeif however is irremediable, as the Senate will greedily swallow the Bill in its present form. This proceeding is the more extraordinary when the President's speech and the answer of the House of Reps. are recollected and compared with it. The third subject is the reduction of the public debt. Hamilton has in an arrogant valedictory Report presented a plan for the purpose. It will require about *30 years* of uninterrupted operation. The fund is to consist of the surpluses of impost and Excise, and the temporary taxes of the last Session which are to be prolonged till 1781.[20] You will judge of the chance of our ever being out of debt, if no other means are to be used. It is to be

---

20. JM seems to have transposed his digits since a later correction, not in his hand, gives the date as 1817; see *PJM*, XV, p. 475.

lamented that the public are not yet better reconciled to direct taxes which alone can work down the debt faster than new emergences will probably add to it. Of this dislike the partizans of the Debt take advantage not only to perpetuate it, but to make a merit of the application of inadequate means to the discharge of it. The plan of Hamilton contained a number of new irredeemabilities, among the remodifications proposed by him. All these have been struck out.

Mr. Christie of the House of Reps. intends to visit England in the interval between the present and next session. He is ambitious of a line from you introducing him to Mr. Pinkney, and has made me his solicitor for it. He is a man of good sense, and second to none in a decided and systematic devotion to Republicanism. Will you oblige us both by inclosing me such a letter. You need not fear its reaching me, as I shall be detained here some time after the adjournment. Adieu

Jefferson to Madison

[Monticello] Feb. 23, 1795

TH: J. TO J. M.

I inclose two letters to the President and Secretary of state open for your perusal and consideration.[21] I pray you to bestow thought on the subject, and if you disapprove it, return me my letters, undelivered, by next post. If you approve of them, stick a wafer in them and have them delivered. I also put under your cover a letter to the Fresco painter from whom you inclosed me one. His not having furnished me with his address obliges me to give you this trouble. Nothing new. Adieu affectionately.

Madison to Jefferson

[Philadelphia ca. Mar. 1, 1795][22]

Bringhurst says he has written to you and will write again. Donath is in Philada. He was disappointed in the importation of his Glass, by the Protest of Bills occasioned by the Yellow fever in Philada. If you still want the Glass, it will be proper to renew your orders to Donath. Letters addressed to him to the care of Jno' Bringhurst, or without that precaution will be pretty sure to get to him.

21. TJ endorsed a proposal to transfer the University of Geneva, recently disestablished by the French Revolution, to Virginia; see *ibid.*, p. 480.
22. For the dating of this unsigned, undated fragment, see *ibid.*, p. 484.

Jefferson to Madison

Monticello Mar. 5, 1795

TH: J. TO MR. MADISON.

Your favor of Feb. 15 is duly recieved and I now inclose the letter for Mr. Christie, which you will be so kind as to deliver to him open or sealed as you think best, and apologize to him for my availing myself of the opportunity of getting the vetch from England which you say is not to be had in Philadelphia.[23] The universal culture of this plant in Europe establishes it's value in a farm, and I find two intervals in my rotation where I can have crops of it without it's costing me a single ploughing. My main object is to turn it in as a green dressing in the spring of the year, having sowed it on the fall fallow. In the mean time, should a short crop of fodder or hard winter call for it as fodder, it is a most abundant and valuable green fodder through the whole winter. We are in despair here for F. Walker. The low practices of his competitor though seen with indignation by every thinking man, are but too successful with the unthinking who merchandize their votes for grog. He is said to be a good republican: but I am told this is the only favorable trait in his character. Adieu affectionately.

Madison to Jefferson

Philadelphia Mar. 23, 1795

DEAR SIR

Your two last favors contained, one of them the letter for Mr. Christie, which has been sent to him; the other accompanied the letters to the President and Mr. Randolph. The two latter were duly delivered also. The President touched on the subject the other day in conversation with me, and has no doubt written to you on it. There are difficulties I perceive in the way of your suggestion, besides the general one arising from the composition of the scientific body, *wholly*[24] out of foreign materials. Notwithstanding the advantages which might weigh in the present case, agst. this objection, I own that I feel its importance. It was not sufficient however to induce me to withold your remarks from the P. as your letter would have authorised me to do. Whilst I am acknowledging your favors, I am reminded of a passage in a former one, which I had proposed to have answered at some length. Perhaps it will be best, at least for the present to say in breif, that reasons of *every* kind, and some of them, of the most *insuperable* as well as *obvious* kind, shut my mind against the

---

23. TJ introduced Gabriel Christie, a Maryland congressman, to Thomas Pinckney, U.S. minister to England; see *ibid.*, p. 487.

24. JM's italics here and below.

admission of any idea such as you seem to glance at. I forbear to say more, because I can have no more to say with respect to myself; and because the great deal that may and ought to be said beyond that restriction will be best reserved for some other occasion, perhaps for the latitude of a free conversation. You ought to be preparing yourself however to hear truths, which no inflexibility will be able to withstand.

I have already told you of my failure to get from E. R. one of your books which has slipped out of his memory as well as his hands. I have since after repeated applications got from Wilson Houdon's [Houard's] Fleta Bracton[25] etc. Mably, he says, he lent to Gallatine with your permission. This was not mentioned however till very lately; and Gallatine is at present in N. Y. As soon as he returns I will renew my efforts. I have procured for you "the Sketches on rotations,["] which I find to be truly a good thing. It was written by Mr. Boardley. The other publications referred to in p. 43. are not to be had of the Booksellers. I propose, if an oppy. offers, to get them thro' some friend who can carry the enquiry to the author himself. I have also procured you the correspondences with Hammond etc. All these with some other things deemed worth your possessing, I shall pack up for a conveyance by water to Richmd. addressing them to the Mercht. there from Staunton, whose name I cannot at this moment recollect.

The Treaty with England arrived soon after the adjournment. It is kept an inpenetrable secret by the Executive. The Senate are Summoned to meet it the 8th. of June. I wish it may not be of a nature to bring us into some delicacies with France, without obtaining fully our objects from G. B. The French it is said are latterly much less respectful than heretofore to our rights on the seas. We have no late private letters from Monroe. His last public ones were no later than Novr. 20. They contained a History of the Jacobin clubs, in the form of an apology for the Convention. Extracts on that subject were immediately put into the Newspapers, and are applied to party purposes generally, particularly in N. Y. where the election of Govr. is on the anvil. Yates and Jay are the candidates. The last accts. from Amsterdam foretell in the next the capture of that place by the French. The inclosed speeches of Pitt and Fox will give you the English politics, and a general view of the crisis in Europe.

I have been detained here by a sick family; and am so at present, by the state of the roads, which are kept bad by the rains and the frosts. I am extremely anxious to be on the journey and shall set out as soon as I can prudently venture. Yrs. always and mo: affecty.

Js. MADISON JR

---

25. For David Houard's editions of *Fleta* and *Britton*, see his *Traités sur les coutumes anglo-normandes,* cited in *PJM*, XV, p. 494. These essays are abbreviated versions of Henry de Bracton's thirteenth-century work *De legibus et consuetudinibus Angliæ.*

Jefferson to Madison

Monticello Apr. 27, 1795

Dear Sir

Your letter of Mar. 23. came to hand the 7th. of April, and notwithstanding the urgent reasons for answering a part of it immediately, yet as it mentioned that you would leave Philadelphia within a few days, I feared that the answer might pass you on the road. A letter from Philadelphia by the last post having announced to me your leaving that place the day preceding it's date, I am in hopes this will find you in Orange. In mine, to which yours of Mar. 23. was an answer I expressed my hope of the only change of position I ever wished to see you make, and I expressed it with entire sincerity, because there is not another person in the US. who being placed at the helm of our affairs, my mind would be so completely at rest for the fortune of our political bark. The wish too was pure and unmixed with any thing respecting myself personally. For as to myself the subject had been thoroughly weighed and decided on, and my retirement from office had been meant from all office high or low, without exception. I can say too with truth that the subject had not been presented to my mind by any vanity of my own. I knew myself and my fellow citizens too well to have ever thought of it. But the idea was forced upon me by continual insinuations in the public papers, while I was in office. As all these came from a hostile quarter, I knew that their object was to poison the public mind as to my motives, when they were not able to charge me with facts. But the idea being once presented to me, my own quiet required that I should face it and examine it. I did so thoroughly and had no difficulty to see that every reason which had determined me to retire from the office I then held, operated more strongly against that which was insinuated to be my object. I decided then on those general grounds which could alone be present to my mind at that time, that is to say, reputation, tranquillity, labor: for as to public duty; it could not be a topic of consideration in my case. If these general considerations were sufficient to ground a firm resolution never to permit myself to think of the office or be thought of for it, the special ones which have supervened on my retirement still more insuperably bar the door to it. My health is entirely broken down within the last eight months; my age requires that I should place my affairs in a clear state; these are sound if taken care of, but capable of considerable dangers if longer neglected; and above all things the delights I feel in the society of my family, and the agricultural pursuits in which I am so eagerly engaged. The little spice of ambition, which I had in my younger days, has long since evaporated, and I set still less store by a posthumous than present name. In stating to you the heads of reasons which have produced my determination, I do not mean an opening for future discussion, or that I may be reasoned out of it. The question is for ever closed with me; my sole object is to avail myself of the first opening ever given me from a friendly quarter (and I could not with decency do it before) of preventing any division or loss of votes, which might be fatal to the Southern[26] interest. If that has any chance of prevailing, it must be by avoiding the loss of a single vote, and by concentrating all it's strength on one object. Who this should be is a question I can more freely discuss with any body than yourself. In this I painfully feel the loss of Monroe. Had he been here I should have been at no loss for a channel thro which to make myself understood, if I have been misunderstood by any body through the instrumentality of Mr. Fenno and his abettors. I long to see you. I am proceeding in my agricultural plans with a slow but sure step. To get under full way will require 4. or 5. years. But patience and perseverance will accomplish it. My little essay in red clover the last year has had the most encouraging success. I sowed then about 40. acres. I have sowed this year about 120. which the rain now falling comes very opportunely on. From 160. to 200. acres will be my yearly sowing. The seed-box described in the Agricultural transactions of New York reduces the expence of seeding from 6/ to 2/3 the acre, and does the business better than is possible to be done by the human hand.[27] May we hope a visit from you? If we may, let it be after the middle of May, by which time I hope to be returned from Bedford. I had had a proposition to meet Mr. Henry there this month to confer on the subject of a convention to the calling of which he is now become a convert.[28] The session of our district court furnished me a just excuse for the time; but the impropriety of my entering into consultation on a measure in which I would take no part, is a permanent one. Present my most respectful compliments to Mrs. Madison and be assured of the warm attachment of dear Sir your's affectionately

Th: Jefferson

26. For a fascinating essay, see James Roger Sharp, "Unraveling the Mystery of Jefferson's Letter of April 27, 1795," *JER* 6 (1986): 411–18. The recipient's copy in the Madison Papers at the Library of Congress shows "Southern" interest; the letterpress or file copy in the Jefferson Papers has that word crossed out and "Republican" written in above the line before "interest." Sharp notes that all the editions of TJ's letters from Lipscomb and Bergh in 1903 back to Ford in 1892–99, to Henry A. Washington in 1853–54 and Thomas Jefferson Randolph in 1829 used the letterpress copy with "Republican" instead of "Southern," although Ford erroneously cited the recipient's copy in the Madison Papers in the Library of Congress as his source. Sharp absolves these editors of changing the letter and concludes that "the letterpress copy in the Jefferson Papers was altered prior to Randolph's 1829 edition. Thus it is likely that Jefferson himself, or Randolph, as the executor of his grandfather's estate, or one of those who assisted him, such as Nicholas P. Trist or James Madison, modified the letter." In 1989, J. C. A. Stagg stated that TJ made the alteration; see *PJM,* XVI, p. 2.

27. TJ referred to Ezra L'Hommedieu's seed box; see Edwin M. Betts, ed., *Thomas Jefferson's Garden Book, 1766–1824,* . . . (Philadelphia, 1944), p. 233.

28. Although a movement to revise the Virginia Constitution of 1776 appeared periodically throughout the 1790s, a state constitutional convention did not meet until 1829. For TJ's decision not to meet with Patrick Henry in 1795, see TJ to Archibald Stuart, Apr. 18, 1795, in Ford, VII, p. 8.

Madison to Jefferson

Orange June 14, 1795

DEAR SIR

I am almost ashamed to be so late in acknowledging your favr. of April 27: but, saying nothing of some unknown cause of its not getting to hand till two weaks or more after its date, I have been in constant expectation and intention of paying my respects in person to Monticello within two or three days and consequently of explaining and justifying my purposes better than it could be done by letter. A succession of incidents has as constantly delayed any visit, till the time has arrived for fulfilling a promised one to a particular relation of Mrs. M. in Hanover about 50 Miles distant. I am the more anxious to have this over, as the season will soon be unsafe in that quarter, and the harvest will require my presence. As soon after my return as possible I will indulge myself with the pleasure of seeing you. I have lately recd. a letter from Monroe of Feby. 25. which he wishes you to see and I shall bring with me.[29] A prior one also of very interesting contents will be also worth your perusal. I have heard nothing yet from Philada. relating to the tenor of the Treaty with G. B.[30] Just about the close of the Session I wrote a coercive letter to Dohrman on the subject of his debt to Mazzei. He answered that he was, just on the rece[i]pt of it, abt. to let me know that the success of some of his efforts wd. soon enable him to close the business. My departure obliged me to put it into the hands of Beckley who was going to N. Y. from whom I learn that D. suspends the payment till a liquidation of the debt can be made, but with an apparent ability and purpose to avoid any delay beyond that. It seems that D. has receipts for part payments to Mazzei subsequent to his deed of Trust to me, and alledges with some probable reason that the sum in the deed was not the real amount of the debt but a round one fully covering and securing the maximum. There are some points also relating to the rate of damages and interest on the protested bills, on which there may be room for negociation. As well as I recollect both were to be settled according to the laws of N. Y. not of Virginia, whether binding in the case or not, in consideration of the indulgence shewn him. I have urged a payment immediately of as much as may be due according to his own shewing, but have recd. no answer. I have several little things for you as your seal etc. with a few pamphlets. Among the latter is a fugitive publication[31]

---

29. James Monroe had sent JM a copy of his letter to Secretary of State Edmund Randolph about his reception in France.

30. The Jay Treaty arrived in Philadelphia on Mar. 7, 1795, but President Washington and Secretary of State Edmund Randolph kept the terms secret pending the special session of the Senate, which was set for June 8; see Jerald A. Combs, *The Jay Treaty: Political Battleground of the Founding Fathers* (Berkeley, 1970), p. 160.

31. JM's anonymous pamphlet entitled *Political Observations* was published on Apr. 20, 1795. In a coded letter to James Monroe on Jan. 26, 1796, he admitted authorship; see *PJM*, XV, pp. 511–34.

answering the misrepre[sen]tations of the Session prior to the last. It was extorted by the intreaties of some friends, just at the close of the session, under a surfeit of politics, and contains about half what was sketched and meant for the press; the nausea of the subject and other circumstances have left the remainder unfinished. I shall bring these articles with me when I pay my visit. Yrs. always and affecy.

Js. MADISON J[R.]

Jefferson to Madison

Monticello July 13, 1795

Th: J. TO J. M.

I send you the inclosed as you may perhaps not have seen it. Return it if you please.[32] I have not yet seen the treaty, but suppose tomorrow's post may perhaps bring it.[33] Mr. and Mrs. Randolph set out the day after tomorrow for the springs, to see if any of them can restore the nearly hopeless state of his health.[34] Nil mihi rescribas. Attamen ipse veni.[35] Vale.

32. Enclosure not found.

33. TJ received a copy of Jay's treaty on July 21; see Malone, III, p. 245.

34. For Martha and Thomas Mann Randolph's visit to restore his health, see *ibid.,* pp. 235–36, and William H. Gaines, Jr., *Thomas Mann Randolph: Jefferson's Son-in-Law* (Baton Rouge, 1966), p. 39.

35. "Yet write nothing back to me; yourself come." Ovid's quotation is cited in *PJM,* XVI, p. 37.

20

THE JAY TREATY, 1795–1796

WHEN JEFFERSON RETIRED from the "hated occupation of politics" at the end of 1793,[1] his departure laid a heavy load on Madison, who shouldered the major burden in transforming the "republican interest" into the Republican party. Labeled by his opponents as "the great man of the party," he was credited by a Connecticut Federalist with "the most personal influence of any man in the house of Representatives." Indeed, Madison, rather than Jefferson, was the early organizer of the Republican party, so much so that it was often referred to as "Madison's Party."[2]

Although Jefferson was not active in party matters during his retirement, Madison kept him well informed about national politics, especially Jay's treaty with Great Britain, the hottest issue of Washington's presidency.[3] The Republicans disliked the use of the chief justice of the United States, the leading member of the federal judiciary, for an executive embassy, and they had long been suspicious of Jay, who a decade earlier had argued that navigation of the Mississippi might be abandoned in negotiations with Spain in exchange for commercial concessions that would be beneficial to eastern shipping.[4] Like Hamilton, he was a staunch Federalist and an admirer of Great Britain.

Throughout the spring of 1795, rumors about the provisions of the treaty that Jay had negotiated the previous fall floated across the Atlantic. Madison's views depended on the most recent news. Although he had been outraged by Jay's "humiliating memorial" to King George III in the fall of 1794, he thought that French military victories would force England to make concessions to the United States. "It is even intimated," he told Jefferson, "that

1. TJ to Mrs. Church, Nov. 27, 1793, in Ford, VI, p. 455.
2. In his excellent analytical study, *The Jeffersonian Republicans: The Formation of Party Organization, 1789–1801* (Chapel Hill, 1957), Noble E. Cunningham, Jr., devotes a chapter to "Madison's Party" between 1793 and 1797; see pp. 67–88.
3. In a letter to Alexander Hamilton, Aug. 31, 1795, President Washington predicted that Jay's treaty would "produce a hot Session"; see Syrett, XIX, p. 205.
4. See JM to TJ, Apr. 28, 1794, above.

satisfactory arrangements will be made on most, if not all the points in question."[5] By the beginning of 1795, he was writing about the high expectations of success from Jay's mission: "It is expected here that he will accomplish much if not all he aims at. It will be scandalous," he added, "if we do not under present circumstances, get all that we have a right to demand."[6]

But as details of the treaty provisions began to leak out, Madison became less sanguine about concessions from England and more fearful of the concessions that Jay might have granted. As early as February 1795, Madison concluded tentatively that "the bargain is much less in our favor than might be expected from the circumstances which co-operated with the justice of our demands." Nonetheless, he thought it wrong to prejudge the issues without the full facts available, even though he suspected that Jay "has been betrayed by his anxiety to couple us with England, and to avoid returning with his finger in his mouth. It is apparent that those most likely to be in the secret of the affair, do not assume an air of triumph."[7]

When Congress adjourned on March 3, 1795, the long-awaited treaty had not yet arrived; but since it was expected momentarily, Washington called a special session of the Senate to consider it on June 8. The president received the treaty on March 7, but he kept it "an inpenetrable secret" until the Senate convened.[8] After Washington submitted the treaty to the Senate, the Federalist majority passed a resolution to continue the secrecy during the deliberations. But after its ratification, a Republican senator slipped a copy of the treaty to a newspaper, and it flew, as Madison noted, "with an electric velocity to every part of the Union."[9]

In the treaty, the United States secured the evacuation of the frontier posts that the British had promised to surrender in 1783; payment for spoliations on American commerce made under the orders-in-council of 1793 and 1794; and a commercial treaty that included the legalization of trade with India and the opening of the British West Indies to small American ships—trade in canoes, according to Madison.[10] The United States promised to pay the pre-Revolutionary claims of British creditors against American citizens, and a mixed arbitration commission was established to fix the amount due. Other matters of controversy, including the disputed Maine boundary between the United States and Canada and the amount to be awarded for spolia-

5. JM to TJ, Nov. 16, 1794, above.
6. JM to TJ, Jan. 11, [1795], above.
7. JM to TJ, Feb. 15, 1795, above.
8. JM to TJ, Mar. 23, 1795, above.
9. JM to James Monroe, Dec. 20, 1795, in Hunt, VI, p. 258. The Senate ratified Jay's treaty on June 24, 1795, and Senator Stevens T. Mason gave it to the press on June 31, 1795. The standard account of the negotiations is Samuel Flagg Bemis, *Jay's Treaty: A Study in Commerce and Diplomacy*, 2d ed. (New Haven, 1962). For domestic repercussions, the best account is Jerald A. Combs, *The Jay Treaty: Political Battleground of the Founding Fathers* (Berkeley, 1970).
10. JM's remark is quoted in Robert Ernst, *Rufus King, American Federalist* (Chapel Hill, 1968), p. 206.

tions, were also referred to arbitration commissions, the beginning of modern arbitration of international disputes. The treaty was silent about compensation for slaves carried off by the British in 1783 and about Indian affairs on the northwestern boundary.

To gain these terms, Jay made concessions on America's claims as a neutral carrier, virtually waiving its "freedom of the seas" doctrine for the duration of the war between England and France. In place of "free ships, free goods," which had been written into all of America's earlier treaties—with France, the Netherlands, Prussia, and Sweden—the treaty accepted the right of the British to seize enemy goods from neutral ships; acquiesced in the operation, though not the principle, of the Rule of 1756, which specified that trade not open in peacetime could not be opened in wartime, "a concession which was to strengthen tremendously the prestige of that arbitrary dictum";[11] and consented to the extension of the contraband list to include foodstuffs under certain conditions. At the same time, Jay failed in his efforts to protect American seamen from impressment.[12]

Other provisions specified that the fur trade should be open to traders from Canada and the United States on both sides of the boundary, except within the limits of the Hudson's Bay Company; that the United States should not export molasses, sugar, coffee, cotton, or other West Indian products, even though some of these were grown in the United States; that there should be no sequestration or confiscation of property in case of war between the countries; that foreign privateers were not to be fitted out in ports of either party, nor were prizes taken by such privateers to be brought in and sold; warships and privateers of either party were to be admitted into the ports of the other, but neither party should receive privateers or prizes of the other's enemy, although nothing in the treaty was to contravene existing treaties, such as the Franco-American alliance. Finally, the United States was barred from raising tariff or tonnage duties on British goods and vessels, although Great Britain could raise duties on American ships equal to those levied on British vessels in American ports. Thus, Great Britain secured during the life of the treaty a guarantee against discriminatory tariff and tonnage duties such as those recommended in Jefferson's commercial report of 1793 and Madison's resolutions of 1794.[13]

Although the Federalists in the Senate were displeased with parts of the treaty, the Senate ratified it with the bare majority required—20 to 10—after rejecting the restrictive article on West Indian trade. With the veil of secrecy lifted, a storm of protest erupted against the treaty. "The first impression," Madison wrote, "was universally and simultaneously against it."[14] When it reached Williamsburg, Bishop James Madison, president of the College of

---

11. Bemis, p. 261.
12. *Ibid.*, pp. 354-60.
13. For the provisions of the treaty, see *ibid.*, pp. 346-73.
14. JM to James Monroe, Dec. 20, 1795, in *PJM*, XVI, p. 168.

William and Mary, wrote in alarm to his cousin: "A vast Feild is now opened to you, and I believe all America looks up to yourself and our Friend Mr Jefferson" to stop the treaty in its tracks.[15]

Madison needed no urging. He thought the treaty "a ruinous bargain" and denounced Jay for granting Great Britain the most-favored-nation status without gaining anything in return. "It seems impossible to screen him from the most illiberal suspicions," he told a New Yorker, "without referring his conduct to the blindest partiality to the British Nation and Govt. and the most vindictive sensations towards the French Republic. Indeed the Treaty from one end to the other must be regarded as a demonstration that the Party to which the Envoy belongs . . . is a British party, systematically aiming at an exclusive connection with the British Governt. and ready to sacrifice to that object as well the dearest interests of our Commerce, as the most sacred dictates of national honor."[16] When Robert R. Livingston urged him to write to Washington opposing the treaty, he refused, but he endorsed Livingston's warning to the president that the treaty would bring on "an immediate rupture with France" that would be "a signal for a civil war at home."[17]

Although Madison later cited the spontaneous petitions that "swarmed from all quarters" urging Washington not to sign the treaty—addresses that he said had been sent "without a possibility of preconcert, or party influence"[18] —he made sure that they continued as part of the Republican campaign against the treaty. In a circular letter to party leaders throughout the country, he condemned the treaty for its acceptance of "the arbitrary maxims" of Great Britain that were hostile to neutral nations in time of war. Such a policy aligned the United States "against the fundamental rights of nations and duties of humanity." Moreover, it made America party to "the scheme of distressing a nation in friendship with this Country, and whose relations to it, as well as the struggles for freedom in which they are engaged, give them a title to every good office not strictly forbidden by the duties of neutrality."

He was highly critical of the article that gave Britain the most-favored-nation status without requiring the withdrawal of unfavorable navigation regulations. "What can be more absurd than to talk of the advantage of securing the *privileges* of sending raw materials to a manufacturing nation, and buying merchandizes which are hawked over the four quarters of the globe for customers?"[19]

---

15. Bishop James Madison to JM, July 25, 1795, *ibid.*, p. 41.

16. JM to Robert R. Livingston, Aug. 10, 1795, *ibid.*, p. 47. William Lord Grenville thought that Jay's treaty created "a permanent union" between Great Britain and the United States; see William Lord Grenville to George Hammond, Nov. 20, 1794, cited in Mary K. Bonsteel Tachau, "George Washington and the Reputation of Edmund Randolph," *JAH* 73 (1986): 24.

17. For Robert R. Livingston to George Washington, Aug. 10, 1795, see John Alexander Carroll and Mary Wells Ashworth, *George Washington: First in Peace* (New York, 1957), p. 268; Brant, III, pp. 425-26; and Ketcham, p. 357.

18. JM to James Monroe, Dec. 20, 1795, in *PJM,* XVI, p. 168.

19. Ketcham, pp. 357-58.

Madison reported to Jefferson that town meetings in Portsmouth, Boston, and Philadelphia had sent unanimous remonstrances to the president. In Richmond, only two individuals "openly espoused the Treaty. . . . In short from all quarters the public voice seems to proclaim the same detestation; except from Alexandria and its neighbourhood where there is some division."[20] In New York, he continued, a Republican rally had silenced Alexander Hamilton with boos and rocks before taking a unanimous vote against the treaty.[21] At another meeting in New York, the militia raised a toast in jest to Jay and Federalist senator Rufus King: "May the cage constructed to coop up the American eagle prove a trap for none but Jays and Kingbirds."[22]

When Hamilton turned from the rostrum to the newspapers, arguing that "the too probable result of a refusal to ratify is war," Jefferson begged Madison to take on his former cabinet colleague: "For god's sake take up your pen, and give [him] a fundamental reply."[23] Jefferson was convinced that "Hamilton is really a colossus to the antirepublican party. Without numbers, he is a host within himself. They have got themselves into a defile, where they might be finished; but too much security on the Republican part, will give time to his talents and indefatigableness to extricate them. We have had only midling performances to oppose to him. In truth, when he comes forward, there is nobody but yourself who can meet him. His adversaries having begun the attack, he has the advantage of answering them, and remains unanswered himself. A solid reply," Jefferson urged, "might yet completely demolish what was too feebly attacked, and has gathered strength from the weakness of the attack."[24]

But Madison demurred, mistakenly thinking that Hamilton needed no reply: "If I mistake not [he] will be betrayed by his anglomany into arguments as vicious and vulnerable as the Treaty itself."[25] Jefferson knew better, predicting that Hamilton would "write an Encyclopedia" in his effort to extricate the Federalists.[26] Jay, with the support of Hamilton and the Federalists, had perpetrated "the boldest act they ever ventured on to undermine the constitution." The treaty was a partisan party measure, Jefferson told Madison: "A bolder party-stroke was never struck. For it certainly is an attempt of a party which finds they have lost their majority in one branch of the legislature"—the

---

20. JM to TJ, Aug. 6, 1795, below.

21. See John C. Miller, *Alexander Hamilton: Portrait in Paradox* (New York, 1959), pp. 424-25.

22. Alfred F. Young, *The Democratic Republicans of New York: The Origins, 1763-1797* (Chapel Hill, 1967), p. 447.

23. For Hamilton's "Camillus" essays, see Syrett, XVIII-XX, *passim;* the quotation is from the first article published on July 22, 1795, *ibid.,* XVIII, pp. 479-89.

24. TJ to JM, Sept. 21, 1795, below.

25. JM to Tench Coxe or A. J. Dallas, Aug. 23, 1795, quoted in Syrett, XVIII, p. 478.

26. TJ to Tench Coxe, Sept. 10, 1795, *ibid.* Hamilton wrote twenty-eight essays and edited ten more written by Senator Rufus King. They have been compared favorably to Hamilton's essays in *The Federalist* by Broadus Mitchell in his *Alexander Hamilton,* 2 vols. (New York, 1962), II, p. 344.

House of Representatives, where Madison's resolutions had been sidetracked for the negotiations—"to make a law by the aid of the other branch, and of the executive, under color of a treaty, which shall bind up the hands of the adverse branch from ever restraining the commerce of their patron-nation."[27]

Late in the summer, Virginia Republicans organized meetings to oppose the treaty in Caroline and Amelia counties and in the cities of Petersburg and Richmond.[28] Jefferson wrote of a protest meeting planned in Albemarle County[29] and was doubly pleased that "Richmond has decided against the treaty."[30] Madison noted that "Mr. Wythe presided at the Richmond Meeting, a circumstance which will not be without its weight, especially as he presided at the former Meeting in support of the Proclamation" of Neutrality.[31]

Throughout most of the summer, Washington withheld his signature from the treaty. When reports reached Philadelphia that British ships had renewed their seizure of American vessels carrying foodstuffs to France, he accepted the advice of Secretary of State Edmund Randolph not to sign until the British revoked their newest order-in-council. But in a bizarre turn of events, Randolph's colleagues in the cabinet, Oliver Wolcott and Timothy Pickering, who had succeeded Hamilton and Knox, forced the ouster of the secretary of state by presenting the president with an intercepted message from the French minister to the United States reporting that Randolph had made "precious confessions," which seemed to implicate him in soliciting a bribe from the French as well as imply that he had been disloyal to Washington in his handling of the Whiskey Rebellion. Acting on this information, Washington decided to sign the treaty that Randolph had suggested that he not sign, then confronted Randolph in a cabinet meeting and forced his resignation.[32]

After Washington signed the treaty, there was a brief lull in the protest meetings, one being canceled in Goochland County in September.[33] During the calm, Madison visited Jefferson at Monticello to consult on a new Republi-

27. TJ to JM, Sept. 21, 1795, below.

28. Harry Ammon, "The Formation of the Republican Party in Virginia, 1789–1796," *J. So. Hist.* 19 (1953): 306.

29. TJ to Thomas Mann Randolph, Aug. 11, 1795, cited in Malone, III, p. 250.

30. TJ to JM, Aug. 3, 1795, below.

31. JM to TJ, Aug. 6, 1795, below.

32. The French dispatch was intercepted by the British navy, then transmitted by Lord Grenville to George Hammond the day after he and Jay signed the treaty that they had just negotiated. Hammond turned it over to Oliver Wolcott and Timothy Pickering, who got the unsuspecting Edmund Randolph to request President Washington's immediate return from Mt. Vernon. For a full account of the mistranslation of the phrase "précieuses confessions" as "precious confessions" instead of "valuable disclosures," see Bonsteel Tachau, 15–34; Irving Brant, "Edmund Randolph, Not Guilty," *WMQ* 7 (1950): 179–98; Carroll and Ashworth, pp. 265–98, 315–36, 635–36; and Combs, pp. 166–69, 193–96.

33. Ammon, 307.

can strategy.³⁴ Although they discussed Randolph's departure from the cabinet and reviewed their historical and archival interests—Madison agreed to loan Jefferson his "Notes on the Debates at the Constitutional Convention"³⁵—they concentrated their attention on plans for a renewed campaign against the treaty in the Virginia legislature in November and in Congress in December.³⁶ The action in the state legislature would lay the groundwork for the contest in Congress.

Madison took the lead in both, first drafting an antitreaty petition for the General Assembly of Virginia, which was published in late October,³⁷ then stopping on November 6 through 8 in Fredericksburg at the invitation of Joseph Jones, a delegate to the Virginia legislature, to discuss the propriety of the General Assembly "declaring their opinion generally of the late Treaty[,] confining themselves to truly exceptionable parts—with equal propriety," Jones wrote in his invitation to Madison, "may they propose an amendment in the constitution to prevent a similar inconvenience in future."³⁸

Thomas Mann Randolph, Jefferson's son-in-law and a member of the assembly, served as a relay man, keeping Madison informed in Philadelphia and Jefferson posted at Monticello. Shortly after the legislature met, the Republicans launched their attack on the treaty by introducing resolutions commending Senators Stevens T. Mason and Henry Tazewell for voting against ratification of the Jay Treaty but praising President Washington's integrity and patriotism, thus acquitting him, according to Randolph, of "all evil intention, but at the same time silently censuring his error."³⁹

Despite strong arguments by John Marshall supporting the constitutionality of a treaty ratified by the Senate and signed by the president, the Republicans in the state legislature carried the test vote on their commendation of the Virginia senators by a margin of 100 to 50. Marshall had admitted the right of the House of Representatives to refuse appropriations to implement the treaty after ratification, and Jefferson was both surprised and pleased that his distant

---

34. JM to TJ, Oct. 18, 1795, below.

35. For references to Edmund Randolph, see JM to TJ, Nov. 8, 1795, below, Dec. 6, 1795, below, and Dec. 27, 1795, below; TJ to JM, Nov. 26, 1795, below. For TJ's interest in preserving historical documents, see Malone, III, pp. 253-54. For JM's loan of his "Notes on the Debates," see JM to TJ, Nov. 8, 1795, below, and *PJM,* X, p. 7.

36. Malone, III, pp. 251-53, says TJ "had no personal share" in the Virginia campaign against the treaty, but see TJ to JM, Nov. 26, 1795, below, and Dec. 3, 1795, below, for his interest in "the first movements of your campaign."

37. See *PJM,* XVI, pp. 62-77.

38. Joseph Jones to JM, Oct. 29, 1795, in *Proceedings* (Massachusetts Historical Society) 25 (1901-2): 150-51. JM visited on Nov. 7, 1795; see JM to TJ, Nov. 8, 1795, below.

39. Thomas Mann Randolph to TJ, Nov. 22, 1795, enclosed in TJ to JM, Nov. 26, 1795, below. The fullest discussion of the Virginia campaign is in Stephen G. Kurtz, *The Presidency of John Adams: The Collapse of Federalism, 1795-1800* (Philadelphia, 1957), pp. 20-30; Thomas J. Farnham, "The Virginia Amendments of 1795: An Episode in the Opposition to Jay's Treaty," *VMHB* 75 (1967): 75-88; and Norman K. Risjord, *Chesapeake Politics, 1781-1800* (New York, 1978), pp. 457-60.

cousin, now serving in the legislature as a Federalist, had conceded "that the whole commercial part of the treaty (and he might have added the whole unconstitutional part of it) rests in the power of the H[ouse] of R[epresentatives]." Jefferson agreed that this "is certainly the true doctrine; and as the articles which stipulate what requires the consent of the three branches of the legislature [Jefferson meant the House, Senate, and president], must be referred to the H[ouse] of R[epresentatives] for their concurrence, so they, being free agents, may approve or reject them, either by a vote declaring that, or by refusing to pass acts." He preferred an explicit rejection as "the most safe and honorable."[40]

On the whole, Jefferson was glad that Marshall, who "has been hitherto able to do more mischief, acting under the mask of republicanism than he will be able to do after throwing it plainly off," had gone into the state legislature. Although Jefferson was worried that Marshall might be able "to embarras the Republican party in the assembly a good deal," Jefferson was sure that Marshall would no longer be able to hide his "profound hypocrisy" behind his "lax lounging manners," which had won him popularity in Richmond and elsewhere. "The plenitude of his English principles," Jefferson predicted, would convince "thinking men in our country" that instead of being a Republican, he was a full-fledged Federalist, a member of "the Alexandrian party and the bigots and passive obedience men of the whole state who have got themselves into the legislature."[41]

After carrying the resolutions praising Senators Tazewell and Mason, the Republican majority in the General Assembly quickly introduced a series of constitutional amendments to be submitted to the other state legislatures as well as Congress. The first sketched the basis for Madison's later opposition in Congress, declaring that no treaty containing provisions within the legislative purview of Congress, such as the control of commerce, could become law until approved by the House of Representatives. In addition, three other amendments slapped at the Senate and John Jay, proposing the reduction of Senate terms from six to three years, specifying that "no person holding the office of a Judge under the United States shall be capable of holding at the same time any other office or appointment whatever," and demanding that impeachment cases be handled in a special tribunal rather than in the Senate.[42] Although Fisher Ames denounced Virginia's amendments as revolutionary, Madison praised the *"firm example"* taken by the Old Dominion.[43]

The Madisons returned to Philadelphia in November, and Jefferson promptly predicted that "the popular branch" of Congress would disapprove

40. TJ to JM, Nov. 26, 1795, below.
41. *Ibid.*
42. Farnham, 84–85.
43. Fisher Ames to Thomas Dwight, Feb. 11, 1796, in Fisher Ames, *Works of Fisher Ames,* ed. Seth Ames, 2 vols. (Boston, 1854), I, p. 186; JM to James Monroe, Dec. 20, 1795, in *PJM,* XVI, p. 170 (JM's italicized words were written in code).

of Jay's treaty "and thus rid us of this infamous act, which is really nothing more than a treaty of alliance between England and the Anglomen of this country against the legislature and people of the United States."[44] And he told Madison that he waited impatiently for a letter from him that would bring news of "the first movements of your campaign, which will be most interesting"—a gross understatement, if ever there was one.[45]

When Congress convened in December 1795, Washington sent a conciliatory message announcing that since notice of the official exchange of ratifications had not yet been received from Great Britain, he would defer a request for legislation to fund the arbitration commissions necessary to implement it.[46] The Senate sent a prompt response to the message, but the House reply was delayed by a disagreement in its committee, which consisted of Madison and two Federalists. Theodore Sedgwick of Massachusetts and Samuel Sitgreaves of Pennsylvania "are strongly for the Treaty," Madison informed his friend, "and wish to favor it, at the same time that they are afraid to hazard direct expressions to that effect." Instead, they wanted to identify the president with the treaty, stress the nation's present prosperity, and warn against war and confusion. To that end, they pushed for a clause, which Madison thought would never be swallowed by the House, affirming that confidence in the president was undiminished, a view "which will be denied by many," Madison lamented, "who sincerely wish it to be the case."[47]

With neither the treaty nor a request for funding before Congress, Madison found the situation "truly perplexing. It is clear," he told Jefferson, "that a majority if brought to the merits of the Treaty are agst. it." But an application to the president would bring him personally into the question, and his popularity might force some Republicans to desert the campaign against the treaty, leaving them in a minority.[48] "Besides the ordinary difficulty of preventing scisms," he confessed, "there is a real obscurity in the constitutional part of the question, and a diversity of sincere opinions about it, which the other side will make the most of it."[49]

As January and February dragged by without official word from Great Britain, tension in Congress mounted to such a height that the House, by a vote of 50 to 38, refused to adjourn for half an hour "to pay the compliment of the day" to the president on his birthday, breaking an annual tradition and revealing the polarization of parties in the House.[50] While Congress marked

44. TJ to Edward Rutledge, Nov. 30, 1795, in Ford, VII, p. 40.
45. TJ to JM, Dec. 3, 1795, below.
46. The British government had to act on the Senate's amendment, which rejected Article 12 on West Indian trade.
47. JM to TJ, Dec. 13, 1795, below.
48. JM to TJ, Dec. 27, 1795, below.
49. JM to TJ, Dec. 13, 1795, below.
50. JM to TJ, Feb. 29, 1796, below.

time, the president rounded out his new cabinet with what Hamilton termed second-rate Federalist appointments "with barely decent qualifications," Oliver Wolcott moving up to secretary of the treasury and Timothy Pickering to secretary of state. "The offices are once more filled," Vice President John Adams observed critically, "but how differently than when Jefferson, Hamilton, Jay, etc. were here!"[51] Madison agreed with his old foe. "Through what official interstice," he asked Jefferson, "can a ray of republican truths now penetrate to the P[resident]?"[52]

Reports of continuing French victories and of bread shortages in Great Britain led Madison to think again of economic coercion as a diplomatic weapon:

In this attitude of things What a noble stroke would be an embargo? It would probably do as much good as harm at home; and would force peace, on the rest of the World, and perhaps liberty along with it. But you know the spell within the Govt., as well as the obstacles to such a measure in the clamors that would be raised among the Merchts. the Millers, and farmers, to say nothing of the Tories etc. who would make more noise than any of them.[53]

Instead of foreign policy, Congress turned to financial matters, establishing a committee of ways and means to investigate revenue needs. Both before and after the Whiskey Rebellion, the excise system had been unproductive "and new excises that will be popular even in the Eastern States do not occur," Madison informed Jefferson. "On the other hand direct taxes, have been so blackened in order to recommend the fiscal policy of indirect ones, and to inspire hatred, and jealousies in the Eastern against the Southern States, and particularly Virginia, that it is doubtful whether the measure, now that it is become necessary, will be borne. . . . Who could have supposed that Hamilton could have gone off in the triumph he assumed, with such a condition of the finances behind him?"[54]

Finally, on March 1, 1796, Washington sent the treaty to Congress, declaring it to be the law of the land but again deferring a request for funds to implement it.[55] An eager freshman Republican congressman, Edward Livingston of New York, then jumped the gun on the following day, requesting the president to transmit to the House copies of the instructions to Jay as well as the correspondence and other documents concerning the treaty. Madison, who had not been consulted, thought the motion too precipitate, writing Jefferson that "the policy of hazarding it is so questionable that he will probably let it sleep or withdraw it. . . . The state of the business as it now presents

51. James T. Flexner, *Washington: The Indispensable Man* (Boston, 1974), pp. 343-44.
52. JM to TJ, Feb. 7, 1796, below.
53. *Ibid.*
54. JM to TJ, Jan. 31, 1796, below.
55. The best accounts of the ratification controversy and the domestic repercussions are in Combs, pp. 171-88, and Cunningham, pp. 77-85.

itself, with the uncertainty of the particular way of thinking in several quarters of the House, make it truly difficult to decide on the course most acceptable to the body of anti-treaty members."[56]

But when the debates began "rather abruptly," Madison joined Albert Gallatin—he called the Pennsylvanian "a real Treasure"—in pressing the Republican views. "The point in debate," he wrote Jefferson, "is the Constitutional right of Congs. in relation to Treaties. There seems at present strong reason to conclude, that a majority will be firm in the doctrine that the House has a Constl. right to refuse to pass laws for executing a Treaty, and that the Treaty power is limited by the enumerated powers" delegated to Congress.[57] The issue boiled down to this: Must members of the House pass money bills automatically to implement a treaty without consulting their own conscience or judgment?

Jefferson could hardly suppress his curiosity. "On the precedent now to be set will depend the future construction of our constitution," he told Monroe in France, "and whether the powers of legislation shall be transferred from the P[resident] Senate and H[ouse] of R[epresentatives] to the P[resident] Senate and Piarningo or any other Indian, Algerine or other chief" negotiating a treaty. "All America is a tip-toe to see what the H[ouse] of Representatives will decide on it."[58] He followed the newspaper accounts of the debates avidly and was so enchanted by Gallatin's speech that he thought it "worthy of being printed at the end of the Federalist, as the only rational commentary on the part of the constitution to which it relates." Gallatin's arguments, Jefferson said, were far more acceptable than those of the Federalists, who contended that the House had no part constitutionally in accepting or rejecting treaties, even though the Constitution required appropriations for implementation to originate in the House. Such a doctrine would "annihilate the whole of the powers given by the constitution" to the popularly elected House. "According to the rule established by usage and common sense of construing one part of the instrument by another, the objects on which the P[resident] and S[enate] may exclusively act by treaty are much reduced, but the field on which they may act, with the sanction of the legislature, is large enough: and I see no harm in rendering their sanction necessary." Jefferson got so carried away that he went one step further. Despite his extensive experience as a negotiator of treaties, he professed that he could see little harm "in annihilating the whole treaty making power, except as to making peace."

Then he leveled his heaviest blast at the treaty. "If you decide in favor of your right to refuse cooperation in any case of treaty," he told Madison, "I should wonder on what occasion it is to be used, if not on one where the rights, the interest, the honor and faith of our nation are so grossly sacrificed,

56. JM to TJ, Mar. 6, 1796, below.
57. JM to TJ, Jan. 31, 1796, below, and Mar. 13, 1796, below.
58. TJ to James Monroe, Mar. 21, 1796, in Ford, VII, p. 67.

where a faction has entered into conspiracy with the enemies of their country to chain down the legislature at the feet of both; where the whole mass of your constituents have condemned this work in the most unequivocal manner, and are looking to you as their last hope to save them from the effects of the avarice and corruption of the first agent, the revolutionary machinations of others, and the incomprehensible acquiescence of the only honest man who has assented to it." As for President Washington, Jefferson hoped that "his honesty and his political errors may not furnish a second occasion to exclaim 'curse on his virtues, they've undone his country.'"[59]

After two weeks of debate, Madison and Gallatin persuaded the House to call on the president for the treaty papers by a vote of 62 to 37.[60] But Washington bluntly refused to submit the documents, denying that the House had a right to see them and citing the still-secret proceedings of the Constitutional Convention to buttress his opinion. Madison was doubly stunned. "The absolute refusal," he told Jefferson, "was as unexpected, as the tone and tenor of the message, are improper and indelicate." He linked the president's appeal to the Constitutional Convention to Hamilton's "Camillus" articles and concluded that "the message came from N. Y. where it was seen that an experiment was to be made at the hazard of the P[resident] to save the faction agst. the Reps. of the people."[61] Even "more extraordinary a great deal than the refusal," Madison added, were the reasons assigned for it, especially Washington's use of the secret journal of the convention, which was "to be kept sacred untill called for by some competent authority. How can this be reconciled," he asked Jefferson, "with the use he has made of it?"[62]

For the first time since the new government had been formed, the Republican members of the House met in caucus to decide on how to deal with the president's refusal to submit to the House the papers he had earlier submitted to the Senate.[63] "I think," Madison told Jefferson, "there will be sufficient firmness to face it with resolutions declaring the Const:l. powers of the House as to Treaties, and that in applying for papers, they are not obliged to state their reasons to the Executive. In order to preserve this firmness however, it is necessary to avoid as much as possible an overt rencontre with the Executive."[64] Madison then drafted two resolutions that denied that the House was claiming any agency in making treaties; instead, it was asserting its right "to judge of the expediency of Treaties stipulating on legislative subjects, and

---

59. TJ to JM, Mar. 27, 1796, below. The first occasion had been Washington's denunciation of the Democratic societies.

60. Brant, III, pp. 434–35, and Combs, pp. 175–76.

61. President Washington had requested Alexander Hamilton's views, but they arrived after the president had sent his message to the House; see Miller, p. 433, and Brant, III, p. 436.

62. JM to TJ, Apr. 4, 1796, and Apr. 11, 1796, below. TJ had borrowed JM's notes on the convention, and JM asked him to check them on this point. For TJ's response of Apr. 17, 1796, see below.

63. Cunningham, p. 82.

64. JM to TJ, Apr. 4, 1796, below.

declaring that it was not requisite in a call for papers to express the use to be made of them."[65] After Thomas Blount of North Carolina introduced these resolutions for Madison, the latter, expecting "a long and obstinate discussion," led off the debate with a lengthy speech, "a free, but respectful review of the fallacy" of Washington's reasoning. In a surprise move, the Federalists called for the question "without a word of argument on the subject. The two resolutions were carried by 57 agst. 35."[66]

With a majority of 63 to 37,[67] the Republicans moved to the final assault on the treaty, urging that appropriations to implement it be refused and proposing that a new treaty be negotiated. "According to present calculation," Madison predicted, "this proposition will be carried by *nearly* the same majority as prevailed in the vote asserting the Rights of the House on the subject of Treaties."[68]

To combat this majority, Hamilton launched a counterattack, appealing to merchants, bankers, and other businessmen to back Jay's treaty and Washington's constitutional arguments. Public rallies produced a rising tide of supportive petitions, and the pressure swayed some Republican congressmen who feared that rejection of the treaty would block British cession of the western posts.[69] Under these circumstances, Madison reported, "the majority has melted, by changes and absence, to 8 or 9 votes. Whether these will continue firm is more than I can decide." He suspected that the Federalists would spin out the debates "for the purpose of calling in the mercantile interference in [its] behalf," citing petitioning campaigns in Philadelphia, New York, Boston, and Baltimore. "The hope of endimnification for past losses, and the fears for their floating speculations [ships and cargoes], which have been arranged on the idea that the Treaty would go into effect, bear down with that class all attention to the general and permanent good of the Country, and perhaps their own real and comprehe[n]sive interest."[70]

Not only were the cities rallying to the treaty. "The Country also is under an operation for obtaining petitions for the Treaty," Madison wrote. Thomas Pinckney had just negotiated a favorable treaty with Spain after that country had withdrawn from the European war as an ally of Great Britain. So fearful was Spain of a rapprochement between the United States and Great Britain as a consequence of Jay's treaty that it had granted free navigation of the Mississippi to Americans. The Federalists argued that the British and Spanish treaties were based on the same constitutional principles, convincing many westerners that the rejection of one meant the rejection of both. "The Western Coun-

---

65. JM to TJ, Apr. 11, 1796, below.
66. *Ibid.*
67. Six latecomers would have joined the 57 voting for the resolutions, and 2 would have joined those voting against; see *ibid.*
68. JM to TJ, Apr. 18, 1796, below.
69. John C. Miller, *The Federalist Era: 1789–1801* (New York, 1960), pp. 174–76.
70. JM to TJ, Apr. 18, 1796, below, and Apr. 23, 1796, below.

ties," Madison observed, "have yielded a number" of petitions in favor of Jay's treaty, "being dextrously alarmed for the Spanish Treaty as involved in the fate of the British."[71] Although the Republican-dominated House treated the treaties separately,[72] the Federalist majority in the Senate, in a move to inflexibly adhere for all or none, talked of tying up the Spanish treaty until the House voted money to implement Jay's treaty.[73]

Economic pressure and the fear of war became the two most effective weapons used by the Federalists in the final stages of combating Madison's campaign against Jay's treaty. "Among other extraordinary manoeuvres," Madison moaned to Jefferson, "the Insurance Companies here [in Philadelphia] and in New Y. stopt business, in order to reduce prices and alarm the public. The Banks," he added, "have been powerfully felt in the progress of the petitions in the Cities for the Treaty. Scarce a mercht. or Trader but what depends on discounts, and at this moment there is a general pinch for money. Under such circumstances, a Bank Director soliciting subscriptions is like a Highwayman with a pistol demanding the purse."[74] In short, he reiterated a week later, "the Banks, the British Merchts. the insurance Comps. were at work in influencing individuals, beating down the prices of produce, and sounding the tocksin of foreign war, and domestic convulsions."[75]

Under such political pressure, the Republican majority slowly disappeared, and Vice President Adams thought that "Mr. Madison looks worried to death. Pale, withered, haggard."[76] When the question of accepting Jay's treaty finally came before the Committee of the Whole, the vote resulted in a 49-to-49 tie, and the chairman, Frederick Muhlenberg, despite being a longtime opponent of the treaty, "decided in the affirmative, saying that in the House it would be subject to modification which he wished." With their majority now doubtful, the Republicans attempted to settle merely for a preamble describing the treaty as objectionable but, under the circumstances, acceptable, if measures were taken for stopping British spoliations and impressments. This move was designed, Madison explained, to make "the pill a bitter one to the Treaty party, as well as less poisonous to the public interest." But party discipline had wilted among the Republicans, and "a few wrongheads . . . thought fit to separate, whereby the motion was lost by one vote. The main question was then carried in favr. of the Treaty by 51 agst. 48."[77]

Jay's treaty was the keystone in the Hamiltonian system of political economy, capping the Federalist program that Madison and Jefferson had opposed

71. JM to TJ, Apr. 18, 1796, below.

72. *Ibid.*

73. JM to TJ, Apr. 23, 1796, below; Miller, *Hamilton,* p. 432; and Combs, p. 180.

74. JM to TJ, Apr. 23, 1796, below.

75. JM to TJ, May 1, 1796, below.

76. John Adams to Abigail Adams, Apr. 28, 1796, cited in Combs, p. 185.

77. JM to TJ, May 1, 1796, below. For a thorough roll-call analysis of congressional voting on the Jay Treaty debate, see Rudolph M. Bell, *Party and Faction in American Politics: The House of Representatives, 1789–1801* (Westport, Conn., 1973), pp. 54–58, 146–49.

from the beginning. Madison was disgusted that the Republican majority had melted away at the critical moment. "The progress of this business throughout has to me been the most worrying and vexatious that I ever encountered," he complained, "and the more so as the causes lay in the unsteadiness, the follies, the perverseness, and the defections among our friends, more than in the strength or dexterity, or malice of our opponents." But he conceded that in the petitioning campaign, the Federalists had won, and he concluded that "an appeal to the people on any pending measure, can never be more than an appeal to those in the neighborhood of the Govt. and to the Banks, the Merchts. and the dependents and expectants of the Govt. at a distance."[78]

With the contest over, Madison's weekly bulletins to Jefferson slowed, even though the congressional session dragged on for another month. "We have had a calm ever since the decision on the Treaty," he informed his friend. The interlude gave him time to analyze the shattering Republican defeat. The cry of war and the long shadow of President Washington's popularity were the ultimate causes. "The people have been every where made to believe that the object of the H. of Reps. in resisting the Treaty was—*War;* and have thence listened to the summons 'to follow where Washington leads.'"[79] In New England especially, the people "have been ready to rise in mass agst. the H. of Reps. Such have been the exertions and influence of Aristocracy, Anglicism, and mercantilism in that quarter, that Republicanism is perfectly overwhelmed, even in the Town of Boston."[80]

Two weeks later, while Congress wrapped up "the remnant of business before them," Madison gave a measured evaluation of the campaign against Jay's treaty, as he looked with foreboding towards the elections of 1796. "A crisis which ought to have been so managed as to fortify the Republican cause, has left it in a very crippled condition; from which its recovery will be the more difficult as the elections in N. Y. Massachussets and other States, where the prospects were favorable, have taken a wrong turn under the impressions of the moment. Nothing but auspicious contingencies abroad or at home, can regain the lost ground."[81]

Frustrated and disillusioned after losing the bitter battle against the Jay Treaty, Madison began to think about retiring from politics. After wrestling with his conscience throughout the summer and fall, he finally announced his decision in December 1796. "Mr. Madison is to retire," President-elect John Adams informed his wife Abigail early in the new year. "It seems the Mode of becoming great is to retire. Madison I suppose after a Retirement of a few years is to become President or V. P. It is marvellous how political Plants grow in the shade."[82]

78. JM to TJ, May 1, 1796, below.
79. JM to TJ, May 9, 1796, below.
80. *Ibid.*
81. JM to TJ, May 22, 1796, below.
82. John Adams to Abigail Adams, Jan. 14, 1797, quoted in *PJM,* XVII, p. xix.

─────────────── THE LETTERS ───────────────

Jefferson to Madison

[Monticello] Aug. 3, 1795

TH: J. TO J. M.

You will percieve by the inclosed that Hamilton has taken up his pen in support of the treaty. (Return it to me.) He spoke on it's behalf in the meeting at New York, and his party carried a decision in favor of it by a small majority. But the Livingstonians appealed to stones and clubs and beat him and his party off the ground.[1] This from a gentleman just from Philadelphia. Adieu.

P. S. Richmond has decided against the treaty. It is said that not even Carrington undertakes to defend it.

Madison to Jefferson

[Orange] Aug. 6, 1795

DEAR SIR

I return the paper covered by your favor of the third, which was handed me by a gentleman who picked it up in Charlottesville. I find that the meeting in N. York was not exactly as represented to you. The Republicans were never outnumbered; and the vote of a very full meeting was finally unanimous in remonstrating agst. the Treaty. The Chamber of Commerce has had a separate meeting and has passed some counteracting Resolutions.[2] In Portsmouth, Boston and Philada. *unanimous* Remonstrances have also issued from Town Meetings and been sent by express to the P[resident]. The silence of the disaffected minorities is easily explained. I understand that Mr. Wythe presided at the Richmond Meeting, a circumstance which will not be without its weight; especially as he presided at the former Meeting in support of the Proclamation. A gentleman who was present says he was told two individuals only in the City, (Hopkins and one of the Marshalls) openly espoused the Treaty. Even Andrews joins in the general denunciation of it. I have a letter from the Bishop which is a Philippic on the subject.[3] In short from all quarters the public voice seems to proclaim the same detestation; except from Alexandria and its neighbourhood where there is some division. Docr. Stuart and the Lees take the

---

1. The fullest discussion of Hamilton's contest with the Republican clan of Livingstons is in Young, pp. 449–54. For Hamilton's "Camillus" essays, see Syrett, XVIII, pp. 475 ff.
2. See Young, pp. 454–55.
3. For Bishop James Madison's letter of July 25, 1795, see *PJM*, XVI, pp. 40–41.

side of the Treaty. I have a letter from Chancellor Livingston which tells me he has taken the liberty of writing a free letter to the P. with a view to impress on him the public sentiment and the consequences of ratifying an act so hostile to the opinions and interests of the people, and to the good understanding with France.[4] The inclosed papers contain some remarks on the Treaty from a hand which will claim attention. They are borrowed, and you may therefore return them by Mr. Jones or any other convenient opportunity. Yrs. affecly.

Js. M. Jr.

Jefferson to Madison

Monticello Sept. 21, 1795

TH: J. TO J. M.

I recieved about three weeks ago a box containing 6. doz. volumes of 283. pages 12mo. with a letter from Lambert, Beckley's clerk, that they came from Mr. Beckley and were to be divided between yourself, J. Walker, and myself. I have sent 2 doz. to J. Walker, and shall be glad of a conveyance for yours. In the mean time I send you by post the title page, table of contents, and one of the pieces, Curtius, lest it should not have come to you otherwise. It is evidently written by Hamilton,[5] giving a first and general view of the subject that the public mind might be kept a little in check till he could resume the subject more at large, from the beginning, under his second signature of Camillus. The piece called 'the Features of the treaty' I do not send because you have seen it in the newspapers. It is said to be written by Coxe, but I should rather suspect by Beckley. The antidote is certainly not strong enough for the poison of Curtius. If I had not been informed the present came from Beckly, I should have suspected it from Jay or Hamilton. I gave a copy or two by way of experiment to honest sound hearted men of common understanding, and they were not able to parry the sophistry of Curtius. I have ceased therefore to give them. Hamilton is really a colossus to the antirepublican party. Without numbers, he is an host within himself. They have got themselves into a defile, where they might be finished; but too much security on the Republican part, will give time to his talents and indefatigableness to extricate them. We have had only midling performances to oppose to him. In truth, when he comes forward, there is nobody but yourself who can meet him. His adversaries having begun the attack, he has the advantage of answering them, and remains unanswered himself. A solid reply might yet completely demolish what was too feebly attacked, and has gathered strength from the weakness of the attack.

4. For Robert R. Livingston's letter to George Washington, July 8, 1795, see George Dangerfield, *Chancellor Robert R. Livingston of New York, 1746–1813* (New York, 1960), pp. 271, 494.
5. The letters of "Curtius" were written by Noah Webster and James Kent; see Young, p. 455.

The merchants were certainly (except those of them who are English) as openmouthed at first against the treaty as any. But the general expression of indignation has alarmed them for the strength of the government. They have feared the shock would be too great, and have chosen to tack about and support both treaty and government, rather than risk the government: thus it is that Hamilton, Jay etc. in the boldest act they ever ventured on to undermine the constitution[6] have the address to screen themselves and direct the hue and cry against those who wished to drag them into light. A bolder party-stroke was never struck. For it certainly is an attempt of a party which finds they have lost their majority in one branch of the legislature to make a law by the aid of the other branch, and of the executive, under color of a treaty, which shall bind up the hands of the adverse branch from ever restraining the commerce of their patron-nation. There appears a pause at present in the public sentiment, which may be followed by a revulsion. This is the effect of the desertion of the merchants, of the President's chiding answer to Boston and Richmond, of the writings of Curtius and Camillus, and of the quietism into which the people naturally fall, after first sensations are over. For god's sake take up your pen, and give a fundamental reply to Curtius and Camillus.

Mr. Randolph and my daughter will be back from the springs in the ensuing week. He is almost entirely recovered by the use of the sweet springs. I expect the execution of your promise to bring Mrs. Madison to see us, with whom we should all be glad to get acquainted. I would have been with you before this, but that I have had almost constant threats of rheumatism so obstinately fixed in it's seat as to render it imprudent for me to move much. Adieu affectionately.

Madison to Jefferson

Orange Oct. 18, 1795

DEAR SIR

On opening the letter forwarded by Pickering, which I omitted at Monticello, because I took for granted that it merely covered, like yours, a copy of the French Constitution, I found a letter from Monroe, of the 30 June, from which the following is an extract. "You will be surprised to hear that the only *Americans*[7] whom I found here, were a *set of New England men connected with Britain and who upon British capital were trading to this country that they are hostile to the French revolution is what you* well know: but that they should be *thriving upon the credit which the efforts* of others in other quarters gain *the American name here you could not expect: that as such they should be in possession of the little*

---

6. TJ first wrote "government," then deleted that word and substituted "constitution"; see *PJM*, XVI, pp. 88–89.
7. This word and the italicized words that follow were written in code.

confidence we had and give a tone to characters on our side of the Atlantick was still less to be expected. But such was the fact. With a few exceptions the *other merchants* are *new made citizens from Scotland. Swan who is a corrupt unprincipled rascal* had by virtue of being the *agent of France* and as we had no *minister and he being tho* (of the latter description) *the only or* most creditable *resident American here had a monopoly* of *the trade of both countries.* Indeed it is believed that he was connected with *the agents* on one side, *and the minister on the other.*[8] I *mention this as a trait worthy your* attention. You will confide this view to *Mr. Jefferson only.* But good may come from it, and especially if *the allurement here will draw them off from the other side of the channel.*" The remainder of the letter is little more than you have probably seen from him.

I have seen Philada. papers down to the 12 inst. One of them contains another letter from E. R. to the P. dated the *8*th. and sent to the press on the 10th applying for a paper refused him by Pickering, intimating that the want of this alone delayed his final statement and notifying the P. that his consent wd. be expected to a publication of it.[9] It appears that the State elections in Pena. will be very warm, and are hinged on the distinction of Treaty and anti Treaty candidates. In Delaware they are over, and have given a Triumph to the Anti Treaty party. The French Constitution has been *unanimously* concluded by the Convention.[10] It is not yet authenticated that war has taken place between England and Spain, but reports and circumstances continue to point at it. Yrs. affectionately

Js. Madison Jr

Madison to Jefferson

Fredericksburg Nov. 8, 1795

Dear Sir

I am thus far on my way to Philada. and shall proceed on the journey this morning. I left with my Father subject to your order the packet of papers promised you. In case of his absence, the overseer will be charged with them. Should you send a special messenger, it will be well to provide agst. much roughness in the carriage, as the papers are in a state not unsusceptible of being

---

8. James Swan had emigrated to Boston from Scotland in 1765, served in the Revolution, and, with the aid of Lafayette, became a contractor in naval supplies in France in 1787. By 1795, he had acquired a controlling share of the U.S. securities owed to France as a part of the Revolutionary war debt. Thus, he was both an agent of the French government and a broker in American securities; see *PJM,* XVI, p. 358. See also Howard C. Rice, "James Swan: Agent of the French Republic, 1794-96," *New England Quarterly* 10 (1937): 464-86.

9. See John J. Reardon, *Edmund Randolph: A Biography* (New York, 1974), pp. 319-22.

10. For the Delaware election, see John A. Munroe, *Federalist Delaware, 1775-1815* (New Brunswick, N.J., 1954), pp. 205-6. For the French constitution of 1795, see Georges Lefebvre, *The French Revolution from 1793 to 1799* (New York, 1964), pp. 160-64.

injured by it.[11] I hear nothing new at this place, except that Wheat is falling in Philada. and consequently so here. Two reason[s] are assigned—the bad quality of the crop—and the English harvest turning out better than was expected. The last cause is no doubt exaggerated, if not forged, but rather in England than here for the papers are full of such paragraphs copied from English papers or English letters. Mr. Randolph's publication is said to be in the press, but has not yet made its appearance. In the mean time Reports continue to circulate to his disadvantage; and I find that malice is busy in attempts to complicate others with his affair. I hope you will not forget to draw on our friend in N. Carolina, for his political anecdotes etc. He will at least in answer to your queries, give you a history of the particular points comprehended in your review. What passed in relation to the Seat of Govt. I know has been entered in his Diary.[12] Yrs. truly

Js. M. Jr.

Jefferson to Madison

[Monticello] Nov. 26, 1795

Your favor from Fredericksburg came safe to hand. I inclose you the extract of a letter I recieved from Mr. R. now in Richmond.[13] Tho you will have been informed of the facts before this reaches you, yet you will see more of the subject by having different views of it presented to you. Though Marshall will be able to embarras the Republican party in the assembly a good deal, yet upon the whole, his having gone into it will be of service. He has been hitherto able to do more mischief, acting under the mask of republicanism than he will be able to do after throwing it plainly off. His lax lounging manners have made him popular with the bulk of the people of Richmond, and a profound hypocrisy with many thinking men in our country. But having come forth in the plenitude of his English principles, the latter will see that it is high time to make him known. His doctrine that the whole commercial part of the treaty (and he might have added the whole unconstitutional part of it) rests in the power of the H. of R. is certainly the true doctrine; and as the

11. At their meeting in Oct., TJ and JM had discussed the preservation of the printed acts of the Virginia assembly as "precious monuments of our . . . history," and JM now supplied "the packet of papers promised you." TJ used the "monuments" phrase in his letter to George Wythe, Jan. 16, 1796, which he enclosed to JM on Jan. 24, 1796; see below. For a statement that JM's packet also included his "Notes on the Debates at the Constitutional Convention," see *PJM*, X, p. 7, and XVI, p. 122; see also JM to TJ, Apr. 4, 1796, below, and TJ to JM, Apr. 17, 1796, below.

12. JM referred to Senator Benjamin Hawkins from North Carolina, who had supported the Compromise of 1790; see *PJM*, XVI, p. 122, and Merritt B. Pound, *Benjamin Hawkins: Indian Agent* (Athens, Ga., 1951), p. 72.

13. For TJ's letter of Nov. 22, 1795, from his son-in-law, Thomas Mann Randolph, see the enclosure from TJ to JM, Nov. 26, 1795, below.

articles which stipulate what requires the consent of the three branches of the legislature, must be referred to the H. of R. for their concurrence, so they, being free agents, may approve or reject them, either by a vote declaring that, or by refusing to pass acts. I should think the former mode the most safe and honorable. The people in this part of the country continue very firmly disposed against the treaty. I imagine the 50 negative votes comprehend the whole force of the Alexandrian party and the bigots and passive obedience men of the whole state who have got themselves into the legislature. I observe an expression in Randolph's printed secret intimating that the President, tho' an honest man himself, may be circumvented by snares and artifices, and is in fact surrounded by men who wish to clothe the Executive with more than constitutional powers. This when public, will make great impression. It is not only a truth, but a truth levelled to every capacity, and will justify to themselves the most zealous votaries, for ceasing to repose the unlimited confidence they have done in the measures which have been pursued. Communicate the inclosed paper, if you please, to Mr. Giles. Our autumn is fine. The weather mild, and intermixed with moderate rains at proper intervals. No ice yet, and not much frost. Adieu affectionately.

ENCLOSURE

[Extract of a Letter from Thomas Mann Randolph to Jefferson]

Richmond Nov. 22, 1795[14]

"Mann Page's motion for a resolution approving the conduct of the minority in the national senate was warmly agitated three whole days, Wednesday, Thursd. and Friday. It was much less ably defended than opposed. John Marshal it was once apprehended would make a great number of converts by an argument which cannot be considered in any other light than an uncandid artifice to prevent what would be a virtual censure of the President's conduct. He maintained *that the treaty in all it's commercial parts was still under the power of the H. of R.* He contended that it was more in the spirit of the constitution for it to be rendered nugatory after it received the sanction of the P. and S. *by the H. of R. refusing it their support,* than for it's existence to be prevented, for it to be stifled in embryo by their declaring upon application from the P. to know their sentiments before he had given it his signature, that they would withhold that support. He compared the relation of the Executive to the Legislative department to that between the states and the Congress under the old confederation. The old Congress might have given up the right of laying discriminating duties in favor of any nation by treaty: it would never have thought of taking before hand the assent of each state thereto. Yet no one would have pretended to deny the power of the states to lay such. This doctrine, I believe, is all that is original in his argument. The sophisms of Camillus, and the nice distinctions of the Examiner[15] made up the rest. It is clear that it was brought forward for the purpose of gaining over the unwary and the wavering. It

14. The text, which is in TJ's hand, is printed from *PJM,* XVI, pp. 135-36.
15. Thomas Mann Randolph referred to William Loughton Smith's *A Candid Examination of the Objections to the Treaty of Amity... between the U. S. and Great Britain...* (Charleston, S.C., 1795), a pamphlet supporting the Jay Treaty.

has never been admitted by the writers in favor of the treaty to the Northward. It's author was disappointed however. Upon a division the vote stood 100. to 50. After the question Charles Lee brought forward a motion of compliment to the P. It was of most uncommon length, which was undoubtedly intended to puzzle: and the word 'wisdom' in expressing the confidence of the house in the P. was so artfully introduced that if the fraudulent design had not been detected in time, the vote of the house, as to it's effect upon the P. would have been entirely done away. A resolution so worded as to acquit the P. of all evil intention, but at the same time silently censuring his error, was passed by a majority of 33. 89 to 56.[16]

Some of the warmest of the victorious party talk of bringing forward a motion for a vote of applause to S. T. Mason. But the more moderate say their triumph is sufficient, and it is supposed this will be dropped."

Jefferson to Madison

[Monticello] Dec. 3, 1795

TH: J. TO J. M.

The inclosed letter came under cover to me from Mde. de Chastellux. As I know not where the Duke de Liancourt is, and have no particular motive for making it the occasion of renewing a slight acquaintance, never valued, I will ask the favor of you to have it handed him.[17] We have no news but the death of Doctr. Gilmer, which happened the night before last. I hear nothing from our assembly. A post or two more I hope will bring us the first movements of your campaign, which will be most interesting. Adieu affectionately.

Madison to Jefferson

Philadelphia Dec. 6, 1795

DEAR SIR

The inclosed letter with a pamphlet under the same cover came to me a few days ago from the post Office with a charge of a dollar postage. I have delayed to forward it till further expence cd. be avoided. The pamphlet I will send by the first good oppy. I have your favor of the 26th. Ult, corroborating the view I had before recd. of matters at Richmond. There is likely to be a Quorum of both Houses of Congress tomorrow. Muhlenberg and Dayton will probably be the candidates for the Chair in the H. of Reps. I can say nothing yet of the complexion of the body, more than has been known from general accts. long ago. With respect to the Cabinet, I am without the least

---

16. For a discussion of this motion, see *PJM,* XVI, p. 136.

17. The duc de La Rochefoucauld-Liancourt later visited Monticello and described it in his *Travels through the United States of North America . . . ,* 2 vols. (London, 1799), II, pp. 69–84.

information. It does not appear that any final step has been taken for filling the vacant Departments. The offer of the Secretaryship of State to P. Henry is a circumstance which I should not have believed without the most unquestionable testimony. Col. Coles tells me Mr. Henry read the letter to him on that subject.[18] It appears that there have been some agitations in Paris produced by the *decree of two thirds,* tacked to the Constitution; but as the Jacobins united with the Convention in crushing them, the crisis was probably the expiring struggle of the Counter revolutionists. From the nature of the Decree, it is not wonderful that it should not have been swallowed without some resistance.[19] Randolph's pamphlet is not yet out. I am told it will appear in a few days. As soon as I can send you a copy you shall have one. Yrs. Affey.

Js. Madison Jr

Madison to Jefferson

Philadelphia Dec. 13, 1795

Dear Sir

I recd. yesterday your favor covering a letter to Monsr. Liancourt which I have put into the hands of Noailles who will attend to the delivery of it.[20] I inclose a copy of the P's speech. The Senate have answered it, as was to be expected. You will see the first fruits of their open doors in the debates it produced.[21] The answer of the House of Reps. will be reported tomorrow. It has been delayed by a disagreement of ideas in the Committee, which consisted of Sedgwick, Sitgreaves and myself. The two former are strongly for the Treaty, and wish to favor it, at the same time that they are afraid to hazard direct expressions to that effect. The policy of that party is to obtain it a quiet passage thro' the present Session, pretending that it is too soon now to meddle with it, as they will hereafter pretend that it is then too late. The means employed are to blazon the public prosperity, to confound the Treaty with the President, and to mouth over the stale topics of war and confusion. The answer as it stands to be reported contains a clause which will put the House of Reps. in a dilemma similar to that forced on the House of Delegates, and I believe will never be swallowed because it is in part notoriously untrue. It affirms the confidence of his fellow Citizens to be undiminished which will be

---

18. For Washington's offer, see Carroll and Ashworth, pp. 312–13, 322.

19. For the Constitution of 1795, see Lefebvre, pp. 160–64. The Two-thirds Decree provided that two-thirds of the 500 incumbent deputies would retain their seats, allowing a gradual transition to the new constitutional regime. Napoleon put down the Paris resistance with a "whiff of grapeshot," a turning point in his career.

20. The vicomte de Noailles was Lafayette's brother-in-law, who emigrated to the United States in 1792; see *PJM,* XVI, p. 164.

21. The Senate met behind closed doors from 1789 until a resolution of Feb. 20, 1794, opened the galleries to the public; see *ibid.*

denied by many who sincerely wish it to be the case. It cannot yet be determined what course the business will take. It seems most probable at present that the answer will be neutralized; and the subject immediately after taken up in a Come. of the whole on the State of the Union; which will have the advantage of disentangleing it from the P. and of accomodating the wishes of some individuals who will be much influenced by the mode. There is pretty certainly a great majority agst. the Treaty on its merits; but besides the ordinary difficulty of preventing scisms, there is a real obscurity in the constitutional part of the question, and a diversity of sincere opinions about it, which the other side will make the most of.[22] Nothing very late from abroad. The provision order has been repealed, but the spoliations go on. The publication of E. R. is not yet out. It is said it will appear the latter end of the present week. Adieu. Yrs. Affy

Js M Jr.

Flour 14 dollrs. and tis thought will rise to 16. The purchases of British agents for the W. India armaments are no doubt one of the causes of this extraordinary rise.

Madison to Jefferson

Philadelphia Dec. 27, 1795

Dear Sir

Mr. R's pamphlet is out and will be forwarded by the first oppy. Altho' I have kept up an enquiry, I have not been able to collect the impression it makes. As it relates to the P[resident] nothing seems to be said: and as it relates to parties in general very little. By Fenno's and Webster's papers, it appears that an effort will be used to run down Mr. R. and if necessary for the purpose to call in the incidents to which his pecuniary embarrassments here exposed him.[23] The speech of the P. will have shewn you the guarded and perplexing shape, in which the Treaty was brought into view. The answer was the result of circumstances which my communications to you explain in part. The silence of it as to the Treaty was an accomodation to the wishes of a few who preferred taking it up by itself afterwards. These individuals have not shewn as much fowardness as was expected, and owing to that cause, and to the acct. of an exchange of Ratifications and the momentary[24] expectation of the Treaty, nothing is yet done on the subject. The situation is truly perplexing. It is clear that a majority if brought to the merits of the Treaty are agst. it. But as the Treaty is not regularly before the House, and an application to the P. brings

22. For the House reply, see Richard E. Welch, Jr., *Theodore Sedgwick: Federalist* (Middletown, Conn., 1965), pp. 142–43, and Carroll and Ashworth, p. 328.
23. Randolph's *Vindication* was published on Dec. 18, 1795.
24. JM mistakenly wrote "momently" but later corrected this to "momentary."

him personally into the question with some plausible objections to the measure, there is great danger that eno' will fly off to leave the opponents of the Treaty in a minority. Enquiries are on foot to ascertain the true state of opinions and the probable turn of votes; and if there be found a firm majority on the right side, an attempt will be made to get at the subject.

There are accts. from Paris to the 5th. of Novr. The new Constitution was taking an auspicious commencement. Monroe's letters to me of Ocr. 23 and 24. give a favorable prospect on that side; as well as with regard to French affairs in general. He confirms the late naval advantages, and speaks of the check on the Rhine as a bagatelle. He knew only from Report, the Ratification of the Treaty by the P. His language breathes equal mortification and apprehension from the event. He says that England would have refused us nothing, and we have yielded every thing; and he cannot but speak as reason dictates. A nation threatened with famine at home, and depending on the forlorn hope of West-India armaments which our market only can feed, was a nation to make rather than receive concessions. I am just told that 97 out of 98 of the Bermuda Judge's decrees agst. our vessels are announced to be reversed in England. This is another proof of Monroe's opinion. The reversal in such a lump must have resulted not from principle, but from policy, as the lumping condemnation proceeded from cupidity. Flour at 14 dolrs. at present. We have had no winter as yet. The weather is now as mild as October. I hope it will assist you agst. your Rheumatic com[plaint.]

Madison to Jefferson

Philadelphia Jan. 10, 1796

DEAR SIR,

The House of Representatives have been latterly occupied with a pretty curious affair. Certain Traders and others, of Detroit, entered into a contract with certain individuals of the United States, for obtaining the peninsula formed by Lakes Huron and Michigan, and containing 20 or 30 millions of acres of valuable land. The traders, by means of their influence over the Indians, were to extinguish the Indian Title; and the other party, by means of their influence, and that of their connexions, with Congress, to extinguish the title of the United States. The Country was to be divided into shares, of which the greater part was to be disposed of by the party who had to deal with Congress. The reason of this, obvious enough in itself, has been sufficiently established by proof. Ever since the session commenced, two of the partners deputed to work the project through Congress have been employed with great industry, opening themselves in different degrees and forms, to different members, according to circumstances. Some of the members, who scented the criminality of the object, waited for a full disclosure. Others, through an eagerness of some sort or other, ran with the tale *first* to the President, and then into the

House of Representatives, without concerting or considering a single step that ought to follow. In consequence of the information to the President, and a representation to the District Judge *of the United States,* a warrant issued, and the offenders were taken into custody by the Marshal. The House could not be prevailed on to take a single day to consider the subject, and a warrant issued from the Speaker, also, by virtue of which the Prisoners were transferred to the Sergeant-at-arms. For the proceedings which have ensued, I must refer you to the newspapers. They ended in the discharge of one of the men, and in the reprimand of the other at the bar, and remanding him to Gaol, where he now lies. In the arguments of the Counsel, and in the debates in the House, the want of jurisdiction in such a case over persons not members of the body was insisted on, but was overruled by a very great majority. There cannot be the least doubt, either of the turpitude of the charge, or the guilt of the accused; but it will be difficult, I believe, to deduce the privilege from the Constitution, or to limit it in practice, or even to find a precedent for it in the arbitrary claims of the British House of Commons. What an engine may such a privilege become, in the hands of a body once corrupted, for protecting its corruptions against public animadversion, under the pretext of maintaining its dignity and preserving the necessary confidence of the public! You will observe that a part of the charge consisted of the slanderous assertion that a majority of the Senate, and nearly a majority of the other House, had embarked in the job for turning a public measure to their private emolument. Apply the principle to other transactions, and the strictures which the press has made on them, and the extent of its mischief will be seen at once. There is much room to suspect that more important characters, both on the British and American sides of this affair, were behind the ostensible parties to it.[25]

The Treaty has not yet been touched. I understand from Mr. Giles that the delay has been explained by him to you. A *copy* of the British ratification arrived lately, and it was hoped a communication of it would have followed. The Executive decided otherwise; and to appease the restlessness of the House of Representatives, Pickering laid the papers before the Speaker, to satisfy him, and enable him to explain the matter to others *individually*. This mode of proceeding does not augment the respect which a more direct and less reserved stile of conduct would inspire, especially as the papers were sufficiently authentic for any use the House of Representatives would be likely to make of them.[26] It is now said that the original is arrived by a British Packet just announced from New York. Having been kept within doors by the badness of the day, I have not ascertained the truth of the account.

---

25. TJ's italics in this paragraph and below. For a brief sketch of the attempt of speculators to obtain huge land grants from Indians during the interregnum between British evacuation and American occupation of Detroit in 1795–96, see F. Clever Bald, *Detroit's First American Decade, 1796–1805* (Ann Arbor, 1948), pp. 12–14; Brant, III, pp. 432–33; and *PJM,* XVI, pp. 175–80.

26. A duplicate of the British ratification of the Jay Treaty reached Philadelphia on Dec. 28, 1795, and JM examined this copy while it was in Speaker Dayton's hands; see *PJM,* XVI, p. 182.

I have letters from Col. Monroe of the 23 and 24 of Octr. His picture of the affairs of France, particularly of the prospect exhibited in the approaching establishment of the Constitution, is very favorable. This, as far as we know, has had an easy birth, and wears a promising countenance. He had not learnt with certainty the ratification of the Treaty by the President, but wrote under the belief of it. His regrets, and his apprehensions, were as strong as might be expected. I have a letter from T. Paine, which breathes the same sentiments, and contains some keen observations on the administration of the Government here. It appears that the neglect to claim him as an American Citizen when confined by Robespierre, or even to interfere in any way whatever in his favor, has filled him with an indelible rancour against the President, to whom it appears he has written on the subject. His letter to me is in the stile of a dying one, and we hear that he is since dead, of the abscess in his side, brought on by his imprisonment.[27] His letter desires that he may be remembered to you.

I inclose a copy of the proceedings relating to the presentation of the French flag. What think you of the President's Jacobinical speech to Adèt?[28]

Randolph's vindication has just undergone the lash of the Author of the "Bone to gnaw."[29] It is handled with much satirical scurrility, not without strictures of sufficient ingenuity and plausibility to aid the plan of running him down. By Mr. Carr, who is now here, we will endeavor to contrive you a copy.

Jefferson to Madison

[Monticello] Jan. 24, 1796[30]

ENCLOSURE
[Jefferson to George Wythe, Jan. 12, 1796]

I recieved last night your letter on the subject of the laws, and certainly will trust you with any thing I have in the world. A waggon was going off this morning from hence to Varina, and I have exerted myself to send them by that. As I have always intended to have my copies bound up so as to make as complete a set as I could, I

---

27. Thomas Paine lived for another thirteen years, dying in 1809.

28. For President Washington's reply to the French minister, see Carroll and Ashworth, pp. 337-38.

29. The author of the attack on Edmund Randolph was William Cobbett. Writing under his pseudonym "Peter Porcupine," he had just published *A New Year's Gift to the Democrats; or, Observations on a Pamphlet Entitled, "A Vindication of Mr. Randolph's Resignation"*; see ibid., p. 336. See also Mary Elizabeth Clark, *Peter Porcupine in America: The Career of William Cobbett, 1792-1800* (Philadelphia, 1939).

30. Letter not found, but JM acknowledged receiving it and the enclosures in his letter of Feb. 7, 1796, below, which summarizes its contents. He later referred to it in his letter to TJ, Apr. 10, 1824, below.

thought it best to do this now, before you begin to make use of them.[31] I have therefore arranged them in to 7. volumes, and propose to make the revisal of 1794. the 8th as you will see by the directions to the book binder. I have ordered the box to be delivered to you, merely that you may open it, see it's contents, and by delivering them to the book binder acquire a right of pressing him to expedite his work. As to all the expences I shall provide for them through the channel of Mr̄ Randolph. When done, take the whole collection, and keep it till it has answered your purpose. I mean to write you a particular statement, of the contents of my collection and it's deficiencies; but this requires more time than the departure of the waggon allows me. It shall follow by post because I am not without hopes you may have some duplicates from which you can spare copies to fill up the chasms of mine.

P.S. Mr̄ Bran has formerly done a good deal of binding for me, and would take pains to serve an old customer well.[32]

ENCLOSURE

Thomas Jefferson, A Statement of the Volumes of the Laws of Virginia, Manuscript and Printed in my possession, Monticello, Jan. 13, 1796

A M.S. marked A. given me by the late Peyton Randolph. It had belonged to his father Sir John Randolph, who had collected papers with a view to write the history of Virginia. It is attested by R. Hickman, and contains the acts of 1623/4 Mar. 5. 35 acts.

M.S. marked ⟨43⟩ purchased of the exrs of the late Peyton Randolph, having been among the collections of Sir John Randolph. From the resemblance of the mark to some I have formerly seen in the Secretary's office, I suspect this to be an original volume of records, probably borrowed by Sr. J. R. It contains the laws from 1629. to 1633.

M.S. marked F. purchased from the admr of Colo. Richard Bland decd. It contains laws from 1639 to 1667.

M.S. marked D. purchased from the admr. of Colo. Richard Bland decd. It contains laws from 1642/3 to 1661/2

M.S. copied by myself of the laws of 1660/1 Mar. 23.

M.S. from the Charles city office, to which it belonged probably. I found it in Lorton's tavern, brought in to be used for waste paper. Much had been already cut off for thread papers and other uses. Debnam, the then clerk very readily gave it to me, as also another hereafter mentioned. It still contains from chap. 31. of the session of 1661/2 to 1702.

M.S. marked B. purchased of the exrs of the late Peyton Randolph. Part of Sr. John Randolph's collection it contains laws from 1662. to 1697.

M.S. appendix to a copy of Pervis's collection from the Westover library, given by the late Colo. W. Byrd to Mr Wayles, whose library came to my hands.

M.S. from the Charles city office, given to me by Debnam as above mentioned. It contains from c. 2 to c. 53. of the laws of 1705.

31. For the use that W. W. Hening made of TJ's printed laws of Virginia in compiling his *Statutes at Large . . . of All the Laws of Virginia . . .* , see E. Millicent Sowerby, *Catalogue of the Library of Thomas Jefferson,* 5 vols. (Washington, 1952–59), II, pp. 255–61. The text of this letter is printed from Sowerby.

32. For an account and an illustration of the bindings, see *ibid.,* pp. 246–54.

M.S. given me by the present John Page of Rosewell. It had belonged to Matthew Page his grandfather who was one of the commissioners of 1705. for revising the laws and was probably furnished with this copy for that work.

Printed laws.
Pervis's collection. This forms the 1st. vol. of any collection of the Printed laws of Virginia.
Revisal of 1732. This forms the 2d. vol.
Revisal of 1748. This is vol. the 3d.
Revisal of 1760. This is vol. the 4th.
Fugitive sheets of the laws of particular sessions bound together from 1734. to 1772. making vol. the 5th.
Ditto . . . . from 1775. to 1783. making vol. the 6th.
Revisal of 1783. by the Chancellors. making vol. 7th.
Revisal of 1794. making vol. 8th.

ENCLOSURE
[Jefferson to George Wythe]

TH: J. TO G. WYTHE   Monticello Jan. 16, 1796

I was so hurried to get ready my collection of printed laws before the departure of the waggon, that I did the work imperfectly. I have since found the laws of 1783. May and Octob. which I should be glad to have added to the end of my 6th volume. If you can procure a copy of those of 1773. I will pray you to add it to the end of the 5th volume, and in both cases to make corresponding changes in the middle one of the three printed labels proposed on these volumes. Indeed I would wish the middle label of the Vth volume to be | Fugitive Sheets. 1734–1773 | and of the VIth to be | Fugitive Sheets 1774–1783 | I chuse to bring down the VIth volume to 1783. that it may terminate at the same period with the Chancellors revisal.

I write you a separate letter which perhaps may lead to the preservation of these laws. Perhaps your friend Mr Taylor, of whom I hear so many good and clever things, may think this business worthy his patronage. Adieu affectionately.

ENCLOSURE
[Jefferson to George Wythe]

Monticello Jan. 16, 1796

In my letter which accompanied the box containing my collection of Printed laws, I promised to send you by post a statement of the contents of the box. On taking up the subject I found it better to take a more general view of the whole of the laws I possess, as well Manuscript as printed, as also of those which I do not possess, and suppose to be no longer extant. This general view you will have in the enclosed paper,[33] whereof the articles stated to be printed constitute the contents of the box I sent you. Those in MS. were not sent, because not supposed to have been within your view, and because some

---

33. The enclosure is TJ's statement of the acts of the Virginia assembly from 1619 through 1783 in his collection, below. Malone, III, p. 254, calls this letter "a classic statement of the desirability of preserving historic documents."

of them will not bear removal, being so rotten, that in turning over a leaf it sometimes falls into powder. These I preserve by wrapping and sewing them up in oiled cloth, so that neither air nor moisture can have access to them. Very early in the course of my researches into the laws of Virginia, I observed that many of them were already lost, and many more on the point of being lost, as existing only in single copies in the hands of careful or curious individuals, on whose death they would probably be used for waste paper. I set myself therefore to work, to collect all which were then existing, in order that when the day should come in which the public should advert to the magnitude of their loss in these precious monuments of our property, and our history, a part of their regret might be spared by information that a portion has been saved from the wreck, which is worthy of their attention and preservation. In searching after these remains, I spared neither time, trouble, nor expense; and am of opinion that scarcely any law escaped me, which was in being as late as the year 1778 in the middle or Southern parts of the State. In the Northern parts, perhaps something might still be found. In the clerk's office in the antient counties, some of these MS. copies of the laws may possibly still exist, which used to be furnished at the public expense to every county, before the use of the press was introduced; and in the same places, and in the hands of antient magistrates or of their families, some of the fugitive sheets of the laws of separate sessions, which have been usually distributed since the practice commenced of printing them. But recurring to what we actually possess, the question is, what means will be the most effectual for preserving these remains from future loss? All the care I can take of them, will not preserve them from the worm, from the natural decay of the paper, from the accidents of fire, or those of removal when it is necessary for any public purposes, as in the case of those now sent you. Our experience has proved to us that a single copy, or a few, deposited in MS. in the public offices, cannot be relied on for any great length of time. The ravages of fire and of ferocious enemies have had but too much part in producing the very loss we are now deploring. How many of the precious works of antiquity were lost while they were preserved only in manuscript? Has there ever been one lost since the art of printing has rendered it practicable to multiply and disperse copies? This leads us then to the only means of preserving those remains of our laws now under consideration, that is, a multiplication of printed copies. I think therefore that there should be printed at public expense, an edition of all the laws ever passed by our legislatures which can now be found; that a copy should be deposited in every public library in America, in the principal public offices within the State, and some perhaps in the most distinguished public libraries of Europe, and that the rest should be sold to individuals, towards reimbursing the expences of the edition. Nor do I think that this would be a voluminous work. The MSS. would probably furnish matter for one printed volume in folio, would comprehend all the laws from 1624 to 1701, which period includes Purvis. My collection of Fugitive sheets forms, as we know, two volumes, and comprehends all the extant laws from 1734 to 1783; and the laws which can be gleaned up from the Revisals to supply the chasm between 1701 and 1734, with those from 1783 to the close of the present century, (by which term the work might be compleated,) would not be more than the matter of another volume. So that four volumes in folio, would give every law ever passed which is now extant; whereas those who wish to possess as many of them as can be procured, must now buy the six folio volumes of Revisals, to wit, Purvis and those of 1732, 1748, 1768, 1783, and 1794, and in all of them possess not one half of what they wish. What would be the expence of the edition I cannot say, nor how much would be reimbursed by the sales; but I am sure it would be moderate, compared with the rates which the public have hitherto paid for printing their laws, provided a sufficient latitude be given as to printers and places. The first step would be to make out a single copy for the MSS., which would employ a clerk about a year or something more, to which expence about a fourth should be added for the collation of the MSS., which would employ 3. persons at a time about half a day, or a day in every week. As I have already spent more time in making myself acquainted with the contents and arrangement of these MSS. than any other person probably ever will, and their condition does not admit their removal to a distance, I will chearfully undertake the direction and superintendence of this work, if it can be done in the neighboring towns of Charlottesville or Milton, farther than which I could not undertake to go from home. For the residue of the work, my printed volumes might be delivered to the Printer.

I have troubled you with these details, because you are in the place where they may be used for the public service, if they admit of such use, and because the order of assembly, which you mention, shews they are sensible of the necessity of preserving such of these laws as relate to our landed property; and a little further consideration will perhaps convince them that it is better to do the whole work once for all, than to be recurring to it by piece-meal, as particular parts of it shall be required, and that too perhaps when the materials shall be lost. You are the best judge of the weight of these observations, and of the mode of giving them any effect they may merit. Adieu affectionately.

ENCLOSURE

Thomas Jefferson, A statement of the particular acts of the assembly of Virginia, in my possesion either M.S. or Printed, and of those not in my possesion and presumed to be lost
[Jan. 16, 1796]

1619.	June.	The first session of assembly ever held in Virginia. Lost.
1620.	May.	Lost.
1622.		Lost.
1623/4	Mar. 5.	I have in M.S.
1626		Lost.
1629.	Oct. 16	
1629/30	Mar. 24.	
1631.	Feb. 21.	
1632.	Sept. 4.	60 acts. ⎫ I have in M.S.
1632/3	Feb. 1.	6. acts.
1633.	Aug. 21.	16. acts.
1639.	Jan. 6.	I have in M.S.
1642.	Apr. 1.	I have the 21st. and 22d. acts in M.S.
1642	[illegible]	A revisal.
1644.	Oct. 1	
1644/5	Feb. 17.	
1645.	Nov. 20.	
1646.	Oct. 5.	
1647.	Nov. 3.	

1648.	Oct. 12.		
1649.	Oct. 10.		
1652.	Apr. 26.		
	Nov. 25.		
1653.	July 5.		I have in M.S.
1654.	Nov. 20.		
1655.	Mar.		
1655/6	Mar. 10.		
1656.	Dec. 1.		
1657/8	Mar. 13.	A revisal.	
1658/9	Mar. 1.		
1659/60	Mar. 13.		
1660.	Oct. 11.		
1660/1	Mar. 23.		
1661/2	Mar. 23.	Chap. 1. to 138. inclusive. Printed.	
1662.	Dec. 2. or 23.	Chap. 1. 2. 3. 4. 5. 6. 7. 8. 9. 10. 11. 12. 13. 15. 17. 18. 21. 23. Printed.	
		14. 16. 19. 20. 22. in M.S.	
1663.	Sep. 10.	Chap. 1. 2. 4. 7. 8. 9. 10. 11. 14. 16. 17. Printed.	
		Chap. 3. 5. 6. 12. 13. 15. 18. in M.S.	
1664.	Sep. 20.	9. acts. Printed.	
1665.	Oct. 10.	Chap. 1. 2. 3. 5. 6. 7. 8. 9. Printed	
		4. 50. in M. S.	
1666.	June 5.	Chap. 2. 3. Printed.	
		1. in M. S.	
	Oct. 23.	Chap. 1. 2. 3. 5. 6. 7. 9. 10. 11. 12. 13. 15. 16. 17. 18. 19. 20. 21. 22. 23. 24. Printed.	
		4. 8. 14. in M. S.	
1667.	Sep. 3.	Chap. 1. 2. 3. 4. Printed	
		5. 6. 7. in M.S.	
1668.	Sep. 17	Chap. 1. 2. 3. 4. 5. 6. 7. 8. 9. Printed.	
1669.	Oct. 20.	Chap. 1. 2. 3. 4. 5. 6. 7. Printed	
		8. 9. in M.S.	
1670.	Oct. 3.	Chap. 1. 2. 3. 4. 5. 6. 7. 8. 9. 10. 12. Printed.	
		11. in. M.S.	
1671.	Sep. 20.	Chap. 1. 4. 5. 6. Printed.	
		2. 3. 7. in M.S.	
1672.	Sep. 24.	Chap. 1. 2. 3. 4. 5. 7. 8. 9. 10. Printed.	
		6. 11. in M.S.	
1673.	Oct. 20.	Chap. 1. 2. 3. 4. 5. Printed.	
		6. 7. in M.S.	
1674.	Sep. 21.	Chap. 1. 3. 4. 6. 7. Printed.	
		2. 5. 8. 9. 10. in M.S.	
1675/6	Mar. 7.	Chap. 3. Printed.	
		1. 2. 4. in M.S.	
1676.	June 5.	Chap. 1. to 20. in M.S.	
1676/7	Feb. 20.	Chap. 4. 6. 7. 8. 9. 10. 11. 13. 14. 16. 17. 20. Printed.	
		1. 2. 3. 5. 12. 15. 18. 19. in MS.	

1677.	Oct. 10.	Chap. 1. 2. 3. 4. 5. 8. 9. 10. 11. 12. Printed. 6. 7. in MS.
1679.	Apr. 25.	Chap. 1. 2. 3. 4. 5. 6. 7. 8. 9. Printed. 10. 11. in MS.
1680.	June 8.	Chap. 1. to 17. Printed.
1682.	Nov. 10.	Chap. 1. to 13. Printed.
1684.	Apr. 16.	Chap. 2. Printed. 1. 3. 4. 5. 6. 7. 8. 9. 10. in MS.
1686.	Oct. 20.	Chap. 1. to 11. in MS.
1691.	Apr. 16.	Chap. 12. Printed. 1. 2. 3. 4. 5. 6. 7. 8. 9. 10. 11. 13. 14. 15. 16. 17. 18. 19. 20. 21. in MS.
1692.	Apr. 11.	Chap. 1. to 7. in MS.
1692/3	Mar. 2.	Chap. 1. to 7. in MS.
1693.	Oct. 10.	Chap. 1. to 5. in MS.
1695.	Apr. 18.	Chap 1. to 6. in MS.
1696.	Sep. 24.	Chap. 1. to 14. in MS.
1697.	Oct. 21.	Chap. 1 in MS.
1698.	Sep. 28.	no law past at this session.
1699.	Apr. 27.	Chap. 1. to 16. in MS.
1700.	Dec. 5.	Chap 1. to 4. in MS.
1701.	Aug. 6.	Chap. 1. to 6. in MS.
1702.	May 30.	Chap. 1. 2. Lost
	Aug. 14.	Chap. 1. a part of it in MS. 2. 3. 4. Lost.
1702/3	Mar 19	no act passed
1704.	Apr. 20	Chap. 1. to 11. Lost
1705.	Apr. 18.	Chap. 1. to 4. Lost.
	Oct. 25.	Chap. 2. 3. 5. 6. 7. 8. 9. 10. 12. 13. 14. 15. 17. 19. 20. 22. 23. 25. 27. 28. 29. 30. 32. 33. 35. 38. 39. 40. 41. 43. 44. 45. 46. 47. 48. 49. 50. 52. 53. Printed. 4. 11. 16. 18. 21. 24. 26. 31. 34. 36. 37. 42. 51. 55. in MS. 1. 54. Lost.
1710.	Oct. 25.	Chap. 3. 4. 5. 8. 11. 12. 13. 14. Printed. 1. 2. 6. 7. 9. 10. 15. 16. 17. in MS.
1711.	Nov. 7.	Chap. 2. 3. Printed. 1. in MS. Here the MSS. end. 4. 5. Lost.
1712.	Oct. 22.	Chap. 4. 5. Printed. 1. 2. 3. 6. 7. Lost.
1713.	Nov. 5.	Chap. 3. 4. 6. 7. 8. Printed. 1. 2. 5. 9. 10. 11. 12. Lost.
1714.	Nov. 16.	Chap. 1. 2. 3. 5. Printed. 4. Lost.
1715.	Aug. 3.	Chap. 1. 2. 3. Lost.

1718.	Apr. 23.	Chap. 1. 3. the substance Printed in Beverley's abridgment. 2. 4. Lost.
1720.	Nov. 2.	Chap. 3. 4. 5. 6. 7. 8. Printed. 1. 2. substance in Beverl. abr. 9. 10. 11. 12. 13. 14. 15. 16. 17. 18. Lost.
1722.	May 9.	Chap. 1. 2. 3. 6. 7. 8. 9. Printed. 4. 5. 10. 11. 12. 13. 14. 15. 16. Lost.
1723.	May 9.	Chap. 2. 4. 8. 10. Printed. 1. 3. 5. 6. 7. 9. 11. 12. 13. 14. 15. Lost.
1726.	May 12.	Chap. 1. 2. 3. 4. 6. 7. 8. Printed. 5. 9. 10. 11. 12. 13. 14. Lost.
1727/8	Feb. 1.	Chap. 3. 5. 6. 7. 8. 9. 10. 11. 12. 13. 14. Printed. 1. 2. 4. 15. 16. 17. 18. 19. 20. 21. 22. Lost.
1730.	May 21.	Chap. 1. 2. 3. 4. 5. 6. 7. 8. 9. 10. 11. 12. 13. 14. 15. 16. 17. 18. 19. Printed. 20. 21. 22. 23. 24. 25. 26. 27. 28. 29. Lost.
1732.	May 18.	Chap. 1. 2. 3. 4. 5. 6. 7. 8. 9. 10. 11. 12. 13. 14. 15. 16. 17. 18. 19. 20. Printed. 21. 22. 23. 24. 25. 26. 27. 28. 29. 30. 31. 32. 33. 34. 35. Lost.

Here begins my collection of the Fugitive sheets of Laws printed for each session.

1734.	Aug. 22.	31. Acts. Printed
1736.	Aug. 5.	25. Acts. Printed.
1738.	Nov. 1.	25. Acts. Printed.
1740.	May 22.	15. Acts. Printed.
	Aug. 1.	1. Act. Printed.
1742.	May 6.	33. Acts. Printed.
1744.	Sep. 4.	46. Acts. Printed.
1745/6	Feb. 20.	30. Acts. Printed.
1746.	July 11.	2 Acts. Lost.
1747.	Mar. 30.	5 Acts. Lost.
1748.	Oct. 27.	Chap. 1. to 55. Printed. also chap. 57. 77. 56. to 89. Lost. (except Chap. 57. 77.)
1752.	Feb. 27.	53. acts. Printed.
1753.	Nov. 1.	28. acts. Printed.
1754.	Feb. 14.	3 acts. Printed.
	Aug. 22.	3. acts. Printed.
	Oct. 17.	7. acts. Printed.
1755.	May 7.	24. acts. Printed.
	Aug. 5.	8. acts. Printed.
	Oct. 27.	6. acts. Printed.
1756.	Mar. 25.	13. acts. Printed.
	Sep. 20.	3. acts. Printed.
1757.	Apr. 14.	30. acts. Printed.
1758.	Mar. 30.	2. acts. Printed.
	Sep. 14.	13. acts. Printed.
	Nov. 9.	1. act. Printed.

1759.	Feb. 22.	34. acts. Printed.
	Nov. 1.	6. acts. Printed.
1760.	Mar. 4.	3. acts. Printed.
	May 19.	Printed.
	Oct. 6.	4. acts. Printed.
1761.	Mar. 5.	31. acts. Printed.
	Nov. 3.	13. acts. Printed.
1762.	Jan. 14.	3. acts. Printed.
	Mar. 30.	7. acts. Printed.
	Nov. 2.	44. acts. Printed.
1763.	May 19.	13. acts. Printed.
1764.	Jan. 12.	13. acts. Printed.
	Oct. 30.	54. acts. Printed.
1766.	Nov. 6.	61. acts. Printed.
1768.	Mar. 31.	7. acts. Printed.
1769.	May 8.	a Convention. no act passed.
	Nov. 7.	89. acts. Printed.
1771.	July 11.	4. acts. Printed.
1772.	Feb. 10.	68. acts. Printed.
1773.	Mar. 4.	16. acts. Lost from my collection.
1774.	May 5.	Dissolved before any act passed.
1775.	June 1.	The last assembly under the Royal government. It was discontinued by not meeting on it's own adjournment, without having passed any law.

Conventions

1775.	July 17.	Ordinances. Printed.
	Dec.	Ordinances. Printed.
1776.	May 6.	Ordinances. Printed.

Assemblies.

	Oct. 7.	Acts. Printed.
1777.	May 5.	Acts. Printed.
	Oct. 20.	Acts. Printed.
1778.	May 4.	Acts. Printed.
	Oct. 5.	Acts. Printed.
1779.	May 3.	Acts. Printed.
	Oct. 4.	Acts. Printed.
1780.	May 1.	Acts. Printed.
	Oct. 16.	Acts. Printed.
1781.	Mar.	
	May 7.	Acts. Printed.
	Nov. 5.	Acts. Printed.
1782.	May 6.	Acts. Printed.
1783.	May 5.	Acts. Printed.
	Oct. 20.	Acts. Printed.

Note that the terms 'Printed' or 'in MS.' means that I have the Laws Printed or in MS.

Madison to Jefferson

Philadelphia Jan. 31, 1796

DEAR SIR

I inclose a letter from Jno. Bringhurst explaining a claim on you for about £17. Pa. Currency, and requesting me to advance it.[34] Taking him to be an honest man in distress, I shall probably venture a compliance with his solicitation, if it should be found that he cannot wait for your orders. In the mean time you can inform me whether the acct. be accurately stated: but if so, you need not forward the money, as it will be equally convenient to me to receive it in Virginia.

The Original of the British Ratification of the Treaty is still to arrive, and we are not likely to be furnished with a copy. Some members are anxious to apply to the President for the communication, and some would take up the subject on its mere notoriety. It is pretty evident however, that either attempt would be defeated by the advantage which the rub agst. the P. in one case, and the informality in the other, would give to the friends of the Treaty, in the discussion, and the pretext they would afford to the insincere or cautious opponents. The Treaty with Spain also is not yet arrived, tho' there is reason for hourly expecting it. The same as to the Treaty with Algiers. You will see in the gazette inclosed a sketch of the debate on the proposition to employ Robinson of Petersburg as Stenographer to the House of Reps. The more the subject is opened, the more the objections are found to be insuperable. There is little doubt that the project will be rejected.[35]

A commmittee of ways and means are employed in investigating our revenues and our wants.[36] It is found that there are between six and seven millions of anticipations due to the Banks, that our ordinary income is barely at par with our ordinary expenditures, and that new taxes must be ready to meet near 1½ millions which will accrue in 1801. The proposition of the Treasury is to fund the anticipations and the foreign debt due in instalments, with an absolute irredeemability for such a period say 20 or 30 years, as will sell the new Stock at par. This is treading as fast on the heels of G. B. as circumstances will permit. It is probable the House will not consent to such an abandonment of the sound principles it has been latterly favoring; but loans at least in some form or other will be indispensable, in order to face the demands

---

34. John Bringhurst was a "fancy goods" merchant in Philadelphia; see *PJM,* XV, p. 468.

35. For the House report on appointing David Robertson as reporter of its debates, see Marion Tinling, "Thomas Lloyd's Reports of the First Federal Congress," *WMQ* 18 (1961): 540. Reporters were not made officers of the House until 1873, when the Government Printing Office began to print the debates.

36. For the creation of the committee, see Patrick J. Furlong, "The Origins of the House Committee of Ways and Means," *WMQ* 25 (1968): 594–600.

on the public until new taxes can be brought into action. With respect to this, the Come. are now in deliberation and embarrassments. The excise system is unproductive, and new excises that will be popular even in the Eastern States do not occur. On the other hand direct taxes, have been so blackened in order to recommend the fiscal policy of indirect ones, and to inspire hatred, and jealousies in the Eastern against the Southern States, and particularly Virginia, that it is doubtful whether the measure, now that it is become necessary, will be borne. Gallatin is a real Treasure in this department of Legislation. He is sound in his principles, accurate in his calculations and indefatigable in his researches. Who could have supposed that Hamilton could have gone off in the triumph he assumed, with such a condition of the finances behind him?

You will see that Govr. Adams has lanced a pretty bold attack agst. the Treaty. The Legislature have not yet answered his speech. Their unhandsome treatment of the Virga. Amendments portends a countertone.[37] Nothing could more than this treatment demonstrate the success with which party calumny has sown animosity and malignity in the State of Massts. agst. a State which feels no return of illwill, and towards which there were formerly in that quarter the strongest habits of cordiality and cooperation. Yrs. always and affey.

Js M. Jr

The navigation project of Genl. Smith waits for a favorable moment of discussion.[38] The Treaty party will make war on it, as secretly levelled at that transaction, and thus endeavor to escape the consequences of sacrificing the obvious interests of the Eastern States.

Madison to Jefferson

Philadelphia Feb. 7, 1796

DEAR SIR

Several mails preceding that of yesterday brought nothing more Southern than Baltimore. This will account for my not receiving your favor of the 24th. Ult, till yesterday.[39] I will make the enquiries and execute the commissions in

---

37. For Massachusetts' rejection of Virginia's antitreaty amendments, see Kurtz, pp. 20-30, and Farnham, 75-88.

38. Samuel Smith, a Baltimore Republican, proposed that the United States not allow foreign ships to transport any goods not grown or produced in the nation to which the ships belonged. The Federalists kept the proposal bottled up in committee; see Frank A. Cassell, *Merchant Congressman in the Young Republic: Samuel Smith of Maryland, 1752–1839* (Madison, Wis., 1971), pp. 62–64.

39. Letter not found.

it with pleasure, and without delay. I am afraid to make the same promise as to the weekly history of what passes in the Govt. behind the curtain; especially as the Cypher might be required for some parts of it. What I can I will do on the subject. I have already made a partial collection of the Tracts you wish. I know not what is meant by the correspondence of Jay and Jefferson; probably it is the correspondence not between them, but between each and others.

I thank you for the Copy of your statement and letter to Mr. Wythe.[40] I value it not only as a gratification to myself; but as another security for the preservation of the document.

Dorhman maintains a silence, that justifies strong suspicions of aversion or inability to pay his debts. I feel no longer any other restraints from resorting to his deed of trust, but that which Mazzei's interest dictates. As yet the land would sell for considerably less than the sum due. The general rise of price which is going on will probably soon remove this difficulty, especially if the Treaty with Spain, shd. have done what is hoped, as to the navigation of the Mississippi.

You will see that the aspect of English affairs grows more and more lowering. The alarm of the Sedition Bills, the bounty on foreign Wheat and *flour*, the detention of the armament fitted up, for the forlorn experiment in the West Indies, are more portentous than any thing previous to these signs of a ripening crisis.[41] The accounts from France are not of very late date, but continue to be auspicious. The Treaties with Algiers and Spain, loiter as that with England did. It is to be hoped this is the only instance in which the parallel holds.

An idea begins to shew itself that an unrestrained exportation of the Bread-articles, threatens a scarcity in our own Country. The large towns will of course be the first seat of such an apprehensions. It is certain that the Crops of Grain in North Carolina failed to such a degree as to start the price of Corn at a dollr. a bushel where it used to sell at ⅓ of a dollar. In Virginia, if the present price be the measure of the quantity, there will be little corn to spare, and probably not a great deal more of wheat. In this State it is turning out more and more in evidence that the crop of Wheat has been very scanty. The Eastern States always require large importations from the others. In N. J. and N. Y. alone, the crops of Wheat appear to have been good; and that is probably exaggeration on the favorable side. Flour at present in this place is rising under the information of the English bounty. All in the Market is said to be bought up, probably by English Agents. It sold a day or two ago, or rather there was offered for it, 14 dollrs. a barrel, and the best informed, speak with confidence of successive rises. In this attitude of things What a noble stroke would be an embargo? It would probably do as much good as harm at home; and would

---

40. See the enclosures of TJ to George Wythe in TJ to JM, Jan. 24, 1796, above.
41. For the English legislation against seditious libels, see Thomas Erskine May, *The Constitutional History of England since the Accession of George III, 1760–1860*, 2 vols. (London, 1880), II, pp. 161–74.

force peace, on the rest of the World, and perhaps liberty along with it. But you know the spell within the Govt., as well as the obstacles to such a measure in the clamors that would be raised among the Merchts. the Millers, and farmers, to say nothing of the Tories etc. who would make more noise than any of them.

I intreat you not to procrastinate, much less abandon your historical task.[42] You owe it to yourself, to truth, to the World. Adieu always yours most affey

---

There is some reason to think that Jno. Rutledge is not right in his mind.[43] Cushing has been put at the head of the Bench, but it is said will decline the pre-eminence. Chase in the place of Blair!!!!—a vacancy remains to be filled. McHenry Secretary at War.[44] Through what official interstice can a ray of republican truths now penetrate to the P.

You will see by the inclosed letter [from J.] B.[45] that I have ad[vanced] him 25 drs. I have already told you that repayment in Virga will [serve] for me as well as [here.]

Jefferson to Madison

Monticello Feb. 21, 1796

TH: J. TO J. M.

I propose to write you a longer letter in answer to your two favors of Jan. 31. and Feb. 7. which came by our last post. But as I may possibly not have time before A's[46] departure, I inclose you a letter to J. Bringhurst, as the perusal of it will answer that article of your letters. When read, be pleased to seal and send it. I thank you as much for your advance to him as if I had really owed it, and if he does not repay it immediately, let me know it and I will do it. I have always considered paiments for my honor, as debts of honor, whether they were right or wrong. Adieu affectionately

---

42. In his unfound letter of Jan. 24, 1796, TJ apparently referred to a historical research topic at which we can only guess; see *PJM,* XVI, pp. 202, 216.
43. Rutledge had tried to drown himself in Dec. 1795; see Maeva Marcus *et al.,* eds., *The Documentary History of the Supreme Court of the United States, 1789–1800,* 3 vols. (New York; 1985), I, pp. 772 ff.
44. For George Washington's appointments of William Cushing as chief justice of the United States, Samuel Chase as associate justice of the Supreme Court, and James McHenry as secretary of war, see Carroll and Ashworth, pp. 339–40.
45. John Bringhurst.
46. TJ may have referred to a Monticello slave; see *PJM,* XVI, p. 229.

Madison to Jefferson

Philadelphia Feb. 21, 1796

DEAR SIR

Since my last I have made enquiry as to Lownes. In general he is well spoken of, in every respect. Old Mr. Howell however, told me he was not a punctual man and was slow in his payments. I then mentioned my reasons for asking him. He proceeded to say that his son dealt in the same article with Lownes, and that if you chose to take your Iron rod here, he would be responsible for the most exact compliance of his son.[47] I next brought Sharpless into view.[48] He spoke of him as a man fully to be relied on, and as a man with whom his son had had some dealings. He said there was but one objection to taking your supplies at short hand from Sharpless, which was that there was very little direct intercourse from Wilmington to Southern ports; that almost every thing exported thence, came first to Philada. I asked whether vessels could not stop there and take in articles; not he said, unless the freight of them was an object. As the order of my enquiries drew out the old gentleman's opinion of Lownes, before he could well feel the interest of his son in the case, his testimony is entitled to respect. I have written to Jno. Bringhurst who resides at Wilmington to get and send me a full acct. of Sharpless and of the terms on which he wd. supply you; but have not yet recd. an answer.

I find as I conjectured that the provision made for the daughters of Degrasse was not in the way of loan but of gift.[49] It would be difficult perhaps to justify the act in either way, by the text of the Constitution. The precedent nevertheless is in favor of Made. de Chattelleux's son. Whether his claim will be viewed with the same indulgence on the score of his father's merits is more than I can venture to decide. The services of De Grasse were critical. Chatelleux you recollect was not a favorite here, tho' the cause may have been erroneous. Congress also were afraid of the Precedent at the time, and endeavored to interweave ingredients of peculiarity. I am really apprehensive that a compliance with the wishes of Made. de Chat: would entail on Us a provision for the families of the whole French army that served in this Country.[50] Congs are occupied with a Bill for selling the Western lands. Opinions are various and

---

47. For Caleb Lownes and Samuel Howell, Sr., Philadelphia iron merchants who supplied TJ with nail rod for his nailery at Monticello, see Edwin M. Betts, ed., *Thomas Jefferson's Farm Book* . . . (Princeton, 1953), pp. 426–28, and Edwin M. Betts, ed., *Thomas Jefferson's Garden Book, 1766–1824,* . . . (Philadelphia, 1944), p. 414.

48. Jonathan Sharpless was a Wilmington blacksmith; see *PJM,* XVI, p. 227.

49. A congressional act in 1795, supplemented by another in 1798, granted $2,000 to each of Admiral de Grasse's four daughters; see *ibid.*

50. The marquise de Chastellux's efforts on behalf of her son were unsuccessful; see *Travels in North America in the Years 1780, 1781 and 1782 by the Marquis de Chastellux,* ed. Howard C. Rice, Jr., 2 vols. (Chapel Hill, 1963), I, pp. 19–23. See also *PJM,* XVI, p. 227.

the result doubtful.⁵¹ The British Treaty not yet before us; nor The Spanish before the Senate, or even arrived as far as I know. The Algerine is come to hand and under the deliberation of the Senate. The history of it contains some curious features, which it is not possible for me to explain in time. In general it costs an immense sum, and the annual tribute is to be pd. in *naval Stores,* infinitely *underated* in the Tariff. The friendly interference of France, tho' applied for and in train, was precluded by the Agent's precipitancy in closing the Treaty; for the hardness of which the apology is that it was the best that could be got.⁵² The letter from Paris in the inclosed paper, is Monroe's, and the latest in date that has been recd from him. The fedl. Court has not yet given judgment in the case of payts. into the Virga. Treasury. Marshall and Cambell were the Counsel on one side, and Lewis and Tilghman on the other.⁵³ Marshal's argument is highly spoken of. Campbell and Ingersol will appear vs. the Carrage tax. Hamilton is here and to join Lee on the other side.

Madison to Jefferson

Philadelphia Feb. 29, 1796

DEAR SIR

The Treaty with Spain arrived on Tuesday last. It adjusts both the boundary and navigation in a very satisfactory manner. I have not yet been able to decide whether, on the latter point it clashes or not with the British Treaty; the article being differently represented by different members of the Senate. Nor am I able to say whether any of the articles come within the objections to the constitutionality of the British Treaty. In what relates to contraband and other points in the law of Nations, I understand it presents an honorable contrast to Jay's stipulations.⁵⁴ The Algerine Treaty has some curious features. Among other's, the sum of one Million paid for the ransom and the peace, does not appear before the Senate, as any part of the Treaty; but has been paid

---

51. For the Land Act of 1796, see Payson J. Treat, *The National Land System, 1785–1820* (New York, 1910), pp. 80–91.

52. JM's italics. For the Algerine treaty, see the excellent account in H. G. Barnby, *The Prisoners of Algiers: An Account of the Forgotten American-Algerian War, 1785–1797* (London, 1966), pp. 123–87. President Washington submitted the treaty to the Senate a week before TJ wrote this letter; the tribute amounted to $24,000 worth of naval stores annually; see *PJM,* XVI, p. 227.

53. JM referred to the case of *Ware* v. *Hylton* (3 Dallas 199), which was argued before the Supreme Court in Feb. 1796. John Marshall and Alexander Campbell, U.S. district attorney for Virginia, served as defendant's counsel, and William Lewis, Edward Tilghman, and Alexander Willocks of Pennsylvania represented the plaintiff; see *ibid.,* p. 225.

54. For the treaty with Spain, see Samuel Flagg Bemis, *Pinckney's Treaty: America's Advantage from Europe's Distresses, 1783–1800,* rev. ed. (New Haven, 1960). President Washington sent the treaty and accompanying material to the Senate on Feb. 26 and 29, 1796.

as a verbal part of the Contract, under the authority of the law of appropriation: So that the most material part of the Treaty has been made by the President and the Legislature, without the Treaty-Agency of the Senate.[55] The British Treaty as finally ratified has been republished in the newspapers from foreign copies, but is still not laid before Congress.

The President's birthday has been celebrated with unexampled splendor. The crisis explains the policy of this. It is remarkable however that the annual motion to adjourn for half an hour to pay the compliment of the day, was rejected this year by 50 vs. 38. altho' last year on the yeas and nays 13 only voted in the negative.[56]

Nothing from abroad. Bringhurst is making enquiry as to Sharpless. Mr. Rittenhouse the same as to the Kitchen Stoves. Adieu

Jefferson to Madison

[Monticello] Mar. 6, 1796

I wrote you Feb. 21. since which I have recd. yours of the same day. Indeed mine of that date related only to a single article in yours of Jan. 31. and Feb. 7. I do not at all wonder at the condition in which the finances of the US. are found. Ham's object from the beginning was to throw them into forms which should be utterly undecypherable. I ever said he did not understand their condition himself, nor was able to give a clear view of the excess of our debts beyond our credits, nor whether we were diminishing or increasing the debt. My own opinion was that from the commencemt of this government to the time I ceased to attend to the subject we had been increasing our debt about a million of D. annually. If Mr. Gallatin would undertake to reduce this chaos to order, present us with a clear view of our finances, and put them into a form as simple as they will admit, he will merit immortal honor. The accounts of the US. ought to be, and may be, made, as simple as those of a common farmer, and capable of being understood by common farmers.[57]

Disapproving, as I do, of the unjustifiable largess to the daurs. of the Ct. de Grasse, I will certainly not propose to rivet it by a second example on behalf of M. de Chastellux' son. It will only be done in the event of such a repetition of the precedent, as will give every one a right to share in the plunder. It is indeed surprizing you have not yet recieved the British treaty in form. I pre-

---

55. For the Algerine treaty, see Ray W. Irwin, *The Diplomatic Relations of the United States with the Barbary Powers* (Chapel Hill, 1931), pp. 71–72.

56. See Carroll and Ashworth, pp. 343–44.

57. Albert Gallatin spent the summer writing *A Sketch of the Finances of the United States,* which confirmed TJ's belief that the national debt had increased; see Raymond Walters, Jr., *Albert Gallatin: Jeffersonian Financier and Diplomat* (New York, 1957), pp. 88–94.

sume you would never recieve it were not your co-operation on it necessary. But this will oblige the formal notification of it to you.

I thank you for your information respecting Lownes. There is one article still necessary to be known from Mr. Howell. Lownes began with credits of 90. days from the time of the departure of the nailrod from Philadelphia (not his delivery of it to the vessel: for that makes a difference sometimes of many weeks) but he afterwards reduced it to 60. days. What would be Mr. Howell's credits? I know that credits in Virginia startle a merchant in Philadelphia; but I presume that Mr. Howel could have confidence enough in me (tho' not personally known to him) to make a trial, and govern himself afterwards according to the result, and to the punctuality with which he would recieve his remittances. I wish to know this, tho' I am not yet decided to drop Lownes, on account of his being a good man, and I like much to be in the hands of good men. There is great pleasure in unlimited confidence. My consumption has now advanced from 3. to 4. tons a quarter. I call for a quarter's supply at once, so that the last quarter's supply is always paid for before the next is called for, or at the very time.[58]

The Spanish treaty will have some disagreeable features, seeds of chicanery and eternal broils, instead of peace and friendship. At a period not long before that, they had been ready to sign one giving us vastly more than we had ever contemplated; particularly in our intercourse with their W. Indies. I by no means think of declining the work we have spoken of. On the contrary, I wish with ardor to begin it, since the change of form into which I propose to put it: the first ideas had always oppressed me from a consciousness of my want both of talents and materials to execute it. But it will be impossible for a year to come; and I am not certain whether, even after the present year, I shall not be obliged to put my farms under such direction as that I should be considered as not here as to them, while I should be here as to my papers. My salutations to Mrs. Madison: friendly esteem to Mr. Giles, Page etc.

P. S. Have you considered all the consequences of your proposition respecting post roads?[59] I view it as a source of boundless patronage to the executive, jobbing to members of Congress and their friends, and a bottomless abyss of public money. You will begin by only appropriating the surplus of the post-office revenues: but the other revenues will soon be called in to their aid, and it will be a scene of eternal scramble among the members who can get the most money wasted in their state, and they will always get most who are meanest. We have thought hitherto that the roads of a state could not be so well

---

58. For TJ's conduct of his nail manufactory, see Malone, III, pp. 217–20.

59. JM had made a motion to have a survey made of the national post road from Maine to Georgia, calling his proposal "the commencement of an extensive work." See Joseph H. Harrison, Jr., "*Sic et non:* Thomas Jefferson and Internal Improvement," *JER* 7 (1987): 338–39, and *PJM,* XVI, pp. 213, 221–22. See also Wesley Everett Rich, *The History of the United States Post Office to the Year 1829* (Cambridge, Mass., 1924), and Carl H. Scheele, *A Short History of the Mail Service* (Washington, 1970).

administered even by the state legislature as by the magistracy of the county, on the spot. What will it be when a member of N. H. is to mark out a road for Georgia? Does the power to *establish* post roads given you by congress, mean that you shall *make* the roads, or only *select* from those already made those on which there shall be a post?[60] If the term be equivocal, (and I really do not think it so) which is the safest construction? That which permits a majority of Congress to go to cutting down mountains and bridging of rivers, or the other which if too restricted may refer it to the states for amendment, securing still due measure and proportion among us, and providing some means of information to the members of Congress tantamount to that ocular inspection which even in our county determinations the magistrate finds can not be supplied by any other evidence? The fortification of harbours was liable to great objection. But national circuumstances furnished some color. In this case there is none. The roads of America are the best in the world except those of France and England. But does the state of our population, the extent of our internal commerce, the want of sea and river navigation, call for such expence on roads here, or are our means adequate to it? Think of all this and a great deal more which your good judgment will suggest, and pardon my freedom.

Madison to Jefferson

Philadelphia Mar. 6, 1796

DEAR SIR

I have recd. your's of [Feb. 21] covering a letter to John Bringhurst which has been forwarded to him. There has not been time enough yet for an answer. The letter promised to myself, in yours, has not come [to] hand. The delay can be sufficiently accounted for by the irregularities of the Southern Mails, particularly South of Baltimore.

The Senate have unanimously ratified the Algerine and Spanish Treaties. The latter was a bitter pill to some for two reasons; first as inviting additional emigrations to the Western Country: secondly, as jostling with the Mississippi article in the British Treaties. The Spanish article is in the words following: "It is likewise agreed that the western boundary of the United States which separates them from the Spanish Colony of Louisiana, is in the middle of the channel or bed of the river Mississippi from the Northern boundary of the said States, to the completion of the 31°. of latitude North of the Equator. And his C. Majesty has likewise agreed that the navigation of the said river in its whole breadth from its Source to the Ocean shall be free only to his subjects and the Citizens of the U. States, unless he should extend this privilege to the subjects of other powers by special Convention." Doubts were expressed by King in the

---

60. TJ's italics.

Senate whether this could be construed into a harmony with the stipulations to G. B. and the pulse of the body felt on the subject with a view to a declaratory proviso to the ratification. It was concluded however not to risk the project, and to presume a construction that would avoid the inconsistency. It seems that Pinkney considered the article as admitting a construction reconcileable with the British article. It is also said that he was offered and refused a proposition expressing or implying our right to the navigation, but more directly clashing with the British Treaties.

The President laid the Treaty before the H. of Reps. on tuesday last about one OClock; and in the afternoon it appeared in a Proclamation in Brown's paper. I am well informed that its publication was concerted with the Printer prior to its communication to the House. Whether an original ratification was recd. as the ground of this proceeding, or the copy heretofore not deemed of sufficient formality has been viewed in a more favorable light I can not undertake to say.[61] I suspect the latter to be the case. Perhaps also the ratification of the Spanish and Algerine Treaties, which contain some stipulations analogous to those complained of as unconstitutional in the British Treaty, may have had weight on the occasion. In general however the Spanish Treaty forms rather a contrast to the British, being more than reciprocal in its essential articles, and on the subject of contraband, and the freedom of goods in free ships, being perfectly satisfactory. A motion has been laid on the table by Mr. Livingston, calling on the President for the instructions to Jay etc. The policy of hazarding it is so questionable that he will probably let it sleep or withdraw it. Notice of direct propositions on the Treaty will probably be given tomorrow. The purport and form of them create much dive[r]sity of ideas among the opponents of the Treaty. The state of the business as it now presents itself, with the uncertainty of the particular way of thinking in several quarters of the House, make it truly difficult to decide on the course most acceptable to the body of anti-treaty members. The other side, of course have no difficulties of this sort to contend with.[62]

The bill for the sale of the back lands makes progress tho' but slowly. Its fate is very uncertain. The proposed aid to the federal City will probably succeed in the event, under the patronage of the P. but in the mean time will no doubt be played off in favor of the Treaty.

The Court has not given judgment yet on the Carriage tax. It is said the Judges will be unanimous for its constitutionality. Hamilton and Lee advocated it at the Bar, agst. Campbell and Ingersoll. Bystanders speak highly of Campbells argument, as well as of Ingersoll's. Lee did not shine, and the great

---

61. When President Washington learned that newspapers in Charleston and Philadelphia had published unofficial copies of the ratifications of Jay's treaty, he sent a copy of the treaty to the House on Mar. 1, 1796, and, on the same day, the *Philadelphia Gazette* published his proclamation dated Feb. 29. The official copy of the British ratification did not arrive until Apr. 22, 1796; see Carroll and Ashworth, pp. 347–48.

62. See Combs, pp. 174–76.

effort of his coadjutor as I learn, was to raise a fog around the subject, and to inculcate a respect in the Court for preceding sanctions, in a doubtful case.

We are three month's without news from France, or even G. Britain. There is a report that one of the Sedition bills has passed the H. of Lords, and is not likely to pass the H. of Commons. There is a paragraph which says that Sweeden and Denmark have prohibited the exportation of Grain. Flour here is abt. 15 dolrs. and Wheat 20/. Adieu Yrs affy.

Js MADISON JR

Madison to Jefferson

Philadelphia Mar. 13, 1796

DEAR SIR

Since my last by the last weekly mail, I have seen Mr Rittenhouse on the subject of the Kitchen Stove.[63] He says that at Lancaster where they were invented and are best known, two only remain in use. They certainly save fuel; but are so much complicated in their operation, as to require particular care, and are liable to the objection of keeping the Kitchen excessively hot. Mrs Rittenhouse intimated that, as several modes of Cookery, roasting boiling etc. were carried on at the same time, it often happened that one of the modes did not keep pace with the other. Mr. R. could not learn the price. He supposed, from the quantity of Iron, that it must be considerable.

We are at length embarked in the discussion of the Treaty, which was drawn in rather abruptly by a proposition calling on the President for papers. The point in debate is the Constitutional right of Congs. in relation to Treaties. There seems at present strong reason to conclude, that a majority will be firm in the doctrine that the House has a Constl. right to refuse to pass laws for executing a Treaty, and that the Treaty power is limited by the enumerated powers. Whether the right ought in the present case to be exerted will be a distinct question on the merits of the Treaty, which have not yet come into discussion. I understand the Treaty party expect success on this question, but despair on every other.

Nothing very late from Europe. The British armament is arriving in the W. Indies, which looks like a postponement of peace. It will augment the call on this Country for provisions, and of course the price. Flour is about 15 dolrs. here at present.

63. For the "Rittenhouse stove," a modification of the Franklin stove, see Brooke Hindle, *David Rittenhouse* (Princeton, 1964), p. 247. Also see JM to TJ, Feb. 29, 1796, above.

Madison to Jefferson

Philadelphia Mar. 21, 1796

DEAR SIR

At the desire of Mr. de Liancourt, I put into his hands this introduction to your remembrance of him as an acquaintance at Paris. He meditates a visit to the Southern States, and expects to have the pleasure of taking Monticello in his route, either in going or returning.[64] I need add nothing to your knowledge of his respectability and virtues, I shall only say that the impression I have of both, induces me to concur cheerfully in the use he now makes of me. With the highest esteem and regard I am Dear Sir Yrs. Affecly.

JS. MADISON JR

Jefferson to Madison

[Monticello] Mar. 21, 1796

Th: Jefferson presents his friendly respects to Mr. Madison and asks the favor of him to procure a safe conveyance for the inclosed letter to Colo. Monroe, which is of great importance public and private, as covering papers of consequence.[65]

Jefferson to Madison

[Monticello] Mar. 27, 1796

Yours of the 13th. is recieved. I am enchanted with Mr. Gallatin's speech in Bache's paper of Mar. 14. It is worthy of being printed at the end of the Federalist, as the only rational commentary on the part of the constitution to which it relates.[66] Not that there may not be objections, and difficult ones, to it, and which I shall be glad to see his answers to: but if they are never an-

64. The duc de La Rochefoucauld-Liancourt later published his *Travels through the United States of North America* . . . in two volumes. His description of his visit to Monticello is in II, pp. 69–84.

65. In his letter to James Monroe of Mar. 21, 1796, in Ford, VII, p. 68, TJ made these observations on the contest over Jay's treaty: "On the precedent now to be set will depend the future construction of our constitution, and whether the powers of legislation shall be transferred from the P[resident,] Senate and H[ouse] of R[epresentatives] to the P[resident,] Senate and Piarningo or any other Indian, Algerine or other chief."

66. The Philadelphia *Aurora* printed Gallatin's speech in favor of Edward Livingston's motion calling on the president to submit to the House documents relating to Jay's treaty; see *PJM,* XVI, p. 281.

swered, they are more easily to be gulped down than those which lie to the doctrines of his opponents, which do in fact annihilate the whole of the powers given by the constitution to the legislature. According to the rule established by usage and common sense of construing one part of the instrument by another, the objects on which the P. and S. may exclusively act by treaty are much reduced, but the field on which they may act, with the sanction of the legislature, is large enough: and I see no harm in rendering their sanction necessary, and not much harm in annihilating the whole treaty making power, except as to making peace. If you decide in favor of your right to refuse cooperation in any case of treaty, I should wonder on what occasion it is to be used, if not on one where the rights, the interest, the honor and faith of our nation are so grossly sacrificed, where a faction has entered into conspiracy with the enemies of their country to chain down the legislature at the feet of both; where the whole mass of your constituents have condemned this work in the most unequivocal manner, and are looking to you as their last hope to save them from the effects of the avarice and corruption of the first agent, the revolutionary machinations of others, and the incomprehensible acquiescensce of the only honest man who has assented to it. I wish that his honesty and his political errors may not furnish a second occasion to exclaim 'curse on his virtues, they've undone his country.' Cold weather. Mercury 26. in the morning. Corn fallen at Richmond to 20/—stationary here. Nicholas sure of his election. R. Jouett and Jo. Monroe in competition for the other vote of the county.[67] Affections to Mrs. M. and yourself. Adieu.

Madison to Jefferson

Philadelphia Apr. 4, 1796

DEAR SIR

I have recd. yours of the 6th. Ult; also your letters for Monroe, Mazzei and Van Staphorsts; and shall have a good conveyance for them in two or three days. I am in some doubt however whether it may not be best to detain those for Mazzei and V. untill you can add the information I am now able to furnish you from Dohrman. He has at length closed the business of Mazzei in a just and honorable manner, by allowing the N. Y. damages on the bills of 20 PerCt. and the N Y. rate of interest, of 7 PerCt. This mode of settlement after deducting the partial payments for which he has receipts, leaves a balance of 3087 dollars, which has been just paid into my hands, and will be disposed of as you shall direct. You will of course lose no time in writing to me on the subject.

67. In the Albemarle County elections for the Virginia House of Delegates on Apr. 4, 1796, Wilson Cary Nicholas won easily, and Joseph J. Monroe, James Monroe's younger brother, defeated Robert Jouett; see *ibid.*

I have not yet heard from Bringhurst on the subject of Sharpless. He has no doubt written to you, according to his promise. I have seen Mr. Howell, who says there would be no difficulty in allowing you the credit you desire, if his son shd. take the place of Lownes.

I was not unaware of the considerations you suggest with regard to the post roads; but do not consider my proposition as involving any dangerous consequences. It is limited to the choice of roads where that is presented, and to the opening them, in other cases, so far only as may be necessary for the transportation of the mail. This I think fairly within the object of the Constn. It had, in fact, become essential that something shd. be done, and something would have been attempted, on a worse principle. If the route shall be once fixt for the post road, the local authorities will probably undertake the improvement etc. of the roads; and individuals will go to work in providing the proper accomodations on them for general use.[68]

The Newspapers will inform you that the call for the Treaty papers was carried by 62 agst. 37. You will find the answer of the President herewith inclosed.[69] The absolute refusal was as unexpected, as the tone and tenor of the message, are improper and indelicate. If you do not at once perceive the drift of the appeal to the Genl. Convention and its journal, recollect one of Camillus's last numbers, and read the latter part of Murray's speech.[70] There is little doubt in my mind that the message came from N. Y. where it was seen that an experiment was to be made at the hazard of the P. to save the faction agst. the Reps. of the people.[71] The effect of this reprehensible measure on the majority is not likely to correspond with the calculation of its authors. I think there will be sufficient firmness to face it with resolutions declaring the Const:l. powers of the House as to Treaties, and that in applying for papers, they are not obliged to state their reasons to the Executive. In order to preserve this firmness however, it is necessary to avoid as much as possible an overt rencontre with the Executive. The day after the message was recd. the bill guarantying the loan for the federal City, was carried thro' the H. of Reps. by a swimming majority.

I have letters from Monroe of the 12 and 20 Jany. The Truce with Austria was demanded by the latter, and was not likely to be renewed. A continuance of the war with England was counted on. The French Govt. was in regular and vigorous operation, and gaining daily more and more of the public confi-

---

68. See Harrison, 339–40. JM's bill was defeated in the Senate.

69. For President Washington's rejection of the House request, see Fitzpatrick, XXXV, pp. 2–5.

70. George Washington cited the "journals of the General convention" to support his claim that the Constitution vested the treaty-making power exclusively in the president and Senate. Alexander Hamilton made the same point in his "Camillus" essays, as did William Vans Murray in his argument against Livingston's motion. See *ibid.*, pp. 4–5; Syrett, XX, pp. 22–24; and Peter P. Hill, *William Vans Murray, Federalist Diplomat: The Shaping of Peace with France, 1797–1801* (Syracuse, 1971), pp. 30–34.

71. President Washington made his decision before he received Hamilton's letter; see Carroll and Ashworth, p. 354.

dence. A forced loan was going on for 25 Mil: sterlg, 12 Mil of wch. was receivable in Assignats at 100 for one; the balance in specie and produce. It is said that the British armament for the West Indies had suffered a *third* Coup de Vent, after leaving the channel, a *third* time.

According to my memory and that of others, the Journal of the Convention was by a vote deposited with the P. to be kept sacred untill called for by some competent authority.[72] How can this be reconciled with the use he has made of it? Examine my notes if you please at the close of the business, and let me know what is said on the subject.[73] You will perceive that the quotation is nothing to the purpose.[74] Most of the majority wd. decide as the Convention did—because they think there may be some Treaties as a Mere Treaty of peace that would not require the Legislative power—a ratification by law also expresses a different idea from that entertained by the House of its Agency. Adieu.

Madison to Jefferson

Philadelphia Apr. 11, 1796

DEAR SIR

Since my last the inclosed was recd. from J. B. The sample of rod must wait for a private conveyance.

Yours of the 27th. has been duly recd. You already know that the call for papers was refused, and reasons assigned more extraordinary a great deal than the refusal. This measure of the Ex. produced two propositions asserting the right of the House to judge of the expediency of Treaties stipulating on legislative subjects, and declaring that it was not requisite in a call for papers to express the use to be made of them. It was expected that a long and obstinate discussion would have attended these defensive measures. Under that Idea I

---

72. JM did not know that President Washington had delivered the convention journal to Secretary of State Pickering on Mar. 19, 1796; see Max Farrand, ed., *The Records of the Federal Convention of 1787*, 4 vols. (New Haven, 1911), III, p. 370.

73. JM had loaned TJ his "Notes on Debates in the Federal Convention"; see JM to TJ, Nov. 8, 1795, above.

74. JM always argued that Washington's citation of the secret journal was neither an accurate nor a justifiable response. After retiring from the presidency, he wrote an analysis of Washington's position, asserting that Washington misjudged the House call for Jay's papers on four grounds. Three boiled down to the claim that the convention vote on Aug. 23, 1787, cited by Washington, did not deal with the issue raised by Livingston since the House was not involved in the ratification of the treaty, but instead was claiming its right to deliberate on provisions that it was called upon to execute. The fourth ground stated that the Constitution's "validity and authority" flowed not from the journal of the Constitutional Convention, but from the state conventions chosen by the people to ratify the document; see Elizabeth Fleet, "Madison's 'Detached Memoranda,'" *WMQ* 3 (1946): 543–45, and *PJM*, XVI, p. 287.

entered into a free, but respectful review of the fallacy of the reasons contained in the Message and the day being nearly spent the Come. rose and an adjt. succeeded. The next morning instead of a reply the question was called for and taken without a word of argument on the subject. The two resolutions were carried by 57 agst. 35, and six members, who not foreseeing the early call for the question had not taken their seats, soon appeared and desired to have their names added to the Majority. This was not permitted by the rules of the House; but the case is explained in the Newspapers. Today is fixed for taking up the Treaties.[75] We shall separate the Spanish and other Treaties from the British, and proceed to make for them the necessary provisions. With respect to the latter, it seems at present probable, that it will be hung up on a recital of the vices of the Treaty itself, the want of information, and the perseverance in seizing our Ships and seamen, which ought to have the same influence on our decision whether viewed as consistent with or an infraction of the Treaty. An Embargo on Indian Corn is proposed, but has not been discussed.[76] Nothing very material from Abroad. Bache is publishing the Treaty Debates in nos. for an 8o. vol: I inclose the 1st. no. under address to Mr. Carr. Adieu

J. M.

Jefferson to Madison

[Monticello] Apr. 17, 1796

DEAR SIR

Yours of the 4th. came to hand the day before yesterday. I have turned to the Conventional history, and inclose you an exact copy of what is there on the subject you mentioned. I have also turned to my own papers, and send you some things extracted from them which shew that the recollection of the P. has not been accurate when he supposed his own opinion to have been uniformly that declared in his answer of Mar. 30. The records of the Senate will vouch this. I happened at the same time with your letter to recieve one from Mazzei giving some directions as to his remittances. I have not time to decide and say by this post how Dohrman's paiment should be remitted according to his desire and existing circumstances, that is to say, whether by bill on Amsterdam to the V. Staphorsts, or by bill on London to himself. I will write to you definitively by next post. We are experiencing a most distressing drought. The ground cannot now be broken with the plough. Our fruit is as yet safe, but the

---

75. For brief discussions, see Robert A. Rutland, *James Madison: The Founding Father* (New York, 1987), pp. 137-43, and Combs, pp. 174-88.

76. The resolution to prevent the exportation of corn and cornmeal, on which the poor relied as a chief source of food, was defeated four days later; see *PJM,* XVI, p. 309.

spring is cold and backward. Corn is at 25/ here, but greatly higher in some parts. Wheat 16/ at Richmond at 90. days. Tobo. 40/. My respects to Mrs. Madison. Adieu affectionately.

ENCLOSURE

Extract verbatim from last page but one, and the last page.[77]

'Mr. King suggested that the journals of the Convention should be either destroyed, or deposited in the custody of the President. He thought, if suffered to be made public, a bad use would be made of them by those who would wish to prevent the adoption of the constitution.

Mr. Wilson preferred the 2d expedient. He had at one time liked the first best: but as false suggestions may be propagated, it should not be made impossible to contradict them.

A question was then put on depositing the journals and other papers of the Convention in the hands of the President, on which

N. H. ay. M. ay. Ct. ay. N. J. ay. Pena. ay. Del. ay. Md. no.[78] Virga. ay. N. C. ay. S. C. ay Georgia ay.

The President having asked what the convention meant should be done with the Journals etc. whether copies were to be allowed to the members if applied for, it was resolved nem: con: "that he retain the Journal and other papers subject to the order of the Congress, if ever formed under the constitution."

The members then proceeded to sign the instrument.' etc.

'In Senate Feb. 1. 1791.

The Commee. to whom was referred that part of the speech of the Pr. of the US. at the opening of the session which relates to the commerce of the Mediterranean, and also the letter from the Secy. of state dated 20th. Jan. 1791. with the papers accompanying the same, reported, Whereupon

Resolved that the Senate do advise and consent that the Pr. of the US. take such measures as he may think necessary for the redemption of the citizens of the US. now in captivity at Algiers, provided the expence shall not exceed 40,000 Dols. and also that measures be taken to confirm the treaty now existing between the U. S. and the emperor of Marocco.'[79]

The above is a copy of a resoln. of Senate referred to me by the P. to prepare an answer to, and I find immediately following this among my papers a press copy from an original written fairly in my own hand ready for the P's signature and to be given in to the Senate the following answer.

'Gent. of the Senate.

I will proceed to take measures for the ransom of our citizens in captivity at Algiers, in conformity with your resoln. of advice of the 1st. inst. so soon as the monies necessary shall be appropriated *by the legislature* and shall be in readiness.

The recognition of our treaty with the new Emperor of Marocco requires also

77. TJ took his extract from the proceeding of Sept. 17, 1787, in JM's "Notes on Debates in the Federal Convention"; see *ibid.*, p. 330.

78. JM inserted an asterisk here and added this footnote: "This negative of Maryland was occasioned by the language of the instructions to the Deputies of that state, which required them to report to the state the *proceedings* of the Convention."

79. TJ quoted from his copy of the Senate executive journal; see *PJM*, XVI, p. 331.

previous appropriation and provision. The importance of this last to the liberty and property of our citizens induces me to urge it on your earliest attention.'[80]

Tho' I have no memm. of the delivery of this to the Senate yet I have not the least doubt it was given in to them and will be found among their records.

I find among my press copies, the following in my hand writing

'The committee to report that the President does not think that circumstances will justify, in the present instance his entering into *absolute* engagements for the ransom of our captives in Algiers, nor calling for money from the treasury, nor raising it by loan, without previous authority from *both branches* of the legislature.' Apr. 9. 1792.[81]

I do not recollect the occasion of the above paper with certainty. But I think there was a commee. appointed by the Senate to confer with the P. on the subject of the ransom, and to advise what is there declined, and that a member of the commee. advising privately with me as to the report they were to make to the house, I minuted down the above, as the substance of what I concieved to be the proper report after what had passed with the Pr. and gave the original to the member preserving the press copy. I think the member was either Mr. Izard or Mr. Butler: and have no doubt such a report will be found on the files of the Senate.

On the 8th. of May following, in consequence of Questions proposed by the Pr. to the Senate, they came to a resolution, on which a mission was founded.

Madison to Jefferson

Philadelphia Apr. 18, 1796

DEAR SIR

My last requested your orders relating to Dohrman's payment to Me for Mazzei; and I impatiently wait for them.

Resolutions have passed for carrying into effect, the Spanish, Indian and Algerine Treaties. The British is now depending. I inclose the proposition in which the opponents of it, will unite. According to present calculation, this proposition will be carried by *nearly* the same majority as prevailed in the vote asserting the Rights of the House on the subject of Treaties.[82] The debate is but just commenced. Those who at first were for a silent question, will probably now spin out time for the purpose of calling in the mercantile interference in behalf. You will see the expedient on foot in this City. The petition of the Merchts. etc. will be signed by 7 or 800 as is said. An adverse petition will be signed by 3 or 4 times that number. In N. Y. and Boston it is hoped the

---

80. TJ quoted from his copy of Washington's message to the Senate on Feb. 22, 1791; see *ibid*.

81. TJ cited his notes of Apr. 9, 1792, on the question of whether the president could negotiate to ransom American captives without the consent of both the Senate and the House; see *ibid*.

82. On Apr. 15, 1796, JM urged the House to refuse appropriations to implement Jay's treaty and proposed that the treaty be renegotiated; see Combs, p. 178.

counter petitioners will equally preponderate. Baltimore which was at first most opposed to the Treaty is become most generally reconciled to the execution. The hope of endimnification for past losses, and the fears for their floating speculations, which have been arranged on the idea that the Treaty would go into effect, bear down with that class all attention to the general and permanent good of the Country, and perhaps their own real and comprehe[n]sive interest. The Country also is under an operation for obtaining petitions for the Treaty. The Western Counties, have yielded a number; being dextrously alarmed for the Spanish Treaty as involved in the fate of the British. I expected to have Sent you my observations on the Presidents Message, which the Printer told me shd. certainly be out this morning.[83] He thought Mr. Iredell's charge and the eccho of the G. Jurey, entitled to priority.[84]

Madison to Jefferson

[Philadelphia] Apr. 23, 1796

DEAR SIR

I inclose another number of the Debates on the Treaty. The subject is still going on in the House, as well as the press. The majority has melted, by changes and absence, to 8 or 9 votes. Whether these will continue firm is more than I can decide. Every possible exertion is made as usual on the other side. A sort of appeal has been made to the people, with an expectation that the mercantile force would triumph over the popular sentiment. In this city the majority of petitioners has appeared agst. the Mercantile party. We do not know the event of the experiment in N. York. Petitions on both sides are running thro' the adjoining States of Delaware, and N. Jersey. Among other extraordinary manoeuvres, the Insurance Companies here and in New Y. stopt business, in order to reduce prices and alarm the public. The Banks have been powerfully felt in the progress of the petitions in the Cities for the Treaty. Scarce a mercht. or Trader but what depends on discounts, and at this moment there is a general pinch for money. Under such circumstances, a Bank Director soliciting subscriptions is like a Highwayman with a pistol demanding the purse. We hope the question will be taken tomorrow. But if carried agst. the Treaty, the game will be played over again in other forms. The Senate will either send it down by itself, or coupled with the Spanish Treaty or both. Nothing of importance from Europe. Adieu.

Js. MADISON JR

83. For JM's observations on Washington's refusal to furnish papers relating to Jay's treaty, see his speech of Apr. 6, 1796, in *PJM,* XVI, pp. 290–301.
84. After Supreme Court Justice James Iredell gave his charge to the Philadelphia grand jury of the federal circuit court, that body urged that Jay's treaty be implemented without delay; see *ibid.,* p. 332.

Jefferson to Madison

[Monticello] Apr. 24, 1796

Yours of the 11th. is recieved, with the letter from Bringhurst.[85] On consideration of all circumstances, I find that the advantages of taking iron from the manufacturer will be more than countervailed by disadvantages. I give up Sharpless therefore. Lownes I must abandon. Above a month ago I wrote to him for an additional ton of rod, merely to furnish a decent occasion to call for nearly that quantity still unfurnished tho paid for so long ago as October last.[86] I find it is not furnished because it was paid for before hand. I therefore conclude to open dealings with Mr. Howel, to whom I have written the inclosed letter, which I have left open for your perusal, merely that understanding the ground of my application, you may have the goodness to call on him, and just make us as it were acquainted in the offset, which will start us with that degree of good understanding that might otherwise require a course of time and dealing to establish. This single office performed, I will give you no further trouble with the business.

With respect to Mazzei's money, I think it safest on the whole to remit it to the Van Staphorsts and Hubbard of Amsterdam, with whom Mazzei is on the best and most confidential terms. I will therefore ask the favor of you to invest it in bills on Amsterdam; not in London bills, as in a former remittance of bills on London payable to the V. S. and H. the drawee availed himself of Mr. Pitt's law forbidding paiment.[87] I will write to V. S. and H. and also to Mazzei by this or the next post, to inform them of what we do, so that you need only put the bills under cover to V. S. and H. and refer them to the explanations they will recieve from me. Nothing new in politics. We are withering under an unparraleled drought. Adieu affectionately.

P. S. I have written the letters to V. S. and H. and P. M.[88] which I will pray you to have forwarded, for which purpose I inclose them.

---

85. In his letter of Apr. 11, 1796, JM enclosed Bringhurst's letter and a sample of iron rods made by Jonathan Sharpless for TJ's nailery.

86. For TJ's use of rod iron at his nailery, see Betts, *Thomas Jefferson's Farm Book,* pp. 426–34.

87. For the financial complications caused by the Batavian Republic's declaration of war on Great Britain in 1795, see *PJM,* XVI, p. 337.

88. It was TJ's letter to Mazzei of Apr. 24, 1796, that created a furor when it was published in the United States in May 1797. See ch. 22, below.

Madison to Jefferson

Philadelphia May 1, 1796

DEAR SIR

I have your favor of the 17 Apl. covering two Extracts one from your notes, the other from mine. The latter corresponds with the recollection which myself, and other members had expressed; and the former with that of Majr. Butler, and with the Journals of the Senate. The Report of the Come. to which you refer, can not be found, tho' Mr. B. says he knows one was made. This enquiry has been set on foot without your name.

The Treaty question was brought to a vote on friday in Come. of Whole. Owing to the absence (*certainly* casual and momentary) of one member, and the illness of another, the Committee were divided 49 and 49. The Chairman (Muhlenberg) decided in the affirmative, saying that in the House it would be subject to modification which he wished. In the House yesterday, an Enemy of the Treaty moved a preamble, reciting "that altho' the Treaty was highly objectionable, yet considering all circumstances, particularly the duration for two years etc., and confiding in the efficacy of measures that might be taken for stopping the Spoliations and impressments etc." For this ingredient, which you will perceive the scope of, all who meant to persevere agst. the Treaty, with those who only yielded for the reasons expressed in it, ought to have united in voting, as making the pill a bitter one to the Treaty party, as well as less poisonous to the public interest. A few wrongheads however thought fit to separate, whereby the motion was lost by one vote. The main question was then carried in favr. of the Treaty by 51 agst. 48.[89] This revolution was foreseen, and might have been mitigated tho' not prevented, if sooner provided for. But some who were the first to give way to the crisis under its actual pressure, were most averse to prepare for it. The progress of this business throughout has to me been the most worrying and vexatious that I ever encountered; and the more so as the causes lay in the unsteadiness, the follies, the perverseness, and the defections among our friends, more than in the strength or dexterity, or malice of our opponents. It is impossible for me to detail these causes to you now. My consolation under them is in the effect they have in riveting my future purposes.[90] Had the preamble condemning the Treaty on its merits, exercising the discretionary power of the House, and requiring from the Ex. a stoppage of the spoliations etc., been agreed to, I have reason to believe, the Treaty party would have felt it a compleat defeat. You will be informed by the newspapers of the means practised for stirring up petitions etc., in favr. of the Treaty. The plan was laid in this City and cir-

---

89. The best summaries of the votes in Congress are in Combs, pp. 178–88, and Carroll and Ashworth, pp. 361–77. On May 6, 1796, Washington signed separate appropriation bills to implement the treaties with Algiers, Great Britain, Spain, and the Northwest Indians; see *PJM,* XVI, p. 344.

90. JM meant that he planned to retire from Congress at the end of his term in Mar. 1797.

culated by a correspondence thro' the Towns every where. In the mean time the Banks, the British Merchts. the insurance Comps. were at work in influencing individuals, beating down the prices of produce, and sounding the tocksin of foreign war, and domestic convulsions. The success has been such as you would suppose. In several neighbouring districts the people have been so deluded as to constrain their Representatives to renounce their opposition to the Treaty. An appeal to the people on any pending measure, can never be more than an appeal to those in the neighbourhood of the Govt. and to the Banks, the Merchts. and the dependents and expectants of the Govt. at a distance. Adieu Affy.

J. M. Jr

Madison to Jefferson

[Philadelphia] May 9, 1796

Dear Sir

I have your letter on the subject of Mr. Howell and seen the old gentleman who interests himself in it. I think it probable you will find reason to be satisfied with the change you have made in your merchant. I have not yet been able to procure bills on Amsterdam for Van Staphorst. They can be got I am told, but not with so much ease or choice, as on London. I shall not intermit my attention to that object.

We have had a calm ever since the decision on the Treaty. Petitions however continue to arrive, chiefly in favr. of the Treaty. The N. England States have been ready to rise in mass agst. the H. of Reps. Such have been the exertions and influence of Aristocracy, Anglicism, and mercantilism in that quarter, that Republicanism is perfectly overwhelmed, even in the Town of Boston. I hope it will prove but a transitory calamity; and that the discovery of the delusion, will ultimately work a salutary effect. The people have been every where made to believe that the object of the H. of Reps. in resisting the Treaty was—*War;* and have thence listened to the summons "to follow where Washington leads." Nothing late from abroad. We expect to adjourn abt. the 20 or 25 inst: Adieu Yrs. affy

Js. Madison Jr

We has [*sic*] just had a most plentiful rain after a drought nearly as severe as that with you.

Madison to Jefferson

Philadelphia May 22, 1796

DEAR SIR

Congress are hurrying through the remnant of business before them, and will probably adjourn about saturday next. Petitions in favor of the Treaty still come in from distant places. The name of the President and the alarm of war, have had a greater effect, than were apprehended on one side, or expected on the other. A crisis which ought to have been so managed as to fortify the Republican cause, has left it in a very crippled condition; from which its recovery will be the more difficult as the elections in N. Y. Massachusetts and other States, where the prospects were favorable, have taken a wrong turn under the impressions of the moment. Nothing but auspicious contingences abroad or at home, can regain the lost ground. Peace in Europe would have a most salutary influence, and accts. just recd. from France revive in some degree the hope of it with the Emperor, which will hasten of course a peace with England. On the other hand, a scene rather gloomy is presented by a letter I have just recd. from Col. M. It is dated Feby. 27. The following extracts form the substance of it.

"About a fortnight past I was informed by *the minister of foreign affairs that the government had at length resolved* how to act *with us in respect to our treaty with England* that *they considered it* as having *violated* or rather *annulled our treaty of alliance with them and taken part with the coalised powers that they had rather have an open enemy than a perfidious friend*—that it was *resolved to send an envoy extra. to the United States to discuss this business with us* and whose *powers would expire with the execution of the trust. I was astonished with the communication and alarmed with its probable consequences.* I told him *it might probably lead to war* and *thereby separate us which was what our enemies wished*—that *it hazarded much and without a probable gain* that from the moment *a person of that character arrived their friends would seem to act under his banner* and which circumstance would *injure their character and lessen their efforts. In truth I did everything in my power to prevent this measure* and in which I am now told by *the minister that I have succeeded* the *Directoire having resolved to continue the ordinary course of representation only.* But thro' this *I hear strong sentiments will be conveyed. The whole of this is made known to the executive by me.*"

"The forced loan was less productive than was expected, *and the embarrassment in the finance extreme.* Some *think another movement at hand but I see no evidence of it* at present. In all calculations on this subject *it ought to be recollected* that the *executive are sound and having the government in their hands are strong.*"

"There are strong symptoms of an actual rupture between us and this country. The *minister the government preferred to have us as open* [enemies] *rather than perfidious friends.* Other proofs occur to shew that *this sentiment has gone deep into their councils.*"

The "Minerva" of N. Y. lately announced, with an affected emphasis, a letter from Paris to N. Y. intimating that influencial persons in the U. S. were urging measures on France, which might force this Country to chuse war agst. England, as the only alternative for war agst. France. It is probable that categorical steps on the part of F. towards us are anticipated as the consequence of what has been effected by the British party here, and that much artifice will be practised by it to charge them in some unpopular form, on its Republican opponents.

Before I leave this I shall make up a parcel of pamphlets etc. for you to be forwarded to Richmond. The inclosed number of the Debates is a continuation which has been regular, I hope the preceding numbers have all arrived safe.

King is appointed Minister to London and Humphreys to Madrid, Pinkney and Short retiring. The vacancy at Lisbon not yet filled.

Madison to Jefferson

[Philadelphia] May 30, 1796

Congress will adjourn the day after to-morrow. News as late as April 8 from London; peace likely to take place between France and England; provisions falling much in price, both in F. and G. B. The moneyed distresses reviving in the latter, and great alarms for a terrible shock to the Banking and Mercantile Houses.

21

THE ELECTION OF 1796

THE FIGHT OVER Jay's treaty was the opening round in the presidential campaign of 1796. Although Madison thought that the Federalist victory in carrying the treaty *"presses hard on the republican interest,"*[1] Jefferson was more optimistic. The treaty had been "a dear bought victory" for the Federalists, he told Monroe. "It has given the most radical shock to their party which it has ever received: and there is no doubt they would be glad to be replaced on the ground they possessed the instant before Jay's nomination extraordinary. They see that nothing can support them but the Colossus of the President's merits with the people, and the moment he retires, that his successor, if a Monocrat, will be overborne by the republican sense of his Constituents, if a republican he will of course give fair play to that sense, and lead things into the channel of harmony between the governors and governed. In the meantime, patience."[2]

The publication of Washington's Farewell Address in September was, as Fisher Ames noted, "a signal, like dropping a hat, for the party racers to start."[3] As early as mid-May, Madison had predicted that the coming campaign would make Jefferson "the *object on one side Adams* apparently *on the other*."[4] Earlier in the year, he had concluded that "the *republicans* knowing that *Jefferson alone* can be *started with hope of success mean to push him*."[5] Except for Madison's exchange with Jefferson in 1795, Jefferson was not consulted about heading the Republican ticket.[6] Nor did Madison write his friend after

---

1. JM to James Monroe, May 14, 1796, in *PJM*, XVI, p. 357; the italicized words were written in code.
2. TJ to James Monroe, July 10, 1796, in Ford, VII, p. 89.
3. Fisher Ames to Oliver Wolcott, Sept. 16, 1796, quoted in Noble E. Cunningham, Jr., *The Jeffersonian Republicans: The Formation of Party Organization, 1789–1801* (Chapel Hill, 1957), p. 93.
4. JM to James Monroe, May 14, 1796, in *PJM*, XVI, p. 358; the italicized words were written in code.
5. JM to James Monroe, Feb. 26, 1796, *ibid.,* p. 232; the italicized words were written in code.
6. See JM to TJ, Mar. 23, 1795, above, and TJ to JM, Apr. 27, 1795, above, for the exchange.

Congress adjourned or make his annual visit to Monticello, even though he spent all summer and most of the fall in Virginia. "I have not seen *Jefferson,*" he explained to Monroe only six weeks before the election, "and have *thought it best to* present *him no opportunity of protesting to* his *friend[s] against* being *embarked in the contest.* Whether *he will get a majority of vote* is *uncertain.*"⁷

Nor was it certain that John Adams would win, especially after Hamilton launched a surreptitious campaign to slide Adams's running mate, Thomas Pinckney, ahead of the New Englander. Although a caucus of Federalist members of Congress had agreed to support Adams for president and Pinckney, who had just returned to the United States after negotiating a popular treaty with Spain, for vice president, the Constitution allowed members of the electoral college to cast votes for two candidates without indicating a preference for president or vice president. Hamilton, therefore, proposed that the Federalist electors support Adams and Pinckney equally in the North, while the electors in Pinckney's home state of South Carolina voted unanimously for Pinckney but withheld a few votes from Adams, making Pinckney president and keeping Adams, no friend to banks, in his post as vice president.⁸

Throughout the election campaign, Jefferson, noting his great "distance from the scene of information and influence,"⁹ maintained an aloof silence while being "pushed" by the Republicans and attacked by the Federalists. But he followed the campaign with mixed feelings, writing after the results were in: "In truth, I did not know myself under the pens of either of my friends or foes. It is unfortunate for our peace, that unmerited abuse wounds, while unmerited praise has not the power to heal. These are hard wages," he added, "for the services of all the active and healthy years of one's life," especially since his name had been brought forward "without concert or expectation on my part; (on my salvation I declare it)."¹⁰

One charge that stung was the claim that Jefferson and the Republicans were subservient to France. The actions of Pierre Adet, Genet's successor as minister to the United States, played into the hands of the Federalists when Adet published a series of documents charging that Jay's treaty violated the Franco-American treaty of 1778 and appealed to the American people for a change in the administration of their government and a return "to sentiments, and to measures, more conformable to the interests of the alliance, and the sworn friendship between the two nations."¹¹ Until then, he threatened, the French would treat American vessels "in the same manner as they suffer the

---

7. JM to James Monroe, Sept. 29, 1796, in *PJM,* XVI, p. 404; the italicized words were written code.

8. Stephen G. Kurtz, *The Presidency of John Adams: The Collapse of Federalism, 1795–1800* (Philadelphia, 1957), pp. 96–113, and John C. Miller, *The Federalist Era: 1789–1801* (New York, 1960), pp. 198–202.

9. TJ to Archibald Stuart, Jan. 4, 1797, in Ford, VII, p. 103.

10. TJ to Edward Rutledge, Dec. 27, 1796, *ibid.,* p. 93.

11. Quoted in Malone, III, pp. 286–87.

English to treat them."[12] The Federalists pounced on this threat, citing Washington's warning in his Farewell Address against foreign influence and linking the Republicans with "the interference of a foreign nation in our affairs."[13]

Although Jefferson never mentioned Adet's intrigue, Madison quickly disowned it and informed Jefferson that "Adêt's Note which you will have seen [in the newspapers], is working all the evil with which it is pregnant. Those who rejoice at its indiscretions and are taking advantage of them, have the impudence to pretend that it is an electioneering manoeuvre, and that the French Govt. have been led to it by the opponents of the British Treaty. Unless the unhapy effect of it here and cause of it in France, be speedily obviated by wise councils and healing measures, the crisis will unquestionably be perverted into a perpetual alienation of the two Countries by the secret enemies of both."[14]

After the elections were over, Adet had sober second thoughts about the man whose candidacy he had hoped to advance: "Mr. Jefferson likes us because he detests England; he seeks to draw near to us because he fears us less than Great Britain; but he might change his opinion of us tomorrow, if tomorrow Great Britain should cease to inspire his fears. Jefferson, although a friend of liberty and learning, although an admirer of the efforts we have made to break our bonds and dispel the cloud of ignorance which weighs down the human race, Jefferson, I say, is American and, as such, he cannot be sincerely our friend. An American is the born enemy of all the European peoples."[15]

After Madison returned in November to his last session of Congress prior to retiring, he began reporting the election results to Jefferson. Before the outcome was clear, he told his friend that "it is not possible yet to calculate with any degree of certainty whether you are to be left by the Electors to enjoy the repose to which you are so much attached, or are to be summoned to the arduous trust which depends on their allotment. It is not improbable," he added, "that Pinkney will step in between the two who have been treated as the principals in the question." Referring to Hamilton's "Jockeyship" to place Pinckney ahead of Adams, he reported that "it is even suspected that this turn has been secretly meditated from the beginning in a quarter where the *leading* zeal for Adams has been affected. This Jockeyship is accounted for by the enmity of Adams to Banks and funding systems which is now become public, and by an apprehension that he is too headstrong to be a fit puppet for the intriguers behind the skreen."[16]

Five days later, the election results were still unknown, but Madison tried

---

12. Cunningham, p. 101.
13. Oliver Wolcott, Jr., to Oliver Wolcott, Sr., Nov. 19, 1796, quoted in Malone, III, p. 288.
14. JM to TJ, Dec. 5, 1796, below.
15. Pierre Adet to the minister of foreign affairs, Dec. 31, 1796, quoted in Malone, III, pp. 289–90.
16. JM to TJ, Dec. 5, 1796, below.

to prepare Jefferson for either the vice presidency or "the primary station, if that should be your lot. The prevailing idea," he continued, "is that Pinkney will have the greatest number of votes: and I think that Adams will be most likely to stand next. There are other calculations however less favorable to both."[17] As the election results became clearer, Madison urged Jefferson to accept the vice presidency, even though "the inadequateness of the importance of the place" did not measure up to the post for which his friends had "pushed" him. "You must prepare yourself therefore to be summoned to the place Mr. Adams now fills," he argued, because "it is expected that as you had made up your mind to obey the call of your Country, you will let it decide on the particular place where your services are to be rendered. . . . On the whole it seems *essential* that you should not refuse the station which is likely to be your lot."

For one thing, Madison continued, it offered the possibility of a reconciliation between Adams and Jefferson, the compatriots of the Revolution, "particularly in *relation to our external system.* You know," he emphasized, "that *his feelings* will not *enslave him to the* example of *his predecessor.* It is certain that his *censures of our paper systems* and the intrigues at *New York for setting P[inckney] above him* have fixed an *enmity with the British faction.* Nor should it pass for nothing, that the true *interest of New England* particularly requires reconciliation with France as the road to her commerce. *Add to the whole that he* is said to speak of *you now in friendly terms* and will no doubt be *soothed by your acceptance of a place subordinate to him*." But Madison could not quite overcome his aversion for Adams, adding that "it must be confessed however that all calculations, are qualified by *his political principles* and *prejudices*."[18]

Breaking his silence on the election, Jefferson repeated his sentiments of 1795, writing that "the first wish of my heart was that you should have been proposed for the administration of the government. On your declining it," he observed, "I wish any body rather than myself: and there is nothing I so anxiously hope as that my name may come out either second or third. These would be indifferent to me; as the last would leave me at home the whole year, and the other two thirds of it."

By Jefferson's calculations, Adams would win. "I have no expectation that the Eastern states will suffer themselves to be so much outwitted as to be made the tools for bringing in P[inckney] instead of A[dams]. I presume they will throw away their second vote." He even foresaw the possibility of a tie between Adams and himself, "a difficulty from which the constitution has provided no issue," especially if the House of Representatives also split evenly in its efforts to break the tie. "In that case," he urged, "I pray you and authorize you fully to sollicit on my behalf that Mr. Adams may be preferred. He has always been my senior from the commencement of our public life, and the expression of

---

17. JM to TJ, Dec. 10, 1796, below.
18. JM to TJ, Dec. 19, 1976, below. The italicized words were written in code.

the public will being equal, this circumstance ought to give him the preference."

But there was also a substantial political reason for not coveting the presidency in 1797. Foreign affairs, he thought, "never wore so gloomy an aspect since the year 83. Let those come to the helm who think they can steer clear of the difficulties. I have no confidence in myself for the undertaking."[19] In a later letter, he elaborated on this theme, writing that Washington was "fortunate to get off just as the bubble is bursting, leaving others to hold the bag. Yet, as his departure will mark the moment when the difficulties begin to work, you will see, that they will be ascribed to the new administration, and that he will have his usual good fortune of reaping credit from the good acts of others, and leaving to them that of his errors."[20]

When the electoral votes were officially tabulated, Adams tallied 71, Jefferson 68, Pinckney 59, and Burr 30. Once the outcome was known, Jefferson assured Madison that he was reconciled "to a relinquishment of the first office" and "acquiescence under the second. As to the first it was impossible that a more solid unwillingness settled on full calculation, could have existed in any man's mind, short of the degree of absolute refusal. The only view on which I would have gone into it for a while," he told his political partner, "was to put our vessel on her republican tack before she should be thrown too much to leeward of her true principles." He confessed that it was difficult to persuade others to believe "one's declarations of a disinclination to honors," but he protested his sincerity. "As to the second," he added, "it is the only office in the world about which I am unable to decide in my own mind whether I had rather have it or not have it. Pride does not enter into the estimate; for I think with the Romans that the General of to-day should be a soldier tomorrow if necessary." And he repeated his views about being in "a secondary position to Mr. Adams. I am his junior in life, was his junior in Congress, his junior in the diplomatic line, his junior lately in our civil government."[21]

Indeed, even before he received Madison's letter urging a reconciliation with Adams, Jefferson had drafted a congratulatory note to the president-elect. He had never doubted that Adams would be elected, he wrote, and he wished that his administration "may be filled with glory and happiness to yourself and advantage to us." Although Jefferson said that he might not be believed, he had "no ambition to govern men," preferring to "leave to others the sublime delights of riding in the storm, better pleased with sound sleep and a warm birth below, with the society of neighbors, friends and fellow laborers of the earth, than of spies and sycophants." In a slashing attack, Jefferson denounced Hamilton's attempt to cheat Adams out of his election "by a trick worthy [of] the subtlety of your arch-friend of New York" and contrasted this

---

19. TJ to JM, Dec. 17, 1796, below.
20. TJ to JM, Jan. 8, 1797, below.
21. TJ to JM, Jan. 1, 1797, below.

attempt to convert friends into "tools to defeat their and your just wishes" with his personal "esteem of the moments when we were working for our independence."[22]

After writing his letter, Jefferson held it until he received Madison's report on Adams's conciliatory stance. He then enclosed it to Madison, suggesting that he forward it unless "any thing should render the delivery of it ineligible in your opinion." "If Mr. Adams can be induced to administer the government on it's true principles," he added, "and to relinquish his bias to an English constitution, it is to be considered whether it would not be on the whole for the public good to come to a good understanding with him as to his future elections. He is perhaps the only sure barrier against Hamilton's getting in."[23]

Madison was delighted that Jefferson had agreed to "a share in the administration." He thought that the closeness of the vote and Jefferson's acceptance would temper the "ostensible protest by this Country agst. Republicanism." But he also squelched Jefferson's letter to the president-elect for several reasons: 1. Adams's cordiality towards Jefferson was well known, and Jefferson's views on Adams had found their way to him; 2. the letter had a general air "which betrays the difficulty of your situation in writing it," an air that might make the wrong impression on the "ticklish" New Englander; 3. Adams might view the denunciation of Hamilton as an effort to drive the wedge even further into the Federalist ranks; 4. the reference to "the sublime delights of riding in the storm" might be taken as a criticism of those who, unlike Jefferson, had no distaste for the helm in the present crisis; 5. the interest of his Republican supporters argued against any depreciation of their efforts in the election; 6. since the direction of Adams's administration might call for forceful opposition in the future by the Republicans, personal pledges of cooperation might be embarrassing if given in written form. Madison readily agreed that the best policy was to cultivate Adams's "favorable dispositions," separating him from the wing led by Hamilton—"his treachery to Adams, will open the eyes of N. England," Madison predicted—and "giving a fair start to his Executive career" without hazarding the future of the Republican party.[24]

Jefferson thanked his friend for not sending his letter to Adams. Although he had not changed his views about Adams, he agreed that "there was a difficultly in conveying them to him, and a possibility that the attempt might do mischief there or somewhere else." Instead, he had responded to a congratulatory note from Senator Langdon of New Hampshire and "said exactly the things which will be grateful to Mr. A[dams] and no more," knowing that they would be shown to Adams.[25]

22. TJ to John Adams, Dec. 28, 1796, enclosed in TJ to JM, Jan. 1, 1797, below.
23. TJ to JM, Jan. 1, 1797, below.
24. JM to TJ, Jan. 8, 1797, below, and Jan. 15, 1797, below.
25. TJ to JM, Jan. 30, 1797, below. Also see Malone, III, pp. 291–94.

Early in January 1797, Madison suggested that Jefferson come to Philadelphia to be sworn in on March 4, even though winter travel would be inconvenient. Madison was not sure that there was a legal necessity for the trip, but he was convinced that there were "so many advantages likely to result from it that I can not help wishing it may be found necessary. If you can not qualify elsewhere, you must come of course, that the danger of an interregnum may be provided against."[26]

Jefferson did not think it necessary to go to Philadelphia to take the oath of office,[27] but he quickly "determined to do it, as a mark of respect to the public, and to do away [with] the doubts which have spread that I should consider the second office as beneath my acceptance. The journey indeed for the month of February is a tremendous undertaking for me, who have not been seven miles from home since my resettlement."[28] He wanted as little formality as possible, however, preferring notification of his election by mail rather than by a delegation of "gentlemen of considerable office."[29] When he arrived in Philadelphia, he wanted "no ceremony whatever," he told Madison. "I shall escape into the city as covertly as possible. If Gov. Mifflin should shew any symptoms of ceremony, pray contrive to parry them."[30]

But Jefferson, who traveled by public stage in an attempt to enter Philadelphia unnoticed, failed to avoid ceremony on his arrival on March 2. Greeted on the outskirts of town by an artillery salute of sixteen rounds, he was accompanied into the city by a military escort carrying a banner welcoming "Jefferson The Friend of the People."[31] He promptly called on John Adams, for he had never "felt a diminution of confidence in his integrity, and retained a solid affection for him."[32] Adams met him cordially, for he had always "believed in his honour, Integrity, his love of Country, and his friends."[33]

On March 3, Jefferson reported, Adams called on him "at Mr. Madison's, where I lodged," to discuss the crisis looming with France.[34] Diplomatic relations between the United States and the French Republic had come to an abrupt halt when Adet's mission as ambassador from France was suspended and Monroe was recalled from France by Washington for failure to support the Jay Treaty. A diplomatic impasse had been created when the French Directory then rejected the new American minister to France, Charles Cotesworth

26. JM to TJ, Jan. 8, 1797, below.
27. TJ to JM, Jan. 30, 1797, below.
28. TJ to JM, Jan. 22, 1797, below.
29. TJ to Henry Tazewell, Jan. 16, 1797, enclosed in TJ to JM, Jan. 16, 1797, below.
30. TJ to JM, Jan. 30, 1797, below.
31. Malone, III, pp. 295–96.
32. TJ to JM, Jan. 22, 1797, below.
33. John Adams to Tristram Dalton, Jan. 19, 1797, in Ford, VII, p. 108n.
34. TJ, "Anas," Mar. 2, 1797, in Ford, I, p. 272; Brant, III, p. 449.

Pinckney, Washington's replacement for Monroe, thus breaking off diplomatic relations and making war possible. Jefferson feared that Hamilton and his followers in Washington's cabinet—"the Executive council," which Adams intended to carry over—favored war with France "and consequent alliance with Great Britain." But he did "not believe Mr. A. wishes war with France. Nor do I believe he will truckle to England as servilely as has been done," he had written to Madison on the eve of his departure for Philadelphia. "If he assumes this front at once and shews that he means to attend to self respect and national dignity with both the nations, perhaps the depredations of both on our commerce may be amicably arrested. I think he should begin first with those who first began with us, and by an example on them acquire a right to redemand the respect from which the other party has departed."[35]

Jefferson must have been startled—and perhaps flattered—when Adams said that his first wish was to send him to Paris but that he supposed that was out of the question. Jefferson agreed. Adams then proposed a bipartisan commission that would include Madison, and he asked Jefferson "to consult Mr. Madison for him." Jefferson agreed to do so, although he saw little hope of success. Six weeks earlier Madison had reported a rumor "that an Envoy Extraordy. was to go to France, and that I was to be the person. I have no reason," he had informed Jefferson then, "to suppose a shadow of truth in the former part of the story; and the latter is pure fiction." Now that fiction had turned to fact, Madison, who had rejected diplomatic posts before and was presently intent on retiring from Congress to live in Virginia with his wife, declined the offer, as Jefferson had expected.[36]

On the eve of his inauguration as vice president, Jefferson, who looked forward to the "tranquil and unoffending station" to which he had been elected, took time out from politics to attend the meeting of the American Philosophical Society for Promoting Useful Knowledge, where he was installed as president of the academy founded by Benjamin Franklin, succeeding the eminent mathematician David Rittenhouse. Happy that the vice presidency promised to be a "tranquil and unoffending station," he anticipated that he would spend "philosophical evenings in the winter, and rural days in the summer."[37]

Three days later, on March 6, Jefferson and Adams dined with Washington before the latter retired to Mt. Vernon. After dinner, as they strolled towards their lodgings, Jefferson informed Adams of Madison's refusal of the diplomatic post in France. A relieved Adams then confessed that political objections had been raised to his conciliatory gesture. The High Federalists in his cabinet, he later wrote, and their colleagues in the Senate objected to his

35. TJ to JM, Jan. 22, 1797, below.
36. TJ, "Anas," Mar. 2, 1797, in Ford, I, pp. 272–73; JM to TJ, Jan. 22, 1797, below.
37. See TJ to Benjamin Rush, Jan. 22, 1797, in Ford, VII, p. 114, and Malone, III, pp. 340–41.

utilizing "the fine talents and amiable qualities and manners of Mr. Madison." "I had said nothing that could possibly displease," the president recalled, "except pronouncing the name Madison."[38]

THE LETTERS

Madison to Jefferson

Philadelphia Dec. 5, 1796

DEAR SIR

It is not possible yet to calculate with any degree of certainty whether you are to be left by the Electors to enjoy the repose to which you are so much attached, or are to be summoned to the arduous trust which depends on their allotment. It is not improbable that Pinkney will step in between the two who have been treated as the principals in the question.[1] It is even suspected that this turn has been secretly meditated from the beginning in a quarter where the *leading* zeal for Adams has been affected. This Jockeyship is accounted for by the enmity of Adams to Banks and funding systems which is now become public, and by an apprehension that he is too headstrong to be a fit puppet for the intriguers behind the skreen. It is to be hoped that P. may equally disappoint those who expect to make that use of him, if the appointment should in reallity light on him. We do not however absolutely despair that a choice better than either may still be made; and there is always the chance of a devolution of the business on the House of Reps. which will I believe decide it as it ought to be decided.

Adêts Note which you will have seen, is working all the evil with which it is pregnant.[2] Those who rejoice at its indiscretions and are taking advantage of them, have the impudence to pretend that it is an electioneering manoeuvre, and that the French Govt. have been led to it by the opponents of the British Treaty. Unless the unhapy effect of it here and cause of it in France, be speedily obviated by wise councils and healing measures, the crisis will unquestionably be perverted into a perpetual alienation of the two Countries by the secret

---

38. TJ, "Anas," Mar. 2, 1797, in Ford, I, p. 273; John Adams, "Letters to the Boston *Patriot*" (1809), cited in Brant, III, pp. 449-50; Malone, III, pp. 296-99.

1. The fullest accounts of Alexander Hamilton's efforts to elevate Thomas Pinckney over both John Adams and TJ are in Kurtz, pp. 96-113, and Manning J. Dauer, *The Adams Federalists* (Baltimore, 1953), pp. 92-111. For a brief sketch, see John C. Miller, *Alexander Hamilton: Portrait in Paradox* (New York, 1959), pp. 444-48.

2. Like Genet, Adet addressed a series of appeals to the American people that denounced the Jay Treaty, announced that the French Republic would "treat the flag of neutrals in the same manner as they shall suffer it to be treated by the English," and favored the election of TJ over Adams; see Kurtz, pp. 126-32, and Alexander De Conde's chapter "Adet's War with Washington's Government" in his *Entangling Alliance: Politics and Diplomacy under George Washington* (Durham, N.C., 1958), pp. 423-55.

enemies of both. The immediate consequences of such an event may be distressing; but the permanent ones to the commercial and other great interests of this Country, form a long and melancholy catalogue. We know nothing of the policy meditated by the Executive on this occasion. The Speech will probably furnish some explanation of it. Yrs. always and affecy.

Js. MADISON JR.

Madison to Jefferson

[Philadelphia] Dec. 10, 1796

DEAR SIR

Exitus in dubio[3] is still the Motto to the election. You *must* reconcile yourself to the secondary as well as the primary station, if that should be your lot. The prevailing idea is that Pinkney will have the greatest number of votes: and I think that Adams will be most likely to stand next. There are other calculations however less favorable to both. The answer to the Presidents Speech is in the hands of Ames, Sitgreaves Smith of Carola. Baldwin and myself.[4] The form is not yet settled. There is a *hope* that it may be got into a form that will go down without altercation or division in the House. Yrs. sincerely

Js. M. JR

Jefferson to Madison

Monticello Dec. 17, 1796

TH: J. TO J. M.

Your favor of the 5th. came to hand last night. The first wish of my heart was that you should have been proposed for the administration of the government. On your declining it I wish any body rather than myself: and there is nothing I so anxiously hope as that my name may come out either second or third. These would be indifferent to me; as the last would leave me at home the whole year, and the other two thirds of it. I have no expectation that the Eastern states will suffer themselves to be so much outwitted as to be made the tools for bringing in P. instead of A. I presume they will throw away their second vote. In this case it begins to appear possible that there may be an equal division where I had supposed the republican vote would have been considerably minor. It seems also possible that the Representatives may be divided. This

---

3. "The issue is doubtful." Ovid's quotation is cited in *PJM,* XVI, p. 425.

4. As a lame-duck congressman, JM did not head the committee on the president's message, but joined Abraham Baldwin as the Republican minority; see Brant, III, p. 447, and John Alexendar Carroll and Mary Wells Ashworth, *George Washington: First in Peace* (New York, 1957), p. 422.

is a difficulty from which the constitution has provided no issue. It is both my duty and inclination therefore to relieve the embarrasment should it happen: and in that case I pray you and authorize you fully to sollicit on my behalf that Mr. Adams may be preferred. He has always been my senior from the commencement of our public life, and the expression of the public will being equal, this circumstance ought to give him the preference. When so many motives will be operating to induce some of the members to change their vote, the addition of my wish may have some effect to preponderate the scale. I am really anxious to see the speech. It must exhibit a very different picture of our foreign affairs from that presented in the Adieu, or it will little correspond with my view of them.[5] I think they never wore so gloomy an aspect since the year 83. Let those come to the helm who think they can steer clear of the difficulties. I have no confidence in myself for the undertaking.

We have had the severest weather ever known in November. The thermometer was at 12°. here and in Goochland, and I suppose generally. It arrested my buildings very suddenly when eight days more would have completed my walls, and permitted us to cover in. The drought is excessive. From the middle of October to the middle of December not rain enough to lay the dust. A few days ago there fell a small rain, but the succeeding cold has probably prevented it from sprouting the grain sown during the drouth. Present me in friendly terms to Messrs. Giles, Venable, Page. Adieu affectionately.

P. S. I inclose a letter for Volney because I do not know where to address to him.

Pray send me Gallatin's view of the finances of the U. S.[6] and Paine's lre. to the President if within the compas of a conveyance by post.[7]

Madison to Jefferson

Philadelphia Dec. 19, 1796

DEAR SIR

The returns from N. Hampshire, Vermont, S. C. and Georga. are still to come in, and leave the event of the Election in some remaining uncertainty. It is but barely possible that Adams may fail of the highest number. It is highly

---

5. George Washington gave his final annual message to Congress on Dec. 7, 1796; see Carroll and Ashworth, pp. 420–22. TJ wanted to compare it with Washington's Farewell Address, which had been published in Sept.

6. *A Sketch of the Finances of the United States* by Albert Gallatin was published in Nov. 1796; see Raymond Walters, Jr., *Albert Gallatin: Jeffersonian Financier and Diplomat* (New York, 1957), pp. 88–94.

7. Thomas Paine, who had dedicated *The Rights of Man* to Washington, attacked the president for supporting Jay's treaty in his *Letter to George Washington*. It appeared serially in the Philadelphia *Aurora* in Oct. and Nov. 1796 before being published as a pamphlet in Feb. 1797; see David Freeman Hawke, *Paine* (New York, 1974), pp. 318–21.

probable, tho' not absolutely certain, that Pinkney will be third only on the list. You must prepare yourself therefore to be summoned to the place Mr. Adams now fills. I am aware of the objections arising from the inadequateness of the importance of the place to the sacrifices you would be willing to make to a greater prospect of fulfilling the patriotic wishes of your friends; and from the irksomeness of being at the head of a body whose sentiments are at present so little in unison with your own. But it is expected that as you had made up your mind to obey the call of your Country, you will let it decide on the particular place where your services are to be rendered. It may even be said, that as you submitted to the election knowing the contingency involved in it, you are bound to abide by the event whatever it may [be]. On the whole it seems *essential*[8] that you should not refuse the station which is likely to be your lot. There is reason to believe also that your neighbourhood to *Adams* may *have a valuable effect on his councils* particularly in *relation to our external system.*[9] You know that *his feelings* will not *enslave him to the* example of *his predecessor.* It is certain that his *censures of our paper systems* and the intrigues at *New York for setting P. above him* have fixed an *enmity with the British faction.* Nor should it pass for nothing, that the true *interest of New England* particularly requires reconciliation with France as the road to her commerce. *Add to the whole that he* is said to speak of *you now in friendly terms* and will no doubt be *soothed by your acceptance of a place subordinate to him.* It must be confessed however that all these calculations, are qualified by *his political principles* and *prejudices.* But they add weight to the *obligation from which you must not withdraw yourself.*

You will see in the answer to the P.s speech, much *room for criticism.* You must, for the present, be *content to know that it resulted from a choice of evils.*[10] His *reply to the* foreign *paragraph indicates a good* effect *on his mind.* Indeed *he cannot but wish to avoid entailing a war on his successor.* The *danger lies in the* fetters *he has put on himself* and *in the irritation* and *distrust of the French government.*

Madison to Jefferson

Philadelphia Dec. 25, 1796

DEAR SIR

I can not yet entirely remove the uncertainty in which my last left the election. Unless the Vermont election of which little has of late been said, should contain some fatal vice, in it, Mr. Adams may be considered as the

---

8. JM's italics.
9. The italicized words in this sentence and those in the rest of the letter were written in code.
10. The House reply praised President Washington's "wisdom and firmness," despite William Branch Giles's attempt to delete these words. The president had expressed his hopes "to maintain cordial harmony" with the French Republic; see Carroll and Ashworth, pp. 421–22.

President elect. Nothing can deprive him of it but a general run of the votes in Georgia, Tenissee and Kentucky in favor of Mr. Pinkney, which is altogether contrary to the best information. It is not even probable that Mr. P. will be the second on the list, the secondary votes of N. Hampshire being now said to have been thrown away on Elseworth: and a greater number consequently required from the states abovementioned than will be likely to fall to his lot. We have nothing new from Europe. The prospect and projects in our foreign Department are under a veil not a corner of which I have been able to lift. I fear the distrust with wch. the French Govt. view the Executive here, and the fetters which the President has suffered himself to put on, will be obstacles to the reconciliation which he can not fail to desire. It is whispered also that the Spanish Minister has intimated the probable dissatisfaction of his Court at the Explanatory Article of the British Treaty. Nor can it be doubted, from the nature of the alliance between that and France, that a common cause will be made in all the steps taken by the latter with respect to this Country. In the mean time the British party are busy in their calumnies for turning the blame of the present crisis from themselves, on the pretended instigations of France, by Americans at Paris; and some of them are already bold eno' to talk of an alliance with England as the resourse in case of an actual rupture with France. The new President whoever he will be will have much in his power; and it is important to make as many circumstances as possible conspire to lead him to a right use of it. There never was greater distress than at this moment in the monied world. Failures and frauds occur daily; And are so much connected with Banks that these Institutions are evidently losing ground in the public opinion.

Jefferson to Madison

[Monticello] Jan. 1, 1797

Yours of Dec. 19. has come safely. The event of the election has never been a matter of doubt in my mind. I knew that the Eastern states were disciplined in the schools of their town meetings to sacrifice differences of opinion to the great object of operating in phalanx, and that the more free and moral agency practised in the other states would always make up the supplement of their weight. Indeed the vote comes much nearer an equality than I had expected. I know the difficulty of obtaining belief to one's declarations of a disinclination to honors, and that it is greatest with those who still remain in the world. But no arguments were wanting to reconcile me to a relinquishment of the first office or acquiescence under the second. As to the first it was impossible that a more solid unwillingness settled on full calculation, could have existed in any man's mind, short of the degree of absolute refusal. The only view on which I would have gone into it for a while was to put our vessel on her republican tack before she should be thrown too much to leeward of her true principles. As to the second, it is the only office in the world about which I am unable to decide in my own mind whether I had rather have it or not have it. Pride does not enter into the estimate; for I think with the Romans that the General of to-day should be a soldier tomorrow if necessary. I can particularly have no feelings which would revolt at a secondary position to Mr. Adams. I am his junior in life, was his junior in Congress, his junior in the diplomatic line, his junior lately in our civil government. Before the receipt of your letter I had written the inclosed one to him.[11] I had intended it some time, but had deferred it from time to time under the discouragement of a despair of making him believe I could be sincere in it. The papers by the last post not rendering it necessary to change any thing in the letter I inclose it open for your perusal, not only that you may possess the actual state of dispositions between us, but that if any thing should render the delivery of it ineligible in your opinion, you may return it to me. If Mr. Adams can be induced to administer the government on it's true principles, and to relinquish his bias to an English constitution, it is to be considered whether it would not be on the whole for the public good to come to a good understanding with him as to his future elections. He is perhaps the only sure barrier against Hamilton's getting in.

Since my last I have recieved a packet of books and pamphlets, the choiceness of which testifies that they come from you. The Incidents of Hamilton's insurrection is a curious work indeed.[12] The hero of it exhibits himself in all the attitudes of a dexterous balance master.

The Political progress is a work of value and of a singular complexion. The eye of the author seems to be a natural achromatic, which divests every object of the glare of colour. The preceding work under the same title had the same merit.[13] One is disgusted indeed with the ulcerated state which it presents of the human mind: but to cure an ulcer we must go to it's bottom: and no writer has ever done this more radically than this one. The reflections into which he leads one are not flattering to our species. In truth I do not recollect in all the Animal kingdom a single species but man which is eternally and

---

11. See the enclosure TJ to John Adams, Dec. 28, 1796, below.

12. TJ referred to Alexander Hamilton's role in the Whiskey Rebellion as described in H. H. Brackenridge, *Incidents of the Insurrection in the Western Parts of Pennsylvania in the Year 1794* (Philadelphia, 1795).

13. James Thomson Callender published Part I of the *Political Progress of Britain; or, An Impartial Account of the Political Abuses in the Government of This Country, from the Revolution in 1688* in Edinburgh in 1792. After emigrating to the United States, he wrote a second part of *The Political Progress of Britain* in 1795, which was republished in Philadelphia in 1796; see Michael Durey, "Thomas Paine's Apostles: Radical Emigres and the Triumph of Jeffersonian Republicanism," *WMQ* 44 (1987): 679, 685. For a critical appraisal of TJ's dealings with Callender, see Worthington C. Ford, ed., *Thomas Jefferson and James Thomson Callender, 1798-1802* (Brooklyn, 1897). Frank Luther Mott, *Jefferson and the Press* (Baton Rouge, 1943), pp. 32-37, presents a more sympathetic account.

systematically engaged in the destruction of it's own species. What is called civilization seems to have no other effect on him than to teach him to pursue the principle of bellum omnium in omnia[14] on a larger scale, and in place of the little contests of tribe against tribe, to engage all the quarters of the earth in the same work of destruction. When we add to this that as to the other species of animals, the lions and tygers are mere lambs compared with man as a destroyer, we must conclude that it is in man alone that Nature has been able to find a sufficient barrier against the too great multiplication of other animals and of man himself, an equilibriating power against the fecundity of generation. My situation points my views chiefly to his wars in the physical world: yours perhaps exhibit him as equally warring in the Moral one. We both, I believe, join in wishing to see him softened. Adieu.

ENCLOSURE
[Jefferson to John Adams]

Dear Sir   Monticello Dec. 28, 1796[15]

The public and the public papers have been much occupied lately in placing us in a point of opposition to each other. I trust with confidence that less of it has been felt by ourselves personally. In the retired canton where I am, I learn little of what is passing: pamphlets I see never; papers but a few; and the fewer the happier. Our latest intelligence from Philadelphia at present is of the 16th. inst. but tho' at that date your election to the first magistracy seems not to have been known as a fact, yet with me it has never been doubted. I knew it impossible you should lose a vote North of the Delaware, and even if that of Pensylvania should be against you in the mass, yet that you would get enough South of that to place your succession out of danger.[16] I have never one single moment expected a different issue: and tho' I know I shall not be believed, yet it is not the less true that I have never wished it. My neighbors, as my compurgators, could aver that fact, because they see my occupations and my attachment to them. Indeed it is possible that you may be cheated of your succession by a trick worthy the subtlety of your arch-friend [Alexander Hamilton] of New York, who has been able to make of your real friends tools to defeat their and your just wishes. Most probably he will be disappointed as to you; and my inclinations place me out of his reach. I leave to others the sublime delights of riding in the storm, better pleased with sound sleep and a warm birth below, with the society of neighbors, friends and fellow laborers of the earth, than of spies and sycophants. No one then will congratulate you with purer disinterestedness than myself. The share indeed which I may have had in the late vote, I shall still value highly, as an evidence of the share I have in the esteem of my fellow citizens. But while, in this point of view, a few votes less would be little sensible, the difference in the effect of a few more would be very sensible and oppressive to me. I have no ambition to govern men. It is a painful and thankless office.

14. "A war of all men against all men." For the use of this quotation from Thomas Hobbes, see *PJM,* XVI, p. 442.

15. For JM's reasons for not delivering TJ's letter to Adams, see JM to TJ, Jan. 15, 1797, below.

16. TJ's estimate was correct. Adams received the unanimous votes of the seven states north of the Delaware River, one from Pennsylvania, three from Delaware, seven from Maryland, one from Virginia, and one from North Carolina.

Since the day too on which you signed the treaty of Paris our horizon was never so overcast. I devoutly wish you may be able to shun for us this war by which our agriculture, commerce and credit will be destroyed. If you are, the glory will be all your own; and that your administration may be filled with glory and happiness to yourself and advantage to us is the sincere wish of one who tho', in the course of our voyage thro' life, various little incidents have happened or been contrived to separate us, retains still for you the solid esteem of the moments when we were working for our independance, and sentiments of respect and affectionate attachment.

TH: JEFFERSON

Jefferson to Madison

[Monticello] Jan. 8, 1797

Yours of Dec. 25. is safely recieved. I much fear the issue of the present dispositions of France and Spain. Whether it be in war or in the suppression of our commerce it will be very distressing and our commerce seems to be already sufficiently distressed through the wrongs of the belligerent nations and our own follies. It was impossible the bank and paper-mania should not produce great and extensive ruin. The President is fortunate to get off just as the bubble is bursting, leaving others to hold the bag. Yet, as his departure will mark the moment when the difficulties begin to work, you will see, that they will be ascribed to the new administration, and that he will have his usual good fortune of reaping credit from the good acts of others, and leaving to them that of his errors.

We apprehend our wheat is almost entirely killed: and many people are expecting to put something else in the ground. I have so little expectations from mine, that as much as I am an enemy to tobacco, I shall endeavor to make some for taxes and clothes. In the morning of the 23d. of Dec. my thermometer was 5°. below 0. and the 24th. it was at 0. On the 26th. of Nov. 22d. of Dec. and this morning it was at 12°. above 0. The last day of Dec. we had a snow 1½ I. deep and the 4th. of this month one of 3. I. deep which is still on the ground. Adieu affectionately.

Madison to Jefferson

Philadelphia Jan. 8, 1797

DEAR SIR

I have recd. your favor of the 17 Ult. The election is not likely to terminate in the equilibrium of votes for which the Constitution has not provided. If the Vermont votes should be valid as is now generally supposed, Mr. Adams will have 71. and you 68. Pinkney being in the rear of both. It is to be hoped that the nicety and in truth the unpropitious casualty, of the choice of Mr. A. will lessen the evil of such an ostensible protest by this Country agst. Republicanism. Your acceptance of a share in the administration will not fail to aid this tendency. It is suggested to me that it will be necessary for you to be here before the adjournment of Congs. in order to be qualified. I have not examined the Constitution and the law on this subject. You will have the means of doing both and of deciding on the question. Altho' I am sensible of the inconveniency of such a trip at this season of the year, yet I see so many advantages likely to result from it that I can not help wishing it may be found necessary. If you can not qualify elsewhere, you must come of course, that the danger of an interregnum may be provided against. The expence would be no objection; and is besides balanced by the effect of the qualification in settling the date of the compensation.

The special communication from the President, on our affairs with France is not yet made. The gloom over them is in no respect diminished. Not a word from Monroe, or any other quarter, relating to his recall; or enabling us to judge on the question whether Pinkney will be received. We wait with anxiety for the light that will probably be thrown on the first point, by the expected communication.

The inclosed paper will give you the foreign news as it has first made its appearance here. A comparison of paragraphs renders the Italian part of it unfavorable to the French very improbable. There may nevertheless be some foundation for it.[17] The French operations agst. our Trade seem to be better authenticated, as well as the renewal of the Algerine warfare. The abortive result of Lord Malmsbury's errand, is also highly probable.[18] I just understand that Spain declared war agst. G. B. on the 8th of Ocr.[19] Adieu

Gallatin's work is a book—and the Letter of Payne to Genl. W. is not within the compass of our privilege. I sent it some time ago in parcels to Mr. Jones, and requested him to forward them to you.

Madison to Jefferson

Philadelphia Jan. 15, 1797

DEAR SIR

The last mail brought me your favor of Jany. 1. inclosing an unsealed one for Mr. A. and submitting to my discretion the eligibility of delivering it. In exercising this delicate trust I have felt no small anxiety, arising by no means

17. For the Austrian attack on Napoleon in Italy, see Georges Lefebvre, *The French Revolution from 1793 to 1799* (New York, 1964), pp. 188–89.
18. *Ibid.* See also Steven T. Ross, *European Diplomatic History, 1789–1815: France against Europe* (New York, 1969), pp. 132–33.
19. On Spain's declaration of war against England, see R. R. Palmer, *The Age of the Democratic Revolution: A Political History of Europe and America, 1760–1800,* 2 vols. (Princeton, 1959–64), II, p. 266.

however from an apprehension that a free exercise of it could be in collision with your real purpose, but from a want of confidence in myself, and the importance of a wrong judgment in the case. After the best consideration I have been able to bestow, I have been led to suspend the delivery of the letter, till you should have an opportunity of deciding on the sufficiency or insufficiency of the following reasons. 1. It is certain that Mr. Adams, on his coming to this place, expressed to different persons a respectful cordiality towards you, and manifested a sensibility to the candid manner in which your friends had in general conducted the opposition to him. And it is equally known that your sentiments towards him personally have found their way to him in the most conciliating form.[20] This being the state of things between you, it deserves to be considered whether the idea of bettering it is not outweighed by the possibility of changing it for the worse. 2. There is perhaps a general air on the letter which betrays the difficulty of your situation in writing it, and it is uncertain what the impression might be resulting from this appearance. 3 It is certain that Mr. A. is fully apprized of the trick aimed at by his pseudo-friends of N. Y: and there may be danger of his suspecting in memento's on that subject, a wish to make his resentment an instrument for avenging that of others. A hint of this kind was some time ago dropped by a judicious and sound man who lives under the same roof, with a wish that even the newspapers might be silent on that point. 4. May not what is said of "the sublime delights of riding in the storm etc." be misconstrued into a reflexion on those who have no distaste to the helm at the present crisis? You know the temper of Mr. A. better than I do: but I have always conceived it to be rather a ticklish one. 5. The tenderness due to the zealous and active promoters of your election, makes it doubtful whether, their anxieties and exertions ought to be depreciated by any thing implying the unreasonableness of them. I know that some individuals who have deeply committed themselves, and probably incurred the political enmity at least of the P. elect, are already sore on this head. 6. Considering the probability that Mr. A.s course of administration may force an opposition to it from the Republican quarter, and the general uncertainty of the posture which our affairs may take, there may be real embarrassments from giving written possession to him, of the degree of compliment and confidence which your personal delicacy and friendship have suggested.

I have ventured to make these observations, because I am sure you will equally appreciate the motive and the matter of them; and because I do not view them as inconsistent with the duty and policy of cultivating Mr. Adam's favorable dispositions, and giving a fair start to his Executive career. As you have, no doubt, retained a copy of the letter I do not send it back as you request.[21] It occurs however that, if the subject should not be changed in your view of it, by the reasons which influence mine, and the delivery of the letter

20. JM did not tell TJ that he had "leaked" the letter to Benjamin Rush, who transmitted its contents to a delighted Adams; see *PJM*, XVI, p. 457.
21. TJ had not retained a copy of his letter to Adams, but he had prepared a "Statement by memory of a letter written to J. Adams. copy omitted to be retained"; see Ford, VII, pp. 97–98.

be accordingly judged expedient, it may not be amiss to alter the date of it; either by writing the whole over again, or authorizing me to correct that part of it.

The special communication is still unmade. It is I am told to be extremely voluminous. I hope, under the sanction of the P.'s reply to our address, that it will be calculated rather to heal than irritate the wounded friendship of the two countries. Yet, I cannot look around at the men who counsel him, or look back at the snares into which he has hitherto been drawn without great apprehensions on this subject. Nothing from France subsequent to the arrival of Pinkney. The negociations for peace you will see are suspended.[22] The accession of Spain to the war enforces the probability that its calamities are not likely yet to be terminated. The late News from the Rhine and from Italy are on the whole favorable to the French. The last battle was on the 27 Ocr. in the Hunspruck, and ended in a victory on their side. The House of Rep: are on direct taxes, which seem to be so much nauseated and feared by those who have created both the necessity and odium of them, that the project will miscarry. Hamilton, you will recollect assured the farmers that all the purposes of the Govt. could be answered without resorting to lands Houses or stock on farms. This deceptive statement with other devices of his administration, is rising up in judgment agst. him and will very probably soon blast the prospects which his ambition and intrigues have contemplated. It is certain that he has lost ground in N. Y. of late; and his treachery to Adams, will open the eyes of N. England.

Jefferson to Madison

Monticello Jan. 16, 1797

Dear Sir

The usual accidents of the winter, ice, floods, rains, have prevented the Orange post from coming to Charlottesville the last postday, so that we have nothing from Philadelphia the last week. I see however by the Richmond papers a probability that the choice of V. P. has fallen on me. I have written the inclosed letter therefore to Mr. Tazewell as a private friend, and have left it open for your perusal. It will explain it's own object and I pray you and Mr. Tazewell to decide in your own discretion how it may best be used for it's object, so as to avoid the imputation of an indecent forwardness in me.

I observe doubts are still expressed as to the validity of the Vermont election. Surely in so great a case, substance and not form should prevail. I cannot suppose that the Vermont constitution has been strict in requiring particular forms of expressing the legislative will. As far as my disclaimer may have any effect, I pray you to declare it on every occasion foreseen or not foreseen by me, in favor of the choice of the people substantially expressed,

22. JM referred to the unsuccessful mission of Lord Malmesbury.

and to prevent the phaenomenon of a Pseudo-president at so early a day.[23] Adieu, yours affectionately

TH: JEFFERSON

ENCLOSURE
[Jefferson to Henry Tazewell]

Dear Sir, Monticello Jan. 16, 1797

As far as the public papers are to be credited, I may suppose that the choice of Vice-president has fallen on me. On this hypothesis I trouble you, and only pray, if it be wrong, that you will consider this letter as not written. I believe it belongs to the Senate to notify the V P of his election. I recollect to have heard, that on the first election of President and Vice President, gentlemen of considerable office were sent to notify the parties chosen. But this was the inauguration of our new government, and ought not to be drawn into example. At the 2d election, both gentlemen were on the spot and needed no messengers. On the present occasion, the President will be on the spot, so that what is now to be done respects myself alone; and considering that the season of notification will always present one difficulty, that the distance in the present case adds a second, not inconsiderable, and may in future happen to be sometimes much more considerable, I hope the Senate will adopt that method of notification, which will always be least troublesome and most certain. The channel of the post is certainly the least troublesome, is the most rapid, and considering also that it may be sent by duplicates and triplicates, is unquestionably the most certain. Inclosed to the postmaster at Charlottesville, with an order to send it by express, no hazard can endanger the notification. Apprehending, that should there be a difference of opinion on this subject in the Senate, my ideas of self-respect might be supposed by some to require something more formal and inconvenient, I beg leave to avail myself of your friendship to declare, if a different proposition should make it necessary, that I consider the channel of the post-office as the most eligible in every respect, and that it is to me the most desirable; which I take the liberty of expressing, not with a view of encroaching on the respect due to that discretion which the Senate have a right to exercise on the occasion, but to render them the more free in the exercise of it, by taking off whatsoever weight the supposition of a contrary desire in me might have in the mind of any member.

Jefferson to Madison

[Monticello] Jan. 22, 1797

Yours of the 8th. came to hand yesterday. I was not aware of any necessity of going on to Philadelphia immediately, yet I had determined to do it, as a mark of respect to the public, and to do away the doubts which have spread

---

23. In Dec. 1796, the Republican press reported that the electoral votes of Vermont, which were equally divided between Adams and Pinckney, were tainted, if not illegal, because Vermont had no state law under which the electors could act. Assuming that Vermont would be deprived of its vote, the Philadelphia *Aurora* predicted that the election would be decided by the House of Representatives in favor of Jefferson; see *PJM,* XVI, pp. 429-30.

that I should consider the second office as beneath my acceptance. The journey indeed for the month of February is a tremendous undertaking for me, who have not been seven miles from home since my resettlement. I will see you about the rising of Congress: and presume I need not stay there a week. Your letters written before the 7th. of Feb. will still find me here. My letters inform me that Mr. A. speaks of me with great friendship, and with satisfaction in the prospect of administering the government in concurrence with me.[24] I am glad of the first information, because tho' I saw that our antient friendship was affected by a little leaven produced partly by his constitution, partly by the contrivance of others, yet I never felt a diminution of confidence in his integrity, and retained a solid affection for him. His principles of government I knew to be changed, but conscientiously changed. As to my participating in the administration, if by that he meant the executive cabinet, both duty and inclination will shut that door to me. I cannot have a wish to see the scenes of 93. revived as to myself, and to descend daily into the arena like a gladiator to suffer martyrdom in every conflict. As to duty, the constitution will know me only as the member of a legislative body: and it's principle is that of a separation of legislative executive and judiciary functions, except in cases specified. If this principle be not expressed in direct terms, yet it is clearly the spirit of the constitution, and it ought to be so commented and acted on by every friend to free government. I sincerely deplore the situation of our affairs with France. War with them and consequent alliance with Great Britain will completely compass the object of the Executive from the commencement of the war between France and England, taken up by some of them from that moment, by others more latterly. I still however hope it will be avoided. I do not believe Mr. A. wishes war with France. Nor do I believe he will truckle to England as servilely as has been done. If he assumes this front at once and shews that he means to attend to self respect and national dignity with both the nations, perhaps the depredations of both on our commerce may be amicably arrested. I think he should begin first with those who first began with us, and by an example on them acquire a right to redemand the respect from which the other party has departed. I suppose you are informed of the proceeding commenced by the legislature of Maryland to claim the South branch of Patowmac as their boundary, and thus, of Albemarle now the central county of the state, to make a frontier. As it is impossible upon any consistent principles and after such a length of undisturbed possession that they can expect to establish their claim, it can be ascribed to no other than an intention to irritate and divide, and there can be no doubt from what bow the shaft is shot. However let us cultivate Pennsylvania and we need not fear the universe. The assembly have named me among those who are to manage this controversy. But I am so averse to motion and contest, and the other members are so fully equal to the

---

24. See Kurtz's chapter "Adams and Jefferson: Friendship and Politics" in his *Presidency of John Adams*, pp. 209–38.

business that I cannot undertake to act in it. I wish you were added to them.²⁵ Indeed I wish and hope you may consent to be added to our assembly itself. There is no post where you can render greater services without going out of your state. Let but this block stand firm on it's basis and Pennsylvania do the same, our union will be perpetual and our general government kept within the bounds and form of the constitution. Adieu affectionately.

Madison to Jefferson

Philadelphia Jan. 22, 1797

DEAR SIR

I have recd. yours of Jany. 8th. You will find by the papers that the communication on French affairs, has been at length made. Being ordered to be printed without being read, I have no direct knowledge of its character.²⁶ Some of the Senate where it has been read in part, represent it as well fitted to convert into an incurable gangrine, the wound which the friendship between the two Republics has suffered. Adding this on our side to the spirit manifested in the language and the proceedings on the other, an awful scene appears to be opening upon us. The only chance to escape it lies in the President-Elect. You know the degree in which I appreciate it. I am extremely apprehensive that he may have been drawn into a sanction to this last step of the Executive, by a complimentary initiation into the business which is soon to devolve on him. This is however apprehension merely; no circumstance being known from which the fact can be inferred. We hear nothing from Monroe or from Pinkney. It has got into the Newspapers that an Envoy Extraordy. was to go to France, and that I was to be the person. I have no reason to suppose a shadow of truth in the former part of the story; and the latter is pure fiction.²⁷ Doctr. Logan has put into my hands a copy of his Agricultural experiments for you which I will forward.²⁸ A vote has passed in favor of a direct tax. The event is notwithstanding doubtful. The Eastern members, after creating the necessity for it, increasing the odium of it, and reproaching their Southn brethren with backwardness in supporting the Govt. are now sneaking out of the difficulty, and endeavouring whilst they get what they wish, to enjoy the popularity of having opposed it.²⁹

25. In addition to TJ, the Virginia House of Delegates appointed John Marshall, Edmund Randolph, Robert Brooke, Ludwell Lee, Bushrod Washington, and John Taylor of Caroline to meet with the Maryland commissioners; see *PJM*, XVI, p. 474.

26. President Washington transmitted a brief message covering a commentary on Franco-American affairs written by Secretary of State Pickering that later appeared as a pamphlet of 100 pages; see De Conde, pp. 482-86.

27. For the report that JM was to be appointed, see Brant, III, pp. 449-51, and *PJM*, XVI, p. 472.

28. George Logan's book on crop rotation had just been published; see *PJM*, XVI, p. 472.

29. For the vote on the direct tax, see Brant, III, p. 448.

Madison to Jefferson

Philadelphia Jan. 29, 1797

DEAR SIR

Yours covering an unsealed letter to Mr. Tazewell came duly to hand, and will be turned to the use you wish. As you take the Philada. Gazette in which the Belligerent answer to Adêts note has been printed in toto, I refer to that for the posture and prospect of things with France.[30] The British party since this overt patronage of their cause, no longer wear the mask. A war with France and an alliance with G. B. enter both into print and conversation; and no doubt can be entertained that a push will be made to screw up the P. to that point before he quits the office. The strides latterly made with so much inconsistency as well as weakness in that direction, prepare us for receiving every further step without surprise. No further discovery has been made of the mind of the P. elect. I can not prevail on myself to augur much that is consoling from him. Nothing from abroad; nor more at home than you will gather from the Newspapers. Adieu. Yrs Affy.

Jefferson to Madison

[Monticello] Jan. 30, 1797

Your's of the 15th. came to hand yesterday. I am very thankful for the discretion you have exercised over the letter. That has happened to be the case which I knew to be possible, that the honest expressions of my feelings towards Mr. A. might be rendered mal-a-propos from circumstances existing and known at the seat of government, but not seen by me in my retired situation. Mr. A. and myself were cordial friends from the beginning of the revolution. Since our return from Europe some little incidents have happened which were capable of affecting a jealous mind like his. The deviation from that line of politics on which we had been united, has not made me less sensible of the rectitude of his heart: and I wished him to know this, and also another truth that I am sincerely pleased at having escaped the late draught for the helm, and have not a wish which he stands in the way of. That he should be convinced of these truths is important to our mutual satisfaction, and perhaps to the harmony and good of the public service. But there was a difficulty in conveying them to him, and a possibility that the attempt might do mischief there or somewhere else, and I would not have hazarded the attempt if you had not been in place to decide upon it's expediency. It is now become unnecessary to

---

30. JM referred to Secretary of State Pickering's lengthy commentary, which accompanied the president's message on French affairs.

repeat it, by a letter I have had occasion to write to Langdon in answer to one from him, in which I have said exactly the things which will be grateful to Mr. A. and no more. This I imagine will be shewn to him.

I have turned to the constitution and laws, and find nothing to warrant the opinion that I might not have been qualified here or wherever else I could meet with a Senator, every member of that body being authorised to administer the oath, without being confined to time or place, and consequently to make a record of it, and to deposit it with the records of the Senate. However I shall come on on the principle which had first determined me, respect to the public. I hope I shall be made a part of no ceremony whatever. I shall escape into the city as covertly as possible. If Govr. Mifflin should shew any symptoms of ceremony, pray contrive to parry them. We have now fine mild weather here. The thermometer is above the point which renders fires necessary. Adieu affectionately.

Madison to Jefferson

Philadelphia Feb. 5, 1797

DEAR SIR

I have recd. yours of [Jan. 22] giving notice that we shall have the pleasure of seeing you here soon, but that letters written before the 7th. would arrive before you leave home.

Nothing occurs to alleviate the crisis in our external affairs. The French continue to prey on our trade. The British too have not desisted. There are accounts that both of them are taking our East-India-men. This is an alarming symtom, there being 60 or 70 vessels from different parts of the U. S. engaged in that trade. Pickering's corrosive letter has not yet been fully printed so as to come before the H of R. It is extremely difficult to decide on the best course to be taken. Silence may be construed into approbation. On the other hand it is not likely that any opportunity will be given for negativing an approving Resolution. And it is at least doubtful whether a vote of positive disapprobation in any form whatever could be safely risked in the House, or if passed whether the public opinion would not be brought to side with the Executive agst. it. It is moreover extremely difficult to shape any measure on the occasion so as to escape the charge either of censuring or advising without a proper warrant from the nature of our Constitutional relation to the Executive. Nor is it unworthy of consideration that there are formidable steps not yet taken by the P. which may be taken before the moment of his exit, which if taken might be efficacious, and which his successor without his sanction would not dare to take.

A bill for collecting the proposed taxes on land etc. is before the committee of ways and means. The difficulties of the subject, the shortness of the time, and the aversion of the Eastern people, render it uncertain whether it will pass or not at the present session. I suspect the policy of the Treasy. Department is to separate the preparatory arrangments, from the actual collection of the tax, and to provide for the former only at present, an expedient not unlikely to succeed, as it will smooth the way for the Eastern members. Some I find who do not disapprove of the plan of direct taxes, are unwilling to fortify the disposition to embroil us with France, by enlarging at the present juncture, our system of revenue.

I reserve for a verbal communication the indications by which we judge of the prospect from the accession of Mr. A. to the Helm. They are not I conceive very flattering.

I just learn that a British packet brings London accts. to Decr. 7. Nothing is as yet given out but that the negociations at Paris have ended in abortion.[31] It is probable that, what is not given out, is not more favorable to G. B. I do not believe that any intelligence has been red. from Monroe or Pinkney subsequent to the arrival of the latter. It is said that the Spaniards are fortifying at the Chickasaw Bluffs. If this be the case, it strengthens the apprehension that they regard the British Treaty with the explanatory article, as superseding the obligation or policy of their Treaty with us. Adieu

Madison to Jefferson

Philadelphia Feb. 11, 1797

DEAR SIR

After several little turns in the mode of conveying you notice of your election, recurrence was had to the precedent of leaving the matter to the Senate, where on the casting vote of Mr. Adams, the notification was referred to the President of the U. States, in preference of the President of the Senate. You will see in the papers the state of the votes, and the manner of counting and proclaiming them. You will see also the intimation given by Mr. A. of the arrangement he has made for taking the oath of office. I understand he has given another intimation which excites some curiosity, and gives rise to several reflections which will occur to you; it is, that he means to take the advice of the Senate on his coming into office whether the offices held during pleasure are or are not vacated by the political demise of his precedecessor? This is the substance. I do not aim at or know the terms, of the question; of which previous notice is thus given that the members of the Senate may the better make up their opinions. What room is there for such a question at all? Must it not have been settled by precedent? On what principle is the Senate to be

---

31. The failure of Lord Malmesbury's mission was reported in a Philadelphia newspaper the next day; see *PJM*, XVI, p. 484.

consulted? If this step be the result of deliberation and system, it seems to shew 1. that the maxims of the British Govt. are still uppermost in his mind. 2 That the practice of his predecessor are not laws to him, or that he considers a second election of the same person as a continuation of the same reign. 3 That the Senate is to be brought more into Executive agency than heretofore.[32]

Accounts have been received of the arrival of Pinkney in France, but not at Paris. Nothing yet from Monroe since he knew of his recall. Every thing relating to that quarter remains in statu quo.

You will find in the inclosed papers that Buonaparte has nearly cut up another austrian army. It is to be hoped that its consequences may force the Emperor to a peace, and thro' him, Great Britain.[33] Adieu

This goes by Mr. Bloodworth son of the Senator from N. Carolina appointed to carry you Notification of your appt.

32. See Kurtz, p. 218.
33. For the subsequent surrender of Austria at Leoben in April, see Lefebvre, pp. 190–92.

22

THE VICE PRESIDENT AND THE FARMER: THE PARTNERS TRADE PLACES AGAIN, 1797

ON MARCH 4, 1797, Jefferson took his oath as vice president in the Senate chamber. Pledging his zealous attachment to the Constitution and the Union, he concluded his brief speech with a tribute to his eminent predecessor, John Adams, with whom he had long enjoyed "a cordial and uninterrupted friendship" and for whom he now prayed that Adams might be "long preserved for the Government, the happiness, and prosperity of our common country." After he was sworn in, the new vice president and the senators moved to the House of Representatives for the inauguration of John Adams and the retirement of George Washington.

The transfer of power from the first president to the second went smoothly. "The change of the Executive here," wrote a South Carolina congressman, "has been wrought with a facility and a calm which has astonished even those of us who always augured well of the government and the general good sense of our citizens. The machine has worked without a creak."[1]

In his inaugural address, Adams promised that he would pursue "the system of neutrality and impartiality among the belligerent powers of Europe" and that he would implement the Jay Treaty while maintaining friendship with the French. To meet the critics who had charged him with political heresies, he reiterated his loyalty to the Constitution and to the republican form of government, declaring that his administration would be without favor to region or party. He was so pleased with his performance the he labeled it with-

---

1. William Loughton Smith to Rufus King, Apr. 3, 1797, in George C. Rogers, junior, *Evolution of a Federalist: William Loughton Smith of South Carolina, 1758–1812* (Columbia, S.C., 1962), p. 296. See also Malone, III, pp. 296–97.

out any show of false modesty as "the sublimest thing ever delivered in America."[2]

The spirit of conciliation was strengthened when the new president and vice president dined with Washington on March 6, before the latter left for Mt. Vernon. Jefferson lingered in Philadelphia for another week, receiving "a thousand visits of ceremony and some of sincerity." On March 13, he returned to Virginia by his usual eastern route.[3]

Madison and his wife, along with her son and younger sister and Madison's sister, returned to Montpellier by the western route through Harpers Ferry. Madison had refused to stand for reelection to Congress, eager to finally retire after twenty years of politics at the state and national levels. Indeed, he warned his father that "if Mr. Jefferson should call and say any thing to counteract my determination" not to run for the Virginia legislature, it was to be viewed as "merely expressive of his own wishes on the subject, and . . . not be allowed to have the least effect. In declining to go into the Assembly, . . . I am sincere and inflexible." He was as eager to settle down with Dolley in Orange County as Jefferson had been to return to Albemarle three years earlier.[4]

Like Jefferson, who was still rebuilding Monticello, Madison and his wife began the remodeling of Montpellier, the home of Madison's parents, which had become their home, adding a portico of Jefferson's design and installing the French furniture shipped over by Monroe.[5] Now that the partners had traded places, with Jefferson in the nation's capital part of each year and Madison enjoying the rural life of a country squire in Virginia, Madison asked his friend to determine "whether there be known in Philad^a any composition for encrusting Brick that will effectually stand the weather: and particularly what is thought of common plaister thickly painted with white lead overspread with sand. I wish to give some such dressing to the columns of my Portico, and to lessen as much as possible the risk of the experiment."[6]

Late in the year, Madison placed a large order with Jefferson's nailery:

---

2. Stephen G. Kurtz, *The Presidency of John Adams: The Collapse of Federalism, 1795–1800* (Philadelphia, 1957), pp. 222–25; Malone, III, pp. 296–98; Peterson, pp. 562–63.

3. Malone, III, pp. 300–1.

4. JM to James Madison, Sr., Mar. 12, 1797, in *PJM*, XVI, p. 500. For TJ's suggestion that JM enter the Virginia assembly, see his letter of Jan. 22, 1797, above.

5. Merrill D. Peterson, *James Madison: A Biography in His Own Words* (New York, 1974), p. 214, and Brant, III, p. 445. See also Conover Hunt, "The Madisons at Montpelier: A President's Duplex in the Virginia Piedmont," in *The American Home: Material Culture, Domestic Space, and Family Life,* to be published as the Proceedings of the 1992 Winterthur Conference.

6. JM to TJ, Apr. 4, 1800, below. Marion du Pont Scott's book *Montpelier: The Recollections of Marion du Pont Scott* (New York, 1976) tells more about Mrs. Scott's interest in horses and racing than about James and Dolley Madison. But she willed Montpellier to the National Trust for Historic Preservation as "an historic shrine . . . to James Madison and his times," and it is now open to the public.

50,000 sixes, 50,000 fours for lathing, and 12,000 brads for flooring. As Jefferson had done while Madison was in Philadelphia, Madison occasionally asked his partner in the capital to buy things for his house, such as 190 windowpanes for French windows and brass hinges for eight doors. A little later, one of Jefferson's skilled workmen came to Montpellier "for plastering and for adjusting stone to the fireplaces." As Madison noted in a letter to Monroe, he was "in the vortex of housebuilding in its most hurried stage." Madison's architectural skill won the praise of Mrs. William Thornton, wife of the architect of the White House, who wrote that Montpellier demonstrated "a taste for the arts which is rarely to be found in such remote and retired situations."[7]

Like Monticello, Montpellier was located in a "retired canton," and Madison quickly settled into the delights of rusticating in rural retirement, not writing to Jefferson for five months.[8] Like Madison, Jefferson hoped to make great progress in remodeling his home during the "delicious spring" of 1797, but President Adams squashed those dreams by calling a special session of Congress on May 15 to meet the growing crisis with France. The vice president left for Philadelphia on May 5, arriving on May 11.[9] He traveled by stage, which, he noted with pleasure, "gives me what I have long been without, an opportunity of plunging into the mixed characters of my fellow-countrymen, the most useful school we can enter into and one which nothing else can supply the want of."

Jefferson had expected his post to be "honorable and easy," and he hoped for "a pretty rapid return of general harmony," if war with France could be avoided.[10] But the political acrimony of the special session quickly changed his mind, as "the roar and tumult of bulls and bears" in Congress shattered any hope for harmony.[11] In reaction to Jay's treaty, the French Directory had recalled its minister to the United States and begun seizing American vessels and confiscating neutral cargoes. In March 1797, it decreed that whenever French vessels captured Americans who had been impressed by the British, the Americans should be treated as pirates and hanged. To dramatize its displeasure with American policy, the Directory also refused to receive Charles Cotesworth Pinckney, the moderate Federalist whom Washington had appointed to replace Monroe as minister to the French Republic, thus breaking off diplomatic relations with the United States until French grievances had been re-

---

7. Brant, III, pp. 458–59. The best discussion of Montpellier, its art, and its furnishings is Conover Hunt-Jones, *Dolley and the "Great Little Madison"* (Washington, 1977).

8. TJ used the "retired canton" phrase in his letter to John Adams, Dec. 28, 1796, enclosed in TJ to JM, Jan. 1, 1797, above.

9. Malone, III, p. 301.

10. TJ to Elbridge Gerry, May 13, 1797, in Ford, VII, p. 120, and TJ to James Sullivan, Feb. 9, 1797, *ibid.*, p. 118.

11. TJ to Edward Rutledge, June 24, 1797, *ibid.*, p. 155.

dressed.¹² The refusal to receive Pinckney and the demand for redress of grievances "without discussion and without investigation," Adams told Congress, "is to treat us neither as allies nor as friends, nor as a sovereign state." Accordingly, he asked Congress to strengthen the nation's army and naval defenses as an aid to a fresh attempt at negotiation in order to preserve peace "compatible with the rights, duties, interests, and honor of the nation."

Adams was also critical of remarks made by French leaders when Monroe departed, viewing these sentiments as even "more alarming than the refusal" to accept Pinckney. "It evinces a disposition to separate the people of the United States from the Government, to persuade them that they have different affections, principles, and interests from those of their fellow-citizens whom they themselves have chosen to manage their common concerns, and thus to produce divisions fatal to our peace." In special remarks directed to the Senate, presided over by Jefferson, he elaborated on this theme, warning the people of the United States to avoid "the direction of foreign and domestic factions."¹³

Jefferson and the Republicans viewed Adams's remarks about "foreign and domestic factions" as a charge that they were pro-French and un-American, and concluded that the president had been won over by the High Federalists in his cabinet; the vice president called these advisers "the Hamiltons by whom he is surrounded."¹⁴ He thought Adams's speech "high toned," although the decision to send a special mission to France was clearly preferable to war, which he feared the "British faction" in the cabinet had first fixed on.¹⁵ "In fact," he wrote an old friend, "I consider the calling of Congress so out of season an experiment of the new administration to see how far and on what lines they could count on its support."¹⁶

After three weeks of inconclusive debates on preparedness measures—"arming the merchantmen, finishing the frigates, fortifying harbors, and making all other military preparations as an aid to negociation"¹⁷—the momentary panic created by Adams's address was checked by events in Europe, Jefferson reported, and the tone of the "British faction" had been "cooling down ever since." "The truth is," he told Aaron Burr, "there is nothing to do, the idea of war being scouted by the events of Europe."¹⁸ The failure of the Bank of England, mutiny in the British fleet, Bonaparte's victories over the Austrians, King George III's desire for peace—Jefferson ticked off events that revived the

12. Alexander De Conde, *The Quasi-War: The Politics and Diplomacy of the Undeclared War with France, 1797-1801* (New York, 1966), pp. 8-17. For a solid biography of Pinckney, see Marvin R. Zahniser, *Charles Cotesworth Pinckney, Founding Father* (Chapel Hill, 1967).

13. Richardson, I, pp. 233-39.

14. TJ to Elbridge Gerry, May 13, 1797, in Ford, VII, p. 120.

15. TJ to JM, May 18, 1797, below.

16. TJ to Peregrine Fitzhugh, June 4, 1797, in Ford, VII, p. 136.

17. TJ to JM, May, 18, 1797, below.

18. TJ to Aaron Burr, June 17, 1797, in Ford, VII, p. 146.

hopes for peace in Congress.[19] In weekly bulletins, the leader of the opposition kept Madison posted on Republican strategy: "The hope . . . is that as the Antirepublicans take the high ground of war, and their opponents are for everything moderate that the most moderate of those who came under contrary dispositions will join them."[20]

Jefferson confessed that those "who have no wish but for the peace of their country, and its independence of all foreign influence, have a hard struggle indeed, overwhelmed by a cry as loud and imposing as if it were true, of being under French influence, and this raised by a faction composed of English subjects residing among us, or such as are English in all their relations and sentiments."[21] In an extraordinary letter to the Federalist candidate for vice president whom he had nosed out in the election, he lamented that partisanship had risen to such heights, although it seemed inseparable from "that degree of freedom which permits unrestrained expression. Political dissension is doubtless a less evil than the lethargy of despotism," he continued, "but still it is a great evil, and it would be as worthy the efforts of the patriot as of the philosopher, to exclude it's influence, if possible, from social life."[22] Alas, the heated debates quickly spilled over from Congress, taking their toll in social circles, he wrote an old friend from Revolutionary days:

> The passions are too high at present, to be cooled in our day. You and I have formerly seen warm debates and high political passions. But gentlemen of different politics would then speak to each other, and separate the business of the Senate from that of society. It is not so now. Men who have been intimate all their lives, cross the streets to avoid meeting, and turn their heads another way, lest they be obliged to touch their hats.[23]

As the presiding officer of the Senate, Jefferson thought that body "higher toned" than the president, and he must have resented signing and transmitting their laudatory response to Adams's speech, even though it slapped directly at the Republicans by suggesting that they might succumb to French attempts "to alienate the affections of our fellow-citizens from their Government." To counteract such efforts, the Senate Federalists pledged to oppose "every attempt to excite dangerous jealousies among us" and thus "convince the world that our Government and your administration of it can not be separated from the affectionate support of every good citizen."[24]

Although Adams appointed three envoys to the special commission to France, he dropped his earlier idea of a bipartisan group, choosing John Marshall of Virginia and Elbridge Gerry of Massachusetts to join C. C. Pinckney

19. See Georges Lefebvre, *The French Revolution from 1793 to 1799* (New York, 1964), pp. 192–94.
20. TJ to JM, May 18, 1797, below.
21. TJ to Horatio Gates, May 30, 1797, in Ford, VII, p. 131.
22. TJ to Thomas Pinckney, May 29, 1797, *ibid.*, p. 128.
23. TJ to Edward Rutledge, June 24, 1797, *ibid.*, pp. 154–55.
24. Richardson, I, p. 241.

of South Carolina, who had been rejected by the French. When Attorney General Charles Lee "consulted a member from Virginia to know whether Marshall would be agreeable," Jefferson wrote Madison, "he named you, as more likely to give satisfaction. The answer was, 'Nobody of Mr. Mad's way of thinking will be appointed.'"[25]

Jefferson applauded the appointment of Gerry, observing that the nomination gave "a spring of hope, which was dead before." "It gave me certain assurance," he wrote the new envoy, "that there would be a preponderance in the mission, sincerely disposed to be at peace with the French government and nation. Peace is undoubtedly at present the first object of our nation. Interest and honor are also national considerations. But interest, duly weighed, is in favor of peace even at the expense of spoliations past and future; and honor cannot now be an object. The insults and injuries committed on us by both the belligerent parties, from the beginning of 1793 to this day, and still continuing, cannot now be wiped off by engaging in war with one of them."[26]

With Madison in retirement, Jefferson quickly assumed command of the Republican party in 1797. He kept track of party votes in the House as well as the Senate, where he counted 18 Federalists, 10 Republicans, and "two wavering votes."[27] When the House ousted Republican John Beckley as clerk by one vote, Jefferson noted "that the republican interest has lost by the new changes."[28] Three weeks later, he confessed that it was "difficult to say whether the Republicans have a majority or not" since votes had "been carried both ways by a difference of from 1. to 6." He was especially critical of three Virginia "renegadoes [who] exactly make that difference."[29] At Francis' Hotel, where he lodged, he was surrounded by "a knot of Jacobins," as a Federalist critic noted, including two senators and four representatives.[30]

As the special session dragged on, Jefferson groaned that "the day of adjournment walks before us like our shadow."[31] He was anxious for adjournment for both policy and personal reasons. He had been the target of Federalist criticism all summer after a garbled version of his private letter to Philip Mazzei, his former neighbor, was published just as the special session of Congress convened. Written in 1796, when Jefferson was at the boiling point over Jay's treaty, the combustible letter was a freewheeling analysis of the changes in the political scene since Mazzei had returned to Italy. "An Anglican monarchical, and aristocratical party has sprung up," he reported, "whose avowed

25. TJ to JM, June 1, [1797], below.
26. TJ to Elbridge Gerry, June 21, 1797, in Ford, VII, pp. 149-50.
27. TJ to JM, June 1, [1797], below.
28. TJ to JM, May 18, 1797, below. On Beckley, see Noble E. Cunningham, Jr., "John Beckley: An Early American Party Manager," *WMQ* 13 (1956): 40-52.
29. TJ to JM, June 8, 1797, below.
30. Malone, III, p. 318.
31. TJ to JM, June 29, 1797, below.

object is to draw over us the substance, as they have already done the forms, of the British government." After praising the republicanism of the mass of the people, he listed their opponents in the new political lineup: the executive, the judiciary, and "all the officers of the government, all who want to be officers, all timid men who prefer the calm of despotism to the boisterous sea of liberty, British merchants and Americans trading on British capitals, speculators and holders in the banks and public funds." "It would give you a fever," he continued in the most critical part of the letter, "were I to name to you the apostates who have gone over to these heresies, men who were Samsons in the field and Solomons in the Council, but who have had their heads shorn by the harlot England." But he thought that Americans would awaken and "preserve the liberty we have obtained only by unremitting labors and perils."[32]

The letter lost—and gained—something in the translation into Italian, then French, and finally back into English. Jefferson first encountered the published version en route to Philadelphia for the special session of Congress and thought that he might have to "take the field of the public papers." The general substance of the letter, he told Madison, "is mine, tho' the diction has been considerably varied in the course of it's translations." He could not disavow it wholly, therefore, nor could he avow it as it stood "because the form was not mine, and, in one place, the substance very materially falsified." For example, the original referred to the "forms" of the British government, by which Jefferson meant "the birth-days, levees, processions to parliament, inauguration pomposities, etc." But the published version used "form," "making me," he complained, "express hostility to the form of our government, that is to say, to the constitution itself." But to go into a public analysis of the word "*form*, used in the singular or plural," would bring on "a personal difference between Genl. Washington and myself," a confrontation that he wanted to avoid since it would embroil him "with all those with whom his [Washington's] character is still popular, that is to say, nine tenths of the people of the U S." For these reasons, he decided "to be entirely silent," but he asked Madison to "advise me what to do, and confer with Colo Monroe on the subject."[33]

After his recall by Washington, Monroe had returned from France during the special session, where he was shunned by the Federalists as the discredited agent of the Republicans and welcomed by the Jeffersonians for having conducted himself with "irreproachable honor and the most dignified sense of duty." Jefferson and fifty Republican congressmen attended an elaborate din-

---

32. The letter is printed in Ford, VII, pp. 72–78. For an account of the letter at the time Jefferson wrote it, and the aftermath, see Malone, III, pp. 267–68, 302–7.

33. TJ to JM, Aug. 3, 1797, below. For TJ's original letter to Philip Mazzei, Apr. 24, 1796, see Ford, VII, pp. 72–78. Mazzei translated it into Italian for a paper in Florence; the French version was translated into French in the Paris *Moniteur;* and this version was retranslated into English by the New York *Minerva* and widely reprinted in the United States. See Malone, III, pp. 302–7. For the *Minerva* version, see Ford, VII, pp. 74–77n.

ner for Monroe at Oeller's Hotel, an action that outraged the Federalists almost as much as Jefferson's Mazzei letter had done.[34]

Although Monroe urged Jefferson to publish a defense of his political views, Madison opposed the move "as a ticklish experiment to say publicly yes or no to the interrogatories of party spirit. It may bring on dilemmas, not to be particularly foreseen, of disagreeable explanations, or of tacit confessions."[35] But Jefferson's silence was viewed by Federalist critics as a confession of guilt, and they blasted the author of the "abominable letter" as a "jesuitical friend of the people." Noah Webster, editor of the New York *Minerva*, and William Cobbett, editor of *Porcupine's Gazette*, called the vice president's opinions treasonous, Porcupine addressing him as "Monsieur Jefferson" and denouncing "thy French-spun theories, thy flimsy philosophy, thy shallow shifting politics."[36]

While Jefferson suffered the political slings in silence, Hamilton rushed into print to preserve his reputation for public probity, confessing to adultery in order to exonerate himself on the charge of corrupt financial transactions. "I see Hamilton has put a short piece into the papers in answer to Callender's publication," Jefferson informed his friend in Orange, "and promises shortly something more elaborate."[37] Madison called the longer pamphlet "a curious specimen of the ingenious folly of its author. Next to the error of publishing at all, is that of forgetting that simplicity and candour are the only dress which prudence would put on innocence." He was particularly critical of Hamilton's "malignant insinuations against others. The one against you," he told Jefferson, "is a masterpiece of folly, because its impotence is in exact proportion to its venom."[38]

Jefferson brushed aside the Hamilton attack, which he viewed as a personal matter, for a far graver political issue raised by a federal grand jury in Richmond during the special session of Congress, one that demonstrated the growing Federalist intolerance of opposition. On May 22, 1797, Supreme Court Justice James Iredell, in his charge to the federal grand jury in Richmond, urged citizens to take "salutary caution" in all discussions of public measures, warning that "some foreign nation . . . [might] foment and take advantage of our internal discords, first making us the dupe and then the prey of an ambition we excited by our divisions." The grand jury promptly responded with a presentment against Samuel J. Cabell, the Republican repre-

---

34. The quotation is from a letter by Albert Gallatin to his wife, June 30, 1797, quoted in Malone, III, p. 324. Also see Noble E. Cunningham, Jr., *The Jeffersonian Republicans: The Formation of Party Organization, 1789–1801* (Chapel Hill, 1957), p. 120. *Porcupine's Gazette* listed the major guests, calling each of them "Monsieur" and labeling Monroe's speech as "Citizen's Reply."

35. JM to TJ, Aug. 5, 1797, below.

36. Malone, III, pp. 302–3, and William Cobbett, *Selections from Cobbett's Political Works*, ed. John M. Cobbett and James P. Cobbett (London, 1835), I (May 1797), p. 150.

37. TJ to JM, July 24, 1797, below.

38. JM to TJ, Oct. 20, 1797, below.

sentative from Jefferson's congressional district, which denounced him for writing a letter to his constituents containing antiadministration remarks "against the happy government of the United States," which tended "thereby to separate the people therefrom, and to increase or produce a foreign influence ruinous to the peace, happiness, and independence of these United States."[39]

Jefferson labeled the presentment a perversion of a legal institution into a political engine, an invitation by federal judges to grand juries "to become inquisitors on the freedom of speech, of writing and of principle of their fellow citizens."[40] Writing to Madison a week later, he said that he hoped to attend the Albemarle court on July 3 to launch an attack on the presentment.[41] Delayed in Philadelphia, he finally left town before Congress adjourned, stopping off to discuss politics with Madison on July 11.

Once he was at Monticello, Jefferson drafted a petition of *"Protest against interference of* [the federal] *Judiciary between Representative and Constituent,"* asserting the natural right of free correspondence between citizen and citizen, a right that was not the gift of municipal law, "but among the objects for the protection of which municipal laws are instituted." The grand-jury action, the vice president argued, was a move designed "to overawe the free correspondence which exists and ought to exist between them [the constituent and his representative], . . . [and] to put the representative into jeopardy of criminal prosecution, of vexation, expense, and punishment before the Judiciary."

Destined for the Virginia assembly, the petition claimed that the presentment was "an infraction of our individual rights as citizens by other citizens of our own State"; it followed, therefore, that "the judicature of this commonwealth is solely competent to its cognizance." Since the federal grand jurors had themselves committed a crime of "the highest and most alarming nature," they should be impeached and punished in order to "secure to the citizens of this commonwealth their constitutional right."[42] Thus, in his headlong effort to protect civil liberty and freedom of expression, Jefferson not only turned to a states' rights defense, but paradoxically proposed to punish Federalist grand jurors for exercising their "natural right of communicating their sentiments to one another by speaking and writing."[43]

39. Griffith J. McRee, *Life and Correspondence of James Iredell,* 2 vols. (New York, 1857), II, pp. 505-10. The Cabell case is discussed in Adrienne Koch and Harry Ammon, "The Virginia and Kentucky Resolutions: An Episode in Jefferson and Madison's Defense of Civil Liberties," *WMQ* 5 (1948): 152-53. For an example of Cabell's letters, see Noble E. Cunningham, Jr., ed., *Circular Letters of Congressmen to Their Constituents, 1789-1829,* 3 vols. (Chapel Hill, 1978), I, pp. xxxvii-xxxix, 67-72.

40. TJ to Peregrine Fitzhugh, June 4, 1797, in Ford, VII, pp. 137-38. For Cabell's reply, see James Morton Smith, *Freedom's Fetters: The Alien and Sedition Laws and American Civil Liberties* (Ithaca, N.Y., 1956), p. 184. The congressman was not prosecuted.

41. TJ to JM, June 15, 1797, below.

42. TJ enclosed his petition in his letter to JM of Aug. 3, 1797, below.

43. TJ used this phrase in his petition, below.

Jefferson sent his petition to Madison and Monroe, proposing that it be circulated in four counties by his nephew Peter Carr (with Jefferson's name kept secret), then presented to the state assembly. The federal presentment—he called it "the case of the grand jury *vs.* Cabell"[44]—had burst upon the special session "just at the moment when Congress was together," he told Madison, and it "produced a great effect both on it's friends and foes in that body, very much to the disheartening and mortification of the latter. I wish this petition, if approved, to arrive there under the same circumstance, to produce the counter-effect so wanting for their gratification."[45]

Madison agreed that it was "of great importance to set the public opinion right with regard to the functions of grand Juries, and the dangerous abuse of them in the federal Courts; nor could a better occasion occur." Although he penciled in a few suggestions so the petition would be "better guarded agst. cavil," he thought that its general tenor "cannot certainly be mended." Nevertheless, he had two worries, one mechanical and one jurisdictional. Could the petition get enough signers, he asked, and should it go to the state assembly, thus "embarking the Legislature in the business"?[46]

Monroe also raised a question about the state legislature acting on a question involving the federal judicial system. But Jefferson persisted, and the House of Delegates passed a resolution denouncing Cabell's presentment as "a violation of the fundamental principles of representation" and "of a natural right of speaking and writing freely."[47] But by failing to take action against the grand jurors, the assembly registered its protest while rejecting Jefferson's proposed method of redress.[48]

——————— THE LETTERS ———————

Jefferson to Madison

Philadelphia May 18 and 19, 1797

I was informed on my arrival here that Genl Pinckney's dispatches had on their first receipt excited in the administration a great deal of passion: that

44. TJ used this phrase in a letter to James Monroe, Sept. 7, 1797, in Ford, VII, p. 171.

45. TJ to JM, Aug. 3, 1797, below. Also see Malone, III, pp. 334–37; Peterson, pp. 605–6; and Noble E. Cunningham, Jr., *In Pursuit of Reason: The Life of Thomas Jefferson* (Baton Rouge, 1987), pp. 210–11.

46. JM to TJ, Aug. 5, 1797, below.

47. Koch and Ammon, 153. A few Republicans voted against the resolution because they opposed a "Legislative censure on the Grand Jury"; see JM to TJ, Jan. 21, 1798, below.

48. The resolutions were not transmitted to the state Senate or to Congress; see Koch and Ammon, 152–53.

councils were held from day to day, and their ill temper fixed at length in war; that under this impression Congress was called: that the tone of the party in general became high, and so continued till the news of the failure of the bank of England.[1] This first gave it a check, and a great one and they have been cooling down ever since, the most intemperate only still asking permission to arm the vessels for their own defence, while the more prudent disapprove of putting it in the power of their brethren and leaving to their discretion to begin the war for us. The impression was too that the executive had for some time been repenting that they had called us, and wished the measure undone. All the members from North as well as South concurred in attesting that negociation or any thing rather than war was the wish of their constitutents. What was our surprise then at receiving the speech which will come to you by this post. I need make no observation to you on it. I believe there was not a member of either house, out of the secret, who was not much disappointed. However some had been prepared. The spirit of supporting the Executive was immediately given out in the lower house and is working there. The Senate admits of no fermentation. Tracy, Laurence and Livermore were appointed to draw an answer for them, Venable, Freeman, Rutledge, Griswold and [Kittera] for the representatives. The former will be reported to day, and will be in time to be inclosed: the other not till tomorrow when the post will be gone. We hope this last will be in general terms, but this is not certain, a majority as is believed (of the commee.) being for arming the merchantmen, finishing the frigates, fortifying harbors, and making all other military preparations as an aid to negociation. How the majority of the house will be is very doubtful. If all were here, it is thought it would be decidedly pacific, but all are not here and will not be here. The division on the choice of a clerk was 41. for Condy, 40 for Beckley.[2] Besides the loss of the ablest clerk in the US. and the outrage committed on the absent members, prevented by the suddenness of the call and their distance from being here on the 1st day of the session, it excites a fear that the republican interest has lost by the new changes. It is said that three from Virginia separate from their brethren. The hope however is that as the Antirepublicans take the high ground of war, and their opponents are for everything moderate that the most moderate of those who came under contrary dispositions will join them. Langdon tells me there is a considerable change working in the minds of the people to the Eastward: that the idea that they have been deceived begins to gain ground, and that were the elections to be now made their result would be considerably different. This however is doubted and denied by others.

1. When it suspended the convertibility of bank notes into specie in Feb. 1797, the Bank of England faltered but did not fail; see J. H. Clapham, *The Bank of England* (London, 1944), pp. 1-5, and R. G. Hawtrey, *Currency and Credit* (London, 1923), pp. 262-85.

2. Beckley had managed Jefferson's campaign in the election of 1796; see Cunningham, "John Beckley," 40-52.

France has asked of Holland to send away our Minister from them and to treat our commerce on the plan of their late decree. The Batavian government answered after due consideration that their commerce with us was now their chief commerce, that their money was in our funds, that if they broke off correspondence with us they should be without resources for themselves, for their own public and for France, and therefore declined doing it. France acquiesced. I have this from the President who had it from his son still at the Hague. I presume that France has made the same application to Spain. For *I know*[3] that Spain has memorialized our Executive against the effect of the British treaty, as to the articles concerning neutral bottoms, contraband, and the Missisipi, has been pressing for an answer and has not yet been able to obtain one. It does not seem candid to have kept out of sight in the speech this discontent of Spain which is strongly and seriously pronounced and to have thereby left it to be imagined that France is the only power of whom we are in danger.

The failure of the bank of England, and the fear of having a paper tender there, has stopped buying bills of exchange. Specie is raked up from all quarters, and remitted for paiments at a disadvantage from risks etc. of 20. per cent. The bankruptcies here have been immense. I heard a sensible man well acquainted with them conjecture that the aggregate of the clear losses on all these added together in all the states would be not less than 10. millions of Dollars, a heavy tax indeed, to which are to be added the Maritime spoliations, and this tax falling on only a particular description of Citizens.

Bills of lading are arrived to a merchant for goods shipped from Bordeaux for this place in a vessel in which *Monroe is coming passenger.* We hope hourly therefore to receive him.[4]

Innes is arrived and that board going to work.[5]

May 19.

The answer of the Senate is reported by the Commee. It is perfectly an echo and full as high toned as the speech. Amendments may and will be attempted but cannot be carried.

Note to me the day you recieve this that I may know whether I conjecture rightly what is our true post day here.

---

3. TJ's italics here and below.

4. TJ's italics. TJ, Albert Gallatin, and Aaron Burr later boarded James Monroe's ship and welcomed him home; see Cunningham, *In Pursuit of Reason,* p. 210.

5. James Innes of Virginia was one of five commissioners on the mixed arbitration panel established by Jay's treaty to deal with American debts owed to British creditors; see Bradford Perkins, *The First Rapprochement: England and the United States, 1795–1805* (Philadelphia, 1955), pp. 48–53.

Jefferson to Madison

Philadelphia June 1, [1797]

DEAR SIR,

I wrote you on the 18th of May. The address of the Senate was soon after that. The first draught was responsive to the speech and higher toned. Mr. Henry arrived the day it was reported,[6] the addressers had not yet their strength around them. They listened therefore to his objections, recommitted the papers, added him and Tazewell to the committee, and it was reported with considerable alterations. But one great attack was made on it, which was to strike out the clause approving everything heretofore done by the Executive. This clause was retained by a majority of four. They received a new accession of members, held a caucus, took up all the points recommended in the speech, except the raising money, agreed the lists of every commee., and on Monday passed the resolutions and appointed the committees, by an uniform vote of 17 to 11. (Mr. Henry was accidentally absent; Ross not then come.) Yesterday they put up the nomination of J. Q. Adams to Berlin which had been objected to as extending our diplomatic establishment. It was approved by 18 to 11. (Mr. Tatnall accidentally absent.) From these proceedings we were able to see that 18 on the one side and 10 on the other, with two wavering votes will decide every question. Schuyler is too ill to come this session, and Gunn has not yet come. Pinckney (the Genl.) John Marshall and Dana are nominated envoys extraordinary to France.[7] Charles Lee consulted a member from Virginia to know whether Marshall would be agreeable. He named you, as more likely to give satisfaction. The answer was, 'Nobody of Mr. Mad's way of thinking will be appointed.'

The representatives have not yet got through their address. An amendment of Mr. Nicholas', which you will have seen in the papers was lost by a division of 46. to 52. A clause by Mr. Dayton expressing a wish that France might be put on an equal footing with other nations was inserted by 52. against 47. This vote is most worthy of notice, because the moderation and justice of the proposition being unquestionable, it shews that there are 47. decided to go all lengths to prevent accomodation. No other members are expected. The absent are two from Massachusetts (not elected) one from Tennissee (not elected) Benton from S. C. (he never attends) and Burgess of N. Carolina. They have received a new orator from the district of Mr. Ames. He is the son of the Secretary of the Senate.[8] They have an accession from

---

6. Senator John Henry of Maryland was a moderate Federalist who was a fellow lodger with TJ at Francis' Hotel; see Malone, III, p. 349.

7. See De Conde, pp. 25–30.

8. Harrison Gray Otis, whom TJ thought "as rhetorical as" Ames, was the new Massachusetts representative; see TJ to Peregrine Fitzhugh, June 4, 1797, in Ford, VII, p. 137.

S. C. also, that State being exactly divided[9] in the H. of Repr. I learned the following facts, which give me real concern. When the British treaty arrived at Charleston, a meeting as you know was called, and a commee. of 19. appointed of whom General Pinckney was one. He did not attend. They waited for him, sent for him; he treated the mission with great hauteur, and disapproved of their meddling. In the course of the subsequent altercations, he declared that his brother T. Pinckney approved of every article in the treaty, under the *existing circumstances.* And since that time, the politics of Charleston have been assuming a different hue.[10] Young Rutledge joining Smith and Harper is an ominous fact as to that whole interest.

Tobacco is at 9. dollars here flour very dull of sale. A great stagnation in commerce generally. During the present uncertain state of things in England the merchants seem disposed to lie on their oars. It is impossible to conjecture the rising of Congress, as it will depend on the system they decide on; whether of preparation for war, or inaction.

In the vote of 46. to 52. Morgan, Macher and Evans were of the majority,[11] and Clay kept his seat, refusing to vote with either. In that of 47 to 52, Evans was the only one of our delegation who voted against putting France on an equal footing with other nations.

P. M. So far I had written in the morning. I now take up my pen to add that the address having been reported to the House, it was moved to disagree to so much of the amendment as went to the putting France on an equal footing with other nations; and Morgan and Macher turning tail (in consequence as is said of having been closeted last night by Charles Lee) the vote was 49. to 50. So the principle was saved by a single vote. They then moved to insist that compensations for spoliations shall be a *sine qua non,* and this will be decided on to-morrow. Yours affectionately.

Jefferson to Madison

Philadelphia June 8, 1797

I wrote you last on the 1st. inst. You will have seen by the public papers that the amendment for putting France on an equal footing with other nations

---

9. John Rutledge, Jr., who had voted for TJ in 1796, had swung over to the Federalists by the middle of 1797; see Rogers, p. 295.

10. TJ viewed General Charles Cotesworth Pinckney as a moderate Federalist and was on good terms with Thomas Pinckney, who was the American envoy to Spain. When the latter returned to South Carolina, he was elected to Congress as a Federalist, succeeding William Loughton Smith; see *ibid.,* p. 304.

11. TJ labeled these three Virginia congressmen "renegadoes" for breaking ranks with the Republicans; see TJ to JM, June 8, 1797, below.

was clogged with another requiring compensation for spoliations. The objection to this was not that it ought not to be demanded but that it ought not to be a sine qua non, and it was feared from the dispositions of the Executive that they would seize it's mention by the representatives as a pretext for making it a sine qua non. The representatives have voted a continuance of the fortifications and a completion and manning of the three frigates. They will probably pass the bills recieved from the Senate prohibiting the exportation of arms and ammunition and for preventing our citizens from engaging in armed vessels. The Senate have also prepared or are preparing bills for raising cavalry, raising a corps of artilleriests, buying 9. more armed vessels, authorizing the Executive to employ them and the frigates as convoys for our commerce, and raising a great provisional army to be called into actual service only in the case of war. All these measures will pass the Senate by a majority of about 18. to 12. probably. That of permitting our merchant vessels to arm was rejected by the committee 3. to 2. Bingham who was of the committee stated to the Senate that he had taken pains to learn the sense of the merchants on this subject and that he had not found one in favor of the permission. Still a part of the Senate are for it, and do not consider it as laid aside. Smith and Harper brought on the same proposition yesterday (being the 5th. of Smith's resolutions) before the representatives. It was amended by changing the word *permitting* to restricting.[12] Another amendment was proposed to add 'except to the Mediterranean and E. Indies.' The day was spent in debate, and no question taken. I believe certainly the general permission will not be given. But what may be the fate of the 3d. 4th. 6th. 7th. and other resolutions is not very certain. We hope favorably. The late victory of Buonaparte and panic of the British government has produced a sensible effect in damping the ardor of our heroes. However they might have been willing at first, partly from inclination, partly from devotion to the Executive, to have met hostilities from France, it is now thought they will not force that nail, but doing of the most innocent things as much as may be necessary to veil the folly or the boldness of calling Congress, be willing to leave the more offensive measures till the issue of the negociation or their own next meeting. This is the most we can hope, and but for the late successes of France and desperate condition of England, it was more than we should have hoped. For it is difficult to say whether the Republicans have a majority or not.[13] The votes have been carried both ways by a difference of from 1. to 6. Our three renegadoes exactly make that difference. Clay proves to

12. TJ's italics. For a brief discussion of William Loughton Smith's resolutions, see Rogers, pp. 300–1. The original resolution did not use the word "permitting," proposing instead "that provision be made . . . for regulating the arming of merchant vessels"; see *Abridgment of the Debates of Congress from 1789 to 1856,* ed. Thomas Hart Benton (New York, 1857), pp. 144, 147. This version was replaced by one stating "that provision be made . . . for restricting the arming of merchant vessels of the United States [to those] bound to the East and West Indies and to the Mediterranean"; see *PJM,* XVII, p. 22.

13. Kurtz, pp. 288–89, notes that "the Federalists had control of both houses of Congress."

be as firm as a rock, having never separated but in the single instance I mentioned in my last letter, when I presume he must have been struck by some peculiar view of the question.

We expect the arrival of Paine daily. Of Monroe we hear nothing, except that he had not left Paris on the 1st. of April.

P. M. This day has been spent in the H. of Representatives in debating whether the restriction of the merchants from arming their vessels except when bound to the Mediterranean or E. Indies, should be taken off as to the W. Indies also. It was determined by 46. against 34. that the W. India vessels should not arm. This is considered as auguring favorably of the other resolutions. The Senate determined to-day 18. to 11 that 9 vessels should be bought, armed etc. by the president. Their cost is estimated at 60,000 D. each. This was on the 2d. reading of the bill. These bills originated in the Senate and going under their sanction to the lower house, while in so vibratory a state, have a very mischievous effect. We expect to rise on Saturday the 17th. I have written for my horses to be at Fredsbg on Sunday the 25th. and I may be with you perhaps on the 26th. or 27th. Adieu.

Jefferson to Madison

Philadelphia June 15, 1797—A.M.

My last was of the 8th inst. I had enclosed you separately a paper giving you an account of Buonaparte's last great victory. Since that we receive information that the preliminaries of peace were signed between France and Austria.[14] Mr. Hammond will have arrived at Vienna too late to influence the terms. The victories lately obtained by the French on the Rhine were as splendid as Buonaparte's. The mutiny on board the English fleet, tho' allayed for the present has impressed that country with terror.[15] King has written letters to his friends recommending a pacific conduct towards France, 'notwithstanding the continuance of her injustices.' Volney is convinced France will not make peace with England, because it is such an opportunity for sinking her as she never had and may not have again. Buonaparte's army would have to march 700. miles to Calais. Therefore, it is imagined the armies of the Rhine will be destined for England.

14. For the surrender of Austria in the Treaty of Leoben, see Lefebvre, pp. 190-92, and Steven T. Ross, *European Diplomatic History, 1789-1815: France against Europe* (New York, 1969), pp. 128-34.
15. See Conrad Gill, *The Naval Mutinies of 1797* (Manchester, Eng., 1913).

The Senate yesterday rejected on it's 2d reading their own bill for raising 4. more companies of light dragoons, by a vote of 15. to 13. Their cost would have been about 120,000 D a year. To-day the bill for manning the frigates and buying 9 vessels @ about 60,000 D each, comes to it's 3d reading. Some flatter us we may throw it out. The trial will be in time to mention the issue herein. The bills for preventing our citizens from engaging in armed vessels of either party, and for prohibitg exportn. of arms and ammunition, have passed both houses. The fortification bill is before the Representatives still. It is thought by many that with all the mollifying clauses they can give it, it may perhaps be thrown out. They have a separate bill for manning the 3. frigates, but it's fate is uncertain. These are probably the ultimate measures which will be adopted, if even these be adopted. The folly of the convocation of Congress at so inconvenient a season and an expense of 60,000 D. is now palpable to everybody; or rather it is palpable that war was the object, since, that being out of the question, it is evident there is nothing else. However nothing less than the miraculous string of events which have taken place, to wit the victories of the Rhine and Italy, peace with Austria, bankruptcy of England, mutiny in her fleet, and King's writing letters recommending peace, could have cooled the fury of the British faction. Even all that will not prevent considerable efforts still in both houses to shew our teeth to France.

We had hoped to have risen this week. It is now talked of for the 24th, but it is impossible yet to affix a time. I think I cannot omit being at our court (July 3.) whether Congress rises or not. If so, I shall be with you on the Friday or Saturday preceding. I have a couple of pamphlets for you, Utrum Horum, and Paine's Agrarian Justice, being the only things since Erskine which have appeared worth notice. Besides Bache's paper there are 2. others now accommodated to country circulation. Gale's (successor of Oswald) twice a week without advertisements at 4. dollars. His debates in Congress are the same with Claypole's. Also Smith proposes to issue a paper once a week, of news only, and an additional sheet while Congress shall be in session, price 4. dollars.

The best daily papers now are Bradford's compiled by Lloyd, and Markland and Cary's. Claypole's you know. Have you remarked the pieces signed Fabius? They are written by John Dickinson.[16]

P. M. The bill before the Senate for equipping the 3 frigates, and buying 9. vessels of not more than 20. guns, has this day passed on it's 3d reading by 16. against 13. The fortification bill before the representatives as amended in commee of the whole, passed to it's 3d reading by 48. against 41. Adieu affectionately, with my best respects to Mrs. Madison.

16. The best study of the Republican press is Donald H. Stewart, *The Opposition Press of the Federalist Period* (Albany, N.Y., 1969). For Dickinson's "Fabius" essays, see Milton E. Flower, *John Dickinson: Conservative Revolutionary* (Charlottesville, 1983), pp. 277–78.

Jefferson to Madison
Philadelphia June 22, 1797

The Senate have this day rejected their own bill for raising a provisional army of 15,000 men. I think they will reject that for permitting private vessels to arm. The Representatives have thrown out the bill of the Senate for raising artillery. They yesterday put off one forbidding our citizens to serve in foreign vessels of war, till Nov, by a vote of 52. to 44. This day they came to a resoln. proposing to the Senate to adjourn on Wednesday the 28th. by a majority of 4. Thus it is now perfectly understood that the convocation of Congress is substantially condemned by their several decisions that nothing is to be done. I may be with you somewhat later than I expected, say from the 1st. to the 4th.

Preliminaries of peace between Austria and France are signed.

Dana has declined the mission to France. Gerry is appointed in his room, being supported in Senate by the republican vote. 6 nays of the opposite description. No news of Monroe or Paine. Adieu. à revoir

Jefferson to Madison
Philadelphia June 29, 1797

The day of adjournment walks before us like our shadow. We shall rise on the 3d. or 4th. of July. Consequently I shall be with you about the 8th. or 9th. The two houses have jointly given up the 9. small vessels. The Senate have rejected at the 3d reading their own bill authorizing the President to lay embargoes. They will probably reject a very unequal tax passed by the Repr. on the venders of wines and spirituous liquors (not in retail). They have past a bill for postponing their next meeting to the constitutional day; but whether the Repr. will concur is uncertain. The Repr. are cooking up a stamp tax which it is thought themselves will reject. The fate of the bill for private armaments is yet undecided in the Senate. The expenses of the session are estimated at 80.000 Doll.

Monroe and family arrived here the day before yesterday, well. They will make a short visit to N. York and then set their faces homewards. My affectionate respects to Mrs. Madison, and salutations to yourself. Adieu.

Jefferson to Madison

Monticello July 24, 1797

In hopes that Mrs. Madison and yourself and Miss Madison will favor us with a visit when Colo Monroe calls on you, I write this to inform you that I have had the Shadwell and Secretary's ford both well cleaned. If you come the lower road, the Shadwell ford is the proper one. It is a little deepened but clear of stone and perfectly safe. If you come the upper road you will cross at the Secretary's ford, turning in at the gate on the road soon after you enter the 3. notched road. The draught up the mountain that way is steady but uniform.

I see Hamilton has put a short piece into the papers in answer to Callender's publication, and promises shortly something more elaborate.[17] I am anxious to see you here soon, because in about three weeks we shall begin to unroof our house, when the family will be obliged to go elsewhere for shelter. My affectionate respects to the family. Adieu.

Madison to Jefferson

Orange Aug. 2, 1797

DEAR SIR

At the desire of Mr. Bringhurst I forward him to Monticello; and make use of the opportunity, the first that has offered, to return you the pamphlet you were so kind as to leave with me. I add to it a late Fredg. paper which has got hold of some important articles of later date than were brought by the last post, and which may therefore be new to you as they were to me. I have had nothing from Monroe since his letter by you. Dawson mentioned on the 10th. that he would be in Virga. in 14 days, but I see by the fête given him in New York that he was there about the middle of the month. I hope you have shared with us in the fine dose of rainey weather which has restored the verdure of the earth; and if followed by the ordinary course of the season, will save our crops of corn from any essential deficit. Mrs. M. joins in respects to the ladies, and the cordiality with which I remain Dear Sir. Yrs. affecy.

Js. MADISON JR

---

17. In *The History of the United States for 1796* (Philadelphia, 1797), James T. Callender accused Hamilton of adultery with Mrs. James Reynolds, whose husband blackmailed him, then accused him of mishandling government funds while he was secretary of the treasury; see John C. Miller, *The Federalist Era, 1789–1801* (New York, 1960), pp. 203–5.

Jefferson to Madison

Th. J. to JM

Monticello Aug. 3, 1797

I scribbled you a line on the 24th ult; it missed of the post, and so went by a private hand. I perceive from yours by Mr. Bringhurst, that you had not received it. In fact, it was only an earnest exhortation to come here with Munroe, which I still hope you will do. In the meantime, I enclose you a letter from him, and wish your opinion on its principal subject.[18] The variety of other topics, the day I was with you, kept out of sight the letter to Mazzei imputed to me in the papers, the general substance of which is mine, tho' the diction has been considerably varied in the course of it's translations from English into Italian, from Italian into French, and from French into English.[19] I first met with it at Bladensburg, and for a moment concieved I must take the field of the public papers. I could not disavow it wholly, because the greatest part was mine, in substance tho' not in form. I could not avow it as it stood, because the form was not mine, and, in one place, the substance very materially falsified. This, then, would render explanations necessary; nay it would render proofs of the whole necessary, and draw me at length into a publication of all (even the secret) transactions of the administration while I was of it; and embroil me personally with every member of the Executive, with the Judiciary, and with others still. I soon decided in my own mind, to be entirely silent. I consulted with several friends at Philadelphia, who, every one of them, were clearly against my avowing or disavowing, and some of them conjured me most earnestly to let nothing provoke me to it. I corrected, in conversation with them, a substantial misrepresentation in the copy published. The original has a sentiment *like* this (for I have it not before me), "they are endeavoring to submit us to the substance, as they already have to the *forms* of the British government;" meaning by *forms,* the birth-days, levees, processions to parliament, inauguration pompisities, etc. But the copy published says, "as they have already submitted us to the *form* of the British," etc. making me express hostility to the form of our government, that is to say, to the constitution itself. For this is really the difference of the word *form,* used in the singular or plural, in that phrase in the English language. Now it would be impossible for me to explain this publicly without bringing on a personal difference between Genl. Washington and myself, which nothing before the publication of this letter has ever done. It would embroil me also with all those with whom his character is still popular, that is to say, nine tenths of the people of the U S.; and what good would be obtained by my avowing the letter

---

18. James Monroe had suggested that TJ make a public acknowledgment of his letter to Mazzei; see Malone, III, p. 304.

19. See Howard R. Marraro, "The Four Versions of Jefferson's Letter to Mazzei," *WMQ* 2d ser., 22 (1942): 23–27.

with the necessary explanations? Very little indeed in my opinion to counterbalance a good deal of harm. From my silence in this instance it can never be inferred that I am afraid to own the general sentiments of the letter. If I am subject to either imputation it is to that of avowing such sentiments too frankly both in private and public, often when there is no necessity for it, merely because I disdain everything like duplicity. Still however I am open to conviction. Think for me on the occasion, and advise me what to do, and confer with Colo Monroe on the subject.

Let me entreat you again to come with him. There are other important things to consult on. One will be his affair. Another is the subject of the petition now enclosed you,[20] to be proposed to our district, on the late presentment of our representative by the grand jury. The idea it brings forward is still confined to my own breast. It has never been mentioned to any mortal, because I first wish your opinion on the expediency of the measure. If you approve it, I shall propose to P. Carr or some other to father it, and to present it to the counties at their General muster. This will be in time for our Assembly. The presentment going in the public papers just at the moment when Congress was together produced a great effect both on it's friends and foes in that body, very much to the disheartening and mortification of the latter. I wish this petition, if approved, to arrive there under the same circumstance, to produce the counter-effect so wanting for their gratification. I would have wished to recieve it from you again at our court on Monday, because P. Carr and Wilson Nicholas will be there, and might also be consulted and commence measures for putting it into motion. If you can return it then with your opinion and corrections it will be of importance. Present me affectionately to Mrs. Madison, and convey to her my entreaties to interpose her good offices and persuasives with you to bring her here, and before we uncover our house, which will yet be some weeks. Salutations and Adieu.

ENCLOSURE
[Jefferson's Petition to the Virginia House of Delegates, Aug. 1797]
To the Speaker and House of Delegates
of the Commonwealth of Virginia, being a Protest against
interference of Judiciary between Representative
and Constituent.

The petition of the subscribers, inhabitants of the counties of Amherst, Albemarle, Fluvanna, and Goochland, sheweth:

That by the constitution of this State, established from its earliest settlement, the people thereof have possessed the right of being governed by laws to which they have

---

20. According to the editors of *PJM*, TJ's draft petition denouncing the federal-circuit-court presentment in May 1797 of Congressman Samuel J. Cabell's circular letters to his constituents "apparently has not survived." The version below is the final draft of TJ's petition to the Virginia House of Delegates; it includes the suggestions made by JM in his letter to TJ of Aug. 5, 1797, below. The House of Delegates adopted the petition on Dec. 28, 1797, by a vote of 92 to 53; see *PJM*, XVII, pp. 33–37.

consented by representatives chosen by themselves immediately: that in order to give to the will of the people the influence it ought to have, and the information which may enable them to exercise it usefully, it was a part of the common law, adopted as the law of this land, that their representatives, in the discharge of their functions, should be free from the cognizance or coercion of the co-ordinate branches, Judiciary and Executive; and that their communications with their constituents should of right, as of duty also, be free, full, and unawed by any: that so necessary has this intercourse been deemed in the country from which they derive principally their descent and laws, that the correspondence between the representative and constituent is privileged there to pass free of expense through the channel of the public post, and that the proceedings of the legislature have been known to be arrested and suspended at times until the Representatives could go home to their several counties and confer with their constituents.

That when, at the epoch of Independence, the constitution was formed under which we are now governed as a commonwealth, so high were the principles of representative government esteemed, that the legislature was made to consist of two branches, both of them chosen immediately by the citizens; and that general system of laws was continued which protected the relations between the representative and constituent, and guarded the functions of the former from the control of the Judiciary and Executive branches.

That when circumstances required that the ancient confederation of this with the sister States, for the government of their common concerns, should be improved into a more regular and effective form of general government, the same representative principle was preserved in the new legislature, one branch of which was to be chosen directly by the citizens of each State, and the laws and principles remained unaltered which privileged the representative functions, whether to be exercised in the State or General Government, against the cognizance and notice of the co-ordinate branches, Executive and Judiciary; and for its safe and convenient exercise, the inter-communication of the representative and constituent has been sanctioned and provided for through the channel of the public post, at the public expense.

That at the general partition of this commonwealth into districts, each of which was to choose a representative to Congress, the counties of Amherst, Albemarle, Fluvanna, and Goochland, were laid off into one district: that at the elections held for the said district, in the month of April, in the years 1795 and 1797, the electors thereof made choice of Samuel Jordan Cabell, of the county of Amherst, to be their representative in the legislature of the general government; that the said Samuel Jordan Cabell accepted the office, repaired at the due periods to the legislature of the General Government, exercised his functions there as became a worthy member, and as a good and dutiful representative was in the habit of corresponding with many of his constituents, and communicating to us, by way of letter, information of the public proceedings, of asking and receiving our opinions and advice, and of contributing, as far as might be with right, to preserve the transactions of the general government in unison with the principles and sentiments of his constituents: that while the said Samuel J. Cabell was in the exercise of his functions as a representative from this district, and was in the course of that correspondence which his duty and the will of his constituents imposed on him, the right of thus communicating with them, deemed sacred under all the forms in which our government has hitherto existed, never questioned or infringed even by Royal judges or governors, was openly and directly violated at a Circuit court of the General Government, held at the city of Richmond, for the district of Virginia, in the month of May of this present year, 1797: that at the said court, A, B, etc., some of whom were foreigners, having been called upon to serve in the office of grand jurors before the said court, were sworn to the duties of said office in the usual forms of the law, the known limits of which duties are to make presentment of those acts of individuals which the laws have declared to be crimes or misdemeanors: that departing out of the legal limits of their said office, and availing themselves of the sanction of its cover, wickedly and contrary to their fidelity[,] to destroy the rights of the people of this commonwealth, and the fundamental principles of representative government, they made a presentment of the act of the said Samuel J. Cabell, in writing letters to his constituents in the following words, to wit: "We, of the grand jury of the United States, for the district of Virginia, present as a real evil, the circular letters of several members of the late Congress, and particularly letters with the signature of Samuel J. Cabell, endeavoring, at a time of real public danger, to disseminate unfounded calumnies against the happy government of the United States, and thereby to separate the people therefrom; and to increase or produce a foreign influence, ruinous to the peace, happiness, and independence of these United States."

That the grand jury is a part of the Judiciary, not permanent indeed, but in office, *pro hac vice*[21] and responsible as other judges are for their actings and doings while in office: that for the Judiciary to interpose in the legislative department between the constituent and his representative, to control them in the exercise of their functions or duties towards each other, to overawe the free correspondence which exists and ought to exist between them, to dictate what communications may pass between them, and to punish all others, to put the representative into jeopardy of criminal prosecution, of vexation, expense, and punishment before the Judiciary, if his communications, public or private, do not exactly square with their ideas of fact or right, or with their designs of wrong, is to put the legislative department under the feet of the Judiciary, is to leave us, indeed, the shadow, but to take away the substance of representation, which requires essentially that the representative be as free as his constituents would be, that the same interchange of sentiment be lawful between him and them as would be lawful among themselves were they in the personal transaction of their own business; is to do away the influence of the people over the proceedings of their representatives by excluding from their knowledge, by the terror of punishment, all but such information or misinformation as may suit their own views; and is the more vitally dangerous when it is considered that grand jurors are selected by officers nominated and holding their places at the will of the Executive: that they are exposed to influence from the judges who are nominated immediately by the Executive, and who, although holding permanently their commissions as judges, yet from the career of additional office and emolument *actually* opened to them of late, whether *constitutionally* or not, are under all those motives which interest or ambition inspire, of courting the favor of that branch from which appointments flow: that grand juries are frequently composed in part of bystanders, often foreigners, of foreign attachments and interests, and little knowledge of the laws they are most improperly called to decide on; and finally, is to give to the Judiciary, and through them to the Executive, a complete preponderance over the legislature, rendering ineffectual that wise and cautious distribution of powers made by the constitution between the three branches, and subordinating to the other two that

---

21. TJ's italics here and later in the petition.

branch which most immediately depends on the people themselves, and is responsible to them at short periods.

That independently of these considerations of a constitutional nature, the right of free correspondence between citizen and citizen on their joint interests, public or private, and under whatsoever laws these interests arise, is a natural right of every individual citizen, not the gift of municipal law, but among the objects for the protection of which municipal laws are instituted: that so far as the attempt to take away this natural right of free correspondence is an offence against the privileges of the legislative house, of which the said Samuel J. Cabell is a member, it is left to that house, entrusted with the preservation of its own privileges, to vindicate its immunities against the encroachments and usurpations of a co-ordinate branch; but so far as it is an infraction of our individual rights as citizens by other citizens of our own State, the judicature of this commonwealth is solely competent to its cognizance, no other possessing any powers of redress: that the commonwealth retains all its judiciary cognisances not expressly alienated in the grant of powers to the United States as expressed in their constitution: that that constitution alienates only those enumerated in itself, or arising under laws or treaties of the United States made in conformity with its own tenor: but the right of free correspondence is not claimed under that constitution nor the laws or treaties derived from it, but as a natural right, placed originally under the protection of our municipal laws, and retained under the cognizance of our own courts.

Your petitioners further observe that though this crime may not be specifically defined and denominated by any particular statute, yet it is a crime, and of the highest and most alarming nature; that the constitution of this commonwealth, aware it would sometimes happen that deep and dangerous crimes, pronounced as such in the heart of every friend to his country and its free constitution, would often escape the definitions of the law, and yet ought not to escape its punishments, fearing at the same time to entrust such undescribed offences to the discretion of ordinary juries and judges, has reserved the same to the cognizance of the body of the commonwealth acting by their representatives in general assembly, for which purpose provision is made by the constitution in the following words, to wit: "The Governor, when he is out of office, and *others* offending against the State, either by mal-administration, corruption, *or other means* by which the safety of the State may be endangered, shall be impeachable by the House of Delegates. Such impeachment to be prosecuted by the Attorney General or such other person or persons as the house may appoint in the general court, according to the laws of the land. If found guilty, he or they shall be either forever disabled to hold any office under government, or removed from such offices *pro tempore,* or subjected to such pains or penalties as the law shall direct."

Considering then the House of Delegates as the standing inquest of the whole commonwealth so established by the constitution, that its jurisdiction as such extends over all persons within its limits, and that no pale, no sanctuary has been erected against their jurisdiction to protect offenders who have committed crimes against the laws of the commonwealth and rights of its citizens: that the crime committed by the said grand jurors is of that high and extraordinary character for which the constitution has provided extraordinary procedure: that though the violation of right falls in the first instance on us, your petitioners and the representative chosen immediately by us, yet in principle and consequence it extends to all our fellow-citizens, whose safety is passed away whenever their representatives are placed, in the exercise of their functions, under the direction and coercion of either of the other departments of government, and one of their most interesting rights is lost when that of a free communication of sentiment by speaking or writing is suppressed: We, your petitioners, therefore pray that you will be pleased to take your constitutional cognizance of the premises, and institute such proceedings for impeaching and punishing the said A, B, etc., as may secure to the citizens of this commonwealth their constitutional right: that their representatives shall in the exercise of their functions be free and independent of the other departments of government, may guard that full intercourse between them and their constituents which the nature of their relations and the laws of the land establish, may save to them the natural right of communicating their sentiments to one another by speaking and writing, and may serve as a terror to others attempting hereafter to subvert those rights and the fundamental principles of our constitution, to exclude the people from all direct influence over the government they have established by reducing that branch of the legislature which they choose directly, to a subordination under those over whom they have but an indirect, distant, and feeble control.

And your petitioners further submit to the wisdom of the two houses of assembly whether the safety of the citizens of this commonwealth in their persons, their property, their laws, and government, does not require that the capacity to act in the important office of a juror, grand or petty, civil or criminal, should be restrained in future to native citizens of the United States, or such as were citizens at the date of the treaty of peace which closed our revolutionary war, and whether the ignorance of our laws and natural partiality to the countries of their birth are not reasonable causes for declaring this to be one of the rights incommunicable in future to adoptive citizens.

We, therefore, your petitioners, relying with entire confidence on the wisdom and patriotism of our representatives in General assembly, clothed preëminently with all the powers of the people which have not been reserved to themselves, or enumerated in the grant to the General Government delegated to maintain all their rights and relations not expressly and exclusively transferred to other jurisdictions, and stationed as sentinels to observe with watchfulness and oppose with firmness all movements tending to destroy the equilibrium of our excellent but complicated machine of government, invoke from you that redress of our violated rights which the freedom and safety of our common country calls for. We denounce to you a great crime, wicked in its purpose, and mortal in its consequences unless prevented, committed by citizens of this commonwealth against the body of their country. If we have erred in conceiving the redress provided by the law, we commit the subject to the superior wisdom of this house to devise and pursue such proceedings as they shall think best; and we, as in duty bound, shall ever pray, etc.

Madison to Jefferson

Orange Aug. 5, 1797

DEAR SIR,

Yours of the 3d arrived safe yesterday. I will converse with Col Monroe, as you desire, on the subject of his letter to you, and listen to all his reasons for the opinion he gives. My present conviction is opposed to it. I have viewed the subject pretty much in the light you do. I consider it, moreover, as a ticklish experiment to say publicly yes or no to the interrogatories of party spirit. It may bring on dilemmas, not to be particularly foreseen, of disagreeable explanations, or of tacit confessions. Hitherto the precedents have been the other way. The late President was silent for many years as to the letters imputed to him, and, it would seem, deposited in the office of State only the answer which the zeal of the Secretary communicated to the public.[22] Mr. Adams has followed the example with respect to Callender's charge, probably well founded, of advising the extermination of the Tories. Col. M. thinks that honest men would be encouraged by your owning and justifying the letter to Mazzei. I rather suspect it would be a gratification and triumph to their opponents; and that out of the unfixed part of the Community more converts would be gained by the popularity of Gen Washington, than by the kind of proof that must be relied on against it.

Wishing to return the "petition, etc." to your Court, as you recommend, I must be brief on that subject. It is certainly of great importance to set the public opinion right with regard to the functions of grand Juries, and the dangerous abuse of them in the federal Courts; nor could a better occasion occur. If there be any doubts in the case, they must flow from the uncertainty of getting a numerous subscription, or of embarking the Legislature in the business. On these points, the two gentlemen you mean to consult can judge much better than I can do. The Petition, in its tenor, cannot certainly be mended. I have noted with a pencil the passages wch. may perhaps be better guarded agst. cavil.

(1) The term "appoint" strictly taken includes the Senate, as well as Executive.

(2) Is it true that the foreign members of the late grand jury lie under *all* the defects ascribed to them? I am a stranger even to their names.

(3) "within the same" Does not impeachment extend to crimes committed elsewhere, by those amenable to our laws?

(4) "such as resided within the American lines during the *whole* war." Wd. not this apply to persons who came here during the war and were faithful to the end of it. Gallatin is an example. Would such a partial disfranchisement of persons already naturalized be a proper precedent? The benefit of stating the evil to the public might be preserved and the difficulty avoided by confining the remedy to future naturalizations, or by a general reference of it to the wisdom of the Legislature. This last may be a good expedient throughout the

---

22. In one of his last official acts as president on his last day in office, George Washington disavowed letters that the British had forged in 1777 to discredit him and the American Revolution. These had been recently reprinted by the Philadelphia *Aurora,* and Washington deposited a statement in the secretary of state's office calling them "a base forgery"; see George Washington to Timothy Pickering, Mar. 3, 1797, in Fitzpatrick, XXXV, pp. 414–16. For a careful account, see James D. Tagg, "Benjamin Franklin Bache's Attack on George Washington," *PMHB* 100 (1976): 191–230.

Petition, in case the assembly cannot be relied on to adopt the specific remedies prayed for.

(5) This change is to avoid the term "expressly" which has been a subject of controversy, and rather decided against by the public opinion.

Your letter of the 24th has come to hand since mine by Mr. B. It is so much our inclination to comply with its invitation that you may be assured it will be done if any wise practicable. I have engagements, however, on hand of sundry kinds which forbid a promise to myself on that head. The situation of my health may be another obstacle. I was attacked the night before last, very severly by something like a cholera morbus or bilious colic, of which, tho' much relieved, I still feel the effects, and it is not quite certain what turn the complaint may take. Adieu affectly,

Js. MADISON JR.

Madison to Jefferson

[Orange] Aug. 24, 1797

DEAR SIR

The inclosed letter for Mr. B. came to my hand last week; but not till the opportunity by the then mail was lost. I hear nothing of Monroe but thro' the Newspapers containing his correspondence with Pickering. As that appears to have been closed on the 31st. of last month, I am in hourly expectation of seeing him. I am also without any late information with respect to the progress of the Committee on Blount and Liston's conspiracy.[23] Dawson wrote me some time ago "that they were going on well, and that he had well grounded reasons, which he could not communicate by letter, to say, that they should bring in some large fish." It is much to be wished none of this description may escape, tho' to be feared that they will be most likely to do so. Mrs. M. offers her respects to the ladies, and joins in my inclination to visit Monticello; but I am so compleatly plunged into necessary occupations of several kinds, that I can[not] positively decide that we shall have that pleasure. Yrs affely

J. MADISON

23. William Blount, Republican senator from Tennessee, was expelled from the Senate on July 8, 1797, for heading up a conspiracy to lead a joint attack of Indians and British adventurers against Spanish possessions in North America. Robert Liston was the British minister to the United States from 1796 to 1800 who collaborated with Blount, paying secret service money to send an agent of Blount's to England. Liston's actions were disavowed by the British government, but TJ and the Jeffersonians always referred to Blount's conspiracy as "Liston's plot" and characterized the Republican Blount's actions as an aberration caused by "the British party who seduced him." See William H. Masterson, *William Blount* (Baton Rouge, 1954), pp. 301–23; Morton Borden, *The Federalism of James A. Bayard* (New York, 1955), pp. 47–61; and Perkins, pp. 99–101.

Madison to Jefferson

[Orange] Oct. 20, 1797

DEAR SIR,

I recd. the inclosed pamphlet from Col. Monroe, with a request that it might be returned to you. The publication under all its characters is a curious specimen of the ingenious folly of its author.[24] Next to the error of publishing at all, is that of forgetting that simplicity and candour are the only dress which prudence would put on innocence. Here we see every rhetorical artifice employed to excite the spirit of party to prop up his sinking reputation; and whilst the most exaggerated complaints are uttered against the unfair and virulent persecutions of himself, he deals out in every page the most malignant insinuations against others. The one against you is a masterpiece of folly, because its impotence is in exact proportion to its venom. Along with the pamphlet is inclosed a letter, which you will be good eno' to have delivered by an early opportunity. Yrs. affecly

J MADISON JR

Madison to Jefferson

Orange Oct. 25, 1797

DEAR SIR

I am placed under circumstances which make it proper I should inform you that Mr. Knapp of Philada. is a candidate for the office of Treasr. to the Mint, vacated by the death of Dr. Way, and is particularly anxious that you should be possessed of that fact, and of the testimony I may be able to give as to his qualifications and character. During several of the last winters I spent in Phida. Mr. K. was a near neighbour, and a familiar intercourse prevailed between our families. I really believe him to be a worthy man, and the line of life he has been in supports the character he bears, of being skilful in the sort of business he aspires to. If you should be invited by any opportunity to say as much to the quarter from which appts. issue, it will be highly acceptable to Mr. K. and ought to be so to me. I have however intimated to him, that I did not expect that your opinion in any way would be asked, and that it would not be proper for you to give it unasked. It is astonishing that it does not occur in these cases that the patronage of those whose politics are adverse to the politics

---

24. In his *Observations on Certain Documents contained in . . . "The History of the United States for the Year 1796," In Which the Charge of Speculation Against Alexander Hamilton, Late Secretary of the Treasury, is Fully Refuted . . .*, Hamilton denied any corrupt dealings as secretary of the treasury and confessed that "my real crime is an amorous connection" with Mrs. Reynolds; see John C. Miller, *Alexander Hamilton: Portrait in Paradox* (New York, 1959), p. 463.

of the administration is more likely to be of injury than service to the suitors for office.

We just have the pleasure of learning that an event has taken place in your family which calls for our joint and warmest congratulations, which we beg you to make acceptable to all to whom [they] are due.[25] Yrs. truly

Js. M. Jr

25. Maria Jefferson married John Wayles Eppes at Monticello on Oct. 13, 1797; see Sarah Nicholas Randolph, *The Domestic Life of Thomas Jefferson* (New York, 1871), p. 246.

23

CRISIS IN FREEDOM: THE XYZ AFFAIR AND THE ALIEN AND SEDITION ACTS, 1798

BY THE SUMMER OF 1797, Jefferson had made the transition from retirement to active leadership of the Republican party, quickly adapting to the role previously played by Madison. In his official capacity as vice president, he presided over the Federalist Senate but was powerless in his anomalous position, being an outsider to the Adams administration. In his unofficial role as party leader, he urged stricter discipline on the Republicans in the House, where leadership had moved from Madison to Albert Gallatin of Pennsylvania, who directed his colleagues as "a well organized and disciplined Corps," according to a Federalist opponent, "never going astray, or doing right even by mistake."[1] Indeed, Oliver Wolcott, Hamilton's successor as secretary of the treasury, recognized the Republican triumverate as "Messrs. Gallatin, Madison, and Jefferson."[2]

A bad cold and an accident involving his younger daughter delayed Jefferson's trip to Philadelphia by a month in the fall of 1797. On the way, he stopped at Montpellier for a brief visit with the Madisons.[3] Once he arrived in the nation's capital, he noted that the political enmities of the special session of Congress had carried over to the regular session. "Party animosities here," he wrote early in 1798, "have raised a wall of separation between those who differ in political sentiments."[4]

While Congress marked time, impatiently awaiting news about the

---

1. Theodore Sedgwick to Rufus King, Apr. 9, 1798, cited in Noble E. Cunningham, Jr., *The Jeffersonian Republicans: The Formation of Party Organization, 1789–1801* (Chapel Hill, 1957), p. 123.
2. Oliver Wolcott to Alexander Hamilton, Apr. 29, 1796, *ibid.*
3. JM to TJ, Dec. 25, 1797, below.
4. TJ to Angelica Church, Jan. 11, 1798, quoted in Malone, III, p. 360.

negotiations in France, there was little to do, and the parties fended for position. In a remarkably detached analysis of the heated political situation, Jefferson described the party system in the terminology of English history: "It is now well understood that two political Sects have arisen within the U. S. the one believing that the executive is the branch of our government which the most needs support; the other that like the analagous branch in the English Government, it is already too strong for the republican parts of the constitution; and therefore in equivocal cases they incline to the legislative powers: the former of these are called federalists, sometimes aristocrats or monocrats, and sometimes tories, after the corresponding sect in the English Government of exactly the same definition: the latter are stiled republicans, whigs, jacobins, disorganizers, etc. . . . Both parties claim to be federalists and republicans, and I believe with truth as to the great mass of them: these appelations therefore designate neither exclusively, and all the others are slanders, except those of whig and tory which alone characterize the distinguishing principles of the two Sects."[5]

Although he classified the mass of the people as both republican—supporters of a republic rather than a monarchy—and federalist—supporters of the Constitution—Jefferson still resorted to designations, especially for leaders, which he labeled slanderous, and his use of the term "Monarchio, Aristocratic Faction" in the Mazzei letter later led to his denunciation on the floor of the House for dangerous political opinions that could lead to "nothing but treason and insurrection."[6]

Gallatin made a vigorous defense of Jefferson's letter, asserting the right of Republicans to express political opinions in opposition to administration policy. "If we complain of the prodigality . . . of the Administration or wish to control it by refusing to appropriate all the money which is asked, we are stigmatized as disorganizers; if we oppose the growth of systems of taxation, we are charged with a design of subverting the Constitution and making a revolution; if we attempt to check the extension of our political connections with European nations, we are branded with the epithet of Jacobins." But the Federalists had inverted things, he argued. "Revolutions and Jacobinism do not flow from that line of policy we wish to see adopted. . . . They exclusively belong to the system we resist; they are its last stage, the last page in the book of the history of governments under its influence."[7]

In their reply to Gallatin, the House Federalists again lambasted Jefferson, calling him a missionary who had imported a "war system" of alliance with France when he returned from his diplomatic post in Paris "to fill a high official station here." To make sure that no one misunderstood his accusation,

---

5. TJ to John Wise, Feb. 12, 1798, in Malone, III, pp. 364–65.

6. Joshua Coit of Connecticut read the garbled version of TJ's Mazzei letter into the congressional record on Feb. 28, 1798; see *ibid*., pp. 366–67.

7. Henry Adams, *The Life of Albert Gallatin* (Philadelphia, 1879), p. 198.

the speaker, Robert Goodloe Harper from South Carolina, attached to the reported debates a footnote designating the vice president as the target of his remarks.[8] As another High Federalist, Senator Theodore Sedgwick from Massachusetts, observed, "More than once he has heard, in debates, and in terms which could not be mistaken, Philippics pronounced against the author of the letter to Mazzei. He is, I have no doubt, the very life and soul of the opposition."[9]

While waiting for news from the three envoys in France, Jefferson fed Madison juicy morsels of political gossip, ranging from the Federalist attempt to expel a Republican representative from Congress to the reverberations set off by a birthday ball in honor of George Washington. When Roger Griswold, a Connecticut Federalist, made a disparaging remark about the Revolutionary war record of Congressman Matthew Lyon, the Vermont Republican replied by spitting in his face. The Federalists then attempted to oust Lyon, carrying a majority vote easily but falling short of the two-thirds necessary to expel "the spitting beast."[10] Jefferson called "the disgusting proceedings in the case of Lyon" to Madison's attention, labeling it a Federalist maneuver "to get rid of his vote" in a closely divided house.[11]

Madison thought that "the affair of Lyon and Griswold is bad eno' [in] every way, but worst of all in becoming a topic of tedious and disgraceful debates in Congress."[12] When Griswold later attacked Lyon on the floor of the House, Madison called the whole episode "extremely disgraceful" but confessed that he was "curious to see how the zealots for expelling Lyon will treat the deliberate riot of Griswold."[13] Jefferson's considered judgment was that "these proceedings must degrade the General government, and lead the people to lean more on their state governments, which have been sunk under the early popularity of the former."[14]

Although the comedic elements of congressmen in combat escaped Jefferson and Madison, they virtually chortled over the dilemma that Federalists faced in dealing with the birthday ball honoring George Washington in 1798. "The late birthnight," the vice president informed his friend gleefully, "has certainly sown tares among the exclusive federals. It has winnowed the grain from the chaff. The sincerely Adamites did not go," nor did the president, Mrs. Adams thinking that a ball for the former president cast her husband into a shadow. "The Washingtonians went religiously, and took the secession of

---

8. Malone, III, pp. 367–68.
9. Theodore Sedgwick to Rufus King, Apr. 9, 1798, *ibid.*, p. 366.
10. Aleine Austin, *Matthew Lyon: "New Man" of the Democratic Revolution, 1749–1822* (University Park, Pa., 1981), pp. 96–108.
11. TJ to JM, Feb. 15, 1798, below.
12. JM to TJ, [Feb. 18, 1798], below.
13. JM to TJ, Mar. 4, 1798, below. A motion to reprimand both men lost by one vote.
14. TJ to JM, Feb. 15, 1798, below. See also John R. Howe, Jr., "Republican Thought and Political Violence of the 1790s," *American Quarterly* 19 (1967): 147–65.

the others in high dudgeon. The one sex [sect] threaten to desert the levees, the other the evening parties." Several New England senators, "Goodhue, Tracy, Sedgwick, etc., did not attend; but the three Secretaries and Attorney General," all Washington appointees carried over into Adams's cabinet, "did."[15] The Republicans, however, "went in number," Jefferson reported, in order "to encourage the idea that the birthnights hitherto kept had been for the General and not the President," thus ending a ceremony associated with royalty.

Madison was pleased that the Republicans had attended the ball since their action was based "on the principle of appropriating it to the person, and not to the office of the late President. It is a pity that the non-attendance of the Adamsites is not presented to the public in such a manner with their names, as to satisfy the real friends of Washington, as well as the people generally, of the true principles and views of those who have been loudest in their hypocritical professions of attachment to him."[16]

Madison, a perpetual critic of Adams, had earlier contrasted the second president most unfavorably with the first. "There never was perhaps a greater contrast between two characters," he observed. Washington "cold considerate and cautious, the other headlong and kindled into flame by every spark that lights on his passions: the one ever scrutinizing into the public opinion, and ready to follow where he could not lead it; the other insulting it by the most adverse sentiments and pursuits: W[ashington] a hero in the field, yet overweighing every danger in the Cabinet. A[dams] without a single pretension to the character of a soldier, a perfect Quixotte as a statesman: the former cheif magistrate pursuing peace every where with sincerity, tho' mistaking the means; the latter taking as much pains to get into war, as the former took to keep out of it."

Warming to his subject, Madison pushed on. "The contrast might be pursued into a variety of other particulars—the policy of the one in shunning connections with the arrangements of Europe, of the other in holding out the U. S. as a makeweight in its Balances of power; the avowed exultation of W. in the progress of liberty every where, and his eulogy on the Revolution and people of France posterior even to the bloody reign and fate of Robespierre—the open denunciations by Adams of the smallest disturbance of the antient discipline order and tranquillity of despotism, etc., etc., etc."[17]

The waiting ended in March. When President Adams announced the failure of the peace mission to France and called for vigorous defense measures to be adopted with promptitude, decision, and unanimity, a political hail-

---

15. TJ to JM, Mar. 2, 1798, below. For the celebration, see Manning J. Dauer, *The Adams Federalists* (Baltimore, 1953), p. 140.
16. JM to TJ, Mar. 12, 1798, below.
17. JM to TJ, [Feb. 18, 1798], below.

storm broke with electric suddenness.[18] (Although the vice president did not know it, Adams had at first drafted a war message but had replaced it with his defense message of March 19.) After Theodore Sedgwick, Federalist whip in the Senate, heard the message, he summarized its political significance: "It will afford a glorious opportunity to destroy faction. Improve it."[19]

Jefferson, who had convinced himself that the unbroken silence of the envoys meant peace, promptly labeled Adams's communication an "insane message." But he knew that the demand for unanimity would push the Republicans to the wall, noting that it had instantly produced a great change in "our political atmosphere": "Exultation on the one side, and a certainty of victory; while the other is petrified with astonishment." President Adams did not call on Congress to declare war, but Jefferson thought that the Federalists were "taking such measures as will be sure to produce war." From his point of view, however, it was impossible "to find any reason in it's favor, resulting from views either of interest or honor, and plausible enough to impose even on the weakest mind; and especially when it would be undertaken by a majority of one or two only."

Indeed, Jefferson thought that the Republicans might have a thin margin, if no one bolted the party or headed for home. "Our Evans," he told Madison, "tho' his soul is wrapt up in the sentiments of this message, yet afraid to give a vote openly for it, is going off to-morrow, as is said. Those who count say there are still 2. members of the other side who will come over to that of peace. If so, the numbers will be for war measures 52. against them 53. if all are present except Evans."

If the Republicans actually had a majority, Jefferson proposed a quick adjournment so that congressmen could "'go home and consult their constituents on the great crisis of American affairs now existing.'" He was sure that this consultation—virtually a referendum—would excite "the whole body of the people from the state of inattention in which they are" and demonstrate that "their safety as well as their rights" rested with the Republicans, who would return to the capital "invigorated by the avowed support of the American people" for peace.[20]

That was wishful thinking, as events quickly demonstrated. Jefferson had woefully underestimated the impact of the president's appeal. Within a week, he wrote that "the decision of the Executive, of two-thirds of the Senate, and half the house of representatives, is too much for the other half of that house." His proposal of adjourning for consultation had been replaced by a Republi-

---

18. Richardson, I, pp. 264-65.

19. Theodore Sedgwick to ———, Mar. 7, 1798, quoted in James Morton Smith, *Freedom's Fetters: The Alien and Sedition Laws and American Civil Liberties* (Ithaca, N.Y., 1956), p. 21. For Adams's draft of the war message, see Page Smith, *John Adams,* 2 vols. (Garden City, N.Y., 1963), II, pp. 954-55.

20. TJ to JM, Mar. 21, 1798, below.

can resolution "'that it is inexpedient to resort to war against the French republic.'" But he was filled with "the most gloomy apprehensions," fearing that "it will be borne down.... In fact the question of war and peace depends now on a toss of cross and pile. If we could but gain this season," he confided to Madison, "we should be saved."[21]

It was Madison who came up with the next Republican tactic. Before war measures were undertaken, he suggested, Adams should be asked to communicate "the intelligence on which such measures are recommended." Just as Congress had pressed Washington for papers relating to Jay's treaty, the House should call for the dispatches relating to the negotiations with France, for it was "facts and proofs," not "the opinion of the P[resident]," that Congress needed to decide on questions of war or peace.[22]

Even before the dispatches were published, Jefferson reported, some of the contents leaked out and created first impressions that were "very disagreeable." The leaks were printed with the "most artful misrepresentations" and "slanderous imputations" that the Republicans were "French partisans," producing "such a shock on the republican mind as has never been seen since our independence."[23] One insinuation involved the vice president directly. "At this moment," he wrote Monroe, "my name is running through all the city as detected in a criminal correspondence with the French directory, and fixed upon me by the documents from our envoys now before the two houses. The detection of this by the publication of the papers, should they be published, will not relieve all the effects of the lie." But he still preferred full publication to "artful misrepresentation" or unbased rumor.[24]

When the dispatches were released in the spring of 1798, a curious circumstance gave the diplomatic confrontation a spy-thriller designation. The XYZ affair took its name from the fact that President Adams withheld the names of the French agents who served as go-betweens for the French foreign minister Talleyrand, calling them Monsieurs X, Y, and Z. The dispatches revealed that Pinckney, Marshall, and Gerry had been treated with contempt by these agents and refused an official reception by Talleyrand until they had disavowed parts of Adams's speech to the special session of Congress in May 1797, offered a large loan to the French Republic, and paid a *doucer*—bribe—to Talleyrand, who offered "to sell his interest and influence with the Directory towards smoothing difficulties with them."[25]

The XYZ revelations "really electrified all classes," according to Fisher

21. TJ to JM, Mar. 29, 1798, below.
22. JM to TJ, Apr. 2, 1798, below.
23. TJ to JM, Apr. 6, 1798, below.
24. TJ to James Monroe, Apr. 5, 1798, in Ford, VII, p. 233.
25. TJ to JM, Apr. 6, 1798, below. The best accounts are in William Stinchcombe, *The XYZ Affair* (Westport, Conn., 1980), and Alexander De Conde, *The Quasi-War: The Politics and Diplomacy of the Undeclared War with France, 1797–1801* (New York, 1966).

Ames, and the nation began immediate preparations for war with France.[26] Secretary of State Timothy Pickering was confident that the publication of the dispatches would end "opposition by Democrats in the House, and French worship . . . outside."[27] Jefferson agreed that the dispatches were "calculated to excite disgust and indignation in Americans generally," without regard to party affiliation.

One aspect of the dispatches also guaranteed "alienation in the republicans particularly." An alphabetical agent had claimed that the American envoys would fail in their attempt to unite the American people in resistance to France's demands for money and an apology from President Adams. "The diplomatic skill of France," Monsieur Y bluntly boasted, "and the means she possesses in your country, are sufficient to enable her, with the French party in America, to throw the blame which will attend the rupture of the negotiations on the Federalists, as you term yourselves, but on the British party, as France terms you."[28]

The envoys replied that the French had miscalculated the party situation in America, and Jefferson agreed. They were so far mistaken about the Republicans, he told Madison, "as to presume an attachment to France and hatred to the Federal party, and not the love of their country, to be their first passion."[29]

One week later, Jefferson told Madison that the Republicans had dropped their resolution against the expediency of war, which, though proper when introduced, was now improper "because to declare that, after we have understood it has been proposed to us to buy peace, would imply an acquiescence under that proposition. All therefore," he counseled, "which the advocates of peace can now attempt, is to prevent war measures *externally*, consenting to every rational measure of *internal* defence and preparation."[30]

In practice, the Republicans tried to draw the line between measures for defense and measures for war. And in case of war, Jefferson observed, the nation would rally against any enemy. "If our house be on fire," he wrote to a neighbor, "without inquiring whether it was fired from within or without, we must try to extinguish it. In that, I have no doubt, we shall act as one man."[31]

Despite this advice, Jefferson found it difficult to concede that the French Directory was directly involved in the "base propositions" revealed in the XYZ affair. These were "very unworthy of a great nation," he said, and he doubted

26. Fisher Ames to Christopher Gore, July 28, 1798, in Fisher Ames, *Works of Fisher Ames*, ed. Seth Ames, 2 vols. (Boston, 1854), I. p. 238.
27. Timothy Pickering to George Washington, Apr. 14, 1798, cited in Smith, *Freedom's Fetters*, p. 7.
28. *Ibid.*, p. 14.
29. TJ to JM, Apr. 6, 1798, below.
30. TJ to JM, Apr. 12, 1798, below.
31. TJ to James Lewis, Jr., May 9, 1798, in Ford, VII, p. 250.

that they could "be imputed to them." To whom, then, could these propositions be attributed? Madison thought that "the conduct of Taleyrand is so extraordinary as to be scarcely credible." If, on the other hand, the demands were true, his depravity, which was not without example, was exceeded only by his stupidity—so much so that Madison doubted that he was responsible for the solicitation of a bribe. "If the evidence be not perfectly conclusive, of which I cannot judge, the decision ought to be agst the evidence, rather than on the side of the infatuation."[32] A week later, he concluded that "whatever probability there may be of individual corruption within the pale of the French Gov^t, the evidence is certainly very insufficient to support such an attack on its reputation in the face of the world."[33] After talking with Monroe, he thought that the transaction by Talleyrand's agents was "a swindling experiment" and the publication of the dispatches, which he had earlier recommended, "a libel on the French Government."[34]

Although Jefferson and Madison gave every benefit of the doubt to the French, they could not quite bring themselves to accept Adams's or the envoys' version of the XYZ affair. "Whatever difference of opinion there may be as to the purity of the French councils," Madison told the vice president, "there will be a general agreement as to the improper views of our own Executive party." Jefferson had already concluded that Adams's speech at the special session of 1797 was "the only obstacle to accommodation, and the real cause of war, if war takes place."[35] As Malone observes, Jefferson, in trying to fix the responsibility for the failure of the diplomatic negotiations with France, "indulged in oversimplification"; his attempt "to blame the recent failure on the American government . . . was labored and injudicious."[36] The same can be said of Madison, who got most of his news, and some of his views, from Jefferson.

The XYZ affair left the public mind "in a state of astonishment" and put the Federalists firmly in control. Things "are at this moment on the creen," Jefferson confessed early in April, tilted definitely towards the Federalists.[37] Adams rode the wave of popular enthusiasm, reveling in such new patriotic songs as "Adams and Liberty" and "Hail, Columbia," which won "the most unbounded applause" at its premier performance in the nation's capital, according to Mrs. Adams. "I suppose the fact to be," a Federalist informed the American minister to Great Britain, "that since man was created and government was formed no public officer has stood higher in the confidence and

32. JM to TJ, Apr. 15, 1798, below.
33. JM to TJ, Apr. 22, 1798, below.
34. JM to TJ, Apr. 29, 1798, below.
35. *Ibid.* and TJ to JM, Apr. 6, 1798, below.
36. Malone, III, p. 374. For a critical account of TJ's "glossing over the XYZ Affair" by "extenuations and half-truths," see Merrill D. Peterson, *Thomas Jefferson and the New Nation* (New York, 1970), pp. 596–97.
37. TJ to JM, Apr. 12, 1798, below.

affection than our present President does." Mrs. Adams confessed that the testimonials applauding the administration's policies were "indeed an incourageing, and gratefull reward" to the president for his exertions. "In short," she wrote, "we are now wonderfully popular except with Bache and Co who in his paper calls the President old, querilous, Bald, blind, cripled, Toothless Adams."[38] At the same time, she wrote that "the Common People say if J[efferson] had been our President, and Madison and Burr our negotiators, we should all have been sold to the French." "All our trouble, and all our difficulty" she ascribed to "those whom the French boast of as their Partizans," men who ought to be "adjudged traitors to their country."[39]

From his isolated post in Virginia, Madison quickly discerned the use that the Federalists would make of the foreign crisis in order to strike at political opposition at home, warning of "the internal views to which they mean also to turn this extraordinary manœuvre." "Perhaps it is a universal truth," he wrote in May, "that the loss of liberty at home is to be charged to provisions against danger, real or pretended, from abroad."[40]

Jefferson confirmed the linkage between defense measures and "internal security," between measures designed to deal with foreign-policy issues and those aimed at "domestic disaffection." As Republicans retreated to the sidelines and waverers went over to the Federalists, he predicted that the "war party" would "carry what they please": renunciation of the Revolutionary war treaties with France; suspension of trade with France and its dependencies; authorization to capture French vessels; formation of a navy and a provisional army; permission to increase the size of the infantry and artillery divisions; and creation of a repressive internal security program.

"One of the war party," he wrote Madison in April, "in a fit of unguarded passion declared some time ago they would pass a citizen [or naturalization] bill, an alien bill, and a sedition bill. Accordingly, some days ago, Coit laid a motion on the table of the H[ouse] of R[epresentatives] for modifying the citizen law. Their threats point at Gallatin, and it is believed they will endeavor to reach him by this bill. Yesterday Mr. Hillhouse laid on the table of the Senate a motion for giving power to send away suspected aliens. This is understood to be meant for Volney and Collot.[41] But it will not stop there when it gets into a course of execution. There is now only wanting, to accomplish the whole declaration before mentioned, a sedition bill, which we shall certainly soon see proposed. The object of that, is the suppression of the whig presses. Bache's has been particularly named. . . . At present," he concluded, "the war

38. Smith, *Freedom's Fetters,* pp. 8-9.
39. *Ibid.*, pp. 15-16.
40. JM to TJ, Apr. 22, 1798, below, and May 13, 1798, below.
41. For Constantin-François Chasseboeuf, comte de Volney, see Gilbert Chinard, *Volney et l'Amérique d'après des documents inédits et sa correspondance avec Jefferson* (Baltimore, 1923); for Victor Collot, see Durand Echeverria, "General Collot's Plan for a Reconnaissance of the Ohio and Mississippi Valleys, 1796," *WMQ* 9 (1952): 512-20.

hawks talk of Septembrizing, Deportation, and the examples for quelling sedition set by the French Executive. All the firmness of the human mind is now in a state of requisition."[42]

When Madison learned of "the success of the war party in turning the Despatches to their inflammatory views," he lamented it as "a mortifying item against the enlightened character of our citizens." But the public response might be only a temporary aberration. "It is to be hoped . . . ," he wrote, "that any arbitrary attacks on the freedom of the press will find virtue eno' remaining in the public mind to make them recoil on the wicked authors. No other check to desperate projects seems now to be left. The sanguinary faction ought not however to adopt the spirit of Robespierre without recollecting the shortness of his triumphs and the perpetuity of his infamy."[43] A short time later, when he received Fenno's Federalist paper from Philadelphia but not Bache's Republican news sheet, he added a postscript to his letter to Jefferson: "I hope the bridle is not yet put on the press."[44]

From his uncomfortable post in the nation's capital, Jefferson watched as "the spirit kindled up in the towns" generated war addresses that came "showering in from New Jersey and the great trading towns." These addresses, however, offering support of administration measures, were understandable, he told Madison, "for indiscreet declarations and expressions of passion may be pardoned to a multitude acting from the impulse of the moment." But President Adams's replies were even "more Thrasonic than the addresses" and seemed to block all hopes for peace.

"Nor is it France alone," the vice president added, "but his own fellow citizens against whom his threats are uttered." In his response to a New Jersey address, the president had denounced " 'the delusions and misrepresentations which have misled so many citizens, [and which] must be discountenanced by authority as well as by the citizens at large.' " Jefferson thought that this censure was directed against the letters from Republican congressmen to their constituents, "which they have been in the habit of seeking after and publishing; while those sent by the Tory part of the house to their constituents, are ten times more numerous, and replete with the most atrocious falsehoods and calumnies. . . . Perhaps," he added, "the P[resident]'s expression before quoted, may look to the Sedition bill which has been spoken of, and which may be meant to put the Printing presses under the Imprimatur of the Executive. Bache is thought a main object of it."[45]

As tempers mounted and party lines hardened, scuffles and fights broke out in the national capital, filling the city on one occasion with so much

---

42. TJ to JM, Apr. 26, 1798, below. For a biography of the leading Republican editor in Pennsylvania, see James Tagg, *Benjamin Franklin Bache and the Philadelphia Aurora* (Philadelphia, 1990).
43. JM to TJ, May 5, 1798, below.
44. JM to TJ, May 13, 1798, below.
45. TJ to JM, May 3, 1798, below.

confusion, Jefferson reported, "that it was dangerous going out." On May 7, nearly 1,200 young men paraded to the president's house, where Adams, in full military dress, welcomed them, listened to their address of support, and thanked them for "their virtuous anxiety to preserve the honor and independence of their country."[46] In reporting the event to Madison, Jefferson observed that "some of the young men who addressed the President . . . mounted the Black (or English) cockade. The next day numbers of the people appeared with the tricolored (or French) cockade. Yesterday being the fast day, the black cockade again appeared, on which the tricolor also showed itself. A fray ensued, the light horse were called in, and the city was . . . filled with confusion from about 6. to 10. o'clock last night." In a follow-up account, Jefferson corrected his report, noting that "in the first moments of the tumults here, . . . the cockade assumed by one party was mistaken to be the tricolor. It was the old blue and red adopted in some places in an early part of the revolution[ary] war. However it is laid aside. But the black is still frequent."[47]

President Adams had proclaimed May 9 as "a day of solemn humiliation, fasting and prayer" throughout the United States, the day the battle of the cockades broke out. Jefferson reported that "the President received 3. anonymous letters"—he suspected that they were "written probably by some of the war men"—"announcing plots to burn the city on the fast-day. He thought them worth being made known, and great preparations were proposed by the way of caution, and some were yielded to by the Governor. Many weak people packed their most valuable movables to be ready for transportation." Except for the fray, which called out the cavalry, however, "the day passed without justifying the alarms. Other idle stories have been since circulated, and the popular mind has not been proof against them."[48]

What the vice president did not know was that one of the three anonymous letters to Adams claimed that resident Frenchmen and domestic traitors were plotting a massacre on Fast Day, listing as the "grandest of all grand Villains that traitor to his country—that infernal Scoundrel Jefferson."[49]

Never an admirer of Adams, Madison read the president's responses to addresses as Jefferson did. He was convinced that they formed "the most grotesque scene in the tragicomedy acting by the Goverm!."[50] "Every answer he gives to his addressers unmasks more and more his principles and views. His

---

46. John Adams, *The Works of John Adams . . .* , ed. Charles Francis Adams, 10 vols. (Boston, 1850–56), IX, pp. 187–88.

47. TJ to JM, May 10, 1798, below, and May 17, 1798, below.

48. TJ to JM, May 17, 1798, below. For John Adams's recollection of Governor Mifflin's calling out "a Patrol of Horse and Foot to preserve the peace" and quell "Terrorism," while TJ "was fast asleep in philosophical Tranquility," see John Adams to TJ, June 30, 1813, in Cappon, II, pp. 346–48.

49. The letter from "A Friend to America and Truth," Apr. 18, 1798, which is in the Adams Papers at the Massachusetts Historical Society (XIX, p. 184), is quoted in Smith, *Freedom's Fetters,* p. 26.

50. JM to TJ, June 10, 1798, below.

language to the young men at Ph[iladelphia] is the most abominable and degrading that could fall from the lips of the first magistrate of an independent people, and particularly from a Revolutionary patriot. It throws some light on his meaning when he remarked to me, 'that there was not a single principle the same in the American and French Revolutions;' and on my alluding to the contrary sentiment of his predecessor expressed to Adêt on the presentment of the Colours, added, 'that it was false let who would express it.' The abolition of Royalty was it seems not one of his Revolutionary principles. Whether he always made this profession," Madison concluded, "is best known to those, who knew him in the year 1776."[51]

The president's addresses won high praise from the Federalists and set the stage for congressional action not only against the external enemy, but what they chose to call the "internal foe." "The answers of the President," wrote Fisher Ames, "have elevated the spirit, and cleared the filmy eyes, of the many. The people have risen *gradatim;* every answer was a step upstairs." Secretary of State Timothy Pickering agreed that "Mr. Adams, in his vigourous answers to the numerous addresses presented to him, enforced by the weight of his official station, as president of the U. States contributed, doubtless, more than any other man to elevate the temper of the nation" to its resistance of France and of the influence of French partisans in America. The crisis with France gave the Federalists an opportunity to equate opposition to the administration's policy with sedition and near-treason. Hamilton was convinced that "many of the leaders of faction will . . . take ultimately a station in the public estimation like that of the Tories of our Revolution."[52]

As the Federalists rammed their repressive legislation through Congress, Jefferson and Madison watched with jaundiced eyes. The vice president thought the alien bill "a most detestable thing," an act "worthy of the 8th or 9th century," that would place aliens "under absolute government." But he was sure the House would pass it, "the majority there being decisive, consolidated, and bold enough to do anything."[53] Madison labeled the alien bill "a monster that must forever disgrace its parents."[54]

But it was the sedition bill that was the most objectionable weapon in the Federalist arsenal, according to Jefferson. "Among other enormities," he told Madison, it "undertakes to make printing certain matters criminal, tho' one of

---

51. JM to TJ, May 20, 1798, below. For a sampling of John Adams's answers to address, see Adams, *Works,* IX, pp. 191–217.

52. Oliver Wolcott, Timothy Pickering, and Alexander Hamilton are quoted in Smith, *Freedom's Fetters,* pp. 20–21. For an analysis of this theme, see Marshall Smelser, "The Federalist Period As an Age of Passion," *American Quarterly* 10 (1958): 391–419.

53. TJ to JM, May 31, 1798, below, and June 7, 1798, below. The reference to the eighth and ninth centuries is in TJ to Thomas Mann Randolph, May 9, 1798, quoted in Smith, *Freedom's Fetters,* p. 53.

54. JM to TJ, May 20, 1798, below.

the amendments to the Constitution has so expressly taken religion, printing presses etc. out of their coercion. Indeed this bill and the Alien bill both are so palpably in the teeth of the constitution as to shew they mean to pay no respect to it."[55]

As the session stretched out and the Federalist program unfolded, the weary vice president decided to go home before Congress adjourned. A sympathetic Madison hoped to have the pleasure "of congratulating you soon, on your release from your painful situation."[56] But Jefferson delayed his departure when he learned that John Marshall had returned from France, for he was anxious to see "whether that circumstance would produce any new projects." He doubted that Marshall was "hot enough" for his Federalist friends, but he thought that they would nevertheless use Marshall's return to further their program.

Indeed, Jefferson soon reported that the Federalists had arranged a hero's welcome for the envoy, who "was received here with the utmost eclat. The Secretary of state and many carriages, with all the city cavalry, went to Frankfort to meet him, and on his arrival here in the evening, the bells rung till late in the night, and immense crowds were collected to see and make part of the shew, which was circuitously paraded through the streets before he was set down at the city tavern. All this was to secure him to their views, that he might say nothing which would expose the game they have been playing."[57]

President Adams sent a special message to Congress, announcing the arrival of the envoy at "a place of safety, where he is justly held in honor." Senators, congressmen, and the vice president visited the Virginian's hotel to congratulate him on his safe return home. But he was not at his lodging when Jefferson called, so Jefferson left a note for his distant kinsman and future nemesis, saying—in a Freudian slip—that he had been "so lucky as to find" that Marshall was out. Whatever Marshall's role with the "war party," Jefferson was convinced that "their system is professedly to keep up an alarm." In his message to Congress, Adams announced that he considered the diplomatic negotiations "at an end" and that he would "never send another minister to France, until he shall be assured that he will be received and treated with the respect due to a great, powerful, free and independent nation."[58]

Marshall's dramatic return gave new impetus to congressional action, just as Jefferson was hoping for adjournment to withdraw "the fire from under a boiling pot."[59] A prominent Federalist observed that the envoy's arrival "will

---

55. TJ to JM, June 7, 1798, below.

56. JM to TJ, June 10, 1798, below.

57. TJ to JM, June 21, 1798, below. For John Marshall's reception, see Albert J. Beveridge, *The Life of John Marshall*, 4 vols. (Boston, 1916-19), II, pp. 343-55.

58. TJ to JM, June 21, 1798, below. See also Smith, *Freedom's Fetters*, pp. 3-8.

59. TJ to JM, June 21, 1798, below.

be of eminent service at this moment, [since] it will tend to urge on energetick measures."⁶⁰ Renouncing the treaties with France by unilateral action, the Federalists took drastic steps that carried the United States into a state of undeclared war with France. To command the augmented army, General Washington was called into federal service as commander in chief, with the army under the field direction of the inspector general, Major General Alexander Hamilton. To meet the expenses of these warlike measures, Congress laid a $2 million direct tax and authorized President Adams to borrow that amount at not more than 6 percent interest in anticipation of tax revenues.[61]

On the weekend of Marshall's arrival, a singular series of events gave the Federalists an opportunity to blast Jefferson on the floor of the House and in the party press for aiding and abetting the one-man peace mission to France by Dr. George Logan of Philadelphia, one of Jefferson's closest friends. The Quaker doctor made his departure something of a "mystery . . . so that his disappearance without notice excited conversation," Jefferson informed his friend in Virginia. "This was seized by the war-hawks, and given out as a secret mission from the Jacobins here to sollicit an army from France, instruct them as to their landing etc. This extravagance," he added, "produced a real panic among the citizens."[62]

"Recall his connections," warned *Porcupine's Gazette,* whose readers did not need to be told that Logan was a seditious envoy from the opposition party; "recollect the situation of this country at this moment, and *tremble for its fate!*" The "infernal design" of this "noted and violent democrat," said the Philadelphia *Gazette,* could only be "the introduction of a French army, *to teach us the genuine value of true and essential liberty* by re-organizing our government, through the blessed operation of the bayonet and guillotine."[63]

Shortly after Logan sailed, Jefferson, who had given him a letter of credence as a visitor to Europe on matters of business, rode to the outskirts of Philadelphia to comfort Mrs. Logan, who found herself "under the ban of political excommunication." "He spoke of the temper of the time," Deborah Logan later recalled, "and the late acts of the legislature with a sort of despair, but said he thought even the shadow of our liberties must be gone if they attempted anything that would injure me."[64]

On the fateful weekend of Marshall's return and Jefferson's visit to Mrs. Logan, Bache published a still secret letter from Talleyrand to the American

---

60. Elias Boudinot to his wife, June 21, 1798, in J. J. Boudinot, *The Life, Public Services, Addresses and Letters of Elias Boudinot, LLD, President of the Continental Congress,* 2 vols. (Boston, 1896), II, p. 141.

61. De Conde, pp. 74–108, and Stephen G. Kurtz, *The Presidency of John Adams: The Collapse of Federalism, 1795–1800* (Philadelphia, 1957), pp. 297–333.

62. TJ to JM, June 21, 1798, below.

63. Frederick B. Tolles, *George Logan of Philadelphia* (New York, 1953), pp. 156–57.

64. Deborah Norris Logan, *Memoir of Dr. George Logan of Stenton,* ed. Frances A. Logan (Philadelphia, 1899), pp. 75–76, and Tolles, pp. 171–72.

envoys, which had been delivered to the publisher by an unidentified person two days before President Adams notified Congress of its receipt by the government. The embarrassing document was Talleyrand's offensive yet conciliatory letter to the American envoys in France—offensive because it virtually dismissed Marshall and Pinckney as accredited negotiators, conciliatory because it offered to continue discussions with the remaining plenipotentiary, Elbridge Gerry.

Citing Bache's unauthorized publication of Talleyrand's letter as a classic example of "the diplomatic skill of France," *Porcupine's Gazette* condemned the Republican editor as an organ of the French, who had printed the letter "for the express purpose of *drawing off the people from the Government,* of exciting discontents, of strengthening Republican opposition, and to procure a *fatal* delay of *preparation for war.*"[65] Bache defended the publication of his "scoop" on the ground that the administration was withholding it in an effort to embroil the United States in an unnecessary war with France.[66]

Robert Goodloe Harper, a South Carolina Federalist, promptly pounced on Bache's publication and Logan's mission as evidence of "a treasonable correspondence, carried on by persons in this country with France, of the most criminal nature." Without naming Logan, he charged that France had secret agents in America who used every means "to excite resistance to measures of our Government, and to raise a spirit of faction in the country favorable to the views of France."[67]

By that time, *Porcupine's Gazette* had learned of Jefferson's visit to Mrs. Logan and raised an incriminating question about the vice president's role in the "treasonable correspondence": "What did he do there? Was it to arrange the Doctor's valuable manuscripts?"[68]

In his final letter to Madison from Philadelphia, Jefferson reported on Harper's linkage of the Logan mission and Bache's publication of Talleyrand's letter, when Harper "gravely announced to the H[ouse] of R[epresentatives] that there existed a traitorous correspondence between the Jacobins here and the French Directory." "This increased the alarm," he told Madison; "their libelists immediately set to work, directly and indirectly to implicate whom they pleased. Porcupine gave me a principal share in it as I am told, for I never read his papers."[69]

In an effort to tie Jefferson to the treasonable plot, Secretary of the Treasury Wolcott made a hurried visit to New York to interview a traveler returning from France with letters addressed to Bache, Monroe, Genet, and "other persons of the same description." He made it clear that he was after the leader

65. Quoted in Smith, *Freedom's Fetters,* pp. 193–94.
66. *Ibid.*, pp. 193–204.
67. Quoted *ibid.*, pp. 102–3.
68. Tolles, pp. 155, 171–72.
69. TJ to JM, June 21, 1798, below.

of the "traitors" by asking repeatedly *"if there were any letters for Mr. Jefferson"* from Talleyrand or the French Directory. The answer was invariably "No."

Failing to link the vice president with the French plot, the cabinet official nevertheless confiscated a personal letter to Jefferson from Fulwar Skipwith, the American consul general in France who had been appointed by Jefferson while he was secretary of state, and seized a packet addressed to Bache, which turned out to be harmless pamphlets on British policy.[70] Wolcott did not mail or deliver Skipwith's letter to Jefferson, nor did he make any use of it in 1798. But his biographer published it in 1846 from the Wolcott Papers in the Connecticut Historical Society, where it yet remains, citing it as one "surrendered to the Executive" rather than seized illegally by Wolcott, and claiming that it furnished "conclusive proofs of the agency of American Jacobins there [in Paris] in instigating the measures of the Directory."[71]

The lack of proof did not stem the Federalist charges against Jefferson. "More and more," Senator Theodore Sedgwick told the American minister to Great Britain, the vice president was becoming "an object of abhorrence and detestation" among "the well disposed."[72] On the day that Jefferson left the nation's capital for Virginia, *Porcupine's Gazette* denounced him as "the head of the democratic frenchified faction in this country," and Noah Webster's paper claimed that in case of a French invasion an American Executive Directory would be established, headed by Jefferson, Madison, Monroe, and Burr.

On the Fourth of July, the day after Jefferson arrived at Monticello, a Federalist rally raised glasses in a toast to the president: "John Adams. May he, like *Samson,* slay thousands of Frenchmen with the *jawbone* of Jefferson."[73]

The Letters

Madison to Jefferson

Orange Dec. 25, 1797

Dear Sir

I have let Col. Monroe know that you were furnished with a draught on a House in Philadelphia for 250 dr and finding that it would be convenient to him, have authorised him to draw on you for that sum. I have also given him a draught on Genl Moylan, of which the inclosed is a letter of advice. I reserve the note of Bailey towards covering the advance made by you unless it should be otherwise settled by Col. Monroe and yourself, as he intimated a desire that

---

70. See Smith, *Freedom's Fetters,* pp. 193–96, and Malone, III, pp. 378–79, 430.

71. George Gibbs, *Memoirs of the Administrations of Washington and Adams, Edited from the Papers of Oliver Wolcott* (New York, 1846), pp. 158–61. If the letter had contained such proof, it seems clear that Wolcott would have introduced it as evidence in 1798.

72. Theodore Sedgwick to Rufus King, July 1, 1798, in Rufus King, *Life and Correspondence of Rufus King,* ed. Charles R. King, 6 vols. (New York, 1894–1900), II, pp. 352–53.

73. Quoted in Smith, *Freedom's Fetters,* p. 14.

it might be. Perhaps it wd. save delay and trouble to Mr. B. if you should find a convenient opportunity to drop a hint to his friend Van Cortland that the note was in your hand; as it is more than probable he may be the channel of taking it up.

According to the bill of nails given in by the workman I shall want from your nailory, 50,000 sixes, 3000 eights, 20,000 tens, 5,000 twentys, and 12,000 flooring Brads.

I shall also want 50,000 fours for lathing, 4,000 sprigs sixes, and 3,000 ditto eights. You can inform me whether these are also made at your shops, or whether it would be better to get them in Philadelphia. I shall write as you suggested to Col. Bell, but it may not be amiss for you to confirm the orders for having the supply prepared for me, according to the above list.

We have had a great proportion of cold weather since you passed us. The therma., however, has not been lower than 10°. It was at this point on the morning of the 21st instant. The drought, also, is equal to the cold. Within the last 31 days the fall of water has been but 1¼ inches only. Of snow there has been none. This cold and dry spell, succeeding the dry fall and late seeding, gives to the wheat fields the worst of appearances.

You will not expect political occurrences from this quarter. The objects of enquiry here are Liston's plot,[1] the envoyship to France, and Monroe's publication. The delay of this last occasions some surprise. I observe that the President has laid hold of the late endemic at the seat of Government as an occasion for getting the prerogative for proroguing the Legislature. Fortunately, the Constitution has provided an important barrier in this case, by requiring a session at least within every year. But still the power may, in unforeseen emergencies, be made an instrument of party or of usurpation, and, it is to be hoped, will not therefore be granted. I have not examined it in a constitutional view, but that also merits attention. Ambition is so vigilant, and where it has a model always in view as in the present case, is so prompt in seizing its advantages, that it cannot be too closely watched, or too vigorously checked.

When you do me the favor to write, let your letters leave Philadelphia in the mail of Friday morning. They will then come without any halt. Adieu.

Jefferson to Madison

[Philadelphia] Jan. 3, 1798

DEAR SIR

Yours of Dec. 25. came to hand yesterday. I shall observe your directions with respect to the post day. I have spoken with the Dept. Post M. Genl. on

---

1. "Liston's plot" was the name which JM and TJ used to refer to the expulsion of Republican Senator William Blount of Tennessee in July 1797 from the U.S. Senate on charges of conspiracy to conquer Spanish territory with British aid; Robert Liston was the British minister to the United States. The question of impeaching Blount was being debated in the Senate. For a brief discussion, see Malone, III, pp. 317–18, 361–62; for a fuller analysis, see Thomas P. Abernethy, *The South in the New Nation, 1789–1819* (Baton Rouge, 1961), pp. 169–216.

the subject of our Fredericksburg post. He never knew before that the Fredsbg printer had taken the contract of the rider. He will be glad if either in your neighborhood or ours some good person will undertake to ride from April next. The price given this year is 330. D. and it will go to the lowest bidder who can be depended on. I understand (tho not from him) that Wyatt will be changed; and in general they determine that printers shall not be postmasters or riders.

Before the receipt of your letter, I had informed Col. Monroe of the paper you had put into my hands for him. The draught was accepted and paiment will be made at the proper term. Genl Van Cortlandt lodging in the same house with me, I had shown him Bailey's note, and he said he would let him know that I was the holder of it.

All the nails you desire can be furnished from Monticello. I will give directions accordingly by my letter of this day. But as we can furnish the whole demand at any time in 3. weeks, and I presume you will not want them till your walls are done, I shall only direct that they go about them whenever they receive notice from you that you will soon want them. If you can give the second notification one month before your actual want, they will be in readiness.

Our weather has been here, as with you, cold and dry. The thermometer has been at 8°. The river closed here the first week of December, which has caught a vast number of vessels destined for departure. It deadens also the demand for wheat. The price at New York is 1.75 and of flour 8.50 to 9.; tobacco 11. to 12. D.; there need be no doubt of greater prices. The bankruptcies here continue: the prison is full of the most reputable merchants, and it is understood that the scene has not yet got to its height. Prices have fallen greatly. The market is cheaper than it has been for 4. years. Labor and house rent much reduced. Dry goods somewhat. It is expected they will fall till they get nearly to old prices. Money scarce beyond all example.

The Representatives have rejected the President's proposition for enabling him to prorogue them. A law is passed putting off the stamp act till July next. The land tax will not be brought on. The Secretary of the Treasury says he has money enough. No doubt these two measures may be taken up more boldly at the next session, when most of the elections will be over. It is imagined the stamp act will be extended or attempted on every possible object. A bill has passed the Rep to suspend for 3. years the law arresting the currency of foreign coins. The Senate propose an amendment, continuing the currency of the foreign gold only. Very possibly the bill may be lost. The object of opposing the bill is to make the French crowns a subject of speculation (for it seems they fell on the President's proclamation to a Dollar in most of the states), and to force bank paper (for want of other medium) through all the states generally. Tench Coxe is displaced and no reason ever spoken of. It is therefore understood to be for his activity during the late election.[2] It is said, that the

---

2. See Kurtz, pp. 291–92. Coxe, who was commissioner of revenue in the Treasury Department, had published essays critical of John Adams during the election of 1796.

people from hence quite to the Eastern extremity are beginning to be sensible that their government has been playing a foul game. In Vermont, Chipman was elected Senator by a majority of one, against the republican candidate. In Maryland, Lloyd by a majority of one, against Winder the republican candidate. Tichenor chosen Governor of Vermont by a very small majority. The house of Representatives of this state has become republican by a firm majority of 6. Two counties, it is said, have come over generally to the republican side. It is thought the republicans have also a majority in the N York H of representatives. Hard elections are expected there between Jay and Livingston, and here between Ross and McKean. In the H of Representatives of Congress, the republican interest has at present, on strong questions, a majority of about half a dozen, as is conjectured, and there are as many of their firmest men absent; not one of the Antirepublicans is from his post.[3] The bill for permitting private vessels to arm, was put off to the 1st Monday in February by a sudden vote, and a majority of five. It was considered as an index of their dispositions on that subject, tho some voted both ways on other ground. It is most evident, that the Antirepublicans wish to get rid of Blount's impeachment. Many metaphysical niceties are handing about in conversation, to shew that it cannot be sustained. To show the contrary, it is evident must be the task of the republicans, or of nobody. Monroe's book is considered as masterly by all those who are not opposed in principle, and it is deemed unanswerable.[4] An answer, however, is commenced in Fenno's paper of yesterday, under the signature of Scipio. The real author not yet conjectured.[5] As I take these papers merely to preserve them, I will forward them to you, as you can easily return them to me on my arrival at home; for I shall not see you on my way, as I mean to go by the Eastern Shore and Petersburg. Perhaps the paragraphs in some of these abominable papers may draw from you now and then a squib. A pamphlet of Fauchet's appeared yesterday.[6] I send you a copy under another cover.

A handbill is just arrived here from N Y, where they learn from a vessel which left Havre about the 9th of Nov, that the emperor had signed the definitive articles, given up Mantua, evacuated Mentz, agreed to give passage to the French troops into Hanover, and that the Portuguese ambassador had been ordered to quit Paris, on account of the seizure of fort St. Julian's by the

---

3. Albert Gallatin thought that the Federalists had a "small majority"; see Cunningham, p. 122.

4. James Monroe's vindication of his conduct as minister to France was entitled *A View of the Conduct of the Executive in the Foreign Affairs of the United States, Connected with the Mission to the French Republic during the Years 1794, 5 and 6.*

5. Ford, VII, p. 190, and Richard Buel, Jr., *Securing the Revolution: Ideology in American Politics, 1789–1815* (Ithaca, 1972), p. 149, state that "Scipio" was Uriah Tracy, Federalist congressman from Connecticut, but TJ attributed it to Attorney General Charles Lee; see TJ to JM, Feb. 8, 1798, below, and Kurtz, p. 292.

6. For a brief discussion of Jean Antoine Joseph Fauchet's "Sketch of the Present State of the Political Relations with the United States of America," see Albert H. Bowman, *The Struggle for Neutrality: A History of the Diplomatic Relations between the United States and France, 1790–1801* (Knoxville, 1974), p. 309.

English, supposed with the connivance of Portugal. Tho this is ordinary mercantile news, it looks like truth.[7] The latest official intelligence from Paris, is from Talleyrand Perigord to the French consul here, (Letombe,) dated Sep 28, saying that our Envoys were arrived, and would find every disposition on the part of his government to accommodate with us. My affectionate respects to Mrs. Madison; to yourself health and friendship. Adieu.

Madison to Jefferson

Orange Jan. 21, 1798

DEAR SIR,

When your favor of the 3rd instant arrived, I was on a journey to the neighborhood of Richmond, from which I did not return till the 18th. The mail on the day following brought me the packet of newspapers under your cover. Col. Bell has written me that the nails ordered, as stated in my last to you, are all ready for me. I had not requested them to be prepared in parcels, as I shall use them, because I want some for out-houses immediately, and I wished to avoid the necessity of more than one trip.

The attack on Monroe's publication evidently issues from, or is aided by, an official source, and is a proof that the latter bites.[8] I have not yet seen a copy of it, and was astonished to learn in Richmond, where I passed a day, that a single copy only had reached that place, which from the length of it, not more than two or three persons had read. By them it was said, that if this did not open the eyes of the people, their blindness must be incurable. If a sufficient number of copies do not arrive there before the adjournment of the Assembly, the only opportunity of circulating the information in this State will be lost for a year, that is, till the subject has lost its flavor. The enormous price, also, was complained of as a probable obstacle to an extensive circulation.

You will have seen in the newspapers the proceedings on the Amherst Memorial, on the Glebes and Churches, and on the proposition for revising the Constitution. The first was the only test of party strength, and so far deceptive as it confounds scrupulous Republicans with their adversaries in the votes against a Legislative censure on the Grand jury.[9]

I did not understand the presentment was vindicated positively by a single member in the debate. The unfavorable accounts as to our three Plenipo's got

---

7. Napoleon forced Austria out of the war, signing the Treaty of Campo Formio on Oct. 18, 1797; see Steven T. Ross, *European Diplomatic History, 1789–1815: France against Europe* (New York, 1969), pp. 124–29.

8. Attorney General Charles Lee wrote pamphlet and newspaper replies to James Monroe's vindication; see Kurtz, p. 292.

9. The Amherst Memorial was TJ's protest against the federal presentment of Congressman Samuel J. Cabell.

to Richmond while I was there, by the way of Norfolk. It seemed to give extreme uneasiness to the warm and well-informed friends of Republicanism, who saw in a war on the side of England, the most formidable means put in the hands of her partizans for warping the public mind towards Monarchy. This consideration certainly merits the strictest regard as an argument for peace, as long as we have a fair choice on the question. The Public will have a right to expect also from our Executive and the negotiators, the fullest communication of every circumstance that may attend the experiment, if it should miscarry. The British Treaty has placed such difficulties in the way of an adjustment, that nothing but the most cordial dispositions on both sides can overcome them; and such have been the indications on the side of our Executive, even during the negociation, that it will not be easily believed, in case of a rupture, that it was not promoted, if not caused, by our own counsels.

We have had a fine spell of open weather, with plentiful rains at proper intervals. This has been favorable to our winter operations, but otherwise to some of those of Nature, particularly in our wheat fields, which continue to present the most unpromising aspect. Accept the most affectionate farewell.

Jefferson to Madison

Philadelphia Jan. 24 and 25, 1798

DEAR SIR,

I wrote you last on the 2d inst, on which day I received yours of Decr 25. I have not resumed my pen, because there has really been nothing worth writing about, but what you would see in the newspapers. There is, as yet, no certainty what will be the aspect of our affairs with France. Either the Envoys have not written to the government, or their communications are hushed up. This last is suspected, because so many arrivals have happened from Bordeaux and Havre. The letters from American correspondents in France have been always to Boston; and the experience we had last summer of their adroitness in counterfeiting this kind of intelligence, inspires doubts as to their late paragraphs. A letter is certainly recieved here by an individual from Talleyrand, which says our Envoys have been heard, that their pretensions are high, that possibly no arrangement may take place, but that there will be no declaration of war by France. It is said that Bournonville has written that he has hopes of an accommodation (3. audiences having then, Nov. 3. been had) and to be himself a member of a new diplomatic mission to this country.[10] On the whole, I am entirely suspended as to what is to be expected.

The representatives have been several days in debate on the bill for foreign

---

10. Charles François Bournonville had served as Genet's secretary in 1793. Talleyrand later sent him as a courier to Philadelphia during the XYZ embroglio; see Bowman, pp. 94, 340.

intercourse. A motion has been made to reduce it to what it was before the extension of 1796. The debate will probably have good effects in several ways on the public mind, but the advocates for the reformation expect to lose the question. They find themselves decieved in the expectation entertained in the beginning of the session, that they had a majority. They now think the majority is on the other side by 2. or 3., and there are moreover 2. or 3. of them absent.

Blount's affair is to come on next. In the mean time the Senate have before them a bill for regulating proceedings in impeachment. This will be made the occasion of offering a clause for the introduction of juries into these trials. (Compare the paragraph in the constitution which says, that the trial of all crimes, *except in cases of impeachment,* [11] shall be by jury, with the viiith amendment,[12] which says, that in *all* criminal prosecutions the trial shall be by jury.) There is no expectation of carrying this; because the division in the Senate is of 2. to 1., but it will draw forth the principles of the parties, and concur in accumulating proofs on which side all the sound principles are to be found.

Very acrimonious altercations are going on between the Spanish minister and the Executive, and at the Natchez something worse than mere altercation. If hostilities have not begun there, it has not been for want of endeavors to bring them on by our agents.

Marshall, of Kentucky, this day proposed in Senate some amendments to the constitution. They were barely read just as we were adjourning, and not a word of explanation given. As far as I caught them in my ear, they went only to modifications of the elections of President and V. President, by authorizing voters to add the office for which they name each, and giving to the Senate the decision of a disputed election of President, and to the Representatives that of Vice President. But I am apprehensive I caught the thing imperfectly, and probably incorrectly.[13] Perhaps this occasion may be taken of proposing again the Virginia amendments, as also to condemn elections by the legislatures themselves, to transfer the power of trying impeachments from the Senate to some better constituted court, etc., etc.[14]

Good tobo here is 13. doll., flour 8.50, wheat 1.50, but dull, because only the millers buy. The river, however, is nearly open, and the merchants will now come to market and give a spur to the price. But their competition will

11. TJ's italics.

12. TJ referred to the Sixth Amendment in the Bill of Rights, which had been the Eighth in the original enumeration adopted by Congress. For the difference between TJ and JM over jury trials in impeachment cases, see Malone, III, pp. 361–62.

13. The proposal by Senator Humphrey Marshall was a forerunner of the Twelfth Amendment; see H. V. Ames, "Proposed Amendments to the Constitution," in *AHA Annual Report for the Year 1896,* 2 vols. (Washington, 1897), II, pp. 77–80, 324–25.

14. For the Virginia amendments, see Thomas J. Farnham, "The Virginia Amendments of 1795: An Episode in the Opposition to Jay's Treaty," *VMHB* 75 (1967): 75–88.

not be what it has been. Bankruptcies thicken, and the height of them has by no means yet come on. It is thought this winter will be very trying. Friendly salutations to Mrs. Madison. Adieu affectionately.

January 25.
I enclose Marshall's propositions. They have been this day postponed to the 1st of June, chiefly by the vote of the anti-republicans, under the acknoleged fear that other amendments would be also proposed, and that this is not the time for agitating the public mind.

Jefferson to Madison
Philadelphia Feb. 8, 1798

I wrote you last on the 25th Ult;[15] since which yours of the 21st has been received. Bache had put 500. copies of Monroe's book on board a vessel, which was stopped by the early and unexpected freezing of the river. He then tried in vain to get them carried by fifties at a time, by the stage. The river is now open here, the vessels have fallen down, and if they can get through the ice below, the one with Bache's packet will soon be at Richmond. It is surmised here that Scipio is written by C. Lee. Articles of impeachment were yesterday given in against Blount. But many knotty preliminary questions will arise. Must not a *formal law*[16] settle the oath of the Senators, forms of pleadings, process against person and goods, etc.? May he not appear by attorney? Must he not be tried by jury? Is a Senator impeachable? Is an ex-Senator impeachable? You will readily conceive that these questions, to be settled by 29. lawyers, are not likely to come to speedy issue.

A very disagreeable question of privilege has suspended all other proceedings for several days. You will see this in the newspapers.

The question of arming was to have come on, on Monday last. That morning, the President sent in an inflammatory message about a vessel taken and burnt by a French privateer, near Charleston. Of this he had been possessed some time, and it had run through all the newspapers. It seemed to come in very *apropos* for spurring on the disposition to arm. However, the question is not come on. In the meantime, the general spirit, even of the merchants, is becoming adverse to it. New Hampshire and Rhode island are unanimously against arming; so is Baltimore. This place becoming more so. Boston divided and desponding. I know nothing of New York; but I think there is no danger of the question being carried, unless something favorable to

---

15. TJ's last letter was dated Jan. 24, although Ford, VII, p. 192, dates it Jan. 25. See also Malone, III, p. 369.
16. TJ's italics here and below.

it is received from our Envoys. From them we hear nothing. Yet it seems reasonably believed that the Executive has heard, and that it is something which would not promote their views of arming. For every action of theirs shews they are panting to come to blows.

Walker's bill will be applied to answer a draught of Colo. Monroe's on Barnes. I have not heard yet from Bailey. I wrote to you about procuring a rider for the Fredsbg post. The proposition should be here by the 14th inst., but I can get it kept open a little longer. There is no bidder yet but Green, the printer. £100 Virga. will be given.

Giles is arrived. My friendly salutations to Mrs. Madison. Adieu affectionately.

Madison to Jefferson

[Orange] Feb. 12, 1798

DEAR SIR

The last mail brought neither letters nor papers from Philadelphia. By the preceding one I received your favor of Jany 24 and a bundle of the gazettes down to the 25th inclusive, with an omission only of that of the 23rd which it may be proper for you to supply in order to keep your set entire. Your account of the probable fortune of the negociations at Paris is less decisively unfavorable than the reports prevailing here. It will be happy if a good issue should result from the crisis. But I have great apprehensions from two sources: 1. the spirit in which the negociation will be conducted on the side of our Executive, if not on the other side also; 2. the real difficultys, which the British Treaty has thrown in the way. It is pretty clear that France will not acquiesce under the advantage which that insidious instrument gives to her enemy, and the House of Representatives at the last session admitted that the condition of the two nations ought to be equalized. How can this now be done? In one of two ways only; either by dissolving the British Treaty, or by stipulating with France that she may plunder us as we have stipulated that Britain may plunder us.

To the first mode the objections on the American side are obvious. To the second, will not France refuse so far to sanction the principle that free ships do *not* make goods free, as to enter into a positive stipulation to that effect, chusing rather to equalize her own situation on the principle of retaliation which indirectly supports instead of surrendering her favorite object. Should this be her course the U. States will have no option but to go directly to war in defense of the British Treaty which was adopted as a defense against war, and in defense of the principle that free ships do *not* make free goods, in opposition both to their own principles and their essential interests—or to go indirectly to war, by using the frigates as convoys and arming private vessels of which the owners and other [?] mariners will often be British subjects under American colors—or to try some defensive regulation of a commercial nature. The first will not be done, because the people are not yet confided in to tolerate it. The last will not be done because it will be difficult to frame such a regulation as will not injure Britain as well as ourselves more than France. The second expedient I conclude therefore will be persisted in; and as there is likely to be a majority ready to back the hostility of the Executive, the best that can be done by the Republicans will be to leave the responsibility on the real authors of whatever evils may ensue.

I am not surprised at the extremity to which the dispute at the Natchez is pushed. I never had a doubt that in proportion as war with France is contemplated, a war with Spain will be provoked by the present administration. The former would not be relished even by the New England privateers, without the prospect of plunder presented by the latter. A war with Spain would also be a most convenient ground for the misdemeanours of Liston and his partizans.

I returned from Albemarle on Monday last, where I consulted with your Nailor on the subject of Sprig's and lathing nails not included in the parcels prepared for me. I found that the cutting machine has never been reestablished, and I did not request that this slight kind of nails should be made in the common way. If you mean however that the machine shall be set up again, or it be a part of your plan to make such nails in the common way, there will be time eno' for either before I shall want them. I was at Mr. Randolph's and found all well there, as you will doubtless learn to be the case from himself.

I was astonished to find that Mr. Monroe himself had not yet seen a printed copy of his publication. In the meantime Scipio's misrepresentations and sophistries are filling the public mind with all the poison which P's malice can distil into it. Where the book is not seen first, and an antidote does not quickly follow from the same center which gives incubation to the poison, innocence and truth can not have fair play.

Present my friendly respects to Mr. Giles who I hear has gone on to Phila also to Mr Tazewell and Mr Dawson. I have been sorry to hear of the ill health of the former. As I perceive by the votes in the Senate that he has resumed his seat, I hope he is well again. Yours always affecty

Jefferson to Madison

Philadelphia Feb. 15, 1798

I wrote you last on the 8th. We have still not a word from our envoys. This long silence (if they have been silent) proves things are not going on very roughly. If they have not been silent, it proves their information if made public would check the disposition to arm. I had flattered myself, from the progress of the public sentiment against arming, that the same progress had taken place in the legislature. But I am assured, by those who have better opportunities of forming a good judgment, that if the question against arming is carried at all, it will not be by more than a majority of two; and particularly, that there will not be more than 4. votes against it from the 5. eastern states, or 5. votes at the utmost. You will have perceived that Dayton is gone over compleatly.[17] He expects to be appointed Secretary of war in the room of McHenry who it is said will retire. He has been told, as report goes, that they would not have confidence enough in him to appoint him. The desire of inspiring them with more seems the only way to account for the eclat which he chuses to give to his conversion. You will have seen the disgusting proceedings in the case of Lyon. If they would have accepted even of a commitment to the Serjeant it might have been had. But to get rid of his vote was the most material object.[18] These proceedings must degrade the General government, and lead the people to lean more on their state governments, which have been sunk under the early popularity of the former. This day the question of the jury in cases of impeachment comes on. There is no doubt how it will go. The general division in the Senate is 22. and 10. And under the probable prospect of what it will forever be, I see nothing in the mode of proceeding by impeachment but the most formidable weapon for the purposes of a dominant faction that ever was contrived. It would be the most effectual one for getting rid of any man whom they consider as dangerous to their views, and I do not know that we could count on one third on an emergency. It depends then on the H. of Representatives, who are the impeachers; and there the majorities are of 1., 2., or 3 only and these sometimes one way and sometimes another. In a question of pure party they have the majority, and we do not know what circumstances may turn up to increase that majority temporarily if not permanently. I know of no solid purpose of punishment which the courts of law are not equal to, and history shows that in England, Impeachment has been an engine more of passion than justice.

A great ball is to be given here on the 22d, and in other great towns of the Union. This is, at least, very indelicate, and probably excites uneasy sensations in some. I see in it however this useful deduction, that the birth days which have been kept have been, not those of the President, but of the General.

I enclose with the newspapers the two acts of parliament passed on the subject of our commerce which are interesting. The merchants here say, that the effect of the countervailing tonnage on American vessels, will throw them completely out of employ as soon as there is peace. The Eastern members say nothing but among themselves. But it is said that it is working like gravel in

---

17. Jonathan Dayton of New Jersey was Speaker of the House.
18. The Federalist attempt to expel Republican congressman Matthew Lyon failed, the 52-to-44 vote falling short of the two-thirds vote necessary for expulsion.

their stomachs. Our only comfort is that they have brought it on themselves. My respectful salutation to Mrs. Madison and to yourself friendship and Adieu.

Madison to Jefferson

[Orange Feb. 18, 1798]

DEAR SIR,

Since my last I have recd. yours of Feby. 8, with a continuation of the Gazettes down to that date, with the exception only mentioned already of the Gazette of Jany. 23. I am glad to find the public opinion to be taking the turn you describe on the subject of arming. For the public opinion alone can now save us from the rash measures of our hot-headed Executive: it being evident from some late votes of the House of Rep^s, particularly in the choice of Managers for the Impeachment, that a majority there as well as in the Senate are ready to go as far as the controul of their constituents will permit. There never was perhaps a greater contrast between two characters than between those of the present President and of his predecessor, altho' it is the boast and prop of the present that he treads in the steps of his predecessor. The one cold considerate and cautious,[19] the other headlong and kindled into flame by every spark that lights on his passions: the one ever scrutinizing into the public opinion, and ready to follow where he could not lead it; the other insulting it by the most adverse sentiments and pursuits: W. a hero in the field, yet overweighing every danger in the Cabinet. A. without a single pretension to the character of a soldier, a perfect Quixotte as a statesman: the former cheif magistrate pursuing peace every where with sincerity, tho' mistaking the means; the latter taking as much pains to get into war, as the former took to keep out of it. The contrast might be pursued into a variety of other particulars—the policy of the one in shunning connections with the arrangements of Europe, of the other in holding out the U. S. as a makeweight in its Balances of power; the avowed exultation of W. in the progress of liberty every where, and his eulogy on the Revolution and people of France posterior even to the bloody reign and fate of Robespierre—the open denunciations by Adams of the smallest disturbance of the antient discipline order and tranquillity of despotism, etc. etc. etc.

The affair of Lyon and Griswold is bad eno' every way, but worst of all in becoming a topic of tedious and disgraceful debates in Congress. There certainly could be no necessity for removing it from the decision of the parties themselves before that tribunal, and its removal was evidently a sacrifice of the dignity of the latter to the party manœuvre of ruining a man whose popularity

19. The editors of *PJM*, XVII, p. 83, note that "someone, possibly John C. Payne," JM's brother-in-law, later scratched out "cold" and interlined "cool."

and activity were feared. If the state of the House suspended its rules in general, it was under no obligation to see any irregularity which did not force itself into public notice. And if Griswold be a man of the sword, he sh^d not have permitted the step to be taken, if not, he does not deserve to be avenged by the House. No man ought to reproach another with cowardice, who is not ready to give proof of his own courage.[20]

I have taken some pains but in vain to find out a person who will engage to carry the Mail from Fred^g to Charlottesville. When I was in the neighbourhood of the latter I suggested the propriety of an effort there for the purpose, but do not know that it will be more successful. Our winter has continued without snow and rather dry, and our Wheat fields wear the most discouraging aspect. Adieu.

Jefferson to Madison

Philadelphia Feb. 22, 1798

Yours of the 12th is recieved. I wrote you last on the 15th, but the letter getting misplaced, will only go by this post. We still hear nothing from our Envoys. Whether the Executive hear, we know not. But if war were to be apprehended, it is impossible our envoys should not find means of putting us on our guard, or that the Executive should hold back their information. No news therefore is good news. The countervailing act, which I sent you by the last post, will confessedly put American bottoms out of employ in our trade with Gr. Britain. So say well-informed merchants. Indeed, it seems probable, when we consider that hitherto, with the advantage of our foreign tonnage, our vessels could only share with the British, and the countervailing duties will, it is said, make a difference of 500. guineas to our prejudice on a ship of 350. tons. Still the Eastern men say nothing.[21] Every appearance and consideration render it probable that on the restoration of peace, both France and Britain will consider it their interest to exclude us from the ocean by such peaceable means as are in their power. Should this take place, perhaps it may be thought just and politic to give to our *native* capitalists the monopoly of our internal commerce. This may at once relieve us from the danger of wars abroad and British thraldom at home.

The news from the Natchez of the delivery of the posts, which you will see in the papers, is to be relied on. We have escaped a dangerous crisis there.[22]

---

20. For the affair of Matthew Lyon and Roger Griswold, see Austin, pp. 96–102.

21. For the best discussion of the British countervailing duties, see Bradford Perkins, *The First Rapprochement: England and the United States, 1795–1805* (Philadelphia, 1955), pp. 76–77.

22. Pinckney's treaty called for Spain to evacuate posts north of the thirty-first parallel, the boundary of West Florida that the United States had claimed since 1783.

The great contest between Israel and Morgan, of which you will see the papers full, is to be decided this day. It is snowing fast at this time, and the most sloppy walking I ever saw. This will be to the disadvantage of the party which has the most invalids. Whether the event will be known this evening, I am uncertain. I rather presume not, and therefore that you will not learn it till next post.[23]

You will see in the papers the ground on which the introduction of the jury into the trial by impeachment was advocated by Mr. Tazewell, and the fate of the question. Reade's motion, which I enclosed you, will probably be amended and established so as to declare a Senator unimpeachable, absolutely. And yesterday an opinion was declared, that not only officers of the state governments but every private citizen of the U S. is impeachable. Whether they will think this the time to make the declaration, I know not, but if they bring it on I think there will be not more than two votes north of the Patowmac against the universality of the impeaching power. The system of the Senate may be inferred from their transactions heretofore, and from the following declaration made to me personally by their oracle.[24] "No republic can ever be of any duration, without a Senate, and a Senate deeply and strongly rooted, strong enough to bear up against all popular storms and passions. The only fault in the constitution of our Senate is that their term of office is not durable enough. Hitherto they have done well, but probably they will be forced to give way in time." I suppose their having done well hitherto, alluded to the stand they made on the British treaty. This declaration may be considered as their text; that they consider themselves as the bulwarks of the government, and will be rendering that the more secure, in proportion as they can assume greater powers. The foreign intercourse bill is set for to-day; but the parties are so equal on that in the Repr. that they seem mutually to fear the encounter.

Tho' it is my intention, and the orders I left were, that the cutting machine should be repaired, yet I think it would not be advisable for you to depend on it, as to your sprigs and lathing nails if you want them before my return: as at my present distance I could not rely sufficiently on the execution of my orders. Immediately on my return my own wants will oblige me to recommence cutting. I imagine that by this time a large cargo of Monroe's book has arrived at Richmond, as the vessel which had them on board got out during the short interval the river was open. My friendly salutations to M͞r͞s Madison and the family. To yourself friendly adieux.

---

23. After Israel Israel, a confirmed Republican, scored a narrow but surprising victory in 1797 over Benjamin Morgan, the Federalist candidate for senator in a district that included Philadelphia and Delaware County, a state Senate investigating committee condemned Israel's election as "illegal and invalid" because unqualified voters had participated. In the runoff election, Morgan won. See the excellent account in Harry Marlin Tinkcom, *The Republicans and Federalists in Pennsylvania, 1790-1801: A Study in National Stimulus and Local Response* (Harrisburg, Pa., 1950), pp. 176-79.

24. On the margin of his copy, TJ wrote "Mr. Adams." For a brief discussion of the English common-law concept of the universality of the impeaching power, see *PJM*, XVII, p. 85.

Jefferson to Madison

Philadelphia Mar. 2, 1798

I wrote you last on the 22d since which I have received yours without date, but probably of about the 18th or 19th. An arrival to the Eastward brings us some news which you see detailed in the papers. The new partition of Europe is sketched, but how far authentic we know not. It has some probability in it's favor. The French appear busy in their preparations for the invasion of England;[25] nor is there any appearance of movements on the part of Russia and Prussia which might divert them from it.

The late birthnight has certainly sown tares among the exclusive federals. It has winnowed the grain from the chaff. The sincerely Adamites did not go. The Washingtonians went religiously, and took the secession of the others in high dudgeon. The one sex [sect] threaten to desert the levees, the other the evening parties. The whigs went in number, to encourage the idea that the birthnights hitherto kept had been for the General and not the President, and of course that time would bring an end to them. Goodhue, Tracy, Sedgwick, etc., did not attend; but the three Secretaries and Attorney General did.[26]

We were surprised, at the close of the last week with a symptom of a disposition to repeal the stamp act. Petitions for that purpose had come from Rhode Island and Virginia, and had been committed to rest with the Ways and Means. Mr. Harper, their chairman, in order to enter on the law for amending it, observed it would be necessary first to put the petitions for repeal out of the way, and moved an immediate decision on them. The Rhode islanders begged and prayed for a postponement, that not expecting that that question was to be called up, they were not at all prepared. But Harper would shew no mercy; not a moment's delay should be allowed. It was taken up, and, on a question without debate, determined in favor of the petitions by a majority of 10. Astonished and confounded, when an order to bring in a bill for repeal was moved, they began in turn to beg for time, 3. weeks, one week, 3. days, 1. day. Not a moment would be yeilded. They made three attempts for adjournment. But the majorities appeared to grow. It was decided, by a majority of 16. that the bill should be brought in. It was brought in the next day, and on the day after passed, sent up to the Senate, who instantly sent it back, rejected by a silent vote of 15. to 12. R. I. and N. Hampshire voted for the repeal in Senate. The act will therefore go into operation July 1 but probably without amendments. However I am persuaded it will be shortlived. It has already excited great commotion in Vermont, and grumblings in Connecticut. But they are

---

25. For the Directory's plan, see E. H. S. Jones, *The Last Invasion of Britain* (London, 1950). On the day that TJ wrote this letter, the Directory abandoned its plans to invade England with Napoleon's army of 56,400 because it had neither the transports nor the escort vessels to cross the Channel; see Ross, pp. 139–45.

26. See Kurtz, pp. 294–95; Dauer, p. 140; and Malone, III, pp. 362–63.

so priest-ridden that nothing is expected from them but the most bigoted passive obedience.

No news yet from our commissioners. But their silence is admitted to augur peace. There is no talk yet of the time of adjourning, tho' admitted we have nothing to do but what could be done in a fortnight or three weeks. When the spring opens and we hear from our commissioners, we shall probably draw pretty rapidly to conclusion.

A friend of mine here wishes to get a copy of Mazzei's Recherches historiques et politiques. Where are they? Salutations and Adieu.

Wheat 1.50. flour 8.50 tobo 13.50.

Madison to Jefferson

[Orange] Mar. 4, 1798

DEAR SIR

Your two favors of the 15 and 22 ult. came to hand by Friday's mail. I can wait without inconvenience for Sprig's etc till you return and reestablish your cutting machine.

Mr. Tazewell's speech is really an able one in defence of his proposition to associate juries with the Senate in cases of impeachment. His views of the subject are so new to me, that I ought not to decide on them without more examination than I have had time for.[27] My impression has always been that impeachments were somewhat sui generis, and excluded the use of Juries. The terms of the amendment to the Constitution are indeed strong, and Mr. T. has given them, as the French say, all their lustre. But it is at least questionable whether an application of that amendment to the case of impeachments would not push his doctrine farther than he himself would be disposed to follow it. It would seem, also, that the reservation of an ordinary trial by a jury must strongly imply that an impeachment was not to be a trial by jury. As removal and disqualification, the punishments within the impeaching jurisdiction, were *chiefly* intended for officers in the Executive line, would it not also be difficult to exclude Executive influence from the choice of juries, or would juries armed with the impeaching power, and under the influence of an unimpeachable Tribunal, be less formidable than the power as hitherto understood to be modified? The universality of this power is the most extravagant novelty that has been yet broached, especially coming from a quarter that denies the impeachability of a Senator. Hardy as these innovators are, I cannot believe they will venture yet to hold this inconsistent and insulting language to the public. If the conduct and sentiments of the Senate on some occasions were to

---

27. TJ had furnished Henry Tazewell with legal references to support the view that impeachment was a criminal prosecution and, therefore, should be tried by a jury; see TJ to Henry Tazewell, Jan. 27, 1798, in Ford, VII, pp. 194-95.

be regarded as the natural and permanent fruit of the institution, they ought to produce not only disgust but despair in all who are really attached to free Government. But I cannot help ascribing some part of the evil to personal characters, and a great deal of it to the present spirit of the Constituents of the Senate. Whenever the State Legislatures resume the tone natural to them, it will probably be seen that the tone of their Representatives will vary also. If it should not, the inference will then be unavoidable that the present constitution of the Senate is at war with the public liberty.

If the countervailing act of G. B. does not open the mouths and eyes both of the Eastern Carriers, it will be a political phenomenon without example. In the year 1789, G. B. had about 230, and America 43 thousand of the tonnage in the mutual trade. The encouragements given by Congress, and which G. B. did not dare to countervail till Jay tied our hands from continuing the advantage on the side of America, have brought up the American share to about one-half. The bounties now secured to the British tonnage will pretty certainly reduce our proportion below its original scantiness.[28] And if the French, as may be expected, should suffer their disgust at the British Treaty to dictate their navigation policy towards us, Jay will have accomplished more than perhaps was ever done by the same personal talents; he will have annihilated the marine of a maritime Country by a single stroke of his pen; and what is still more extraordinary recd. the plaudits of the victims whom he has sacrificed.

I am curious to see how the zealots for expelling Lyon will treat the deliberate riot of Griswold. The whole affair has been extremely disgraceful; but the dignity of the Body will be wounded, not by the misconduct of individual members, which no public body ought to be answerable for, but by the misconduct of itself, that is of a majority, and it is to be feared that the majority in this case are ready for every sacrifice to the spirit of party which infatuates them. The greatest sinners among them are Sewall and Harper, who forced the offensive business on the House.

We have had lately $4\frac{1}{2}$ inches of snow. On the 22nd, however, the day on which it was snowing, as you observe in your letter, it was throughout fair here. On the 21st, day and night together, there fell $\frac{5}{8}$ of an inch, and on the night of the 23rd, $\frac{1}{8}$ of an inch of rain. Yours always and affecy.

Madison to Jefferson

[Orange] Mar. 12, 1798

Dear Sir

I have recd. your favor of Mar. 2 with a continuation of the gazettes, with an omission however of Feby 23. I apprized you before of a like omission of Jany. 23.

---

28. JM later added an asterisk here and inserted this note: "This prevented by the war in Europe and the neutrality of the U.S."

I think the Whigs acted very properly in attending the Birth-night, on the principle of appropriating it to the person, and not to the office of the late President. It is a pity that the non-attendance of the Adamsites is not presented to the public in such a manner with their names, as to satisfy the real friends of Washington, as well as the people generally, of the true principles and views of those who have been loudest in their hypocritical professions of attachment to him.

The proceedings relative to the Stamp act mark strongly two things: one, that the public feeling is not as is pretended in unison with [all?] the measures of the Government; the other that it will whenever it shewes itself, direct immediately the course of the H. of Rep^s and no doubt finally the Senate also. The Eastern votes for the repeal are a demonstration of both these truths.

The enclosed paper contains all the information I possess on the subject of Mazzei's cargo of books. Notwithstanding the lapse of time I have never had a single return of sales. Whilst Congress sat in New York, I repeatedly enquired of Rivington, without learning that any had taken place. I beg you to preserve and return the paper.

We have had warm and dry weather for 10 days till yesterday, which gave us a fine rain. The wheat fields in general retain their sickly countenance. In many places it is thought impossible to replace the seed, and it seems certain that the ensuing crop will be very short, whatever change for the better may happen in the residue of the season. Great efforts are generally on foot for crops of Tobo.

Jefferson to Madison

Philadelphia Mar. 15, 1798

I wrote you last on the 2d instt. Your's of the 4th is now at hand. The public papers will give you the news of Europe. The French decree making the vessel friendly or enemy, according to the hands by which the cargo was manufactured has produced a great sensation among the merchants here.[29] It's operation is not yet perhaps well understood; but probably it will put our shipping out of competition, because British bottoms, which can come under convoy will alone be trusted with return cargoes. Our's losing this benefit would need a higher freight out, in which therefore they will be underbid by the British. They must then retire from the competition. Some no doubt will try other channels of commerce, and return cargoes from other countries. This effect would be salutary. A very well-informed merchant too (a Scotsman, entirely in the English trade) told me he thought it would have another good

29. On Jan. 18, 1798, the Directory adopted a decree authorizing seizure of neutral ships that carried any article produced in England or her colonies and barred from French ports any vessel that had visited a British port en route; see Bowman, pp. 320–21.

effect, by checking and withdrawing our over-extensive commerce and navign (the fruit of our neutral position) within those bounds to which peace must necessarily bring them. That this being done by degrees will probably prevent those numerous failures produced generally by a peace coming on suddenly. Notwithstanding this decree, the sentiments of the merchants become more and more cooled and settled down against arming. Yet it is believed the Representatives do not cool; and tho' we think the question against arming will be carried, yet probably by a majority of only 4. or 5. Their plan is, to have convoys furnished for our vessels going to Europe, and smaller vessels for the coasting defence. On this condition, they will agree to fortify Southern harbours, and build some gallies. It has been concluded among them, that if war takes place, Wolcott is to be retained in office, that the P. must give up McHenry, and as to Pickering they are divided, the Eastern men being determined to retain him, their middle and Southern brethren wishing to get rid of him. They have talked of Genl. Pinckney as successor to McHenry. This information is certain. However, I hope that we shall avoid war and save them the trouble of a change of ministry. The P has nominated J Q Adams Commissioner Plenipoty to renew the treaty with Sweden.[30] Tazewell made a great stand against it, on the general ground that we should let our treaties drop, and remain without any. He could only get 8. votes against 20. A trial will be made to-day in another form, which he thinks will give 10. or 11. against 16. or 17. declaring the renewal inexpedient. In this case, notwithstanding the nomination has been confirmed, it is supposed the P would perhaps not act under it, on the probability that more than a third would be against the ratification. I believe however that he would act, and that a third could not be got to oppose the ratification. It is acknoleged we have nothing to do but to decide the question about arming. Yet not a word is said about adjourning, and some even talk of continuing the session permanently; others talk of July and August. An effort however will soon be made for an early adjournment. My friendly salutations to Mrs. Madison; to yourself affectionate adieux.

Jefferson to Madison

Philadelphia Mar. 21 and 22, 1798

I wrote you last on the 15th. Since that, yours of the 12th is recieved. Since that too a great change has taken place in the appearance of our political atmosphere. The merchants, as before, continue, a respectable part of them, to wish to avoid arming. The French decree operated on them as a sedative, producing more alarm than resentment; on the Representatives, differently. It

---

30. Samuel Flagg Bemis, *John Quincy Adams and the Foundations of American Foreign Policy* (New York, 1949), p. 92.

excited indignation highly in the war party, tho' I do not know that it had added any new friends to that side of the question. We still hoped a majority of about 4. but the insane message which you will see in the public papers has had great effect.[31] Exultation on the one side, and a certainty of victory; while the other is petrified with astonishment. Our Evans, tho' his soul is wrapt up in the sentiments of this message, yet afraid to give a vote openly for it, is going off to-morrow, as is said. Those who count say there are still 2. members of the other side who will come over to that of peace. If so, the numbers will be for war measures 52. against them 53. if all are present except Evans.

The question is, what is to be attempted, supposing we have a majority? I suggest two things: 1. As the President declares he has withdrawn the Executive prohibition to arm, the Congress should pass a Legislative one. If that should fail in the Senate, it would heap coals of fire on their head. 2. As to do nothing, and to gain time, is everything with us, I propose that they shall come to a resolution of adjournment 'in order to go home and consult their constituents on the great crisis of American affairs now existing.' Besides gaining time enough by this to allow the descent on England to have it's effect here as well as there, it will be a means of exciting the whole body of the people from the state of inattention in which they are; it will require every member to call for the sense of his district by petition or instruction; it will shew the people with which side of the House their safety as well as their rights rest, by shewing them which is for war and which for peace; and their representatives will return here invigorated by the avowed support of the American people. I do not know however whether this will be approved, as there has been little consultation on the subject. We see a new instance of the inefficacy of Constitutional guards. We had relied with great security on that provision which requires two-thirds of the Legislature to declare war.[32] But this is completely eluded by a majority's taking such measures as will be sure to produce war.

I wrote you in my last, that an attempt was to be made on that day in Senate to declare an inexpediency to renew our treaties. But the measure is put off under a hope of it's being attempted under better auspices.

To return to the subject of war, it is quite impossible, when we consider all it's existing circumstances, to find any reason in it's favor, resulting from views either of interest or honour, and plausible enough to impose even on the weakest mind; and especially; and when it would be undertaken by a majority of one or two only. Whatever then be our stock of charity or liberality we must resort to other views. And those so well known to have been entertained at Annapolis and afterwards at the grand convention by a particular set of men, present themselves as those alone which can account for so extraordinary a degree of impetuosity. Perhaps instead of what was then in contemplation, a

31. In his message of Mar. 19, 1798, President Adams, after announcing the refusal of France to recognize officially the American peace negotiators, called for vigorous defense measures.

32. TJ was mistaken on this point; only a majority vote is necessary. See his correction in TJ to JM, Apr. 19, 1798, below.

separation of the union, which has been so much the topic to the Eastward of late, may be the thing aimed at.

I have written so far, two days before the departure of the post. Should anything more occur to-day or to-morrow, it shall be added.

22^d

At night. Nothing more.

Jefferson to Madison
Philadelphia Mar. 29, 1798

I wrote you last on the 21st. Your's of the 12th, therein acknoleged, is the last recd. The measure I suggested in mine of adjourning for consultation with their constituents was not brought forward; but on Tuesday 3. resolutions were moved, which you will see in the public papers. They were offered in committee, to prevent their being suppressed by the previous question, and in the commee on the state of the Union to put it out of their power, by the rising of the commee and not sitting again, to get rid of them. They were taken by surprise, not expecting to be called to vote on such a proposition as 'that it is inexpedient to resort to war against the French republic.'[33] After spending the first day in seeking on every side some hole to get out at, like an animal first put into a cage, they gave up that resource. Yesterday they came forward boldly, and openly combated the proposition. Mr. Harper and Mr. Pinckney pronounced bitter Philippics against France, selecting such circumstances and aggravations as to give the worst picture they could present. The latter, on this, as in the affair of Lyon and Griswold, went far beyond that moderation he has on other occasions recommended. We know not how it will go. Some think the resolution will be lost, some, that it will be carried; but neither way by a majority of more than 1. or 2. The decision of the Executive, of two-thirds of the Senate, and half the house of representatives, is too much for the other half of that house. We therefore fear it will be borne down, and are under the most gloomy apprehensions. In fact the question of war and peace depends now on a toss of cross and pile. If we could but gain this season, we should be saved. The affairs of Europe would of themselves relieve us. Besides this there can be no doubt that a revolution of opinion in Massachusetts and Connecticut is working. Two whig presses have been set up in each of those States.

There has been for some days a rumor that a treaty of alliance offensive and defensive with Gr. Britain, is arrived. Some circumstances have occasioned it to be listened to; to wit, the arrival of Mr. King's Secretary, which is affirmed, the departure of Mr. Liston's secretary, which I know is to take place on Wednesday next, the high tone of the executive measures at the last and

33. For the Sprigg resolutions of Mar. 27, 1798, see De Conde, pp. 70–71.

present session, calculated to raise things to the unison of such a compact, and supported so desperately in both houses in opposition to the pacific wishes of the people and at the risque of their approbation at the ensuing election. Langdon yesterday in debate mentioned this current report. Tracy in reply declared he knew of no such thing, did not believe it, nor would be it's advocate. The Senate are proceeding on the plan communicated in mine of Mar. 15. They are now passing a bill to purchase 12. vessels of from 14. to 22. guns. which with our frigates are to be employed as convoys and guarda costas. They are estimated, when manned and fitted for sea, at 2. millions. They have past a bill for buying one or more founderies. They are about bringing in a bill for regulating private arming, and the defensive works in our harbors have been proceeded on some time since.

An attempt has been made to get the Quakers to come forward with a petition, to aid with the weight of their body the feeble hand of peace. They have with some effort got a petition signed by a few of their society. The main body of their society refuse it. McLay's peace motion in the assembly of Pennsylvania was rejected with an unanimity of the Quaker vote, and it seems to be well understood that their attachment to England is stronger than to their principles of their country. The revolution war was a first proof of this. Mr. White, from the federal city, is here, soliciting money for the buildings at Washington. A bill for 200.000 D has passed the H R, and is before the Senate, where it's fate is entirely uncertain. He is become perfectly satisfied that Mr. A is radically against the government's being there. Goodhue[34] (his oracle) openly said in commee in presence of White, that he knew the government was obliged to go there, but they would not be obliged to stay there. Mr. A said to White, that it would be better that the President should rent a common house there to live in; that no President would live in the one now building. This harmonizes with Goodhue's idea of a short residence. I write this in the morning, but need not part with it till night. If anything occurs in the day it shall be added.

P. M. Nothing material has occurred. Adieu.

Madison to Jefferson

[Orange] Apr. 2, 1798

DEAR SIR,

Since my last, I am in debt for your two favors of the 15th and 22, the Gazettes of the 3, 6 7 and 8 Ulto, with a regular continuation to the 22d—two statements from the Treasury Department, and Paine's letter to the French people and armies.

---

34. Benjamin Goodhue was a Federalist senator from Massachusetts from 1796 to 1800; see David Hackett Fischer, *The Revolution of American Conservatism: The Federalist Party in the Era of Jeffersonian Democracy* (New York, 1965), p. 249.

The President's message is only a further development to the public, of the violent passions, and heretical politics, which have been long privately known to govern him. It is to be hoped however that the H. of Rep^s will not hastily eccho them. At least it may be expected that before war measures are instituted, they will recollect the principle asserted by 62 vs. 37, in the case of the [Jay] Treaty, and insist on a full communication of the intelligence on which such measures are recommended. The present is a plainer, if it be not a stronger case, and if there has been sufficient defection to destroy the majority which was then so great and so decided, it is the worst symptom that has yet appeared in our Councils. The constitution supposes, what the History of all Govts demonstrates, that the Ex. is the branch of power most interested in war, and most prone to it. It has accordingly with studied care, vested the question of war in the Legisl. But the Doctrines lately advanced strike at the root of all these provisions, and will deposit the peace of the Country in that Department which the Constitution distrusts as most ready without cause to renounce it. For if the opinion of the P. not the facts and proofs themselves are to sway the judgment of Congress in declaring war, and if the President in the recess of Congr^s create a foreign mission, app^t the minister, and negociate a War Treaty, without the possibility of a check even from the Senate, untill the measures present alternatives overruling the freedom of its judgment; if again a Treaty when made obliges the Legis. to declare war contrary to its judgment, and in pursuance of the same doctrine, a law declaring war, imposes a like moral obligation, to grant the requisite supplies until it be formally repealed with the consent of the P. and Senate, it is evident that the people are cheated out of the best ingredients in their Gov^t, the safeguards of peace which is the greatest of their blessings.

I like both your suggestions in the present crisis. Congress ought clearly to prohibit arming, and the P. ought to be brought to declare on what ground he undertook to grant an indirect licence to arm. The first instructions were no otherwise legal than as they were in pursuance of the law of Nations, and consequently in execution of the law of the land. The revocation of the instructions is a virtual change of the law, and consequently a usurpation by the Ex. of a legislative power. It will not avail to say that the law of Nations leaves this point undecided, and that every nation is free to decide it for itself. If this be the case, the regulation being a Legislative not an Executive one, belongs to the former, not the latter Authority; and comes expressly within the power "to define the law of Nations" given to Congress by the Constitution. I do not expect however that the Constitutional party in the H. of R. is strong eno' [to] do what ought to be done in the present instance. Your 2^d idea that an adjournment for the purpose of consulting the constituents on the subject of war, is more practicable because it can be effected by that branch alone if it pleases, and because an opposition to such a measure will be more striking to the public eye. The expedient is the more desirable as it will be utterly impossible to call forth the sense of the people generally before the season will be over, especially as the Towns, etc. where there can be most despatch in such an operation are on the wrong side, and it is to be feared that a partial expression of the public voice, may be misconstrued or miscalled, an evidence in favor of the war party. On what do you ground the idea that a decln of war requires ⅔ of the Legislature? The force of your remark however is not diminished by this mistake, for it remains true, that measures are taking or may be taken by the Ex. that will end in war, contrary to the wish of the Body which alone can declare it.

Jefferson to Madison
                                              Philadelphia Apr. 5, 1798

I wrote you last on the 29th ult; since which I have no letter from you. These acknolegments regularly made and attended to will shew whether any of my letters are intercepted, and the impression of my seal on wax (which shall be constant hereafter) will discover whether they are opened by the way. The nature of some of my communications furnishes ground of inquietude for their safe conveyance. The bill for the federal buildings labors hard in Senate, tho' to lessen opposition the Maryland Senator himself proposed to reduce the 200.000 D to one-third of that sum. Sedgwick and Hillhouse violently opposed it. I conjecture that the votes will be either 13. for and 15. against it, or 14. and 14. Every member declares he means to go there, but tho' charged with an intention to come away again, not one of them disavowed it. This will engender incurable distrust.

The debate on Mr. Sprigg's resolutions has been interrupted by a motion to call for papers. This was carried by a great majority.[35] In this case, there appeared a separate squad, to wit, the Pinckney interest, which is a distinct thing, and will be seen sometimes to lurch the President. It is in truth the Hamilton party, whereof P is only made the stalking horse.[36] The papers have been sent in and read, and it is now under debate in both houses, whether they shall be published. I write in the morning, and if determined in the course of the day in favor of publication, I will add in the evening a general idea of their character. Private letters from France, by a late vessel which sailed from Havre Feb. 5. assure us that France classing us in her measures with the Swedes and Danes, has no more notion of declaring war against us than them. You will see a letter in Bache's paper of yesterday which came addressed to me. Still the fate of Sprigg's resolutions seems in perfect equilibrio.

35. The vote was 65 to 27; see Kurtz's chapter "Political Consequences of the XYZ Papers" in his *Presidency of John Adams,* pp. 284–306.
36. Thomas Pinckney of South Carolina, Adams's running mate who lost the vice presidency to TJ, was a congressman from Charleston.

You will see in Fenno two numbers of a paper signed Marcellus. They promise much mischief, and are ascribed, without any difference of opinion, to Hamilton. You must, my dear Sir, take up your pen against this champion. You know the ingenuity of his talents, and there is not a person but yourself who can foil him. For heaven's sake, then take up your pen, and do not desert the public cause altogether.

Thursday evening. The Senate have, to-day, voted the publication of the communications from our envoys. The House of Repr. decided against the publication by a majority of 75 to 24. The Senate adjourned over to-morrow (good Friday), to Saturday morning; but as the papers cannot be printed within that time, perhaps the vote of the H of R may induce the Senate to reconsider theirs. For this reason, I think it my duty to be silent on them. Adieu.

Jefferson to Madison

[Philadelphia] Apr. 6, 1798

So much of the communications from our envoys has got abroad, and so partially, that there can now be no ground for reconsideration with the Senate. I may therefore consistently with duty do what every member of the body is doing. Still I would rather you would use the communication with reserve till you see the whole papers. The first impressions from them are very disagreeable and confused. Reflection however and analysis resolves them into this. Mr. A's speech to Congress in May is deemed such a national affront, that no explanation on other topics can be entered on till that, as a preliminary is wiped away by humiliating disavowals or acknolegments. This working hard with our envoys, and indeed seeming impracticable for want of that sort of authority, submission to a heavy amercement (upwards of a million sterl.) was, at an after meeting suggested as an alternative which might be admitted if proposed by us. These overtures had been through informal agents; and both the alternatives bringing the envoys to their ne plus, they resolve to have no more communication through inofficial characters, but to address a letter directly to the government, to bring forward their pretensions. This letter had not yet however been prepared. There were, interwoven with these overtures some base propositions on the part of Taleyrand through one of his agents, to sell his interest and influence with the Directory towards smoothing difficulties with them in consideration of a large sum (50.000 £ sterl.) and the arguments to which his agent resorted to induce compliance with this demand, were very unworthy of a great nation (could they be imputed to them) and calculated to excite disgust and indignation in Americans generally, and alienation in the republicans particularly, whom they so far mistake as to presume an attachment to France and hatred to the Federal party, and not the love of their country, to be their first passion. No difficulty was expressed towards an adjustment of all differences and misunderstandings or even ultimately a paiment for spoliations, if the insult from our Executive should be first wiped away. Observe that I state all this from only a single hearing of the papers, and therefore it may not be rigorously correct. The little slanderous imputation before mentioned has been the bait which hurried the opposite party into this publication. The first impressions with the people will be disagreeable, but the last and permanent one will be, that the speech in May is now the only obstacle to accommodation, and the real cause of war, if war takes place. And how much will be added to this by the speech of November, is yet to be learnt. It is evident however on reflection, that these papers do not offer one motive the more for our going to war. Yet such is their effect on the minds of wavering characters, that I fear that to wipe off the imputation of being French partisans, they will go over to the war measures so furiously pushed by the other party. It seems indeed as if they were afraid they should not be able to get into war till Great Britain will be blown up, and the prudence of our countrymen from that circumstance have influence enough to prevent it. The most artful misrepresentations of the contents of these papers were published yesterday, and produced such a shock on the republican mind as has never been seen since our independence. We are to dread the effects of this dismay till their fuller information.[37] Adieu.

P. M. Evening papers have come out since writing the above. I therefore inclose them. Be so good as to return Brown's by post, as I keep his set here. The representations are still unfaithful.

Jefferson to Madison

Philadelphia Apr. 12, 1798

I wrote you two letters on the 5th [and 6th] inst; since which I have recd yours of the 2d. I send you, in a separate package, the instructions to our envoys and their communications. You will find that my representation of their contents, from memory, was substantially just. The public mind appears still in a state of astonishment. There never was a moment in which the aid of an able pen was so important to place things in their just attitude. On this depend the inchoate movement in the Eastern mind, and the fate of the elections in that quarter, now beginning and to continue through the summer. I would not propose to you such a task on any ordinary occasion. But be

---

37. The best discussions of the negotiations are in Stinchcombe, *The XYZ Affair,* and Bowman, pp. 306-59.

assured that a well digested analysis of these papers would now decide the future turn of things which are at this moment on the creen. The merchants here are meeting under the auspices of Fitzsimmons to address the President and approve his propositions. Nothing will be spared on that side.

Sprigg's first resolution against the expediency of war, proper at the time it was moved, is now postponed as improper, because to declare that, after we have understood it has been proposed to us to buy a peace, would imply an acquiescence under that proposition. All therefore which the advocates of peace can now attempt, is to prevent war measures *externally*, consenting to every rational measure of *internal* defence and preparation.[38] Great expences will be incurred; and it will be left to those whose measures render them necessary, to provide to meet them. They already talk of stopping all paiments of interest, and of a land tax. These will probably not be opposed. The only question will be how to modify the land tax. On this there may be great diversity of sentiment. One party will want to make it a new source of patronage and expence. If this business is taken up it will lengthen our session. We had pretty generally, till now, fixed on the beginning of May for adjournment. I shall return by my usual routes, and not by the Eastern shore, on account of the advance of the season. Friendly salutations to Mrs. Madison and yourself. Adieu.

Madison to Jefferson

[Orange] Apr. 15, 1798

DEAR SIR,

My last answered yours of the 21, since which I recd on friday last your three favors of the 29 Ult. of Apl 5 and 6. I have no reason to suspect that any of your letters have miscarried, or been opened by the way. I am less able to say whether mine have all reached you, as I have generally written them in haste, and neglected to keep a note of their dates. I will thank you to mention in your acknowledgement of this, whether you recd one from me inclosing a letter to F. A. Muhlenburg, and whether he certainly rec^d it. It related to a case of humanity and required an answer which has never come to hand.

The effect of the P's speech in F. is less to be wondered at, than the speech itself with other follies of a like tendency is to be deplored. Still the mode and degree of resisting them is rather meeting folly with folly, than consulting the true dignity and interest which ought to prescribe such cases. The conduct of Taleyrand is so extraordinary as to be scarcely credible.[39] I do not allude to its

38. TJ's italics.
39. Charles-Maurice de Talleyrand-Périgord had spent two years in the United States and was widely acquainted with both Republican and Federalist leaders, including JM. See *PJM,* XVII,

depravity, which however heinous, is not without examples. Its unparalleled stupidity is what fills one with astonishment. Is it possible that a man of sagacity as he is admitted to be, who has lived long eno. in this Country to understand the nature of our Govt, who could not be unaware of the impossibility of secrecy and the improbability of success in pursuing his propositions thro' the necessary forms, who must have suspected the Ex. rather of a wish to seize pretexts for widening the breach between the two Republics, than to make use of any means however objectionable to reconcile their differences; who must have been equally suspicious of the probable inclination of some one or other of the Envoys—is it possible, that such a man under such circumstances, could have committed both his character and safety, by such a proposition? If the evidence be not perfectly conclusive, of which I cannot judge, the decision ought to be agst. the evidence, rather than on the side of the infatuation. It is easy to foresee however the zeal and plausibility with which this part of the despatches will be inculcated, not only for the general purpose of enforcing the war measures of the Ex. but for the particular purpose of diverting the public attention from the other more important part, which shews the speech and conduct of the P. to be now the great obstacle to accomodation. This interesting fact must nevertheless finally take possession of thinking minds; and strengthen the suspicion, that whilst the Ex. were pursuing ostensible plans of reconciliation, and giving instructions which might wear that tendency, the success of them was indirectly counter-worked by every irritation and disgust for which opportunities could be found in official speeches and messages, answers to private addresses harangues in Congress and the vilest insults, and calumnies of Newspapers under the patronage of the Government. The readyness with which the papers were communicated and the quarter proposing the call for them, would be entitled to praise, if a mass of other circumstances did not force a belief that the view in both, was more to inflame than to inform the public mind. It is not improbable that the influence of the first impressions in checking the rising spirit in N. England, and bearing up the party of Jay in N. Y. whose re-election is brought into danger by the pestilent consequences experienced from his Treaty, had considerable share in the motive.

The negative declaration proposed by Mr. S.[40] is liable to so many specious objections, that I shall be surprised if a willing majority does not take advantage of them. In ordinary cases, the mode of proceeding is certainly ineligible. But it seems equally obvious that cases may arise, for which that is the proper one. Three of these occur, where there does not appear any room to doubt on the subject. 1. Where nothing less than a declaration of pacific

---

p. 258; Hans Huth and Wilma Pugh, "Talleyrand in America As a Financial Promoter, 1794-96," in *AHA Annual Report for the Year 1941*, 2 vols. (1942), II, pp. 1-176; and Edwin R. Baldridge, "Talleyrand's Visit to Pennsylvania, 1794-1796," *Pennsylvania History* 36 (1969): 145-60.

40. JM referred to Sprigg's resolutions.

intentions from the department entrusted with the power of war, will quiet the apprehensions of the constituent body, or remove an uncertainty which subjects one part of them to the speculating arts of another. 2. Where it may be a necessary antidote to the hostile measures or language of the Ex. Departmt. If war sentiments be delivered in a speech to Congress which admits of a direct answer, and the sentiments of Congress be against war it is not doubted that the counter sentiments might and ought to be expressed in the answer. Where an extra message delivers like sentiments, and custom does not permit a like explanation of the sentiments of the Legislature, there does not appear any equivalent mode of making it, except that of an abstract vote. 3. Where public measures or appearances, may mislead another nation into distrust of the real object of them, the error ought to be corrected; and in our Gov.^t where the question of war or peace lies with Congress, a satisfactory explanation cannot issue from any other Department. In Govts where the power of deciding on war is an Ex. prerogative it is not unusual for explanations of this kind to be given either on the demands of foreign Nations, or in order to prevent their improper suspicions. Should a demand of this sort be at any time made on our Gov.^t—the answer must proceed, [if thro' an Executive functionary]⁴¹ from the war prerogative, that is, from Congr—and if an answer could be given, on demand, a declaration without a demand may certainly be made with equal propriety, if there be equal occasion for it.

The discovery of Mr. A.'s dislike to the City of Washington will cause strong emotions. What sort of conscience is that which feels an obligation on the Gov^t to remove thither, and a liberty to quit it the next day? The objection to the magnificence of the President's House belongs to a man of very different principles from those of Mr. A. The increase of expence therefore without a probable increase of salary in proportion, must be the real ground of objection.

I have looked over the two papers which you consider as so threatening in their tendency. They do not, I own, appear to me exactly in the same light; nor am I by any means satisfied that they are from the pen you ascribe them to. If they are, there certainly has been a disguise aimed at in many features of the stile. I differ still more from you as to the source from which an antidote, if necessary, ought to come. But waiving every thing of that sort, there is really a crowd and weight of *indispensable* occupations, on my time, which it would be very tedious to explain, but wch I pledge myself, will justify me in leaving such tasks to others, not only commanding more time for them, but in every respect more favorably situated for executing them with advantage and effect. And it is with no small pleasure I observe that some pens are employed which promise the public all the lights with respect to their affairs, which can be conveyed to them thro' the channels of the press.

It is now become certain that not half crops of wheat can be made. Many

---

41. At a later date, JM inserted the remarks in brackets; see *PJM,* XVII, p. 114.

will not get back more than their seed, and some not even that. We have lately had a severe spell of N. E. rain, which in this neighbourhood swept off at least 15 Per C! of the Catch;[42] and from accts in different directions it appears to have been equally fatal. We are at present in the midst of a cold N. W. spell, which menaces the fruit. The tops of the Blue Mountains are tinged with snow, and the Therm^r this morning was at 31°. It does not appear however that the mischief is yet done. The coming night, if no sudden change takes place, must, I think, be fatal.

If Mr. Bailey has not yet taken up his note, be so good as to have the inclosed forwarded to him.

Jefferson to Madison

[Philadelphia] Apr. 19, 1798

I wrote you last on the 12th and then acknoleged your last at hand of the 2^d inst. The sensations first occasioned by the late publications have been kept up and increased at this place. A petition from the merchants and traders and others was so industriously pushed as to have obtained a very extensive signature. The same measure is pursuing in New York. As the election of their governor comes on next Tuesday, these impressions will just be in time to affect that. We have no information yet of their effect to the Eastward. In the meantime petitions to Congress against arming from the towns of Massachusetts were multiplying. They will no doubt have been immediately checked. The P.'s answer to the address of the merchants here you will see in Fenno of yesterday. It is a pretty strong declaration that a neutral and pacific conduct on our part is no longer the existing state of things. The vibraters in the H. of R. have chiefly gone over to the war party. Still if our members were all here, it is believed the naval-bill would be thrown out. Giles, Clopton, and Cabell are gone. The debate began yesterday, and tho' the question will be lost, the effect on the public mind will be victory. For certainly there is nothing new which may render war more palatable to the people. On the contrary the war-members themselves are becoming alarmed at the expences, and whittling down the estimates to the lowest sums. You will see by a report of the Secretary at war which I inclose you that he estimates the expences of preparation at seven millions of Dollars; which it is proposed to lower to about 3. millions. If it can be reduced to this, a stoppage of public interest will suffice and is the project of some. This idea has already knocked down the public paper, which can no longer be sold at all. If the expences should exceed 3. m. they will undertake a land tax. Indeed a land tax is the decided resource of many, perhaps of a

---

42. "Catch" refers to the germination of a field crop, which makes replanting unnecessary; see *ibid.*, p. 115.

majority. There is an idea of some of the Connecticut members to raise the whole money wanted by a tax on salt; so much do they dread a land tax. The middle or last of May is still counted on for adjournment.

Col° Innes is just arrived here, heavily laden with gout and dropsy. It is scarcely thought he can ever get home again.[43] The principles likely to be adopted by that board have thrown the administration into deep alarm. It is admitted they will be worse than the English, French, and Algerine depredations added together. It is even suggested that, if persevered in, their proceedings will be stopped. These things are not public.

Your letter, by occasioning my recurrence to the constitution, has corrected an error under which a former one of mine had been written. I had erroneously conceived that the declaration of war was among the things confided by the Constitution to *two thirds* of the legislature.[44] We are told here that you are probably elected to the state legislature. It has given great joy, as we know your presence will be felt anywhere, and the times do not admit of the inactivity of such talents as yours. I hope therefore it is true, as much good may be done by a proper direction of the local force. Present my friendly salutations to Mrs. Madison and to yourself affectionately adieu.

P.M. The enclosed was sealed before I recollected that I have mentioned a *petition* instead of *an address* to the President, which is to be corrected. A nomination for Govr. Secretary and three judges to the Missisipi territory is in sent to the Senate, four of whom are agents, or interested in the land speculations of that country, two of them bankrupt speculators, and the 5th. unknown. The Senate demur, and are going into an enquiry. The nomination of George Matthews governor, Millar of Connecticut Secretary, Wetmore of Mass. Clarke of Missi district (a merchant who married a daughter of Adam Hoops) and Tilton of New Hampshire judges.

Madison to Jefferson

[Orange] Apr. 22, 1798

DEAR SIR,

My last was on the 15th. and acknowledged your preceding letters. I have since recd. that of the 12th. under the same cover with the Gazettes; and the instructions and despatches under a separate cover. The interruptions of company, added to the calls of business, have not left me time as yet to read over the whole of those papers. A glance at them, with the extracts given to their contents, fully account for the state of astonishment produced in the public

---

43. James Innes died later in 1798, after serving briefly on the joint commission to settle claims of British creditors owed by American debtors before the Revolution; see Jane Carson, *James Innes and His Brothers of the F. H. C.* (Charlottesville, 1965).

44. See TJ to JM, Mar. 21, 1798, above.

mind. And yet the circumstance that ought to astonish most, perhaps, is the publication of them by the Executive and Senate. Whatever probability there may be of individual corruption within the pale of the French Gov^t, the evidence is certainly very insufficient to support such an attack on its reputation in the face of the world, even if we could separate the measure from its inevitable effect in blasting every chance of accommodation, if it should reach France before terms shall be finally settled. After this stroke in the politics of those two branches of our Govt., no one who has not surrendered his reason, can believe them sincere in wishing to avoid extremities with the French Republic; to say nothing of the internal views to which they mean also to turn this extraordinary manœuvre. There has not been time for any impressions on the public sentiment in this quarter, which the Despatches are calculated to make. The first will no doubt pretty much correspond with those made elsewhere. But the final impressions will depend on the further and more authentic developments, which cannot be far behind, and which may by this time be arrived where you are. I find that in several places the people have turned out with their protests agst. the war measures urged by the Ex. Whether the proceeding will be general, I cannot pretend to decide. In this County a petition is to be handed about, which will I presume be pretty fully signed, if sufficiently circulated; unless the disaffected few among us should be emboldened by the present crisis to circulate along with it, the impressions emanating from the Despatches, which may stop the hands of wavering or cautious people.

Altho' the thermometer on the mornings of the 15 and 16 inst. was at 31 and 32°, the fruit was not materially injured except in low situations: but having sunk during the night following to 24° vegitation of every kind seemed to feel the blow. The Peaches and Cherries appear to [be] totally destroyed, and most of the apples. Even the young Hickory leaves are in considerable proportion compleatly killed. The weather has since been more natural to the season.

Jefferson to Madison

Philadelphia Apr. 26, 1798

I wrote you last on the 19th since which your's of the 15th is recieved. I well remember the recieving that which inclosed a letter to Muhlenburg, but do not exactly recollect how I sent it. Yet I have no doubt I sent it by my servant, that being my constant practice. Your note for Baily I showed to Genl Van Cortlandt who was going to N. York. On his return he told me he would pay the note himself before the rising of Congress, since which I have said nothing to him more, as I doubt not he will do it. Not knowing however the precise object of your letter to Bailey, I have sent it to the post office.

The bill for the naval armament (12. vessels) passed by a majority of about 4 to 3 in the H of R. All restrictions on the objects for which the vessels should be used were struck out. The bill for establishing a department of Secretary of the navy was tried yesterday, on its passage to the 3d reading and prevailed by 47. against 41. It will be read the 3d time to-day.[45] The Provisional army of 20,000. men will meet some difficulty.[46] It would surely be rejected if our members were all here. Giles, Clopton, Cabell and Nicholas are gone, and Clay goes to-morrow. He received here news of the death of his wife. Parker is completely gone over to the war party. In this state of things they will carry what they please. One of the war party, in a fit of unguarded passion declared some time ago they would pass a citizen bill, an alien bill, and a sedition bill.[47] Accordingly, some days ago, Coit laid a motion on the table of the H of R for modifying the citizen law. Their threats point at Gallatin, and it is believed they will endeavor to reach him by this bill. Yesterday Mr. Hillhouse laid on the table of the Senate a motion for giving power to send away suspected aliens. This is understood to be meant for Volney and Collot. But it will not stop there when it gets into a course of execution. There is now only wanting, to accomplish the whole declaration before mentioned, a sedition bill, which we shall certainly soon see proposed. The object of that, is the suppression of the whig presses. Bache's has been particularly named. That paper and also Cary's totter for want of subscriptions. We should really exert ourselves to procure them, for if these papers fall, republicanism will be entirely brow beaten. Cary's paper comes out 3 times a week, @ 5 D. The meeting of the people which was called at New York, did nothing. It was found that the majority would be against the Address. They therefore chose to circulate it individually. The committee of ways and means have voted a land tax. An additional tax on salt will certainly be proposed in the House, and probably prevail to some degree. The stoppage of interest on the public debt will also perhaps be proposed, but not with effect. In the meantime, that paper cannot be sold. Hamilton is coming on as Senator from N. Y.[48] There has been so much contrivance and combination in that, as to shew there is some great object in hand. Troup the district judge of N. York, resigns towards the close of the session of their assembly. The appointment of Mr. Hobart, then Senator, to succeed Troup, is not made by the President till after the assembly had risen. Otherwise, they would have chosen the Senator in place of Hobart. Jay then names Hamilton Senator, but not till a day or two before his own election as Governor was to come on, lest the unpopularity of the nomination

---

45. See Marshall Smelser, *The Congress Founds the Navy, 1787–1798* (Notre Dame, 1959).

46. For the split within the Federalist party over John Adams's preference for the navy and Alexander Hamilton's and the High Federalists' preference for the army, see Kurtz, pp. 307–33, who calls the difference "the most significant single issue" of Adams's presidency.

47. For the enactment of the Alien and Sedition Laws, see Smith, *Freedom's Fetters,* pp. 22–155.

48. Governor John Jay appointed Alexander Hamilton as senator, but Hamilton promptly refused the post.

should be in time to affect his own election. We shall see in what all this is to end; but surely in something. The popular movement in the eastern states is checked as we expected, and war addresses are showering in from New Jersey and the great trading towns. However we still trust that a nearer view of war and a land tax will oblige the great mass of the people to attend. At present, the war hawks talk of Septembrizing, Deportation, and the examples for quelling sedition set by the French Executive.[49] All the firmness of the human mind is now in a state of requisition. Salutations to Mrs. Madison; to yourself, friendship and adieu.

P.M. The bill for the naval department is passed.

Madison to Jefferson

[Orange] Apr. 29, 1798

DEAR SIR,

My last was on the 22d. Yours recd. by the last mail was of the 19th inst. The despatches have not yet come sufficiently to the knowledge of the bulk of the people to decide the impression which is to result from them. As far as I can infer from the language of the few who have read the newspapers, there will be a general agreement as to the improper views of our own Executive party, whatever difference of opinion there may be as to the purity of the French councils. Indeed the reflexion of others, as well as my own traces so many absurdities and improbabilities in many of the details that the injustice seems equal to the temerity of publishing such a libel on the French Government. Col. Monroe lodged with me last night on his way to the District Court at Fred^g. He considers the transaction as evidently a swindling experiment, and thinks the result will bring as much derision on the Envoys, as mischief on the Country. I am sorry to learn that the naval bill is likely to be carried, and particularly that any of our friends should by their leaving Congs. be accessory to it. The public sentiment here is unquestionably opposed to every measure that may increase the danger of War. Petitions expressive of it will be signed by all to whom they are presented, with such exceptions only as may be guessed at. It appears however that the crisis is over for their effect on Congs., if there were a disposition there to listen to them.

I take the liberty of subjoining a list of a few articles not to be got out of Philadelphia, and so important to my present object that I break through every restraint from adding to the trouble of which you have more than enough.[50] I hope the commission may be facilitated by your previous acquaint-

---

49. The coup d'état of Sept. 4, 1797, purged the French government of dissenters, many of whom were deported to French Guiana; see *PJM,* XVII, p. 122.

50. See Robert A. Rutland, *James Madison: The Founding Father* (New York, 1987), p. 154.

ance with the places at which they are to be had, and that you will be able to make use of the time of others chiefly for the purpose. If J. Bringhurst should be in the way, he will readily relieve you from all attention to the details. I wish them to be forwarded to "Fredg. to the care of Robert Dunbar, Esq., at Falmouth." The enclosed draught will be a fund for the purchase. Adieu. Affectionately.

		Inches
100	Panes Window Glass	15½ by 12½
80	ditto	12⅝ by 12½ do
10	do	17½ by 9½ do

3 Brass locks of good size and quality—3 do of smaller size, with screws etc.
Brass spiral hinges for 8 doors with do.

Jefferson to Madison

Philadelphia May 3, 1798

I wrote you last on the 26th; since which yours of the 22d of April is recieved acknoleging mine of the 12th; so that all appear to have been received to that date. The spirit kindled up in the towns is wonderful. These and N. Jersey are pouring in their addresses, offering life and fortune. Even these addresses are not the worst things, for indiscreet declarations and expressions of passion may be pardoned to a multitude acting from the impulse of the moment. But we cannot expect a foreign nation to shew that apathy to the answers of the President, which are more Thrasonic than the addresses. Whatever chance for peace might have been left us after the publication of the dispatches, is compleatly lost by these answers. Nor is it France alone but his own fellow citizens against whom his threats are uttered. In Fenno of yesterday you will see one wherein he says to the Address from Newark, 'the delusions and misrepresentations which have misled so many citizens, must be discountenanced by authority as well as by the citizens at large;' evidently alluding to those letters from the representatives to their constituents, which they have been in the habit of seeking after and publishing; while those sent by the Tory part of the house to their constituents, are ten times more numerous, and replete with the most atrocious falsehoods and calumnies.[51] What new law they will propose on this subject, has not yet leaked out. The citizen bill sleeps.

51. For a superb collection of congressmen's letters to their constituents, see Noble E. Cunningham, Jr., ed., *Circular Letters of Congressmen to Their Constituents, 1789–1829*, 3 vols. (Chapel Hill, 1978).

The alien bill proposed by the Senate has not yet been brought in. That proposed by the H. of R. has been so moderated, that it will not answer the passionate purposes of the war gentlemen. Whether therefore the Senate will push their bolder plan, I know not. The provisional army does not go down so smoothly in the R. as it did in the Senate. They are whittling away some of it's choice ingredients; particularly that of transferring their own constitutional discretion over the raising of armies to the President. A commee. of the R. have struck out his discretion, and hang the raising of the men on the contingencies of invasion, insurrection, or declaration of war. Were all our members here, the bill would not pass. But it will probably as the House now is. It's expence is differently estimated from 5. to 8. millions of dollars a year. Their purposes before voted require 2. millions above all the other taxes, which therefore are voted to be raised on lands, houses and slaves. The provisional army will be additional to this. The threatening appearances from the Alien bills have so alarmed the French who are among us, that they are going off. A ship, chartered by themselves for this purpose will sail within about a fortnight for France with as many as she can carry. Among these I believe will be Volney, who has in truth been the principal object aimed at by the law.[52] Notwithstanding the unfavorableness of the late impressions, it is believed the New York elections, which are over, will give us two or three republicans more than we now have. But it is supposed Jay is re-elected. It is said Hamilton declines coming to the Senate. He very soon stopped his Marcellus. It was rather the sequel that was feared than what actually appeared. He comes out on a different plan in his Titus Manlius, if that be really his.[53] The appointments to the Missisipi territory were so abominable that the Senate could not swallow them. They referred them to a commte to inquire into characters, and the P withdrew the nomination and has now named Winthrop Sergeant Governor, Steele of Augusta in Virginia, Secretary, Tilton and —— two of the Judges, the other not yet named. As there is nothing material now to be proposed, we generally expect to rise in about three weeks. However I do not yet venture to order my horses. My respectful salutations to Mrs. Madison. To yourself affectionate friendship, and adieu.

Perhaps the Ps expression before quoted, may look to the Sedition bill which has been spoken of, and which may be meant to put the Printing presses under the Imprimatur of the Executive. Bache is thought a main object of it.

Cabot, of Massachusetts, is appointed Secretary of the navy.[54]

It is said Hamilton declines coming to the Senate.

52. See Chinard, *Volney et l'Amérique.*
53. For a brief discussion of Alexander Hamilton's essays as "Titus Manlius," see Dauer, pp. 147, 219, and Syrett, XXI, p. 381.
54. George Cabot of Massachusetts did not accept the assignment, and President Adams appointed Benjamin Stoddert of Maryland.

Madison to Jefferson

[Orange] May 5, 1798

DEAR SIR,

I have to thank you for your favor of the 26th ult. My last was of the 29th. The success of the war party in turning the Despatches to their inflammatory views is a mortifying item against the enlightened character of our citizens. The analysis of the Despatches by Sidney cannot fail to be an effectual antidote, if any appeal to sober reflection can prevail against occurrences which are constantly addressing their imaginations and feelings. The talents of this writer make it lucky that the task has not been taken up by other hands.[55] I am glad to find in general that everything that good sense and accurate information can supply is abundantly exhibited by the newspapers to the view of the public. It is to be regretted that these papers are so limited in their circulation, as well as that the mixture of indiscretions in some of them should contribute to that effect. It is to be hoped however that any arbitrary attacks on the freedom of the press will find virtue eno' remaining in the public mind to make them recoil on the wicked authors. No other check to desperate projects seems now to be left. The sanguinary faction ought not however to adopt the spirit of Robespierre without recollecting the shortness of his triumphs and the perpetuity of his infamy. The contrivance of Jay for reproducing Hamilton into office and notice suggests, no doubt, a variety of conjectures. If the contrivance is to be ascribed chiefly to Jay, it probably originated in the alarm into which the consequences of the Treaty have thrown its author, and the new demand for the services of its champion. Events have so clearly demonstrated the great objects of that Treaty to have been to draw us into a quarrel with the enemies of G. B. and to sacrifice our navigation to hers, that it will require greater efforts than ever to skreen the instrument and author much longer from the odium due to them. The late acts of the B. Par^t would before this, have unmasked the character of the Treaty, even to the people of N. England, if adventitious circumstances had not furnished its partizans with fresh dust for their eyes. A tax on land, with a loss of market for its produce, will put their credulity and blindness to a test that may be more dreadful to the Deluders.

We have had a dry spell latterly which succeeding the effects of the frost, will affect every species of crop that depends on the favor of the season. I write to Mr. Dawson by this post for a small balance, between 30 and 40 dollars, which I beg you to receive. Should the funds in your hands admit, you will further oblige me by having my brother William's name subscribed to Carey's paper, and paying the necessary advance; the paper to be sent to Orange Ct. House.

---

55. For a reference to "Sidney's" essays in Bache's *Aurora*, see Buel, p. 164, and *PJM*, XVII, p. 127.

Jefferson to Madison

[Philadelphia] May 10, 1798

I wrote you last on the 3d. inst while yours of Apr. 29 is recieved. A day or two after I arrived here J. Bringhurst called on me. Since that moment I have never seen him nor heard of him. He cannot therefore be here. But I have put your letter and draught into the hands of Mr Barnes, and desired him to get Bohemian glass from Donath. I will myself look to the locks and hinges. But both articles would have been better with further explanation. 'Brass locks.' Do you mean mortise locks, or locks cased in brass and to be screwed on the outside of the door. The former are generally preferred, but require a thick door. 'Brass spiral hinges.' I do not know what these are by that name; but perhaps the shop keepers can tell me. If you mean the dove-tail rising hinge, which raises the door as it opens, I can assure you from my own experience as well as that of others that they do not answer. The weight of the door raised by the dovetail joint wears it out very soon, and often (if there happens any little obstruction) burst off the axis. The hinges now universally used are 5 inch butt hinges screwed on the edge of the door with stout screws. They show only the joint which is of polished iron. Mortise brass hinges are still somewhat in use. They show only their joint. As I shall probably be here till you can send an answer to this, if you do it by return of post, I will defer getting the locks and hinges, in hopes of further explanation.

No bill has passed since my last. The alien bill now before the Senate you will see in Bache.[56] I shall make no comment on it. The first clause was debated through the whole of Tuesday. To judge from that we cannot expect above 5. or 6. votes against it. We suppose the lower house will throw it out and proceed on that which they have prepared. The bill for the provisional army is under debate. It will probably pass or be rejected by a very minute majority. If our members were here it would be rejected with ease. The tax on lands, slaves and houses is proceeding. The questions on that will only be of modification. The event of the N. York elections is not yet absolutely known, but it is still believed we have gained 2. more republicans to Congress. Burr was here a day or two ago. He says they have got a decided majority of Whigs in their state H. of R. He thinks that Connecticut has chosen one Whig, a Mr. Granger, and calculates much on the effect of his election. An election here of town officers for Southwark, where it was said the people had entirely gone over to the tory side, showed them unmoved. The Whig ticket was carried by 10. to 1. The informations are so different as to the effect of the late dispatches on the people here that one does not know what to conclude: but I am of opinion they are little moved. Some of the young men who addressed the President on

---

56. For the Senate "Act Concerning Aliens," or the Alien Friends Law, which was published in the *Aurora* on May 8, 1798, see Smith, *Freedom's Fetters,* pp. 50–53.

Monday mounted the Black (or English) cockade. The next day numbers of the people appeared with the tricolored (or French) cockade. Yesterday being the fast day, the black cockade again appeared, on which the tricolor also showed itself. A fray ensued, the light horse were called in, and the city was so filled with confusion from about 6. to 10. o'clock last night that it was dangerous going out. I write in the morning and therefore know nothing of the particulars as yet, but as I do not send my letter to the post office till night, I shall probably be able by that time to add some details. It is also possible some question may be taken which may indicate the fate of the provisional army. There is a report which comes from Baltimore of peace between France and England on terms entirely dictated by the former. But we do not hear how it comes, nor pay the least attention to it.

P. M. By the proceedings in Senate today I conclude the alien bill will pass 17 to 6. The Provisional army has been under debate in the lower house. A motion was made to strike out the first section confessedly for the purpose of trying the fate of the bill. The motion was lost by 44. to 47. Had all the members in town been present, and the question in the house instead of the committee, the vote would have been 45. against the bill and 46. for it.

No further particulars about the riot appear.

Barnes has recieved for you from Moylan 158.22 which he will place to your credit in account. The ironmongers to whom I have been since writing in the morning know nothing of *spiral hinges*.

Madison to Jefferson

[Orange] May 13, 1798

Dear Sir,

I have recd. your favor of the 3d Inst. My last acknowledged your preceding one. The successful use of the Despatches in kindling a flame among the people, and of the flame in extending taxes, armies, and prerogative, are solemn lessons, which I hope will have their proper effect when the infatuation of the moment is over. The management of foreign relations appears to be the most susceptible of abuse of all the trusts committed to a Government, because they can be concealed or disclosed, or disclosed in such parts and at such times as will best suit particular views; and because the body of the people are less capable of judging, and are more under the influence of prejudices, on that branch of their affairs, than of any other. Perhaps it is a universal truth that the loss of liberty at home is to be charged to provisions against danger, real or pretended, from abroad. The credit given to Mr. Adams for a spirit of conciliation towards France is wonderful, when we advert to the history of his irritations, from the first name in the Envoyship, down to his last answer to the addressers. If he finds it thus easy to play on the prepossessions of the people for their own Gov^t against a foreign, we ought not to be disappointed if the same game should have equal success in the hands of the Directory.

We have had little or no rain for a month, and the evil has been increased by much windy and cold weather. The thermometer yesterday morning was at 38°, and the frost such as to kill the leaves of tender trees in low situations. I hope now you will soon be released from the thorny seat in which you are placed, and that I shall not be disappointed of the pleasure of seeing you on your way. You must so arrange your time as to be able to ride a mile while with me to see a threshing-machine I have lately built on Martin's plan.[57] It is worked and attended by five or six hands at most, and I think promises more for general use than all the other modifications. I shall not describe it, because your own inspection will so soon give you a more perfect idea of it. Yours always and affey.

Js MADISON JR.

I recd. no paper by last mail but Fenno's. I hope the bridle is not yet put on the press.

Jefferson to Madison

[Philadelphia] May 17, 1798

My last to you was of the 10th. Since that I have recieved yours of the 5th. I immediately sent a note to Carey to forward his paper to your brother as you desired. The first vote of any importance on the alien bill was taken yesterday. It was on agreeing to the 1st section, which was carried by 12. to 7. If all the Senators in town had been present it would have been 17. to 7. The Provisional army gets along. The Rep. have reduced the 20. to 10. M.[58] They have struck out the clauses for calling out and exercising 20,000 militia at a time. The 1st Volunteer clause has been carried by a great majority. But endeavours will be made to render it less destructive and less injurious to the militia. I shall enclose you a copy of the land-tax bill. In the first moments of the tumults here, mentioned in my last, the cockade assumed by one party was mistaken to be the tricolor. It was the old blue and red adopted in some places in an early part of the revolution war. However it is laid aside. But the black is still frequent. I am a little apprehensive Burr will have miscalculated on Granger's election in Connecticut. However it is not yet known here. It was expected Hillhouse would have been elected their Lt. Govr. but Treadwell is chosen. We know nothing more certain yet of the New York elections. Hamilton

---

57. For Thomas C. Martin's threshing machine, see Edwin M. Betts, ed., *Thomas Jefferson's Farm Book* . . . (Princeton, 1953), pp. 74–75.

58. 10,000.

declined his appointment as Senator, and Jay has named North, a quondam aid of Steuben. All sorts of artifices have been descended to, to agitate the popular mind. The President received 3. anonymous letters (written probably by some of the war men) announcing plots to burn the city on the fast-day. He thought them worth being made known, and great preparations were proposed by the way of caution, and some were yielded to by the Governor. Many weak people packed their most valuable movables to be ready for transportation. However the day passed without justifying the alarms.[59] Other idle stories have been since circulated, and the popular mind has not been proof against them. The addresses and answers go on. Some parts of Maryland and of this state are following the example of N. Jersey. The addresses are probably written here; those which come purely from the country are merely against the French, those written here are pointed with acrimony to party. You will observe one answer in which a most unjustifiable mention has been made of Monroe, without the least occasion leading to it from the address.[60] It is now openly avowed by some of the Eastern men that Congress ought not to separate. And their reasons are drawn from circumstances which will exist through the year. I was in hopes that all efforts to render the sessions of Congress permanent were abandoned. But a clear profit of 3. or 4. Dollars a day is sufficient to reconcile some to their absence from home. A French privateer has lately taken 3. American vessels from York and Phila. bound to England. We do not know their loading, but it has alarmed the merchants much. Wheat and flour are scarcely bought at all. Tobacco, old, of the best quality, has long been 14. D. My respects to Mrs. Madison and to the family. Affectionate adieus to yourself.

P.M. The Provisional army bill has this day passed to it's 3d. reading. The volunteer corps remains a part of it.

Madison to Jefferson

[Orange] May 20, 1798

DEAR SIR

Your favor of the 3d. was acknowledged in my last. I am now to thank you for that of the 10th. You must ascribe my inaccuracy as to the locks and hinges partly to myself and partly to my workman. Four of the doors will be thick eno'

---

59. TJ did not know that the letters warned against plots by resident Frenchmen and domestic traitors, headed by the "grandest of all grand Villains"—"that infernal Scoundrel Jefferson"; see Smith, *Freedom's Fetters,* p. 26.

60. In answering an address from the inhabitants of Lancaster, Pennsylvania, on May 8, 1798, President Adams had called James Monroe "a disgraced minister, recalled in displeasure for misconduct." For the role played by Adams's answers to public addresses in fostering the alien and sedition system, see *ibid.,* pp. 16–21. A selection of Adams's replies is printed in John Adams, *The Works of John Adams,* . . . ed. Charles Francis Adams, 10 vols. (Boston, 1850–56), IX, pp. 182–236.

for mortise locks which I accordingly prefer and of the quality which you think best. Three of the doors will be about 1 ¼ inch thick only. If this thickness be insufficient for the mortise locks, I must get the favor of you to order brass locks of moderate size to be screwed on the outside. There will be also 2 outside folding doors about the thickness of 1 ¾ inch for which I wish you to order such locks and Bolts as you better judgment may chuse. "Spiral hinges" were a misnomer for the dovetail rising hinge. Your objection to that sort is so decisive that I can not hesitate to change it for the 5 inch Butt hinge, showing an iron joint. The 7 doors and two folding doors will require 22 hinges, or 33 if more than two be thought necessary for all the doors, or 30 if more than two for the thick and two only for the 1 ¼ doors. Being disappointed in getting pullies for windows in Fredg, I must extend my tax on your kindness to the procuring that supply also. Three dozen will be wanted, of about 1 ⅜ inch diameter. The brass pullies I suppose are the proper sort, but relying more on your knowledge than my own or my workman's, I must beg you to substitute a better if there be one.

The Alien bill proposed in the Senate is a monster that must forever disgrace its parents. I should not have supposed it possible that such an one could have been engendered in either House, and still persuade myself, that it cannot possibly be fathered by both. It is truly to be deplored that a standing army should be let in upon us by the absence of a few sound votes. It may however all be for the best. These addresses to the feelings of the people from their enemies, may have more effect in opening their eyes, than all the arguments addressed to their understandings by their friends. The President, also, seems to be co-operating for the same purpose. Every answer he gives to his addressers unmasks more and more his principles and views. His language to the young men at Ph^a is the most abominable and degrading that could fall from the lips of the first magistrate of an independent people, and particularly from a Revolutionary patriot. It throws some light on his meaning when he remarked to me, "that there was not a single principle the same in the American and French Revolutions;" and on my alluding to the contrary sentiment of his predecessor expressed to Adêt on the presentment of the Colours, added, "that it was false let who would express it." The abolition of Royalty was it seems not one of his Revolutionary principles. Whether he always made this profession is best known to those, who knew him in the year 1776.

The turn of the elections in N. Y. is a proof that the late occurrences have increased the noise only and not the number of the Tory party. Besides the intrinsic value of the acquisition, it will encourage the hopes and exertions in other States. You will see by the Newspapers the turn which a Townmeeting took in Fredericks^{bg} I forgot to acknowledge the pamphlet containing the last Despatch from the Envoys recd with your letter of the 10th. It is evidently more in the forensic than Diplomatic stile, and more likely in some of its reasonings to satisfy an American Jury than the French Government. The defence of the provision article is the most shallow that has appeared on that subject. In some instances the reasoning is good, but so tedious and tautologous as to insult the understanding as well as patience of the Directory, if really intended for them, and not for the partial ear of the American public.[61] The want of rain begins to be severely felt, and every appearance indicates a continuance of it. Since the 10th of April there has fallen but one inch of water, except a very partial shower of less than ½ an inch. Adieu. Affec.[ly]

Jefferson to Madison

[Philadelphia] May 24, 1798

My last was of the 17th since which yours of the 13th is recieved. The Alien bill of the Senate still hangs before them. Some of it's features have been moderated, which has so much disgusted it's warmest friends that some of them have declared they will vote against it, so that I think it possible they may reject it. They appear to be waiting for one from the house of repr. worse I think than theirs, which got on to it's third reading; but in that stage was recommitted by a majority of 2. yesterday. I suppose it will be softened a little on the recommitment. The Senate yesterday passed their bill for capturing any French cruiser, who shall have taken our vessels, or who shall be found hovering on our coast for that purpose. Sitgreaves's resolutions proposed to the H. of R. of nearly the same tenor were yesterday debated but no question taken. If these bills pass, and place us in a state of war, it may truly be ascribed to the desertion of our members. Of 14. who are absent, 10 are from the republican side of the house. Had every one been in his place not a single one of the dangerous measures carried or to be carried would have prevailed. Even the provisional army would have been rejected, for it was carried but by a majority of 11. The absentees are Freeman, Skinner, Livingston, S. Smith, Nicholas, Giles, Cabell, Clay, Finlay, and Swanwick sick. The news from Amsterdam from our Consul Bourne, which you will see in the papers, has every appearance of truth. The war men however are very unwilling to have it believed. The flame kindled by the late communications, has from the nature of them, and the unparalleled industry of the war party, spread more even in the country than I had expected. Addresses continue to be poured in on us. I mentioned in my last the P's attack on Monroe. His friends here think that nothing can save him from the impression of that, but his coming into the H. of R. taking his stand on that independent theatre, from which his countrymen will see what are his principles. It has been said Cabell will give place to him. On that hypothesis I have counselled him strongly to come to the next session. Such a recruit is immensely wanted here. It is believed we have gained 2. members in

---

61. JM referred to John Marshall's reply to Talleyrand of Jan. 27, 1798, which President Adams had transmitted to Congress on May 4, 1798; see Bowman, p. 329.

the N. York election. Salutations to the family and friendly Adieu to yourself.

Mr. Adams in conversation in the Statehouse yard with Blair McLanachan, declared that such was his want of confidence in the faith of France, that were they to agree to a treaty ever so favorable, he should think it his duty to reject it.

P.M. Sitgreaves' resolns. were moved to be postponed to a very distant day in June. The question was this day lost 53. to 40. Had all been here it would have been carried.

Tracy (one of the war-commte. of the Senate) told Anderson yesterday that he had drawn a bill for declaring our Treaty with France void and commencing hostilities, but the commee. thought the bill now past by the Senate would answer the same end and give less alarm.

Stockton told Tazewell yesterday he should be for a declaration of war before Congress should separate. It is now declared by several Senators that they would not accept any treaty which France could offer.

Madison to Jefferson

[Orange] May 27, 1798

DEAR SIR,

I have duly recd. yours of the 17th, accompanied by the Direct tax bill, which I have not yet been able to run thro'. Everything I perceive is carried as the war party chuse. They will of course be the more responsible for consequences. The disposition to continue the Session is a proof that the operation of the irritating proceedings here on those of France is expected to furnish fresh fuel for the popular flame and to favor the success of the Executive projects in the Legislature. It is to be deplored that we have no authentic and impartial channel thro' which the true state of things in Europe, particularly in France, can reach the public mind of this Country. The present temper of the Envoys cannot fail to discolour all that passes thro' them; and if this were not the case, the obvious policy of the Ex. is a compleat bar to the disclosure of all other than inflammatory communications.

The inclosed accurate and authentic view of that "stupendous fabric of human wisdom" which Mr. A. idolizes so much, deserves I think the public attention at the present moment. At the request of Callender, I promised several years ago to send it to him, but never could lay my hand on it till a few days ago when it fell in my way without being sought for.[62] If you have an oppy, and think it worth while, you can let the public have a sight of it; and for

---

62. In his response, TJ called JM's paper on the British constitution "the petition for the reform of the British parliament"; see TJ to JM, June 7, 1798, below. It was probably a *Petition praying for a Reform in Parliament, presented to the House of Commons by Charles Grey, Esq. on Monday, 6th May, 1793 . . . ,"* in *PJM*, XVII, p. 138.

the reason just mentioned, I could wish if there be no objection that it might pass thro' his hands. As the paper is of some value, it may be well to preserve it, in case it should not be republished, or in case a part only should be so.

There have been pretty extensive, but not universal rains since my last. This neighbourhood has been but barely touched by them. I have not heard from yours. Adieu. Affely.

J M Jr.

Jefferson to Madison

Philadelphia May 31, 1798

I wrote to you last on the 24th, since which yours of the 20th is recieved. I must begin by correcting two errors in my last. It was false arithmetic to say that two measures therein mentioned to be carried by majorities of 11., would have failed if the 14. absentees (wherein a majority of 6 was ours) had been present. Six coming over from the other side would have turned the scale, and this was the idea floating in my mind, which produced the mistake. The 2d error was in the version of Mr. A's expression, which I stated to you. His real expression was 'that he would not unbrace a single nerve for any treaty France could offer; such was their entire want of faith, morality,' etc.

The bill from the Senate for capturing French armed vessels found hovering on our coast was past in two days by the lower house without a single alteration; and the Ganges, a 20-gun sloop fell down the river instantly to go on a cruise. She has since been ordered to New York, to convoy a vessel from that to this port. The Alien bill will be ready to day, probably, for it's 3d. reading in the Senate. It has been considerably mollified, particularly by a proviso saving the rights of treaties. Still it is a most detestable thing. I was glad in yesterday's discussion to hear it admitted on all hands that laws of the U S subsequent to a treaty, controul it's operation, and that the legislature is the only power which can controul a treaty. Both points are sound beyond doubt. This bill will unquestionably pass the H. of R, the majority there being decisive, consolidated, and bold enough to do anything. I have no doubt from the hints dropped, they will pass a bill to declare the French treaty void. I question if they will think a declaration of war prudent, as it might alarm, and all it's effects are answered by the act authorizing captures. A bill is brought in for suspending all communication with the dominions of France, which will no doubt pass. It is suspected they mean to borrow money of individuals in London, on the credit of our land tax, and perhaps the guarantee of Gt Britain. The land tax was yesterday debated, and a majority of 6. struck out the 13th. section for the classification of houses and taxing them by a different scale from the lands. Instead of this is to be proposed a valuation of the houses and lands together. Macon yesterday laid a motion on the table for adjourning on the 14th. Some think they do not mean to adjourn; others, that they wait first the return of the envoys, for whom it is now avowed the brig Sophia was sent. It is expected she would bring them off about the middle of this month. They may therefore be expected here about the 2d week of July. Whatever be their decision as to adjournment, I think it probable my next letter will convey orders for my horses and that I shall leave this place from the 20th to the 25th of June; for I have no expectation they will actually adjourn sooner. Volney and a ship-load of others sail on Sunday next. Another ship-load will go off in about 3. weeks. It is natural to expect they go under irritations calculated to fan the flame. Not so Volney. He is most thoroughly impressed with the importance of preventing war, whether considered with reference to the interests of the two countries, of the cause of republicanism, or of man on the broad scale. But an eagerness to render this prevention impossible leaves me without any hope. Some of those who have insisted that it was long since war on the part of France, are candid enough to admit that it is now begun on our part also.

I enclose for your perusal a poem on the alien bill, written by Mr. Marshall. I do this as well for your amusement as to get you to take care of this copy for me till I return; for it will be lost by lending, if I retain it here, as the publication was suppressed after the sale of a few copies, of which I was fortunate enough to get one. Your locks, hinges, etc., shall be immediately attended to. My respectful salutations and friendship to Mrs. Madison, to the family, and to yourself. Adieu.

P. S. The President, it is said, has refused an Exequatur to the Consul General of France, Dupont.[63]

P. P. S. This fact is true. I have it this moment from Dupont, and he goes off with Volney to France in two or three days.

Madison to Jefferson

[Orange] June 3, 1798

DEAR SIR,

Friday's mail brought me your favor of May 24. The letter from S. Bourne had previously reached us thro' a Fred^g paper. It is corroborated I find by several accounts from different sources. These rays in the prospect will if I can judge from the sensations in this quarter, have an effect on the people very different from that which appears in the public councils. Whilst it was expected

---

63. Victor du Pont had been transferred from Charleston to the Philadelphia consulate to succeed Joseph Philippe Letombe as consul general, but President Adams refused to grant him an exequatur; see Bowman, p. 322.

that the unrelenting temper of France would bring on war, the mask of peace was worn by the war party. Now that a contrary appearance on the side of France is intimated, the mask is dropped, and the lye openly given to their own professions by pressing measures which must force France into War. I own I am not made very sanguine by the reported amendment in the posture of our Negociators, first because the account may not be very correct, and next because there are real difficulties to be overcome, as well as those which the pride of one or other of the parties may create, not to mention the probable arrival of what has passed here before the scene is closed there. But the palpable urgency of the Ex. and its partizans to press war in proportion to the apparent chance of avoiding it, ought to open every eye to the hypocrisy which has hitherto deceived so many good people. Should no such consequence take place it will be a proof of infatuation which does not admit of human remedy. It is said, and there are circumstances which make me believe it, that the hot-headed proceedings of Mr. A. are not well relished in the cool climate of Mount Vernon.[64] This I think may fairly be inferred from the contrast of characters and conduct, but if it has been expressed it must have been within a very confidential circle. Since my last there has been a sequel of fine and extensive rains. We have had a tolerable, tho' not an equal or sufficient share of them. Your neighbourhood I fancy has fared better.

If Barnes has not sent off the Glass pullies etc. please to order as much of the proper chord as will be wanted for the latter. Very aff^y y^r

Js. M. Jr.

Jefferson to Madison

Philadelphia June 7, 1798

I wrote you last on the 31st. since which yours of the 27th. of May is received. The alien bill when we had nearly got through it, on the 2d reading (on a report from the committee of the whole) was referred to a special committee. by a vote of it's friends (12) against 11. who thought it could be rejected on the question for the 3d reading. It is reported again very much softened, and if the proviso can be added to it, saving treaties, it will be less objectionable than I thought it possible to have obtained. Still it would place aliens not protected by treaties under absolute government. They have brought into the lower house a sedition bill, which among other enormities, undertakes to make printing certain matters criminal, tho' one of the amendments to the Constitution has so expressly taken religion, printing presses etc. out of their coercion. Indeed this bill and the Alien bill both are so palpably in

---

64. JM was wrong about Washington's attitude. Washington supported the Federalist domestic and foreign policies, and soon headed the army being raised; see Marshall Smelser, "George Washington and the Alien and Sedition Laws," *AHR* 59 (1954): 322–34.

the teeth of the constitution as to shew they mean to pay no respect to it. The citizen bill passed by the lower house sleeps in a Committee of the Senate.[65] In the mean time Callendar, a principal object of it, has eluded it, by getting himself made a citizen. Volney is gone. So is Dupont, the rejected consul. The bill suspending intercourse with the French dominions will pass the Senate today with a small amendment. The real object of this bill is to evade the counter-irritations of the English who under the late orders for taking all vessels from French ports, are now taking as many of our vessels as the French. By forbidding our vessels to go to or from French ports we remove the pabulum for these violations of our rights by the English, undertaking to do the work for them ourselves in another way. The tax on lands, houses and slaves is still before the H. of R. They have determined to have the houses and lands valued separately though to pay the same tax ad valorem, but they avow that when they shall have got at the number and value of houses, they shall be free hereafter to tax houses separately, as by an indirect tax. This is to avoid the quotaing of which they cannot bear the idea. Rogueries under a quotaing law can only shift the burthen from one part to another of the same state; but relieve them from the bridle of the quota and all rogueries go to the relief of the states. So odious is the quota to the N. E. members that many think they will not pass the bill at all. The question of adjournment was lost by two votes. Had our members been here it would have been carried and much mischief prevented. I think now they will make their session permanent. I have therefore in my letters of today ordered my horses to be at Fredsbg on the 24.th and shall probably be with you on the 25th or 26th. I send you further communications from our envoys. To these I believe I may add on good grounds that Pinckney is gone with his family into the south of France for the health of his daughter, Marshal to Amsterdam (but whether coming here for instructions or not is a secret not entrusted to us) and Gerry remains at Paris. It is rumored and I believe with probability that there is a schism between Gerry and his colleagues. Perhaps the directory may make a treaty with Gerry, if they can get through it before the brig Sophia takes him off. She sailed the 1st of April. It is evident from these communications that our envoys have not the least idea of a war between the two countries; much less than their dispatches are the cause of it. I mentioned to you in my last that I expected they would bring in a bill to declare the treaty with France void. Dwight Foster yesterday brought in resolutions for that purpose, and for authorizing general reprisals on the French armed vessels: and such is their preponderance by the number and talents of our absentees withdrawing from us that they will carry it.[66] Never was any event so important to this country since it's revolution, as the issue of the invasion of England. With that we shall stand or fall.

    Colo. Innes's situation is desperate. Every day now is expected to be his

---

65. The "citizen bill" became the Naturalization Act of 1798; see Smith, *Freedom's Fetters,* pp. 22–49, 435–38.

66. Congress formally abrogated the Franco-American treaties of 1778 on July 7, 1798.

last. The petition for the reform of the British parliament enclosed in your last shall be disposed of as you desire. And the first vessel for Fredericksburg will carry your locks, hinges, pullies and glass. My respectful salutations to Mrs. Madison and the family, and friendship and Adieus to yourself.

Madison to Jefferson

[Orange] June 10, 1798

DEAR SIR,

I have duly recd. your favor of the 31 Ult: and am glad to find mine are recd as regularly as yours. The law for capturing French privateers may certainly be deemed a formal commencement of hostilities, and renders all hope of peace vain, unless a progress in amicable arrangements at Paris not to be expected, should have secured it agst the designs of our Goverm! If the Bill suspending commerce with the French Dominions passes as it doubtless will, the French Government will be confirmed in their suspicion begotten by the British Treaty, of our coalition in the project of starving their people; and the effect of the measure will be to feed the English at the expence of the farmers of this Country. Already flour is down, I hear at 4 dollars a barrel. How far the views of the Gov! will be answd by annihilating the ability to pay a land tax at the very moment of imposing it, will be best explained by the experim! Looking beyond the present moment it may be questioned whether the interest of G. B. will be as much advanced by the sacrifice of our trade with her enemies as may be intended. The use of her manufactures here depends on our means of payment, and these on the sale of our produce to the markets of her enemies. There is too much passion, it seems in our Councils to calculate consequences of any sort. The only hope is that its violence by defeating itself may save the Country. The answers of Mr. Adams to his addressers form the most grotesque scene in the tragicomedy acting by the Goverm! They present not only the grossest contradictions to the maxims measures and language of his predecessor and the real principles and interests of his Constituents, but to himself. He is verifying compleatly the last feature in the character drawn of him by Dr. F. however his title may stand to the two first, "Always an honest man, often a wise one, but sometimes wholly out of his senses."

I thank you for the offspring of the Senatorial Muse, which shall be taken care of. It is truly an unique. It is not even prose run mad.

Monroe is much at a loss what course to take in consequence of the wicked assault on him by Mr. A. and I am as much so as to the advice that ought to be given him. It deserves consideration perhaps that if the least occasion be furnished for reviving Governmental attention to him, the spirit of party revenge may be wreaked thro' the forms of the Constitution. A majority in the H. of R. and ⅔ of the Senate seem to be ripe for everything. A temperate and dignified animadversion on the proceeding, published with his name, as an appeal to the candor and justice of his fellow Citizens, agst the wanton and unmanly treatment, might perhaps be of use. But it w^d be difficult to execute it in a manner to do justice to himself, and inflict it on his adversary, without clashing with the temper of the moment. Hoping for the pleasure of congratulating you soon, on your release from your painful situation, I close with the most affectionate assurance that I am yours

J M JR.

Jefferson to Madison

[Philadelphia] June 14, 1798

I wrote you last on the 7th since which yours of the 3d. is recieved. Your next (which I shall still be here to recieve) will probably acknolege mine of May 31. and will perhaps be your last as you could see by mine of the 7th. that I should leave this on the 20th. which I still propose. The new citizen or naturalization bill is past the Senate also. It requires 14 years residence to make a citizen. It had friends in both parties. The Whigs apprehended that the success of the invasion of England would drive all their aristocracy here. Their opponents believing still in the final failure of the revolution of France and the safety of England, apprehended a deluge of the democrats of both countries. We were within one vote however in the Senate of striking out *14* years and inserting *7*. Langdon who would have been for it had previously declined voting on the bill at all, because he had just taken his seat. His vote would have divided the Senate 12. and 12. The bill for suspending intercourse with the French dominions is signed by the President. The bill for assessing lands houses and slaves came up to the Senate yesterday. The classification of houses had been struck out of it. The second bill, for laying the tax on these subjects, is still before the R. The Senate have brought in a bill authorizing the President to accept of any number of armed vessels, not exceeding 12, and carrying not less than 22. nine pounders, which any individual may build and cede on terms he shall approve, by way of loan. But neither the terms as to interest or paiment of the principal, nor the maximum of size are limited, but a proposition to limit was rejected. Some treated the apprehension that large ships might be obtained as chimerical, while others wished they might be all of the line, and at least 3, 4, or a half a dozen 74s. This bill is in fact to open a loan in the form of ships. Harper has brought in resolutions for authorizing the President to borrow money for the excess of this year's expenses, above the taxes. No other limitation of sum. I do not believe we can borrow any considerable sum but in London. Some think the bank of the US. may lend as far as a couple of millions. The opinion of their connection with the government has already sunk their shares from 23. to 20. while those of Pennsylvania have risen from 23. to 29. above par. The British captures of our vessels have multiplied greatly. Our stopping intercourse with France will keep that portion of our vessels out of their way. They will still take those bound to Dutch and Spanish ports.

The committees of the two houses appointed jointly to propose a time of adjournment have not yet reported; so that it is still uncertain whether and when they will adjourn. My horses are to meet me at Fredericksburg on Sunday the 24th. Whether I can reach you the next day is uncertain. Probably not. Innes is still living. He has been carried into the country.

The window cord shall be added to the other articles. No vessel for Fredericksburg has yet occurred. This of course will be my last to you from hence. Friendly salutations to Mrs Madison, the family and yourself and affectionately Adieu.

P.S. Flour at Baltimore 4.50 D. here 5 D. The farmers of this state have almost universally their last year's crop wheat and flour still in their own hands.

P.M. The joint committee for adjournmt have reported that they think it not improbable that Congress may adjourn from the middle of July to the 1st. of October, but they do not think it prudent to fix a day at present.

Jefferson to Madison

Philadelphia June 21, 1798

Yours of the 10th inst is recieved. I expected mine of the 14th. would have been my last from hence, as I had proposed to have set out on the 20th. But on the morning of the 19th, we heard of the arrival of Marshall at New York, I concluded to stay and see whether that circumstance would produce any new projects. No doubt he there recieved more than hints from Hamilton as to the tone required to be assumed. Yet I apprehend he is not hot enough for his friends. Livingston came with him from New York. M. told him they had no idea in France of a war with us. That Taleyrand sent passports to him and Pinckney, but none for Gerry. Upon this, Gerry staid, without explaining to them the reason. He wrote however to the President by Marshall, who knew nothing of the contents of the letter. So that there must have been a previous understanding between Taleyrand and Gerry. M. was received here with the utmost eclat. The Secretary of state and many carriages, with all the city cavalry, went to Frankfort to meet him, and on his arrival here in the evening, the bells rung till late in the night, and immense crowds were collected to see and make part of the shew, which was circuitously paraded through the streets before he was set down at the city tavern. All this was to secure him to their views, that he might say nothing which would expose the game they have been playing. Since his arrival I can hear of nothing directly from him, while they are disseminating through the town things, as from him, diametrically opposite to what he said to Livingston. Dr Logan, about a fortnight ago, sailed for Hamburg. Tho for a twelvemonth past he had been intending to [go to] Europe as soon as he could get money enough to carry him there, yet when he had accomplished this, and fixed a time for going, he very unwisely made a mystery of it, so that his disappearance without notice excited conversation. This was seized by the war-hawks, and given out as a secret mission from the Jacobins here to sollicit an army from France, instruct them as to their landing etc. This extravagance produced a real panic among the citizens, and happening just when Bache published Taleyrand's letter, Harper on the 18th gravely announced to the H. R. that there existed a traitorous correspondence between the Jacobins here and the French Directory; that he had got hold of some threads and clues of it, and would soon be able to develope the whole. This increased the alarm; their libellists immediately set to work, directly and indirectly to implicate whom they pleased. Porcupine gave me a principal share in it as I am told, for I never read his papers. This state of things added to my reasons for not departing at the time I intended. These follies seem to have died away in some degree already.[67] Perhaps I may renew my purpose by the 25th. Their system is professedly to keep up an alarm. Tracy at the meeting of the joint committee for adjournment declared it necessary for Congress to stay together to keep up the inflammation of the public mind, and Otis expressed a similar sentiment since. However they will adjourn. The opposers of adjournment in Senate, yesterday agreed to adjourn on the 10th. of July. But I think the 1st. of July will be carried. That is one of the objects which detains myself as well as one or two more of the Senate who had got leave of absence. I imagine it will be decided to-morrow or next day. To separate Congress now will be withdrawing the fire from under a boiling pot.

Your commissions here are all in readiness, but no vessel for Fredericksburg has yet occurred. My respectful salutations to Mrs. Madison, and the family, and cordial friendship to yourself.

P. M. A message to both houses this day from the Pr. with the following communications.

Mar. 23. Pickering's letter to the envoys directing them if they are not actually engaged in negociation with authorized persons, or not conducted bona fide and not merely for procrastination, to break up and come home, and at any rate to consent to no loan.

Apr 3. Talleyrand to Gerry. He supposes the other two gentlemen, perceiving that their known principles are an obstacle to negociation, will leave the republic, and proposing to renew the negociations with Gerry immediately.

---

67. For a balanced discussion of Logan's peace mission, see Frederick B. Tolles, "Unofficial Ambassador: George Logan's Mission to France, 1798," *WMQ* 7 (1950): 3-25.

Apr 4. Gerry to Taleyrand. Disclaims a power to conclude anything separately, can only confer informally and as an unaccredited individual, reserving to lay everything before the government of the U S. for approbation.

Apr 14. Gerry to the President. He communicates the preceding and hopes the President will send other persons instead of his collegues and himself, if it shall appear that anything can be done.

The President's message says that as the instructions were not to consent to any loan, he considers the negociation as at an end; and that he will never send another minister to France until he shall be assured that he will be received and treated with the respect due to a great, powerful, free and independant nation.

A bill is brought into the Senate this day, to declare the treaties with France void, prefaced by a list of grievances in the style of a manifesto. It passed to the 2d. reading by 14. to 5.

A bill for punishing forgeries of bank paper, passed to the 3d. reading by 14 to 6. Three of the 14. (Laurence, Bingham and Read) bank directors.

24

THE KENTUCKY AND VIRGINIA RESOLUTIONS AND AMERICAN CIVIL LIBERTIES, 1798–1799

BY JUNE 27, 1798, Jefferson had had enough. After the XYZ disclosures, he had watched as repressive actions directed against domestic disaffection were drafted and defended in Congress as measures of national defense. Through April, May, and June, as the policy of proscription unfolded, he had stuck to his post, serving as "a fair mark for every man's dirt."[1] "You should know the rancorous passions which tear every breast here," he told his daughter, "even of the sex which should be a stranger to them. Politics and party hatreds destroy the happiness of every being here. They seem, like salamanders, to consider fire as their element." After the alien bills were introduced, he wrote: "I never was more home-sick, or heart-sick. The life of this place is peculiarly hateful to me, and nothing but a sense of duty and respect to the public could keep me here a moment."[2]

But he swallowed his pride and was forced by virtue of his position as presiding officer of the Senate to sign the Alien Friends Act, a bill that he later called "that libel on legislation."[3] Determined not to be a party to a sedition law designed to throttle political discussion in the critical years before the election of 1800, he decided to leave the capital after concluding that "my presence here is useless to the public." Having "neither ears to hear, eyes to see, or tongue to speak, but as the Senate direct me," he could do nothing to turn the tide which seemed to him to threaten civil liberty, freedom of political action, and constitutional government. In such a helpless situation, his son-in-

---

1. TJ to Peregrine Fitzhugh, Feb. 23, 1798, in Ford, VII, p. 208.
2. TJ to Martha Jefferson Randolph, May 17, 1798, Edgehill-Randolph Papers, University of Virginia, and TJ to John Wayles Eppes, May 6, 1798, *ibid*.
3. TJ to Joseph Priestley, Mar. 21, 1801, in Ford, VIII, p. 22.

law responded, no one could expect him to remain only "to behold the detestable triumph of principles which your heart has always abhorred and your head opposed."[4]

As he boarded the stage for his long journey home, Jefferson carried two indelible impressions with him. On the day before, the Federalists, without waiting for Congress to pass a sedition law, had arrested Benjamin Franklin Bache, editor of the nation's leading Jeffersonian newspaper, for seditious criticism of the president and executive government, boldly claiming federal common-law jurisdiction over the alleged crime. On the same day, the vice president had presided over the Senate and listened in shocked silence as Senator James Lloyd's draconic treason and sedition bill was read in the Senate.

Although President Adams had not called for a declaration of war against France nor had Congress voted such a declaration, Lloyd designated the government and people of France as enemies of the United States and declared that adherence to them or giving them aid and comfort was treason—the first and only time in American history that a legislative attempt has been made to establish by law the concept of treason in peacetime. Another section of the bill branded as "seditious or inflammatory" any expressions tending to produce a belief among the citizenry that the federal government had been led to pass any law by motives "hostile to the constitution, or liberties and happiness of the people." Fine and imprisonment would await any person who attempted to defame the president or any federal court by declarations "directly or indirectly tending to criminate their motives in any official transactions."[5]

In a parting shot laden with sarcasm, the Federalist *Gazette of the United States* urged the vice president to reconsider his decision to depart. "Pray stay a little longer and aid the public councils with your wisdom; leave not your country at this critical period when it is seeking the most effectual means of self-preservation." Doubtful that such patriotic motives would persuade Jefferson "to tarry a day or two," "Pliny" suggested that the vice president consider the reeling Republican cause: "Recollect that your friend Bache is just now prosecuted for some of his many false and scandalous stories concerning the Government of the United States which he has published in the Aurora—the same newspaper . . . which your fellow laborers in the iniquitous work of alienating the affections and confidence of the people from the administration of their government, have used for their engine—the same," the writer concluded ominously, which possessed "a direct intercourse with the office of

---

4. TJ to Thomas Mann Randolph, May 24, 1798, Jefferson Papers, Library of Congress, and Thomas Mann Randolph to TJ, June 10, 1798, Edgehill-Randolph Papers, University of Virginia. For the relationship between Randolph and TJ, see William H. Gaines, Jr., *Thomas Mann Randolph: Jefferson's Son-in-Law* (Baton Rouge, 1966).

5. For the Bache indictment, see James Morton Smith, *Freedom's Fetters: The Alien and Sedition Laws and American Civil Liberties* (Ithaca, N.Y., 1956), pp. 196–204. For Lloyd's bill, see *ibid.*, pp. 107–10.

foreign affairs at Paris." "A friend in need," the author twitted, "is a friend indeed."[6]

Jefferson had predicted that the suppression of Republican presses—Bache's in particular—was the object of any sedition legislation passed by the Federalists.[7] Lloyd's sedition bill, amended by striking out the section on treason, passed the Senate as Philadelphia celebrated the Fourth of July. Senator Stevens Thomson Mason of Virginia informed Jefferson that debate was drowned out by "the drums Trumpets and other martial music which surrounded us." Most of the Federalist senators watched the military parade "with their bodies out of the windows and could not be kept to order." But when the Republicans attempted to postpone the question or adjourn, the Federalists rejected both moves and voted for the bill despite the "uproar and confusion." "Its passage through the Senate," Senator Henry Tazewell of Virginia lamented, "is an unauspicious event to have happened on the 4th of July." But, as Mason pointed out, "there seemed to be a particular solicitude to pass it on that day."[8]

In the House debates on Lloyd's sedition bill, John Allen of Connecticut tried to link the vice president to Bache, whose articles, he charged, were "the tocsin of insurrection." *Porcupine's Gazette* also implicated Jefferson as a confidential adviser to the indicted newspaperman; both were part of a treasonable conspiracy that constituted an internal threat to the nation. Leaving Jefferson unnamed, Allen repeated the charges in the House in an innuendo understood by all: "I do not walk the streets arm-in-arm, I hold no midnight conference, I am not daily and nightly closeted with the editor."[9]

When Samuel Smith, a Republican congressman from Maryland, called his attention to the accusation, Jefferson gave a factual reply to the charge of being closeted with Bache and others. "If the receipt of visits in my public room, the door continuing free to every one who should call at the same time, may be called *closeting*, then it is true that I was *closeted* with every person who visited me; in no other sense is it true as to any person." He readily admitted that he occasionally received visits from Bache, a man of ability "and of principles the most friendly to liberty and our present form of government. Mr. Bache," he added, "has another claim on my respect, as being the grandson of Dr. Franklin, the greatest man and ornament of the age and country in which he lived." Although Jefferson despised the vilification poured on him by Porcupine, Fenno, and others, he needed no sedition law to shield him from

---

6. "Pliny" to TJ, June 26, 1798, in the Philadelphia *Gazette of the United States* (June 27, 1798).

7. TJ to JM, Apr. 26, 1798, May 3, 1798, and June 7, 1798, above.

8. Henry Tazewell to TJ, July 5, 1798, and Stevens Thomson Mason to TJ, July 6, 1798, quoted in Smith, p. 111. After the Senate struck out the treason provisions in Lloyd's bill, the author worked unsuccessfully for "a declaration of war, which I look upon as necessary to enable us to lay our hands on traitors"; see James Lloyd to George Washington, July 4, 1798, *ibid.*, p. 110.

9. On this episode, see *ibid.*, pp. 113–19.

criticism. He thought it "an injury to which duty requires every one to submit whom the public think proper to call to it's councils," and he, therefore, refused "to suffer calumny to disturb my tranquility."[10]

More than any other letter he wrote in 1798, Jefferson's reply to Congressman Smith shows the deep impression that the Federalist system of repression had made on him for his personal safety. The continuing attempt to implicate him with Bache demonstrated again that "the spirit of party hostility and rage" was more virulent than ever. In an extraordinary testament, he informed Smith of his firm resolution to meet any assault on the principles of freedom or his own personal integrity without flinching. He had always willingly expressed his political principles to everyone. "They are the same I have acted on from the year 1775 to this day, and are the same, I am sure, with those of the great body of the American people."

But Jefferson believed that the Federalists were deluding the people and would press their temporary majority so hard that it would create "much particular mischief. There is no event, therefore, however atrocious, which may not be expected. I have contemplated every event which the Maratists of the day can perpetrate," he concluded, "and am prepared to meet every one in such a way, as shall not be derogatory either to the public liberty or my own personal honor."[11]

In such a defiant mood, Jefferson began preparing his attack on the repressive Alien and Sedition Laws, an effort designed to rally the American people to "rejudge those who, at present, think they have all judgment in their own hands."[12] Three of these laws had been enacted while Jefferson was presiding over the Senate. The Naturalization Act nearly tripled the residence requirement for aliens to become naturalized citizens, raising it from five to fourteen years.[13] The Alien Enemies Law became a permanent wartime statute but was not invoked at this time since Congress did not declare war against France. The Act Concerning Aliens, sometimes called the Alien Friends Law, was designed for the temporary crisis with France and could be used in peace or war. It gave the president extraordinary power over aliens, establishing guilt by suspicion for a two-year period and authorizing the chief executive to order the deportation of any foreigner he deemed dangerous to the peace and safety of the United States or whom he suspected of being concerned in treasonable

10. TJ to Samuel Smith, Aug. 22, 1798, in Ford, VII, pp. 275–80.

11. *Ibid.* Jean-Paul Marat, a vitriolic journalist during the French Revolution, "invented the language of the Terror," erased the line between political opposition and treason, and demanded a purge of "200,000 heads." See François Furet and Mona Ozauf, eds., *A Critical Dictionary of the French Revolution* (Cambridge, Mass., 1989), pp. 137–50, 244–51.

12. Ford, VII, p. 278.

13. TJ wrote JM that "we were within one vote . . . in the Senate of striking out *14* years and inserting *7.*" Had that vote been given, it would have divided the Senate evenly, and TJ, as the tiebreaker, would have voted for the shorter term; see TJ to JM, June 14, 1798, above.

or secret machinations against the government. The Sedition Law, which Congress passed after Jefferson had returned to Monticello, was aimed at "internal enemies" and "domestic traitors" who published "false, scandalous, and malicious writing or writings" against the government, Congress, or the president, or sought to bring them into contempt or disrepute or to excite against them the hatred of the people of the United States. It was to expire on March 3, 1801, the final day of Adams's administration.[14]

While Jefferson remained in Philadelphia, he and Madison had corresponded about the progress of the Federalists' system of political intolerance, which was aimed at the Republican party, Republican congressmen, and Republican newspapers. On his way home, Jefferson stopped at Montpellier on July 2 and 3, where the two friends had plenty of time to review "the reign of witches" and discuss the most effective means of protest.[15] In all probability, they discussed two sets of resolutions challenging the constitutionality of the Alien and Sedition Laws, with Jefferson assigned the responsibility of writing the set for North Carolina and Madison agreeing to write the Virginia resolutions; Jefferson later agreed to send his set to Kentucky.[16] As he had in the case of the Cabell presentment by federal grand jurors, Jefferson proposed to use the state legislatures as the most effective and least vulnerable mouthpieces for the protests, leaving the authors unknown except to the middlemen who introduced the resolutions. Indeed, he renewed his attack on the Cabell presentment by drafting a new petition that urged the Virginia legislature to reform its method of jury selection so that both grand juries and trial juries remained "the true tribunal of the people."

To replace the policy of allowing state courts or their agents to select jurors, he proposed the popular election of a pool of jurors in districts, with assignment to particular juries to be made by lot as necessary. Since the federal judiciary law followed state practices, he thought it likely that federal grand jurors might also become elective in Virginia if the state altered its laws, thereby affording further protection to "persecuted man."[17] Thus, the Virginia and Kentucky resolutions were a continuation of the campaign to defend civil liberties and protect the rights of opposition parties launched the previous year after the presentment of Congressman Cabell.[18]

14. The laws are printed in Smith, pp. 435–42. See also Marshall Smelser, "The Jacobin Phrenzy: Federalism and the Menace of Liberty, Equality, and Fraternity," *Review of Politics* 13 (1951): 457–82.

15. TJ used this phrase in his letter to John Taylor, June 4, 1798, in *Massachusetts Historical Society Collections* 7th ser., 1 (1900): 61–64.

16. For TJ's linking of North Carolina with Virginia, see *ibid*. For TJ's approval for directing the resolutions to Kentucky, see TJ to Wilson Cary Nicholas, Oct. 5, 1798, in Ford, VII, pp. 281–82.

17. TJ to JM, Oct. 26, 1798, below, encloses TJ's petition on the election of jurors.

18. See Adrienne Koch and Harry Ammon, "The Virginia and Kentucky Resolutions: An Episode in Jefferson and Madison's Defense of Civil Liberties," *WMQ* 5 (1948): 152–54.

Except for Jefferson's stopover with the Madisons on July 2 and 3, the two friends exchanged neither visits nor letters until late October.[19] But they read the newspapers carefully and received periodic reports from senators and congressmen, learning about the common-law indictments of Bache and John Daly Burk, editor of the New York *Time Piece,* both charged prior to the enactment of the Sedition Law.[20] On July 12, Senator Tazewell sent Jefferson the final text of the Sedition Law passed by Congress; it arrived at Monticello at the end of July.

Although Jefferson had consistently stated that the war fever would generate its own remedy, the repressive language of the Sedition Act forced him to reconsider his passive policy. Without waiting for any indictments under the Alien or the Sedition Law, Jefferson began composing his resolutions of protest, completing them by the end of September. As he had in the 1797 presentment petition, he seems to have drafted the resolutions without consulting anyone, then submitted them to his neighbor Wilson Cary Nicholas, a member of the Virginia Senate and the only Virginian to know the exact tenor of the resolutions before they left the state. Intended for North Carolina, the resolutions were diverted to Kentucky when Nicholas gave them to John Breckinridge, a former neighbor of Jefferson's, now a member of the Kentucky legislature, who was visiting friends in Albemarle County. Before leaving Kentucky, Breckinridge had spearheaded a grass-roots protest movement against the suppressive legislation, and he was confident that the Kentucky legislature would adopt Jefferson's resolutions. Nicholas relied on his judgment, and so did Jefferson. "I entirely approve of the confidence you have reposed in Mr. Brackinridge," he told Nicholas, characteristically misspelling his former neighbor's name, "as he possesses mine entirely."[21] Breckinridge gave solemn assurances that Jefferson's name as author would be kept secret.

In his letter approving these arrangements, Jefferson suggested that Nicholas show the resolutions to Madison, whom Nicholas planned to visit. "You know of course that I have no secrets from him," Jefferson added. "I wish him therefore to be consulted as to these resolutions."[22] However, illness prevented Nicholas from visiting Madison before Breckinridge took the draft to

---

19. Adrienne Koch, *Jefferson and Madison: The Great Collaboration* (New York, 1950), p. 187, suggests that "there were probably frequent meetings and secret messages exchanged, which may have been instantly destroyed and were never recorded in Jefferson's epistolary ledger, in order to guard the secrecy they so much required."

20. For the *Burk* case, see Smith, pp. 204-20. TJ dismissed the Federalist claim that the federal courts had common-law jurisdiction without specific legislative action as an "audacious, barefaced and sweeping pretention"; see TJ to Edmund Randolph, Aug. 18, 1799, in Ford, VII, pp. 383-84.

21. TJ to Wilson Cary Nicholas, Oct. 5, 1798, *ibid.,* pp. 281-82. See also James Morton Smith, "The Grass Roots Origins of the Kentucky Resolutions," *WMQ* 27 (1970): 237-38, and Lowell Harrison, *John Breckinridge, Jeffersonian Republican* (Louisville, 1969), pp. 75-78. Breckinridge later served as attorney general in TJ's cabinet.

22. TJ to Wilson Cary Nicholas, Oct. 5, 1798, in Ford, VII, pp. 281-82.

Kentucky,[23] so Madison did not read them until he visited Jefferson late in October.[24] At about the same time, Jefferson informed Senator Stevens Thomson Mason that he thought "some of the State legislatures will take strong ground" against the Alien and Sedition Laws.[25]

Considering the Sedition Law to be "a nullity as absolute and as palpable as if Congress had ordered us to fall down and worship a golden image,"[26] Jefferson denounced the Federalist legislation as unconstitutional usurpations of rights reserved to the states or to the people. The Constitution ratified by the states was not based on the principle of unlimited submission to the federal government. Only enumerated powers had been delegated to the general government. Whenever that government assumed powers not delegated to it, therefore, its acts were "unauthoritative, void, and of no force." Moreover, the First Amendment specifically prohibited Congress from making any law respecting an establishment of religion, or prohibiting the free exercise thereof, or abridging the freedom of speech or of the press, "thereby guarding in the same sentence," he argued, "and under the same words, the freedom of religion, of speech, and of the press: insomuch, that whatever violates either throws down the sanctuary which covers the others, and that libels, falsehood and defamation, equally with heresy and false religion, are withheld from the cognizance of federal tribunals."

Standing as expressions of political opinion and nothing more, Jefferson's resolutions would have been a searing indictment of Federalist political philosophy and public policy, a solid defense of freedom, civil liberty, and self-government. But in constructing a theoretical framework for his attack on usurpation, he set forth the compact theory of the Union and a states' rights argument justifying the legislature's right not only to criticize federal measures, but also to judge their validity and enforceability. Since the Union originated as a compact among the states, he argued, and since the contracting parties had created no final arbiter of the Constitution (the doctrine of judicial review had not yet been established), each party had "an equal right to judge for itself, as well of infractions as of the mode and measure of redress." With inexorable logic flowing from this premise, Jefferson concluded that acts that went beyond the delegated powers were unconstitutional and that the rightful remedy was nullification.

Jefferson did not say that the rightful remedy was the constitutional remedy, however. Instead, that remedy was based on natural right: "Every state has a natural right in cases not within the compact . . . to nullify of their own authority all assumptions of power by others within their limits." But he backed off from this essentially revolutionary and extraconstitutional step,

23. Harrison, p. 76, and Brant, III, p. 460.
24. TJ to JM, Oct. 26, 1798, below, mentions the visit.
25. TJ to Stevens Thomson Mason, Oct. 11, 1798, in Ford, VII, p. 283.
26. TJ used this phrase in a letter to Abigail Adams, July 22, 1804, in Cappon, I, p. 275.

suggesting instead that Kentucky communicate its views to the other contracting parties—that is, the other states—inviting them to declare "whether these acts are or are not authorized by the federal compact." He expressed confidence that "the co-states, recurring to their natural right in cases not made federal," would concur in declaring these acts void and of no force, and would each take measures "providing that neither . . . shall be exercised within their respective territories."[27]

This sweeping claim in the name of states' rights, had it been implemented, would have placed Kentucky in open defiance of federal laws; it was an extreme argument that was potentially as dangerous to the Union as the oppressive laws were to individual liberty. But Kentucky did not go that far. Although Breckinridge introduced Jefferson's resolutions with only a few changes, he dropped all references to nullification and any suggestion that the obnoxious laws could not be enforced within the state. Instead, he followed the lead that he and the local leaders of the earlier county protests in the state had proposed, calling for a double-barreled campaign to repeal the "unconstitutional and obnoxious acts." The resolutions were to be transmitted to the Kentucky senators and representatives in Congress, who were to work for repeal, and the governor was instructed to send them to the legislatures of the other states to gain their concurrence in requesting "repeal at the next session of Congress."

Madison did not see Jefferson's draft until it had been dispatched to Kentucky. He first read Jefferson's resolutions while he was visiting Monticello in October, but Jefferson did not send him a copy until November 17, the day that Governor James Garrard signed the Kentucky resolutions. Jefferson suggested that his draft could serve as a model for Virginia. "I think we should distinctly affirm all the important principles they contain, so as to hold to that ground in future, and leave the matter in such a train as that we may not be committed absolutely to push the matter to extremities, and yet may be free to push as far as events will render prudent."[28]

Like Breckinridge, the judicious Madison did not think it prudent to go as far as Jefferson had gone. The Virginia resolutions were shorter, more moderate, and quieter in tone. They were more carefully couched in Madison's understanding of the constitutional tradition; they made no reference to natural law theory and, therefore, omitted any mention of the "rightful remedy" of nullification, a word that Madison came to abhor. They opened with a declaration of warm attachment to the Union of the States created by the constitutional compact; denounced the Alien and Sedition Acts as "alarming infractions" of the Constitution; cited other federal measures that enlarged governmental powers and threatened "to transform the present republican

27. For TJ's draft and fair copy of the Kentucky resolutions, see Ford, VII, pp. 289–309. For the fair copy that TJ sent to JM, see the enclosure in TJ to JM, Nov. 17, 1798, below.

28. TJ to JM, Nov. 17, 1798, below. For solid discussions, see Malone, III, pp. 395–409, and Brant, III, pp. 452–71.

system of the United States, into an absolute, or at best a mixed monarchy"; and proposed that the legislature "interpose" by urging the other states to concur in declaring the obnoxious laws unconstitutional and to take necessary and proper measures for cooperating with Virginia "in maintaining the authorities, rights, and liberties, reserved to the States respectively, or to the people."[29]

Wilson Cary Nicholas again served as the intermediary, going to Montpellier to pick up Madison's draft (and agreeing to keep Madison's authorship secret), stopping off at Monticello for consultation with Jefferson, and then transmitting the resolutions to John Taylor for introduction in the Virginia assembly. By that time, Jefferson had learned that the first victim of the Sedition Law was the Republican congressman from Vermont, Matthew Lyon of spitting fame, whom the Federalists had tried to expel from Congress. The conviction of an elected representative of the people for having critically commented on President Adams in a letter to his constituents made a tremendous impression on the vice president, who might be threatened with the same treatment if one of his critical letters were intercepted.[30] To Taylor, who was to introduce Madison's resolutions, Jefferson confessed, "I know not which mortifies me most, that I should fear to write what I think or my country bear such a state of things. Yet Lyon's judges, and a jury of all nations, are objects of national fear."[31]

After three days of mulling over Lyon's conviction, Jefferson decided to make his friend's draft tougher, bringing it into line with his own resolutions. Without consulting Madison, he suggested that Nicholas add a phrase that Madison had carefully avoided, stating "that the said acts are, and were ab initio, null, void and of no force, or effect."[32] Both Nicholas and Taylor liked the change, and Taylor introduced the altered resolutions in the Virginia House of Delegates in December 1798. But the Madisons were visiting Dolley's relatives near Richmond, and it seems clear that he rejected Jefferson's harder line, for Taylor struck out the modification and restored Madison's original wording just before the final vote.[33]

Madison then explained to his friend the grounds for differing on proposed remedies by states in cases of unconstitutional acts: "Have you ever considered thoroughly the distinction between the power of the *State* and that of the *Legislature,* on questions relating to the federal pact. On the supposition that the former is clearly the ultimate Judge of infractions, it does not follow that the latter is the legitimate organ especially as a Convention was the

---

29. For JM's draft of the Virginia resolutions of 1798, see Hunt, VI, pp. 326–31, and *PJM,* XVII, pp. 188–90.
30. For the trial of Lyon, see Smith, *Freedom's Fetters,* pp. 221–46.
31. TJ to John Taylor, Nov. 26, 1798, in L. and B., X, p. 63.
32. TJ to Wilson Cary Nicholas, Nov. 29, 1798, in Ford, VII, pp. 312–13.
33. Brant, III, pp. 462–63.

organ by which the compact was made. This was a reason of great weight for using general expressions that would leave to other States a choice of all the modes possible of concurring in the substance, and would shield the Gen. Assembly agst. the charge of Usurpation in the very act of protesting agst the usurpations of Congress."[34]

In no instance since their exchange of views on "the earth belongs to the living" did the Father of the Constitution differ so fundamentally with the Author of the Declaration of Independence. He always argued that his resolutions were a constitutional mode of redress, a solemn expression of opinion that looked to repeal, which would require majority action rather than action by a single state as a "natural right"—essentially a revolutionary right—to nullify federal laws within its territory. Although the Virginia resolutions were a declaration by the legislature, they asserted the power of the states, "cooperating with this State," to take "the necessary and proper measures" against unconstitutional laws. Kentucky altered Jefferson's original draft to call for repeal by majority action, even though that legislature retained Jefferson's declaration that each state "has an equal right to judge for itself, as well of infractions as of the mode and measure of redress."[35]

Madison took seriously Jefferson's cautionary note that they should be flexible in choosing the tactics to implement their strategy of state protests, and he, like Jefferson, tried to "leave the matter in such a train as that we may not be committed absolutely to push the matter to extremities." Both men used states' rights arguments as sticks to beat off what they considered federal violations of individual rights and civil liberties. They obviously agreed on the diagnosis of the disease, but they differed on the rightful remedy even while they sought to push "a political resistance for political effect," as Jefferson later phrased it.[36]

While the Kentucky and Virginia resolutions were being circulated to Congress and the state legislatures, Jefferson returned to Philadelphia for the winter session of Congress, arriving on Christmas Day, 1798. Although Congress continued to press preparedness measures, Jefferson thought that the "XYZ fever" had cooled, with public opinion swinging towards the Republicans. Looking to the future, he observed that "it is on the progress of public opinion we are to depend for rectifying the proceedings of the next Congress. The only question," he told Madison, "is whether this [session] will not carry things beyond the reach of rectification."

But he was heartened by the petitions and remonstrances against the Alien and Sedition Laws pouring in from New York, New Jersey, and Pennsylvania, for he feared that if Virginia stood alone, the federal government might

34. JM to TJ, Dec. 29, 1798, below.

35. Both Jefferson's and Kentucky's resolutions used the terms "state" or "states" instead of "legislature," which is used in both of these sets and in the Virginia resolutions only when directing that the resolutions be communicated to the other state legislatures.

36. Peterson, p. 615. See also Koch and Ammon, 145–76.

attempt "to coerce her."[37] The best strategy for the Republican party, therefore, was "firmness on our part, but a passive firmness. . . . Anything rash or threatening might check the favorable dispositions of these middle states and rally them again around the measures which are ruining us."[38]

Jefferson urged Madison to write short, hard-hitting essays for the Republican press, and Madison responded promptly with "a few observations" on "Foreign Influence," which Jefferson submitted to the Philadelphia *Aurora* for anonymous publication on January 23, 1799. The essay "met such approbation," a delighted Jefferson wrote, "as to have occasioned an extraordinary impression of that day's paper."[39] So popular was the piece that to the "extraordinary first impression, they have been obliged to make a second, and of an extraordinary number." Jefferson praised Madison's essay, along with other articles in the *Aurora,* as the sort of thing "the public want. . . . They wish to hear *reason* instead of *disgusting blackguardism*. The public sentiment being now on the creen and many heavy circumstances about to fall into the republican scale, we are sensible that this summer is the season for systematic energies and sacrifices. The engine," he emphasized, "is the press. Every man must lay his purse and his pen under contribution. As to the former, it is possible I may be obliged to assume something for you.[40] As to the latter, let me pray and beseech you to set apart a certain portion of every post day to write what may be proper for the public. . . . You can render such incalculable services in this way as to lessen the effect of our loss of your presence here."[41]

Even before he had received Jefferson's plea for more articles, Madison had mailed off a forceful essay, which appeared in the *Aurora* on February 23, 1799, as "Political Reflections" by "A Citizen of the United States." An appreciative Jefferson, who had sent it to the Republican newspaper, labeled the essay "precious."[42]

On December 26, 1798, the day after Jefferson's arrival in Philadelphia, Representative Roger Griswold of Connecticut proposed an amendment to the Sedition Act to punish anyone who usurped the executive authority of the government of the United States by commencing or carrying on any correspondence with the governments of any foreign prince or state relating to

37. For the suggestion by General Hamilton that the United States Army be moved towards Virginia to be used "to subdue a *refractory and powerful State*," see John C. Miller, *Alexander Hamilton: Portrait in Paradox* (New York, 1959), pp. 489-92; Manning J. Dauer, *The Adams Federalists* (Baltimore, 1953), pp. 208-10, 214-15; and Stephen G. Kurtz, *The Presidency of John Adams: The Collapse of Federalism, 1795-1800* (Philadelphia, 1957), pp. 316-17.

38. TJ to JM, Jan. 30, 1799, below.

39. JM sent his observations to TJ on Jan. 12, 1799, below, and TJ acknowledged them on Jan. 30, 1799, below. For the article, see *PJM,* XVII, pp. 211-20.

40. TJ committed JM for $100 to support Republican newspapers; see TJ to JM, Feb. 19, 1799, below.

41. TJ to JM, Feb. 5, 1799, below.

42. See JM to TJ, Feb. 8, 1799, below, and TJ to JM, Feb. 19, 1799, below. The essay is in *PJM,* XVII, pp. 237-43.

controversies or disputes with the United States.⁴³ It was aimed at George Logan, but it gave the Federalists another opportunity to denounce "the contriver of this mission," the vice president, even though Congressman Harper's attempt to read the Mazzei letter into the congressional record was ruled out of order.⁴⁴ Everyone, Jefferson assured Madison, understood the Federalists' strategy: "The real views in the importance they have given to Logan's enterprise are mistaken by nobody."⁴⁵ By linking Logan, the agent, to Jefferson, the contriver, and identifying both with the "French party," they hoped to undermine popular support for the Republican party and opposition to the Federalist program. As a British observer noted, "This situation of [the] Vice President is rendered uneasy to him by the state of politics, as he presides over the Senate and they annoy him by their remarks frequently."⁴⁶

Although Congress passed the Logan Act, the Federalist tactics boomeranged, and Jefferson informed Madison that Dr. Logan had been elected to the Pennsylvania legislature, soundly defeating Frederick Augustus Muhlenberg, former Speaker of the Federalist House of Representatives. Moreover, Congressman Matthew Lyon, running for office from the Vermont jail cell where he was serving out his sentence for sedition, had been reelected to Congress handily. "His majority," Jefferson announced with pleasure, "is great. Reports vary from 600. to 900." And he passed along some political gossip about a petition that had been "presented to the President, signed by several thousand persons in Vermont, praying a remitment of Lyon's fine. He asked the bearer of the petition if Lyon himself had petitioned, and being answered in the negative, said, 'penitence must precede pardon.'"⁴⁷

As Congress was expanding the army and navy—Jefferson listed the *existing* army of 5,000, the *additional* army of 9,000, the *eventual* army of 30,000, the *volunteer* army of 75,000, and the navy of 12 vessels⁴⁸—President Adams was evaluating official as well as informal peace feelers from France. On February 18, 1799, he announced what Jefferson called "the event of events," the appointment of a new peace mission to France to resume the negotiations that had broken off after the XYZ affair. As Abigail Adams told her husband, nothing that he had done as president had "so universally electrified the public."⁴⁹

---

43. TJ to JM, Jan. 3, 1799, below.
44. Frederick B. Tolles, *George Logan of Philadelphia* (New York, 1953), pp. 185–204, and Malone, III, pp. 430–31.
45. TJ to JM, Jan. 16, 1799, below.
46. Patricia Holbert Menk, "D. M. Erskine: Letters from America, 1798–1799," *WMQ* 6 (1949): 281.
47. TJ to JM, Jan. 3, 1799, below. For JM's views on Lyon, see JM to TJ, Jan. 12, 1799, below. For Lyon's reelection, see Smith, *Freedom's Fetters*, pp. 241–46.
48. TJ to JM, Feb. 5, 1799, below, and Feb. 19, 1799, below.
49. Quoted in Alexander De Conde, *The Quasi-War: The Politics and Diplomacy of the Undeclared War with France, 1797–1801* (New York, 1966), p. 184.

Jefferson obviously agreed. "Yesterday," he wrote with delight to Madison, "the P[resident] nominated to the Senate W. V. Murray M[inister] P[lenipotentiary] to the French republic and adds that he shall be instructed not to go to France without direct and unequivocal assurances from the Fr[ench] government that he shall be recieved in character, enjoy the due privileges and a minister of equal rank title and power, be appointed to discuss and conclude our controversies by a new treaty. This," he added, "had evidently been kept secret from the Feds of both Houses, as appeared to their dismay."[50] To Madison he confided: "Never did a party shew a stronger mortification, and consequently that war had been their object." But the Hamiltonian phalanx was strong enough to pressure Adams to add two additional envoys and to delay their departure until France had given assurances of their proper reception, a move that Jefferson viewed as an attempt to put off the day of reconciliation.[51]

As if to demonstrate their frustration, the Federalists closed out the session of Congress with what the vice president called "a scandalous scene" in the House. Knowing that they had the votes to carry their report rejecting the petitions against the Alien and Sedition Laws, "they held a Caucus and determined that not a word should be spoken on their side in answer to anything which should be said on the other." Indeed, they drowned out the Republican speakers by entering "into loud conversations, laugh, cough, etc., so that for the last hour of these gentlemen's speaking they must have had the lungs of a vendue master to have been heard. . . . It was impossible to proceed," he concluded, and the Federalists carried their report endorsing the Alien and Seditions Laws by a vote of 52 to 48.[52]

─────────────── THE LETTERS ───────────────

Jefferson to Madison

[Monticello] Oct. 26, 1798

The day after you left us, I sat down and wrote the petition I mentioned to you. It is not yet correct enough, and I enclose you a copy to which I pray your corrections, and to return it by the next post, that it may be set in motion. On turning to the judiciary law of the U. S. I find they established the designation of jurors *by lot or otherwise as NOW practised in the several states;*

---

50. TJ to JM Feb. 19, 1799, below.
51. TJ to JM, Feb. 26, 1799, below.
52. *Ibid.*

should this prevent, in the first moment the execution of so much of the proposed law, as respects the federal courts, the people will be in possession of the right of electing jurors as to the state courts, and either Congress will agree to conform their courts to the same rule, or they will be loaded with an odium in the eyes of the people generally which will force the matter through.

I will send you a copy of the other paper by Richardson.[1] Do not send for him till Monday sennight, because that gives us another post-day to warn you of any unexpected delays in winding up his work here for the season, which, tho' I do not foresee, may yet happen. Adieu affectionately.

ENCLOSURE
[Jefferson's Petition on the Election of Jurors]

[Oct. 1798]

To the General Assembly of the Commonwealth of Virginia

The Petition of sundry persons inhabitants of the county of Albemarle and citizens of the said commonwealth respectfully sheweth.

That though civil govmt. duly framed and administered be one of the greatest blessings and most powerful instruments for procuring safety and happiness to men collected in large societies, yet such is the proneness of those to whom it's powers are necessarily deputed to pervert them to the attainment of personal wealth and dominion and to the utter oppression of their fellow-men, that it has become questionable whether the condition of our aboriginal neighbors, who live without laws or magistracies, be not preferable to that of the great mass of the nations of the earth who feel their laws and magistrates but in the weight of their burthens: that the citizens of these United states, impressed with this mortifying truth when they deposed the abusive government under which they had lived, founded their new forms, as well particular as general, in this fact and principle, that the people themselves are the safest deposit of power, and that none therefore should be trusted to others which they can competently exercise themselves: that their own experience having proved that the people are competent to the appointment or election of their agents, that of their chief executive magistrates was reserved to be made at short periods, by themselves, or by others chosen by themselves: as was also the choice of their legislatures, whether composed of one or more branches: that in the Judiciary department, sensible that they were inadequate to difficult questions of law, these were in ordinary cases, confided to permanent judges, but reserving to juries only, extraordinary cases where a bias in the permanent judge might be apprehended,[2] and where honest ignorance would be safer than per-

---

1. TJ's enclosure was his petition on the election of jurors, a follow-up to Congressman Samuel J. Cabell's presentment by a Federalist grand jury in 1797. The "other paper," which he failed to enclose, was his draft of the Kentucky resolutions; he mailed it to JM on Nov. 17, 1798, below. Richard Richardson was a bricklayer, plasterer, and stone cutter at Monticello whom TJ loaned on occasion to JM; see Malone, III, p. 241.

2. After receiving JM's suggestions of Oct. 31, 1798, TJ revised the preceding section on the powers of juries and judges as follows: "that in the Judiciary department, sensible that they were inadequate to difficult questions of law, these were generally confided to permanent judges, but reserving to juries the decision both of law and fact where in their opinion bias in the permanent judge might be apprehended"; see *PJM,* XVII, p. 172.

verted science: and reserving to themselves also the whole department of facts, which constitutes indeed the great mass of judiciary litigations: that the wisdom of these reservations will be apparent on a recurrence to the history of that country from which we chiefly emigrated, where the faint glimmerings of liberty and safety now remaining to the nation are kept in feeble life by the reserved powers of the people only: that in the establishment of the trial by jury however a great inconsistence has been overlooked in this and some other of the states, or rather has been copied from their original without due attention: for while the competence of the people to the appointmt even of the highest executive and of the legislative agents is admitted and established, and their competence to be themselves the triers of Judiciary facts, the appointmt of the special individuals from among themselves who shall be such triers of fact, has not been left in their hands, but has been placed by law in officers, dependent on the executive or judiciary bodies: that triers of fact are therefore habitually taken in this state from among accidental bystanders and too often composed of foreigners attending on matters of business, and of idle persons collected for purposes of dissipation; and, in cases interesting to the powers of the public functionaries, may be specially selected from descriptions of persons to be found in every country, whose ignorance or dependance renders them pliable to the will and designs of power: that in others of these states, [and particularly in those to the eastward of the union,]³ this germ of rottenness in the institution of juries has been carefully excluded, and their laws have provided with laudable foresight for the appointment of jurors by select men chosen by the people themselves: and to a like restitution of principle and salutary precaution against the abuse of power by the public functionaries, who never did yet in any country fail to betray and oppress those for the care of whose affairs they were appointed, by force if they possessed it, or by fraud and delusion if they did not, your petitioners pray the timely attention of their legislature, while that legislature (and with a heartfelt satisfaction the petitioners pronounce it) are still honest enough to wish the preservation of the rights of the people, and wise enough to circumscribe in time the spread of that gangrene, which sooner than many are aware, may reach the vitals of our political existence.

And lest it should be supposed that the popular appointmt of jurors may scarcely be practicable in a state so extensive and circumstanced as ours, your petitioners will undertake to suggest one mode, not presumg to propose it for the adoption of the legislature, but firmly relying that their wisdom will devise a better: they observe then that by a law already passed for the establishment of schools, provision has been made for laying off every county into districts or precincts; that this division which offers so many valuable resources for the purposes of information, of justice, of order and police, may be recurred to for the object now in contemplation, and may be completed for this purpose where it has not been done for the other, that the inhabitants of every precinct may meet at a given time and place in their precinct, and in the presence of the constable or other head officer of the precinct, elect from among themselves some one to be a juror; that from among those so chosen in every county, some one may be designated by lot, who shall attend the ensuing session of the federal court within the state, to act as grand and petty jurors, one of these from every senatorial district being designated by lot for a grand juror, and the residue attending to serve as petty jurors, to

3. This clause was struck out of the petition by TJ.

be in like manner designated by lot in every particular case: that of the others so chosen in every county composing a district for the itinerant courts of this commonwealth, so many may be taken by lot as shall suffice for grand and petty juries for the district court next ensuing their election: and the residue so chosen in each county may attend their own county courts for the same purposes till another election, or, if too numerous the supernumeraries may be discharged by lot: and that such compensation may be allowed for these services as, without rendering the office an object worth canvassing, may yet protect the juror from actual loss: That an institution on this outline, or such better as the wisdom of the General assembly will devise, so modified as to guard it against the intrigue of parties, the influence of power, or irregularities of conduct, and further matured from time to time as experience shall develope it's imperfections, may long preserve the trial by jury, in its pure and original spirit, as the true tribunal of the people, for a mitigation in the execution of hard laws when the power of preventing their passage is lost, and may afford some protection to persecuted man, whether alien or citizen, which the aspect of the times warns we may want.

And your petitioners, waiving the expression of many important considerations which will offer themselves readily to the reflection of the general assembly, pray them to take the premises into deep and serious consideration and to do therein for their country what their wisdom shall deem best, and they, as in duty bound, shall ever pray etc.

Madison to Jefferson

[Orange] Oct. 31, 1798

DEAR SIR

I return the draught recd. by the last post, with one or two very small alterations. The interlineated "or an allotted portion thereof," seems to suggest that the whole no. might be so great as to beget objections to the expence which are always formidable in such cases. I have doubted whether the terms "ordinary" and "extraordinary" sufficiently marked the boundary between the power of the Judge and of Jurys over points of law, and whether they do not yield too much of the strict right of the latter in case they chuse to exert it. But you are so much better able to decide on this subject than myself, that I have not ventured to note any precise amendment. I shall not send for Richardson sooner than you propose; but shall then hope for the use of him for some time for plaistering as well as adjusting the Stone to the fireplaces. The state of the business under Mason increases my dependence on the auxiliary. Mr. R. will please to bring with him such utensils as he will need. Yrs. affecy.

Js. MADISON JR.

The Thermr. at Sunrise Ocr. 30—22°
31. 26.

Jefferson to Madison

[Monticello] Nov. 3, 1798

Yours of Oct. 31 has been duly recieved and the corrections suggested are thankfully adopted. The petition will be offered for signature at our court the day after tomorrow. Richardson has been in a great measure prevented doing any thing this week by the weather, which has been too cold for laying mortar. He has still 2. or 3. days work of that kind to do, which is indispensable, and about as long a job for kilning some bricks which we must secure in an unburnt state through the winter. We must therefore beg you to put off sending for him till Saturday next.

Yesterday's papers bring us an account of Lyon of Vermont being indicted before Judge Patterson under the Sedition act. Possibly your papers may not mention the issue. He was found guilty, fined 1000. D. and adjudged to 4. months imprisonment. He was immediately committed. The words called seditious were only general censures of the proceedings of Congress and of the President. Affectionate respects to Mrs. Madison your father and family. Adieu

P.S. Your nails are ready

Jefferson to Madison

Monticello Nov. 17, 1798

Mr. Richardson has been detained by several jobs indespensible to the progress of the carpenters, and to the securing what is done against winter. When will Whitten be done with you? Or could you by any means dispense with his services till I set out for Philadelphia? My floors can only be laid while I am at home, and I can not get a workman here. Perhaps you have some other with you or near you who could go on with your work till his return to you. I only mention these things that if you have any other person who could enable you to spare him a few weeks, I could employ him to much accommodation till my departure in laying my floors. But in this consult your own convenience only.

I enclose you a copy of the draught of the Kentucky resolves.[4] I think we should distinctly affirm all the important principles they contain, so as to hold to that ground in future, and leave the matter in such a train as that we may

---

4. For TJ's press copy of his file copy of the Kentucky resolutions, a duplicate of the copy which John C. Breckinridge carried to Kentucky, see below. For an earlier draft, TJ's fair or file copy, and the resolutions adopted by the Kentucky legislature, see Ford, VII, pp. 289-309.

not be committed absolutely to push the matter to extremities, and yet may be free to push as far as events will render prudent. I think to set out so as to arrive in Philadelphia the Saturday before Christmas. My friendly respects to Mrs. Madison, to your father and family; health, happiness and adieu to yourself.

40. lbs. of IVd. nails @ 14½d per lb. were sent this morning, being all we had. They contained (according to the count of a single pound) 314 × 40 = 12,560.

ENCLOSURE
[Jefferson's Draft of the Kentucky Resolutions of 1798]

[Sept.? 1798]

1. *Resolved,* That the several States composing the US. of America are not united on the principle of unlimited submission to their general government; but that by a compact under the style and title of a Constitution for the US. and of amendments thereto, they constituted a general government for special purposes, delegated to that government certain definite powers, reserving, each state to itself, the residuary mass of right to their own self-government; and that whensoever the General government assumes undelegated powers, it's acts are unauthoritative, void, and of no force: that to this compact each state acceded as a state, and is an integral party, it's co-states forming, as to itself, the other party: that the government created by this compact was not made the exclusive or final judge of the extent of the powers delegated to itself; since that would have made it's discretion, and not the constitution, the measure of its powers; but that, as in all other cases of compact among powers having no common judge, each party has an equal right to judge for itself, as well of infractions as of the mode and measure of redress.

2. *Resolved,* That the constitution of the US. having delegated to Congress a power to punish treason, counterfeiting the securities and current coin of the US. piracies and felonies committed on the high seas, and offences against the law of Nations, and no other crimes whatsoever, and it being true as a general principle, and one of the Amendments to the constitution having also declared, that "the powers not delegated to the U S. by the constitution, nor prohibited by it to the states, are reserved to the states respectively, or to the people," therefore the act of Congress, passed on the 14th day of July, 1798, and intituled "An Act in addition to the act intituled An Act for the punishment of certain crimes against the U. S." as also the act passed by them on the [27th] day of June, 1798, intituled "An Act to punish frauds committed on the bank of the US." (and all their other acts which assume to create, define or punish crimes, other than those so enumerated in the Constitution,) are altogether void, and of no force; and that the power to create, define and punish such other crimes is reserved, and of right appurtains solely and exclusively to the respective states, each within its own territory.

3. *Resolved,* that it is true as a general principle, and is also expressly declared by one of the Amendments to the Constitution, that "the powers not delegated to the US. by the constitution, nor prohibited by it to the states, are reserved to the states respectively, or to the people"; and that no power over the freedom of religion, freedom of speech, or freedom of the press being delegated to the US. by the constitution, nor prohibited by it to the states, all lawful powers respecting the same did of right remain, and were reserved, to the states or the people: that thus was manifested their

determination to retain to themselves the right of judging how far the licentiousness of speech and of the press may be abridged without lessening their useful freedom, and how far those abuses which cannot be separated from their use should be tolerated, rather than the use be destroyed; and thus also they guarded against all abridgment by the U.S. of the freedom of religious opinions and exercises, and retained to themselves the right of protecting the same, as this state, by a law passed on the general demand of it's citizens, had already protected them from all human restraint or interference: And that in addition to this general principle and express declaration, another and more special provision has been made by one of the amendments to the constitution which expressly declares that "Congress shall make no law respecting an establishment of religion, or prohibiting the free exercise thereof, or abridging the freedom of speech or of the press": thereby guarding in the same sentence, and under the same words, the freedom of religion, of speech, and of the press: insomuch, that whatever violates either throws down the sanctuary which covers the others, and that libels, falsehood and defamation, equally with heresy and false religion, are withheld from the cognizance of federal tribunals: that, therefore, the act of Congress of the US. passed on the 14th. day of July, 1798, intituled "An Act in addition to the act intituled An Act for the punishment of certain crimes against the US." which does abridge the freedom of the press, is not law, but is altogether void, and of no force.

4. *Resolved,* that alien friends are under the jurisdiction and protection of the laws of the state wherein they are; that no power over them has been delegated to the US. nor prohibited to the individual states distinct from their power over citizens: and it being true as a general principle, and one of the amendments to the constitution having also declared that "the powers not delegated to the US. by the constitution, nor prohibited by it to the states, are reserved to the states respectively, or to the people," the act of the Congress of the US. passed on the   day of July, 1798, intituled "An Act concerning Aliens," which assumes powers over Alien-friends, not delegated by the constitution, is not law, but is altogether void, and of no force.

5. *Resolved,* that in addition to the general principle, as well as the express declaration, that powers not delegated are reserved, another and more special provision, inserted in the constitution from abundant caution, has declared that "the migration or importation of such persons as any of the states now existing shall think proper to admit, shall not be prohibited by the Congress prior to the year 1808"; that this commonwealth does admit the migration of Alien-friends, described as the subject of the said act concerning aliens: that a provision against prohibiting their migration, is a provision against all acts equivalent thereto, or it would be nugatory; that to remove them when migrated, is equivalent to a prohibition of their migration, and is therefore contrary to the said provision of the Constitution, and void.

6. *Resolved,* that the imprisonment of a person under the protection of the laws of this commonwealth on his failure to obey the simple *order* of the President to depart out of the US. as is undertaken by said act intituled "An Act concerning Aliens," is contrary to the constitution, one Amendment to which has provided that "no person shall be deprived of liberty without due process of law." And that another having provided that "in all criminal prosecutions the accused shall enjoy the right to public trial, by an impartial jury, to be informed of the nature and cause of the accusation, to be confronted with the witnesses against him, to have compulsory process for obtaining witnesses in his favor, and to have the assistance of counsel for his defence," the same act, undertaking to authorize the President to remove a person out of the US.

who is under the protection of the law, on his own suspicion, without accusation, without jury, without public trial, without confrontation of the witnesses against him, without hearing witnesses in his favor, without defence, without counsel, is contrary to the provision also of the constitution, is therefore not law, but utterly void, and of no force. That transferring the power of judging any person, who is under the protection of the laws, from the courts to the President of the US. as is undertaken by the same act concerning Aliens, is against the article of the constitution which provides that "the judicial power of the United States shall be vested in courts, the judges of which shall hold their offices during good behavior" and that the said act is void for that reason also. And it is further to be noted that this transfer of judiciary power is to that magistrate of the general government who already possesses all the Executive, and a negative on all Legislative powers.

7. *Resolved,* That the construction applied by the General government (as is evidenced by sundry of their proceedings) to those parts of the constitution of the US. which delegate to Congress a power "to lay and collect taxes, duties, imposts and excises, to pay the debts and provide for the common defence and general welfare of the US." and "to make all laws which shall be necessary and proper for carrying into execution the powers vested by the constitution in the government of the US. or in any department or officer thereof," goes to the destruction of all limits prescribed to their power by the constitution: that words meant by the instrument to be subsidiary only to the execution of limited powers, ought not to be so construed as themselves to give unlimited powers, nor a part to be so taken as to destroy the whole residue of that instrument: that the proceedings of the General government under color of these articles, will be a fit and necessary subject of revisal and correction, at a time of greater tranquility, while those specified in the preceding resolutions, call for immediate redress.

8th. *Resolved,* that a committee of conference and correspondence be appointed, who shall have in charge to communicate the preceding resolutions to the legislatures of the several states, to assure them that this commonwealth continues in the same esteem for their friendship and union which it has manifested from that moment at which a common danger first suggested a common union: that it considers union, for specified national purposes, and particularly for those specified in the late federal compact, to be friendly to the peace, happiness and posperity of all the states; that faithful to that compact, according to the plain intent and meaning in which it was understood and acceded to by the several parties, it is sincerely anxious for it's preservation: that it does also believe, that to take from the states all the powers of self-government, and transfer them to a general and consolidated government, without regard to the special delegations and reservations solemnly agreed to in that compact, is not for the peace, happiness or prosperity of these states; and that therefore this commonwealth is determined, as it doubts not its co-states are, to submit to undelegated, and consequently unlimited powers in no man, or body of men, on earth: that in cases of an abuse of the delegated powers, the members of the general government being chosen by the people, a change by the people would be the constitutional remedy; but, where powers are assumed which have not been delegated, a nullification of the act is the rightful remedy: that every state has a natural right in cases not within the compact (casus non fœderis) to nullify of their own authority all assumptions of power by others within their limits: that, without this right, they would be under the dominion, absolute and unlimited, of whosoever might exercise this right of judgment for them: that nevertheless this commonwealth, from motives of regard and respect for its co-states, has wished to communicate with them on the subject; that with them alone it is proper to communicate, they alone being parties to the compact, and solely authorized to judge in the last resort of the powers exercised under it, Congress being not a party, but merely the creature of the compact, and subject, as to it's assumptions of power, to the final judgment of those by whom, and for whose use, itself, and it's powers were all created and modified: that if the acts before specified should stand, these conclusions would flow from them; that the General government may place any act they think proper on the list of crimes, and punish it themselves whether enumerated or not enumerated by the constitution as cognizable by them; that they may transfer it's cognizance to the President, or any other person, who may himself be the accuser, counsel, judge and jury, whose *suspicions* may be the evidence, his *order* the sentence, his *officer* the executioner, and his breast the sole record of the transaction: that a very numerous and valuable description of the inhabitants of these states being, by this precedent, reduced, as Outlaws, to the absolute dominion of one man, and the barrier of the constitution thus swept away for us all, no rampart now remains against the passions and the power of a majority in Congress to protect from a like exportation, or other more grievous punishment the minority of the same body, the legislatures, judges, governors and counsellors of the states, nor their other peaceable inhabitants, who may venture to reclaim the constitutional rights and liberties of the states and people, or who for other causes, good or bad, may be obnoxious to the views, or marked by the suspicions of the President, or be thought dangerous to his or their elections or other interests public or personal: that the friendless alien has indeed been selected as the safest subject of a first experiment; but the citizen will soon follow, or rather, has already followed; for already has a Sedition act marked him as it's prey: that these and successive acts of the same character, unless arrested at the threshold, necessarily drive these states into revolution and blood, and will furnish new calumnies against republican government, and new pretexts for those who wish it to be believed that man cannot be governed but by a rod of iron: that it would be a dangerous delusion, were a confidence in the men of our choice to silence our fears for the safety of our rights; that confidence is everywhere the parent of despotism; free government is founded in jealousy, and not in confidence; it is jealousy and not confidence which prescribes limited constitutions, to bind down those whom we are obliged to trust with power: that our constitution has accordingly fixed the limits to which, and no further, our confidence may go: and let the honest advocate of confidence read the Alien and Sedition acts, and say if the Constitution has not been wise in fixing limits to the government it created, and whether we should be wise in destroying those limits. Let him say What the government is, if it be not a tyranny, which the men of our choice have conferred on our President, and the President of our choice has assented to, and accepted over the friendly strangers, to whom the mild spirit of our country and it's laws have pledged hospitality and protection: that the men of our choice have more respected the bare *suspicions* of the President than the solid rights of innocence, the claims of justification, the sacred force of truth, and the forms and substance of law and justice: in questions of power, then, let no more be heard of confidence in man, but bind him down from mischief by the chains of the constitution. That this commonwealth does therefore call on its co-states for an expression of their sentiments on the acts concerning aliens, and for the punishment of certain crimes herein before specified, plainly declaring whether these acts are or are not authorized by the federal compact? And it doubts not that their sense will be so enounced as to prove their attachment unaltered to limited government, whether general or particular; and that the rights and liberties of their co-states will be exposed to no dangers by remaining embarked in a common bottom with their own: that they will concur with this commonwealth in considering the said acts as so palpably against the constitution as to amount to an undisguised declaration that that compact is not meant to be the measure of the powers of the General government, but that it will proceed in the exercise, over these states, of all powers whatsoever; that they will view this as seizing the rights of the states, and consolidating them in the hands of the General government, with a power assumed to bind the States, (not merely in the cases made federal [casus fœderis] but) in all cases whatsoever, by laws made, not with their consent, but by others against their consent; that this would be to surrender the form of government we have chosen, and to live under one deriving it's powers from its own will, and not from our authority, and that the co-states, recurring to their natural right in cases not made federal, will concur in declaring these acts void and of no force, and will each take measures of its own for providing that neither these acts, nor any others of the general government, not plainly and intentionally authorized by the constitution, shall be exercised within their respective territories.

9th. *Resolved,* that the said committee be authorized to communicate, by writing or personal conferences, at any times or places whatever, with any person or persons who may be appointed by any one or more of the co-states to correspond or confer with them; and that they lay their proceedings before the next session of assembly.

Madison to Jefferson

[Orange] Dec. 11, 1798

DEAR SIR

According to your favor by Mr. Richardson, I expect the pleasure of seeing you in the course of the present Week. Be so good as to bring a memorandum from your nailery of the amount of my debt to it.[5] I had hoped that you were possessed of the aid of Mr. Chuning and his young men, but the Bearer Mr. W. Whitten tells me the contrary. Mr. C. left this saturday was two weeks, and promised to ride up to Monticello the day following. It has been impossible to spare L. Whitten. He has been under the spur to keep the way prepared for the Plasterers, and to finish off a number of indispensable jobbs always overlooked till the execution is called for. The Fredg paper of the 7th inst: contains the official confirmation from Nelson of the destruction of the French fleet[6] as first brought from Cadiz. Adieu Affecly.

Js. MADISON JR

Please to forward the inclosed safely.

5. TJ's partial endorsement on the back of the letter (the first line has been worn off) reads as follows: ". . . he inclosed me a draught on Moylan with orders to apply £48-11-3. balance for nails./See Memn. book, 1799. Jan. 9. J. Barnes credits me 161.875 = £48-11-3 for Mr Madison"; see JM to TJ, Dec. 29, 1798, below.

6. News of Admiral Horatio Nelson's defeat of the French fleet off the coast of Egypt on Aug. 1 did not reach London until Oct. 1; see *PJM,* XVII, p. 184.

Madison to Jefferson

[Montpellier] Dec. 29, 1798

DEAR SIR,

I inclose a draught on Genl. Moylan, out of which you will be pleased to pay yourself the price of the Nails, £48-11. 3*d.*, Va. Cy to let Barnes have as much as will discharge the balance I owe him, and to let what may remain lie till I write to you again.

The P's speech corresponds pretty much with the idea of it which was preconceived. It is the old song with no other variation of the tune than the spirit of the moment was thought to exact.[7] It is evident also that he rises in his pitch as the ecchoes of the S. and H. of R. embolden him, and particularly that he seizes with avidity that of the latter flattering his vigilance and firmness agst. illusory attempts on him, without noticing, as he was equally invited, the allusion to his pacific professions. The Senate as usual perform their part with alacrity in counteracting peace by dextrous provocations to the pride and irritability of the French Govt. It is pretty clear that their answer was cooked in the same shop with the speech. The finesse of the former calculated to impose on the public mind here, and the virulence of the latter still more calculated to draw from France the war, which cannot be safely declared on this side, taste strongly of the genius of that subtle partizan of England who has contributed so much to the public misfortunes. It is not difficult to see how A. could be made a puppet thro the instrumentality of creatures around him, nor how the Senate could be managed by similar artifice.[8]

I have not seen the Result of the discussions at Richmond on the alien and sedition laws. It is to be feared their zeal may forget some Considerations which ought to temper their proceedings. Have you ever considered thoroughly the distinction between the power of the *State* and that of the *Legislature,* on questions relating to the federal pact. On the supposition that the former is clearly the ultimate Judge of infractions, it does not follow that the latter is the legitimate organ especially as a Convention was the organ by which the compact was made. This was a reason of great weight for using general expressions that would leave to other States a choice of all the modes possible of concurring in the substance, and would shield the Genl. Assembly agst. the charge of Usurpation in the very act of protesting agst the usurpations of Congress. I have not forgotten my promise of McGeehee's prices, but cd not conveniently copy them for the present mail. Always affly Yrs.

J. MADISON JR.

---

7. Adams called for an extension of the defense measures adopted in the summer of 1798 and rejected a new diplomatic mission to France "without more determinate assurances that he will be received"; see Ralph Adams Brown, *The Presidency of John Adams* (Lawrence, Kans., 1975), pp. 90–91, and Kurtz, pp. 344–45.

8. For Hamilton's influence with Adams's cabinet and with the High Federalists in Congress, see Kurtz, p. 345, who notes, however, that the president rewrote "the vital wording on the question of recognizing French advances" towards negotiations.

Jefferson to Madison

Philadelphia Jan. 3, 1799

I have suffered the post hour to come so nearly on me, that I must huddle over what I have more than appears in the public papers. I arrived here on Christmas day, not a single bill or other article of business having yet been brought into Senate. The P's speech, so unlike himself in point of moderation, is supposed to have been written by the military conclave, and particularly Hamilton.[9] When the Senate gratuitously hint Logan to him, you see him in his reply come out in his genuine colors. The debates on that subject and Logan's declaration you will see in the papers.[10] The republican spirit is supposed to be gaining ground in this State and Massachusetts. The tax gatherer has already excited discontent. Gerry's correspondence with Taleyrand, promised by the Presidt at the opening of the session, is still kept back. It is known to shew France in a very conciliatory attitude, and to contradict some executive assertions. Therefore it is supposed they will get their war measures well taken before they will produce this damper. Vans Murray writes them that the French government is sincere in their overtures for reconciliation and have agreed, if these fail, to admit the mediation offered by the Dutch govnt.[11] In the mean time the raising the army is to go on, and it is said they propose to build twelve 74's. Insurance is now higher in all the commercial towns against British than French capture. The impressment of seamen from one of our armed vessels by a British man of war has occasioned Mr. Pickering to bristle up it is said. But this cannot proceed to any effect. The capture by the French of the Retaliation (an armed vessel we had taken from them) will probably be played off to the best advantage. Lyon is re-elected. His majority is great. Reports vary from 600. to 900. Logan was elected into the Pensylva. legislature against F. A. Muhlenburg by 1256 to 769. Livermore has been re-elected in N. Hampshire by a majority of 1. in the lower and 2. in the upper house.

Genl Knox has become bankrupt for 400,000 D, and has resigned his military commission. He took in Genl Lincoln for 150,000 D, which breaks him. Colo Jackson also sunk with him.

It seems generally admitted, that several cases of the yellow fever still exist

---

9. The ranking generals in the new provisional army were George Washington, Alexander Hamilton, and Charles Cotesworth Pinckney; they attended the opening of Congress when President Adams addressed both houses of Congress on Dec. 8, 1798. See Brown, p. 90, and Albert H. Bowman, *The Struggle for Neutrality: A History of the Diplomatic Relations between the United States and France, 1790–1801* (Knoxville, 1974), pp. 364–65.

10. After George Logan returned from his peace mission from France, President Adams called for a law to punish the "temerity and impertinence of individuals affecting to interfere in public affairs between France and the United States . . . and intended to impose upon the people and separate them from their government"; see Tolles, p. 184.

11. For the offer of the Batavian Republic to mediate the conflict between France and the United States, see Bowman, pp. 343–44, 365–66.

in the city, and the apprehension is, that it will re-appear early in the spring. You promised me a copy of McGee's bill of prices. Be so good as to send it on to me here. Tell Mrs. Madison her friend Made d' Yrujo, is as well as one can be so near to a formidable crisis. Present my friendly respects to her, and accept yourself my sincere and affectionate salutations. Adieu.

I omitted to mention that a petition has been presented to the President, signed by several thousand persons in Vermont, praying a remitment of Lyon's fine. He asked the bearer of the petition if Lyon himself had petitioned, and being answered in the negative, said, 'penitence must precede pardon.'

Madison to Jefferson

[Orange] Jan. 12, 1799

DEAR SIR,

According to a promise in my last, I enclose a copy of the rates at which M'Gehee works. I enclose, also, a few observations on a subject which we have frequently talked of, which are submitted to your entire disposal, in whole or in part, under the sole reserve of the name of the author.[12] In Gordon's History, Vol. IV, p. 399-400, is a transaction that may, perhaps, be properly referred to in the debate on the alien bill. Among other names is that of Sedgwick, to a protest against a bill subjecting to banishment, without trial by jury. It does not appear clearly whether the exiles were under the character of aliens or Citizens. If under the former, the case is in point.

In the hurry of my last, I suspect that I overrated the payments expected from Moylan and Lewis. Should they be short of the objects to which they are appropriated, I will make up the deficiency on notice. We have lately had a few days of intense cold, and now the weather is in the opposite extreme. The Thermometer on Sunday morning last was at 6° and on Monday within the Bulb. Our post had not arrived at the usual hour on Wednesday, and I have not since heard from the office. We are consequently without any late intelligence of your proceedings. I have been disappointed in seeing no step taken in relation to Lyon.[13] He is clearly within his privilege, and it ought to be claimed for him. In the case of Wilkes, the Judges were unanimously of opinion that a libel did not take away his privilege, altho' it is there less definite than with us. The House of Commons voted differently, but it was the vote of a faction, and therefore of less weight than the other authority. Adieu

12. TJ disposed of JM's observations by having them published in the Philadelphia *Aurora* on Jan. 23, 1799, under the title "Foreign Influence." See *PJM,* XVII, pp. 211-20; also see TJ to JM, Jan. 30, 1799, below, and Feb. 5, 1799, below.

13. After serving his sentence under the Sedition Act, Congressman Matthew Lyon returned to the House of Representatives, where the Federalists attempted to expel him as "a notorious and Seditious person"; see Aleine Austin, *Matthew Lyon: "New Man" of the Democratic Revolution, 1749-1822* (University Park, Pa., 1981), p. 127.

Jefferson to Madison

Philadelphia Jan. 16, 1799

The forgery lately attempted to be plaid off by Mr. H. on the house of representatives, of a pretended memorial presented by Logan to the French government, has been so palpably exposed as to have thrown ridicule on the whole of the clamours they endeavored to raise as to that transaction. Still however their majority will pass the bill. The real views in the importance they have given to Logan's enterprise are mistaken by nobody.[14] Mr. Gerry's communications relative to his transactions after the departure of his colleagues, tho' he has now been returned 5. months, and they have been promised to the house 6. or 7. weeks, are still kept back. In the meantime, the paper of this morning promises them from the Paris papers. It is said they leave not a possibility to doubt the sincerity and the anxiety of the French government to avoid the spectacle of a war with us.[15] Notwithstanding this is well understood, the army and a great addition to our navy are steadily intended. A loan of 5. millions is opened at 8. per cent. interest! In a rough way we may state future expences thus annually. Navy 5½ millions (exclusive of it's outfit) army (14,000 men) 6½ millions, interest of national debt (I believe) about 4. millions, interest of the new loan 400,000. Which with the expences of government will make an aggregate of about 18,000,000. All our taxes this year have brought in about 10½ millions, to which the direct tax will add 2. millions, leaving a deficit of between 5 and 6. millions. Still no addition to the taxes will be ventured on at this session. It is pretty evident from the proceedings to get at the measure and number of windows in our houses that a tax on air and light is meditated, but I suppose not till the next session. The bankrupt bill was yesterday rejected by a majority of three. The determinations of the British commissioners under the treaty (who are 3. against 2. of ours) are so extravagant, that about 3. days ago ours protested and seceded. It was said yesterday they had come together again. The demands which will be allowed on the principles of the British majority will amount to from 15. to 20. millions of Dollars. It is not believed that our government will submit to it, and consequently that this must again become a subject for negociation.[16] It is very evident the British are using that part of the treaty merely as a political engine.

14. For an account of Robert Goodloe Harper's attack on Logan, see Tolles, pp. 188–99. The "pretended memorial by Logan" was written by Richard Codman, a friend of the Federalist leader Harrison Gray Otis.

15. President Adams sent Gerry's letters to Congress on Jan. 18, 1799. They confirmed TJ's views and were instrumental in shaping the president's change of policy in February; see De Conde, pp. 168–73, and Bowman, pp. 360–63.

16. For the breakdown of the joint commission on pre-Revolutionary debts, which was established by Jay's treaty and which met in Philadelphia, see Bradford Perkins, *The First Rapprochement: England and the United States, 1795–1805* (Philadelphia, 1955), pp. 117–20.

Notwithstanding the pretensions of the papers of the danger and destruction of Buonaparte, nothing of that is believed. It seems probable that he will establish himself in Egypt, and that is, at present at least, his ultimate object. Ireland also is considered as more organized in her insurrection and stronger than she has been hitherto.

As yet no tobacco has come to this market. At New York the new tobo is at 13. D. Georgia has sent on a greater quantity than had been imagined, and so improved in quality as to take the place of that of Maryland and the Carolines. It is at 11. D. while they are about 10. Immense sums of money now go to Virginia. Every stage is loaded. This is partly to pay for last year's purchases, and partly for the new.

In a society of members, between whom and yourself is great mutual esteem and respect, a most anxious desire is expressed that you would publish your debates of the Convention. That these measures of the army, navy and direct tax will bring about a revulsion of public sentiment is thought certain, and that the constitution will then receive a different explanation. Could those debates be ready to appear critically, their effect would be decisive. I beg of you to turn this subject in your mind. The arguments against it will be personal; those in favor of it moral; and something is required from you as a set-off against the sin of your retirement.

Your favor of Dec 29. came to hand Jan. 5. seal sound. I pray you always to examine the seals of mine to you, and the strength of the impression. The suspicions against the government on this subject are strong. I wrote you Jan 5. Accept for yourself and Mrs. Madison my affectionate salutations and Adieu.

Madison to Jefferson

Orange Jan. 25, 1799

I have recd. your favor of the 3d. inst: but not till the day before yesterday. The same mail brought me two parcels of the newspapers, one of which was due two mails and the other one mail sooner. The papers due at the time did not come. You see therefore the uncertain footing of the conveyance. I should be more willing to ascribe the delays to the season of the year, if there were not proofs that there has been no entire failure of the post, and that the complaint is applicable to letters as well as newspapers. All that I have recd. from Mr. Dawson have been several weeks in the passage. The two recd. along with yours were of the 2d. and 3d. instant. I have already intimated to you that Wednesday is the proper day for your letters to leave Philada. in order to avoid a halt by the way. I sent you some time ago the promised state of McGehees' prices. Some of them he signified were put down without being clear that they were the customary ones. But in general he considered them as rather below the standard of your neighborhood, than above it.

I have long been anxious to know the real complexion of Gerry's report to the Executive. Several symtoms concur with your information, that it does not favor the position which our Govt wished to take. Among them is a letter from a person who says he had been shown Gerry's journal. If truth shall be found to have been suppressed or mistated in order to trick the public into a war or an army, it will be one of the most daring experiments that has been made on the apathy of the people. You do not say whether the narrow escape of Livermore proceeded from a Republican rival or the mere declension of his personal consequence. On the former supposition the State of N. Hampshire must be on the point of abandoning the party it has hitherto been among the foremost in supporting. I see by the vote of the Senate of N. C. on the subject of the Alien and Sedition laws, that great progress has been made in that State towards throwing its weight into the scale of the administration.[17] What is understood to be the true result of the late elections for Congress? I have never seen a full return of it either for Massts. or S. Carolina or Georgia. I have no late information as to the prospect in the doubtful districts of this State. The opinion still prevails that Marshal will be disappointed; but it is agreed that the maximum of effort will be used in his favor, and we know that in that case, the issue must be attended with some uncertainty.[18] The proceedings at Richmond find their way to you immediately from thence better than I can give them to you. Indeed I do not receive them myself, but slowly and through casual opportunities. Adieu with the sincerest affection

Js Madison Jr

I have never yet learnt whether the death of Yard was a true or false report. What is the fact?

Jefferson to Madison

[Philadelphia] Jan. 30, 1799

My last to you was of the 16th. since which yours of the 12th. is recieved and it's contents disposed of properly. These met such approbation as to have occasioned an extraordinary impression of that day's paper.[19] Logan's bill is

17. When the Kentucky resolutions of 1798 were circulated to the state legislatures, the North Carolina Senate had them read and laid on the table, then adopted an address endorsing President Adams's conduct. Although the details of the House action is uncertain, it passed a resolution calling for Congress to repeal the Alien and Sedition Laws; see Frank Maloy Anderson, "Contemporary Opinion of the Virginia and Kentucky Resolutions, Part II," *AHR* 5 (1900): 235–36, and *PJM,* XVII, p. 22.

18. John Marshall won by about 100 votes; see William Stinchcombe, *The XYZ Affair* (Westport, Conn., 1980), p. 127.

19. The Philadelphia *Aurora* published JM's article "Foreign Influence" on Jan. 23, 1799; see *PJM,* XVII, pp. 214–20.

passed. The lower house, by a majority of 20. passed yesterday a bill continuing the suspension of intercourse with France, with a new clause enabling the President to admit intercourse with the rebellious negroes under Toussaint, who has an agent here, and has thrown off dependence on France.[20] The H of R have also voted 6. 74's and 6. 18's, in part of the additional navy, say 552 guns, which in England would cost 5,000 D, and here 10,000, consequently more than the whole 5. millions for which a loan is now opened at 8. per cent. The maintenance is estimated at £1,000 lawful a gun annually. A bill has been this day brought into the Senate for authorizing the P. *in case of a declaration of war or danger of invasion by any European power* to raise an *eventual*[21] army of 30. regiments, infantry, cavalry and artillery in addition to the *additional* army, the *provisional* army, and the corps of volunteers, which last he is authorized to brigade, officer, exercise, and pay during the time of exercise.[22] And all this notwithstanding Gerry's correspondence recently recd. and demonstrating the aversion of France to consider us as enemies. All depends on her patients standing the measures of the present session, and the surrounding *her* islands with our cruisers and capturing their armed vessels on her own coasts. If this is borne awhile, the public opinion is most manifestly veering in the middle states, and was even before the publication of Gerry's correspondence. In New York, Jersey, and Pensylvania, every one attests this, and Genl Sumpter, just arrived, assures me that the republicans in S C have gained 50. per cent in numbers since the election, which was in the moment of the X Y Z. fever. I believe there is no doubt the republican governor would be elected here now, and still less for next October. The gentlemen of N C seem to be satisfied that their new delegation will furnish but 3. perhaps only 2. anti-republicans; if so, we shall be gainers on the whole. But it is on the progress of public opinion we are to depend for rectifying the proceedings of the next Congress. The only question is whether this will not carry things beyond the reach of rectification. Petitions and remonstrances against the alien and sedition laws are coming from various parts of N. Y. Jersey and Pensyva: some of them very well drawn. I am in hopes Virginia will stand so countenanced by those States as to repress the wishes of the government to coerce her, which they might venture on if they supposed she would be left alone. Firmness on our part, but a passive firmness, is the true course. Anything rash or threatening might check the favorable dispositions of these middle states and rally them again around the measures which are ruining us.

Buonaparte appears to have settled Egypt peaceably and with the consent of the inhabitants, and seems to be looking towards the E. Indies where a most formidable cooperation has been prepared for demolishing the British power.

20. See De Conde, pp. 135–36.

21. TJ's italics here and below.

22. For the differences among the eventual army, the additional army, the provisional army, the volunteer army, and the regular army, see Richard H. Kohn, *Eagle and Sword: The Federalists and the Creation of the Military Establishment in the United States, 1783–1802* (New York, 1975), pp. 219–38.

I wish the affairs of Ireland were as hopeful, and the peace with the north of Europe.[23]

Nothing new here as to the price of tobo, the river not having yet admitted the bringing any to this market. Spain being entirely open to ours, and depending on it for her supplies during the cutting off of her intercourse with her own colonies by the superiority of the British at sea, is much in our favor.

I forgot to add that the bill for the *eventual* army authorizes the President to borrow 2. millions more. Present my best respects to Mrs. Madison, health and affectionate salutations to yourself. Adieu.

Jefferson to Madison

[Philadelphia] Feb. 5, 1799

I wrote you last on the 30th Jan since which yours of the 25th is recd. At the date of my letter I had only heard the bill for the eventual army read once. I concieved it additional to the *Provisional*[24] army etc. I must correct the error. The bill for the provisional army (about 10,000 men) expires this session without having been carried into execution. The eventual army (about 30,000) is a substitute. I say *about* 30,000 because some calculate the new establishment of a regiment we are now passing to a little over, and some a little under 1,000. officers and privates. The whole land army contemplated is the *existing* army 5000. the *additional* army 9000. the *eventual* army 30,000. and the *volunteer* army, the amount of which is not known. But besides that it is 44,000 men, and nobody pretends to say that there is from any quarter the least *real* danger of invasion. These may surely be set down at 500 dollars per annum a man, though they pretend that the existing army costs but 300. The reason of that is that there are not actually above 3000. of them, the 5,000 being merely on paper.

The bill for continuing the suspension of intercourse with France and her dependencies is still before the Senate, but will pass by a very great vote. An attack is made on what is called Toussaint's clause, the object of which, as is charged by the one party and *admitted* by the other, is to facilitate the separation of the island from France. The clause will pass however, by about 19. to 8. or perhaps 18. to 9. Rigaud at the head of the people of color maintains his allegiance. But they are only 25,000 souls, against 500,000. the number of the blacks. The treaty made with them by Maitland is (if they are to be separated

---

23. For a brilliant account of the Irish upheaval against Great Britain, see Thomas Pakenham, *The Year of Liberty: The Story of the Great Irish Rebellion of 1798* (Englewood Cliffs, N.J., 1970).

24. TJ's italics here and below.

from France) the best thing for us. They must get their provisions from us. It will indeed be in English bottoms, so that we shall lose the carriage. But the English will probably forbid them the ocean, confine them to their island, and thus prevent their becoming an American Algiers.[25] It must be admitted too, that they may play them off on us when they please. Against this there is no remedy but timely measures on our part, to clear ourselves, by degrees, of the matter on which that leven can work.

The opposition to Livermore was not republican. I have however seen letters from New Hampshire from which it appears that the public sentiment there is no longer progressive in any direction, but that at present it is dead water. That during the whole of their late session not a word has been heard of Jacobinism, disorganization etc. no reproach of any kind cast on the republicans, that there has been a general complaint among the members that they could hear but one side of the question, and the great anxiety to obtain a paper or papers which would put them in possession of both sides. From Massachusetts and R. I. I have no information. Connecticut remains rivetted in her political and religious bigotry.

Baldwin is elected by the legislature of Georgia a Senator for 6. years in the room of Tatnal, whose want of firmness had produced the effect of a change of sides.

We have had no report of Yard's being dead. He is certainly living.[26]

A piece published in Bache's paper on *foreign influence,* has had the greatest currency and effect. To an extraordinary first impression, they have been obliged to make a second, and of an extraordinary number.[27] It is such things as these the public want. They say so from all quarters, and that they wish to hear *reason* instead of *disgusting blackguardism.* The public sentiment being now on the creen and many heavy circumstances about to fall into the republican scale, we are sensible that this summer is the season for systematic energies and sacrifices. The engine is the press. Every man must lay his purse and his pen under contribution. As to the former, it is possible I may be obliged to assume something for you. As to the latter, let me pray and beseech you to set apart a certain portion of every post day to write what may be proper for the public. Send it to me while here, and when I go away I will let you know to whom you may send so that your name shall be sacredly secret. You can render such incalculable services in this way as to lessen the effect of our loss of your presence here. I shall see you on the 5th and 6th of March. Affectionate salutations to Mrs. Madison and yourself. Adieu.

---

25. For the treaty between Maitland and Toussaint, see Thomas O. Ott, *The Haitian Revolution, 1789–1804* (Knoxville, Tenn., 1973), pp. 100–4.

26. James Yard, whom TJ had appointed as U.S. consul general to St. Croix, Danish West Indies, in 1791, occasionally acted as a wine merchant for JM; see *PJM* (SS ser.), I, p. 30.

27. JM's essay "Foreign Influence" was originally published in the Philadelphia *Aurora* on Jan. 23, 1799.

Madison to Jefferson

[Orange] Feb. 8, 1799

DEAR SIR

I did not receive your last favor of the 16th Ult° till the mail after it was due, with the further delay of its coming by the way of Charlottesville. The last mail brought me not a single Newspaper, tho' it was before in arrears. That there is foul play with them I have no doubt. When it really happens that the entire Mass cannot be conveyed, I suspect that the favorite papers are selected, and the others laid by; and that when there is no real difficulty the pretext makes room for the same partiality. The idea of publishing the Debates of the Convention ought to be well weighed before the expediency of it, in a public as well as personal view be decided on. Besides the intimate connection between them, the whole volume ought to be examined with an eye to the use of which every part is susceptible. In the Despotism at present exercised over the rules of construction, and the counter reports of the proceedings that would perhaps be made out and mustered for the occasion, it is a problem what turn might be given to the impression on the public mind. But I shall be better able to form and explain my opinion by the time, which now approaches when I shall have the pleasure of seeing you. And you will have the advantage of looking into the sheets attentively before you finally make up your own. I have had a glance at Gerry's communications and P[ickering]s Report on it. It is impossible for any man of candor not to see in the former, an anxious desire on the part of France for accommodation, mixed with the feelings which Gerry satisfactorily explains. The latter displays a narrow understanding and a most malignant heart. Taken however in combination with preceding transactions, it is a link that fits the chain. The P. could not do less in his speech than allow France an option of peace, nor his Minister do more than to insult and exasperate her if possible into a refusal of it.[28]

Inclosed is a letter to Barnes with two orders which I hope will suffice both for you and him. Should there be any deficit I can now make it up here on your return where possibly it may be more convenient for you to receive it. I inclose also a few more observations which are submitted to your discretion, under the usual reservation. They were sketched prior to the arrival of P's Report, to which they may appear to have reference; or they might have assumed still more of that aspect.[29] The impression of your Seals have not been very distinct, but there has been no other suspicious circumstance attending

---

28. For Adams's release of Gerry's notes on Feb. 2, 1799, see Kurtz, pp. 344-53.

29. TJ submitted JM's observations to the Philadelphia *Aurora,* which published them on Feb. 23, 1799, under the title "Political Reflections" by "A Citizen of the United States." See *PJM,* XVII, pp. 212, 237-43; see also TJ to JM, Feb. 19, 1799, below.

them. I put into the letter to Barnes, the last of them that you may judge yourself of the appearance.

If you find it not inconvenient in your strolls to buy me a cheap diamond [for cutting glass] and bring it with you, I shall be obliged to you to take that trouble. An indifferent one which I owned was lost, and I wish to replace it.

Jefferson to Madison

[Philadelphia] Feb. 12, 1799

I wrote you last on the 5th. which acknoleged yours of Jan. 25. the last at hand. Yesterday the bill for 6.74's and 6.18's passed the H. of R. by 54. against 42. And the bill for a new organization of the army (into regiments of about 1,000.) passed the Senate. The bill continuing the suspension of intercourse with France and her dependencies has passed both houses, but the Senate struck out the clauses permitting the President to extend it to other powers. Toussaint's clause however was retained. Even South Carolinians in the H. of R. voted for it. We may expect therefore black crews, and supercargoes and missionaries thence into the southern states; and when that leven begins to work, I would gladly compound with a great part of our northern country, if they would honestly stand neuter. If this combustion can be introduced among us under any veil whatever, we have to fear it. We shall this day pass the retaliation bill. It recites and is expressly founded on the French arret of Oct. 29. 98, communicated to us by the President. It came out from Sedgwick and Stockton in debate that they had had it from the Secy. of state that he had received a letter from Mr. King informing him of the suspension of that arret. Yet tho' they knew we were legislating on it, the P. has not communicated it; and the retaliators insist on passing the bill.[30] It is now acknoleged on all hands, denied on none, and declared by the insurance companies that during the last 6. months the British depredns. have far exceeded the French.[31] King has been appointed to enter into a treaty with Russia at London and Phocion Smith was yesterday confirmed by the Senate as Envoy extray and M. P. to Constantinople to make a like treaty with the Turks. To chuse the moment of a coalition between the Turks, Russians and English against France, to unite us by treaty with that body as openly as they intend to pro-

30. For the retaliation act against French naval attacks, see Kurtz, p. 352, and Bowman, p. 366.
31. The Insurance Company of North America listed American damages from British vessels at $280,000 and from French privateers at $260,000; see Kurtz, p. 352. Between 1796 and 1798, insurance rates on American shipping bound for the Caribbean increased fivefold as a result of seizures by England and France; see De Conde, pp. 124-25.

pose, cannot be misconstrued. I send you under a separate cover the French originals of Gerry's communcns, one of G. N.'s pamphlets[32] and the Treasury statements of exports and imports of the last year. Adieu.

P. S. No letter you could write after your receipt of this will find me here.

P.M. The vessel called the Retaliation, formerly French property taken by us, armed and sent to cruise on them, retaken by them and carried into Guadaloupe, arrived here this morning with her own capt. crew etc. They say that new commrs. from France arrived at Guadaloupe, sent Victor Hughes[33] home in irons, liberated this crew, said to the capt that they found him to be an officer of the US. bearing their commission, possessed of a vessel called the Retaliation then in their port; that they should not enquire into any preceding fact, but that he was free with his vessel and crew to depart: that as to differences with the US. commrs. were coming out from France to settle them; in the mean time no injury should be done to us or our citizens. This was known to every Senator when we met; the Retaliation bill came on, on it's passage, and was passed with only 2. dissenting voices, 2 or 3. who would have dissented happening to be absent.

Jefferson to Madison

[Philadelphia] Feb. 19, 1799

I wrote to you last on the 11th. Yesterday the bill for the *eventual*[34] army of 30 regiments (30.000) and 75.000. volunteers passed the Senate. By an amendment, the P was authorized to use the volunteers for every purpose for which he can use militia, so that the militia are rendered compleatly useless. The friends of the bill acknoleged that the volunteers are a *militia,* and agreed that they might properly be called the Presidential militia. They are not to go out of their state without their own consent. Consequently all service out of the state is thrown on the constitutional militia, the Presidential militia being exempted from doing duty with them. Leblanc an agent from Desfourneaux of Guadaloupe came in the Retaliation. You will see in the papers Desfourneaux's letter to the President which will correct some immaterial circumstances of the statement in my last. You will see the truth of the main fact that the vessel and

---

32. The pamphlet, entitled *A Letter from George Nicholas to His Friend in Virginia* (Lexington, Ky., 1798), was a defense of the Kentucky resolutions; see Malone, III, pp. 412–13.

33. Victor Hughes, a French merchant in Saint Domingue, lost a fortune when Toussaint l'Ouverture ousted the French. After returning to France, he was dispatched to Guadaloupe and recaptured the island from the British in 1794, serving as governor until he was replaced by General Edmé-Étienne Borne Desforneaux in Nov. 1798; see *PJM,* XVII, pp. 233, 236.

34. TJ's italics here and below.

crew were liberated without condition. Notwithstanding this, they have obliged Leblanc to recieve the French prisoners and to admit in the papers the terms, 'in *exchange* for *prisoners* taken from us,' he denying at the same time that they considered them as *prisoners,* or had any idea of *exchange.* The object of his mission was not at all relative to that; but they chuse to keep up the idea of a cartel, to prevent the transaction from being used as evidence of the sincerity of the French govent towards a reconciliation. He came to assure us of a discontinuance of all irregularities in French privateers from Guadaloupe.[35] He has been recieved very cavalierly. In the meantime, a *consul general* is named to St. Domingo; who may be considered as our minister to Toussaint.[36]

But the event of events was announced to the Senate yesterday. It is this. It seems that soon after Gerry's departure overtures must have been made by Pichon, French chargé d'affaires at the Hague, to Murray. They were so soon matured, that on the 28th of Sep. 98, Taleyrand writes to Pichon, approving what had been done, and particularly of his having assured Murray that *whatever* Plenipotentiary the govent of the U S. should send to France to end our differences would undoubtedly be recieved with the respect due to the representative of a *free, indepndt and powerful nation;* declaring that the President's instructions to his envoys at Paris, if they contain the whole of the American government's intentions, announce dispositions which have been always entertained by the Directory, and desiring him to communicate these expressions to Murray in order to convince him of the sincerity of the French government and to prevail on him to transmit them to his government. This is dated Sep 28. and may have been received by Pichon Oct 1. And near 5. months elapse before it is communicated. Yesterday, the P. nominated to the Senate W. V. Murray M. P. to the French republic and adds that he shall be instructed not to go to France without direct and unequivocal assurances from the Fr. government that he shall be recieved in character, enjoy the due privileges and a minister of equal rank title and power, be appointed to discuss and conclude our controversies by a new treaty.[37] This had evidently been kept secret from the Feds of both Houses, as appeared by their dismay. The Senate have passed over this day without taking it up. It is said they are graveled and divided; some are for opposing, others do not know what to do.[38] But in the meantime, they

35. Edmé-Étienne Borne Desforneaux was France's governor-general of Guadaloupe. During the quasi war at sea, the French captured the *Retaliation,* a former French sloop of war of twelve guns that had earlier been taken by the American navy and renamed. Desforneaux subsequently released the American captain and seamen and sent President Adams a letter denying enmity towards the United States; see De Conde, pp. 126-29, 418.

36. For the mission of Edward Stevens as consul general to Santo Domingo, see *ibid.,* pp. 136-40.

37. For the negotiations leading to Adams's action, see *ibid.,* pp. 142-80, and Bowman, pp. 334-66. For TJ's reaction, see Malone, III, pp. 434-36.

38. For the conflict between the High Federalists and the Adams Federalists, see Dauer, pp. 212-38.

have been permitted to go on with all the measures of war and patronage, and when the close of the session is at hand it is made known. However it silences all arguments against the sincerity of France, and renders desperate every further effort towards war. I enclose you a paper with more particulars. Be so good as to keep it till you see me, and then return it as it is the copy of one I sent to another person, and is the only copy I have.

Since I began my letter I have recieved yours of Feb. 8. with it's enclosures. That referred to my discretion is precious, and shall be used accordingly.

Affectionate salutations to Mrs. M. and yourself, and adieu

P. S. I have committed you and your friends for 100. D. I will justify it when I see you.

ENCLOSURE
Extract of a letter from Taleyrand to Pichon, chargé d'affaires of France at the Hague, dated Paris Sep. 28. 98.

——[']I am thoroughly convinced that should explanations take place with confidence between the two cabinets, irritation would cease, a crowd of misunderstandings would disappear and the ties of friendship would be more strongly united as each party would discover the hand which sought to disunite them.

—According to these bases, (a reference to former correspondence) you were right to assert that whatever Plenipotentiary the government of the US. might send to France to put an end to the existing differences between the two countries wod. be undoubtedly recieved with the respect due to the representative of a free, independent and powerful nation.

I cannot persuade myself, citizen, that the American govmt. need any further declarations from us to induce them, in order to renew the negotiation, to adopt such measures as would be suggested to them by their desire to bring the differences to a peaceable end. If misunderstandings on both sides have prevented some explanations from reaching that end, it is presumable that, those misunderstandings being done away, nothing henceforth will bring obstacles to the reciprocal dispositions. The President's instructions to his envoys at Paris, which I have only known by the copy given you by Mr. Murray and recieved by me July 9. announce, if they contain the whole of the American government's intentions, dispositions which could only have added to those which the Directory have always entertained, and notwithstanding the posterior acts of that governmt., notwithstanding the irritating and almost hostile measures they have adopted, the Directory has manifested it's perseverence in the sentiments deposited both in my correspondence with Mr. Gerry and in my letter to you of the 11th. Fructidor, and which I have herein before repeated in the most explicit manner. Carry therefore, citizen, to Mr. Murray those positive expressions, in order to convince him of our sincerity, and prevail upon him to transmit them to his government.'

Extract from the President's message to Senate of Feb. 18. nominating W. Vans Murray M. P. of the US. to the French republic. 'He will be instructed that he shd. not go to France without direct and unequivocal assurances from the French government signified by their minister of foreign relations that he shall be recieved in character, shall enjoy the privileges attached to his character by the Law of nations and that a minister of equal rank, title and power shall be appointed to treat with him, to discuss and conclude all controversies between the two republics by a treaty.'

Observe the date of Taleyrand's letter, Sep. 28. Pichon would recieve it Oct. 1. A matter of such importance could not be near 5. months coming here. The P. then has probably been possessed of it before Congress met and has kept it back that the measures of war and influence might not be prevented.

Do not let this paper get into the press, or go out of your hand: but avail yourself of it's substance as you please.

Jefferson to Madison

Philadelphia Feb. 26, 1799

My last to you was of the 19th. It acknoleged yours of the 8th. In mine, I informed you of the nomination of Murray. There is evidence that the letter of Taleyrand was known to one of the Secretaries, therefore probably to all. The nomination, however, is declared by one of them to have been kept secret from them all. He added that he was glad of it, as, had they been consulted, the advice would have been against making the nomination. To the rest of the party however the whole was a secret till the nomination was announced. Never did a party shew a stronger mortification, and consequently that war had been their object. Dana declared in debate (as I have from those who were present) that we had done everything which might provoke France to war; that we had given her insults which no nation ought to have borne; and yet she would not declare war. The conjecture as to the Executive is that they recieved Taleyrand's letter before or about the meeting of Congress;[39] that not meaning to meet the overture effectually, they kept it secret, and let all the war measures go on, but that just before the separation of the Senate, the P. not thinking he could justify the concealing such an overture, nor indeed that it could be concealed, made a nomination hoping that his friends in the Senate would take on their own shoulders the odium of rejecting it. But they did not chuse it. The Hamiltonians would not, and the others could not, alone. The whole artillery of the phalanx therefore was plaid secretly on the P. and he was obliged himself to take a step which should parry the overture while it wears the face of acceding to it. (Mark that I state this as conjecture; but founded on workings and indications which have been under our eyes.) Yesterday, therefore, he sent in a nomination of Oliver Elsworth, Patrick Henry and W. Vans Murray, Envoys Ext. and M. P. to the French Republic, but declaring the two former should not leave this country till they should recieve from the French

39. TJ was less than generous to Adams, who apparently received on Feb. 1, 1799, Talleyrand's letter of Sept. 28, 1798, in a dispatch from William Vans Murray of Oct. 7, 1798. Adams sent it to the Senate on Feb. 18, 1799, and TJ enclosed it to JM on Feb. 19, 1799; see De Conde, p. 174.

Directory assurances that they should be received with the respect due by the law of nations to their character etc.[40] This, if not impossible, must at least keep off the day, so hateful and so fatal to them, of reconciliation, and leave more time for new projects of provocation. Yesterday witnessed a scandalous scene in the H. of R. It was the day for taking up the report of their commee against the Alien and Sedition laws etc. They held a Caucus and determined that not a word should be spoken on their side in answer to anything which should be said on the other. Gallatin took up the Alien and Nicholas the Sedition laws; but after a little while of common silence, they began to enter into loud conversations, laugh, cough, etc., so that for the last hour of these gentlemen's speaking they must have had the lungs of a vendue master to have been heard. Livingston however attempted to speak. But after a few sentences the Speaker called him to order and told him what he was saying was not to the question. It was impossible to proceed. The question was taken and carried in favor of the report 52 to 48. The real strength of the two parties is 56. to 50.[41] But two of the latter have not attended this session. I send you the report of their committee.

I still expect to leave this on the 1st and be with you on the 7th of March. But it is possible I may not set out till the 4th. and then shall not be with you till the 10th. Affectionately adieu.

ENCLOSURE
Congressional Report Defending the Alien and Sedition Laws

Feb. 21, 1799[42]

The committee to whom were referred the memorials of sundry inhabitants of the counties of Suffolk and Queen, in the State of New York; of Essex county, in New Jersey; of the counties of Philadelphia, York, Northampton, Mifflin, Dauphin, Washington, and Cumberland, in Pennsylvania; and of the county of Amelia, in Virginia, complaining of the act entitled "An act concerning aliens," and other late acts of Congress, submit the following report:

It is the professed object of these petitions to solicit a repeal of two acts passed during the last session of Congress, the one "An act concerning aliens," the other "An act in addition to an act for the punishment of certain crimes against the United States," on the ground of their being unconstitutional, oppressive, and impolitic.

The committee cannot, however, forbear to notice that the principal measures hitherto adopted for repelling the aggressions and insults of France have not escaped animadversion.

Complaints are particularly directed against the laws providing for a navy; for augmenting the army; authorizing a provisional army and corps of volunteers; for laying a duty on stamped vellum, parchment, and paper; assessing and collecting direct taxes; and authorizing loans for the public service.

---

40. For the maneuvers of the High Federalists that led Adams to add Ellsworth and Henry to the peace mission, see *ibid.*, pp. 181–85. For the delay in sending the mission, see Kurtz, pp. 374–89.
41. See Malone, III, pp. 413–14.
42. The report is printed from *ASP, M,* I, pp. 181–84.

With these topics of complaint, in some of the petitions, are intermingled invectives against the policy of the Government from an early period, and insinuations derogatory to the character of the Legislature and of the administration.

While the committee regret that the public councils should ever be invited to listen to other than expressions of respect, they trust that they have impartially considered the questions referred to their examination, and formed their opinions on a just appreciation of their merits, with a due regard to the authority of Government and the dispassionate judgment of the American people.

The act concerning aliens, and the act in addition to the act entitled an act for the punishment of certain crimes, shall be first considered.

Their *constitutionality* is impeached. It is contended that Congress have no power to pass a law for removing aliens.

To this it is answered, that the asylum given by a nation to foreigners is mere matter of favor, resumable at the public will. On this point abundant authorities might be adduced, but the common practice of nations attests the principle.

The right of removing aliens, as an incident to the power of war and peace, according to the theory of the constitution, belongs to the Government of the United States. By the fourth section of the fourth article of the constitution, Congress is required to protect each State from invasion; and is vested by the eighth section of the fifth article with power to make all laws which shall be proper to carry into effect all powers vested by the constitution in the Government of the United States, or in any department or officer thereof; and to remove from the country, in times of hostility, dangerous aliens, who may be employed in preparing the way for invasion, is a measure necessary for the purpose of preventing invasion, and, of course, a measure that Congress is empowered to adopt.

The act is said to be unconstitutional, because to remove aliens is a direct breach of the constitution, which provides, "by the ninth section of the first article, that the migration or importation of such persons as any of the States shall think proper to admit shall not be prohibited by the Congress prior to the year 1808."

To this it is answered, first, that this section in the constitution was enacted solely in order to prevent Congress from prohibiting, until after a fit period, the importation of slaves, which appears from two considerations: First, that the restriction is confined to the States which were in existence at the time of establishing the constitution; and, secondly, that it is to continue only twenty years; for neither of which modifications could there have been the least reason, had the restriction been intended to apply, not to slaves particularly, but to all emigrants in general.

Secondly, It is answered, that to prevent emigration in general, is a very different thing from sending off, after their arrival, such emigrants as might abuse the indulgence, by rendering themselves dangerous to the peace or safety of the country; and that if the constitution in this particular should be so construed, it would prevent Congress from driving a body of armed men from the country, who might land with views evidently hostile.

Thirdly, that as the constitution has given to the States no power to remove aliens during the period of their limitation under consideration, in the mean time, on the construction assumed, there would be no authority in the country empowered to send away dangerous aliens, which cannot be admitted; and that on a supposition that the aforesaid restrictive clause included every description of emigrants, the different sections must receive such a construction as shall reconcile them with each other; and, according to a fair interpretation of the different parts of the constitution, the section cannot be considered as restrictive on the power of Congress to send away dangerous foreigners in times of threatened or actual hostility. And though the United States, at the time of passing this act, were not in a state of declared war, they were in a state of partial hostility, and had the power, by law, to provide, as by this act they have done, for removing dangerous aliens.

This law is said to violate that part of the constitution which provides that the trial of all crimes, except in cases of impeachment, shall be by jury; whereas, this act invests the President with power to send away aliens on his own suspicion, and thus to inflict punishment without trial by jury.

It is answered, in the first place, that the constitution was made for citizens, not for aliens, who of consequence have no rights under it, but remain in the country, and enjoy the benefit of the laws, not as matter of right, but merely as matter of favor and permission; which favor and permission may be withdrawn, whenever the Government charged with the general welfare shall judge their further continuance dangerous.

It is answered, in the second place, that the provisons in the constitution relative to presentment and trial of offences by juries, do not apply to the revocation of an asylum given to aliens. Those provisions solely respect crimes, and the alien may be removed without having committed any offence, merely from motives of policy or security. The citizen, being a member of society, has a right to remain in the country, of which he cannot be disfranchised, except for offences first ascertained, on presentment and trial by jury.

It is answered, thirdly, that the removal of aliens, though it may be inconvenient to them, cannot be considered as a punishment inflicted for an offence, but, as before remarked, merely the removal from motives of general safety, of an indulgence which there is danger of their abusing, and which we are in no manner bound to grant or continue.

The "Act in addition to an act entitled an act for the punishment of certain crimes against the United States," commonly called the "sedition act," contains provisions of a two-fold nature: first, against seditious acts; and, second, against libellous and seditious writings. The first have never been complained of, nor has any objection been made to its validity. The objection applies solely to the second; and on the ground, in the first place, that Congress have no power by the constitution to pass any act for punishing libels, no such power being expressly given; and all powers not given to Congress being reserved to the States, respectively, or the people thereof.

To this objection it is answered, that a law to punish false, scandalous, and malicious writings against the Government, with intent to stir up sedition, is a law necessary for carrying into effect the power vested by the constitution in the Government of the United States and in the Departments and officers thereof, and, consequently, such a law as Congress may pass; because the direct tendency of such writings is to obstruct the acts of the Government by exciting opposition to them, to endanger its existence, by rendering it odious and contemptible in the eyes of the people, and to produce seditious combinations against the laws, the power to punish which has never been questioned; because it would be manifestly absurd to suppose that a Government might punish sedition, and yet be void of power to prevent it by punishing those acts which plainly and necessarily lead to it; and because, under the general power to make all laws proper and necessary for carrying into effect the powers vested by the constitution in the Government of the United States, Congress has passed many laws for which no express provision can be found in the constitution, and the constitutionality of which has never been questioned; such as the first section of the act now under consideration, for punishing seditious combinations; the act passed during the present session for punishing persons who, without authority from the Government, shall carry on any correspondence relative to foreign affairs with any foreign Government; the act for the punishment of certain crimes against the United States, which defines and punishes misprision of treason; the tenth and twelfth sections, which declare the punishment of accessaries to piracy, and of persons who shall confederate to become pirates themselves, or to induce others to become so; the fifteenth section, which inflicts a penalty on those who steal or falsify the record of any court of the United States; the eighteenth and twenty-first sections, which provide for the punishment of persons committing perjury in any court of the United States, or attempting to bribe any of their judges; the twenty-second section, which punishes those who obstruct or resist the process of any court of the United States; and the twenty-third, against rescuing offenders who have been convicted of any capital offence before those courts; provisions, none of which are expressly authorized, but which have been considered as constitutional, because they are necessary and proper for carrying into effect certain powers expressly given to Congress.

It is objected to this act, in the second place, that it is expressly contrary to that part of the constitution which declares that "Congress shall make no law respecting an establishment of religion, or prohibiting the free exercise thereof, or abridging the liberty of the press." The act in question is said to be an abridgment of the liberty of the press, and therefore unconstitutional.

To this it is answered, in the first place, that the liberty of the press consists, not in a license for every man to publish what he pleases, without being liable to punishment if he should abuse this license to the injury of others, but in a permission to publish, without previous restraint, whatever he may think proper, being answerable to the public and individuals for any abuse of this permission to their prejudice; in like manner as the liberty of speech does not authorize a man to speak malicious slanders against his neighbor, nor the liberty of action justify him in going by violence into another man's house, or in assaulting any person whom he may meet in the streets. In the several States the liberty of the press has always been understood in this manner, and no other; and the constitution of every State, which has been framed and adopted since the declaration of independence, asserts "the liberty of the press;" while in several, if not all, their laws provide for the punishment of libellous publications, which would be a manifest absurdity and contradiction, if the liberty of the press meant to publish any and every thing, without being amenable to the laws for the abuse of this license. According to this just, legal, and universally admitted definition of "the liberty of the press," a law to restrain its licentiousness, in publishing false, scandalous, and malicious libels against the Government, cannot be considered as an "abridgment" of its "liberty."

It is answered, in the second place, that the liberty of the press did never extend, according to the laws of any State, or of the United States, or of England, from whence our laws are derived, to the publication of false, scandalous, and malicious writings against the Government, written or published with intent to do mischief, such publications being unlawful and punishable in every State; from whence it follows, undeniably, that a law to punish seditious and malicious publications is not an abridgment of the "liberty of the press;" for it would be a manifest absurdity to say that a man's liberty was abridged by punishing him for doing that which he never had a liberty to do.

It is answered, thirdly, that the act in question cannot be unconstitutional, because it makes nothing penal that was not penal before, and gives no new powers to the court, but is merely declaratory of the common law, and useful for rendering that law more generally known and more easily understood. This cannot be denied, if it be admitted, as it must be, that false, scandalous, and malicious libels against the Government of the country, published with intent to do mischief, are punishable by the common law; for, by the second section of the third article of the constitution, the judicial power of the United States is expressly extended to all offences arising under the constitution. By the constitution, the Government of the United States is established, for many important objects, as *the Government of the country;* and libels against that Government, therefore, are offences arising under the constitution, and consequently are punishable at common law by the courts of the United States. The act, indeed, is so far from having *extended* the law, and the power of the court, that it has abridged both, and has enlarged instead of abridging the "liberty of the press:" for, at common law, libels against the Government might be punished with fine and imprisonment at the discretion of the court, whereas the act limits the fine to two thousand dollars, and the imprisonment to two years; and it also allows the party accused to give the *truth* in evidence for his justification, which, by the common law, was expressly forbidden.

And lastly, it is answered, that had the constitution intended to prohibit Congress from legislating at all on the subject of the press, which is the construction whereon the objections to this law are founded, it would have used the same expressions as in that part of the clause which relates to religion and religious tests; whereas the words are wholly different: "Congress," says the constitution, amendment 3rd, "shall make no law *respecting* an establishment of religion, or *prohibiting* the free exercise thereof or *abridging* the freedom of speech, or the press." Here it is manifest that the constitution intended to prohibit Congress from legislating at all on the subject of *religious establishments,* and the prohibition is made in the most express terms. Had the same intention prevailed respecting the press, the same expressions would have been used, and Congress would have been "prohibited from passing any law *respecting* the press." They are not, however, "prohibited" from legislating at all on the subject, but merely from *abridging* the liberty of the press. It is evident they may legislate respecting the press, may pass laws for its regulation, and to punish those who pervert it into an engine of mischief, provided those laws do not "abridge" its "liberty." Its *liberty,* according to the well-known and universally admitted definition, consists in permission to publish, without previous restraint upon the press, but subject to punishment afterwards for improper publications. A law, therefore, to impose previous restraint upon the press, and not one to inflict punishment on wicked and malicious publications, would be a law to abridge the liberty of the press, and, as such, unconstitutional.

The foregoing reasoning is submitted as vindicating the validity of the laws in question.

Although the committee believe that each of the measures adopted by Congress during the last session is susceptible of an analytical justification on the principles of the constitution, and national policy, yet they prefer to rest their vindication on the true ground of considering them as parts of a general system of defence, adapted to a crisis of extraordinary difficulty and danger.

It cannot be denied that the power to declare war, to raise and support armies, to provide and maintain a navy, to suppress insurrections, and repel invasions, and also the power to defray the necessary expense by loans or taxes, is vested in Congress. Unfortunately for the present generation of mankind, a contest has arisen, and rages with unabated ferocity, which has desolated the fairest portions of Europe, and shaken the fabric of society through the civilized world. From the nature and effects of this contest, as developed in the experience of nations, melancholy inferences must be drawn, that it is unsusceptible of the restraints which have either designated the objects, limited the duration, or mitigated the horrors of national contentions. In the internal history of France, and in the conduct of her forces and partisans in the countries which have fallen under her power, the public councils of our country were required to discern the dangers which threatened the United States, and to guard not only against the usual consequences of war, but also against the effects of an unprecedented combination to establish new principles of social action, on the subversion of religion, morality, law, and government. Will it be said, that the raising of a small army, and an eventual provision for drawing into the public service a considerable proportion of the whole force of the country was, in such a crisis, unwise or improvident?

If such should be the assertion, let it be candidly considered whether some of our fertile and flourishing States did not, six months since, present as alluring objects for the gratification of ambition or cupidity as the inhospitable climate of Egypt. What then appeared to be the comparative difficulties between invading America and subverting the British power in the East Indies? If this was a professed, not real object of the enterprise, let it be asked, if the Sultan of the Ottoman empire was not really the friend of France, at the time when his unsuspecting dependencies were invaded; and whether the United States were not, at the same time, loaded with insults and assailed with hostility? If, however, it be asserted that the system of France is hostile only to despotic or monarchical Governments, and that our security arises from the form of our constitution, let Switzerland, first divided and disarmed by perfidious seductions, now agonized by relentless power, illustrate the consequences of similar credulity. Is it necessary at this time to vindicate the naval armament? Rather may not the inquiry be boldly made, whether the guardians of the public weal would not have deserved and received the reproaches of every patriotic American, if a contemptible naval force had been longer permitted to intercept our necessary supplies, destroy our principal source of revenue, and seize, at the entrance of our harbors and rivers, the products of our industry destined to our foreign markets? If such injuries were at all to be repelled, is not the restriction which confined captures by our ships solely to armed vessels of France a sufficient proof of our moderation?

If, therefore, naval and military preparations were necessary, a provision of funds to defray the consequent expenses was of course indispensable; a review of all the measures that have been adopted since the establishment of the Government will prove that Congress have not been unmindful of the wishes of the American people, to avoid an accumulation of the public debt; and the success which has attended these measures affords conclusive evidence of the sincerity of their intentions. But to purchase sufficient quantities of military supplies to establish a navy, and provide for all the contingencies of an army, without recourse to new taxes and loans, was impracticable; both measures were, in fact, adopted. In devising a mode of taxation, the convenience and ease of the least wealthy class of the people were consulted as much as possible; and, although the expenses of assessment have furnished a topic of complaint, it is found that the allowances are barely sufficient to ensure the execution of the law, even aided as they are by the disinterested and patriotic exertions of worthy citizens; besides, it ought to be remembered that the expenses of organizing a new system should not, on any principle, be regarded as a permanent burden on the public.

In authorizing a loan of money, Congress have not been inattentive to prevent a permanent debt; in this particular, also, the public opinion and interest have been consulted. On considering the law, as well as the manner in which it is proposed to be carried into execution, the committee are well satisfied in finding any excess in the immediate charge upon the revenue is likely to be compensated by the facility of redemption which is secured to the Government.

The alien and sedition acts, so called, form a part, and in the opinion of the committee an essential part, in these precautionary and protective measures adopted for our security.

France appears to have an organized system of conduct towards foreign nations, to bring them within the sphere and under the dominion of her influence and control. It has been unremittingly pursued under all the changes of her internal polity. Her means are in wonderful coincidence with her ends: among these, and not least successful, is the direction and employment of the active and versatile talents of her citizens abroad as emissaries and spies. With a numerous body of French citizens and other foreigners, and admonished by the passing scenes in other countries, as well as by aspects in our own, knowing they had the power, and believing it to be their duty, Congress passed the law respecting aliens, directing the *dangerous* and *suspected* to be removed, and leaving to the *inoffensive* and *peaceable* a safe asylum.

The principles of the sedition law, so called, are among the most ancient principles of our Governments. They have been ingrafted into statutes, or practised upon as maxims of the common law, according as occasion required. They were often and justly applied in the revolutionary war. Is it not strange that now they should first be denounced as oppressive, when they have long been recognised in the jurisprudence of these States?

The necessity that dictated these acts, in the opinion of the committee, still exists.

So eccentric are the movements of the French Government, that we can form no opinion of their future designs towards our country. They may recede from the tone of menace and insolence to employ the arts of seduction, before they astonish us with their ultimate designs. Our safety consists in the wisdom of the public councils, a co-operation on the part of the people with the Government, by supporting the measures provided for repelling aggressions, and an obedience to the social laws.

After a particular and general review of the whole subject referred to their consideration, the committee see no ground for rescinding these acts of the Legislature. The complaints preferred by some of the petitioners may be fairly attributed to a diversity of sentiment naturally to be expected among a people of various habits and education, widely dispersed over an extensive country; the innocent misconceptions of the American people will, however, yield to reflection and argument, and from *them* no danger is to be apprehended.

In such of the petitions as are conceived in a style of vehement and acrimonious remonstrance, the committee perceive too plain indications of the principles of that exotic system which convulses the civilized world. With this system, however organized, the public councils cannot safely parley or temporize, whether it assumes the guise of patriotism to mislead the affections of the people; whether it be employed in forming projects of local and eccentric ambition, or shall appear in the more generous form of open hostility, it ought to be regarded as the bane of public as well as private tranquillity and order.

Those to whom the management of public affairs is now confided, cannot be justified in yielding any established principles of law or government to the suggestions of modern theory; their duty requires them to respect the lessons of experience, and transmit to posterity the civil and religious privileges which are the birthright of our country, and which it was the great object of our happy constitution to secure and perpetuate.

Impressed with these sentiments, the committee beg leave to report the following resolutions:

Resolved, That it is inexpedient to repeal the act passed the last session, entitled "An act concerning aliens."

Resolved, That it is inexpedient to repeal the act passed the last session, entitled "An act in addition to the act entitled 'An act for the punishment of certain crimes against the United States.'"

Resolved, That it is inexpedient to repeal any of the laws respecting the navy, military establishment, or revenue of the United States.

25

THE RESOLUTIONS RENEWED, 1799

*J*EFFERSON LEFT PHILADELPHIA on March 1, 1799, and when he reached his home he found the north end of Monticello still without a roof. "It seems," he wrote his daughter, "as if I should never get it inhabitable." But by April, when he paid off his roofer, the house had been covered, and he turned to the laying of floors in his evolving home.[1] His mind was still on the boiling cauldron of politics, however, even when he was writing to a friend in Italy: "Every course of life doubtless has its difficulties; but in the stormy ocean of public life the billows are more furious, the blasts more deadly, than those which assail the bark moored in a retired port."[2]

Stormy or not, Madison decided to leave retirement for politics in April 1799 after learning that Patrick Henry, by now a confirmed Federalist and a supporter of the Alien and Sedition Laws, planned to run for the Virginia legislature.[3] On the day that Jefferson wrote about "the stormy ocean of public life," Madison was elected once again to the General Assembly as a delegate from Orange County.[4]

For almost six months—between March and late August—Madison and Jefferson exchanged no letters. Throughout January and February 1799, while Jefferson was in Philadelphia, both men suspected that their mail was being tampered with. "The suspicions against the government on this subject," Jefferson cautioned, "are strong." When Madison failed to receive his newspapers on time, he concluded "that there is foul play with them." A close inspection of the seals on Jefferson's letters showed that they were not "very distinct," Madison added, "but there has been no other suspicious circumstance attending them."[5]

1. Malone, III, pp. 241–42.
2. TJ to Charles Bellini, Apr. 24, 1799, *ibid.,* p. 436.
3. Brant, III, p. 465, and Robert A. Rutland, *James Madison: The Founding Father* (New York, 1987), p. 159.
4. Ketcham, p. 398.
5. See TJ to JM, Jan. 16, 1799, above, and JM to TJ, Jan. 25, 1799, above, and Feb. 8, 1799, above.

Late in the summer, Jefferson invited Madison to Monticello to "consider a little together what is to be done" about renewing the resolutions of the previous year. "That the principles already advanced by Virginia and Kentuckey are not to be yielded in silence, I presume we all agree." On a hot August day, Madison visited Jefferson to pick up a load of nails and, more importantly, to coolly dissuade him from some extreme views set forth in his hastily scribbled note of invitation.[6] He favored an answer to the states and to the committee in Congress that had endorsed the Alien and Sedition Acts, arguing that these laws violated the Constitution and exercised "powers over us to which we have never assented." Like Jefferson, he wanted to "express in affectionate and conciliatory language our warm attachment to union with our sister-states, and to the instrument and principles by which we are united." But Madison thought that Jefferson had pushed his compact theory too far when he said that "we are willing to sacrifice to this [Constitution] every thing except those rights of self government[,] the securing of which was the object of that compact." For from that exception flowed Jefferson's fateful—perhaps fatal—theory of "scission," or secession. If the Republicans failed to rally the people around "the true principles of our federal compact," Jefferson had argued, we should then "sever ourselves from that union we so much value, rather than give up the rights of self government which we have reserved, and in which alone we see liberty, safety and happiness."[7]

After consulting with Madison, Jefferson quickly retreated from his extremist position, quietly revising his proposals for joint action by Virginia and Kentucky. In a letter to his neighbor Wilson Cary Nicholas, the intermediary in 1798 and again in 1799, he omitted his suggestion about severing "ourselves from [the] union" and modified his stance about reserving "the rights resulting to us from these palpable violations of the constitutional compact by the Federal government." Although he repeated this phrase tentatively to Nicholas, he noted Madison's objections and conceded that he would "recede readily, not only in deference to his judgment, but because as we should never think of separation but for repeated and enormous violations, so these, when they occur, will be cause enough of themselves."[8]

Madison and Jefferson planned at least one more meeting before the state legislator went to Richmond and the vice president to Philadelphia. But Jefferson, acting on the advice of Monroe, canceled his trip to Montpellier at the last moment, fearful that a local Federalist snooper "would make it a subject of some political slander, and perhaps of some political injury. I have yeilded to

---

6. For the order of nails, see JM to TJ, [Aug. 14, 1800], below.

7. TJ to JM, Aug. 23, 1799, below. JM's copy has a note in his hand saying that a visit "took the place of an answer to the letter."

8. TJ to Wilson Cary Nicholas, Sept. 5, 1799, in Ford, VII, pp. 389-92. For a discussion of the Kentucky resolutions of 1799, which uses the word "nullification," see Adrienne Koch and Harry Ammon, "The Virginia and Kentucky Resolutions: An Episode in Jefferson and Madison's Defense of Civil Liberties," *WMQ* 5 (1948): 166-69. They are printed in Ethelbert Dudley Warfield, *The Kentucky Resolutions of 1798: An Historical Study* (New York, 1894), pp. 123-26.

his representations," Jefferson confessed, "and therefore shall not have the pleasure of seeing you till my return from Philadelphia.... I regret it the more too, because from the commencement of the ensuing session, I shall trust the post offices with nothing confidential, persuaded that during the ensuing twelve-month [leading to the election of 1800] they will lend their inquisitorial aid to furnish matter for new slanders."[9]

In lieu of a personal meeting to discuss party strategy in the coming campaign, Jefferson sketched his ideas for Madison, now that President Adams had authorized a new peace mission to France:

Our objects, according to my ideas, should be these. 1. Peace even with Great Britain. 2. A sincere cultivation of the Union. 3. The disbanding of the army on principles of economy and safety. 4. Protestations against violations of the true principles of our constitution, merely to save them, and prevent precedent and acquiescence from being pleaded against them; but nothing to be said or done which shall look or lead to force, and give any pretext for keeping up the army.

Jefferson wanted to do nothing to unite the Federalist factions—the Adamsites, who supported the second peace mission to France, and the Hamiltonians, who supported the army commanded by the New Yorker. "We should leave to them alone," he counseled, "to manage all those points of difference which they may chuse to take between themselves, only arbitrating between them by our votes, but doing nothing which may hoop them together." To promote their continuing dialogue, Jefferson asked his friend to send his "ideas as fully as you can give them as to State as well as Federal matters."[10]

Jefferson returned to Philadelphia on December 28, 1799, lodging at Francis' Hotel until the middle of May 1800. Madison had planned to pop a last-minute note to Jefferson before the latter departed, but "a dysenteric attack which laid me up for about a week" prevented that. Despite his continuing "state of debility," Madison went to Richmond for the winter session of the state legislature, where he became chairman of the committee to prepare a vindication of the resolutions that he had written secretly the year before, defending them against "the replies of the other States, and the sophistries from other quarters," including the congressional defense of the Alien and Sedition measures. Madison promptly sent his friend a draft of his report,[11] a brilliant exposition that argued that the Sedition Law was unconstitutional; that free speech and a free press are fundamental to republican government— indeed, that "the right of freely examining public characters and measures" is "the only effectual guardian of every other right"; that a popular, or free, form of republican government cannot be libeled; that the federal government pos-

---

9. TJ to JM, Nov. 22, 1799, below. Also see James Monroe to JM, Nov. 22, 1799, in Hamilton, *Writings of Monroe*, III, pp. 159–60.
10. TJ to JM, Nov. 26, 1799, below.
11. JM to TJ, Dec. 29, 1799, below, and Jan. 4, 1800, below.

sessed no jurisdiction over common-law crimes; and that the First Amendment superseded the common law on speech and press, guaranteeing freedom of both against the federal government, which had no authority to abridge them.

To support this argument, he noted that freedom of religion and freedom of the press were "both included in the same amendment, made at the same time, and by the same authority." He concluded, therefore, that "liberty of conscience and the freedom of the press, were *equally* and *completely* exempted from all authority whatever of the United States." The relationship of a free press to a free, elective, and responsible government made political criticism essential for an informed electorate to make intelligent decisions. The resolutions of 1798 had been based on that proposition; they were expressions of political opinion "unaccompanied with any other effect, than what they may produce . . . by exciting reflection." Unlike judicial decisions, which were judges' legal opinions, they could not be "carried into immediate effect by force." Instead, they were legitimate verbal appeals that called on the other states for their concurrence "in making a like declaration."[12] Madison's report of 1800 has been hailed by Leonard Levy as "a characteristically brilliant exposition" of "uncommon authority," "a major step in the evolution of the meaning of the free speech-and-press clause."[13]

While the legislature was discussing his report, Madison fired off five brief bulletins to keep Jefferson informed, writing in mid-January that both houses had approved it. In Philadelphia, the vice president waited impatiently for an official copy so that he could rush it into print as part of the Republican party's campaign literature. In February, he complained to Monroe, who had recently been elected governor of Virginia, that he had not yet received an official copy.[14] When Monroe finally sent him a copy in March, Jefferson had "a great impression made," which "has been sold off, and dispersed into the other states."[15]

Less than a week after the adoption of his "Report on the Resolutions" in January 1800, Madison attended a caucus with 93 Republican members of the state legislature to create a party organization to support Jefferson's campaign in the presidential race. Madison had already informed Jefferson that the legislature would change the state election laws, replacing district elections of presidential electors with a statewide general ticket in an effort "to give Virg^a

---

12. Madison's report of 1800 is printed in Hunt, VI, pp. 341–406, and in *PJM,* XVII, pp. 303–51.

13. See Leonard W. Levy, *Legacy of Suppression: Freedom of Speech and Press in Early American History* (Cambridge, Mass., 1960), pp. 273, 282. Levy's views have also undergone an evolution of sorts. In the paperback edition of his book, he used his original subtitle as the new title: *Freedom of Speech and Press in Early American History* (New York, 1963). A quarter of a century later, he revised the book, retitled it again, and retained his appraisal of Madison's report; see his *Emergence of a Free Press* (New York, 1985), pp. 315, 325.

14. TJ to James Monroe, Feb. 6, 1800, in Ford, VII, p. 424.

15. TJ to James Monroe, Mar. 26, 1800, in Adrienne Koch, *Jefferson and Madison: The Great Collaboration* (New York, 1950), pp. 204–5.

fair play."[16] Along with such "venerable patriots" as George Wythe and Edmund Pendleton, Madison headed the general ticket and served as chairman of the Orange County committee, which cooperated with the five-man state central committee coordinating the campaign.[17]

In addition to the assault on Federalist policy in Madison's report, the Virginia legislature adopted the Giles Resolutions, a set of instructions directing Virginia's congressional delegation to vote for the repeal of the Alien and Sedition Laws, the disbanding of the army, and the rejection of a federal common-law jurisdiction.[18] Jefferson and Madison had discussed these matters in August, especially the question of a federal common law of crimes. According to Jefferson, this latter claim was the most dangerous one ever made by the Federalists on behalf of federal jurisdiction. "All their other assumptions of un-given powers have been in detail. The bank law, the treaty doctrine, the sedition act, the alien act . . . etc., etc., have been solitary, unconsequential, timid things, in comparison with the audacious, barefaced and sweeping pretention to a system of law for the U S, without the adoption of their legislature, and so infinitely beyond their power to adopt." If these claims by some judges and many Federalists should prevail, the Republican leader emphasized, "consolidationists" would overleap the enumerated powers of Congress and open an unbounded field of federal jurisdiction. "Who could have conceived in 1789," he asked, "that within ten years we should have to combat such windmills."[19]

On the foreign front, the optimistic Jefferson reaffirmed his hopes for Adams's second peace mission, watching carefully the progress of the envoys on the one hand and the internal developments in France on the other. Napoleon Bonaparte's overthrow of the French Republic and establishment of a "Dictatorial consulate," coupled with French attacks on American commerce and the earlier congressional abrogation of the French treaties, convinced him that American policy could no longer be tied to European quarrels. "It is very material," wrote this long-time admirer of the French Revolution, "for the . . . [people] to be made sensible that their own character and situation are materially different from the French; and that whatever may be the fate of republicanism there, we are able to preserve it inviolate here. . . . Our vessel is moored at such a distance, that should theirs blow up, ours is still safe, if we will but think so."[20]

---

16. See JM to TJ, Jan. 12, 1800, below, and Jan. 18, 1800, below. For TJ's approval of this move, see his letter to James Monroe, Jan. 12, 1800, in Ford, VII, p. 401.

17. Noble E. Cunningham, Jr., *The Jeffersonian Republicans: The Formation of Party Organization, 1789–1801* (Chapel Hill, 1957), pp. 150–52, 196; Malone, III, p. 461; Ketcham, pp. 403–4.

18. JM to TJ, Jan. 9, 1800, below, Jan. 12, 1800, below, and Jan. 18, 1800, below.

19. TJ to Edmund Randolph, Aug. 18, 1800, in Ford, VII, pp. 383–87. The best discussion of whether there was a federal common-law jurisdiction is Stephen B. Presser's "A Tale of Two Judges: Richard Peters, Samuel Chase, and the Broken Promise of Federalist Jurisprudence," *Northwestern University Law Review* 73 (1978): 27–111.

20. TJ to John Breckinridge, Jan. 29, 1800, in Ford, VII, pp. 417–18.

Madison agreed that the rise of Napoleon and "the late defection of France has left America the only Theatre on which true liberty can have a fair trial."[21] He watched the denouement of the French Republic with regret, but he accepted the "melancholy evidence . . . that the destiny of the Revolution is transferred from the Civil to the military authority. Whether the lesson will have the proper effect here in turning the public attention to the danger of military usurpations, or of intrigues between political and military leaders," he wrote his friend, "is more than I can say. A stronger one was perhaps never given, nor to a Country more in a situation to profit by it."[22]

Jefferson also worried about military usurpation, especially after Hamilton succeeded to the command of the provisional army following General Washington's death in December 1799. He feared that "our Buonaparte, surrounded by his comrades in arms," might make domestic use of the army, stepping in "to give us political salvation in his own way."[23]

Washington's death and the rising hope for President Adams's peace mission undermined the provisional army, and Congress began to dismantle it in 1800 with bipartisan support, a sure indication, Jefferson reported, that the Federalists were "of a more moderate temper than for some time past." In his first letter after arriving in Philadelphia (this one went by private hand), he confided to Madison that "the Feds begin to be very seriously alarmed about their election next fall. Their speeches in private, as well as their public and private demeanor to me indicate it strongly." Then, in an astute analysis of the coming vote in the fall, he appraised the prospects of a Republican victory that would put him in the new president's house in Washington, along with a Republican Congress. After weighing all the states, he concluded that "we may say that if the *city* election of N. York is in favor of the Republican ticket, the issue will be republican."[24]

As gloom settled over the Federalists, they turned to political skulduggery. "The horrors which they evidently feel at the approach of the Electoral epoch," Madison predicted, "are a sufficient warning of the desparate game by which they will be apt to characterize the interval."[25] "The rapid progress of public sentiment warns them of their danger," Jefferson observed, "and they are passing laws to keep themselves in power."[26] Senator James Ross of Pennsylvania introduced an electoral-count bill in a bold attempt to alter by legislation rather than amendment the constitutional system for deciding disputed elections for president and vice president. A thoroughly partisan measure, the

---

21. JM to TJ, Apr. 4, 1800, below.

22. JM to TJ, Feb. 14, 1800, below.

23. TJ to Thomas Mann Randolph, Feb. 2, 1800, in Ford, VII, pp. 422–23. A year earlier, following the adoption of the Virginia resolutions of 1798, Hamilton had suggested that the army be used to "put Virginia to the test of resistance"; see Alexander Hamilton to Theodore Sedgwick, Feb. 2, 1799, in Syrett, XXII, pp. 452–54.

24. TJ to JM, Mar. 4 (with Mar. 8 postscript), 1800, below.

25. JM to TJ, Apr. 20, 1800, below.

26. Peterson, p. 631.

bill gave absolute power to a "Grand Committee of Thirteen," including six members from each house, both dominated by Federalist majorities, and the chief justice of the United States, Oliver Ellsworth, whom President Adams had appointed to the second peace mission to France. This committee would meet in secret session, inspect the electoral certificates from the states, determine which electoral votes to count and which to disallow, throw out votes they considered to be illegal, and decide on who should be president according to their tally. Since there was to be no appeal from the committee's decision, Congress would have abdicated its constitutional role in counting the electoral vote.[27] The Senate passed the electoral-count bill, Jefferson reported, after it had "struck out the clause limiting the powers of the electoral committee, and extended it to *all* subjects of inquiry," making it even worse than the original version.[28]

The House of Representatives also passed the bill but amended it to require a joint vote of both houses for the acceptance of the Grand Committee's report.[29] When the Senate held out for absolute control, the bill died, but the Federalists in the Senate "remained undismayed to the last. Firm to their purposes, regardless of public opinion, and more disposed to coerce than to court it," Jefferson noted, "not a man of their majority gave way in the least."[30]

Madison was appalled by the "group of daring experiments presented by our public Councils" and accused the Federalists of resorting to every strategy "that may afford a chance of prolonging their ascendency."[31] When he read the Ross bill, he denounced the "licentiousness" of the Senate in "constructive perversions of the Constitution. . . . Indeed such an unbridled spirit of construction as has gone forth in sundry instances, would bid defiance to any possible parchment securities against usurpation." If the Federalists followed Ross's lead, he added, "we shall soon have to look into our code of laws, and not the Charter of the people, for the form as well as the powers of our Government." Given this instance of legislative interference in the constitutional method of electing a president, he thought it "impossible to say, how far the choice of the Ex[ecutive] may be drawn out of the Constitutional hands, and subjected to the management of the Legislature. The danger is the greater," he concluded, "as the Chief Magistrate, for the time being may be bribed into the usurpations by so shaping them as to favor his re-election."[32] A

---

27. James Morton Smith, *Freedom's Fetters: The Alien and Sedition Laws and American Civil Liberties* (Ithaca, N.Y., 1956), pp. 288–89, and Malone, III, pp. 463–64. Manning J. Dauer, *The Adams Federalists* (Baltimore, 1953), p. 244, notes that "Congress abdicated all control" under the Senate bill.

28. TJ to L. W. Tazewell, Apr. 10, 1800, quoted in Smith, p. 300.

29. The vote is tabulated in Dauer, pp. 317–20.

30. TJ to JM, May 12, [1800], below.

31. JM to TJ, Apr. 20, 1800, below.

32. JM to TJ, Mar. 15, 1800, below.

Philadelphia observer, somewhat more detached, wrote that Congress was like "a conclave of cardinals, intriguing in the election of a Pope."[33]

The Republican press, led by the Philadelphia *Aurora*, blasted the supporters of the Ross bill as "the party hostile to the popular interest," who wished "to destroy the popular authority and to engross every power which the people enjoy by the right and constitution in the hands of a few." When the *Aurora* published the text of the Ross bill, citing it as "an offspring of this spirit of faction secretly working," the Senate condemned the editor, William Duane, without a hearing, for writing a seditious libel that was a "high breach of the privileges" of the Senate."[34]

The proposed proceeding in the Senate presented the vice president with a disconcerting dilemma. Should he preside over a kangaroo-court prosecution of the nation's leading Republican editor whom the Senate had already judged guilty of printing a seditious libel, a concept that he despised? Choosing his official duties over his personal views, he signed the warrant for Duane's appearance, informing Madison noncommitally that "we have this day also decided in Senate on the motion for overhauling the editor of the Aurora. It was carried, as usual, by about 2. to 1."[35] In response to the Senate's summons, Duane appeared before the Senate but requested that he be represented by counsel. The Senate agreed to allow legal assistance but imposed three conditions: there could be no challenge to the Senate's jurisdiction in the case, and defense counsel could be heard only in denial of any facts charged against the editor or "in excuse and extenuation of his offence."

Duane's lawyers, Alexander Dallas and Thomas Cooper, refused to represent their client under such restrictions, Cooper writing that he would not "appear before the senate with *their gag in my mouth*" as "a tame and manacled assistant."[36] Thus deprived of legal assistance, Duane notified the vice president as presiding officer of the Senate that he would decline to appear and subsequently went into hiding. The Senate then declared the editor guilty of contempt and directed the vice president to sign a warrant for his arrest. Jefferson again did his duty, but Duane evaded arrest, editing the *Aurora* from his hideaway. Ten days later, Jefferson informed Madison that "they have not yet taken him."[37]

Duane reported that Jefferson's signature on his arrest warrant was a matter of form, if not another Federalist trick. The vice president had no vote except in case of a tie, so he was no more accountable for the warrant "than for

---

33. Peterson, p. 626.

34. Smith, pp. 289–94. Senator Uriah Tracy of Connecticut took the lofty position that the actions of the Senate could not be questioned anywhere at any time by anyone; see *ibid.*, p. 291.

35. TJ to JM, Mar. 8 postscript to Mar. 4, 1800, below.

36. Two weeks later, Cooper was arrested for seditious libel; see Smith, p. 316.

37. TJ to JM, Apr. 4, 1800, below. For a biography of Duane, see Kim Tousley Phillips, *William Duane: Radical Journalist in the Age of Jefferson* (New York, 1989).

the Sedition Law, or Mr. Ross's law for regulating elections, etc., a measure expressly designed to prevent Mr. Jefferson being elected President of the United States." If the measure passed, he added, Jefferson would have to sign it, even though the Senate's revised version was much worse than the draft printed by Duane.

While the *Duane* case was before the Senate, Jefferson exercised one of his rare opportunities to cast a tie-breaking vote. When a group of Duane's backers presented a petition and remonstrance to the Senate suggesting that it reconsider its action against the editor, the Federalists moved to table it without a reading; but the vote resulted in an even split. Jefferson broke the tie, and the petition, protesting the Senate's action as a second kind of unwritten Sedition Law, was read. After rejecting the plea, the Senate, on the eve of adjournment, requested President Adams to initiate a prosecution of the elusive editor under the Sedition Act.[38]

As the election of 1800 heated up, the Federalists stepped up the prosecutions under the Sedition Law, with the strictest enforcement coming in such thoroughly Federalist states as those in New England or those where Federalist supremacy was threatened by the rising Republicans, as in Pennsylvania and New York. All eight proceedings in 1800, except for the case against James T. Callender in Virginia, were instituted in these areas: three in New York; two in Pennsylvania, where Duane's lawyer, Thomas Cooper, was indicted two weeks after his refusal to appear before the Senate; and one each in Vermont and Connecticut. All involved Republican editors and propagandists, although none stooped so low as the 1799 prosecution of an inebriated Republican in New Jersey for a ribald reference to the president's posterior.[39] As Jefferson noted, "the onset on the presses is to cripple and suppress the Republican efforts during the campaign which is coming on. In the meantime their own batteries are teeming with every falsehood they can invent for defamation."[40]

Only two days before Cooper's indictment, Jefferson had sent 96 copies of Cooper's *Political Arithmetic*, a ponderous pamphlet on political economy written from a Republican point of view, to his campaign manager in Virginia for distribution to the county committees. Although Cooper's pamphlet could hardly be considered seditious, Jefferson told the manager, "I trust yourself only with the secret that these pamphlets go from me. You will readily see what a handle would be made by my advocating their contents."[41]

This letter, like most of Jefferson's letters in 1800, went by private hand rather than through the postal system, a continuing precaution based on his

---

38. Smith, pp. 288–306, and Malone, III, pp. 463–66.

39. For a summary of the enforcement of the Sedition Law, see Smith, pp. 176–87; for the New Jersey case, see *ibid.*, pp. 270–74.

40. Peterson, p. 630.

41. TJ to Philip Norborne Nicholas, Apr. 7, 1800, in Ford, VII, p. 439. For an analysis of Cooper's pamphlet, see Dumas Malone, *The Public Life of Thomas Cooper, 1783–1839* (New Haven, 1926), pp. 98–101.

"knowing that a campaign of slander is now open upon me, and believing that the postmasters will lend their inquisitorial aid to fish out any new matter of slander they can [to] gratify the powers that be."[42]

Madison thought that the Federalists had overplayed their hand and offered an optimistic appraisal of Republican prospects in April 1800. "The spirit manifested in the Senate steadily, and in the other House occasionally, however mischievous in its immediate effects, cannot fail I think to aid the progress of reflection and change among the people. In this view," he wrote reassuringly to his friend, "our public malady may work its own cure, and ultimately rescue the republican principal from the imputation brought on it by the degeneracy of the public Councils. Such a demonstration of the rectitude and efficacy of popular sentiment, will be the more precious," he added, since Napoleon's seizure of power had ended the experiment in republicanism in France, leaving "America the only Theatre on which true liberty can have a fair trial."[43]

Jefferson agreed with Madison's appraisal of popular sentiment, observing that the tide of "of public opinion sets so strongly against the federal proceedings, that this melted off" the Federalists majorities in Congress, particularly in the House of Representatives. "On the whole," he wrote at the end of the congressional session in May 1800, "the federalists have not been able to carry a single strong measure in the lower house the whole session. When they met, it was believed they had a majority of 20. But many of these were new and moderate men, and soon saw the true character of the party to which they had been well disposed while at a distance."[44] The continuing intransigence of the Senate meant, however, that "our scenes here can never be pleasant," although he concluded that the session had been "less stormy, less painful than during the XYZ paroxysms."[45]

Just before Congress adjourned, a congressional caucus of Republicans nominated Jefferson for president and chose Aaron Burr of New York as his running mate. The Federalists also held a congressional caucus and chose Adams and Charles Cotesworth Pinckney of South Carolina, the XYZ envoy, as their standard-bearers, pledging to support them equally. In a letter to the Federalist Speaker of the House, General Hamilton explained that "to support *Adams* and *Pinckney* equally is the only thing that can possibly save us from the fangs of *Jefferson*."[46]

In his last letter from Philadelphia, Jefferson informed his son-in-law that Adams had fired two of Hamilton's cohorts from his cabinet, replacing Secre-

---

42. Peterson, p. 626.
43. JM to TJ, Apr. 4, 1800, below.
44. TJ to JM, May 12, [1800], below.
45. TJ to Martha Jefferson Randolph, Apr. 22, 1800, in Sarah Nicholas Randolph, *The Domestic Life of Thomas Jefferson* (New York, 1871), p. 225.
46. Alexander Hamilton to Theodore Sedgwick, May 4, 1800, in Syrett, XXIV, pp. 452–53.

tary of State Timothy Pickering with John Marshall, thus confirming publicly the split in the Federalist party into Adamsite and Hamiltonian wings. Indeed, he heard that the "hocus-pocus maneuvers" of the Federalists might be a ploy by the Hamiltonians and the High Federalists to give Pinckney preference over Adams.[47] As Congress adjourned for the last time in Philadelphia prior to its move to Washington, Jefferson could hardly wait to get home to give Madison the news "which could not be confided to paper."[48]

---------------------- THE LETTERS ----------------------

Jefferson to Madison

Monticello Aug. 23, 1799

With this you will receive the IV^d nails desired in your memorandum, that is to say 25. lb weighing about 2½ lb. to the ~~M~~ [thousand]. Probably they yield something more than a thousand to that weight, not being so uniform as they ought to be. We are now working up some remnants of hoops of different breadths till the arrival of a supply of proper size from Philadelphia. They are ⅓ per pound consequently come cheap. The error in the nails sent before was Mr McGehee's as I entered the memorandum in my book from his dictation, and he saw them weighed out according to that.

Mrs. Madison tells me that Lumsden your plasterer, lives about 10. or 15. miles from you and that an opportunity may perhaps be found of conveying him a letter.[1] I trouble you with one, open, which when read be so good as to seal and forward by any opportunity you approve.

I inclose you a letter I received from W. C. Nicholas three days ago.[2] It is so advantageous that Virginia and Kentuckey should pursue the same tract on this occasion, and a difference of plan would give such advantage to the Consolidationers that I would immediately see you at your own house, but that we have a stranger lying ill here, whose state has been very critical, and who would suffer in spirits at least if not substantially by my absence. I shall not answer Mr. N's letter till Thursday next. Perhaps you could take a ride about that

---

47. See Malone, III, pp. 475–76. For Pickering, see Gerard H. Clarfield, *Timothy Pickering and American Diplomacy, 1795–1800* (Columbia, Mo., 1969).

48. TJ to JM, Apr. 4, 1800, below.

1. After visiting relatives who lived in Albemarle County, Dolley Madison stopped at Monticello on her way home; see *PJM*, XVII, p. 258.

2. Wilson Cary Nicholas planned to visit Kentucky and promised to carry any suggestions that TJ made about reiterating the Kentucky resolutions of 1798; see Koch, pp. 196–98.

time, so as to have a meeting here with him on Sunday sennight, the day preceding our court. I dare say he will not go before court, and if you could drop him a line by post he would certainly meet you, and let us consider a little together what is to be done. Not that I should prepare anything, but the opportunity is certainly a valuable one of producing a concert of action. I will in the mean time give you my ideas to reflect on. That the principles already advanced by Virginia and Kentuckey are not to be yielded in silence, I presume we all agree. I should propose a declaration or Resolution by their legislatures on this plan. 1st. Answer the reasonings of such of the states as have ventured into the field of reason, and that of the Committee of Congress. Here they have given us all the advantage we could wish. Take some notice of those states who have either not answered at all, or answered without reasoning. 2. Make a firm *protestation* against the principle and the precedent; and a *reservation* of the rights resulting to us from these palpable violations of the constitutional compact by the Federal government, and the approbation or acquiescence of the several co-states; so that we may hereafter do, what we might now rightfully do, whenever repetitions of these and other violations shall make it evident that the Federal government, disregarding the limitations of the federal compact, mean to exercise powers over us to which we have never assented. 3. Express in affectionate and conciliatory language our warm attachment to union with our sister-states, and to the instrument and principles by which we are united; that we are willing to sacrifice to this every thing except those rights of self government the securing of which was the object of that compact: that not at all disposed to make every measure of error or wrong a cause of scission, we are willing to view with indulgence [and] to wait with patience till those passions and delusions shall have passed over which the federal government have artfully and successfully excited to cover it's own abuses and to conceal it's designs; fully confident that the good sense of the American people and their attachment to those very rights which we are now vindicating will, before it shall be too late, rally with us round the true principles of our federal compact. But determined, were we to be disappointed in this, to sever ourselves from that union we so much value, rather than give up the rights of self government which we have reserved, and in which alone we see liberty, safety and happiness.

These things I sketch hastily, only as topics to be enlarged on, and wishing you to consider on them or what else is best to be done. At any rate let me hear from you by the post or before it if you can.[3] Adieu affectionately.

---

3. JM noted on this letter that a visit "took the place of an answer to the letter." For JM's influence in moderating TJ's more extreme views, see *ibid.*, pp. 199–201.

Madison to Jefferson

[Orange] Nov. 2, 1799

DEAR SIR

The Bearer Mr. Polk is a Portrait Painter and a kinsman of Mr. Peale of Philada. He visits Monticello with a wish to be favored with a few hours of your sitting for his pencil.[4] Having no acquaintance with you he asks the aid of a line towards obtaining one, and this will be presented to you for the purpose. With perfect sincerity I am yours

Js. MADISON JR

Madison to Jefferson

[Orange] Nov. 3, 1799

DEAR SIR

Be so good as to let Col. Monroe have the inclosed as early as may be convenient.[5] Have you fixed the time of your setting out for Philadelphia? I wish much for the pleasure of seeing you on your way, but if you do not aim to be there at the beging. of the session, I shall probably lose the opportunity.[6] As something however may depend on circumstances and arrangements, it will be convenient for me to learn your intended movements. Adieu Yrs. truly

Js. MADISON JR.

Jefferson to Madison

Monticello Nov. 22, 1799

DEAR SIR,

I have never answered your letter by Mr. Polk,[7] because I expected to have paid you a visit. This has been prevented by various causes, till yesterday, being the day fixed for the departure of my daur. Eppes. My horses were ready for me to have set out to see you. An accident postponed her departure to this

---

4. Charles Peale Polk painted portraits of James Madison, Sr., and JM's mother, Nelly Conway Madison, at Montpellier. They are now owned by the Maryland Historical Society; see *PJM*, XVII, p. 275.

5. Enclosure not found.

6. TJ called off his visit to Montpellier at the suggestion of James Monroe; see TJ to JM, Nov. 22, 1799, below.

7. For Polk's Portrait of TJ, which the artist completed on Nov. 5, see Alfred L. Bush, "The Life Portraits of Thomas Jefferson," in *Jefferson and the Arts: An Extended View,* ed. William Howard Adams (Washington, 1976), pp. 50–53.

day, and my visit also. But Colo. Monroe dined with us yesterday, and on my asking his commands for you, he entered into the subject of the visit and dissuaded it entirely, founding the motives on the espionage of the little wretch in Charlottesville, who would make it a subject of some political slander, and perhaps of some political injury. I have yeilded to his representations, and therefore shall not have the pleasure of seeing you till my return from Philadelphia. I regret it sincerely, not only on motives of affection but of affairs. Some late circumstances change considerably the aspect of our situation, and must affect the line of conduct to be observed. I regret it the more too, because from the commencement of the ensuing session, I shall trust the post offices with nothing confidential, persuaded that during the ensuing twelve-month they will lend their inquisitorial aid to furnish matter for new slanders. I shall send you as usual printed communications, without saying anything confidential on them. You will of course understand the cause.

In your new station[8] let me recommend to you the jury system: as also the restoration of juries to the court of Chancery, which a law not long since repealed, because "the trial by jury is troublesome and expensive." If the reason be good, they should go through with it, and abolish it at common law also. If P. Carr is elected in the room of W.N. he will undertake the proposing this business and only need your support. If he is not elected, I hope you will get it done otherwise. My best respects to Mrs Madison, and affectionate salutations to yourself.

TH. JEFFERSON

Jefferson to Madison

[Monticello] Nov. 26, 1799

I omitted in my letter of the 23d [22d] to say any thing on the subject of Mr Wirt; which however was necessary only for form's sake, because I had promised it. You know he is a candidate for the clerkship of your house, you know his talents, his worth, and his republicanism; and therefore need not my testimony, which could otherwise be given for him in the strongest form on every point. The desirable object is to have the exact measure of every man's properties, and give it to the best. I suppose it is thought time that the republicans should know that offices are to be given exclusively to their opponents by their friends, no longer. It is advantage enough to the Feds to possess the exclusive patronage of the administration; and so long as they go on the

---

8. JM returned to the Virginia legislature in Dec. 1799. The "jury system" referred to TJ's efforts to substitute the election of jurors and their assignment to jury duty by lot instead of appointment; see TJ to JM, Oct. 26, 1798, above, and Jefferson's petition on the election of jurors, above.

exclusive principle, we should do the same.⁹ I mentioned that new circumstances would require consideration as to the line of conduct these would require from us. Our objects, according to my ideas, should be these. 1. Peace even with Great Britain. 2. A sincere cultivation of the Union. 3. The disbanding of the army on principles of economy and safety. 4. Protestations against violations of the true principles of our constitution, merely to save them, and prevent precedent and acquiescence from being pleaded against them; but nothing to be said or done which shall look or lead to force, and give any pretext for keeping up the army. If we find the Monarchical party really split into pure Monocrats and Anglo-monocrats, we should leave to them alone to manage all those points of difference which they may chuse to take between themselves, only arbitrating between them by our votes, but doing nothing which may hoop them together. The post which leaves Richmond on the 9th. of Dec. will be the last by which I can recieve letters here. By that time you will be able to form a tolerable judgment of the complexion of your house, and I shall be very happy to recieve your ideas as fully as you can give them as to State as well as Federal matters. Health and affectionate salutations to Mrs Madison and yourself.

Madison to Jefferson

Richmond Dec. 29, 1799

DEAR SIR,—

My promise to write to you before your leaving Albemarle was defeated by a dysenteric attack which laid me up for about a week, and which left me in a state of debility not yet thoroughly removed. My recovery has been much retarded by the job of preparing a vindication of the Resolutions of last Session agst the replies of the other States, and the sophistries from other quarters. The Committee made their report a few days ago, which is now in the press and stands the order of the day for thursday next. A set of Resolutions proposed by Mr. Giles, instructing the Senators to urge the repeal of the unconst^l acts, the disbanding of the army, and a proper arrangement of the militia, are also in the press, and stand the order of the same day for the same Committee. It is supposed that both these papers, the latter perhaps with some modifications, will go through the H. of Delegates. The Senate, owing to inattention and casualties, is so composed as to render the event there not a little uncertain. If an election, to fill the vacancy of Mr. H. Nelson who lately resigned, should send Mr. Andrews in preference to his competitor Mr. Saunders, I am told that the parties will be precisely in equilibrio, excepting only one or two

---

9. William Wirt, a Richmond lawyer, replaced John Stuart, a Federalist, as clerk of the Virginia House of Delegates; see *PJM*, XVII, p. 281. See also Michael L. Oberg, "William Wirt and the Trials of Republicanism," *VMHB* 99 (1991): 305–26.

whom circumstances now and then on particular questions, transfer from the wrong to the right side. It is hoped that this contingent fund of votes, will be applicable to the Vindication.[10] On other important questions, there is much less expectation from it. There is a report here that the Legislature of N. Carolina now in session, have voted the Resolutions of Virginia under their table. The report is highly improbable, and I do not believe it. But it is impossible to calculate the progress of delusion, especially in a State where it is said to be under systematic management, and where there is so little either of system or exertion opposed to it.[11] We had a narrow escape yesterday from an increase of pay to the members, which would have been particularly unseasonable and injurious both within and without the State. It was rejected on the third reading by a small majority; and was so much a favorite, with the distant members particularly, that I fear it has left them in rather an ill humour.

The late course of foreign events has probably made the same impression everywhere.[12] If it should not render France less anxious to meet our advances, its good effects will be felt every way. If our Executive and their Envoys be sincere in their pacific objects, it will perhaps supply by their increased anxiety what may be lost on the other side. But there can be little confidence after what has been seen, that the negociation would be influenced by this temper of the Envoys, instead of that which perverted it in the hands of their predecessors. This possibility of failure in the diplomatic experiment, will present the most specious obstacle to an immediate discharge of the army. It would be useful for the Assembly to know how this matter is viewed where you are. Mr. Dawson will be good eno' to write me on the subject. I intended to have written to him by this mail; but my time has been taken from me till the closing of the mail is approaching. Yrs. affecly,

J M. JR.

Madison to Jefferson

Richmond, Jan. 4, 1800

DEAR SIR,—

My last covered a copy of the Report on the Resolutions of last year. I now inclose a copy of certain resolutions moved by Mr. Giles, to which he means to add an instruction on the subject of the intercourse law which has been so injurious to the price of our Tob°. It is not improbable that the

---

10. For the passage of JM's report of 1800 on the Virginia resolutions of 1798, see Koch, pp. 202–7.

11. See Frank Maloy Anderson, "Contemporary Opinion of the Virginia and Kentucky Resolutions, Part II," *AHR* 5 (1900): 235–36.

12. On Nov. 9, 1799, Napoleon's coup d'état overthrew the Directory and established the Consulate, with Bonaparte as first consul.

Resolutions when taken up, may undergo some mollifications in the spirit and air of them. The Report has been under debate for two days.[13] The attacks on it have turned cheifly on an alledged inconsistency between the comment now made, and the arguments of the last session, and on the right of the Legislature to interfere in any manner with denunciations of the measures of the Genl Gov^t.

The first attack has been parried by an amendment admitting that different constructions may have been entertained of the term "States" as "parties" etc. but that the sense relied on in the report must be concurred in by all. It is in fact concurred in by both parties. On examination of the Debates of the last session, it appears that both were equally inaccurate and inconsistent in the grounds formerly taken by them. The attack on the right of the Legislature to interfere by declaration of opinion will form a material point in the discussion. It is not yet known how far the opposition to the Report will be carried into detail. The part relating to the Common law it is said will certainly be combated. You will perceive from this view of the matter, that it is not possible to guess how long, we shall be employed on it. There will in the event be a considerable majority for the Report in the House of Delegates, and a pretty sure one in the Senate. Can you send me a copy of Preistly's letters last published. Adieu

J. M. Jr

Madison to Jefferson

[Richmond] Jan. 9, 1800

DEAR SIR,

The question on the Report printed, was decided by 60 for and 40 agst it, the day before yesterday, after a debate [of] five days. Yesterday and today have been spent on Mr. Giles' propositions, which with some softenings will probably pass, by nearly the same vote. The Senate is in rather a better state than was expected. The Debate turned almost wholly on the right of the Legislature to protest. The Constitutionality of the Alien and Sedition Acts and of the C[ommon] Law was waived. It was said that the last question would be discussed under Mr. Giles' propositions; but as yet nothing has been urged in its favour[.] It is probable however that the intention has not been laid aside. I thank you for the pamphlets. Adieu Yrs affy.

Js. MADISON JR.

---

13. For brief discussions of JM's report of 1800 on the Virginia resolutions of 1798, see Brant, III, pp. 467–71, and Ketcham, pp. 399–403. For a critical analysis of JM's defense, see Levy, *Emergence of a Free Press,* pp. 312–25.

Madison to Jefferson

Richmond Jan. 12, 1800

DEAR SIR,

My last informed you of the result of the debates on the justifying Report of the Select Committee. I am now able to add that of Mr. Giles's resolutions. The question on the whole was decided in the affirmative by a little upwards of a hundred against less than fifty. The vote was rather stronger on some of the particular resolutions, for example the instruction for disbanding the army. The alien sedition and Tobacco instructions passed without a count or a division. That relating to the common law, passed unanimously with an amendment qualifying it in the words of the paragraph in the Justifying Report under which certain defined parts of the C. L. are admitted to be the law of the U. S. This amendment was moved by the minority on the idea that it covers the doctrine they contend for. On our side it is considered as a guarded exposition of the powers expressed in the Const^n and those necessary and proper to carry them into execution. I am not able to say in what manner they misconstrue the definition, unless they apply the term "adopt" to the "Court" which would be equally absurd and unconstitutional. The Judges themselves will hardly contend that they can *adopt* a law, that is, make that law which was before not law. The difference in the majority on the Report and the resolutions, was occasioned chiefly by the pledge given agst the former by the members who voted agst the Resolutions of last year. The resolutions also underwent some improvements which reconciled many to them who were not satisfied with their first tone and form. It is understood that the present assembly is rather stronger on the republican side than the last one: and that a few favorable changes have taken place in the course of the session. It is proposed to introduce to-morrow a bill for a general ticket in chusing the next Electors.[14] I expect to leave this in a week; so that your subsequent favors will find me in Orange.

Shew this to Mr. Dawson. Adieu.

Madison to Jefferson

Richmond Jan. 18, 1800

DEAR SIR,

Since my last the Senate have agreed to the *Report* and the *Resolutions* by 15 to 6. To the latter, they made an amendt. to the definition of the portion of

---

14. Virginia adopted a general ticket of presidential electors instead of choosing them by districts, as had been done since 1789. See Cunningham, pp. 145–50; Richard Beeman, *The Old Dominion and the New Nation, 1788–1801* (Lexington, Ky., 1972), pp. 221–22; and Norman K. Risjord and Gordon DenBoer, "The Evolution of Political Parties in Virginia, 1782–1800," *JAH* 60 (1974): 983–84.

C. L. in force in the U. S. by inserting the words "by Congress" after the word "adopted," in order to repel the misconstruction which led the minority to concur in that particular resolution as it passed the H. of D.[15] The amend^t was agreed to by 82 to 40. The plan of a Genl Ticket was so novel that a great n^o who wished it, shrunk from the vote, and others apprehending that their Const^{ts} [Constituents] would be still more startled at it voted agst it, so that it passed by a majority of 5 votes only. The event in the Senate is rather doubtful; tho' it is expected to get thro'. As the avowed object of it is to give Virg^a *fair play*, I think if passed into a law, it will with proper explanations become popular. I expect to get away ab^t the middle of the week. The Assembly will rise perhaps at the end of it; tho' possibly not so soon. I forgot to tell you that a renewed effort to raise the pay of the members to 3 d^{rs} has succeeded; a measure wrong in principle, and which will be hurtful in its operation. I have desired Barnes to pay you a balance in his hands, out of which you will please to pay yourself the balance due to your Nailory. Adieu. Yrs. affly.

J. M. Jr

Madison to Jefferson

Orange Feb. 14, 1800

DEAR SIR,

My last to you was from Rich[mon]d; your last to me is just recd. covering the Bill for drawing Jurors by lot.[16] The plan proposed by the Bill is a great improvement on the regulation in force here. I cannot say, whether it may have the same merit every where. This subject was not wholly forgotten during our late session. A Bill was even prepared on it, by one of our State Judges.[17] But subjects deemed more immediately interesting, diminished so much the attention of some whose agency in carrying it thro' was essential, that the bill was never introduced.

We see by the late papers that a new scene is presented on the French Theatre, which leaves the dénôuement more a problem than ever. The characters and professions of some of the leading actors furnish a hope that monarchy may not be their object, but melancholy evidence appears that the destiny of the Revolution is transferred from the Civil to the military authority. Whether the lesson will have the proper effect here in turning the public

15. For a brief discussion of JM's views on whether there was a federal common law, see Levy, *Emergence of a Free Press,* pp. 315–25. For a general discussion, see Presser, 27–111.

16. TJ did not write a covering letter; see TJ to JM, Mar. 4, 1800, below. Charles Pinckney introduced a bill in the U.S. Senate on Jan. 31, 1800, "to establish an uniform code of drawing juries by lot"; see *PJM,* XVII, p. 364.

17. St. George Tucker drafted the bill for reforming the jury system; see *ibid.*

attention to the danger of military usurpations, or of intrigues between political and military leaders, is more than I can say. A stronger one was perhaps never given, nor to a Country more in a situation to profit by it.

We have had, for two weeks and more, snow on the ground from 15 to 20 inches deep, which has blockaded every body within his own doors. Adieu.

I was a subscriber for Trumbull's prints, which I find are now in America.[18] Can you tell me where and how I am to get them and what is to be pd. in addition to the payments at subscribing. I wish to know also whether they are to be delivered in frames.

Jefferson to Madison

Philadelphia Mar. 4 and 8, 1800

I have never written to you since my arrival here, for reasons which were explained. Your's of Dec. 29. Jan. 4. 9. 12. 18. and Feb. 14. have therefore remained unacknoleged. I have at different times enclosed to you such papers as seemed interesting. To-day I forward Bingham's amendment to the election bill formerly enclosed [to] you, Mr. Pinkney's proposed amendmnt. to the const'n, and the report of the Ways and Means.[19] B[ingham's] amendmt. was lost by the usual majority of 2. to 1. A very different one will be proposed, containing the true sense of the Minority, viz. that the two houses, voting by heads, shall decide such questions as the constitution authorizes to be raised. This may probably be taken up in the other house under better auspices, for tho' the federalists have a great majority there, yet they are of a more moderate temper than for some time past. The Senate however seem determined to yeild to nothing which shall give the other house greater weight in the decision on elections than they have.

Mr. Pinckney's motion has been supported, and is likely to have some votes, which were not expected. I rather believe he will withdraw it, and propose the same thing in the form of a bill; it being the opinion of some that such a regulation is not against the present constitution. In this form it will stand a better chance to pass, as a majority only in both houses will be neces-

---

18. Prints made from John Trumbull's engravings of his paintings *The Battle of Bunker Hill* and *The Death of General Montgomery at the Attack on Quebec* were published in 1798, and the artist presented a set to Congress in Sept. 1798; see John Trumbull, *The Autobiography of Colonel John Trumbull, Patriot-Artist, 1756–1843*, ed. Theodore Sizer (New Haven, 1953), p. 219.

19. Enclosures not found. The "election bill" referred to Senator Ross's electoral-count bill; see Smith, pp. 288–300. See also Richard Buel, Jr., *Securing the Revolution: Ideology in American Politics, 1789–1815* (Ithaca, 1972), pp. 208–11. Charles Pinckney's proposed amendment would have barred any federal judge from holding another federal appointment while in office; see *PJM*, XVII, p. 370.

sary. By putting off the building of the 74's and stopping enlistments, the loan will be reduced to 3½ millions. But I think it cannot be obtained. For though no new bankruptcies have happened here for some weeks, or in New York, yet they continue to happen in Baltimore, and the whole commercial race are lying on their oars, and gathering in their affairs, not knowing what new failures may put their resources to the proof. In this state of things they cannot lend money. Some foreigners have taken asylum among us, with a good deal of money, who may perhaps chuse that deposit. Robbins's affair has been under agitation for some days.[20] Livingston made an able speech of 2½ hours yesterday. The advocates of the measure feel it's pressure heavily; and tho' they may be able to repel L[ivingston's] motion of censure, I do not believe they can carry Bayard's of approbation.

The landing of our envoys at Lisbon will risk a very dangerous consequence, insomuch as the news of Truxton's aggression will perhaps arrive at Paris before our commissioners will.[21] Had they gone directly there, they might have been two months ahead of that news. We are entirely without further information from Paris. By letters from Bordeaux, of Dec. 7, tobo was then from 25 to 27 D. pr. cwt. Yet did Marshall maintain on the non-intercourse bill, that it's price at other markets had never been affected by that law. While the navigating and provision states who are the majority can keep open all the markets, or at least sufficient ones for their objects, the cries of the tobacco makers, who are the minority and not at all in favor, will hardly be listened to. It is truly the fable of the cat pulling the nuts out of the fire with the monkey's paw; and it shows that G. Mason's proposition in the convention was wise, that on laws regulating commerce, two thirds of the votes should be requisite to pass them. However, it would have been trampled under foot by a triumphant majority.

Mar. 8.

My letter has lain by me till now, waiting Mr. Trist's departure. The question has been decided to-day on Livingston's motion respecting Robbins, 35. for it, about 60. against it. Livingston, Nicholas, and Gallatin distin-

20. The Robbins affair involved Jonathan Robbins, a sailor who claimed to be an American victim of British impressment. After having a search made of the town records of Danbury, Connecticut, Robbins's alleged place of birth, President Adams directed the federal court in Charleston, South Carolina, to turn him over to the British navy, which charged him with mutiny. The Republicans then attacked the administration for pro-British leanings; see Donald H. Stewart, *The Opposition Press of the Federalist Period* (Albany, N.Y., 1969), pp. 242–47. Robbins later confessed that he was Thomas Nash, a British subject; see Cunningham, p. 175. For a brilliant and exhaustive reexamination, see Ruth Wedgwood, "The Revolutionary Martyrdom of Jonathan Robbins," *Yale Law Journal* 100 (1990): 229–368.

21. On Feb. 1, 1800, Captain Thomas Truxton, commanding the *Constellation,* won a running battle with the heavier French frigate, *La Vengeance,* the last major naval battle of the half war with France; see Alexander De Conde, *The Quasi-War: The Politics and Diplomacy of the Undeclared War with France, 1797–1801* (New York, 1966), pp. 209–10.

guished themselves on one side, and J. Marshall greatly on the other. Still it is believed they will not push Bayard's motion of approbation. We have this day also decided in Senate on the motion for overhauling the editor of the Aurora. It was carried, as usual, by about 2. to 1. H. Marshall voting of course with them, as did and frequently does Anderson of Tennessee, who is perfectly at market. It happens that the other party are so strong, that they do not think either him or Marshall worth buying.

As the conveyance is confidential, I can say something on a subject which, to those who do not know my real dispositions respecting it, might seem indelicate. The Feds begin to be very seriously alarmed about their election next fall. Their speeches in private, as well as their public and private demeanor to me indicate it strongly. This seems to be the prospect. Keep out Pennsylva, Jersey, and N. York, and the rest of the states are about equally divided; and in this estimate it is supposed that N. Carolina and Maryland added together are equally divided. Then the event depends on the 3. middle states before mentd. As to them, Pennsylva passes no law for an election at the present session. They confide that the next election gives a decided majority in the two houses when joined together. M'Kean therefore intends to call the legislature to meet immediately after the new election to appoint electors themselves. Still you will be sensible there may arise a difficulty between the two houses about voting by heads or by houses.

The republican members here from Jersey are entirely confident that their two houses, joined together, have a majority of republicans; their council being republican by 6. or 8. votes, and the lower house federal by only 1. or 2. And they have no doubt the approaching election will be in favor of the republicans. They appoint electors by the two houses voting together.

In N. York all depends on the success of the city election which is of 12. members, and of course makes a difference of 24. which is sufficient to make the two houses, joined together, republican in their vote. Govr. Clinton, Genl. Gates, and some other old revolutionary characters, have been put on the republican ticket. Burr, Livingston, etc. entertain no doubt on the event of that election. Still these are the ideas of the republicans only in these three states, and we must make great allowance for their sanguine views. Upon the whole, I consider it as rather more doubtful than the last election, in which I was not decieved in more than a vote or two. If Pennsylvania votes, then either Jersey or New York giving a republican vote, decides the election. If Pennsylva does not vote, then New York determines the election. In any event, we may say that if the *city* election of N. York is in favor of the Republican ticket, the issue will be republican; if the federal ticket for the city of N York prevails, the probabilities will be in favor of a federal issue, because it would then require a republican vote both from Jersey and Pennsylva to preponderate against New York, on which we could not count with any confidence. The election of New York being in April, it becomes an early and interesting object.

It is probable the landing of our envoys in Lisbon will add a month to our session; because all that the Eastern men are anxious about, is to get away before the possibility of a treaty's coming in upon us.

You must consider the money you have in Mr. Barnes' hands as *wholly* at your disposal. I have no note here of the amount of our nail account; but it is small and will be quite as convenient to me to recieve after I go home. Present my respectful salutations to Mrs. Madison and be assured of my constant and affectionate esteem.

Madison to Jefferson

[Orange] Mar. 15, 1800

DEAR SIR,

Since my last I have been favored with the following inclosures.—The Bill relating to Electors, Ramsay's oration, the Report on ways and means, a motion by Bingham, and the resolution for excluding the Judges from other offices.

It is not to be denied that the Const^n might have been properly more full in prescribing the election of P. and V. P. but the remedy is an amendment to the Const^n, and not a legislative interference. It is evident that this interference ought to be and was meant to be as little permitted as possible; it being a principle of the Const^n that the two departments should be independent of each other, and dependent on their Constituents only. Should the spirit of the Bill be followed up, it is impossible to say, how far the choice of the Ex. may be drawn out of the Constitutional hands, and subjected to the management of the Legislature. The danger is the greater, as the Chief Magistrate, for the time being may be bribed into the usurpations by so shaping them as to favor his re-election. If this licentiousness in constructive perversions of the Constitution, continue to increase, we shall soon have to look into our code of laws, and not the Charter of the people, for the form as well as the powers of our Government. Indeed such an unbridled spirit of construction as has gone forth in sundry instances, would bid defiance to any possible parchment securities against usurpation.

I understand that the general ticket law is represented at Phil^a as generally unpopular. I have no reason to believe this to be the fact. On the contrary, I learn that the information collected at Richmond on this subject is satisfactory to the friends of the law.

The ground has been covered for six weeks with snow; and there is still a remnant of it. It has given a very unusual backwardness to all the preparations for the ensuing crops, but we hope for some amends from its influence on the winter grain.

Jefferson to Madison

Philadelphia Mar. 25, 1800

Yours of the 15th is safely recieved. I percieve by that that I had by mistake sent you Ramsay's Eulogy instead of Cooper's smaller pamphlet, which therefore I now inclose merely for the last paper in it, as the two first were in the copy I first sent you. I inclose also Mr. Nicholas's amendment this day proposed to the bill concerning President and V. P. formerly sent you. We expect it will be rejected by 17. to 13. in Senate, but that it may be brought forward in the lower house with better prospects. We have nothing from Europe but what you will see in the newspapers. The Executive are sending off a frigate to France; but for what purposes we know not. The bankrupt law will pass. A complimentary vote of a medal to Truxton will pass.[22] A judiciary law adding about 100,000 D. to the annual expense of that department is going through the H. of R. A loan of 3½ millions will pass. The money it is said will be furnished by some English houses. Bankruptcies continue at Baltimore; and great mercantile distress and stagnation here. The Republican spirit beginning to preponderate in Pennsa, Jersey and N. Y. and becoming respectable in Mass. N. Hampsh. and Connect. Of R. I. and Vermont I can say nothing. There are the strongest expectations that the Republican ticket will prevail in the city election of N. Y. Clinton, Gates and Burr are at the head of it. It's success decides the complexion of that legislature. We expect Gouvr. Morris to be chosen by the present legislature a Senator of the U. S. in the room of Watson resigned. The legislature here parted in a state of distraction; their successors, as soon as chosen, will be convened: but it is very questionable if the Senate will not still be obstinate. We suppose Congress will rise in May. Respectful and affectionate salutations to Mrs. Madison and yourself. Adieu.

Madison to Jefferson

[Orange] Apr. 4, 1800

DEAR SIR

Your favor by Mr Trist was duly handed to me, since which I have rec^d the Report on imports under your cover, and yesterday your favor of the 25 ult.: accompanied with the Pamphlet and Mr Nicholas's motion on the Electoral Bill, which appears to be so fair and pertinent, that a rejection of it in favor of

---

22. For accounts of Republican opposition to the Federalist-sponsored bankruptcy law of 1800, see Morton Borden, *The Federalism of James A. Bayard* (New York, 1955), pp. 62–72; Charles Warren, *Bankruptcy in United States History* (Cambridge, Mass., 1935); Peter J. Coleman, *Debtors and Creditors in America: Insolvency, Imprisonment for Debt, and Bankruptcy, 1607–1900* (Madison, 1974), pp. 18–21; and Buel, pp. 207–8.

any other modification proposed, must fix a new brand on the Authors. The spirit manifested in the Senate steadily, and in the other House occasionally, however mischievous in its immediate effects, cannot fail I think to aid the progress of reflection and change among the people. In this view our public malady may work its own cure, and ultimately rescue the republican principal from the imputation brought on it by the degeneracy of the public Councils. Such a demonstration of the rectitude and efficacy of popular sentiment, will be the more precious, as the late defection of France has left America the only Theatre on which true liberty can have a fair trial. We are all extremely anxious here to learn the event of the Election in N. Y. on which so much depends. I have nothing to add to what I have already said on the prospect with us. I have no reason whatever to doubt all the success that was expected. If it should *fall in your way*,[23] you will oblige me by inquiring whether there be known in Philad? any composition for encrusting Brick that will effectually stand the weather: and particularly what is thought of common plaister thickly painted with white lead overspread with sand. I wish to give some such dressing to the columns of my Portico, and to lessen as much as possible the risk of the experiment. Affectionately Yrs

JS. MADISON JR

Jefferson to Madison

[Philadelphia] Apr. 4, 1800

Christopher McPherson, better known as M̄r Ross's man Kitt,[24] proposing to go to Charlottesville direct, I shall put into his care a packet of books and a letter left in my room for you, by somebody, while I was out, without information as to the quarter from whence they came. I observe them addressed to the care of the Governor Monroe. I suppose Kitt will carry on the letter; but as he goes in the stage to Fredsb͞g, he will leave the books there with M̄r Maury.

Capt Barry in the frigate US. arrived last night. Our envoys landed Nov. 27 at Lisbon from whence their secretaries proceeded by land to Paris. The principals reimbarked Dec. 21. for Lorient but after long beating against contrary winds in the bay of Biscay, they landed at Corunna Jan. 11. and sent a

23. JM's italics.

24. Christopher McPherson was the son of a slave woman named Clarinda and of Charles McPherson, a Scots merchant in Louisa County, Virginia. After being sold to David Ross, a Richmond merchant, McPherson was trained as a clerk. Ross emancipated him in 1792 and retained him as a clerk until 1799. In 1800, McPherson became a clerk in the High Court of Chancery. For a description of his reception at Montpellier, where he dined with the Madisons "and enjoyed a full share of the Convers[ation]," see Edmund Berkeley, Jr., "Prophet without Honor: Christopher McPherson, Free Person of Color," *VMHB* 77 (1969): 180–90.

courier to Paris for their passports. They proceeded to Burgos, and there recieved their passports from Paris, with a letter from Taleyrand expressing a desire to see them at Paris, and assuring them that the form of their credentials addressed to the Directory would be no obstacle to their negociation.[25] Murray was already at Paris. The letters from our envoys to the Executive, brought by Capt Barry, are dated at Burgos Feb. 10. They would have about 800. miles to Paris, where they will have arrived probably about the 1st week in March and by the 1st. week of May we may expect to hear of their reception. The frigate Portsmouth is about sailing from N. York to France, the object a secret.

The H. of R. having voted to adjourn the 1st Monday in May, the Senate this day postponed taking up the resolution for a fortnight. Still I think we shall adjourn the 1st or 2nd week in May. The Senate yesterday rejected $\overline{\text{Mr}}$ Pinckney's bill against appointing judges to any other offices. They have this day rejected a bill from the H. of R. for removing military troops from the place of election on the day of an election. You will have seen their warrant to commit Duane. They have not yet taken him. The President has nominated a third Major General to our 4000. men (Brookes of Mass.) and 204. promotions and appointments of officers are now before the Senate for approbation, to make the officers for 16. regiments compleat.[26] It will all be justified and confirmed.

Dupont de Nemours has been here on a visit from New York. He will settle there or at Alexandria. He promises me a visit with Madame Dupont, and will pay his respects to you on his way. He is one of the very great men of the age.[27] I am to go by Chesterfield to take my daughter Eppes home with me. This will deprive me of the pleasure of seeing you on the way; but not I hope of seeing you at Monticello where a great deal can be said to you which could not be confided to paper. Accept my affectionate salutations and assurances of attachment for $\overline{\text{Mrs}}$ Madison and yourself. Adieu.

JAMES MADISON

Madison to Jefferson

[Orange] Apr. 20, 1800

DEAR SIR,

Since my last, I have been favored with yours by Christo^r McPherson. It brought me the first agreeable information of the prospect held out by our Envoys. The posture of Europe, tho' dreadful to humanity in general, will I

---

25. See Albert H. Bowman, *The Struggle for Neutrality: A History of the Diplomatic Relations between the United States and France, 1790–1801* (Knoxville, 1974), p. 390, and De Conde, pp. 223–24.

26. See Stephen G. Kurtz, *The Presidency of John Adams: The Collapse of Federalism, 1795–1800* (Philadelphia, 1957), p. 397.

27. *The Correspondence of Jefferson and du Pont de Nemours, 1798–1817* (Boston, 1930), has been edited by Dumas Malone.

trust enforce the disposition of France to come to a proper adjustment with us. And notwithstanding the group of daring experiments presented by our public Councils, I also trust that they will not venture on either a direct refusal, or a palpable evasion of this result. Still however the situation of the party bent on war is such, that every stratagem ought to be suspected that may afford a chance of prolonging their ascendency. The horrors which they evidently feel at the approach of the Electoral epoch are a sufficient warning of the desperate game by which they will be apt to characterise the interval. In my next I shall be able to give you some partial information of the temper of the people here, as it will be shewn by our State election, which takes place on the 23 inst. I find that considerable exertion is used to raise prejudices agst. the measures of the last session of Assembly, especially the novel mode of appointg. Electors. I am not possessed however of any evidence of their success that deserves attention.

I sincerely wish Mr. Dupont may fulfil his promise to you and that I may come in for a participation of the visit. I beg you to make him sensible of the particular pleasure I shall feel in an opportunity of testifying to him at my own house the high esteem I entertain for his genius and virtues.

As your return to Virginia will soon take place and I am anxious to obtain some little remittances due to me from Philada., I must trouble you with the two inclosed draughts, and request that you will be good eno' to bring the proceeds with you. That on Lewis, I have not made payable to Barnes, because some personalities would make it unpleasing to him; and no other person occurring, I have left it to you to make use of any one you may find convenient. I wish it not to be put on any footing that may lead to legal proceedings in case he should not comply with the order, altho' there is not the slightest shadow for his hesitation. May I trouble you also to have the note to the Editor handed to him, and the advance of five dollars paid to him.

I will write you again by next post, being much hurried by being just returned from an absence for some days from home.

Madison to Jefferson

[Orange] Apr. 27, 1800

DEAR SIR

My last acknowledged yours by Christ: McPherson. I have nothing more to add, but the accts. I have from the elections in a few neighboring Counties. In this Davis and Barbour have succeeded: in the adjoing one, Hill and Early: In Louisa Yancy and Garland Anderson Jr—in Culpeper the two former ones. You will probably learn from Albemarle that F. Walker and a Mr. Garland have prevailed agst. Woods and Brown. If the whole state bears any likeness to the above sample of it, the patrons of usurpation and aristocracy will have little encouragement in this quarter. I am sorry that I am not to have the pleasure of seeing you on your way home. I wish nevertheless that you will be good eno'

[to] take charge of the money, if any should be obtained for me before you set out. Should Mr. W. Nicholas intend me the pleasure of calling, he would be a good hand to hasten its receipt.[28] Yrs. affcly.

Js. Madison Jr

Jefferson to Madison

Philadelphia May 12, [1800]

Dear Sir,

Congress will rise today or tomorrow. Mr. Nicholas proposing to call on you, you will get from him the Congressional news. On the whole the federalists have not been able to carry a single strong measure in the lower house the whole session. When they met, it was believed they had a majority of 20. But many of these were new and moderate men, and soon saw the true character of the party to which they had been well disposed while at a distance. The tide too of public opinion sets so strongly against the federal proceedings, that this melted off their majority, and dismayed the heroes of the party. The Senate alone remained undismayed to the last. Firm to their purposes, regardless of public opinion, and more disposed to coerce than to court it, not a man of their majority gave way in the least; and on the electoral bill they *adhered* to John Marshal's amendment, by their whole number;[29] and if there had been a full Senate there would have been but 11. votes against it, which includes H. Marshall who has voted with the republicans this session.

I have delivered to Mr Nicholas 160. dollars for you recieved from Mr Lewis, and he will recieve 123. dollars for you from Mr Barnes paid by Moylan. I deliver him also 110. D. in gold for your father, part of 160.38. delivered me for him by Mr Hurt. Mr Hurt had not been able to get it in small money. I therefore made interest at the mint for 50. D. in dimes and half dimes, which Mr Nicholas not being able to take, I shall carry with me and have ready to deliver on my arrival at Monticello.

Mr Anthony tells me there is a guinea and a half for every print of J. Trumbal's to be paid by those subscribers who paid half on subscribing. Your prints are not sent here. He supposes them sent to some place in Virginia.[30] I have wished very much to see La Trobe in order to come at him as to a coating for your columns, but it has not been in my power. I spoke on the subject with

---

28. Wilson Cary Nicholas had been elected to the Senate by the Virginia legislature at the end of 1799, following the death of Henry Tazewell.

29. Despite TJ's slap at John Marshall, the rejection of the Ross electoral-count bill by the House was due largely to Marshall's moderation as the Federalist floor leader, according to the Speaker of the House; see Theodore Sedgwick to Rufus King, May 11, 1800, in Rufus King, *Life and Correspondence of Rufus King,* ed. Charles R. King, 6 vols. (New York, 1894–1900), III, pp. 237–38.

30. Joseph Anthony, Jr., a Philadelphia silversmith, handled the sale of John Trumbull's prints; see *PJM,* XVII, p. 388. For Trumbull's prints, see Irma B. Jaffe, *John Trumbull: Patriot-Artist of the American Revolution* (Boston, 1975), pp. 186–87.

W. Hamilton of the Woodlands who has skill and experience on the subject. From him I got only that common plaster would not do. He whitewashes his brickwork.³¹ In L. Burlington's edition of Palladio he tells us that most of the columns of those fine buildings created by Palladio are of brick covered with stucco, and stand perfectly.³² I know that three fourths of the houses in Paris are covered with plaister and never saw any decay in it. I never enquired into its composition; but as they have a mountain of plaister of Paris adjoining the town, I presume it to be of that. I imagine a coat of the thickness of a knife blade would do on brick, which should cost little. I presume your plaisterer Wash could do it well.

I recieved from J. Bringhurst for Mrs Madison a letter which I delivered to Mr Nicholas. Also a small package containing, I think he said, a watch-chain and other things, and another containing a book. If Mr Nicholas can take the former, I will send it by him. If not, I will find room for it in my trunk. I am so streightened however that I have been obliged to put the book into a trunk which goes round by sea.

I have this day paid 5. dollars at the Aurora office for Capt Winston, as you desired. I hope I shall see you soon after my return either at your own house or Monticello or both. Accept assurances of constant and affectionate esteem to Mrs Madison and yourself from Dear Sir Your sincere friend and serv^t

TH: JEFFERSON

---

31. William Hamilton's estate the Woodlands was on the Schuykill River near Philadelphia, and TJ thought its gardens "the only rival I have known in America to what may be seen in England"; see John C. Greene, *American Science in the Age of Jefferson* (Ames, Iowa, 1984), p. 50.

32. TJ, a confirmed Palladian, owned four editions of Andrea Palladio's *Four Books of Architecture;* see E. Millicent Sowerby, *Catalogue of the Library of Thomas Jefferson,* 5 vols. (Washington, 1952–59), IV, pp. 359–61, 363–64, 380. See also Mario Di Valmarana, ed., *Palladian Studies in America,* I: *Building by the Book* (Charlottesville, 1984), for a discussion of the relationship between English and American Palladianism. For an analysis of the 1738 edition dedicated to Lord Burlington, which TJ owned, see Harold Francis Pfister, "Burlingtonian Architectural Theory in England and America," *Winterthur Portfolio* 11 (1976): 123–51.

THE ELECTION OF 1800 AND THE CRISIS OF SUCCESSION

ON MAY 15, 1800, JEFFERSON LEFT PHILADELPHIA for the last time, knowing that the nation's capital would move to the District of Columbia in the autumn. He hoped to skirt Richmond and, therefore, avoid becoming "a manniquin of ceremony," stopping instead with his daughter and son-in-law at their home nearby. Although he avoided ceremony at his country retreat, he could not avoid politics. Early in May, the editor of the *Virginia Federalist* had reported erroneously that James T. Callender, a virulent critic of President Adams, was staying at Monticello, a charge denied by the Republican newspaper, the Richmond *Examiner,* on May 16. One week later, the federal grand jury indicted Callender for publishing seditious libels in his pamphlet *The Prospect before Us,* a campaign document that labeled Adams "a hoary headed incendiary" and urged the election of Jefferson: "Take your choice . . . between Adams, war and beggary, and Jefferson, peace and competency." Describing the author as "a person of wicked, depraved, evil disposed, disquiet and turbulent mind and disposition," the indictment charged him with designing to defame the president by writing false, scandalous, and malicious statements with intent to bring him into contempt.[1]

On the day after the indictment and two days before the arrest of Callender, Governor Monroe, who had earlier predicted to the vice president that the Federalists would attempt to enforce the Sedition Law in Virginia as an electioneering trick, asked him if it would be proper to employ public counsel

---

1. For the Callender trial, see James Morton Smith, *Freedom's Fetters: The Alien and Sedition Laws and American Civil Liberties* (Ithaca, N.Y., 1956), pp. 334–58, and Malone, III, pp. 471–72, 477. For the relationship between TJ and Callender, see Charles A. Jellison, "That Scoundrel Callender," *VMHB* 67 (1959): 295–306. For a biography of Callender, see Michael Durey, *"With the Hammer of Truth": James Thomson Callender and America's Early National Heroes* (Charlottesville, 1990).

to defend Callender and "give an eclat to a vindication of the principles of the State." At the same time, he pledged that he would maintain order in the city, although he expected that "the people will behave with dignity on the occasion and give no pretext for comments to their discredit." Jefferson, who was still at his daughter's home, replied promptly that it was "essentially just and necessary that Callender should be substantially defended. Whether in the first stage by publick interference"—by state-appointed counsel—"or private contributors, may be a question."[2]

Jefferson did not linger in Richmond for Callender's trial and conviction.[3] Instead, he took his younger daughter, who had lost her first child, to Monticello to spend the summer. There he sat out the presidential campaign, knowing that it would "be as hot as that of Europe. But happily indeed in ink only; they in blood."[4] In a contest characterized by the most vicious personal attacks in the history of presidential elections,[5] he maintained an active interest as a relatively detached and comparatively silent observer.[6]

Jefferson kept a running tally of the electoral vote, beginning with the Republican upset of the Federalists in New York in April, the first real test of party strength. He had earlier predicted that a win there would mean a national victory. Hamilton feared the same result and tried to tamper with the New York returns after Burr's efforts led to a Republican triumph. In an urgent letter to Governor John Jay, he asked him to reconvene the lame-duck Federalist legislature to alter the state's election law and, thus, reverse the election results. If the governor let the election stand, Hamilton warned frantically, it would mean "the OVERTHROW of the GOVERNMENT . . . a REVOLUTION, after the manner of BONAPARTE." "In times like these in which we live," he assured Jay, "it will not do to be overscrupulous." His proposal had one other merit, he added: it would "insure a majority of votes in the United States for a Federal candidate." Every legal and constitutional step, he argued, should be taken "to prevent an atheist in religion, and a fanatic in politics, from getting possession of the helm of state."[7]

During the summer lull, Jefferson resumed his rebuilding of Monticello

---

2. James Monroe to TJ, May 25, 1800, and May 24, 1800, in Hamilton, *Writings of Monroe*, III, p. 180, and TJ to James Monroe, May 26, 1800, in Ford, VII, p. 448. The defense counsel, which included the attorney general of Virginia, the clerk of the House of Delegates, and the governor's son-in-law, contributed their services; see Smith, p. 346.

3. Callender's sentence was to expire on Mar. 3, 1801, Adams's last day in office and the day the Sedition Law was to expire.

4. Peterson, p. 629.

5. For sprightly accounts, see C. O. Lerche, Jr., "Jefferson and the Election of 1800: A Case Study in the Political Smear," *WMQ* 5 (1948): 467–91, and Charles E. O'Brien, "The Religious Issue in the Presidential Campaign of 1800," *Essex Institute Historical Collections* 107 (1971): 82–93.

6. For solid accounts of the election, see Malone, III, pp. 476–92, and Peterson, pp. 634–42.

7. Alexander Hamilton to John Jay, May 7, 1800, in Syrett, XXIV, pp. 464–66. Jay rejected Hamilton's proposal; see James Morton Smith, "Alexander Hamilton, the Alien Act, and Seditious Libels," *Review of Politics* 16 (1954): 305–33.

and continued to supply Madison with nails for the remodeling of Montpelier. In July, the Madisons visited Jefferson, and the vice president and the farmer squared their financial accounts, which had slipped into some disarray as they concentrated their attention on politics.[8] Although Jefferson spent part of the summer completing his *Manual of Parliamentary Practice,* which laid down rules for the conduct of the Senate, he scanned the newspapers carefully, calling Madison's attention to a series of Federalist toasts at a Fourth of July celebration in Raleigh, North Carolina.[9] But he wrote only one other letter to Madison that summer, expressing some anxiety about the peace mission to France and evaluating reports on the Republican presidential vote—North Carolina, a bare majority; Georgia, unanimous; New Jersey, favorable; South Carolina, "unanimous either with them or against them: but not certainly which." He discounted reports about Connecticut, the most rigid of the Federalist states, turning Republican. "That," he wrote, "is impossible," even though republicanism there was rising with unexpected rapidity, as it was in Massachusetts, still a Federalist stronghold.[10]

Madison passed along his budget of political intelligence—Pennsylvania was uncertain; New Jersey, favorable; Maryland, "neither flattering, nor altogether hopeless"; and South Carolina, "rather ominous, but . . . soon [to] be relieved by an overbalance of republicanism" in the backcountry, which would offset the federalism of Charleston.[11] And from Burr's future son-in-law, he heard, incorrectly, that Rhode Island was "on the right side." But Jefferson's running mate was worried about party solidarity in supporting him "for the secondary station," fearful that "the requisite concert may not sufficiently pervade the several States."[12] In Virginia, the elections had been successful "beyond expectation"—Jefferson carried Orange County 340 to 7—and Madison looked forward eagerly to his "electoral errand" to Richmond in December, when he and the other electors on the Republican general ticket would cast their ballots unanimously for Jefferson and Burr.[13]

By November, it was clear that the presidential election would be decided by the vote in South Carolina. There, the Republican campaign committee was headed by Senator Charles Pinckney, a cousin of the Federalist vice-presidential candidate. In order to safeguard his reports to Jefferson from interception in the spy-ridden postal system,[14] he enclosed them in a letter addressed

8. TJ to JM, July 20, 1800, below, and JM to TJ, [ca. Aug. 14, 1800], below.
9. TJ to JM, July 20, 1800, below. See also TJ, *Jefferson's Parliamentary Writings: "Parliamentary Pocket-Book" and A Manual of Parliamentary Practice,* ed. Wilbur Samuel Howell, in *PTJ,* 2d ser. (Princeton, 1988). Howell calls the *Manual,* which was published in 1801, "the most enduring of any book by any American President or Vice President."
10. TJ to JM, Sept. 17, 1800, below.
11. JM to TJ, Oct. 1, 1800, below, and JM to TJ, ca. Nov. 11, 1800, below.
12. JM to TJ, Oct. 21, 1800, below.
13. JM to TJ, ca. Nov. 11, 1800, below.
14. TJ mentions the "prying season" in his letter to JM, Dec. 19, 1800, below.

to Madison. Thus it was that Madison had the pleasant privilege of handing Jefferson the letter that informed him that he would be the next president of the United States. The fateful letter arrived at Montpellier on November 24, just before Jefferson stopped overnight with the Madisons on his way to Washington, the nation's new capital. Together they read Pinckney's assurance that "we shall have a decided majority in our Legislature," which would choose the state's presidential electors.[15] Both knew that the South Carolina vote guaranteed a Republican victory, and Jefferson promptly offered and Madison accepted the post of secretary of state. They also discussed other appointments, including that of Albert Gallatin of Pennsylvania as secretary of treasury and Robert R. Livingston or Samuel Smith of Maryland as secretary of the navy.[16] And they wrestled with the difficulty of "mak[in]g app[ointmen]ts with[ou]t a Senate, in case of resignations *prior to March 4*."[17]

The election in South Carolina, as Jefferson observed after getting settled in Washington, "has in some measure decided the great contest." He qualified his remarks because, through a quirk in the electoral system and the steadiness of party discipline, the campaign had resulted in "an absolute parity between the two republican candidates," giving Jefferson and Burr 73 votes each, Adams 65, and Pinckney 64.[18] This unexpected result, he lamented, "has produced great dismay and gloom on the republican gentlemen here, and equal exultation on the federalists, who openly declare they will prevent an election, and will name a President of the Senate, *pro tem*," from their lame-duck majority, "by what they say would only be a *stretch* of the constitution."

Under these circumstances, Jefferson predicted, the month of February, set for the official electoral count, "will present us storms of a new character." The way to prevent the Senate "stretch" was to follow the constitutional method of referring the decision to the House to vote by state delegations, and, by his quick calculation, seven of the sixteen states could be counted on to vote right, leaving two necessary to make a majority of nine. "It is thought by some that Baer of Maryland, and Linn of N[ew] J[ersey] will come over. Some even count on Morris of Vermont. But you must know," he told the veteran legislator, "the uncertainty of such a dependence under the operation of caucuses and other federal engines." Nonetheless, he seemed confident that the House would choose him over Burr, and he pressed Madison to come to

15. Pinckney's three-part letter to TJ, written on Oct. 12, 16, and 26, 1800, is printed in *AHR* 4 (1898): 111–16. For Pinckney's cover letter to JM, Oct. 26, 1800, see *ibid.*, 116–18. TJ endorsed Pinckney's letter as having been received on Nov. 24, 1800, the night TJ stayed with the Madisons; see his Personal Account Books for Nov. 24, 1800, University of Virginia Library photostats, and JM to TJ, ca. Nov. 11, 1800, below. In his Epistolary ledger, however, TJ mistakenly listed it as having been received on Nov. 24 in Washington, although he did not reach the capital until Nov. 27; see the University of Virginia Library photostats.
16. See TJ to JM, Dec. 19, 1800, below.
17. See JM's inquiry in his letter to TJ, Jan. 10, 1801, below.
18. One Rhode Island elector cast his vote for John Jay.

Washington in time for his inauguration. Once his election was confirmed, he proposed "to aim at a candid understanding with Mr. A[dams]," hoping "to induce in him dispositions liberal and accommodating."[19]

While Madison was in Richmond making sure that the Virginia electors cast a unanimous vote for Jefferson and Burr equally—he was anxious to offset Burr's fear that the southern states might not pursue "the requisite concert" in supporting him for the vice presidency, he learned officially that South Carolina's vote had indeed fixed "the event of a Republican President." But his count also indicated that there might be a tie, in which case it would "devolve on the H[ouse] of Reps. to make the discrimination." In such an event, he thought—perhaps too optimistically—that "a proper one will be made." Since the vote in four Republican states—Georgia, North Carolina, Tennessee, and Kentucky—was not yet known, however, he hoped, as Burr's agent had suggested, that the foresight of some of the electors would lead one or more of them to withhold a vote from Burr.[20]

But as the final votes trickled in, it became clear, as Jefferson reported the day after Christmas, that "the result is a perfect parity between the two republican characters. The Feds appear determined to prevent an election," he added, but they had switched from the president *pro tem* of the Senate to John Jay, whom Adams had recently appointed chief justice to succeed Oliver Ellsworth, who had resigned and was still in France resting up after the peace mission. Another possibility was John Marshall, who had succeeded Pickering as secretary of state after Adams cleaned his cabinet of Hamiltonians. Jefferson discounted these maneuvers, however, still thinking that nine of the sixteen congressional delegations would cast their vote for the people's choice.[21]

Two days after Jefferson wrote Madison, the constitutional machinery ground into action. On December 28, 1800, the official returns from the states were delivered to the vice president as presiding officer of the Senate, and Jefferson reported their arrival to Secretary of State John Marshall.[22] But the electoral-vote certificates could not be opened and counted until February 11, 1801, as the law prescribed. During the prolonged uncertainty, the political pot stayed at a constant boil in Washington, demonstrating, as Albert Gallatin observed, that "the majority drink naught but politics, and by not mixing with men of different or more moderate activities, they inflame one another."[23] Madison could hardly believe that there could be an "attempt to strangle the election of the people, and smuggle into the Chief Magistraey the creature of a faction. It would seem that every individual member, who has any standing or

19. TJ to JM, Dec. 19, 1800, below.
20. JM to TJ, Dec. 20, 1800, below.
21. TJ to JM, Dec. 26, 1800, below.
22. Malone, III, p. 495.
23. Peterson, p. 644.

stake in society, or any portion of virtue or sober understanding must revolt at the tendency of such a manœuver."[24]

But reality led him to look at the two options mentioned by Jefferson, "an interregnum in the Executive, or of a surreptitious intrusion into it." Either event would create a constitutional crisis. "Will it be best to acquiesce in a suspension or usurpation of the Executive authority till the meeting of Cong^s" ten months later, in December 1801? Or should Jefferson and Burr summon the new Congress "by a joint proclamation or recommendation"? Madison favored the latter move because "the prerogative of convening the Legislature must reside in one or [the] other of them, and if both concur, must substantially include the requisite will. The intentions of the people would undoubtedly be pursued." He hoped, however, "that all such questions will be precluded by a proper decision of nine States in the H[ouse] of R[epresentatives]."[25]

About the time that Jefferson received this letter, the Federalists in the lame-duck House, which had been elected at the height of the XYZ fever, met in caucus and decided to support Burr.[26] President Adams was appalled that the Federalists would back Burr and suffer "the humiliation of seeing this dexterous gentleman rise, like a balloon, filled with inflammable air, over their heads." Hamilton also preferred Jefferson to Burr, whom he labeled "the Catiline of America." However, the Federalists paid little attention to these leaders, who had sniped at each other in internal party bickering throughout the election campaign.[27]

Jefferson wrote only one letter to Madison during this protracted waiting period, for he dared not "through the channel of the post hazard a word to you on the subject of the election. Indeed," he added, "the interception and publication of my letters exposes the republican cause as well as myself personally to so much obloquy that I have come to a resolution never to write another sentence of politics in a letter."[28]

Throughout the period of uncertainty, Jefferson presided evenhandedly over the Senate every day it met. The Senate debated ratification of the new treaty with France, known as the Convention of 1800, which was designed to end the quasi war and restore diplomatic relations between France and the United States.[29] After John Jay rejected his reappointment as chief justice of the United States, President Adams nominated, and the Senate confirmed,

24. JM to TJ, Jan. 10, 1801, below.
25. *Ibid.*
26. Malone, III, p. 499.
27. *Ibid.*, p. 500.
28. TJ to JM, Feb. 1, 1801, below.
29. See Albert H. Bowman, *The Struggle for Neutrality: A History of the Diplomatic Relations between the United States and France, 1790–1801* (Knoxville, 1974), pp. 415–20. After the Senate ratified the convention, President Adams appointed Senator James A. Bayard as minister to France. When Bayard rejected his appointment, Adams left the exchange of ratifications to his successor.

John Marshall, the secretary of state, for that post. Jefferson watched as the Senate passed the Judiciary Act of 1801 and presided while that body confirmed a flurry of last-minute Federalist appointments as judges, viewing the rush as an attempt to buttress Federalist control of the only branch of government they retained after losing the other two in the recent election. Of the enlarged judiciary, staffed by the outgoing Federalists to a man, he dreaded "this above all the measures meditated," he told Madison, "because appointments in the nature of freehold render it difficult to undo what is done."[30]

On February 11, 1801, the members of the House met jointly with the Senate to watch Jefferson open the election certificates, hand them to the tellers for tallying, then announce the totals, which had been known for two months. The next morning Jefferson scribbled a hasty note to Madison at 7:00 A.M., announcing that "the H. of R. has been in conclave ever since 2. oclock yesterday. At 10 P.M. 17. ballots had been tried, and were invariably 8. [for Jefferson] 6. [for Burr] and 2. divided."[31] The voting continued throughout the night at intervals of half an hour to an hour until the sleepy representatives decided in the early morning hours of February 12 to suspend the balloting from 7:00 A.M. until noon. "And after trying a few more ballots with the same effect," Jefferson reported, they "suspended it again till 11 a.m. tomorrow." The twenty-eighth ballot was taken on Thursday, two more on Friday the thirteenth, and three on Valentine's Day. In a note to Governor Monroe on Sunday, Jefferson reported that "four days of balloting have produced not a single change of a vote."[32] As the tension mounted, he confessed to his daughter that "the scene passing here makes me pant to be away from it: to fly from the circle of cabal, intrigue and hatred, to one where all is love and peace."[33] Two more ballots followed on the sixth day. And on the seventh day, February 17, on the thirty-sixth ballot, Jefferson prevailed.

The next day, the president-elect wrote Madison a brief explanation, "notwithstanding the suspected infidelity of the post." Three things influenced the Federalist hard-liners: "the impossibility of electing B[urr,] the certainty that a legislative usurpation would be resisted by arms, and a recourse to a Convention to reorganize and amend the government."[34] In a raucous caucus—"a consultation on this dilemma," Jefferson called it—the Federalists had to decide "whether it would be better for them to come over in a body, and go with the tide of the times, or by a negative conduct suffer the election

---

30. TJ to JM, Dec. 26, 1800, below. For JM's analysis of the convention of 1800, see JM to TJ, Jan. 10, 1801, below.

31. TJ to JM, Feb. 12, 1801, below.

32. TJ to James Monroe, Feb. 15, 1801, in Ford, VI, pp. 490-91. See also Peterson, p. 649.

33. TJ to Maria Eppes, Feb. 15, 1801, Jefferson Papers of the University of Virginia, 1732-1828 (Microfilm, Reel 5).

34. TJ told Governor Monroe that "the very word convention gives them the horrors, . . . in the present democratic spirit of America"; see TJ to James Monroe, Feb. 15, 1801, in L. and B., X, p. 201.

to be made by a bare majority, keeping their body entire and unbroken, to act in phalanx on such ground of opposition as circumstances shall offer." The diehards opted for the negative approach: "Morris of V[ermont] withdrew, which made Lyon's vote that of his State. The 4 Maryland Federalists put in 4. blanks which made the positive tickets of their colleagues the vote of the state. S. Carolina and Delaware," previously for Burr, "put in [6.] blanks," he concluded. "So there were 10. states for one candidate, 4. for another, and 2. blanks." Jefferson was convinced that the action of the Federalists, by their negative and tardy act of withholding their votes, amounted to "a declaration of war, on the part of this band." According to James A. Bayard, the lone representative from Delaware who engineered the tiebreaker, the Federalists, after deciding that Burr could not be elected, concluded that the only reason for supporting him thereafter was "to exclude Jefferson at the expense of the Constitution."[35]

There was one consolation, however, Jefferson informed the future secretary of state. The hard-liners in Congress had isolated themselves from their party members at the grass-roots level. "Their conduct appears to have brought over to us the whole body of the Federalists, who being alarmed with the danger of a dissolution of the government, had been made most anxiously to wish [for] the very administration they had opposed, and to view it when obtained as a child of their own." These "quondam leaders" in Congress, he thought, had abandoned the mass of the Federalists, who were "aggregated under other banners. Even Hamilton and Higginson have been partisans for us. This circumstance, with the unbounded confidence which will attach to the new ministry as soon as known, will start us on high ground."[36]

Madison was relieved to hear of the House's action although he confessed that the result "was generally looked for in this quarter. It was thought not probable that the phalanx would hold out agst the general revolt of its partizans out of doors and without any military force to abet usurpation. How fortunate," he added thankfully, "that the latter has been withheld: and what a lesson to America and the world, is given by the efficacy of the public will when there is no army to be turned agst it!"[37]

---

35. The quotation by Bayard is in Malone, III, p. 504; also see *ibid.,* IV, pp. 3–14. For Bayard's role, see Morton Borden, *The Federalism of James A. Bayard* (New York, 1955), pp. 80–93, and John S. Pancake, "Aaron Burr: Would-Be Usurper," *WMQ* 8 (1951): 204–13.

36. TJ to JM, Feb. 18, 1801, below.

37. JM to TJ, Feb. 28, 1801, below. See Morton Grodzins, "Political Parties and the Crisis of Succession in the United States: The Case of 1800," in *Political Parties and Political Development,* ed. Joseph La Palombara and Myron Weiner (Princeton, 1966), pp. 303–27, for a fascinating discussion.

THE LETTERS

Jefferson to Madison

Monticello June 13, 1800

DEAR SIR

In my last letter to you from Philadelphia I mentioned that I had sent for yourself by Mr. Nicholas 160 Doll. recd. from Lewis, and 110. Doll. for your father part of the 160.38 delivered to me by Mr Hurt for him. The remaining 50. D. I brought and have here in half dimes ready to be delivered. I mentioned also that Mr Nicholas would recieve from Barnes Genl. Moylan's money (123. Dol. if my memory is right.) All this I hope has been right. I was charged by Barnes with 270. D. for Mrs Key in this neighborhood. He had made up the parcels and labelled them. I gave that of 270. D. labelled by him for you, to Mr Nicholas, as above mentd. Yet when I came to open here the one he had labelled, *externally* for Mrs Key, I found the *internal* divided into two parcels and labelled the one 160. D. for you and 110. D. for your father. Not doubting that he had committed an error in cross-dividing the external labels, and the sum happening to be precisely the same, I delivered the money to Mrs. Key. It would have been more satisfactory to me if a similar discovery of disagreement between the external and internal labels of the other parcel had been observed. But Mr Nicholas tells me he returned that parcel to Barnes and took paper instead of it. However it suffices that yourself and your father have recieved your 270. D.

I have here also for Mrs Madison 2. small packets, about the size of letters and a third, containing a book, is on it's way in a trunk of mine which left Philadelphia about the 26th. Ult. by water. I have not yet heard of it's arrival in Richmond. I am not without hopes that you will soon recieve these things *here* yourselves. At present and for some days you would find Dr. and Mrs Bache with us. On Monday we expect Mr and Mrs Hollins on their return from Warren to Baltimore. Tho' late occurrences have been wonderful, and furnish much matter for consideration; yet they are beyond the limits of a letter and not proper for one which is to go through the post office. There seems now to be one possibility which would furnish matter for [a] very interesting consultation between us, and a consultation much to be desired: and unless you should find it convenient to come here soon, I propose to myself the pleasure of seeing you at your own house. But this cannot be till Mr Eppes and my daughter, who are to leave tomorrow, return again; which will not be until after his harvest. They take the wheels of my chair to equip the Phaeton for them. Perhaps I may be able to borrow a chair in the neighborhood, tho' I do not know of one at present. Should it be convenient for Mrs Madison and yourself to solve the difficulty it will be sooner done and more to our gratification. Mr Randolph and my daughter will participate in the pleasure of your company here. Accept my sincere and affectionate attachments to Mrs Madison and yourself. Adieu

Jefferson to Madison

Monticello July 20, 1800

TH:J. TO J. MADISON.

Since you were here I have had time to turn to my accounts, and among others undertook to state the one with you: but was soon brought to a nonplus, by observing that I had made an entry Aug. 23. 99. of nails delivered for you, but left the particulars and amount blank till Mr Richardson should give them in to me. Whether he omitted this, or I to enter them I cannot tell, nor have either of us the least recollection what they were. I am in hopes I may have sent you a bill of them, as I generally do if I see the messenger before departure. But sometimes I omit this. At any rate I am in hopes that either from the bill or the recollections of those who used them you may be able to fill up the blank in the inclosed account, conjecturally at least. I recieved from Mr. Barnes in Jan. a credit of 69.23 D on your account. Not having the amount of nails, I could not tell what I ought to have recieved, but I remember that my idea at the time was that it must be a good deal more than you owed me, and that of course there would be a balance to return you: this shall be instantly done on recieving either your statement or conjecture of the amount, which I pray you to do.[1]

I see in Gale's paper of July 8. an account of the 4th. of July as celebrated at Raleigh. The Governor presided at the dinner. Among the toasts were the following. The U. S. may they continue free, sovern. and indepdt. not influenced by foreign intrigue, nor distracted by internal convulsions. The Pres. of the US. May his countrymen rightly appreciate his distinguished virtue patriotism, and firmness. The V.P. of the US. The militia of the US. May the valor of the souldier be combined with the virtue of the citizen. The Navy of the US. The benifits which have arisen from it's infant efforts is a just presage of it's future greatness and usefulness. The freedom of the press without licentiousness. The friends of religion and order. May they always triumph over the supporters of infidelity and confusion, etc. My respects to Mrs Madison. Adieu affectionately

1. For TJ's nailery, see Edwin M. Betts, ed., *Thomas Jefferson's Farm Book* . . . (Princeton, 1953), pp. 426–28.

James Madison to Th: Jefferson for nails

						Dr.		
						£	s	d
1799.	July 25.	to	23 lb. IVs	} @ 14½		1-	9-	0
			1. lb. inch brads					
			500. 1½ I. brads @	12½ per lb.			3-	8
			26. lb. X ds. @	11½		1-	4-	11
			35. lb. XVId. brads @ 10½			1-	10-	7½
	Aug. 23.	to						
		Cr.						
1800.	Jan. 28.	By credit with J. Barnes 69.23D = £20.15.5.						

Madison to Jefferson

[Orange ca. Aug. 14, 1800]

DEAR SIR

I have had an opportunity since my return of seeing Mr. McGee on the subject of the nails used by him last summer and of collecting through him the information of his brother who brought down the parcell delivered in July. They concur in saying that the Spriggs. the X. and XVI d alone formed that parcel and that the XVI d. were not brads but nails owing to a mistake in executing the order. I recollect myself that no brads were recd. because the disappointment was felt at the time, and the floor of the Portico was laid with brads made in my father's shop, and a remainder of the Stock procured the preceding year. The IV d. cut nails, are accounted for by Mrs M. and the driver of my carriage, who brought them down in Augst. The precise date is not recollected but from circumstances it must have been in an advanced Stage of the month. A part of them were used in lathing the ceiling of the Portico. The balance is still on hand. It would seem therefore that you have enumerated all the nails sent: and that by filling the blank in Augst. with a transfer to that time, of the IV d. charged in July, the account will probably stand right.[2] As this explanation however rests mainly on memory, it must yield to any better evidence that may be found. None such is within my possession. I have a letter from Mr. Dawson dated Hager's Town July 28: in which he says that the choice of Delegates in Maryland is to be made on the first Monday in Octr. that the contest in all the counties is uncommonly warm, that he thinks it more than probable the majority will be of the administration party, and that in such event, it is understood the Legislature will be immediately called together for the purpose of appointg Electors. Adieu

J. M. JR

2. TJ manufactured "4d. 6d. 8. 10. 12d. 16d. 18. d 20d. 24d. [and] 30d." nails and "6d. brads"; see *ibid.*, p. 428.

Jefferson to Madison

Monticello Aug. 29, 1800

DEAR SIR

Before the receipt of your last favor, Mr McGehee had called on me, and satisfied me that the entry of nails delivered in Aug. and left blank was really of nails charged in July and not then delivered. The misconception on my part arose from imperfect entries made on the reports of Mr Richardson who generally delivered out the nails. I am chagrined at it's having been the cause of my holding the whole of the 69.23 D. of your order on Barnes, when so inconsiderable a portion of it was for me. I now send a statement of our account and the balance of £13-7-2 shall be sent by Mr Barber from our court unless a more direct conveyance occurs.

I have recieved no letters of particular information since you were here: nor do I learn any thing lately respecting N. Carolina. The republican papers of Massachusetts and Connecticut continue to be filled with the old stories of deism, atheism, antifederalism etc. as heretofore and are very silent as to Pinckney.

P. Carr yesterday lost his son; and his daughter is understood to be hopeless. Mr Trist has at length made a purchase of lands, those on which James Kerr lived, on the road to Mr Divers's, @ 7. D. the acre. A purchaser has offered for Colo. Monroe's land above Charlottesville @ 6. D. He came from Loudon, with a Mr Craven, recommended to me as a tenant by Genl. Mason. Craven has rented 5. fields of me of 100. acres each on this side of the river, with all the negroes belonging to the plantation (18 workers) stock, etc. at £350 a year for 5. years. I had before nearly compleated the leasing all my lands on the other side the river. My nailery and the erecting my mill are now to be my chief occupations. I hope to rent the latter advantageously. Lands are rising sensibly here. Several are wanting to buy, and there is little for sale. I imagine we shall hardly be summoned to Washington before the fixed time of meeting. Present my respects to Mrs Madison, and affectionate salutations to yourself.

TH JEFFERSON

James Madison junr. to Th: Jefferson

					Dr.		
					£	s	d
1799	July 25	To	23. lb IVd nails	@ 14½	1-	9-	0
	Aug 23		1. lb inch brads				
			500. 1½ brads @ 12½ pr. Ct			3-	8
			26. lb. X" @ 11½		1-	4-	11
			35. lb XVId brads @ 10½		1-	10-	7½

			Dr.		
			£	s	d
1800.	May 12.	To pd. for Aurora for J. Winston by yr order	1-	10	
	Aug. 10.	To remitted S. T. Mason for Holt etc. by your order	1-	10	
		balance due J. M.	13-	7-	2
			20-	15-	4½
	Jan.	By your order on J. Barnes 69.23	20-	15-	4½

Jefferson to Madison

Monticello Sept. 17, 1800

Dear Sir,

I now send by Bp. Madison the balance which should have gone from our last court by Mr. Barber: but not seeing him the first day of the court, that breaking up on the first day, contrary to usage [and] universal expectation, Mr. Barber was gone before I knew that fact.

Is it not strange the public should have no information of the proceedings and prospects of our envoys in a case so vitally interesting to our commerce? That at a time when, as we suppose, all differences are in a course of amicable adjustment, Truxton should be fitted out with double diligence that he may get out of port before the arrival of a treaty, and shed more human blood merely for the pleasure of shedding it?

I have a letter from Mr. Butler in which he supposes that the Republican vote of N. Carolina will be but a bare majority. Georgia he thinks will be unanimous with the republicans; S. C. unanimous either with them or against them: but not certainly which. Dr. Rush and Burr give favorable accounts of Jersey. Granger and Burr even count with confidence on Connecticut. But that is impossible. The revolution there indeed is working with very unexpected rapidity: before another Congressional election it will probably be complete. There is good reason to believe Massachusetts will increase her republican vote in Congress, and that Levi Lincoln will be one. He will be a host in himself; being undoubtedly the ablest and most respectable man of the Eastern states.[3] Health, respect affection.

Th. Jefferson

D	C
44.	53.

3. TJ later appointed Lincoln as his first attorney general.

Madison to Jefferson

[Orange ca. Sept. 23, 1800]

DEAR SIR

I recd. by Bishop M. the 44.D 53.C commited to his care. The silence which prevails as to the negociations of our Envoys is not less surprising to my view than to yours. We may be assured however that nothing of a sort to be turned to the party objects on the anvil has been recd. unless indeed the publication shd. be delayed for a moment deemed more critically advantageous. As we are left to mere conjectures, the following have occurred to me. The long continuance of the Envoys at Paris of itself indicated that difficulties of some sort or other have sprung up or been created. As the French govt. seems to have provided for the future security of our commerce by repealing the decrees under which it had been violated, and as the ultimatum of the Ex. explained by former instructions permitted a waver at least of claims for past spoliations, it would seem that no insuperable obstacles would be likely to arise on these articles. In looking for other solutions, my attentions have fallen on the articles contained in the Treaty of 1778 relating 1. to free ships freeing their cargoes. 2 to the permissions granted to prizes 3. to convoys. That a difficulty may have happened on the first, is rendered not improbable by the late transactions with Prussia. The 2d. is suggested by the circumstances under which the stipulation was sought and obtained by G. B. and the 3d. by the late occurrences and combinations in Europe. Should any one or more of these conjectures be just, the explanation will also coincide with the reports from different quarters, which speak of the Treaty of 78 as at the bottom of the impediments, and if so it seems more likely that they would be found in such parts of it as have been alluded to, than in the guaranty which cannot be needful to France, and which her pride would be more ready to reject than to claim.[4] I cannot but flatter myself, that your letter from Mr B[utler] is to be otherwise explained than by admitting the accuracy of his information. Mr. Dawson now with me has a letter from Macon of Aug. 15 which with apparent confidence promises 9 Repub. votes in N. C. and in general seems to be pleased with the present temper of it. As to S. C. I learn in various ways that there is thought to be no danger there, and that the adverse party openly relinquish expectation. From the North your intelligence will be later as well as better than mine. Yrs always and affecly.

Js. MADISON JR.

---

4. For a discussion of the negotiations, which began on Apr. 2, 1800, and ended on Sept. 29, 1800, see Bowman, pp. 393–414.

Madison to Jefferson

[Orange] Oct. 1, 1800

DEAR SIR

Mr. Trist left with me yesterday on his way home, the inclosed pamphlet which I return to him thro' your hands that you may have an oppy. of perusing it, in case a copy should not yet have reached you. I understand from Mr. T. who left Philada. on Monday the 22d. that the prospect of a vote by Pennsa. was rather clouded by the uncertainty of the elections in one or two of the Senatorial districts. He seems to think that a favorable vote from N J. may be expected. The idea collected by him as to Maryland in his passage thro' that State, is neither flattering, nor altogether hopeless. In general he speaks of the impression among all parties as strong in favor of republican issue to the main question. In the federal City he was told by Mr. R. Harrison, that late accounts had come to hand, which tho' not official were credited, that our Envoys in consequence of the form taken by the negociations, were on board the vessel which was to bring them home, and had refused the invitation of Buonaparte to stay three days longer.[5] No particulars whatever were explained by Mr. H. nor any indications given of the effect of the intelligence on the feelings of the Cabinet

You will do well in making your arrangements for the arrival of the Hessian fly among you next season. Many fields sown this fall in our neighborhood, must be resown or given up for some other crop, and a little to the North of us the destruction is still greater. Yrs. affcy.

Js. MADISON JR.

Madison to Jefferson

[Orange] Oct. 21, 1800

DEAR SIR

This will be handed you by M.̲ Altson of S. Carolina,[6] who proposes to call at Monticello on his return from a Northern tour. He will probably be well known to you by other introductions; but those which he has brought to me, as well as a short acquaintance with him make me feel an obligation to add mine. He appears to be intelligent, sound in his principles, and polished in his manners. Coming fresh from N. Y. through Pen.ª and Maryl.ᵈ he will be able to furnish many details on late occurrences. The fact of most importance mentioned by him and which is confirmed by letters I have from Burr and Gilston, is that the vote of Rho: Island will be assured on the right side. The

---

5. This was a false rumor. The Convention of 1800 was signed at 2:00 A.M. on the day this letter was written, although it is dated Sept. 30; see *ibid.*, p. 413.

6. Joseph Allston married Theodosia Burr, daughter of vice-presidential candidate Aaron Burr.

latter gentleman expresses much anxiety and betrays some jealousy with respect to the *integrity* of the Southern States in keeping the former one in view for the secondary station. I hope the event will skreen all the parties, particularly Virginia from any imputation on this subject: tho' I am not without fears, that the requisite concert may not sufficiently pervade the several States. You have no doubt seen the late Paris Statement, as well as the comment on it by observator who is manifestly Hamilton.[7] The two papers throw a blaze of light on the proceedings of our administration and must I think, co-operate with other causes, in opening thoroughly the eyes of the people. Sincerely yours

Js. Madison Jr.

Jefferson to Madison

Monticello Nov. 9, 1800

Dear Sir

This will be handed you by Mr Erwin, a gentleman of Boston, with whom I became acquainted last winter in a letter of introduction from old Saml. Adams. He is sensible, well informed and strongly republican, wealthy and well allied in his own state and in England. He calls to pay his respect to you. I inclose you two letters which the Govr. sent me by him for perusal. It is a pity that a part of one of them was not put into the papers, to show the effects our maniac proceedings have had, and were intended to have. When perused, be so good as to re-inclose them to the Governor by the same bearer.

I think it possible that Mr [John] Adams may put some foolish things into his speech on the possibility of it's being his valedictory one; and that this may give the Senate an opportunity again of shewing their own malice. I propose therefore to give time for the speech and answer to be over before I arrive there. At present I think of being with you on Friday the 21st. on my way. I have a great deal to do however before I can get away. The Republicans in Charleston have lost 11. out of 15. in their city election. The country is said to be firm. But this I imagine cannot be counted on, considering local and personal interests and prejudices. Nor do I rely on what Govr. Fenner of R. I. said to Mr Alston. You know that 2. of the 3. counties of Delaware elected Fedl. representatives to their legislature. Health and affection

Th. Jefferson

P.S. I send by Mr Erwin 9. copies of Callendar's Prospect forwarded me for you.[8]

---

7. Alexander Hamilton's comments as "Observator" were published in the New York *Spectator* on Oct. 8, 1800; they are reprinted in Syrett, XXV, pp. 131–39. Hamilton argued that a treaty with France was unnecessary and that the two nations could "pass into a state of peace in fact on the basis of the law of nations."

8. George W. Erving, whose name TJ consistently misspelled, later held diplomatic posts under TJ and JM. In his pamphlet *The Prospect before Us,* James T. Callender, who labeled John Adams a

Madison to Jefferson

[Orange] ca. Nov. 11, 1800

Dear Sir,

Yours by Mr. Erwin was delivered by him safe, with the two letters inclosed. I forwarded them by him this morning, as you desired, to the Governor.[9] They confirm, in substance, the state and difficulty of the negociation, as presented by the late statement under the Paris head. The observations on the delays carried out by the Ex. and the favorable moment lost thereby, are interesting, and deserve the public attention, if they could be properly submitted to it. I have suggested the idea to the Governor.

The accts. from S. Carolina are rather ominous, but I trust we shall soon be relieved by an overbalance of republicanism in the upper elections. To the most unfavorable suppositions, we can as yet oppose the hopes presented by Pennsylva. and the chance that a competency of votes may be obtained in spite of defections in the former State. I inclose a hand-bill lately published in Maryland, and industriously circulated there and to the Southwd. You will probably be surprized at one of the documents included in it. Mr. Duval expresses considerable fears of its tendency, but I cannot view the danger in so serious a light. I am glad to find you do not mean to postpone your journey to Washington later than the 21st, as I wish much to see you on the way, and shall set out for Richmd. if called thither on the electoral errand as is probable, at least 8 or 9 days before the legal day. The elections as far as I have learned are successful beyond expectation. In this County the votes were 340 odd to 7, and in a number of other Counties in the most commanding majorities. Even in Frederick, I hear the difference was nearly as 3 to 1. Yrs. affly.

Js Madison Jr.

Jefferson to Madison

Washington Dec. 19, 1800

Dear Sir,

Mrs. Brown's departure for Virginia enables me to write confidentially what I could not have ventured by the post at this prying season.[10] The elec-

---

"hoary headed incendiary," argued that the election of 1800 presented a choice between "Adams, war, and beggary, and Jefferson, peace and competency"; see Smith, *Freedom's Fetters,* pp. 339-40.

9. James Monroe was governor of Virginia. He had told JM that Erving had warned against Burr's ambitions, suggesting that TJ's election should be "secured against [any] accident which might otherwise give us in the first station, a friend we did not intend to place there"; James Monroe to JM, Nov. 6, 1800, in Presidential Papers Microfilm: James Madison Papers.

10. Mrs. Brown was "probably Mrs. Catherine Brown of Philadelphia. Her daughter, Mary Brown, married Hore Browse Trist in April 1799"; see *PJM,* XVII, p. 445.

tion in S. Carolina has in some measure decided the great contest. Tho' as yet we do not know the actual votes of Tenissee, Kentucky and Vermont yet we believe the votes to be on the whole, J. 73. B. 73. A. 65. P. 64. Rhode isld withdrew one from P. There is a possibility that Tenissee may withdraw one from B. and Burr writes that there may be one vote in Vermont for J. But I hold the latter impossible, and the former not probable; and that there will be an absolute parity between the two republican candidates. This has produced great dismay and gloom on the republican gentlemen here, and equal exultation on the federalists, who openly declare they will prevent an election, and will name a President of the Senate, *pro tem.* by what they say would only be a *stretch* of the constitution. The prospect of preventing this, is as follows. G. N. C. T. K. V. P. and N. Y. can be counted on for their vote in the H. of R. and it is thought by some that Baer of Maryland, and Linn of N. J. will come over. Some even count on Morris of Vermont. But you must know the uncertainty of such a dependance under the operation of caucuses and other federal engines. The month of February therefore will present us storms of a new character. Should they have a particular issue, I hope you will be here a day or two, at least, before the 4th of March. I know that your appearance on the scene before the departure of Congress, would assuage the minority, and inspire in the majority confidence and joy unbounded, which they would spread far and wide on their journey home. Let me beseech you then to come with a view of staying perhaps a couple of weeks, within which time things might be put into such a train, as would permit us both to go home for a short time for removal. I wrote to R. R. L. by a confidential hand three days ago. The person proposed for the T. has not come yet.[11]

Davie is here with the Convention, as it is called; but it is a real treaty, and without limitation of time.[12] It has some disagreeable features, and will endanger the compromitting us with G B. I am not at liberty to mention it's contents, but I believe it will meet with opposition from both sides of the house. It has been a bungling negociation. Elsworth remains in France for his health. He has resigned his office of C. J. Putting these two things together we cannot misconstrue his views. He must have had great confidence in Mr. A's continuance to risk such a certainty as he held. Jay was yesterday nominated Chief Justice. We were afraid of something worse. A scheme of government for the territory is cooking by a committee of each house under separate authorities but probably a voluntary harmony. They let out no hints. It is believed that the judiciary system will not be pushed as the appointments, if made by the present administration, could not fall on those who create

11. TJ offered the post of secretary of the navy to Robert R. Livingston. Albert Gallatin was the person proposed for the Treasury Department.
12. Although Chief Justice Oliver Ellsworth headed the peace mission, he decided to spend the winter in England, so William R. Davie brought the convention home. William Vans Murray, the third negotiator, returned to his post at The Hague.

them.[13] But I very much fear the road system will be urged. The mines of Peru would not supply the monies which would be wasted on this object, nor the patience of any people stand the abuses which would be incontroulably committed under it. I propose, as soon as the state of the election is perfectly ascertained, to aim at a candid understanding with Mr. A. I do not expect that either his feelings, or his views of interest will oppose it. I hope to induce in him dispositions liberal and accommodating. Accept my affectionate salutations.

Madison to Jefferson

Orange Dec. 20, 1800

Dear Sir,

I did not write to you from Richmond, because I was considerably indisposed during my stay there, and because I could communicate to you nothing that would not reach you with equal speed through other channels. Before I left that place, the choice of electors in S. Carolina had been recd. by the Govr. in a letter from Col. Hampton, and was understood by all parties to fix the event of a Republican President. The manner in which the Electors have voted in that State, in Va., Maryland, Penna., and N.Y., makes it probable that the Vice President will also be republican. If the States of Georgia, N. C., Tene., and Kentucky, should follow these examples, it will even devolve on the H. of Reps. to make the discrimination. There can be no danger I presume but that in such an event a proper one will be made; but it is more desirable that it should be precluded by the foresight of some of the Electors. Gelston of N. Y. assures me that there are two if not three States in which something to this effect may be looked for, but he does not name the States. Govr. Davie passd thro' Richmond whilst I was there. I happened not to see him, however, nor did I learn from others what complexion he seemed disposed to give to the business of his mission.

It was my intention to send by you my subscription money for Lyon, as well as Smith,[14] and my memory leaves me at a loss whether I did so or not. I rather suspect that it was not done. Will you be so good as to recollect and let me know; and if it be in no respect out of your way, you will further oblige me by making the advance to him for me. It shall be replaced as soon as possible. He was promised that the sum of 5 Dollars should be forwarded by you, and

---

13. TJ misjudged the situation. The Judiciary Act of 1801 created twenty-three new federal judgeships and expanded the number of marshals and justices of the peace, which President Adams filled with Federalists.

14. JM made contributions to two Republican newspapers that had been recently founded in the District of Columbia: the *Friend of the People*, edited by James Lyon, son of Congressman Matthew Lyon, and the *National Intelligencer*, edited by Samuel Harrison Smith; see *PJM*, XVII, p. 447.

the disappt. may be as inconvenient to him as disagreeable to me. I observe an answr. to Hamilton's pamphlet by a Citizen of N. York, as advertized in Washington. If this be not the piece published in the Aurora under the name of *Aristides,* I would thank you for a copy. I received a copy of H's pamphlet lately under cover from Mr. Steele. My Rheumatic complaint has sensibly increased on me of late. I am trusting for a remedy to temperance and flannel. Wishing you an exemption from the like and all other evils I remain Dear Sir yrs. affely.

Js. MADISON JR.

Jefferson to Madison

[Washington] Dec. 26, 1800

All the votes have now come in, except of Vermont and Kentuckey, and there is no doubt that the result is a perfect parity between the two republican characters. The Feds appear determined to prevent an election, and to pass a bill giving the government to Mr. Jay, appointed Chief Justice, or to Marshall as Secy of state. Yet I am rather of opinion that Maryland and Jersey will join the 7. republican majorities. The French treaty will be violently opposed by the Feds. The giving up the vessels is the article they cannot swallow. They have got their judiciary bill forwarded to commitment. I dread this above all the measures meditated, because appointments in the nature of freehold render it difficult to undo what is done. We expect a report for a territorial government which is to pay little respect to the rights of man.

Your's of the 20th came safely to hand. I am almost certain that you sent money by me to Lyon, which he sent to me for and recieved as soon as he heard I was arrived. As I was merely the bearer I did not take a receipt. I will inquire into it, and do what is necessary. No answer yet from R. R. L. Cordial and affectionate salutations. Adieu.

Madison to Jefferson

[Orange] Jan. 10, 1801

DEAR SIR,

Mrs Browne having been detained at Fredg for some time, I did not receive your favor of the 19th in time to be conveniently acknowledged by the last mail. The succeeding one of the 26th came to hand on the 7th instant only, a delay that fixes blame on the post office either in Washington or Fredg. In all the letters and most of the Newspapers which I have lately rec^d thro' the post office, there is equal ground for complaint.

I find that the vote of Kentucky establishes the tie between the Repub: characters, and consequently throws the result into the hands of the H. of R. Desperate as some of the adverse party there may be, I can scarcely allow myself to believe that enough will not be found to frustrate the attempt to strangle the election of the people, and smuggle into the Chief Magistracy the creature of a faction. It would seem that every individual member, who has any standing or stake in society, or any portion of virtue or sober understandg must revolt at the tendency of such a manœuvre. Is it possible that Mr. A. sh^d give his sanction to it if that should be made a necessary ingredient? or that he would not hold it his duty or his policy, in case the present House should obstinately refuse to give effect to the Constn, to appoint, which he certainly may do before his office expires as early a day as possible, after that event, for the succeeding House to meet, and supply the omission. Should he disapp^t a just expectation in either instance, it will be an omen, I think, forbidding the steps towards him which you seem to be meditating. I would not wish to discourage any attentions which friendship, prudence, or benevolence may suggest in his behalf, but I think it not improper to remark, that I find him infinitely sunk in the estimation of all parties. The follies of his administration, the oblique stroke at his Predecessor in the letter to Coxe, and the crooked character of that to T. Pinkney,[15] are working powerfully agst him. Added to these causes is the pamphlet of H. which, tho' its recoil has perhaps more deeply wounded the author, than the object it was discharged at, has contributed not a little to overthrow the latter staggering as he before was in the public esteem.[16]

On the supposition of either event, whether of an interregnum in the Executive, or of a surreptitious intrusion into it, it becomes a question of the first order, what is the course demanded by the crisis. Will it be best to acquiesce in a suspension or usurpation of the Executive authority till the meeting of Cong^s in De^r next, or for Congs to be summoned by a joint proclamation or recommendation of the two characters havg a majority of votes for President. My present judgment favors the latter expedient. The prerogative of convening the Legislature must reside in one or other of them, and if both concur, must substantially include the requisite will. The intentions of the people would undoubtedly be pursued. And if, in reference to the Const^n, the

---

15. For Adams's dismissal of Tench Coxe for pro-Jeffersonian leanings, see Stephen G. Kurtz, *The Presidency of John Adams: The Collapse of Federalism, 1795–1800* (Philadelphia, 1957), pp. 291–92, and Jacob E. Cooke, *Tench Coxe and the Early Republic* (Chapel Hill, 1978), pp. 304–8. During the election campaign of 1800, Republican newspapers published a letter from Adams to Coxe, written in May 1792, which impugned the character of Thomas Pinckney, American minister to Great Britain. When Pinckney demanded an explanation, Adams published an apology in the Philadelphia *Aurora;* see *PJM,* XVII, p. 456.

16. In his *Letter from Alexander Hamilton concerning the Public Conduct and Character of John Adams,* which he published on the eve of the election of 1800, Hamilton was critical of "the disgusting egotism, the distempered jealousy, and the ungovernable indiscretion of Mr. Adams's temper."

proceeding be not strictly regular, the irregularity will be less in form than any other adequate to the emergency; and will lie in form only rather than substance; whereas the other remedies proposed are substantial violations of the will of the people, of the scope of the Constitution, and of the public order and interest. It is to be hoped however that all such questions will be precluded by a proper decision of nine States in the H. of R.

I observe that the French Convention is represented as highly obnoxious to the Senate. I should not have supposed that the opposition would be hinged on the article surrendering public vessels.[17] As the stipulation is mutual it certainly spares our pride, sufficiently to leave us free to calculate our interest, and on this point there cannot be a difference of opinion. I was less surprised at the obstacle discovered in the British Treaty, the letter of which combined with the repeal of the French Treaty, beget a suspicion that in some quarters at least the present posture of things has been long anticipated. It is certain however that the Convention leaves G. B. on a better footing than the B. Treaty placed her, and it is remarkable that E. D.[18] and Murray, should have concurred in the arrangement, if it have any real interference with bona fide engagements to G. B. It may be recollected that the privilege given to British prizes was not purchased like that to French prizes, by any peculiar services to us; and never had any other pretext, than the alledged policy of putting the two great rival nations of Europe as nearly as possible on an equal footing. Notwithstanding this pretext for the measure, H. in his late pamphlet acknowledges the error of it. It would be truly extraordinary if a measure intended for this equalizing purpose, should be construable into an insuperable barrier to the equality proposed. It is of vast moment both in a domestic and foreign view, that the Senate should come to a right decision. The public mind is already sore and jealous of that body, and particularly so of the insidious and mischievous policy of the British Treaty. It is strongly averse also to war, and would feel abhorrence of an unjust or unnecessary war with any nation. It is much to be wished that these facts may not be disregarded in the question before the Senate. If there be anything fairly inadmissible in the Convn it would be better to follow the example of a qualified ratification, than rush into a provoking rejection. If there be anything likely, however unjustly, to beget complaints or discontents on the part of G. B. early and conciliatory explanations ought not to be omitted. However difficult our situation has been made, justice and prudence will it is hoped, steer us through it peacefully. In some respects the task is facilitated at the present moment. France has sufficiently manifested her friendly disposition, and what is more, seemed to be duly impressed with the interest she has in being at peace with us. G. B. however intoxicated with her maritime ascendency, is more dependent every day on our commerce for her resources, must for a considerable length of time

---

17. The Convention of 1800 stipulated that each country would restore the naval vessels captured from the other; see Alexander De Conde, *The Quasi-War: The Politics and Diplomacy of the Undeclared War with France, 1797–1801* (New York, 1966), p. 254.

18. "E." was Oliver Ellsworth, and "D." was William R. Davie.

look in a great degree to this Country, for bread for herself, and absolutely for all the necessaries for her islands. The prospect of a Northern Confederacy of Neutrals cannot fail, in several views, to inspire caution and management towards the U. S., especially as in the event of war or interruption of commerce with the Baltic, the essential article of naval Stores can be sought here only. Besides these cogent motives to peace and moderation, her subjects will not fail to remind her of the great pecuniary pledge they have in this Country, and which under any interruption of peace or commerce with it, must fall under great embarrassments, if nothing worse.

As I have not restrained my pen from this hasty effusion, I will add for your consideration one other remark on the subject. Should it be found that G. B. means to oppose pretensions drawn from her Treaty, to any part of the late one with F. may she not be diverted from it, by the idea of driving us into the necessity of soothing France, by stipulations to take effect at the expiration of the Treaty with G. B. and that w^d be a bar to the renewal of the latter. Or in case the pretensions of G. B. should defeat the Treaty now before the Senate, might not such an expedient be made a plaister for the wound given to F?

My health still suffers from several complaints, and I am much afraid that any changes that may take place are not likely to be for the better. The age and very declining state of my father are making also daily claims on my attention, and from appearances it may not be long before these claims may acquire their full force. All these considerations mingle themselves very seriously with one of the eventual arrangements contemplated. It is not my purpose however to retract what has passed in conversation between us on that head.[19] But I cannot see the necessity, and I extremely doubt the propriety, should the contest in hand issue as is most probable, of my anticipating a relinquishment of my house. I cannot but think, and feel that there will be an awkwardness to use the softest term, in appearing on the political Theatre before I could be considered as regularly called to it, and even before the commencement of the authority from which the call would proceed. Were any solid advantage at stake, this scruple might be the less applicable, but it does not occur that the difference of not very many days, can be at all material. As little can I admit that the circumstance of my participation in the Ex. business, could have any such effect on either the majority or minority as has occurred; or if a partiality in any particular friends would be gratified by a knowledge of such an arrangement, that the end would not be as well attained by its being otherwise made known to them that it was to take place, as by its being announced by my appearance on the spot. I only add that I am sensible of the obligation of respecting your conclusion whatever it may finally be, but I cannot but hope that it may be influenced by the considerations which I have taken the liberty to hint. Very affecly. and respectfully I am Dr. Sir Yrs.

You may recollect a difficulty suggested in mak^g app^{ts} with$^!$ a Senate, in case of resignations *prior to March* 4. How have you solved it?

19. JM had accepted the post of secretary of state when TJ visited Montpellier on Nov. 24, 1800.

Jefferson to Madison

[Washington] Feb. 1, 1801

I have not written to you since the letter by Mrs. B. Yours of Jan. 10 is recieved, and your own wishes are entirely acquiesced in as to time. Clermont has refused.[20] I think to adopt your idea at Baltimore.[21] I dare not through the channel of the post hazard a word to you on the subject of the election. Indeed the interception and publication of my letters exposes the republican cause as well as myself personally to so much obloquy that I have come to a resolution never to write another sentence of politics in a letter.

The inclosed came under a blank cover to me, and I broke it open and read it through, and till I was folding it up to put away, I did not discover your name on the back of it, and consequently that it was destined for you.[22] I hope your health is getting better. I think nothing more possible than that a change of climate, even from a better to a worse, and a change in the habits and mode of life, might have a favorable effect on your system. I shall be happy to hear that your father is rallying. The approaching season will be favorable for that. Present my respectful attachments to Mrs. Madison and accept affectionate assurances of friendship to yourself. Adieu.

Jefferson to Madison

Washington Feb. 12, 1801 7 A.M.

TH. J. TO JAS. MADISON

The H. of R. has been in conclave ever since 2. oclock yesterday. At 10. P.M. 17. ballots had been tried, and were invariably 8. 6. and 2. divided. I have not heard from the Capitol this morning. I can venture nothing more by the post but my affectionate salutations[23] to yourself and Mrs Madison.

P.S. 1. P.M. The H. or R. suspended the balloting from 7. to 12. this morning, and after trying a few more ballots with the same effect, suspended it again till 11 a. m. tomorrow.

20. Clermont was the name of Robert R. Livingston's estate on the Hudson.
21. Samuel Smith of Baltimore was offered the cabinet position of secretary of the navy.
22. The letter was from James T. Callender; see JM to TJ, Feb. 28, 1801, below.
23. Later in the afternoon, TJ learned that ten more ballots had been taken after the first postponement, making a total of twenty seven, and he sent this information, in an almost identical note to this point, to Philip Norborne Nicholas, the manager of the Republican presidential campaign in Virginia, omitting the postscript. In addition, he sent it to Mann Page, John Page, Governor James Monroe, John Wayles Eppes, Thomas Mann Randolph, Colonel Nicholas

Jefferson to Madison

Washington Feb. 18, 1801

Notwithstanding the suspected infidelity of the post, I must hazard this communication. The minority in the H. of R. after seeing the impossibility of electing B. the certainty that a legislative usurpation would be resisted by arms, and a recourse to a Convention to reorganize and amend the government, held a consultation on this dilemma, Whether it would be better for them to come over in a body, and go with the tide of the times, or by a negative conduct suffer the election to be made by a bare majority, keeping their body entire and unbroken, to act in phalanx on such ground of opposition as circumstances shall offer? We know their determination on this question only by their vote of yesterday. Morris of V. withdrew, which made Lyon's vote that of his State. The 4 Maryland Federalists put in 4. blanks which made the positive tickets of their colleagues the vote of the state. S. Carolina and Delaware put in blanks. So there were 10. states for one candidate, 4. for another, and 2. blanks. We consider this therefore as a declaration of war, on the part of this band. But their conduct appears to have brought over to us the whole body of the Federalists, who being alarmed with the danger of a dissolution of the government, had been made most anxiously to wish the very administration they had opposed, and to view it when obtained as a child of their own. They see too their quondam leaders separated fairly from them, and themselves aggregated under other banners. Even Hamilton and Higginson have been partisans for us. This circumstance, with the unbounded confidence which will attach to the new ministry as soon as known, will start us on high ground. Mr. A. embarrasses us. He keeps the offices of State and War vacant, but has named Bayard M. P. to France, and has called an unorganized Senate on the 4th. of March. As you do not like to be here on that day, I wish you could come within a day or two after. I think that between that and the middle of the month we can so far put things under way, as that we may go home to make arrangements for our final removal. Come to Conrad's where I will bespeak lodgings for you.

Yesterday Mr. A. nominated Bayard to be M. P. of the U S. to the French republic; to-day Theophilus Parsons Atty Genl of the U S. in the room of C. Lee, who with Keith Taylor *cum multis aliis* [with many others]; are appointed judges under the new system. H. G. Otis is nominated a district attorney. A vessel has been waiting for some time in readiness to carry the new minister to France. My affectionate salutations to Mrs. Madison and yourself. Adieu.

Lewis, Peter Carr, Dr. William Bache, and Archibald Stuart. He also enclosed a copy of Thomas Paine's pamphlet *Compact Maritime* to JM and the other addresses; see *PJM* XVII, p. 465.

Madison to Jefferson

[Orange] Feb. 28, 1801

DEAR SIR,

Your favor of the 1st instant was to have been acknowledged a week ago, but the irregularity of the post occasioned by high waters has delayed it to the present opportunity. I have now to acknowledge your two subsequent ones of the 12th and 19th [18th]. In compliance with the last, I had proposed to leave home in a few days, so as to be with you shortly after the 4th of March. A melancholy occurrence has arrested this intention. My father's health for several weeks latterly seemed to revive, and we had hopes that the approach of milder seasons would still further contribute to keep him with us. A few days past however he became sensibly worse, and yesterday morning rather suddenly, tho' very gently the flame of life went out. It is impossible for me now to speak of my movements with precision. Altho' the exact degree of agency devolving on me remains to be known, a crowd of indispensable attentions must necessarily be due from me. In this posture of things I can only say that I shall wait the return of the post after this reaches, by which I hope to learn whether your intended continuance at Washington will admit, and the state of things will require, my being there before you leave it. By this information I shall be governed, unless imperiously controuled by circumstances here.

The conduct of M[r] A. is not such as was to have been wished or perhaps, expected. Instead of smoothing the path for his successor, he plays into the hands of those who are endeavoring to strew it with as many difficulties as possible; and with this view does not manifest a very squeamish regard to the Const[n]. Will not his app[ts] to offices, not vacant actually at the time, even if afterwards vacated by acceptances of the translations, be null?

The result of the contest in the H. of R. was generally looked for in this quarter. It was thought not probable that the phalanx would hold out ag[st] the general revolt of its partizans out of doors and without any military force to abet usurpation. How fortunate that the latter has been witheld: and what a lesson to America and the world, is given by the efficacy of the public will when there is no army to be turned ag[st] it!

I observe that a Com[e] is app[d] to enquire into the effects of the late fires[24] This is no doubt proper; but does not I think promise much. More is to be expected from the scrutinies of honest heads of Dep[ts], aided by the documents and other evidences which they will have time and the best means of examining. I take for granted one of the first steps of the new adm[n] will be to institute returns, particularly in the Navy and war dep[ts], of the precise state in which

---

24. The late fires included one of Nov. 8, 1800, in the War Department and another of Jan. 20, 1801, in the Treasury Department. The Republicans at first charged that they were incendiary, but the report of the congressional committee found no evidence for the charge. The report of Feb. 28, 1801, which was presented by John Nicholas, a Republican congressman from Virginia, is in *ASP, M,* I, pp. 247–52.

every circumstance involved in them, comes into the new hands. This will answer the double purpose of enabling the public to do justice both to the authors of past errors and abuses and the authors of future reforms.

I rec^d a few days ago the inclosed letter from Mr. Page. Altho' there are parts of it, which might well be omitted in the transmission to you, yet the length of the proper extracts tempts me to shun the trouble of making them. In justice to Doc^r Tucker, I say with pleasure, that I have always regarded him as a man of the greatest moral and political probity, truly attached to Republican principles, of a very ingenious mind, extensive information, and great exactitude in his ideas and habits of business; and, consequently well fitted for public service.[25]

The letter from Callendar seems from its contents to have been meant for you, tho. superscribed to me.[26] Most affectionately I am Dr. Sir yrs.

Js. Madison Jr.

25. TJ appointed Dr. Thomas Tudor Tucker of South Carolina as treasurer of the United States; see *PJM,* XVII, p. 476.

26. Callender had been convicted under the Sedition Act. His Feb. letter to JM has not been found, but he mentioned it in his letter to JM, Apr. 27, 1801; see *PJM* (SS ser.), I, pp. 117, 120. On the day he was inaugurated, TJ sent word to Callender that his $200 fine would be remitted as soon as possible (TJ to George Jefferson, Mar. 4, 1801, cited in Malone, IV, pp. 207-8), then pardoned him on Mar. 16. But the U.S. marshal in Virginia, a lame-duck Federalist, was slow to repay the fine, and Callender turned against TJ; see Smith, *Freedom's Fetters,* pp. 356-58, and Noble E. Cunningham, *The Jeffersonian Republicans in Power: Party Operations, 1801-1809* (Chapel Hill, 1963), pp. 250-53.

27

THE REVOLUTION OF 1800

ON MARCH 4, 1801, Chief Justice John Marshall administered the oath of office to Thomas Jefferson, the first president to be inaugurated in the young nation's new capital on the Potomac. The president-elect had walked from his nearby boardinghouse to the Senate chamber, where he had presided as vice president, accompanied by an escort of Alexandria militia, a cadre of congressmen, and two of Adams's cabinet officers. Adams himself had left Washington at 4:00 A.M., fleeing on the early morning stage. Aside from the parade of riflemen and the discharge of artillery, there was no pomp or ceremony, and the simplicity of the proceedings seemed to stress the Republican "revolution," a theme implicit in Jefferson's inaugural address.

The new president had had about two weeks to work on his speech, a bit less time than he had had to compose the Declaration of Independence, but he had completed it early enough to have it printed and ready for distribution the moment his auditors walked out of the Senate chamber. That was an appropriate and thoughtful gesture since he spoke so softly that few in the crowded room could hear his words.[1]

But those who listened or read learned that Jefferson's "essential principles of our government" turned on the concepts set forth in the Declaration, which he had written, and in the federal Constitution and Bill of Rights, which Madison had done so much to mold. These principles "should be the creed of our political faith—the text of civic instruction," the twin principles of federal union and republican freedom. He affirmed the "sacred" principle of majority rule but added "that though the will of the majority is in all cases to prevail, that will, to be rightful must be reasonable; that the minority possess their equal rights, which equal law must protect, and to violate would be oppression." And since both the majority and the minority were made up of individuals, he emphasized the protections of individual liberty, stressing the

---

1. See Malone, IV, pp. 3–4, 17, and Noble E. Cunningham, Jr., *The Process of Government under Jefferson* (Princeton, 1978), pp. 8–11.

need for "the diffusion of knowledge and arraignment of all abuses at the bar of public reason," then listing the four freedoms: "freedom of religion, freedom of press, freedom of person under the protection of the habeas corpus, and trial by juries impartially selected."

A "bright constellation" of principles followed: "equal and exact justice to all men, of whatever state or persuasion, religious or political; peace, commerce, and honest friendship with all nations—entangling alliances with none; the support of the State governments in all their rights, as the most competent administrations for our domestic concerns and the surest bulwarks against antirepublican tendencies; the preservation of the General Government in its whole constitutional vigor, as the sheet anchor of our peace at home and safety abroad; a jealous care of the right of election by the people—a mild and safe corrective of abuses which are lopped by the sword of revolution where peaceable remedies are unprovided; . . . economy in the public expense, that labor may be lightly burdened; . . . [and] encouragement of agriculture, and of commerce as its handmaid."

Referring to the campaign of 1800 as a contest of opinion, Jefferson observed that it had been decided by the voice of the people under the rules of the Constitution. Accordingly, all would, "of course, arrange themselves under the will of the law, and unite in common efforts for the common good." The peaceful transfer of political power from one party to another was "the vital principle of republics" and a rejection of the only alternative, an appeal to force, which was "the vital principle and immediate parent of despotism." In distinguishing between principles and opinions, he wrote a conciliatory passage in an effort to wipe out any lingering fears of republicanism and to convert the mass of Federalists to his principles: "But every difference of opinion is not a difference of principle. We have called by different names brethren of the same principle. We are all republicans: we are all federalists."[2]

He had already called for a restoration to social intercourse of "that harmony and affection without which liberty and even life itself are but dreary things. And let us reflect that, having banished from our land that religious intolerance under which mankind so long bled and suffered, we have yet gained little if we countenance a political intolerance as despotic, as wicked, and capable of as bitter and bloody persecutions." In a free government, error of opinion could be tolerated. In a reference to the frenzy of 1798, he wrote:

If there be any among us who would wish to dissolve this Union or to change its republican form, let them stand undisturbed as monuments of the safety with which error of opinion may be tolerated where reason is left free to combat it. I know, indeed, that some honest men fear that a republican government can not be strong, that this Government is not strong enough; but would the honest patriot, in the full tide of successful experiment, abandon a government which has so far kept us free and firm on

---

2. When this surprising statement appeared in print, the nouns were often capitalized: "We are all Republicans: we are all Federalists."

the theoretic and visionary fear that this Government, the world's best hope, may by possibility want energy to preserve itself? I trust not. I believe this, on the contrary, the strongest Government on earth. I believe it is the only one where every man, at the call of the law, would fly to the standard of the law, and would meet invasions of the public order as his own personal concern. Sometimes it is said that man can not be trusted with the government of himself. Can he, then, be trusted with the government of others? Or have we found angels in the forms of kings to govern him? Let history answer this question."[3]

Later that day, Mrs. Samuel Harrison Smith, whose husband had printed Jefferson's inaugural address for instant distribution, observed that she had "this morning witnessed one of the most interesting scenes, a free people can ever witness. The changes of administration, which in every government and in every age have most generally been epochs of confusion, villainy and bloodshed, in this our happy country take place without any species of distraction, or disorder."[4] For the first time in the nation's history, political power had been peaceably transferred from one party to another.[5]

Two days after his inaugural, Jefferson wrote that the ship of state had been through a rough storm but was now on "her republican tack, and she will now show by the beauty of her motion the skill of her builders."[6] Two weeks later, noting again that the storm was subsiding, he made broader claims for the "revolution of 1800": "We can no longer say there is nothing new under the sun. For this whole chapter in the history of man is new. The great extent of our Republic is new. Its sparse habitation is new. The mighty wave of public opinion which has rolled over it is new. But the most pleasing novelty is, it's so quickly subsiding over such an extent of surface to it's true level again. The order and good sense displayed in this recovery from delusion, and in the momentus crisis which lately arose, really bespeak a strength of character in our nation which augurs well for the duration of our Republic; and I am much better satisfied now of it's stability than I was before it was tried."[7]

As early as November 1800, Madison had agreed to serve in Jefferson's old post as secretary of state, thus reuniting them in the nation's capital. Jefferson had tried to persuade his friend to come to Washington before the inauguration, but the future secretary of state thought there would be "an awkwardness to use the softest term, in appearing on the political Theatre before I could be considered as regularly called to it, and even before the commencement of the authority from which the call would proceed."[8] Despite an attack of rheumatism that was worsening, he agreed to join the new president shortly after the

3. TJ's inaugural address is in Richardson, I, pp. 321–24, and Ford, VIII, pp. 1–6.
4. Mrs. Samuel Harrison Smith to Susan B. Smith, Mar. 4, 1801, in Margaret Bayard Smith, *The First Forty Years of Washington Society, Portrayed by the Family Letters of Mrs. Samuel Harrison Smith...*, ed. Gaillard Hunt (New York, 1906), pp. 25–26.
5. Daniel Sisson, *The American Revolution of 1800* (New York, 1974), is the fullest treatment.
6. TJ to John Dickinson, Mar. 6, 1801, in Ford, VIII, pp. 7–8.
7. TJ to Joseph Priestley, Mar. 21, 1801, *ibid.*, p. 22.
8. TJ to JM, Dec. 19, 1800, above, and JM to TJ, Jan. 10, 1801, above.

inaugural, but late in February his father died, making that impossible.⁹

Jefferson had already discussed the makeup of his administrative family with Madison. The other department heads included Secretary of the Treasury Albert Gallatin, who, as Jefferson noted, "though unappointed, has stayed till now to give us the benefit of his counsel"; Secretary of War Henry Dearborn; and Attorney General Levi Lincoln, whom Jefferson had earlier praised as "undoubtedly the ablest and most respectable man of the Eastern states."¹⁰ Lincoln, the president informed Madison, also "has undertaken the duties of your office per interim, and will continue till you can come." Benjamin Stoddert, who had served as head of the Navy Department in Adams's administration, accommodated Jefferson "by staying till I could provide a successor. This I find next to impossible," he added, listing successive turndowns from Robert R. Livingston of New York, who later served as minister to France, Congressman Samuel Smith of Maryland, and Senator John Langdon of New Hampshire. Nonetheless, he assured Madison that "we shall have an agreeable society here, and," in the sparsely settled capital, "not too much of it."

While wrestling with personnel problems, Jefferson managed to find housing for the Madisons shortly before he moved to the President's House on March 19.¹¹ After persuading Samuel Smith to take the navy assignment temporarily, Jefferson left Lincoln and Dearborn to represent the administration while he returned to Monticello to attend to personal affairs and pack books and furnishings.¹² He stopped overnight with the Madisons on April 3 en route to Monticello and again on April 26 on his return trip to Washington.¹³ Madison's continuing illness prevented the Madisons from accompanying Jefferson on their first trip to the new capital.

As soon as he returned to Washington, the president sent Madison a quick note about road conditions, complaining that "the Bull run hill is really the worst I ever saw on a public road," worse even than Little's Lane, where a wagon was stuck when he came by and where he doubted that "any four-wheeled carriage could then have got through the spot where the waggon was without stalling." Since he was expecting the Madisons in time for a four o'clock dinner, he had made arrangements to have local farmers help them up the hill.¹⁴

During their first month in Washington, the Madisons moved in as Jefferson's guests in the President's House. Late in May, they moved to temporary quarters, leaving the president and his private secretary, Meriwether Lewis, to rattle around in the huge house, as Jefferson said, like two mice in a

---

9. JM to TJ, Feb. 28, 1801, above. See also Brant, IV, pp. 36-38, and *PJM* (SS ser.), I, pp. 1-2.
10. TJ to JM, Sept. 17, 1800, above.
11. TJ to JM, Mar. 12, 1801, below, and Malone, IV, pp. 29-35. JM's commission as secretary of state, Mar. 5, 1801, is printed below.
12. TJ to JM, Mar. 26, 1801, below.
13. Brant, IV, pp. 40-41.
14. TJ to JM, Apr. 30, 1801, below.

church.[15] In the fall, the Madisons decided on a new house next to the one that Jefferson had earlier lined up for them, "some two or three hundred yards" from Madison's office.[16]

Jefferson and his colleagues quickly worked out operating procedures based on the his experience in Washington's cabinet and his observations of the Adams government, and he came to dominate his administration even more than either of his predecessors had done. Unlike Adams, who had inherited Washington's cabinet, which was more loyal to Hamilton than to him, Jefferson chose advisers who were loyal to him and to whom he was loyal. After six months of working together, he told Madison and the other department heads that he was sure that his conduct "must have proved, better than a thousand declarations would, that my confidence in those whom I am so happy as to have associated with me, is unlimited, unqualified, and unabated. I am well satisfied that everything goes on with a wisdom and rectitude which I could not improve [on]. If I had the Universe to chuse from, I could not change one of my associates to my better satisfaction."[17]

After reviewing the Washington and Adams experience, Jefferson decided that he wanted "not only the best, but also an uniform course of proceeding, as to manner and degree." Under Adams, who took "long and habitual absences from the seat of government," there was a tendency towards ministerial independence, with governmental affairs parceled out among four independent heads, "drawing sometimes in opposite directions." He preferred the Washington model:

Letters of business came addressed sometimes to the President, but most frequently to the heads of departments. If addressed to himself, he referred them to their proper department to be acted on: if to one of the Secretaries, the letter, if it required no answer, was communicated to the President simply for his information. If an answer was requisite, the Secretary of the department communicated the letter and his proposed answer to the President. Generally they were simply sent back, af[ter] perusal, which signified his approbation. Sometimes he returned them with an informal note, suggesting an alteration or a query. If a doubt of any importance arose, he reserved it for conference. By this means he was always in accurate possession of all facts and proceedings in every part of the Union, and to whatsoever department they related; he formed a central point for the different branches, preserved an unity of object and action among them, exercised that participation in the gestion [?] of affairs which his office made incumbent on him, and met himself the due responsibility for whatever was done.[18]

Since the president was ultimately responsible for the mode, manner, and substance of administrative decisions, Jefferson, who disliked dissension and

---

15. Malone, IV, p. 40.
16. TJ to JM, Mar. 12, 1801, below. The house was located at what is now 1333 F Street N.W.; see Brant, IV, p. 43. See also *PJM* (SS ser.), I, pp. 112-13.
17. TJ to JM and the heads of departments, Nov. 6, 1801, below.
18. *Ibid.*

avoided controversy whenever possible, achieved unity in the executive branch through collegial discussions, running cabinet meetings like a seminar session, working towards consensus, with room for dissent, while avoiding wrenching divisions that might move in the direction of ministerial independence.

Unlike Hamilton, who saw administration as a powerful engine, Jefferson saw it as a well-oiled wheel with the president as the central hub, which made things move forward. In his daily dealings with his department heads, as in the occasional cabinet meetings, he had an informal touch, using suggestions instead of commands, sorting out the important from the routine, and making decisions after weighing alternatives carefully.

The Washington method, he confessed, "gave indeed to the heads of departments the trouble of making up, once a day, a packet of all their communications for the perusal of the President; it commonly also retarded one day their dispatches by mail: but, in pressing cases, this injury was prevented by presenting that case singly for immediate attention; and it produced [for] us in return the benefit of his sanction for every act we did."[19] As the administrative head of the government, President Jefferson served as the chief executive officer whose sanction gave final authority to public policy.[20]

During the summer of 1801, Jefferson and his colleagues faced four pressing problems: peace and war—peace with France and war with Tripoli—and appointments and pardons. Just before Adams left office, he announced the end of the quasi war with France and said that he would leave the exchange of ratifications of the Convention of 1800 to his successor.[21] The Senate had ratified the treaty but had deleted one article and added another that required agreement by the French. Jefferson quickly dispatched the documents to France, and William Vans Murray, American minister at The Hague, conducted the negotiations. If these negotiations were delayed for any reason, Robert R. Livingston, Jefferson's choice as minister to France, would take over negotiations, following Jefferson's contingency plans: "Suppose we were to instruct Livingston in case he finds on arrival in Paris that the ratification is withheld," he wrote the secretary of state, "that he propose the single article for the restitution of prizes, and say to them that with every disposition towards them of perfect friendliness and free commerce, we are willing to trust, without a treaty to the mutual interests of the two countries for dictating the terms of our commercial relations, not doubting that each will give the best terms in practice to the other, that on the expiration of the British treaty we shall probably do the same with that nation, and so with others. Unless indeed events should render it practicable to sign a short formula merely explanatory or amendatory of the L[aw] of Nations in a few special articles. The being in freedom to refuse entrance in time of war to armed ships, or prizes, to refuse or

19. *Ibid.*
20. See Cunningham, pp. 27-47, and Robert M. Johnstone, Jr., *Jefferson and the Presidency: Leadership in the Young Republic* (Ithaca, 1978).
21. Alexander De Conde, *The Quasi-War: The Politics and Diplomacy of the Undeclared War with France, 1797-1801* (New York, 1966), pp. 292-93.

send off ministers and consuls in time of war, is a most desirable situation in my judgment."[22] Late in the fall, Jefferson learned that the French had ratified the treaty modifications, and after the Senate approved, he proclaimed the convention in effect in December, thus restoring normal diplomatic relations between France and the United States.[23]

While speeding peace with France, Jefferson and Madison turned towards war with the piratical powers of the Mediterranean. Jefferson had first dealt with the Barbary States while he was in France in the 1780s and as secretary of state in the 1790s. Although the United States had entered into formal treaties with the four pirate states of Algiers, Morocco, Tunis, and Tripoli, purchasing peace with presents and annual tributes, not much had changed during the past fifteen years. Jefferson had always opposed paying tribute, as he noted in a letter to Madison: "I am an enemy to all these douceurs, tributes and humiliations.... I know that nothing will stop the eternal increase of demand from these pirates but the presence of an armed force, and it will be more economical and more honorable to use the same means at once for suppressing their insolencies."[24]

Accordingly, the president ordered Commodore Richard Dale to take a naval squadron of four vessels to protect American commerce in the Mediterranean, and the secretary of state informed American diplomatic representatives in the area of the new policy of "exhibiting to the Barbary powers a naval force from the United States."[25] By the time it arrived, the pasha of Tripoli, outraged that Algiers had extorted a higher tribute than he, had declared war on the United States. When the president heard of Tripoli's action, he thought it a pity that Dale "did not know of the war" when he sailed, or "he might have taken their admiral and his ship" at Gibraltar.[26]

The issues of war and peace took relatively little time compared with questions of appointments and removals, reformation and reconciliation, spoils and principle. These problems were both delicate and tough—delicate to balance and tough to resolve. Nonetheless, Jefferson quickly laid down his guidelines, even before Madison came to the capital in May, deciding to make as few removals as possible, thus wooing the Federalists, and to replace all ousted officials with deserving democrats, thus rewarding the Republicans.

He was especially upset by Adams's last-minute effort to pack the federal service, particularly the judiciary, with Federalists. Adams had made a series of

22. TJ to JM, Sept. 12, 1801, below. JM agreed on the need to get Livingston "on the ground as soon as possible"; see JM to TJ, Sept. 16, 1801, below.

23. Malone, IV, pp. 35–36.

24. TJ to JM, Aug. 28, 1801, below.

25. JM to American consuls, Mediterranean, May 21, 1801, in *PJM* (SS ser.), I, p. 209.

26. TJ to JM, Sept. 12, 1801, below. See the short note by Robert A. Rutland and associates, "Dispatching a Naval Squadron to the Mediterranean, 20–21 May 1801," in *PJM* (SS ser.), I, pp. 197–99. The best account of the contest with the Barbary powers is William M. Fowler, Jr., *Jack Tars and Commodores: The American Navy, 1783–1815* (Boston, 1984). See also the incisive summary in Abraham D. Sofaer, *War, Foreign Affairs and Constitutional Power: The Origins* (Cambridge, Mass., 1976), pp. 208–24.

"midnight appointments," which the lame-duck Senate worked overtime on March 3, 1801, to confirm before Jefferson moved from presiding officer there to the presidency the next day. Jefferson considered as "nullities" all appointments to offices held at presidential pleasure if Adams made them after December 12, 1800, the date when the election results became known in Washington. He had no qualms, he told Madison, about removing men "indecently appointed and not yet warm in the seat of office."[27] As he later told Abigail Adams, all such appointees were "my most ardent political enemies, from whom no faithful cooperation could ever be expected, and laid me under the embarrasment of acting thro' men whose views were to defeat mine; or to encounter the odium of putting others in their places. It seemed but common justice to leave a successor free to act by instruments of his own choice."[28] Since he considered Adams's action in this category of officeholders as null and void, he hardly considered his refusals to honor these appointments as removals.[29]

But federal officials guilty of negligence or official misconduct not only could be, but ought to be, removed. Delinquency in accounts, electioneering, picking packed juries, and pressing prosecutions for party purposes became grounds for ousting customs collectors, federal marshals, and district attorneys who, Jefferson was convinced, had acted improperly in their enforcement of the Sedition Act. Republican replacements of biased district attorneys and federal marshals seemed "the only shield for our Republican citizens against the federalism of the courts."[30]

Except for these two limited categories for removals, however, Jefferson decided that officeholders should not be removed for differences of political opinion, although he hoped to establish a better balance between Republican and Federalist officeholders. He estimated that Washington and Adams had appointed about 600 federal civil servants but counted only 6 Republicans in office when he was inaugurated.[31] And he noted that vacancies without removals seldom occurred: "those by death are few; by resignation none." Accordingly, he made sure that all appointments went to Republicans, and the letters between the president and the secretary of state in the late summer of 1801 are peppered with references to applicants for jobs as diverse as the district attorney in the territory of Mississippi to the American consul in St. Petersburg in Russia.[32]

---

27. TJ to JM, Aug. 13, 1801, below.
28. TJ to Abigail Adams, June 13, 1804, in Cappon, I, p. 270.
29. See Carl Prince, "The Passing of the Aristocracy: Jefferson's Removals of the Federalists, 1801–1805," *JAH* 57 (1970): 563–75, and Cunningham, pp. 165–87.
30. TJ to Archibald Stuart, Apr. 8, 1801, in Ford, VIII, pp. 46–47.
31. Marshall Smelser, *The Democratic Republic, 1801–1815* (New York, 1968), p. 49. See also Carl Prince, *The Federalists and the Origins of the U.S. Civil Service* (New York, 1977).
32. See TJ to JM, Aug. 13, 1801, below, Aug. 22, 1801, below, Aug. 28, 1801, below, Sept. 12, 1801, below, and JM to TJ, Aug. 26, 1801, below, Aug. 27, 1801, below, Sept. 16, 1801, below, [Sept. 17, 1801], below. The best discussion of TJ and patronage appointments is Noble E.

Although the Sedition Law had expired about twelve hours before Jefferson was inaugurated, two victims were still in prison, and a prosecution against the leading Republican editor was still pending. Jefferson promptly pardoned the prisoners, James T. Callender and David Brown, and canceled the proceedings against William Duane, editor of the Philadelphia *Aurora*.[33]

Jefferson and Madison each made one other personal decision of importance in the summer of 1801. They decided not to stay in Washington during the dog days of August and September, beating a retreat from the heat to Monticello and Montpellier and shuttling official dispatches between Virginia and Washington.[34] Just before Madison left the nation's capital, he suffered "a slight bilious interruption," but, he assured a colleague, "if I can get into the pure air which I breathe at home, without a return of the attack, I shall have a more flattering prospect than I have had for nearly two years past."[35] Jefferson was even more emphatic about the healthiness of the summer air in Virginia. To Albert Gallatin, who remained in Washington throughout the summer, he wrote from Monticello: "I consider it as a trying experiment for a person from the mountains to pass the two bilious months on the tide-water. I have not done it these forty-years, and nothing should induce me to do it" now.[36]

─────────────── THE LETTERS ───────────────

Jefferson to Madison

[Washington Mar. 5, 1801]

Thomas Jefferson, President of the United States of America,
To all who shall see these presents, Greeting:

Know Ye, That reposing especial trust and confidence in the patriotism, integrity and abilities of James Madison of Virginia, I have nominated, and, by and with the advice and consent of the Senate, do appoint him Secretary of State, and do authorize

---

Cunningham, Jr., *The Jeffersonian Republicans in Power: Party Operations, 1801–1809* (Chapel Hill, 1963), pp. 30–70.

33. For the decision by Jefferson and his cabinet, see "Notes on Procedures on Prosecutions under Sedition Act," Mar. 9, 1801, cited in James Morton Smith, *Freedom's Fetters: The Alien and Sedition Laws and American Civil Liberties* (Ithaca, 1956), pp. 268–69. For Callender's pardon, see *ibid.,* p. 358. Brown had been sentenced to eighteen months in jail, the longest term imposed under the Sedition Law. Although his term had expired, he remained in jail because he was unable to pay his fine; see *ibid.,* pp. 257–70. For Duane, see *ibid.,* pp. 303–6. See also JM to TJ, Aug. 26, 1801, below, and TJ to JM, July 17, 1801, below, July 19, 1801, below, Aug. 22, 1801, below.

34. JM left on or about July 29, and TJ left on July 30; see *PJM* (SS ser.), I, p. xxxi.

35. JM to Levi Lincoln, July 25, 1801, *ibid.,* p. 476. See also Brant, IV, pp. 43–44.

36. TJ to Albert Gallatin, Sept. 18, 1801, in Ford, VIII, p. 95.

and empower him to execute and fulfil the duties of that office according to law; and to have and to hold the said office with all the powers, privileges and emoluments to the same of right appertaining unto him the said James Madison during the pleasure of the President of the United States for the time being.

In Testimony whereof I have made these letters patent, and caused the seal of the United States to be hereto affixed. Given under my hand, at the City of Washington, this fifth day of March, in the year of our Lord one thousand eight hundred and one, and of the Independence of the United States of America, the twenty fifth.

TH: JEFFERSON

By the President:
    Levi Lincoln
        Acting as Secretary of State.

Madison to Jefferson

[Orange] Mar. 7, 1801

DEAR SIR

Since my last which went by the mail in course, the papers of my deceased father have been opened. His will was made thirteen years ago, since which two of my brothers have died, one of them leaving a large number of children mostly minors, and both of them intestate. The will itself, besides the lapsed legacies, does not cover all the property held at the time; and valuable parcels of property were acquired subsequent to the will. The will is also ambiguous in some important points, and will raise a variety of questions for legal opinions if not controversies. Another circumstance in the case is that some memorandums preparatory to considerable alterations in the will were left in his hand writing; to which is to be added verbal intimations in his last moments of others wished by him. As the event took place also prior to the 1st. of March, an immediate division may be required if the parties interested so chuse. From this explanation you will judge of the task devolved on me as Extr., and in the other relations in which I stand; especially as much must necessarily be done by amicable negociations concessions and adjustments; and will be indulgent enough to combine it with the political lien to which I have subjected myself. I wait with anxiety for your answer to my last which I expect by the mail of wednesday next. I have nothing to add to that, but a repetition of the assurances with which I am most respectfully and affectionately your friend and servt.

JS. MADISON.

Jefferson to Madison

Washington Mar. 12, 1801

DEAR SIR

I offer you my sincere condolances on the melancholy loss, which has detained you at home: and am entirely sensible of the necessities it will have imposed on you for further delay. Mr. Lincoln has undertaken the duties of your office per interim, and will continue till you can come. Genl. Dearborn is in the War Department. Mr. Gallatin, though unappointed, has staid till now to give us the benefit of his counsel. He cannot enter into office till my return, and he leaves us tomorrow. In the mean time Dexter continues. Stoddert also accomodated me by staying till I could provide a successor.[1] This I find next to impossible. R. R. L. first refused. Then Genl. Smith refused. Next Langdon. I am now returning on Genl. Smith, but with little confidence of success. If he will undertake 6. months or even 12. months hence, I will appoint Lear in the mean time. He promised, if Langdon would take it for 6. months, he would in that time so dispose of his business as to come in. This makes me hope he may now accept in that way. If he does not, there is no remedy but to appoint Lear permanently.[2] He is equal to the office if he possessed equally the confidence of the public. What a misfortune to the public that R. Morris has fallen from his height of character. If he could get from confinement, and the public give him confidence, he would be a most valuable officer in that station and in our council.[3] But there are two impossibilities in the way. I have ordered my chair and horses to meet me at Heron's on the 22d. inst. not that I count on being there punctually on that day, but as near it as I can.[4] I shall be at home a fortnight. I hope you will find it convenient to come on when I do or very soon after. Dr. Thornton means to propose to rent his house to you. It will be some two or three hundred yards distant from your office, but also that much nearer towards the Capitol.[5] We shall have an agreeable society here, and not too much of it. Present my esteem to Mrs. Madison and accept yourself assurances of my constant and sincere attachment

TH: JEFFERSON

1. As the leading Republican congressman in the preceding volatile session of Congress, Gallatin had fought Federalist measures vigorously, and TJ feared that the partisan Senate over which he had presided as vice president would not confirm Gallatin as secretary of the treasury. TJ, therefore, gave him a recess appointment on May 14, and the newly elected Senate, now safely Republican, confirmed him in Dec. 1801. Samuel Dexter and Benjamin Stoddert were temporary carryovers from the Adams cabinet; see Malone, IV, pp. 33–34.

2. TJ finally filled the Navy Department in July by appointing Robert Smith, brother of Senator Samuel Smith, of Baltimore. See Thom M. Armstrong, *Politics, Diplomacy, and Intrigue in the Early Republic: The Cabinet Career of Robert Smith, 1801–1811* (Dubuque, 1991).

3. Morris was in debtor's prison after his land-speculating schemes collapsed.

4. Heron's was in Culpeper; see *PJM* (SS ser.), I, p. 13.

5. William Thornton was designer of the U.S. Capitol and a District of Columbia commissioner; see *ibid.*

Jefferson to Madison

Washington Mar. 26, 1801

TH: J. TO J. M.

I am still here. Three refusals of the Naval Secretaryship have been re[c]ieved, and I am afraid of recieving a 4th. this evening from Mr. Jones of Phila. In that case Genl. Smith has agreed to take it pro tempore, so as to give me time; and I hope the moment it is in either his or Jones's hands, to get away; but this may be yet three four or five days. Lincoln is doing the duties of your office. He and Dearborn will remain here. Health, respect and affectionate attachment.

Jefferson to Madison

Monticello Apr. 17, 1801

TH: J. TO J. MADISON.

I shall be with you on the 25th. unless health or weather prevent. But if you propose leaving home sooner for Washington, do not let my coming prevent you. Only, in that case, if convenient, lodge word at Gordon's,[6] or write me by next post, that you will be gone; as I should then wish to lengthen my day's journey. I have not been able to look yet into my newspapers, but I presume yours contain all mine do. My respectful compliments to Mrs. Madison, and affectionate attachment to yourself.

TH: JEFFERSON

Madison to Jefferson

[Orange Apr. 22, 1801]

DEAR SIR

Your favor of the 17th. came to hand by the last mail. You will find us at home on saturday. It would have been expedient on some accounts to have set out before that day, but it has been rendered impossible by several circumstances, particularly by an attack on my health which kept me in bed 3 or 4 days, and which has not yet permitted me to leave the House. I hope to be able to begin the journey by sunday or monday at farthest and to get as far as Capt Winston's the first day. I should have been glad to have taken a ride to Mon-

---

6. Gordon's Tavern was in Gordonsville on the road between Charlottesville and Washington; see *ibid.*, p. 102.

ticello during the Court especially as it would have given me an interview with Mr. E. Randolph whom I wished to consult on some law points, but it was first inconvenient and then impossible.

Jefferson to Madison

Monticello Apr. 25, 1801

TH: J. TO J. M.

I received yesterday your's of the 22d. and learn with regret that you have been so unwell. This and the state of the [country, the river and] roads should delay your departure, at least till the weather is better. I should have set out this morning, but it is still raining, and the river all but swimming at the last ford. If these circumstances are more favorable tomorrow I shall then set out, or whenever they become so, as I do not like to begin a journey in a settled rain. Contrive, if you can, to let it be known at Gordon's if you shall be gone, as I could then continue on the direct road, which is better as well as shorter. My best respects to Mrs. Madison and affectionate esteem and attachment to yourself.

TH: JEFFERSON

Jefferson to Madison

Washington Apr. 30, 1801

TH: J. TO J. M.

I hasten the return of the bearer that he may meet you at Brown's and convey you information as to the road. From Songster's I tried the road by Ravensworth, which comes into the turnpike road 4½ miles below Fairfax courthouse. There are about 2 miles of it which I think cannot be passed by your carriage without oversetting; and consulting with Colo. Wren who knows both roads, he says there is no comparison; that you must absolutely come by Fairfax courthouse, all that road being practicable till you come to Little's lane, which you have to encounter whatever way you come. I passed it yesterday, a waggon being then stuck fast in it, nor do I suppose any four-wheeled carriage could then have got through the spot where the waggon was without stalling. But two days of wind and sun will by tomorrow make immense odds in it; so that I hope you will be able to pass it.

I met with Mr. Gaines and a Mr. Brawner at Brown's. They live near. I spoke of the difficulty of your getting up the Bull run hill. They agreed together to take each a horse and draw your carriage up. Accept their offer by all means: as however steady your horses, they will be in the utmost peril of baulking; and should they once begin there are other bad hills sufficient to make them give you a great deal of vexation. The Bull run hill is really the worst I ever saw on a public road. Still let nothing tempt you to go by Centerville as on that rout the whole is cut by waggons into Mudholes. From Brown's to Fairfax court house you have 14. miles of very firm road, only hilly in the beginning. You had better start as soon as you can see to drive, breakfast at Colo. Wren's, and come on here to dinner. We shall wait for you till 4. oclock.[7] My respects to Mrs. Madison and affectionate esteem to yourself.

Jefferson to Madison

Washington May 9, 1801

SIR

A person of the name of Thompson, of Amherst county in Virginia has asked my interference for the recovery of his son John Thompson understood to be impressed on board the Squirrel a British vessel of war. The inclosed letter gave him the first information he has recieved from him for some time past, for so long a time indeed that he had apprehended he was dead. He thinks the letter not written by his son, but by some mess mate who had got ashore. But I was not certain whether this was not said as an excuse to cover the illiterate composition of the letter. The father is known to me to be a native of Virginia, having been a fellow-collegian of mine: and the name subscribed to the letter, it's address, and it's contents, prove so as not to be doubted, that he in whose name it is written is not an impostor.[8] As nothing more than his identity and citizenship can be justly requisite to obtain his liberation, I will pray you to take such measures as may be efficacious for his recovery and restoration to his family. Accept my cordial and respectful salutations.

TH: JEFFERSON

Jefferson to Madison

Washington June 20, 1801

DEAR SIR

I observe a great number of contracts for carrying the mails are advertised to be made within a short time hence, and for 4. years. I suppose the principal reason for making such long contracts is the trouble which would be so often

---

7. JM arrived in Washington on Friday, May 1, presumably in time for dinner; see *ibid.*, p. 127.
8. John Thompson attended William and Mary while TJ was studying law in 1763; see *ibid.*, p. 149.

recurring to the post office, if they were shorter. This should have it's just weight: but it may be doubted whether contracts for so long a time as 4. years do not produce greater evils. But however this may be decided hereafter, for the present I am disposed to believe that a shorter term would be better for once. I have long been persuaded that we might greatly increase the rapidity of the movements of the mails; and have had it in contemplation to propose this when we get ourselves a little clear of more pressing business. But we shall be precluded by the 4. year contracts. I suggest to your consideration therefore the expediency of making the ensuing contracts for one year only, to give us time to try whether a more rapid conveyance be not practicable. The time for making the contracts being close at hand, an immediate determination seems necessary.[9] Accept assurances of my affectionate esteem and respect

TH: JEFFERSON

Jefferson to Madison

[Washington] June 20, 1801

The application of William Greetham for a Mediterranean pass for a vessel owned here, tho built abroad, being unauthorised by practice, tho' perhaps not by law, and concerning the departments of both the State and Treasury, I ask the favor of Mr. Madison and Mr. Gallatin to give me their opinions thereon.[10] At the same time I communicate to them what passed on the subject of passports under General Washington's administration, when the question was first taken up.

TH: JEFFERSON

Madison to Jefferson

[Washington ca. June 24, 1801]

DEAR SIR

I suggested some time ago to Col. Habersham the objections to a Contract for 4 years for carrying the mail.[11] His reply was that frequent contracts would not only be very troublesome, but by lessening the value of contracts, discourage good undertakers. He added that a clause in the contracts reserved

9. For mail contracts, see Wesley Everett Rich, *The History of the United States Post Office to the Year 1829* (Cambridge, Mass., 1924).

10. JM's opinion has not been found, but Gallatin's is summarized in *PJM* (SS ser.), I, p. 331.

11. Joseph Habersham of Georgia had been appointed postmaster general by George Washington in 1795.

to him a right at all time to make any of regulations he might chuse, making at the same time an equivalent change in the compensation. Still, however, the conversation, left him as I thought under the impression that the term of the contracts was to be shortened. I will renew the subject with him as soon as I can.

Presuming that the grounds stated for the pardon of Freeman were intended for the files only not for the instrument of the Pardon, the latter will be made out without specifying them.[12] One of them, viz. that reciting the character of the testimony, may be delicate, both as it respects the Witness and the Court. The precedent of stating in the pardon the grounds of it, may also be embarrassing, as the omission may produce criticism, and the real grounds tho' good, be often of a nature unfit or difficult to be precisely stated. With assurance of the most perfect respect and attachment I remain Yrs.

JAMES MADISON

Jefferson to Madison

[Washington] June 24, 1801

Th: Jefferson returns to Mr. Madison Erving's letter to Genl. Dearborne, and approves of a commission to him as Consul at London. Where to find a competent successor for Lisbon he knows not, unless Gilman, who refused St. Domingo, will accept this. Perhaps Genl. Dearborne can judge. The place must be reserved for a man of real diplomatic abilities.[13] Marchant's case will be the subject of further consultation with Mr. Madison. Th: J. sends a letter from Pierpoint Edwards for Messrs. Madison, Gallatin and Dearborne, ad legendum, and to be returned.[14] The Hippè begins to be felt. As soon as the qualms of this are a little assuaged, another broken dose should be given. He sends to the same gentlemen Mr. Paul's application for a door keeper's place and Mr. Jones's for a clerk's or some other place. Knowing how they are overrun with these things, it is with reluctance he troubles them with them: but as those places are not within his cognisance, he must either refer the applications, or reject them, which would be thought hard, and might sometimes deprive the offices of an application of value. He makes this apology for the future as well as past references of this kind.

12. Lewis Freeman had been convicted of altering a note of the Bank of the United States. TJ pardoned him on June 20, 1801; see *PJM* (SS ser.), I, p. 342.
13. After having appointed George William Erving of New York to the consular post in Lisbon, TJ commissioned him instead as consul at London. Nicholas Gilman of New Hampshire had been recommended by Henry Dearborn; see *ibid.*, pp. 343–44.
14. Edwards described Federalist reaction in Connecticut to TJ's replacement of the Federalist collector of the port with a Republican; see Malone, IV, pp. 75–79.

Jefferson to Madison

[Washington] July 15, 1801

Whether prizes and the proceeds of them taken after the date of the treaty with France can be restored by the Executive, or need an act of the legislature?

The constitution has authorised the ordinary legislature alone to declare war against any foreign nation. If they may enact a perfect, they may a qualified war, as was done against France. In this state of things they may modify the acts of war, and appropriate the proceeds of it. The act authorising the capture of French armed vessels and dividing and appropriating their proceeds, was of this kind.

The constitution has given to the President and Senate alone the power (with the consent of the foreign nation) of enacting peace. Their treaty for this purpose is an absolute repeal of the declaration of war, and of all laws authorising or modifying war measures. The treaty with France had this effect. From the moment it was signed all the acts legalising war-measures ceased ipso facto; and all subsequent captures became unlawful. Property wrongfully taken from a friend on the high sea is not thereby transferred to the captor. In whatever hands it is found, it remains the property of those from whom it was taken; and any person possessed of it private or public, has a right to restore it. If it comes to the hands of the Executive they may restore it: if into those of the legislature (as by formal paiment into the treasury) they may restore it. Whoever, private or public, undertakes to restore, takes on themselves the risk of proving that the goods were taken without the authority of law, and consequently that the captor had no right to them. The Executive, charged with our exterior relations, seems bound, if satisfied of the fact, to do right to the foreign nation, and take on itself the risque of justification. Submitted to Mr. Madison's consideration.

Th: J.

[Addendum]

To the preceding observations it may be added that the stipulation to restore vessels taken after the treaty is only pro majori cautelâ;[15] as, without that, the right to demand and the duty to restore, would equally exist.

Nor is the objection good that till ratificn. the treaty is not compleat: because when ratified, it is confirmed ab initio.

These observns. respect only vessels taken after the signature of the treaty. But it is said there is one vessel taken before the treaty but not yet condemned.

---

15. "For greater caution; by way of additional security. Usually applied to some act done, or some clause inserted in an instrument, which may not be really necessary, but which will serve to put the matter beyond any question"; see *PJM* (SS ser.), I, p. 417, citing *Black's Law Dictionary* (St. Paul, 1979), p. 1092.

I suspect this will stand on very different ground. By the law of nature, property is transferred by the act of capture, which act is compleat when the victory is absolute. The act of Congress July 9. 1798. says 'all armed vessels *captured* shall *accrue*[16] to the captors, and on due condemnation shall be distributed etc.' This confirms the natural law. The property vests by the capture; the condemnation is only the declaration of a fact, to wit, that the capture was rightful, and a partitioning among the owners. If condemnation was an act of war, it would be made unlawful by the treaty: but it seems to be a mere municipal act or decision between inter-claiming citizens. If the property was definitively transferred by the capture under an existing act of the legislature who were competent to the passing that act, it may be doubted whether the Presidt. and Senate, can retrospectively annul that. The legislature can; and they ought in good faith to the foreign nation to make the restitution; but also to give indemnificn. to the captors, whose legal acquisition is taken from them for the purposes of public peace.

Jefferson to Madison

[Washington ca. July 17, 1801]

It is objected that the act of Congress Mar. 3. 1800. c. 14. sect. 1. 2. entitles a citizen owner of a vessel to restitution until the vessel has been condemned by competent authority on paying salvage to the captor. Every man, by the law of nature, and every fellow citizen by compact, is bound to assist another against violence to his person or property. Tho' therefore by the law of nature the property of the sufferer has past to his enemy by capture, yet if it be retaken, most states, if it belong to their own citizen, and is retaken by their own citizen, oblige him to restore it, on recieving paiment for the risk and trouble of recapture. This is done by the 1st. and 2d. sections of the act. In the like manner if the property taken belonged to a friend, and was retaken by their citizen, they compel restitution, provided the laws of the friend would in the like case have compelled restitution to them. This is the object of the 3d. section of the act beforementd. As some limit however is necessary to the claim of restitution, some nations have determined it when the property was carried infra presidia of the enemy: or into their fleet, or after a pernoctatio, or 24 hours; some not till condemnation in a competent court. The latter is the English rule, and Congress in the act beforementioned has adopted it for the US. But the circumstance of condemnation is thereby made material only in the case of goods taken by an enemy from a fellow-citizen or friend and retaken

16. TJ's italics.

and restitution claimed, or in the case of enemy's property taken, and an inter-claim of partition among the captors. And the intervention of a court is made necessary in these cases, only on behalf of the rights of the friend or citizen; not out of any tenderness to the rights of the enemy whose property has been taken; not to save that to him in any case. Suppose a citizen of the US. had sole taken a French armed vessel, and without carrying her into court at all, a treaty of pacification had been made containing no provision for restitution. The law of nature says the property was transferred by the capture, and no law of the US. has made it necessary for a sole-owner to go into any court. Surely, after the peace, the former French owner, could not recover the property in our courts. The result of this is that adjudication is not necessary to secure the property in the captor but in the cases of recapture, or of contending parceners: that the transfer is compleat without it, by the mere act of capture.

But while it is clear enough that an enemy cannot claim the benefit of these acts requiring adjudication in certain cases, because not made for him, yet the doubt remains whether the treaty made by the president and Senate was not competent to render adjudication a necessary circumstance, even in favor of the enemy. The treaty has certainly done this, and retro-actively. Their competence depends on the extent we give to the words of the constitution empowering them 'to make treaties.' These words are very indefinite: but surely we must never admit them to be of universal comprehension: and if we must *of necessity* give them some definite extent, I do not know a more rational one than 'to those things usually settled by treaty.' The question then assumes this shape. Is the restitution of property rightfully taken in war, among the usual subjects of treaty?

Madison to Jefferson

[Washington July 17, 1801]

The following memoranda, and the inclosed letter from Mr. Dallas will present to the President the state of the information in the office of State on the subject of the indictmt. under the sedition act agst. Duane, at the request of the Senate.[17] The President will observe, that another prosecution agst. him, at *Common law,* is pending in the same Court.

---

17. For Duane's difficulties with the Senate and his subsequent indictment under the Sedition Act, see ch. 25, above. His case was set for trial in the federal circuit court in Oct. 1801; see Smith, pp. 288–306.

16. May. 1800.	Mr: Lee's letter to Mr. Ingersol directing prosecution vs Duane *for libel* on the Senate, agreeably to Resoln. of Senate
25. March. 1801.	Mr. Lincoln's letter to Mr. Dallas for stayg. prosecutions under *sedition law,* except *that vs. Duane* requested by Senate
31. March.	Mr. Dallas's answer (inclosed)
9. April	Mr. Lincoln's reply—authorizing him to engage Counsel at public expence—is at a loss what direction to give as to the prosecution *at common law,* for violating Liston's letters,[18] the President being absent—recommends a continuance of the cause, which is sd. to have taken place.

Lord Mansfield's state of the doctrine of Capture and condemnation will be seen p. 692-3-4. of 2 Bur. herewith sent.[19] The act of Congs. Mar. 3. 1800 as to salvage in cases of recaptures, enters into the enquiry. Contrary to the act referred to by Mr. Jefferson—it favors the necessity of condemnation, at least in Sec. 3. concerning alien friends. In the case of recaptures of the property of Citizens, to whom national protection is due the restitution might be construed into an indemnification for witholding the necessary protection.

Jefferson to Madison

[Washington] July 19, 1801

TH: J. TO MR. MADISON.

With respect to the prosecutions against Thomas and others[20] for a misdemeanor at *Common law* we ought to presume the judges will do right, and to give them an opportunity of doing so. The Executive ought not to sit in previous judgment on every case and to say whether it shall or shall not go

18. Duane had also been indicted at common law in 1800 for libeling Robert Liston, the British minister to the United States, when he published two stolen letters that Liston had mailed to his government. They were published in the Philadelphia *Aurora* on July 13 and 15, 1799, and reported on the possibility of war with France and the coordination of British and American policy towards Toussaint L'Ouverture, thus demonstrating, according to the editor, an improper "intimacy between a *foreign* minister and the directors of American affairs"; see *PJM* (SS ser.), I, pp. 131-32, 442, and Smith, p. 301.

19. Ruling in a case of the loss of a British ship to a belligerent, Mansfield observed that the moment between capture and the transfer of property rights to the captor by condemnation proceedings was arbitrary, and he cited "great Incertainty and Variety of Notions" among nations and commentators. To clarify the issue and establish a legal precedent, he ruled in 1758 that "if the Ship taken by an enemy *escapes* from the Enemy, or is *retaken;* or if the Owner *redeems* (ransoms) the Capture; his Property is thereby *revested*"; see *PJM* (SS ser.), I, p. 424, citing James Burrow's *Report of Cases Adjudged in the Court of King's Bench*..., 2d ed., 5 vols. (London, 1771-80), II, p. 693.

20. Daniel and Joseph Thomas, George Piper, and William Duane were indicted for purloining and publishing dispatches of Robert Liston, the British minister to the United States; see JM to TJ, July 17, 1801, above.

before the judges. I think therefore this case ought to go on to trial, without interference of the Executive till the judges shall actually have done wrong.

But the prosecution against Duane being under the *Sedition law,* on which the judges have given repeated decisions, we know we shall have to control them ultimately, and therefore may as well do it at once, to save to all parties the expence and trouble of trial. This prosecution may therefore be absolutely withdrawn.[21]

Jefferson to Madison

Monticello Aug. 7, 1801

Th: Jefferson presents his affectionate salutations to Mr. Madison and sends him the inclosed which will explain itself. He hopes to see him and family at Monticello when most convenient to themselves; and observes for his information that the road through Shadwell is put into fine order, the right hand at issuing from the ford on this side to be greatly preferred to the left. The road by Milton is all but impassable. Health and respect.

Madison to Jefferson

[Orange Aug. 11, 1801]

DEAR SIR

Docr. Rose being about to call at Monticello I prefer a conveyance by him to the mail for the papers herewith inclosed, as I shall thereby be saved the necessity of having a messenger at the Ct. House in time to catch the arrival of the post.

I have red. yours of the 7th. inst.[22] Having been before applied to by a letter from Hembold on the subject of printing the laws in his German newspaper, I had authorized Mr. Wagner to have it done, with an understanding that the preference was not to influence a further decision on the place and the press most eligible for the purpose. I was not at the time acquainted with the character or principles of the man, and it had been suggested that Lancaster or Reading, as more central might be more proper sources of publication.[23]

21. See Smith, pp. 303–6. On July 20, 1801, JM directed A. J. Dallas, the federal district attorney for Pennsylvania, to enter a nolle prosequi upon the sedition indictment found against Duane.

22. Letter not found. Dr. Robert H. Rose, a local physician, was married to JM's sister, Francis Taylor Madison; see *PJM,* I, p. 211, VIII, p. 67.

23. George Helmbold, Jr., was the publisher of the *Neue Philadelphia Correspondenz;* see Clarence S. Brigham, *History and Bibliography of American Newspapers, 1690–1820,* 2 vols. (Worcester, Mass., 1947), II, pp. 926–27.

Among the papers sent for perusal you will find the letter from Thornton as to the quoad prize carried into Boston. I send Wagner's sketch of an answer.[24] If you think it proper to meet the pretension under the British Treaty now rather than to wait the result of depending questions, you will to please signify it: as well as whether the ground taken by Wagner be *substantially* approved. Perhaps a more concise reply in the first instance might be better. Perhaps also the advantages of silence under present circumstances may balance the objection of its fostering an inadmissible claim.[25] You will find also a letter from N. Webster. It is observable that he does not directly combat the principle of distribution laid down in your reply to the Remonstrance.[26] You will be so good as to return his letter with such of the other papers as would encumber your files, or be more properly placed in mine.

Mrs. M. offers her affectionate compliments to the Ladies of your family and looks with pleasure to the opportunity of visiting them, which cannot at present be fixt to a day or even to a week, but will probably be pretty soon. She also joins in the best respects we can both offer to yourself. Yrs with respectful attachment

JAMES MADISON

Jefferson to Madison

Monticello Aug. 13, 1801

DEAR SIR,

Doctr. Rose delivered me last night the letter with which you charged him, and I have thought it better to attend to it's contents at once before the arrival of the load of other business which this morning's post will bring. Pinckney's, Orr's, Livermore's, Howell's, Webster's, Murray's, Otis's, Graham's and Thornton's letters, with Wagner's sketch of an answer to the latter

24. Jacob Wagner, who had been chief clerk in the State Department during the Adams administration, was retained by JM and remained in office until 1807, when he resigned to edit a Federalist newspaper in Baltimore; see Cunningham, *Process of Government under Jefferson,* p. 178.

25. Edward Thornton was the British chargé d'affaires to the United States. He had written about the British snow *Windsor,* which was transporting 122 French, Swedish, and Danish prisoners of war to England when the captives mutinied, seized control of the ship, and took it into Boston. Thornton claimed that the *Windsor* was now a French prize, having been captured by a predominantly French crew; and since the Convention of 1800 had not yet been ratified with France, the Jay Treaty required the United States to expel the ship; see *PJM* (SS ser.), I, pp. 268–71, and Brant, IV, pp. 61–62.

26. For Noah Webster's letter to JM, see *PJM* (SS ser.), I, pp. 436–41. After TJ removed Elizur Goodrich, one of President Adams's midnight appointees, as collector in New Haven, Connecticut, and replaced him with Samuel Bishop, a Republican, the merchants of the town sent a remonstrance to the president protesting his action. In his reply, TJ stated that the new national majority should have a proportionate share of political offices; see Malone, IV, pp. 75–80. For TJ's policy on appointments and removals, see Cunningham, *Process of Government under Jefferson,* pp. 165–87.

are all returned herewith. Reed's papers being voluminous have not been read.

I thought a commission as District attorney had been forwarded to Howell: if so, his letter is not intelligible to me, where he says he is ready prepared to quit his office when a more deserving person shall be thought of. That he would have preferred himself to Barnes as judge is evident enough.[27]

Tho' I view Webster as a mere pedagogue of very limited understanding and very strong prejudices and party passions, yet as editor of a paper and as of the Newhaven association, he may be worth stroking. His letter leaves two very fair points whereon to answer him. 1. the justice of making vacancies in order to introduce a participation of office. 2. That admitted, the propriety of preventing men indecently appointed and not yet warm in the seat of office from continuing, rather than to remove those fairly appointed and long in possession. As to Goodrich and Bishop it would be like talking to the deaf to say anything to a man as immovably biassed as he is.

Thornton's letter is the same I have seen before I left Washington. When we consider that our minister has to wait months and years for an answer to the most trifling or most urgent application to his government, there would be no indecency to decline answering so crude an application as this respecting the prize, which he does not know if it be prize or not, brought into Boston *as the newspapers say.*[28] I think it better to avoid determining, with foreign ministers, hypothetical cases. They may by stating possible cases, so employ us as to leave no time for those which are actual. The actual furnish occupation enough for our whole time. Perhaps the case of giving or refusing asylum for prizes may never arise. Yet if we predetermine it, we shall be led into all the altercation and discussion which would be necessary were we obliged to decide it. I think therefore the answer to Thornton might be that his letter being hypothetical presents two questions, calling for very different considerations, both of which it cannot now be necessary to determine. That both are founded on newspaper information only, which is too uncertain ground for the government to act on: and that so soon as certain information shall be received that any such case has happened and what the exact nature of the case is, we will do on it what shall be right.[29]

I have been reading Schlegel's pamphlet [on neutral rights] with great attention. It contains a great deal of sound information. He does not however prove that in cases uncontroulled by treaty, the nations of Europe (or a single one of them in a single case) have practised on the principle, as a principle of natural law, that free bottoms make free goods. His own facts shew that the principle practised on in the earliest times was that an enemy's goods in a friend's bottom are lawful prize: that on an attempt by the Dutch to introduce the other principle, it was overborne by Lewis XIV and by England, and the

---

27. TJ appointed David Howell, a Providence lawyer who had served with JM in the Continental Congress in 1782–83, as U.S. district attorney for Rhode Island, after appointing his predecessor, David Leonard Barnes, as federal district judge; see *PJM* (SS ser.), I, pp. 59, 173.

28. TJ's italics.

29. For TJ's decision on the *Windsor,* see his letter to JM, Aug. 22, 1801, below.

old principle adhered to. Still it does not follow but that a sound principle may have been smothered by powerful states acting on a temporary interest, and that we have always a right to correct antient errors, and to establish what is more conformable to reason and convenience. This is the ground we must take.

I shall rejoice to see Mrs. Madison, yourself and the chess heroine here.[30] Observe that the governor is at Richmond every other Saturday. He goes down this day and will be back on Tuesday. Accept assurances of my affectionate friendship.

Jefferson to Madison

Monticello Aug. 14, 1801

DEAR SIR

I wrote yesterday to you, before the arrival of the post. That brought some blank commissions which I have signed and now forward. Mr Wagner's note will explain them.

The abuses and waste of public money in the military and naval departments have been so gross, that I do not think we can avoid laying some of them before Congress. I inclose you information of one which is not to be neglected. I have desired further information. I expect it will be found to have originated in Toussard who was a protegé of Knox's.[31]

Of 6. patients inoculated with the kine pox on the 7th inst. one shews considerable symptoms of having taken the disease. I yesterday performed 6. more inoculations from matter recieved from Boston and some from England viâ Boston. I learn that Dr Gant's efforts have all failed. Health and affectionate attachment.

TH: JEFFERSON

Madison to Jefferson

[Orange] Aug. 16, 1801

DEAR SIR,

Mrs. Tudor (the lady of Judge Tudor of Boston) with her son, intending to be at Monticello this evening or tomorrow, I intrust to them the inclosed papers, which will thus reach you a little earlier, than if detained for the mail,

---

30. The "chess heroine" was Dolley Madison's sister, Anna Payne; see *PJM* (SS ser.), II, p. 42.

31. TJ enclosed a letter that alleged that fortifications built in Newport, Rhode Island, during the quasi war with France had been constructed under a rigged contract recommended by President Adams "for the purpose of benefiting Genl. [Henry] Knox," a leading Federalist who supplied the army with timber and lime from his Maine properties. Although the letter was signed with a pseudonym, it was written by John Rutledge, Jr., a South Carolina Federalist; see Robert K. Tatzlaff, *John Rutledge Jr.: South Carolina Federalist, 1766–1819* (New York, 1982), pp. 216–20.

by which I shall again write you. In the mean time I remain Yours most respectfully and affly.

                    JAMES MADISON

Madison to Jefferson

[Orange, Aug. 18, 1801]

DEAR SIR

    Inclosed herewith are several letters and papers for perusal. Among the former you are troubled with another from Thornton. You will observe that the Declaration of the Master of the British Vessel carried into Boston, states only that the Prisoners were French Spanish Danish etc. etc. without saying whether they were taken in the French service, or that of their respective countries. This circumstance, and the distinction between a prize of such a description and one made by a ship of war or privateer, or even a letter of marque, seem to admit an easy reply to Thornton, in general terms, that the case is not considered as within the purview of the Treaty, but will be attended to on the principles applicable to it. What these may require deserves both inquiry and consideration. The Books which I have and have looked into take no specific notice of such a capture. In whatever light it be regarded, it cannot, if out of the stipulation in the British Treaty, fall within that of the French either antient or recent. We seem to be free therefore to permit the vessel to continue or to order her away as may be expedient, unless the law of nations prescribe one or the other course, or the instructions of 1793. impose one or the other, on our consistency. The law of nations, as far as I recollect, prescribes nothing more than an equality in the neutral towards the beligerent nations. The restrictions of 1793. have the same object, as far as antecedent Treaties would allow.[32] The question results, whether the late order for the departure of the Spanish prize,[33] be not sufficiently analogous to require a like one in the present case, even if it be ascertained that the prize was made by

---

32. In the struggle to maintain neutrality between France and England, President Washington and TJ had endeavored to maintain the belligerents on an equal footing in 1793, even though the United States was bound by treaty obligations to France. By 1801, the treaties with France had been abrogated, but the United States now had treaty obligations with Great Britain. Both in 1793 and 1801, the distinction among public vessels, men-of-war, and certain private vessels—especially armed merchantmen that had taken prizes—was difficult to define; see Brant, IV, pp. 61–62.

33. In June, a Spanish armed merchantman with a British prize in tow sailed up the Delaware River and began unloading its American cargo. Thornton claimed that the Spanish ship belonged to an ally of France and operated as a privateer, making its reception in an American port a violation of Jay's treaty, which obliged the United States to expel it. The administration directed the Spanish merchantman to order the departure of its British prize but allowed the merchantman to remain in port, despite protests by Thornton that it should be required to depart also. But under Pinckney's treaty with Spain, the vessel was allowed to make nonmilitary repairs and complete unloading the American-owned cargo aboard; see *PJM* (SS ser.), I, pp. 270–71.

French Prisoners only. Should this be your determination and it be deemed of importance to avoid the delay of a week, you can drop a line to the Secretary of the Treasury, directing him to give the proper word on to the Collector at Boston; or in case the delay be not of importance, I can on receiving your determination transmit it to Mr. G. by the evening mail. You will find under cover to Mr Wagner an answer to the Danish Resident, which if approved you will please to forward.

We cannot yet fix the time which is to give us the pleasure of seeing Monticello. We have been in expectation of a visit from some of our distant friends which has not yet been executed, and we are without information when it will be, or whether it has been laid aside. It is probable we shall know more on the subject in a few days, and we shall then decide, having regard to your hint as to the periods observed by the Governour in dividing his time between Richmond and Albemarle. Always and affect^{ly} yours

JAMES MADISON

Jefferson to Madison

Monticello Aug. 22, 1801

DEAR SIR

Your's of the 18th. is recieved, and I now return all the papers which accompanied it, (except those in Bingham's case) and also the papers inclosed in that of the 16th.

The case of the British Snow Windsor taken by the prisoners she was carrying and brought into Boston is new in some circumstances. Yet I think she must fairly be considered as a prize made on Great Britain, to which no shelter or refuge is to be given in our ports, according to our treaty. A vessel may be made prize of by persons attacking from another vessel, or from the shore, or from within itself. It is true the masters declaration is that the prisoners were French, Swedes, Dutch, Danes, Spaniards and one American, without saying in the French service; but the French, Dutch and Spaniards were enemies, and the others must have been in enemy's service or they were pirates. The case of the Spanish prize sent away may be urged on us, and I see no reason why we should attempt an exception to the general rule for this singular and small description of cases. I hardly imagine Pichon will object to it, further than to strengthen the force of a precedent which is in the long run to be so much in favor of France and Spain, who are captured ten times where they are once captors. Still, wishing you to revise this opinion of mine, I refer it back to yourself to give the order for departure, or any other answer you think best.[34]

---

34. The *Windsor*, which had been captured "from within itself," was ordered out of Boston, underscoring the government's policy of not giving sanctuary to belligerent ships; see *ibid*. L. A. Pichon was the French chargé d'affaires in Washington.

Toussaint's offence at our sending no letters of credence with Mr Lear is not regular. Such letters are never sent with a Consul, nor to a subordinate officer. The latter point, I doubt not, is that of the offence.[35]

Poinsette's application requires attention as a precedent. A frigate is going on public service. We give a passage to our own minister and his suite. That is in rule. A French chargé (Le Tombe) asks a passage. He is allowed it with the consent of Mr Livingston. This too is in rule as a matter of comity, and a return for similar civilities from that nation. In 1782.3. I was to have gone in the Romulus, on the offer of the French minister. They actually went to the expence of building a round house for my sole accomodation. But have we a right to give passages generally to private individuals whenever a public vessel is passing from one place to another? What would the public vessels become in that case? It is true I have given Thomas Paine a passage in the Maryland: but there is a clear enough line between Thomas Paine and citizens in general.[36] If Mr Poinsette could get Mr Livingston to recieve him as one of his suite, there would be no inconvenience in the precedent. These are my hasty thoughts on the subject. Be so good as to weigh and correct them. And do in it what you think right.

Do you know if Mr Dallas has commenced another prosecution against Duane on behalf of the Senate? Either this should be done, or an official opinion given against it. Perhaps it would be best to do it, and leave to juries and judges to decide against it's being sustainable.[37]

What would you think of Clay of Philadelphia for the Consulship of Lisbon? It has been suggested that he might perhaps accept it. We cannot expect a man of better talents. If you have no reason in opposition to it, I will have it proposed to him privately through the channel which suggested it.

Is it not worthy of consideration whether we should not, through Mr Livingston, propose to Prussia to exchange the new articles inserted in our late treaty for the old ones of the former omitted in it? The change was excessively against her will, and places us in a disgraceful position as to interesting principles of public law.[38]

35. For Toussaint's reaction, see De Conde, pp. 314–15.

36. TJ offered Paine the opportunity to take passage on the return trip of the public vessel that had brought Congressman John Dawson to France with the ratification of the Convention of 1800, but Paine did not accept the offer; see Malone, IV, p. 194.

37. Duane requested a dismissal of his indictment, and TJ directed that the prosecution under the Sedition Act be discontinued. But he also suggested that a new proceeding be instituted against Duane on whatever other law might deal with the offense of criticizing the Senate. The grand jury found no such law other than the recently expired Sedition Law and refused to return an indictment; see Smith, pp. 301–5.

38. The "old articles," which asserted that "free ships make free goods," were abandoned in the 1799 treaty that John Quincy Adams negotiated with Prussia, then an ally of Great Britain. This brought the "new articles" in that treaty into conformity with the articles in Jay's treaty; see Samuel Flagg Bemis, *John Quincy Adams and the Foundations of American Foreign Policy* (New York, 1949), pp. 93–95.

There is a Charles D. Coxe (brother in law of Tenche) so well recommended for a Consulship that I wish he could be gratified.

Bingham's case shall be the subject of the next letter. Respect and attachment to Mrs Madison and Miss Payne; affectionate friendship to yourself.

TH: JEFFERSON

Madison to Jefferson

[Orange] Aug. 26, 1801

DEAR SIR

I have duly rec^d yours of Aug. 22. with the papers sent with it. I have heard nothing from Dallas on the subject of another prosecution agst Duane. It is to be presumed that he will either commence it, or let us know his reason for not doing so. Should further silence take place, I will jog his attention. I know nothing of Clay personally. All I know thro' others is in his favor, and speak him well adapted to the station you have thought of for him. C. D. Coxe can have Madiera, if you determine against Pintard. No other place occurs as so clearly disposable.

I inclose herewith the communications brought me by the last mail. I have signed the exequatur requested by Mr Olsen, that if a grant of it should be decided, there may be no delay. He seems to have had in view some thing less formal. It is odd that Soderstrom should still proceed in Danish Business, knowing as he must the presence of Olsen, and being himself too, without any regular authority from that Gov^t [39]

Consul Eaton you will find has taken another *extraordinary* step. Wagner's explanation of it with his own letter, leaves me nothing to add on the subject, farther than that I have signified my opinion that under the choice of difficulties, the least will be to ship the powder and ball requested by the Dey of Algiers. As there is little room for doubting his continuance at peace, it may not be amiss to take the opp^y. to make another payment to him; and there will be less trouble and loss in doing it in these articles than any other. I have also signified that the contract of Eaton must as the lesser evil be fulfilled, but that it ought to be done in a way if possible, that may throw the expence on himself, if hereafter so determined. The private commission as to the Timber, and the equivocal one as to the Cattle I have desired Mr Wagner not to meddle with.

---

39. JM first heard that "a gentleman named Olson" had arrived from Denmark to serve as the Danish minister to the United States. His name was Peder Blicher Olsen; see Sören J. M. P. Fogdall, *Danish-American Diplomacy, 1776–1920,* vol. VIII of the University of Iowa Studies in the Social Sciences (Iowa City, 1922), pp. 30, 35, 157. Until the arrival of the Danish minister, Richard Söderström, Swedish consul general in the United States, had represented the Danish government; see *ibid.,* p. 296.

Can you give me any information towards an Answer to the letter from Mr Starke. I recollect nothing on the subject.⁴⁰

I have desired Mr Wagner to send you copy of the last letters from the Dep.^t of State to Mr Eaton with such other information as he might enable you to give your answer to the Bey of Tunis with care and precision. It is probable you may find it convenient to allude to the jewels preparing for him in London. Yours respectfully and Affec.^y

JAMES MADISON

Madison to Jefferson

[Orange] Aug. 27, 1801

DEAR SIR

I sent you yesterday by Doc.^r Bache a packet rec.^d by the mail of last week, that it might the less interfere with what you recieve directly.⁴¹ I avail myself of another private opportunity to forward the communications rec.^d by the mail of yesterday, by which means the further advantage will be obtained, of gaining a week in those cases which require your sanction, and which need not go back thro' my hands.

Among the communications you will find Thornton again on our hands, and with a case that seems to compel us to meet the question whether the British Treaty is to operate ag.st French Ships with prizes, as well as those of other nations. It is more than probable that another privateer which has arrived in N. Carolina with a British prize, though called in the Newspapers Spanish will be found to be French and will soon double the demand for a decision of that question. Will it be best to give in the first instance a particular and argumentative, or a more general and categorical answer to Mr Thornton. It may be a consideration in favor of the latter that we have no reason to suppose that his Gov.^t enters into his construction of the Treaty of 1794. Yours truly etc.

JAMES MADISON

I forgot to mention St Petersburg as vacant for a Consul. If Coxe will go there, it would be more convenient than to give him Madiera, which may be eligible for others.

---

40. Theodore Stark of Frederick County, Virginia, had applied for the position of Mississippi territorial attorney; see Clarence E. Carter, ed., *The Territorial Papers of the United States,* 28 vols. (Washington, 1934–75), *Mississippi,* V, p. 655.

41. Dr. William Bache was the grandson of Benjamin Franklin and the brother of Benjamin Franklin Bache, the publisher of the Philadelphia *Aurora,* who died of yellow fever in 1798; see Randolph Shipley Klein, ed., *Science and Society in Early America: Essays in Honor of Whitfield J. Bell, Jr.* (Philadelphia, 1986), pp. 58, 60. At TJ's suggestion, he bought a farm in Albemarle County near Monticello; see *PJM* (SS ser.), II, p. 70.

Jefferson to Madison

Monticello Aug. 28, 1801

DEAR SIR

Your's of the 26th. by Doctr. Bache came duly to hand: and I now return you all the papers you inclosed except the commission for the Marshal of New Jersey, which I retain till I see you, which Dr. Bache gives me hopes will be the ensuing week, and I suppose will of course be the day after tomorrow, as you will then be free from the pressure of the post. I inclose with those papers, for perusal, a letter and memorial from a Mr Joseph Allen Smith, of whom I know nothing more than these papers inform me. You will be sensible that in his assumption of diplomatic functions he has not shewn much diplomatic subtlety. He seems not afraid of Logan's law in our hands. Of Mr Starke's application for the attorney's place of Missisipi I recollect nothing; and not having here my bundle of applications for office I can ascertain nothing. But I am persuaded he has not applied to me: and consequently it must have been to our predecessors. This would afford a reason the more for enquiries concerning him before we decide about him. This shall be reserved for conversation when we meet.

I feel a scruple at signing the recital of a falshood in the Exequatur for Olsen, to wit, 'the having seen his commission'. It would bind us to admit his credentials let them be what they will; and be an useless departure from fact. I think with you that he desires much less, and what is perfectly admissible; and consequently that it would be better to write him a very civil letter yielding exactly what he asks.

What are the delays in the performance of our stipulations of which the Bey of Tunis, and Eaton complain? I thought we had not only complied with the treaty, but were doing considerably more. I have read Eaton's correspondence, and form a very respectable opinion of his understanding. I should be disposed to do so too of his honesty: but how, to these two qualities, can we reconcile his extraordinary mission of this vessel? If nothing sinister appears on the enquiry Mr Wagner is making, he should be made to understand that the administration will not admit such unauthorised and useless waste of the public money.[42] As to the cattle and timber, I would leave them to be sent or not by those charged with them. I am an enemy to all these douceurs, tributes and humiliations. What the laws impose on us let us execute faithfully; but nothing more. I think it would be well to engage Mr Wagner (who is fully competent to it) to make up, for the eye of Congress a full statement of every expence which our transactions with the Barbary powers has occasioned, and of what we still owe, that they may be enabled to decide, on a full view of the subject,

---

42. William Eaton, American consul at Tunis, had chartered a brig to carry his warning that the bashaw of Tripoli was planning a war against American commerce; see *PJM* (SS ser.), I, pp. 78–82, and Gardner W. Allen, *Our Navy and the Barbary Corsairs* (Boston, 1905), pp. 59–88.

what course they will pursue. I know that nothing will stop the eternal increase of demand from these pirates but the presence of an armed force, and it will be more economical and more honorable to use the same means at once for suppressing their insolencies.

I think with you we had better send by Eaton's vessel the powder and ball wanting for Algiers.

I have recieved information through a single hand from one of Bainbridge's lieutenants, that Bainbridge himself connived at the impressment of the George Washington, and perhaps received a douceur. As soon as we hear of an actual hostility by Tripoli I think that Cathcart should be sent to Algiers, and O'Brian permitted to retire [?]. These two men have completely shewn themselves to be what I concieved of them on a pretty full acquaintance in Philadelphia.[43]

Would it not be well to instruct our agents resident where there have been British admiralty courts to collect all the cases, which can be authenticated, of the enormities of those courts? I am persuaded it must be the groundwork of a demand on our part of stipulations from that country entirely novel in their nature, and which nothing but the disgrace of their proceedings can extort from them. But they are indispensably necessary for us. We are surely never more to submit to such ruinous degradations again. In hopes of seeing you soon I conclude with assurances of sincere and affectionate friendship

TH: JEFFERSON

P. S. I send Bingham's case to Mr Lincoln.[44]

Madison to Jefferson

[Orange] Sept. 11, 1801

DEAR SIR

The mail of Wednesday brought the dispatches from France which ought to have come in the preceding one. I inclose them with sundry other letters etc. They would have been sent yesterday but an express could not readily be procured. I have engaged the Bearer a free Negro of good character to deliver them to you as early today as he can accomplish the ride. He is to recieve a dollar and a half per day, counting a day for going, the like for returning, and adding the time he may be detained. As it may not be convenient for you to read the papers in time to return them, with any directions you may wish, by the post of tomorrow, you can keep him as long as may be necessary. I shall be

---

43. This paragraph, which is obliterated in the recipient's copy, has been transcribed from TJ's file copy.

44. The *Bingham* case involved a prize ship captured by a Massachusetts privateer during the American Revolution; see Robert C. Alberts, *The Golden Voyage: The Life and Times of William Bingham, 1752–1804* (Boston, 1969), pp. 78–79, 365–67, 417–18.

glad to have the letters back which require answers that may be prepared for the mail in course.

The complaint I brought with me from Monticello proved more slight than I apprehended. It has kept me however little fit for business since my return, and I do not yet find myself in the state to be desired. I shall nevertheless take up the subject of instructions for M^r. L that no delay may happen. Be so good as to let me know when the Boston will be ready, and any account if any you have as to Mr Livingston's forwardness for embarking. I have not yet rec^d from Wagner some papers required to assist my agency in the case. Nor do I recollect that the commission and letters of Credence were signed before we left Washington. Perhaps these may have gone on to you yesterday. As it has been objected to Murray that he had no *special* commission, it might not be amiss to add one to Mr L. if it could be done without delay.

Bishop Madison and Doctor Jones being with me, and understanding that I am sending a Messenger to Monticello, charge me to tender you their particular respects. With the sincerest attachment I am Dear Sir Yours

JAMES MADISON

Jefferson to Madison

Monticello Sept. 11, 1801

DEAR SIR

I have no letter from you by the mail, whence I conclude I may possibly recieve something by private conveyance. A letter from Miss Paine to Virginia Randolph saying nothing of your health makes me hope it is reestablished. I inclose you a letter from Genl Saml Smith with Barney's letter to him. It contains matters worthy of some attention. I do not believe that Murray would endeavor to defeat the treaty.[45] On the contrary I believe he would be anxious to get it through. However the more I reflect on it the more I am satisfied it's non-ratification is unimportant, and will give us all the benefits of peace and commercial relations without the embarrasments of a treaty.

You will recieve by this post my letter to the Bey of Tunis, and one to Rob. R. Livingston on Neutral rights; both open, and to be forwarded. I have recieved no letter by this post from M$\bar{r}$ Gallatin which augurs ill of the situation of his family, as he has had occasion to write me weekly on a great variety of matter. Accept assurances of my constant and affectionate esteem and great respect.

TH: JEFFERSON

---

45. Joshua Barney, an American sea captain who had commanded a French privateer, charged that William Vans Murray was delaying the exchange of ratifications of the Convention of 1800, which Murray had helped negotiate; see De Conde, p. 319.

Jefferson to Madison

Monticello Sept. 12, 1801

DEAR SIR,

Yours of yesterday was delivered by your express about 5. o'clock in the evening. My occupations for the departing post have prevented my answering instantly.

No commission nor letter of credence was signed for Mr. Livingston before we left Washington. I think the Boston has not yet left Boston for New York. I presume therefore that we can sign those papers in time after our return to Washington. I suspect, on view of Murray's letters, that the real obstacle to the ratification is nothing more than a desire to obtain an express renunciation of the demand of indemnities. If this be the case it will probably be ratified on that condition. On the established principle that everything is abandoned which is not provided for in a treaty of peace, the express abandonment would not be necessary if the 2d article is expunged.[46] Suppose we were to instruct Livingston in case he finds on arrival in Paris that the ratification is withheld, that he propose the single article for the restitution of prizes, and say to them that with every disposition towards them of perfect friendliness and free commerce, we are willing to trust, without a treaty to the mutual interests of the two countries for dictating the terms of our commercial relations, not doubting that each will give the best terms in practice to the other, that on the expiration of the British treaty we shall probably do the same with that nation, and so with others. Unless indeed events should render it practicable to sign a short formula merely explanatory or amendatory of the L. of Nations in a few special articles. The being in freedom to refuse entrance in time of war to armed ships, or prizes, to refuse or send off ministers and consuls in time of war, is a most desirable situation in my judgment.

I wonder to see such an arrearage from the Department of State to our bankers in Holland.[47] Our predecessors seem to have levied immense sums from their constituents merely to feed favorites by large advances, and thus to purchase by corruption an extension of their influence and power. Their just debts appear to have been left in the background. I understood that the advance to Genl. Lloyd was to relieve his distress, and the contract a mere cover for letting him have the benefit of the 5,000 D. What would you think of agreeing to annul the contract on his previous *actual reimbursement* of the money?

I think we may conclude with tolerable certainty that the Tripolitans had

---

46. For the provisions of the Convention of 1800, see *ibid.*, pp. 351–72. The second article postponed negotiations on French indemnities for seizure of American ships and abrogation of the Franco-American treaties of 1778 and 1788 until a more convenient time; see *ibid.*, pp. 288–93, 311–20.

47. For the Dutch loan of 500,000 francs negotiated on Mar. 1, 1801, see Pieter J. Van Winter, *American Finance and Dutch Investment, 1780–1805*, 2 vols. (New York, 1977), II, pp. 1082–83.

not taken any of our vessels before Dale's arrival at Gibraltar. What a pity he did not know of the war, that he might have taken their admiral and his ship.

Mr. Church does not exactly ask for a restoration of his consulship at Lisbon: But I am inclined to think it the very best step we can take.[48] However this may be a subject of conversation when we meet. I am happy to hear your complaint has been so slight. I hope the great change in the weather since last night will secure us against the return of any more very hot weather. My respects to the ladies, and sincere and affectionate esteem to yourself.

P. S. All the papers are returned except Davis' letter recommending a collector for the Ohio district.

Madison to Jefferson

[Orange] Sept. 16, 1801

DEAR SIR

The Messenger delivered me about 9 o'C. on Saturday evening the packet with your letters of Sep.r 11 and 12. I join in your opinion that the suspicions of Murray in the letters inclosed in the former are too harsh to be probable. Still his situation may produce feelings and views not coincident with ours, and strengthens the policy of getting the Chancellor on the ground as soon as possible. I hear nothing of the Boston frigate. Perhaps the mail of [to]day may bring some account of her movements. I shall take care that no delay shall be chargeable on me; though I have been very little in a condition since I got home for close application of any sort. I have not been under the necessity of lying up, or renouncing current attentions, but have felt too much of the "Malaise" for any thing beyond them. I return the letters from S. Smith and B. and forward a letter from D.r Thornton. I have one from him myself, which I shall answer by saying that on the receipt of M's resignation you had fixt on a successor, and closed the door to further applications.[49] I find that the idea of H's appointment had leaked out, and that his pretensions were not regarded by the Doc.r as a bar to his own. I inclose also a letter from F. Preston which speaks itself the objects of the Writer. I believe him to be a man of worth, of good understanding, and in a position to have some knowledge of Indian affairs. With these qualifications he might be a fit Associate of Hawkins and Wilkinson, should Pickens decline and his being a Virginian has no objection. I have with me M.r Davis of N. Y. whom I presume to be the candidate for an office in that City. As he has but just arrived, I have not had conversation eno'

---

48. Edward Church had been dismissed as American consul to Lisbon during the Adams administration; see Edward Church to JM, June 23, 1801, in *PJM* (SS ser.), I, p. 340.

49. Samuel Meredith resigned as treasurer of the United States in Oct. 1801; see Malone, IV, p. 56. TJ appointed Thomas Tudor Tucker as treasurer and Richard Harison as auditor; see *ASP, M*, I, p. 304, and Cunningham, *Process of Government under Jefferson*, pp. 325–32.

with him to find out whether he means to visit Monticello. I conjecture that to be his primary object. He brings me an introduction from Ed. Livingston and from him only.⁵⁰ Yours always most affectionately and respectfully

JAMES MADISON

Madison to Jefferson

[Orange Sept. 17, 1801]

DEAR SIR

I make use of the opp^y. by Mr Davis to forward you the contents of the weekly packet rec^d. yesterday from the Office of State. Having had time scarcely to read some of the communications, I am unable, if there were occasion, to submit comments on them. Mr Wagner writes that Mr Graham left Washington on Saturday last with the papers relating to the Mission of Mr Livingston, and was to be with me on Monday evening past. As he is not yet arrived, I think it not improbable that he may have gone by to Monticello with an intention to take me in his way back. I inclose a letter from Genl. Gates, concurring in the recommendations of Mr Davis.

Mr Graham has this moment arrived, and has brought me sundry documents some of which I am obliged to sign without reading, as they will be subject to your revision, and I sh^d otherwise lose the opp^y. by Mr Davis. Mr Graham declines proceeding further than Orange.⁵¹ The inclosed very confidential letter from D W Clinton was brought by Mr G. very apropos to be forwarded to you. Adieu Y^{rs} most aff^y. and rsp^y.

JAMES MADISON

I send a newspaper copy of the French Convention.

Jefferson to Madison

Monticello Sept. 18, 1801

DEAR SIR

Your favor of the 16th. by post and 17th by Mr. Davis have been duly received. He has not yet opened himself to me; but I shall assure him that

---

50. Matthew L. Davis, a friend of Burr, sought the post of naval officer in New York but was not appointed; see Gaillard Hunt, "Office-seeking during Jefferson's Administration," *AHR* 3 (1898): 270–91.

51. John Graham, whom JM called "a young man of intelligence and very estimable character from Kentucky," became private secretary to Charles Pinckney, American minister to Spain; see *PJM* (SS ser.), I, p. 279.

nothing can be said here on the subject, nor determined on but when we shall be together at Washington. I have a letter from Mr. Gallatin whose only doubt is whether Rogers should be removed. If he is, he seems clear Davis had better have the appointment. I think it shall be better to postpone an answer to Govr. Clinton on Brants proposition till we can be together at Washington. In fact it belongs to the War department.[52] Genl. Pickens is arrived at S. W. point which answers Mr. Preston's application. I wrote to the Secretary of War [Navy] Sep. 5 to have the Boston expedited. I have a letter from him dated Baltimore Sep. 10: he had not then received mine. He had just lost his eldest son. It is pretty evident we shall be at Washington in time to dispatch papers for the Chancellor. For that reason I retain the several commissions signed by you and forwarded yesterday, not being satisfied which we had better use. I am satisfied we ought not to keep Murray there on so slender a business. I count fully myself the 1st. Consul will ratify on condition of an abandonment of spoliations on our part. If he does not, would it not be better to give the Chancellor a power to execute the article for the restitution of prizes, and leave to the Senate whether any new modifications shall be agreed to? You know my opinion as to the importance of the ratification. But all this shall be the subject of consultation when we meet. I return all your papers except those applying for offices, which I imagine had better be in my bundle. I shall see you on Saturday or Sunday if you be not gone. My respects to the ladies and affectionate attachment to yourself.

TH: JEFFERSON

Madison to Jefferson

[Orange] Sept. 23, 1801

DEAR SIR

Having sent you by M.[r] Davis the communications rec.[d] by the mail of last week, I have none to make you at present. You will find me at home, on Saturday or Sunday, when I hope to be able to fix the day for following you to Washington. The dispatches for M.[r] Livingston will be ready by the time I shall have the pleasure of seeing you. My conversation with M.[r] Graham who staid a day or two with me, and appears to be a sensible and steady young man, has suggested some ideas for enlarging the instructions to M.[r] Pinkney on the subject of Louisiana, which I will also put in form by the time of your arrival. With the most respectful attachments I remain Dear Sir Y.[rs]

JAMES MADISON

---

52. The Iroquois chieftain Joseph Brant had written to Governor Clinton of New York asking if an Indian settlement on American soil would be acceptable to the U.S. government; see Isabel Thompson Kelsay, *Joseph Brant, 1743–1807: Man of Two Worlds* (Syracuse, 1984), p. 622.

Jefferson to Madison

[Washington Sept. 21 – Dec. 11, 1801?]⁵³

to the preceding observations it may be added that the stipulation to restore vessels taken after the treaty is only pro major cautela [for greater caution], as without that the right to demand and the duty to restore, would equally exist.

Nor is the objection good that till ratifcn the treaty is not compleat because when ratified, it is confirmed ab initio.

These observations respect only vessels taken after the signature of the treaty. But it is said there is one vessel taken before the treaty but not yet condemned. I suspect this will stand on very different ground. By the law of nature, property is transferred by the act of capture, which act is compleat when the victory is absolute. The act of Congress July 9. 1798. says 'all armed vessels *captured* shall *accrue* to the captors, and on due condemnation shall be distributed etc.' This confirms the natural law. The property vests by the capture; the condemnation is only the declaration of a fact, to wit, that the capture was rightful, and a partitioning among the owners. If condemnation was an act of war, it would be made unlawful by the treaty but it seems to be a mere municipal act or decision between inter-claiming citizens.

If the property was definitively transferred and the capture [made] under an existing act of the legislature who were competent to the passing that act, it may be doubted whether the Presidt. and Senate can retrospectively annul that.

The legislature can, and it ought in good faith to the foreign nation to make the restitution, but also to give indemnification to the captors, whose legal acquisition is taken from them for the purposes of public peace.

Madison to Jefferson

Orange Oct. 3, 1801

DEAR SIR

Mr. Kemble followed you on tuesday afternoon, with the dispatches for Mr. Livingston and Mr. Pinkney, and I hope arrived in time to get them to N.

---

53. This fragment of a memorandum refers to the Convention of 1800, which ended the quasi war between the United States and France. Negotiated by envoys appointed by President John Adams, it was ratified by the Senate with reservations in Feb. 1801, on the eve of TJ's inauguration. When James A. Bayard, Adams's appointee to negotiate the exchange of ratifications, declined the mission, TJ instructed William Vans Murray, American minister to the Netherlands and one of the envoys who had negotiated the convention, to handle the exchange of ratifications. News of the French ratification reached the United States on Sept. 29, the ratified treaty arrived at the end of November, TJ submitted it to the Senate on Dec. 11, the Senate ratified on Dec. 19, and TJ proclaimed it as the law of the land on Dec. 21, 1801. Articles III and IV specified that ships or property captured by either nation "shall be mutually restored"; see *Treaties and Other International Acts of the United States of America,* ed. Hunter Miller, 8 vols. (Washington, 1931–1948), II, pp. 459–62, and De Conde, pp. 254–55, 293, 311–20, 353–55.

York before the frigate could sail. By detaining him, no time was lost as he was employed in making fair copies, otherwise to be made in the office, and as by reposing himself and his horse he could return the more expeditiously.[54] The distribution of the slaves among the Legatees and the subsequent interchanges among them for the accomodation of both have consumed the whole of this week. The sales of personal articles etc. will begin on monday, and I had hoped would have ended on the same day. It is now understood that it will employ two days. I shall not lose a moment in hastening thereafter my departure and journey.[55] The delay would give me much concern if it were not unavoidable, and if I did not flatter myself that no public inconvenience would flow from it[.] With the most respectful attachment I am sin[cerely] yours

JAMES MADISON

Jefferson to Madison

[Washington] Nov. 5, 1801

TH. J. TO J. M.

Will you consider whether a copy of the inclosed sent to each head of department would be best; or to avail myself of your kind offer to speak to them. My only fear as to the letter is that they might infer a want of confidence on my part. But you can decide on sounder views of the subject than my position may admit. [If] you prefer the latter, modify any expressions which you may think need it. Health and affection.

Jefferson to Madison

Washington Nov. 6, 1801

Circular to the heads of departments, *and Private.*

DEAR SIR

Coming all of us into Executive office new, and unfamiliar with the course of business previously practised, it was not to be expected we should in the first outset adopt, in every part, a line of proceeding so perfect as to admit no amendment. The mode and degrees of communication particularly between the President and heads of departments have not been practised exactly on the same rule in all of them. Yet it would certainly be more safe and satisfactory for ourselves as well as the public, that not only the best, but also an uniform course of proceeding, as to manner and degree, should be ob-

54. Hazen Kimball was a clerk in the State Department; see *PJM* (SS ser.), I, p. 350.
55. JM was handling the settlement of his father's estate.

served. Having been a member of the first administration under Genl. Washington, I can state with exactness what our course then was. Letters of business came addressed sometimes to the President, but most frequently to the heads of departments. If addressed to himself, he referred them to their proper department to be acted on: if to one of the Secretaries, the letter, if it required no answer, was communicated to the President simply for his information. If an answer was requisite, the Secretary of the department communicated the letter and his proposed answer to the President. Generally they were simply sent back, af[ter] perusal, which signified his approbation. Sometimes he returned them with an informal note, suggesting an alteration or a query. If a doubt of any importance arose, he reserved it for conference. By this means he was always in accurate possession of all facts and proceedings in every part of the Union, and to whatsoever department they related; he formed a central point for the different branches, preserved an unity of object and action among them, exercised that participation in the gestion of affairs which his office made incumbent on him, and met himself the due responsibility for whatever was done.

During Mr Adams's administration, his long and habitual absences from the seat of government rendered this kind of communication impracticable, removed him from any share in the transaction of affairs, and parcelled out the government in fact among four independent heads, drawing sometimes in opposite directions. That the former is preferable to the latter course cannot be doubted. It gave indeed to the heads of departments the trouble of making up, once a day, a packet of all their communications for the perusal of the President; it commonly also retarded one day their dispatches by mail: but, in pressing cases, this injury was prevented by presenting that case singly for immediate attention; and it produced us in return the benefit of his sanction for every act we did. Whether any change of circumstances may render a change in this procedure necessary, a little experiment will shew us. But I cannot withold recommending to the heads of departments that we should adopt this course for the present, leaving any necessary modifications of it to time and trial.

I am sure my conduct must have proved, better than a thousand declarations would, that my confidence in those whom I am so happy as to have associated with me, is unlimited, unqualified, and unabated. I am well satisfied that everything goes on with a wisdom and rectitude which I could not improve. If I had the Universe to chuse from, I could not change one of my associates to my better satisfaction. My sole motives are those before expressed as governing the first administration in chalking out the rules of their proceeding; adding to them only a sense of obligation imposed on me by the public will, to meet personally the duties to which they have a[ppointed me.] If this mode of proceeding shall meet the approbation of the heads of departments, [it may] go into execution without giving them the trouble of an answer: if any other can be suggested which would answer our views, and add less to their labours, that will be a sufficient reason for my preferring it to my own proposition, to the substance of which only, and not to the form, I attach any importance.

Accept for yourself particularly, my dear Sir, assurances of my constant and sincere affection and respect.

TH: JEFFERSON

Jefferson to Madison

[Washington] Nov. 12, 1801

Will you give this enclosed a serious revisal, not only as to matter, but diction? Where strictness of grammar does not weaken expression, it should be attended to in complaisance to the purists of New England. But where by small grammatical negligences, the energy of an idea is condensed, or a word stands for a sentence, I hold grammatical rigor in contempt. I will thank you to expedite it, and to consider, as you go along, in the documents promised, which of them go from your office, and to have them prepared in duplicates with a press copy of one of the duplicates for me.[56]

Genl. Hurd's commission is still wanting.[57]

The inclosed letter etc. from Read was sent me by Mr Gallatin.[58] I inclose it merely that you may have your eye on the establishment of these agents. Be so good as to return it immediately to Mr. Gallatin.

Jefferson to Madison

[Washington Nov. ——, 1801]

TH. J. TO J. M.

Will you be so good as once more to revise this? Altho' I have not entirely obliterated all the passages which have been thought objectionable, yet I have very much reduced and smoothed them. Still verbal and minor corrections of style or sentiment will be thankfully received and made.

---

56. TJ enclosed the draft of his first annual address to Congress on Dec. 8, 1801, to JM, Gallatin, and Smith for their comments; see Ford, VIII, pp. 108–25. His most important alteration was the deletion of his condemnation of the Sedition Act, which he had planned to call a "palpable and unqualified contradiction to the constitution" and, therefore, "a nullity." Although JM's response has not been found, Brant, IV, p. 58, credits him with persuading TJ to omit it. Cunningham, *Process of Government under Jefferson*, p. 76, criticizes Brant's claim for Madison and credits Smith and Gallatin as being responsible for TJ's action.

57. John Heard was later nominated as marshal for New Jersey.

58. James Read was seeking appointment as port collector of Wilmington, North Carolina; see *PJM* (SS), II, p. 237.

Madison to Jefferson

[Washington Nov. 16, 1801]

J. Madison presents his respects to the President with a letter from Col. Burr and another from Col. Humphreys. The latter is a duplicate, with an exception of the postscript. J.M. has been so much indisposed since Saturday evening that he could not call on the President, as he wished, in order to consult his intentions as to M.̲ Thornton's letter. If the President proposes to make it the subject of conversation among the heads of Dep.̲ṭ̲ṣ̲ it is suggested whether it may not be best to hasten a meeting in order that no room may be given by delay, for inferring that hesitation existed as to the proper answer. A continuance of J. M's indisposition will deprive him and M.̲ṛ̲ṣ̲ M. of the pleasure of dining with the President today. Monday Morning

Jefferson to Madison

[Washington] Nov. 22, 1801

TH. J. TO J.M.

The Virginia resolution inclosed was [sent], I am sure, in full confidence that you would contribute your counsel as well as myself.[59] I have only relieved you from the labour of the premier ebauche. I must [ask] you to consider the subject thoroughly, and either make the inclosed what it should be, or a new draught. It should go without delay, because I shall desire Monroe, if there is any thing in it he does not like, to send it back for alteration. And a fortnight is the whole time allowed for this[.] Best wishes and affections.

Madison to Jefferson

Washington Dec. 8, 1801

SIR,

I have the honor to transmit here-with two copies of the second census (except for the State of Tennessee, which is not yet received,) and to notice the

---

59. Following Gabriel's Rebellion, a slave uprising in Virginia in 1800, several leaders were executed. As an alternative to the death penalty, the legislature authorized Governor James Monroe to sell outside the boundaries of the United States all other slaves convicted of conspiracy or other crimes. When the governor asked the president for assistance, Jefferson offered to investigate the possibility of a refuge in Africa; see Harry Ammon, *James Monroe: The Quest for National Identity* (New York, 1971), pp. 186–88, 198–99. The most thorough analysis is in Douglas R. Egerton, *Gabriel's Rebellion: The Virginia Slave Conspiracies of 1800 and 1802* (Chapel Hill, 1993).

following deviations from the law under which it was taken, affecting the uniformity of some of the returns.[60]

The return for the counties of Dutchess, Ulster and Orange, in the district of New-York, was not received at this office until the 21st of September last.

The return for a portion of Baltimore County, in the district of Maryland, was not received until the 19th ult. The return for the Western District of Virginia was not received in its present form, until the 20th of October last.

The Marshal for the district of South-Carolina did not take the oath prescribed by law, until three days after the date of this return.

In the return for the Indiana Territory, the population of some of its settlements is grouped together, instead of being divided into classes.

It is proper that I should add, that I have no reason to suppose that the above irregularities have happened from culpable neglect in the Marshals themselves.

I have added to these copies an aggregate schedule of the returns from each district and territory. With perfect respect, I remain, Your most obedient servant,

JAMES MADISON

60. TJ transmitted the enclosures to Congress with his presidential message of Dec. 8, 1801; see Richardson, I, p. 327.

AN INTERLUDE OF PEACE, 1801–1802

*L*ATE IN LIFE, Jefferson claimed that the revolution of 1800 "was as real a revolution in the principles of our government as that of 1776 was in its form; not effected indeed by the sword, as that, but by the rational and peacable instrument of reform, the suffrage of the people."[1] In his quest for a symbolic removal of "monocratic" features from the presidency, Jefferson decided to submit his first annual message to Congress in writing and have it read by a clerk, rather than reading it in person. In his opinion, the customary communication by the president seemed too imitative of the monarch's remarks from the throne, and its abolition underscored a new republican simplicity that contrasted with "relics" from the past. Moreover, it eliminated the need for both houses of Congress to prepare replies to the address and for the president to return his replies to their replies.

Jefferson's decision on this point, like his decision to abolish levees and other pomp and ceremony, was based on his criticism of royal and aristocratic practices as improper for a republic, a view reenforced by his observations while he was in France.[2] A Pennsylvania congressman quickly applauded Jefferson for eliminating "all the pomp and pageantry, which once dishonored our republican institutions" and for sparing the public the spectacle of a president "drawn to the Capitol by six horses . . . and gaped at by a wondering multitude."[3]

Republican simplicity was also the theme of Jefferson's first message to Congress. The federal government, he wrote, was "charged with the external

---

1. TJ to Spencer Roane, Sept. 6, 1819, in L. and B., XV, p. 212.
2. See Charles Warren, "How the President's Speech to Congress Was Instituted and Abandoned," in *Odd Byways of American History* (Cambridge, Mass., 1942), pp. 136–58, and Malone, IV, pp. 90–95.
3. Michael Leib to Lydia Leib, Dec. 9, 1801, cited in Noble E. Cunningham, Jr., *In Pursuit of Reason: The Life of Thomas Jefferson* (Baton Rouge, 1987), p. 247.

and mutual relations only of these states," while the great field of human concerns—the "principal care of our persons, our property, and our reputation"—was left with the states. From his point of view, the federal organization was "too complicated, too expensive," with offices and officers multiplied unnecessarily.[4]

Fortunately, the Convention of 1800 had restored peace with France, and the Treaty of Amiens had restored peace in Europe, thus removing the only real threat to the success of Jefferson's domestic policies: reduction of army and naval expenditures; abolition of internal taxes, thus eliminating a swarm of tax collectors; inauguration of a debt-reduction program that would pay off the national debt in fifteen years; and specific, instead of general, appropriations, which had allowed Hamilton so much leeway. Jefferson also had two other goals: the repeal of the Judiciary Act of 1801[5] and the replacement of the Naturalization Act of 1798 with the more liberal law of 1795, which Madison had written.[6]

But Jefferson was no repudiationist. With the exception of the judiciary and internal taxes, he made no move to dismantle the Federalist financial system but instead turned to the difficult task of reducing the debt while eliminating internal taxes. "When this government was first established," Jefferson wrote after being in office less than a year, "it was possible to have kept it going on true principles, but the contracted, English, half-lettered ideas of Hamilton, destroyed that hope in the bud. We can pay off his debt in 15 years: but we can never get rid of his financial system. It mortifies me," he confessed, "to be strengthening principles which I deem radically vicious, but this vice is entailed on us by the first error. In other parts of our government I hope we shall be able by degrees to introduce sound principles and make them habitual. What is practicable must often controul pure theory: and the habits of the governed determine in a great degree what is practicable."[7]

Jefferson's deference to "the habits of the governed" pushed him in a democratic direction. He was sure that the repeal of the Federalist Judiciary Act was "unquestionably pleasing to the people generally," and he thought that documentation on the number of court cases handled each year "would rally the public opinion again to what is right, should that any where have been shaken by the volumes of misrepresentations which have been published, and shew we are not to be dismayed by any thing of that kind."[8]

Always solicitous of public opinion, Jefferson remained attentive and re-

---

4. TJ's first message to Congress, on Dec. 8, 1801, is in Ford, VIII, pp. 109–25. This statement is on p. 120.

5. For the repeal, see Malone, IV, pp. 110–35, and Richard E. Ellis, *The Jeffersonian Crisis: Courts and Politics in the Young Republic* (New York, 1971; rpt. New York, 1974), pp. 36–52.

6. The residence requirement dropped from fourteen years to five; see James H. Kettner, *The Development of American Citizenship, 1608–1870* (Chapel Hill, 1978), pp. 239–47.

7. TJ to Pierre-Samuel du Pont de Nemours, Jan. 18, 1802, in Ford, VIII, p. 127.

8. TJ to JM, Sept. 6, 1802, below. Also see TJ to JM, Feb. 26, 1802, below, and JM to TJ, [Feb. 26, 1802,] below.

sponsive to the public will, and he identified the work of the Republican Congress with "the desires of the people." Towards the end of the session in the spring of 1802, he wrote that "they have reduced the army and navy to what is barely necessary. They are disarming executive preponderance, by putting down one-half of the offices of the United States, which are no longer necessary. These economies have enabled them to suppress all the internal taxes, and still to make provision for the payment of the public debt as to discharge that in eighteen years. They have lopped off a parasitic limb, planted by their predecessors on their judiciary body for party purposes; they are opening the doors of hospitality to fugitives from the oppressions of other countries; and" (shifting from the Congress as "they" to the administration as "we") "we have suppressed all those public forms and ceremonies which tended to familiarize the public eye to the harbingers of another form of government."[9]

Although the president and the secretary of state continued to discuss domestic political issues in 1801 and 1802, most of their correspondence concentrated, as one would expect, on diplomatic matters, with Napoleon's ambitions in the Western Hemisphere and war with the Barbary pirates taking up most of their attention. During the upheavals of the French Revolution, a black statesman, Toussaint l'Ouverture, who held a commission in the French army, led a slave revolt in Santo Domingo, freeing the slaves and establishing an autonomous government virtually free from French control. During the quasi war with France, the United States and England opened trade with Toussaint, and President Adams sent a consular representative to promote commerce.[10] On taking office, Jefferson appointed Tobias Lear, formerly private secretary to President Washington, as commercial agent in 1801, and Madison directed Lear to pursue "an amicable and conciliatory line of conduct, regulated by the principle of neutrality, towards all powers, internally or externally connected with the island."[11]

When Napoleon gained power in France, he linked the fate of Santo Domingo to the future of Louisiana. In an effort to revive the French Empire in the New World, he concluded a secret treaty with Spain that retroceded the old French colony of Louisiana to France in exchange for the "Kingdom of Etruria," an enlarged Tuscan state to be created for the son-in-law of the king of Spain. He then took advantage of the Peace of Amiens, signed on October 1, 1801, to dispatch a French army, commanded by his brother-in-law General Charles Leclerc, to reconquer Santo Domingo and pave the way for the occupation of Louisiana, which would serve as the granary for the French Empire in the Western Hemisphere.

9. Peterson, p. 702.
10. Bradford Perkins, *The First Rapprochement: England and the United States, 1795–1805* (Philadelphia, 1955), pp. 106–10.
11. Brant, IV, p. 63.

An Interlude of Peace, 1801–1802

Within three months of Jefferson's inauguration, word reached the president and the secretary of state that Louisiana had been ceded. "You have probably heard the rumour," Madison informed Wilson Cary Nicholas, "of a cession of Louisiana to France, by a late and latent Treaty with Spain. . . . The subject engages our attention, and the proceedings deemed most suited to the complexity of the case, and the contrariety of interests and views involved in it, will be pursued."[12]

Jefferson and Madison agreed that the replacement of weak Spanish control by an energetic French policy under the dictatorial and antirepublican Bonaparte would bring the two nations into daily collisions that might force a closer connection between the United States and Great Britain. "The day that France takes possession of New Orleans," Jefferson wrote in a private letter to the American minister in France, ". . . we must marry ourselves to the British fleet and nation."[13]

Shortly after Jefferson wrote this letter, Madison learned that the French army in Santo Domingo had bogged down, a victim of black rebels and yellow fever, and he informed the president that instead of a quick French victory, "a protracted if not a doubtful warfare" was more likely, forming "a very powerful obstacle to the execution of the [Louisiana] project."[14] Through the remainder of the year, the president and the secretary of state followed a program of watchful waiting, biding their time for negotiation but never deviating from the position Madison had adopted in 1780, when he first wrote the American demand for a free port at the mouth of the Mississippi.

While the French project in the New World was sputtering, the Spanish governor at New Orleans, by his arbitrary action, irritated Jefferson so much that the president resorted to undiplomatic language in his complaint to the secretary of state: "Indeed I wish we could once get the European powers to give to their diplomatic representatives here such provisional authorities as would enable them to controul the conduct of their governors in whatever relates to us. We are too far from Europe to dance across the ocean for attendance at their levees whenever these pigmy kings in their colonies think proper to injure or insult us."[15]

The "pigmy kings" of the Barbary powers continued their "bickerings" with the United States in 1802, with Morocco joining Tripoli briefly in levying war on American commerce.[16] "Hostility is a less evil than so degrading an abandonment of the ground rightfully taken by us," Madison argued, and he pressed for sending additional naval vessels to the Mediterranean, despite the

---

12. JM to Wilson Cary Nicholas, July 10, 1801, in *PJM* (SS ser.), I, p. 394. Also see JM to TJ, Sept. 23, 1801, above.

13. TJ to Robert R. Livingston, Apr. 18, 1802, in L. and B., X, pp. 312–15, and Malone, IV, pp. 249–61.

14. JM to TJ, May 7, 1802, below, and JM to Robert R. Livingston, cited in Brant, IV, p. 78.

15. TJ to JM, Aug. 30, 1802, below.

16. See JM to TJ, Aug. 20, 1802, below.

rising costs that threatened the administration's economy drive.[17] Jefferson sided with Madison and the secretary of the navy in overriding Secretary of the Treasury Gallatin's objections. Indeed, the president concluded, "if peace with Morocco does not take place this year, I should think it proper that we should undertake forming a permanent league of the powers at war, or who may from time to time get into war[,] with any of the Barbary powers."[18]

Until he could confirm "that we are no longer on a footing of amity with Morocco," Jefferson debated whether to send the annual tribute, which included gun carriages as gifts to the pirates, or to send additional warships to make war on them. He delayed writing the emperor, he confessed, "because when one has nothing to write about it is difficult to find the end to begin at." But ten days later, the president concluded that "the demand of the emperor of Morocco is so palpably against reason and the usage of nations that we may consider it as a proof either that he is determined to go to war with us at all events, or that he will always make common cause with the Barbary powers when we are at war with any of them." If peace could not be restored with Morocco, Madison suggested that "neither of the frigates in the Mediterranean in a condition to remain ought to be recalled. I should prefer," he told Jefferson, "if circumstances admitted, that the force there ought rather to be increased."[19]

Jefferson's decision to use force against the pirates in the Mediterranean reflected the views he had formed fifteen years earlier. Although he continued the payment of tribute to Algiers, Tunis, and Morocco under treaties negotiated during the Washington and Adams administrations, he thought that these payments and those by his predecessors were wasted. "There is no end to the demand of these powers, nor any security in their promises," he concluded. "The real alternative before us is whether to abandon the Mediterranean or to keep up a cruise in it, perhaps in rotation with other powers."[20] As he told Madison, "Tho' armed by Congress to employ the frigates largely, it was in confidence we would not do it lightly."[21]

Nor did the president and the secretary of state take their tasks lightly. Both spent long hours each day at their desks, pouring over dispatches and personally penning detailed replies, setting a demanding administrative routine at the beginning of the Republican "revolution." "It keeps me from 10 to 12 and 13 hours a day at my writing table," Jefferson told his son-in-law, "giving me an interval of 4 hours for riding, dining and a little unbending."[22]

17. JM to TJ, [Aug. 14, 1802,] below.
18. TJ to JM, Aug. 23, 1802, below. TJ favored "a liberal attention . . . to the interests of Sweden in the Mediterranean"; see Gardner W. Allen, *Our Navy and the Barbary Corsairs* (Boston, 1905), pp. 88–124.
19. See TJ to JM, July 30, 1802, below, Aug. 6, 1802, below, Aug. 9, 1802, below, and Aug. 16, 1802, below, and JM to TJ Aug. 14, 1802, below.
20. TJ to Wilson Cary Nicholas, June 11, 1801, in Ford, IX, pp. 264–65.
21. TJ to JM, Aug. 30, 1802, below.
22. TJ to Thomas Mann Randolph, Nov. 16, 1801, cited in Cunningham, p. 251.

The Letters

Madison to Jefferson

[Washington Dec. 10, 1801]

J. M. hav^g recieved notice this afternoon of the opp^y by a packet, has hastily written to Mr King. The President will please to read it and return it as soon as possible, that if approved, it may be got into the Mail tonight, with^t which the opp^y will be lost.
Thursday night.

Madison to Jefferson

[Washington] Dec. 24, [1801]

J. Madison's respectful compliments to the President
It appears that the Sec^y of State, the Sec^y of the Treasury, and the Attorney General were app^d commiss^{rs} to settle with Georgia,[1] by their names, but with their official titles annexed. On the resignation of Col. Pickering, Mr Marshall was app^d *in his room,* No resignation of his Commission for the Georgia business being referred to or implied. It seems to have been understood, that altho' these public offices were app^d as private individuals, these Commissions ceased with their official characters, and consequently the three Commissions are at present vacant.

Jefferson to Madison

Washington Dec. 29, 1801

Having no confidence that the office of the private secretary of the President of the US. will ever be a regular and safe deposit for public papers or that due attention will ever be paid on their transmission from one Secretary or President to another, I have, since I have been in office, sent every paper, which I deem mearly public, and coming to my hands, to be deposited in one of the offices of the heads of departments, so that I shall never add a single

---

1. In 1798, Georgia agreed to appoint state commissioners to negotiate with a federal commission for the transfer of that state's western land claims, which led to an agreement on Apr. 24, 1802.

paper to those now constituting the records of the President's office; nor, should any accident happen to me, will there be any papers in my possession which ought to go into any public office. I make the selection regularly as I go along, retaining in my own possession only my private papers, or such as, relating to public subjects, were meant still to be personally confidential for myself. Mr Meredith the late treasurer in obedience to the law which directs the Treasurer's accounts to be transmitted to remain with the President, having transmitted his accounts, I send them to you to be deposited for safe keeping in the Domestic branch of the office of Secretary of State, which I suppose to be the proper one. Accept assurances of my affectionate esteem and high regard.

TH: JEFFERSON

Jefferson to Madison

Washington Dec. 29, 1801

circular

DEAR SIR

To compleat the roll of governmental officers on the plan inclosed will give the departments some serious trouble; however it is so important to present to the eye of all the constituted authorities, as well as of their own constituents, and to keep under their eye, the true extent of the machine of government, that I cannot but recommend to the heads of departments to endeavor to fill up each, their portions of the roll as compleatly as possible and as early too, that it may be presented to the legislature.[2] Health and affectionate respect.

TH: JEFFERSON

P. S. As the Postmaster general has a part to perform, will you instruct him accordingly? I inclose a spare copy of the papers which you can hand him.

Madison to Jefferson

Washington [Dec. 1801]

Salaries and Compensations to the Secretary of State,
his Clerks, and the offices, acting
in connection with the Department of State.

Department of State

James Madison, Secretary, annual salary, by the ball, which will expire on the 3rd. March next, $5,000, after which it will be 3500

2. TJ sent the roll to Congress on Feb. 17, 1802. For the tabular compilation of officers and employees in the executive branch, see Noble E. Cunningham, Jr., *The Process of Government under Jefferson* (Princeton, 1978), pp. 325–27. For a complete list of employees with their compensation, see *ASP, M,* I, pp. 260–319.

For the hire of clerks of whom at present he has at present six, viz. Jacob Wagner, Christopher S. Thom, John C. Miller, Stephen P. Calonton, William Crawford, and Daniel Brent, there is provided by law $5950, in addition to which there was appropriated for the present year 15 per cent. making together $6842.50; for the last quater the said clerks were compensated at the rate of (per annum) 5350.00

Minister to Foreign Countries

Rufus King, to London, Salary per annum	9000
His private Secretary	1350
Robert R. Livingston, to Paris	9000
Thomas Sumter jr. his Secretary of Legation	1350
Charles Pinckney, to Madrid	9000
John Graham, his Secretary of Legation	1350

Consuls

Richard O'Brien, Consul General at Algiers	4000
William Eaton, Consul at Tunis	2000
James L. Cathcart, ditto to Tripoli	2000
James Simson, ditto at Morocco	2000

Note. None of the other Consuls receive Salaries, but they are allowed a commission in their lawful disbursements, not exceeding five per cent.

Agents

George W. Erving, Agent at London for managing claims in prize cases	2000
Fulwar Skipwith, Agent at Paris for same purpose	2000
David Lenox, Agent at London for the relief of Seamen	3000

William Savage, Agent at Jamaica, for the same purpose, a commission of five per cent. on his disbursements

Commissioners under the 7th. article of the treaty of Amity etc. with Great Britain

Christopher Gore and William Pinkney @ £1500 Stl. each and half the salary of Mr. Trumbull the fifth Commissioner at the same rate,—together—	$16,650

Madison to Jefferson

[Washington 1801?]

Opinion on the powers of special
U. S. diplomatic emissaries.

Gouverneur Morris was appointed to London by a letter from Genl. Washington to enquire into the objections to the execution of the treaty of peace and on what terms G. Britain would enter into a treaty of commerce. Mr. M. was expected to be in London at or near the time when the letter would arrive there. I once enquired to the Auditor's office out of what fund he was compensated, but was informed that it did not appear he had any allowance. I conjectured however that the answer was given before due search was made.

John Q. Adams was ordered from the Hague to London to exchange the ratifications of the Br. treaty. He was allowed his expenses.

Samuel Sitgreaves, one of the Commissioners under the 6th. article of the Br. treaty, was sent to London to assist Mr. King in stating and removing the difficulties which had occurred at the Boards.

I do not find upon record, after the slight search I have made, that his allowances are specified, but I think I cannot be mistaken in stating them to be a continuance of his salary as Commissioner and repayment of his expenses.

Mr. Dawson's mission [to France] is to[o] fresh in memory as not to need a statement.

In our barbary affairs, frequent instances have occurred of special agencies and powers in their nature diplomatic being vested in persons holding consular commissions, such as the appointment of Joel Barlow by an arrangement between Messrs. Monroe and Humphreys to assist in conducting the Barbary negotiations, in consequence of which he exercised personally and by substitution very important and costly diplomatic functions.

Messrs. Eaton, O'Brien and Cathcart were authorized by the President to negotiate alterations in the treaty with Tunis in pursuit of which Eaton and Cathcart proceeded to that city and executed that charge. The case of Mr. Davis at Tunis, without any commission, is well understood.

The expenses of the barbary negotiations was paid or payable out of the funds appropriated for that purpose.

Jefferson to Madison

[Washington 1801?]

A commission of Judge of the orphan's court of Alexandria to be made out for George Gilpin.

Th. J.

Jefferson to Madison

[Washington 1801?]

William Bellinger Bullock
Joseph Welscher
Edward Stebbins
John Postal Williamson

} All of Savanna, to be Commissioners of bankruptcy for Georgia

Madison to Jefferson

Washington Jan. 11, 1802

SIR,

I have the honor to lay before you an estimate of the sum necessary to be appropriated for carrying into effect the Convention between the United States of America and the French Republic of the 30th of Sept. 1801. I have the honor to be, Sir, Your most Obt Sert.

JAMES MADISON

ENCLOSURE

[Estimate of the expenses necessary for carrying into effect the convention between the United States of America and the French republic]

For captures made prior to the date of the treaty, on which no final condemnation had then passed, and of which the property was brought into the United States,	$137,770
For captures made subsequent to the date of the treaty,	70,351
For captures, where the property was not brought into the United States nor any condemnation had,	122,156
For cases of capture not at present known, and for a possible excess of the indemnities to be paid, above the estimate; say,	19,723
	$350,000

NOTE. The sum of two thousand dollars per annum, to cover the allowance to an agent at Paris, to perform the office of soliciting the claims for restitution under the convention, has been included in the general estimate for the service of the year 1802.

The repairs put upon the corvette Berceau, before her delivery to the French republic, are not included in the above estimate: they amounted to $32,839 54.

Jefferson to Madison and Mrs. Madison

[Washington] Jan. 26, 1802

Th: Jefferson requests the favor of Mr. Mrs. Madison's and family's company to dinner the day after tomorrow at half after three oclock.

Madison to Jefferson

Washington Feb. 16, 1802

SIR

I have the honor to enclose a letter from the Secretary of the Treasury to me, together with the documents accompanying it, containing an account of the monies drawn out of the Treasury under the several appropriations made for defraying the expenses incident to the intercourse with the Mediterranean powers, and statements of the credits obtained or claimed at the Treasury by the persons to whom they were advanced.

It would have been very desireable to separate the whole amount expended into the several subordinate heads of expense, intimated in the close of the Secretary's letter: but apprized of your wish to communicate, as soon as possible, such information as that letter affords, I forbear to detain it, especially as an opinion of the present scantiness of materials to effect the separation referred to, does not encourage the hope of its being rendered perfect. With the highest respect, I have the honor to be, Sir, Your most obed. servt.

JAMES MADISON

Madison to Jefferson

Washington Feb. 25, 1802

The Secretary of State has the honor to lay before the President of the United States, copies of the following documents, viz.

A Schedule containing a statement of the suits, in the Circuit Court for Maryland, ending with November term last.

A similar statement of suits in the District Court for Kentucky, ending with March term last.

A certificate of the Clerk of the Circuit Court for West Tennessee (and who was the Clerk of the late District Court for Tennessee) respecting the suits in the Courts of the United States within that State.

The two last mentioned papers are intended as corrections of the document referred to in your Message to Congress at the opening of the present session, as containing a statement of the suits in the Courts of the

An Interlude of Peace, 1801–1802

United States: and the first mentioned Schedule to supply an omission in it.

This occasion being adapted to the purpose, the Secretary takes leave to mention some other imperfections of the document referred to in the Message.

In Massachusetts 14 common Law suits being omitted at October term 1797, the whole number of common law suits should be 244 instead of 230; the aggregate of all the suits, 323 instead of 320; and the number of suits decided, discontinued, dismissed and not prosecuted 282 instead of 283.

In Virginia, the aggregate should be 2162 instead of 2048; and the number decided, discontinued, dismissed and not prosecuted 1831 instead of 1717.

In North Carolina the aggregate should be 629 instead of 495, and the number decided, discontinued, dismissed and not prosecuted 495 instead of 361.

And in South Carolina the aggregate should be 882 instead of 1143 and the number decided, discontinued, dismissed and not prosecuted 621 instead of 571.

None of the above variations affect the whole number of causes stated to be depending in either of the Districts except that of Kentucky, to which an addition of 21 is made by the second statement received: but Maryland adds to the whole 69 of such causes. That the aggregate is not materially varied is also apparent from the annexed recapitulation.

It would be unnecessary to explain with minuteness how these errors originated; it is sufficient to observe that they arose partly from inexact statements returned to this Office by the Clerks of the Courts, and partly in analyzing and adding the numbers contained in the returns and transcribing the result. All which is respectfully submitted.

JAMES MADISON

Recapitulation of the suits in the circuit courts of the United States, and the district courts for Maine, Kentucky, and Tennessee.

	Instituted.	*Depending.*
New Hampshire,	114	7
Rhode Island,	275	10
Massachusetts,	323	41
Maine,	9	3
Connecticut,	354	38
Vermont,	278	64
New York and Albany,	106	—
New Jersey,	104	14
Eastern district of Pennsylvania,	1,061	174
Western district of Pennsylvania,	none	none
Delaware,	163	16
Maryland,	279	69
Kentucky,	870	246

	Instituted.	Depending.
Eastern district of Virginia,	2,162	331
Western district of Virginia—not completely organized.		
North Carolina,	629	134
South Carolina,	495	261
Georgia,	897	147
Districts of E. and W. Tennessee,	*239	†74
District of Ohio—not organized.		
	8,358	1,629
Former recapitulation made,	8,276	1,539
Difference,	82	90

*There is reason to suppose this number exceeds the truth, but how much is uncertain.
†This number includes eleven new suits, brought between April term, 1801, and 10th July following.

Jefferson to Madison

[Washington] Feb. 26, 1802

TH: J. TO J.M.

Will you see if the inclosed is right, and make any alterations in it you think for the better? particularly is the expression *lately recieved* true? or should the word *lately* be left out?[3]

Madison to Jefferson

[Washington Feb. 26, 1802]

The word *lately* is true as it refers to the returns of Maryland and Kentucky—that from the former being an *original* statement—that from the latter a corrective one. The message seems unexceptionally proper.

3. In his first annual message to Congress on Dec. 8, 1801, TJ had relied on statistics, compiled by JM, relating to the number of cases instituted or pending in U.S. courts since 1789; see TJ to JM, Nov. 12, 1801, above. One commentator calls it "a highly inaccurate and hastily prepared statement"; see Ellis, p. 41. After receiving a corrected tabulation from JM on Feb. 26, 1802, TJ sent Congress the new totals, listing 8,358 cases instituted, 82 more than the original total, and 1,629 pending, 90 more than the earlier count; see *ASP, M,* I, p. 320. His purpose was to cast doubt on the expansion of the federal judicial system under Adams and pave the way for the repeal of the Judiciary Act of 1801. JM's reply of Feb. 26, 1802, below, was written at the bottom of TJ's request.

Madison to Jefferson
Washington Mar. 29, 1802

The Secretary of State, to whom has been referred by the President of the United States a Resolution of the House of Representatives of the 23d Inst., requesting the President to communicate to that House such information as he may have received relative to the Copper mines on the South side of Lake Superior, in pursuance of a Resolution of the 16th. April 1800, authorising the appointment of an Agent for that purpose, begs leave to lay before him the Copy of a letter of the 24th. September 1800, from the late Secretary of State to Richard Cooper Esqr., of Cooper's Town in the State of New York, appointing him an Agent, in pursuance of the last mentioned Resolution—and the Copy of one from the Attorney General of the United States, of the 30th. March 1801, at that time acting as Secretary of State, to the said Richard Cooper, signifying to him that as the Resolution in question contemplated an execution of the work and a report thereof, in time for the consideration of Congress at its next Session, and this had not been done, it was thought necessary to suspend the further prosecution of it, and that he was accordingly to do so. The Secretary also begs leave to lay before the President copies of sundry other letters on this subject, which, together with those mentioned above, serve to give a view—of the whole transaction, so far as this Department has had an agency in it, tho' they do not afford the particular information required by the Resolution referred to the Secretary of State, by the President. All which is respectfully submitted.

JAMES MADISON

Madison to Jefferson
Washington Apr. 16, 1802

The Secretary of State, to whom has been referred, by the President of the United States, a resolution of the Senate, passed on the 12th day of this month, requesting the President to cause to be laid before the Senate the amount of claims preferred under the seventh article of the treaty of amity, commerce, and navigation with Great Britain, and of the sums awarded by the commissioners, and paid by the British Government, and a statement of the principles adopted by the said commissioners in their proceedings under the said article, thereupon respectfully submits the following report to the President:

That, agreeably to an estimate made on the 9th of May, 1798, by Samuel Cabot, Esq., at that time an agent of the United States, under the seventh article of the said treaty, the claims preferred under that article amounted to the sum of one million two hundred and fifty thousand pounds sterling. The document herewith submitted to the President, containing a general statement of moneys received on awards of the commissioners, will show the sums awarded by them, and paid by the British Government, under the article in question of the said treaty.

It does not appear, from any researches which the Secretary has been able to make, that the precise principles on which the commissioners have proceeded, can be otherwise deduced than from the awards made in the several cases which have been decided. Any statement of them in detail is presumed not to be within the intention of the resolution.

All which is respectfully submitted:

JAMES MADISON.

Statement of moneys received by awards of the Commissioners acting under the seventh article of the British Treaty.

	£	s.	d.	£	s.	d.
Received by Samuel Bayard, on eleven cases				21,744	13	5¼
Of this sum, was taken to repay the public advances, which appear to have been made only in these three cases, viz:						
Farmer, Osborn,	243	4	9			
Sally, Choate,	395	10	6			
Rising Sun, Rositer,	4	9	6	643	4	9
Net sum received by claimants,				21,101	8	8¼
Received by Samuel Williams, on seventeen awards,				36,857	0	11½
From this deducted for public advances which, appear to have been paid only in these cases, viz:						
Fair Lady, Lillibridge,	25	0	0			
Lydia, Rinkers,	20	0	0			
Bethia, Lothrop,	201	1	0			
	46	19	0			
	25	0	0			
Sally, Burchmore,	243	19	6			
Two Brothers, Calley,	251	17	5	813	16	11
Net sum received by claimants,				36,043	4	0½
Received by claimants from Mr. Bayard,				21,101	8	8½
From Mr. Williams,				36,043	4	0½
Twelve awards, amount received by private agents,				36,610	8	11
These are all that have been paid to private agents, so far as I can discover from documents in my possession, nor does Mr. Williams know of any more.						
Total received by claimants, on the awards of the commissioners.—Forty cases,				93,755	1	7¼

Amount of public advances,	1,457	1	8
And in one case, viz: Eliza, Borrowdaile, where proceeds were received by private agent,	25	0	0
	1,482	1	8

It would appear that, of the whole forty cases, decided as above, public advances have been made only in nine; upon each of those cases it is probable there were also several expenses paid by the claimants: these, as well as what was paid in the remaining thirty-one cases, as also in seventeen which were dismissed by the Board, it is impossible to ascertain.

London, December 1, 1801.　　　　　　　　　　　　George W. Erving, *Agent*.

It appeared, by the statment of my predecessor, that only seventeen cases were dismissed by the Board; but, by a particular examination of documents furnished me by the clerk of the Board, I find that there were, in fact, thirty-one cases dismissed.

December 1.　　　　　　　　　　　　　　　　　　　　　　　　G. W. E.

Madison to Jefferson

Washington Apr. 18, 1802

The Secretary of State respectfully reports to the President the information requested by the Resolution of the House of Representatives, of the 8th of January last relative to Spoliations committed on the Commerce of the United States, under Spanish authority; and also, relative to the imprisonment of the American Consul at Saint Jago de Cuba.

This Report has been delayed longer than was wished: but the delay has been made unavoidable by the sickness and absence of the Chief Clerk in this Department, who had partially gone through the necessary researches, and could most readily have compleated them.

JAMES MADISON

Madison, Albert Gallatin, and Levi Lincoln to Jefferson

Washington Apr. 26, 1802

SIR:

We have the honor to enclose a copy of an agreement entered into between the commissioners of the United States and those of Georgia, in pursuance of the act, entitled "An act supplemental to the act, entitled An act for an amicable settlement of limits with the State of Georgia, and authorizing the establishment of a Government in the Mississippi territory."

The nature and importance of the transaction have induced the insertion of a clause which renders it necessary that the subject should be communicated to Congress, during their present session.

We have the honor to be, very respectfully, sir, your obedient servants,

JAMES MADISON,
ALBERT GALLATIN,
LEVI LINCOLN.

The President of the United States.

Articles of agreement and cession, entered into on the twenty-fourth day of April, one thousand eight hundred and two, between the commissioners appointed on the part of the United States, by virtue of an act, entitled "An act for an amicable settlement of limits with the State of Georgia, and authorizing the establishment of a Government in the Mississippi territory" and of the act supplemental to the last mentioned act, on the one part, and the commissioners appointed on the part of the State of Georgia, by virtue of an act, entitled "An act to carry the twenty-third section of the first article of the constitution into effect," and of the act to amend the last mentioned act, on the other part.

Article I. The State of Georgia cedes to the United States all the right, title, and claim, which the said State has to the jurisdiction and soil of the lands situated within the boundaries of the United States, south of the State of Tennessee, and west of a line, beginning on the western bank of the Chattahoochee river, where the same crosses the boundary line between the United States and Spain; running thence up the said river Chattahoochee, and along the western bank thereof, to the great bend thereof, next above the place where a certain creek or river, called "Uchee," (being the first considerable stream on the western side, above the Cussetas and Coweta towns) empties into the said Chattahoochee river; thence, in a direct line, to Nickajack, on the Tennessee river; then crossing the said last mentioned river; and thence, running up the said Tennessee river, and along the western bank thereof, to the southern boundary line of the State of Tennessee; upon the following express conditions, and subject thereto; that is to say:

First, That out of the first net proceeds of the sales of the lands thus ceded, which net proceeds shall be estimated by deducting, from the gross amount of sales, the expenses incurred in surveying, and incident to the sale, the United States shall pay, at their treasury, one million two hundred and fifty thousand dollars to the State of Georgia, as a consideration for the expenses incurred by the said State, in relation to the said territory; and that, for the better securing as prompt a payment of the said sum as is practicable, a land office, for the disposition of the vacant lands thus ceded, to which the Indian title has been, or may hereafter be extinguished, shall be opened within a twelvemonth after the assent of the State of Georgia to this agreement, as hereafter stated, shall have been declared.

Secondly, That all persons who, on the twenty-seventh day of October, one thousand seven hundred and ninety-five, were actual settlers within the territory thus ceded, shall be confirmed in all the grants legally and fully executed prior to that day, by the former British Government of West Florida, or by the Government of Spain, and in the claims which may be derived from any actual survey or settlement made under the act of the State of Georgia entitled "An act for laying out a district of land, situate on the river Mississippi, and within the bounds of this State, into a county, to be called Bourbon," passed the seventh day of February, one thousand seven hundred and eighty-five.

Thirdly, That all the lands ceded by this agreement to the United States shall, after satisfying the above mentioned payment of one million two hundred and fifty thousand dollars to the State of Georgia, and the grants recognized by the preceding condition, be considered as a common fund, for the use and benefit of the United States Georgia included, and shall be faithfully disposed of for that purpose, and for no other use or purpose whatever provided, however, that the United States, for the period, and until the end of one year after the assent of Georgia to the boundary established by this agreement shall have been declared, may, in such manner as not to interfere with the abovementioned payment to the State of Georgia, nor with the grants hereinbefore recognized, dispose of or appropriate a proportion of the said lands, not exceeding five millions of acres, or the proceeds of the said five millions of acres, or of any part thereof, for the purpose of satisfying, quieting, or compensating, for any claims other than those hereinbefore recognized, which may be made to the said lands, or to any part thereof. It being fully understood that, if an act of Congress making such disposition or appropriation shall not be passed into a law within the abovementioned period of one year, the United States shall not be at liberty thereafter to cede any part of the said lands on account of claims which may be laid to the same, other than those recognized by the preceding condition, nor to compensate for the same; and in case of any such cession or compensation, the present cession of Georgia to the right of soil over the lands thus ceded or compensated for shall be considered as null and void, and the lands thus ceded or compensated for shall revert to the State of Georgia.

Fourthly, That the United States shall, at their own expense, extinguish, for the use of Georgia, as early as the same can be peaceably obtained, on reasonable terms, the Indian title to the country of Talassee, to the lands left out by the line drawn with the Creeks, in the year one thousand seven hundred and ninety-eight, which had been previously granted by the State of Georgia, both which tracts had formally been yielded by the Indians; and to the lands within the forks of Oconee and Ocmulgee rivers; for which several objects the President of the United States has directed that a treaty should be immediately held with the Creeks; and that the United States shall, in the same manner, also extinguish the Indian title to all the other lands within the State of Georgia.

Fifthly, That the territory thus ceded shall form a State, and be admitted as such into the Union, as soon as it shall contain sixty thousand free inhabitants, or at an earlier period, if Congress shall think it expedient, on the same conditions and restrictions, with the same privileges, and in the same manner, as is provided in the ordinance of Congress of the thirteenth day of July, one thousand seven hundred and eighty-seven, for the Government of the Western territory of the United States; which ordinance shall, in all its parts, extend to the territory contained in the present act of cession, that article only excepted which forbids slavery.

Art. II. The United States accept the cession above mentioned, and on the conditions therein expressed: and they cede to the State of Georgia whatever claim, right, or title, they may have to the jurisdiction or soil of any lands lying within the United States, and out of the proper boundaries of any other State, and situated south of the southern boundaries of the States of Tennessee, North Carolina, and South Carolina, and east of the boundary line hereinabove described, as the eastern boundary of the territory ceded by Georgia to the United States.

Art. III. The present act of cession and agreement shall be in full force as soon as the Legislature of Georgia shall have given its assent to the boundaries of this cession: provided, that the said assent shall be given within six months after the date of these presents; and provided, that Congress shall not, during the same period of six months, repeal so much of any former law as authorizes this agreement, and renders it binding and conclusive on the United States: but if either the assent of Georgia shall not be thus given, or if the law of the United States shall be thus repealed, within the said period of six months, then, and in either case, these presents shall become null and void.

In faith whereof the respective commissioners have signed these presents, and affixed hereunto their seals. Done at the city of Washington, in the District of Columbia, this twenty-fourth day of April, one thousand eight hundred and two.

JAMES MADISON, [L. S.]
ALBERT GALLATIN, [L. S.]
LEVI LINCOLN, [L. S.]
Commissioners on the part of the United States.

JAMES JACKSON, [L. S.]
ABRAH. BALDWIN, [L. S.]
JOHN MILLEDGE, [L. S.]
Commissioners on the part of the State of Georgia.

J. Franklin, *Senator of the United States for North Carolina,*
Samuel A. Otis, *Secretary of the Senate of the United States,*   Witnesses.
John Beckley, *Clerk of the House of Representatives of the United States.*

Jefferson to Madison

[Washington] Apr. 29, 1802

Th Jefferson asks the favor of the heads of the Departments to examine and consider the charges of Col. Worthington against Govr. St. Clair with the answer of the latter and the documents in support or in validation of the charges; and to favor him with their opinion in writing on each charge distinctly, whether "established" or "not established," and whether those "established" are sufficiently weighty to render the removal of the Governor proper

TH JEFFERSON.[4]

---

4. For the criticism by Thomas Worthington and the Republicans in territorial Ohio of Arthur St. Clair, governor of the Northwest Territory, see Alfred Byron Sears, *Thomas Worthington: Father of Ohio Statehood* (Columbus, 1958), pp. 79–93, and Andrew R. L. Cayton, *The Frontier Republic: Ideology and Politics in the Ohio Country, 1780–1825* (Kent, Ohio, 1986), pp. 72–80.

Jefferson to Madison

[Washington] May 5, 1802

TH: J. TO J. MADISON

I think it is Dean Swift who says that a present should consist of something of little value, and which yet cannot be bought for money. I send you one strictly under both conditions. The drawing was made by Kosciuszko for his own use, and the engraving also I believe.[5] He sent me four copies, the only ones which have come to America. The others I give to my family, and ask yourself and M̄rs̄ Madison to accept of the one now sent.

Madison to Jefferson

private

Washington May 7, 1802

DEAR SIR

M.ͬ Lear arrived here the day before yesterday a few minutes after your departure. He confirms the information as to the imprisonment of Cap.ͭ Rodgers and Davidson.[6] Inclosed is a copy of le Clerc's explanation on the subject, of my letter to Pichon with his answer, and of a letter to M.ͬ Livingston which I shall forward to Philad.ᵃ this morning, that it may overtake the dispatches already in the hands of M.ͬ Dupont. The other information given by M.ͬ Lear is that the state of things in S.ͭ Domingo augurs a protracted if not a doubtful warfare, that the ports abound, and superabound with every accessary, that money has lately arrived both from France and from the Havanna, that the irritations between the French and the Americans are occasioned by faults on both sides, and that there probably is a mixture of antirepublican venom in those of the French. From a confidential communication made to him, it appears that the idea in the Army is that Republicanism is exploded, that Monarchy must be forced, and that Buonaparte is the proper successor to the cashiered dynasty, but that it is the party etc. not the nation that wishes this revolution.

M.ͬ Smith is not yet returned from Baltimore. M.ͬ Gallatin left us this morning. Gen.ˡ Dearborn will go for a few days to Philad.ᵃ on Monday or tuesday.

I inclose a recommendation of A Collector for Amboy, that in case you

---

5. For the portrait of TJ by Tadeusz Kościuszko, see Alfred L. Bush, "The Life Portraits of Thomas Jefferson," in *Jefferson and the Arts: An Extended View,* ed. William Howard Adams (Washington, 1976), pp. 45–48. See also Edward P. Alexander, "Jefferson and Kościuszko: Friends of Liberty and of Man," *PMHB* 92 (1968): 87–103.

6. Leclerc seized American cargoes to supply French troops in Santo Domingo. For his treatment of Rodgers and Davidson, see Brant, IV, pp. 76–81.

decide in your absence, all the candidates for that vacancy may be before you. With the most respectful attachment I remain yours

JAMES MADISON

Jefferson to Madison

Monticello May 9, 1802

TH: J. TO J. MADISON.

The road through Ravensworth is rendered absolutely impassable for a four wheeled carriage by a single change made lately by one of the Mr Fitzhughs in his plantation. You must not therefore attempt it, but go on to Fairfax C. H. and there turn off to Songster's. Bull run is now passed at an excellent ford, and the hills by a great deal of work have been made quite good. The road between Elkrun church and Norman's ford is bad, as it generally is, but it will be better by the time you come on. All the rest is fine.

I think Mr Wagner should be instructed to take decisive measures for having a sheet of the laws printed daily till done. A person direct from Kentucky, tells me a person of known credit had reached there from New Orleans which he left March 6, and affirms a French governor had arrived there, without troops, and had taken possession of the government. He was so positive that if we have nothing later from thence, I should think it possible.[7] Adieu affectionately.

Madison to Jefferson

private

Washington May 11, 1802

DEAR SIR

I have nothing new since my last either from Europe or the W. Indies. The elections in N. York are not yet finally known. It is suggested that the efforts of the minority have prevailed beyond the apprehensions of the majority. Cabot accepts his mission on the terms proposed to him. I have just recd. letters from Erving shewing the turn which the affair took in London, to be such as was conjectured. The compatibility of his agency with an Assessorship was denied by the Commissioners and made the ground of rejecting him. The Controversy ended in his relinquishing his pretensions, and of course he is prepared for the ground on which we have placed him. He is evidently sound with King and the B   , but professes a superiority to all personal considera-

---

7. The report was false.

tions when in the way of his public duty. I inclose a solicitation for office according to the wish of the candidate. I inclose also a letter from S. Sayre which will deserve no other attention than as it brings to view the necessity of thinking of proper persons for the service he recommends himself for.[8] I am at a loss for proper characters myself, and I do not find that any are particularly in the view of those more capable of pointing them out. My horses are not yet arrived. Y.^{rs} always most respectfully and affectionately

JAMES MADISON

Yrujo has just delivered me a long narration of a riot in Philad.^a which ended in an insulting destruction of a Spanish flag in the harbour, for which he claims due reparation to the honor of his Master. He suggests that a reward be proclaimed for the apprehension of the offenders, which of itself will heal the wound[?], if the offenders can not be traced. I shall consult Mr Lincoln in the case. My first thought is that a letter be written to Govr McKean, on the idea of its not being within federal cognizance.[9]

Jefferson to Madison

Monticello May 14, 1802

TH. J. TO J. MADISON

    I wrote you on the 9th but whether the new post had got into motion at that time I know not. It related chiefly to the roads. Yesterday I recieved yours of the 7th. and 11th. It really seems doubtful whether the conduct of Le Clerc proceeds from the extravagance of his own character, or from a settled design in his government. So many things lately wear the latter appearance that one cannot be without suspicion. Your letter to Livingston will give them an opportunity of developing their views. The fact respecting the insult on the Spanish flag deserves enquiry. I believe the fray began by one of the crew knocking down a peace officer, whereupon the sheriff and posse took the whole crew, and had them committed, taking possession of the ship in the meanwhile for safekeeping. This I have collected from the newspapers and some anonymous letters sent me on the occasion. If the state government will take it up, it will be best to give it that direction.

    Sayre's letter is highly impudent.

    I recieved from your office some commissions to sign. Such as you had signed I now return to the office. The others I have thought it would be shortest to inclose to yourself to be left at Orange C. H. Affectionate esteem and respect.

8. For Sayre's unsuccessful campaign for a government post, see John R. Alden, *Stephen Sayre: American Revolutionary Adventurer* (Baton Rouge, 1983), pp. 189–91.

9. Don Carlos Martínez d'Yrujo was the Spanish minister to the United States. He was the son-in-law of Governor McKean of Pennsylvania.

Madison to Jefferson

[Washington May 21, 1802]

Extract of a letter from Wm Eaton to James Leander Cathcart, dated May 21st 1802.[10]

"It is favorable to us here that the Captures of Tunisian merchant-men Complained of, have all been done by the Swedes. This Circumstance relieves me from incalculable perplexities with this Gov^t.

Lieutenant Sterett assures me that seven days ago the Bashaw Cissi Mohammed was at Malta waiting the arrival of our Squadron—Captain McNeill signifies to me by letter of the 17th Inst, that this is by arrangement between them."

Jefferson to Madison

Monticello May 24, 1802

DEAR SIR

Our postrider having mistaken his day, brought us no mail on Thursday last. Yesterday I recieved a double one. In it were the inclosed letters. Those from Dupont and Granger are forwarded for your perusal, and I will recieve them again when I see you at your own house. The one from Dallas to yourself on Jackson's case I recieved from Mr Brent: the recommendation of the Attorney of the district, and of the jury, and the circumstances of the case seem to be a good foundation of pardon, which I would wish to have issued therefore unless you disapprove it. They do not mention when the execution is to be; but probably it would be well to lose no time lest the pardon should get too late. If your clerks have it in readiness I will sign it on my arrival in Washington which will be in six days from this time. I will be with you on Thursday or Friday at farthest, unless rain prevents, and take your commissions for Washington. I have forbidden any mail to be forwarded to me later than the one recieved yesterday. Present my best respects to the ladies, and accept my affectionate salutations yourself.

TH: JEFFERSON

---

10. Eaton was consul at Tunis. Cathcart, who had been consul at Tripoli, escaped to Leghorn, Italy, after the war with Tripoli began in 1801. Lieutenant Andrew Sterett commanded the *Enterprise* and Captain Daniel McNeill the *Boston* in the Mediterranean. For Eaton's attempts to place "the Bashaw Cissi Mohammed," Hamet Karamanli, on the throne of Tripoli, from which he had been removed by his usurping brother, see Louis B. Wright and Julia H. Macleod, *The First Americans in North Africa: William Eaton's Struggle for a Vigorous Policy against the Barbary Pirates, 1799–1805* (Princeton, 1945).

Madison to Jefferson

Washington June 19, 1802

Opinion on charges exhibited against Governor St. Clair, by Colonel Worthington

The President having called on the heads of Departments for their opinion in writing whether certain charges made by Col. Worthington against Governor S? Clair be or be not established; and whether such as are established, be sufficiently weighty to render the removal of the Governor proper? the Secretary of State respectfully submits his opinion as follows;

Charge 1. Forming new Counties and fixing their seats of justice by his sole authority.

The fact is admitted and its legality contended for. The reasons given are unsatisfactory to the judgment of the Secretary of State; but he cannot undertake to say that they have so little plausibility as to preclude a difference of opinion.

Ch. 2^d. "Putting a negative on useful and necessary laws."

It appears that the Negative had been exercised in many cases, and in some probably, where the laws would have been salutary. The discretion however involved in the case of this power, requires stronger and clearer abuses of it, than are shewn, to justify a hasty or rigorous condemnation.

Ch. 3. "Taking illegal fees."

In the case of ferry licences the charge seems undeniable. In that of tavern licences, an act is found in the code of the Territory, authorizing the fees, but there is reason to believe that a latitude of construction or rather an abuse of power in which the Gov? himself participated, was employed in the adoption of the Act. With respect to the Marriage fees, it is affirmed that a legal authority also exists. As the volume of laws however referred to on this point cannot be consulted, no opinion will be given either on the tenor or the origin of the Act.

The taking of illegal fees is in itself an abuse of power, of so deep a die, as, unless mitigated by powerful circumstances, to justify a rigorous proceeding against the author of it and as to be altogether excusable under no circumstances.

Ch. 4. "Negativing a bill abolishing fees, and passing one giving the Gov? a sum meant by the Legislature as a substitute for them."

This charge involves questions which it would be difficult to unravel, and perhaps improper to decide.

Ch. 5. "Concurring in the plan of changing the Constitutional boundaries of the proposed states N. W. of the Ohio."

The fact is certain, and the attempt of the Governor to explain [are] obscure and unsatisfactory.

Ch. 6. "Appointing his son Attorney General, by an illegal commission during good behaviour." The fact is admitted without being palliated by the explanations given by the Governour.

Ch. 7. "Attempting to influence certain judiciary proceedings."

This charge as far as it can be judged of by what appears, can not be considered as established. In one at least of the transactions referred to the conduct of the Governor was justified by that of the Justices.

Ch. 8. "Appointing to offices requiring residence in one county, persons residing in another."

The fact here may be true, and conduct of the Gov.r free from blame. If the offices were incompatible, the second appointment might be made on the presumption that the first could be relinquished. To judge fully of the case it ought also to be known what the law of the territory is with respect to the residence and deputyship of the different officers.

Ch. 9. "Neglecting to organize and discipline the Militia."

This charge is not established.

Ch. 10. "Hostility to republican form of Government."

The circumstances under which expressions to this effect are understood to have been used, and under which the evidence of them appears to have been collected, render it improper to lay stress on this charge.

Upon the whole, it appears that altho' the conduct of the Governor has been highly culpable in sundry instances, and sufficiently so in the particular cases of Commissioning his son during good behaviour, and in what relates to fees, to plead for a removal of him from his office, yet considering the revolutionary and other interesting relations in which he has stood to the public, with other grounds on which some indulgence may be felt for him, it is the opinion of the Secretary of State, that it will be proper to leave him in possession of his office under the influence of a salutary admonition.[11]

JAMES MADISON

Jefferson to Madison

[Washington] July 19, 1802

Henry Warren (of Mass) to be Collector of Marblehead v. Samuel R. Gerry
William Lyman of Massachusetts to be Collector of Newbury port, vice Dudley A. Tyng

11. On behalf of the president, JM sent Governor St. Clair a letter of reprimand on June 23, 1802; it is printed in Randolph C. Downes, "Thomas Jefferson and the Removal of Governor St. Clair in 1802," *Ohio Archeological and Historical Publications* 36 (1927): 71–72. For a thoughtful unraveling of the political, social, cultural, and geographical tensions on the frontier, see Andrew R. L. Cayton, "Land, Power, and Reputation: The Cultural Dimension of Politics in the Ohio Country," *WMQ* 47 (1990): 266–86.

William R. Lee of Massachus: to be collector of Salem and Beverley vice Joseph Hiller
Peter Muhlenburg of Pensylvania to be Collector of vice George Latimer
John Page of Virginia to be Collector of Petersburg v. William Heth.
Tenche Cox of Pensylvania to be Supervisor of Pensylvania v. Peter Muhlenburg.

Perhaps it may be better to inclose blank commissions to Mr. Gallatin in all the cases, to be filled up and sent out by him, all together, on his return.

TH: JEFFERSON

Madison to Jefferson

Washington July 22, 1802

DEAR SIR

On consultation with the Secretary of the Navy, it has been concluded that the public service will be favored by sending the ship the General Greene, with the provisions and gun-carriages destined for the Mediterranean, instead of chartering a private vessel for the occasion. It has occurred also that as the period at which an annual remittance to Algiers will become due, will arrive before the ship will get to that place, it may be found proper that another thirty thousand dollars should be sent as an experimental measure for avoiding the stipulated and expensive tribute of Stores.[12] Should the substitute be accepted, it will be a saving to the U. States. Should it be rejected, time will be gained for the other remittance. I have written to Mr Gallatin on the subject, and requested him to make preparation for having the money ready in case your approbation should be signified to him. You will recollect no doubt that if a letter from you to the Emperor of Morocco, should be decided on, as a companion to the gun carriages, it must be forwarded in time for the sailing of the Ship. May I ask the favor of you to leave it open for the perusal of Mr Sampson, that it may serve as an explanation and instruction to him in the case.[13] The ship will probably sail from this place in about 20 days from this date.

I observe in the papers that one of the Commiss^{rs} of Bankruptcy for Philad^a has been taken off by the fever. I have not heard lately from M^r. Wagner, but think it not improbable that the vacancy will attract the attention of himself and his friends, and that it may be properly bestowed on him, if no particular claim to it be in the way. With the most respectful attachment I remain Dr Sir Yrs.

JAMES MADISON

12. Under the treaty of 1795 with Algiers, the annual tribute in naval stores was three years in arrears. JM proposed a cash payment instead; see Allen, pp. 56–57, and Marshall Smelser, *The Democratic Republic, 1801–1815* (New York, 1968), p. 58.
13. "Mr. Sampson" was James Simpson, consul at Algiers; see Wright and Macleod, pp. 111, 127.

Jefferson to Madison

Monticello July 30, 1802

DEAR SIR

Your's of July 22. came to hand on the 25th the day of my arrival here. I think the proposition to tender another 30,000. D. to Algiers a very judicious one, and have therefore written to Mr Gallatin to take measures in conjunction with yourself to make the remittance by the General Greene. I have not yet written to the Emperor of Morocco, because when one has nothing to write about it is difficult to find the end to begin at. I will sketch something before next post, and inclose it for your attention with a blank sheet signed, over which they may write the letter.

You are now I presume in the middle of your journey and must have had a good deal of rain. This will be directed to await in Orange for your return. Present me respectfully to the ladies, and be assured of my affectionate esteem.

TH: JEFFERSON

P.S. Not knowing whether the inclosed letters have passed through your hands I forward them to you instead of returning them to the office from whence I recieved them.

Madison to Jefferson

Washington July 30, 1802

DEAR SIR

I inclose several letters for you put into my hand by Mr Pichon, with some communications of his own, which are proper to be forwarded along with them. Inclose[d] also a letter from M^r. Jones at Gaudaloupe, and two others declining commissions of Bankruptcy.

My departure from this place, suspended for a day by preparations for the Mediterranean business stated in my last, has since been prevented by the lameness of a horse which obliges me to leave him behind and to purchase another. Having been this long detained, and understanding that Mr Gallatin will be here to night or tomorrow, I am inclined to submit to a little further delay for the chance of seeing him. By Sunday at farthest I hope to be on the road, and in about 10 days from that date to be at home.

Nothing has occurred at this place since you left it which deserves mention. With the most respectful attachment I remain yours

JAMES MADISON

Jefferson to Madison

Monticello Aug. 1, 1802

Th: Jefferson returns the inclosed commission, with his signature, to the Secretary of state's office. He presumes it is to be delivered to Mr̄ Gallatin. A commission is wanting for John Selman of the North Western territory,[14] as Commissioner in the subject of Symmes's lands in the room of Goforth resigned.[15]

He begs leave to observe too that Mr̄ Scott's commission as Marshal of Virginia, signed July 8. but dated July 1. had not been recieved by him on the 25th of July, and that the business of the offices is at a stand.

Jefferson to Madison

Monticello Aug. 6, 1802

Dear Sir

I now return you the letters of Mr̄ Pichon, and of Jones; also those of Van Poleran and Thos Sumter. The letter to be written to Van Poleran should be so friendly as to remove all doubt from the Batavian government that our suppression of that mission proceeds from any other motive than of domestic arrangement and economy[16]

I inclose you a draught of a letter to the Emperor of Morocco, which make what it should be and send to your office to be written over the blank I have signed.[17] A letter from Mr Short dated Norfolk July 24. gives me reason to expect him here hourly. Present my respects to the ladies, and accept assurance of my constant and affectionate esteem and respect.

Th: Jefferson.

---

14. John Selman was appointed commissioner of Symmes's land claims in Ohio; see JM to TJ, Oct. 18, 1802, below.

15. William Goforth of Cincinnati was elected president pro tem of the Ohio constitutional convention; see Sears, p. 94.

16. Sumter was secretary of legation in France. As part of his economy drive, TJ had reduced the foreign missions of the United States to Great Britain, France, and Spain. R. G. Polanen was minister of the Batavian Republic to America; see Malone, IV, p. 102, and *PJM* (SS ser.), I, pp. 480-81.

17. TJ's draft letter to the emperor of Morocco is too illegible to transcribe.

Jefferson to Madison

Monticello Aug. 9, 1802

DEAR SIR

The inclosed letter from Mr. Simpson our Consul in Marocco was forwarded to me from your office by yesterday's post. The demand of the emperor of Morocco is so palpably against reason and the usage of nations that we may consider it as a proof either that he is determined to go to war with us at all events, or that he will always make common cause with the Barbary powers when we are at war with any of them. His having ordered our Consul away is at any rate a preliminary of so much meaning that the draught of the letter I had forwarded you for him, as well as the sending him the gun carriages, are no longer adapted to the state of things. On this subject I should be glad of your opinion, as also of what nature should be the orders now to be given to our officers in the Mediterranean.

The Boston frigate is expected to return: there will then remain in the Mediterranean the Chesapeake, Morris, the Adams, Campbell, and the Constitution, Murray; one of which perhaps would have been recalled, as two are thought sufficient for the war with Tripoli, especially while Sweden cooperates In the present state of things would it not be adviseable to let the three remain or does it seem necessary to send another?

I inclose you a letter from Richard Law dated New London. I suppose he may be the District judge and should be answered. The proper notification of the Commrs. of bankruptcy to the judges seems to be their commission exhibited by themselves to the court, as is done in the case of a Marshal, the only other officer of a court appointed by us. Accept assurances of my constant and affectionate esteem.

TH: JEFFERSON

P.S. A letter from Capt Morris informs us he had gone over to Tangier, but hed not yet had any communication with the government: but that he should absolutely refuse the passports.

Madison to Jefferson

Orange Aug. 11, 1802

DEAR SIR

I reached home just before dark this evening, after the most fatiguing journey I ever encountered, having made the tour I proposed over the mountains, and met with every difficulty which bad roads and bad weather could inflict. As this must be at the Court House early in the morning, I have only time to inclose you some dispatches from Mr. Livingston which I recd. the night before I left Washington, and decyphered on the journey, with some others which I found here on my arrival and have but slightly run over. The inclosed patent may be sent with your signature to the office without returning thro' my hands. Your favor of the 30th ult: I also found here on my arrival. Yrs with respectful attachment

JAMES MADISON

Jefferson to Madison

Monticello Aug. 12 [13], 1802

TH: J. TO MR MADISON

The post having made it night before his arrival yesterday and my mail extraordinarily voluminous, I have been able to read and now return you the inclosed papers only. Mr Livingston's shall come by the next mail. I do not like this mistake of Capt McNeil's, and fear it will be very embarrassing.[18] Other dispatches oblige me to close here with assurances of my affectionate esteem and respect.

Madison to Jefferson

Orange Aug. 14, 1802

DEAR SIR

I rec^d last evening your two favors of the 9 and 13th [19] Before I left Washington I wrote to Simpson approving his refusal of passports in the cases required by the Emperor, and understood that the instructions from the Navy Dept. to Comodore Morris were founded on the same principle. It is to be inferred therefore that we are no longer on a footing of amity with Morocco, and I had accordingly retained your letter, and concurred in the provisional step taken for stopping the gun carriages.[20] As it is possible however that things may take a more favorable turn in that quarter, I have desired Mr Brent to forward, with the quickest attention, whatever accounts may arrive, and

18. Captain Daniel McNeill had transported Robert R. Livingston, the new American minister to France, then reported to the American squadron dispatched to the Mediterranean to blockade Tripoli. TJ learned that he had reportedly engaged a Tunisian squadron, although Tunis was a friendly nation. He was relieved of his command and later dismissed from service on Oct. 27, 1802, under the naval reduction act of 1801; see Dudley W. Knox, ed., *Naval Documents Related to the United States Wars with the Barbary Powers, 1785–1807,* 7 vols. (Washington, 1935–48), II, pp. 233, 257, 307.

19. *PJM* has redated TJ's letter of Aug. 12 as Aug. 13.

20. The emperor of Morocco had requested passports to send grain through the American blockade to Tripoli. When these were refused, Morocco declared war on the United States on June 17, 1802; see Wright and Macleod, p. 111.

also to let me know the day, as soon as it can be done, on which the General Greene is to sail. Should it be found that peace with Morocco can not be preserved or restored without the concession demanded by him, my opinion decides that hostility is a less evil than so degrading an abandonment of the ground rightfully taken by us.[21] As a consequence of this opinion, I concur in that which your quere intimates, that neither of the frigates in the Mediterranean in a condition to remain ought to be recalled. I should prefer if circumstances admitted, that the force there ought rather to be increased, and with the greater reason as the blunder of McNeil may endanger the footing on which we stand with Tunis. May it not be proper, as soon as authentic information of this occurrence comes to hand, that something of a healing nature should be said from the Gov^t to the Bey, in addition to the explanations which will no doubt be made from the naval Commander.

The letter from Law the District Judge of Connecticut, was preceded by one to me from a Comiss^r of Bankruptcy at Boston, representing the objection of Davis the D. Judge there, to proceed without such a notification as is proposed by Law. Viewing as you do the Commission itself, as the most authentic of all notifications, I did not give any answer, presuming that the scruples of the Judge would yield to further reflection. The letter from Law shall be answered to the effect which you suggest.

Among the papers now inclosed are applications from the Mech^{ts} of Boston and Philad^a for an interposition in behalf of their vessels etc. detained in Spanish America. This is a delicate subject, and must be so handled as well for their interest as for the honor and dignity of the Gov^t I suppose they may be told that Spain does not object to a Board for deciding on our complaints and that Mr P. will endeavor to give it latitude eno' for all just cases. The sending a public ship, as suggested by Fitzsimmons, seems to have no rational object and to be of an injurious tendency. Y^{rs} with respectful attachment

JAMES MADISON

Jefferson to Madison

Monticello Aug. 16, 1802

DEAR SIR

I now return all the papers recieved from you by this post, except those relating to our affairs at Buenos Ayres.

M^r. Boudinot's provisional measures for taking care of the mint on shutting it up appear entirely proper. The 5th alone seems imperfect, as I do not see why a positive conclusion should not have been formed as to the care of the bullion, the most important part of the charge. I presume the bank of the US. would have recieved that as well by the papers, keys etc. However it is too late

---

21. Peace with Morocco was restored in Aug. 1802; see *ibid.*

to say any thing on that subject, and I have no doubt that effectual care has in the end been taken.[22]

With respect to Commissioners of bankruptcy at Fredericksburg, you are sensible that if we were to name Commissioners over the whole face of every state in the Union, these nominations would be infinite, and 99 in 100. of them useless. To draw some line therefore was necessary. We have accordingly confined our nominations to the greater commercial towns only. I am sensible however that bankruptcies may happen in small towns and even in the country, and that some regulation should be provided to check what may be had more conveniently than to that of referring the case to the commissioner of the large cities who may be distant. What would you think of writing a circular instruction to the district attornies of the US. to notify us when any case arises too distant for the established comm^{rs} to take up, sending us at the same time a recommendation of proper persons to act in that case, whom, or such others who may be preferred, may be commissioned to act in that special case? He should inform the judges of this instruction so that they will apply to him to procure commissioners in any cases before them. The delay of this will be trifling. Or will you propose anything you may like better? Accept assurances of my affectionate esteem and respect.

TH: JEFFERSON

Jefferson to Madison

Monticello Aug. 17, 1802

DEAR SIR

I now return you the papers forwarded by the merchants of Philadelphia and Boston on the subject of the wrongs they complain of at Buenos Ayres. I observe that they have not gone into a developement of the subject. Two or three cases are opened with some degree of detail; as to the rest we have only a list of the ships for which our interference is claimed. But in cases where a hair's breadth of difference makes the thing right or wrong, full details are requisite. I think we ought to be informed what was the extent and what was to constitute the termination of the indulgences granted to Neutrals under which these vessels have ventured there: as also the specific circumstances under which every vessel went. Spain had a right, according to the practice established, to give to those indulgences what duration she thought proper, only not withdrawing them so suddenly and on such short notice as to make the indulgence a trap to catch our vessels. Reasonable time should be allowed them to settle their affairs. On this last ground only can we urge any claim against Spain. We should therefore have a precise statement of the case of

---

22. In Apr. 1802, the House passed a bill to abolish the mint as part of the Republican economy drive, but the bill failed to pass in the Senate; see George Adams Boyd, *Elias Boudinot, Patriot and Statesman, 1740–1821* (Princeton, 1952), pp. 241–42.

every vessel, and strike off from the list all those which cannot be brought within the limits of the indulgences, urging, under the authority of the government, only such cases as are founded in right. There seems to have been a great breach of faith by individuals, Spanish subjects: for these their courts should be open to us: or perhaps these cases could be got before the Commn. proposed by Mr. Pinkney in the Algesiras depredations. I hazard these reflections that you may consider whether a detailed statement of cases should not be called for from the merchants, lest we should be committing ourselves in behalf of mere interloping and contraband adventures. Accept assurances of my constant affection and respect.

TH: JEFFERSON

Madison to Jefferson

Orange Aug. 18, 1802

DEAR SIR

Your favor of the 16th came duly to hand with the papers to which it referred. I now forward others rec^d by the last mail.

I have signified to Mr Sumpter that his resignation was acquiesced in, and have used a language calculated to satisfy him that he retains the good opinion of the Executive.[23] What is to be said to Mr Livingston on his request that he may app^t a private Secretary, and fill provisionally consular vacancies? Considering the disposition of a Secretary of Legation, acting as private Sec^y to view himself on the more important side, and of the Minister to view and use him on the other, it is to be apprehended, that there may be difficulty in finding a successor to Mr Sumter who will not be likely to be infected with the same dissatisfaction. I am not aware that the other proposition of Mr L. is founded in any reason claiming equal attention. Yours with respectful attachment

JAMES MADISON

Madison to Jefferson

[Orange] Aug. 20, 1802

DEAR SIR

The inclosed letters will shew the object of the Bearer Mr Baker. From his conversation I find that, placing Bourdeaux and Gibralter out of view, he wishes to be app^d as Consul, to Minorca, where, he says a Consul will be

---

23. Sumter's official reason for resigning as secretary of legation was his refusal to become Livingston's personal secretary, but he told the minister he was unwilling to mix "the public and private agency of claims" against France. For differing interpretations, see Brant, IV, pp. 95, 101, and George Dangerfield, *Chancellor Robert R. Livingston of New York, 1746–1813* (New York, 1960), pp. 382–83.

admitted, since that it is again under the Spanish Government, and where he observes a Consul may be of use to the U. States, particularly during our bickerings with the Barbary powers. I find from his conversation also that he is a native of Minorca, whilst under British Gov.^t but that he has been in the U. States about six years and is an American Citizen. Nothing has passed between us that can influence his expectations or calculations, of the result of his pursuit. Always with affectionate respects Y.^{rs}

JAMES MADISON

Jefferson to Madison

Monticello Aug. 23, 1802

DEAR SIR

Yesterday's post brought me, as I suppose it did you, information of the Emperor of Morocco's declaration of war against us, and of the capture of a merchant vessel of ours (the Franklin, Morris) off cape Palos by a Tripoline as is said in a new York letter, but a Moroccian as I am in hopes from the place, and the improbability of a Tripoline being there.[24] The letter to the Emperor and the gun carriages are of course to be stopped, and I have approved a proposition from Mr Smith to send another frigate which he says can be ready in two weeks, in addition to the New York. These with those already there, and the Swedes,[25] are surely sufficient for the enemies at present opposed to us. These are the only alterations made in the arrangements we had agreed on. I have desired Mr Smith to recommend a liberal attention in our officers to the interests of Sweden in the Mediterranean, and if peace with Morocco does not take place this year, I should think it proper that we should undertake forming a permanent league of the powers at war, or who may from time to time get into war with any of the Barbary powers. Accept assurance of my constant and affectionate esteem.

TH: JEFFERSON

Madison to Jefferson

[Orange] Aug. 25, 1802

DEAR SIR

Yours of the 23.^d has been duly rec.^d Mr Brent[26] had informed me that copies of the letters from the Mediterranean had been sent to you by Mr Smith, and therefore I did not send the originals by express. The declaration of

---

24. For the capture of the *Franklin* by a Tripolitanian corsair, see Allen, pp. 111–12.

25. Sweden was at war with Tripoli and cooperated with the American squadron in blockading Tripoli; see *ibid.*, p. 108.

26. Daniel Brent was a clerk in the State Department; see *PJM* (SS ser.), I, pp. 349–50.

a rupture by the Emr. of Morocco, put me at a loss what to say to Simson on the subject of the gun carriages, and how to decide as to the letter you left with me. As the event however was anticipated when you were here, as a necessary consequence of Morris's concurrence [?] in the refusal of Simson, and of the instructions sent from the Navy Dept. by the Adams, I concluded that the gun carriages ought still to go, subject to the discretionary and conciliatory use of Morris and Simson, and have written to Simson on that supposition. I was the more inclined to this opinion, by the anxiety and the ideas of the Secretary of the Treas^y. Reasoning in a similar manner, I sent on to Mr Brent your letter to the E. of M. with an erasure of the last paragraph, and some little alteration besides, with a request that the Secretaries present would decide what ought to be done; and have in my letter to Simson given him like discretion over it, as I gave him with respect to the gun carriages. In pursuance now of your decision agst sending either, I shall write by the next mail to have a postscript added by Mr Brent signifying that change that has taken place. Nothing appears in the communications to me, relative to the affair between the Boston and the Tunisian cruisers. In my letters to Cathcart Eaton OBrian and Simson, I have spoken of it as report believed here, and have fashioned my instructions accordingly particularly those to Eaton. I find from Gavino's letter to me, that the capture of the American vessel, was ascribed to a pirate, and not to a cruiser of Tripoli or Morocco. With most respectful attachment I remain Y^{rs}

JAMES MADISON

Jefferson to Madison

Monticello Aug. 27, 1802

DEAR SIR

I inclose you a letter from W. Hampton and Fontaine Maury on the subject of apprehensions that the negroes taken from Guadaloupe will be pushed in on us. It came to me under the superscription of Mr Brent, so may not have been seen by you. Would it not be proper to make it the subject of a friendly letter to M. Pichon. Perhaps Govr. Clinton should also recieve some mark of our attention to the subject.[27]

I received under the same cover a letter from Israel Smith to you on the subject of Commrs. of bankruptcy for Vermont. I had been expecting a General recommendation from him and Bradley. I therefore make this the occasion of reminding them of it.

Of the blank commissions of bankruptcy which came to me with your signature, I signed and sent two to Mr Brent to be filled with the names of

27. General Leclerc sent eighteen or nineteen shiploads of black leaders, including Toussaint l'Ouverture, from Santo Domingo to France in June 1802. Two vessels in this fleet carried Negroes and mulattoes from Guadaloupe; see Shelby T. McCloy, *The Negro in France* (Lexington, Ky., 1961), pp. 106–8.

Wm. Cleveland and [blank] Killam of Salem.[28] The rest you will recieve herewith.

I have no further news from the Mediterranean. Genl. Dearborn has been unwell and quitted Washington. Gallatin not well and gone to New York. His 2d. clerk sick, Miller also, and Harrison unwell and gone away. There seems to be much sickness begun there. Mr Short left Washington on Saturday last, and comes here by the way of the Berkley springs. Pichon does not come. Accept assurances of my affectionate esteem and respect.

TH: JEFFERSON

Madison to Jefferson

[Orange, ca. Aug. 29, 1802]

DEAR SIR

Yours of the 27. came duly to hand. I had rec^d the letter from W. Hampton and Fr. Maury. I had proposed to observe to them, that the case fell wholly within the State laws, and that it was probable the several Governors would be led to attend to it by the correspondence between the Mayor of N.Y. and the French consul and Admiral. It had occurred also that it might not be amiss for the President to intimate to the Sec^y of the Treasury, a circular letter from that Dept. to the officers of the Customs, calling on their vigilance as a co-operation with the State authorities in inforcing the laws agst the smugling of slaves. As a further measure a letter may be written to Mr Pichon as you suggest, and whatever else you think proper from me shall also be attended to.

I inclose several land patents which you will please to send, with your sanction, to Mr Brent; also a letter from Govr McKean and another from James Yard; to which is added a letter from a Mr Cochran, which gives some ideas and facts which will repay the perusal. I need not observe that the answer to his inquiry will transfer his hopes of patronage from the fed^l Gov^t to the State Gov^{ts}

What is decided on the subject of our Tob^o by Leiper, and what are to be the prices and paym^{ts} if he is to burn it? Y^{rs}. always with respect and attachment

JAMES MADISON

Jefferson to Madison

Monticello Aug. 30, 1802

DEAR SIR

Your two favors of the 25th. and blank were recieved yesterday; and all the papers forwarded me are returned by this post. I must pray you to direct an

---

28. William Cleveland and Mr. Killam were appointed commissioners of bankruptcy for Salem, Massachusetts; see JM to TJ, [Oct. 18, 1802,] below.

extract from so much of Mr Clarke's letter as relates to the dissatisfaction of the Chickasaw chief with the Spanish governor, to be taken and sent to Genl. Dearborn to whom I have written on the subject.[29] Mr Clarke's letter cuts out a considerable job for us, but the several matters are so important that I think a detailed instruction should be sent to Mr Pinckney. Indeed I wish we could once get the European powers to give to their diplomatic representatives here such provisional authorities as would enable them to controul the conduct of their governors in whatever relates to us. We are too far from Europe to dance across the ocean for attendance at their levees whenever these pigmy kings in their colonies think proper to injure or insult us.

Be so good as to order a commission from your office for John Shore of Virginia as successor to Heath at Petersburg.[30] The stile of the office must be obtained from the treasury: also a commission for Abraham Bloodgood for Albany,[31] for which Mr Gallatin will apply.

On the suggestion in the newspapers that Simpson is recalled to Marocco, I have suggested to Mr Smith, *if it be known certainly before the John Adams sails,* to consider whether we ought not to retain her. Tho' armed by Congress to employ the frigates largely, it was in confidence we would not do it lightly. I wish you to consider whether it would not be useful, by a circular to the clerks of the federal courts, to call for a docket of the cases decided in the last twelvemonth, say from July 1. 1801. to July 1. 1802. to be laid before Congress. It will be satisfactory to them, and to all men to see how little is to be done by the federal judiciary, and will effectually crush the clamour still raised on the suppression of the new judges. I think it a proper document to be furnished annually, as it may enable us to make further simplifications of that corps. I have written to Mr Gallatin respecting the Guadaloupe negroes. Accept assurances of my affectionate friendship.

TH: JEFFERSON

P. S. I before mentioned to you what I had written to Lieper on the subject tho. I have recd no answer. The same letter said something of his disappointment of office. I suspect it has not pleased him. I own I have thought something of his silence, were it only on account of the use Callender is making of his name.[32]

---

29. Daniel Clark, Jr., was an American merchant in New Orleans who served at various times as consular agent; see Arthur P. Whitaker, *The Mississippi Question, 1795–1803: A Study in Trade, Politics, and Diplomacy* (New York, 1934), p. 143.

30. John Shore became collector for Petersburg, Virginia; see JM to TJ, [Oct. 18, 1802,] below.

31. Abraham Bloodgood became surveyor for the port of Albany, New York; see *ibid.*

32. For the dating of this postscript, see *PJM* (SS ser.), I, p. 127.

Madison to Jefferson

[Orange] Sept. 1, 1802

DEAR SIR

The mail not having returned from Milton when my messenger left the Court House on Monday evening, and it having been inconvenient to send thither at any time since, I can not now acknowledge any favor which may have come from you since my last. Among the letters inclosed is one from Higginson seconding the application from Philad^{ia} for your patronage to a demand on the viceroy of the La Plata provinces. The measure as proposed seems to be inadmissable on several grounds, but I shall be glad to have your sanction if you think it proper, to a refusal. Yours with respectful attachment

JAMES MADISON

Jefferson to Madison

Monticello Sept. 3, 1802

DEAR SIR

Yours of the 1st was received yesterday. I now return the letters of Higginson Davis etc. praying that a public vessel may be sent to demand their vessels of the Viceroy of La Plata, indemnity for the detention and a full performance of existing contracts with the Spanish merchants of La Plata. It would certainly be the first instance of such a demand made by any government from a subordinate. Certainly we have never sent a ship on such an errand. I cannot also but regret the observations made in mine of the 17th [33] that among the papers sent you by the merchants there were but two or three cases so specified as that we could form any judgment about them, and even for these some very material confirmation was wanting to shew that they went under license, all commerce with a Spanish colony being primâ facie contraband. As to the other cases they named only the ships and masters, which cannot but excite some doubts of contraband. I see no reason for departing from the regular course and committing our peace with Spain by a vapouring demand of what, for any thing which has been shewn, may turn out to have been smuggling adventures. The merchants must pursue their own measures in the first place, and for such cases as they shall shew to have been contrary to right, we must aid them with our interposition with the Spanish government. In the mean time Mr Pinckney should be desired to look into the cases should they go there, satisfy himself of those which are right, ask redress for them, abandoning those evidently illicit: except indeed so far as sudden changes of their regulations may have entrapped a bonâ fide trader.

33. Letter not found.

I send you an answer from Lieper recieved yesterday. I suppose he meant this answer to my proposition as an answer to your's also, altho' the cases differed in a material circumstance. Accept my affectionate esteem and respect.

TH: JEFFERSON

Madison to Jefferson

[Orange] Sept. 3, 1802

DEAR SIR

I have duly rec^d yours of the 30th ult. with the several papers to which it refers. I have directed the commissions for Shore and Bloodgood to be made out, and have sent the extract from Clark's letter as you required to Genl. Dearborn. He had however been made acquainted with it, by Mr. Brent, before the letter was forwarded to me. May it not be as well to let the call for the Dockets be a rule of Congress, as there is no specific appropriation for the expence, and a regular call by the Ex. might not be regarded as within any contingent fund? To this consideration it may be added that the Ex. have no power over the Clerks of the Courts, and that some of them might refuse to comply from a dislike to the object. When the object was not known, there was a manifest repugnance in some instances. Your final determination in the case shall be pursued. I have thought also that it might be as well to postpone till the reassembling at Washington any general regulation with regard to the appointment of Commissioners of Bankruptcy; but shall in this case also cheerfully conform to your pleasure.

Mr Brent informs me that he has sent you copies of Eaton's letter of May 25-27. and Cathalan's[34] of June 10. It does not seem necessary that the communications of the former should be made the subject of further instructions till we receive further accts. from other sources. Thornton you will see is renewing the subject of the Snow Windsor. May he not be told that the remedy lies with the Courts, and not with the Ex. The absence of the vessel can no more be a bar to it, than the sale was. It seems proper however that the irregularity in sending the vessel out without the legal clearance should be prevented. The law is I believe defective on this point. The correspondent referred to in Steel's letter is, I take it, Mr Brown the Kentucky Senator. Yours with respectful attachment

JAMES MADISON

---

34. Stephen Cathalan, Sr., was the American commercial agent in Marseilles in 1787, and Étienne Cathalan is listed in 1802; see *PTJ,* XI, pp. 507-9, and *ASP, M,* I, p. 307. Étienne was probably the son of Stephen, Sr., who had shipped the Levant and Piedmont rice that TJ had arranged to smuggle out of Italy in 1787.

Jefferson to Madison

Monticello Sept. 6, 1802

DEAR SIR

Your's of the 3.ᵈ came to hand yesterday.[35] I am content that the questions relative to Commissioners of bankruptcy and dockets should remain until we meet: altho' I think there are reasons of weight for not leaving the latter for Congress to do, for that would be abandoning it. The repeal of that law[36] has been unquestionably pleasing to the people generally; and having led Congress to it, we owe to them to produce the facts which will support what they have done. It would rally the public opinion again to what is right, should that any where have been shaken by the volumes of misrepresentations which have been published, and shew we are not to be dismayed by any thing of that kind. Perhaps our directions may better go to the district attornies to procure the dockets. They have a right as individuals to demand them. I believe we need ask only the *cases determined* during the year. This would be very short indeed.

I do not sufficiently recollect the particulars of the Snow Windsor to be exact on that subject. But I know that I had not a doubt as to the justice of what we concluded before, nor do I see any thing in Mr Thornton's letter to create a doubt. We did our duty in ordering the vessel away. The delays which followed [were] such as the vigilance of no government can prevent: and the treaty at length placed her at liberty. If delays are to be paid for by a government, what have we not to demand from Great Britain? I think with you we should shew our sincerity by prosecuting for the deportation of the vessel without a clearance, as far as the laws justify.

I have written to Mr Smith to stop the John Adams. The war being returned to it's former state against Tripoli only, we should reduce our force to what had been concluded on as to that power, as soon as we learn the state of things with Tunis. In the mean time the New York will go on.

Mr̄ Steel's labours to shew he is agreeable to the Gov.ʳ shew pretty clearly the reverse, independent of the Governor's own evidence. Accept my affectionate esteem and respect.

TH: JEFFERSON

Madison to Jefferson

[Orange ca. Sept. 7, 1802]

DEAR SIR

Yours of the 6.ᵗʰ instant was duly brought by the last mail.

I inclose under cover to M.ʳ Brent, the answer to the Merch.ᵗˢ of Boston

---

35. Letter not found.
36. TJ referred to the repeal of the Judiciary Act of 1801.

and Philadᵃ, which if approved you will be so good as to seal and send on to him. I inclose also a letter from Mʳ Brent to me, for the sake of the explanation it gives relative to the consulate at Nante. If Mʳ Grant should not go, it is to be recollected that the vacancy there has been thought of for Mʳ Patterson whose appointment to l'Orient interferes with the situation of Mr. Vail.

Docʳ Thornton and his family are with us;[37] and I believe mean to pay their respects to Monticello before their return.[38] We shall ride up at the same time, if my absence from home should not be forbidden by circumstances which I am endeavoring to deprive of that tendency. With respectful attachment I remain Yours

JAMES MADISON

Jefferson to Madison

Monticello Sept. 10, 1802

DEAR SIR

Yours by yesterday's post is recieved. The letter to Higginson and others is entirely approved, and is sealed and forwarded to Mr̄ Brent. The Consulate at Nantes must be disposed of according to our former arrangement. I do not know whether the Mr Lynch recommended is the one who was living at Nantes when I was in France, or his son. Of that one there is something not favourable resting in my mind, altho' I cannot recollect the particulars.[39] But Patterson's claims are certainly superior.[40]

I recᵈ from Mr Brent extracts from the letters of Chancʳ Livingston and Sumpter concerning the resignation of the latter. I presume he does not wait for a formal permission, but suppose it had better be sent. I inclose you a commission of bankruptcy for your signature. It is to correct an error of having given a former one to a person of the same surname, for which this is now substituted. Mr̄ Brent reminds me of a parcel of blanks he sent for signature. I remember signing them, and sending them either to yourself or him.

We shall be very happy to see yourself, family, and Dʳ and Mrs Thornton here. The Govʳ is up at present; goes home on Thursday (16ᵗʰ) and returns on Tuesday (21st.). When you get to the fork of the road at Will Becks's, the other side of Milton, a turn of the road forces you to the river at Milton, and

---

37. For the Thorntons' visit to the Madisons, see Brant, IV, p. 44.

38. For the Thorntons' and Madisons' visit to Monticello, see Malone, IV, p. 166, and Jack McLaughlin, *Jefferson and Monticello: The Biography of a Builder* (New York, 1988), pp. 14–34.

39. TJ had met Anthony Lynch while on his tour through southern France in 1787. Lynch had pressed claims against Thomas Barclay, who served as consul to France, commissioner to Morocco, and agent for the state of Virginia between 1781 and 1787, resulting in Barclay's imprisonment for debt in France. TJ considered Barclay "an honest and honourable debtor" and Lynch and other creditors "the counterpart of Shylock in the play"; see TJ to JM, June 20, 1787, above. See also *PTJ*, XI, pp. 493–500, 552, 669–71, and Louis Gottschalk, *Lafayette between the American and the French Revolution, 1783–1789* (Chicago, 1950), p. 330.

40. William Patterson was vice consul at L'Orient, France; see *ASP, M*, I, p. 307.

when there it is better to cross there and come round along the public road on this side the river, my private one being hardly wide enough and safe for a carriage, altho' my waggons and carts do pass it. This adds a couple of miles to the length of the journey. With my best respects to the ladies accept assurances of my constant and affectionate friendship.

TH: JEFFERSON

P.S. I notify the offices at Washington that the post which leaves that place on the 24th. inst. is the last by which any thing should be forwarded to me here.

Madison to Jefferson

[Orange] Sept. 11, 1802

DEAR SIR

Yours of the 10th is duly rec^d. I answered by duplicates Mr Sumter's resignation as soon as it had been submitted to you. Mr Livingston's request that he may app^t a successor has not yet been answered. It is probable he will expect to know your determination in the first letter that may be written to him. The blanks of which Mr Brent reminded you, came to me from you some time ago, and were sent on to him with my signature.

You will recieve herewith two letters from Mr Livingston of May 28. and June 8th and one from Mr King of June 20th I am glad to find that Otto is to share in the negociations concerning Louisiana, because it is probable he may retain the original policy of France on that subject, and because his destination to this country gives him an interest in a policy that will be welcome to us. The arrival of Dupont also will be very apropos.[41] The reasoning of M^r. L. to the Spanish Minister, has a certain degree of force, but if not managed cautiously may commit us in other points of view.

We can not yet fix the day of our visit to Monticello. Yours as ever

JAMES MADISON

Jefferson to Madison

Monticello Sept. 13, 1802

DEAR SIR

I now return you the papers which came in your letter of the 11th. I am not satisfied that the ground taken by the Chancellor Livingston is advantageous. For the French government and the Spanish have only to grant him all he asks (and they will in justice and policy do that at once) and his mouth must

---

41. Pierre-Samuel du Pont de Nemours carried to Livingston JM's official instructions about Louisiana negotiations as well as TJ's private note that threatened an alliance with Great Britain if France persisted in its attempt to reestablish a presence in the Mississippi Valley; see Malone, IV, pp. 254–58.

be shut: because after-sought objections would come from him to great disadvantage. Whereas the true and solid objection remains in full force after they shall have the merit of granting all he asks.⁴²

Judge Law's letter can be nothing more than an effort to save himself from the appearance of retreating. The Commissioners will surely exhibit their appointments to him, in the expectation of being called into action. If they do not the District Attorney (according to what I propose) will on the application of the judge ask appointments from us.

I inclose you a letter from the Mayor of New York, who asks a guard or guards from us to prevent the French blacks from escaping into the country. If a guard to their hospital would suffice, that could be admitted under the provisions of the Quarantine law: and Genl. Dearborne (with whom I concur) seems disposed to this. I think therefore to leave to his discretion to order the guard. But I think it would be well that you should write a friendly explanation to Mr Pichon, to whom it might otherwise wear an unfriendly aspect. I cannot but view this case as still lying substantially within the police of the states, and that we have only small and incidental relations with it; viz, as within the cases of contraband or smuggling.

Colo. Monroe has in contemplation to carry his family down on Thursday, not to return. Mr Short and Bishop Madison arrived here yesterday. We shall hope to see you here before Monroe goes, as I think an interview with him would not be unuseful. Will you be pleased to order a commission for Wm. Carey to be collector of York vice Wm. Reynolds dead? Accept my affectionate salutations.

P.S. Return Livingston's letter to the War office.

Madison to Jefferson

[Orange] Sept. 15, 1802

DEAR SIR

I have duly rec^d. yours of the 13th I had been apprised of the application by the Mayor of N.Y. for a guard. Considering as you do, that the federal Gov^t have only an incidental connection with the case of the French Negroes, I have waited for more particular information concerning them, before writing to Pichon, who I learnt from Mr Brent, and also from himself, was exerting himself to get them away. His plan was to ship them to France, but he was at a loss for the means. I had my fears that if prematurely pressed on the subject, it might lead to applications for aid. The mail of tomorrow, I hope will bring me from Mr Brent an answer to some enquiring which will assist in framing a proper letter to him.

I am sorry to learn that Col. Monroe is so soon to leave Albemarle with

---

42. Dangerfield, pp. 331–36, summarizes Livingston's remarks to the Spanish minister about Louisiana.

his family. I had assured myself that I should see him on our visit to his neighborhood, as your letter intimated that he would not leave it till tuesday next. We propose to be with you, accompanied by D̲r̲ Thornton, his lady and her mother, on saturday evening, and still hope the opp.y may not be lost. It will add to the satisfaction to find Bishop Madison as well as M̲r̲. Short at Monticello. I shall direct a commission to be made out for Mr. Cary to take the place of M̲r̲. Reynolds. Yours as ever

JAMES MADISON

Jefferson to Madison

Monticello Sept. 17, 1802

DEAR SIR

I recieved yesterday your's of the 15th In the hope of seeing you here tomorrow I return no papers. I will pray you not to fail in your visit. I have rec̲d̲ a letter from M̄r̄ R. Smith disapproving of the countermand of the John Adams for reasons detailed; and one from Mr Gallatin disapproving of the original order for her sailing. (He had not then, Sep. 9. heard of the countermand) The vessel now awaits our decision, which I have delayed till the next post, in order to consult with you on the subject. This renders it interesting that you should preserve your purpose of coming tomorrow, when I shall be happy to recieve your's and D̲r̲ Thornton's families and friends. B̲P̲ Madison is gone. Col̲o̲ Monroe was to go off yesterday; but I have not heard whether his family is gone or not. If not, he will be back on Tuesday. But I rather expect they are gone. D̲r̲ Bache has broken up housekeeping, ready for his departure. Accept my affectionate salutations.

TH: JEFFERSON

Jefferson to Madison

Monticello, Sept. 27, 1802

DEAR SIR

Unexpected delays in getting my carriage ready will render it impossible for me to leave this till Thursday or Friday, probably Friday; and as you will be gone or going by that time, and we shall meet so soon in Washington, I shall not have the pleasure of seeing you at your own house, but get on as far as the day will let me. M̄r̄ Gallatin left N. York on the 21st and expected to be at Washington before the 30th My respects to the ladies and affectionate salutations to yourself.

TH: JEFFERSON

Jefferson to Madison

[Washington] Oct. 8 [?], 1802

Commissioners of bankruptcy for Vermont.
- Samuel Prentiss
- Darius Chipman
- Richard Skinner
- Mark Richards
- Reuben Atwater
- James Elliot
- Oliver Gallop

Commissions to be made out

TH. JEFFERSON

Also Commission for Robert [torn]kran to be Marshal of S. Carolina vice Charles Blockran resigned

TH. J.

Madison to Jefferson

[Washington Oct. 18, 1802]

Memorandum for the President of commissions issued from July 28 to date

Peter Muhlenberg,	Collector of the Customs for the District of Penns^a Comm^n dated	28 July 1802
William R. Lee,	Collector for Salem & Beverly—	31 July—
Daniel Bissell,	D^o for Massac—	11 Aug^t —
D^o D^o	Inspector of the Revenue for D^o	11th —
Joseph Farley	D^o Collector for the District of Waldoborough	} 25 Aug^t
D^o D^o	Inspector of the Revenue for D^o	
John Gibaut,	Collector for Gloucester	25 Aug^t.
George Wentworth,	Inspector of the Revenue for Portsmouth	} 25 Aug^t
D^o D^o	Surveyor for the same—— ——	
Joseph Wilson,	Collector for the District of Marblehead	} 25 Aug^t
D^o D^o	Inspector for the port of Marblehead	

An Interlude of Peace, 1801–1802

Ralph Cross,	Collector for Newburyport—	25 Aug.ᵗ
Abraham Bloodgood,	Surveyor for the Port of Albany	} 28 Aug.ᵗ
D.º D.º	Inspector for D.º	
John Shore	Collector for Petersburg	6 Sep.ᵗ
~~William Carey,~~	~~D.º for Yorktown~~	
	~~Virg.ʸ~~	~~10 Sep.ᵗ~~ (declined to accept)
Thomas Archer,	Collector for Yorktown—	11 Oct.
D.º D.º	Inspector of the Revenue for	
	D.º	11.ᵗʰ
Robert Anderson New,	Collector for the District of	
	Louisville Dated	11.ᵗʰ Oct.
Robert Anderson New,	Inspector of the Revenue for	
	the port of Louisville	11.ᵗʰ Oct.
~~Joseph Wood,~~	Register of the Land office at	
	Marietta—	26 Aug.ᵗ—
	Commissioners of Bankruptcy	
William Cleveland	for Salem in the District of	
——Killam	Massac.ᵗˢ— The two first	
Joseph Story	are dated the 27 Aug.ᵗ 1802	
	the latter 13 Sep.ʳ	
Tench Coxe,	Supervisor of the Revenue for	
	the District of Penns.ᵃ	July 28. 1802.
—— John Selman,	Com͞m͞r on Symme's land	
	Claims (permanent)	Aug.ᵗ
Note— Thomas Monroes	Com͞m͞n is dated	June 2.ᵈ 1802 (permanent).

Jefferson to Madison

[Washington] Nov. 18, 1802

Will you give the inclosed a serious perusal, and make such corrections, in matter and manner as it needs, and that without reserve, and with as little delay as possible, as I mean to submit it in like manner to the other gentlemen, singly first, and then together. The part respecting the treasury department is not yet prepared. A concluding paragraph is also to be added, when we see if any other matter is to be inserted.[43]

Jefferson to Madison

[Washington] Dec. 2, 1802

TH: J. TO MR. MADISON

Mr. Nimms the Commr. of bkrptcy appointed for Norfolk whose Christian name was left blank, is named "James."

---

43. For TJ's second annual message to Congress, delivered on Dec. 15, 1802, see Richardson, I, pp. 342–46.

Madison to Jefferson

Washington Dec. 21, 1802

The Secretary of State to whom the Resolution of the House of Representatives of the United States of the 17th. inst. was referred by the President, has the honor to enclose to him the letters and communications annexed from the Governor of the Mississippi Territory, the Governor of Kentucky and from Wm. E Hulings formerly appointed Vice Consul of the United States at New Orleans. In addition to this information on the subject of the Resolution, it is stated from other sources that on the 29th. of October American vessels from sea remained under the prohibition to land their cargo and that the American produce carried down the Mississippi could be landed only on paying a duty of 6 per cent with an intimation that this was a temporary permission. Whether in these violations of Treaty the officer of Spain at New Orleans has proceeded with or without orders from his Government, can not as yet be decided by any positive testimony, but it ought not to be omitted in the statement here made that other circumstances concur with the good faith and friendship otherwise observed by His Catholic Majesty in favouring a belief that no such orders have been given.

JAMES MADISON

Jefferson to Madison

[Washington ca. 1802]

A Commission of Judge of the orphan's court of Alexandria to be made out for George Gilpen

TH. J.

29

"THIS AFFAIR OF LOUISIANA," 1803

"Every eye in the U. S. is now fixed on this affair of Louisiana," President Jefferson informed Robert R. Livingston, American minister in France. Writing in the spring of 1802, Jefferson thought that "perhaps nothing since the revolutionary war has produced more uneasy sensations through the body of the nation."[1] Dispatching this letter by Pierre-Samuel du Pont de Nemours, who was returning to France on business but agreed to serve as an intermediary in the Louisiana negotiation, the president informed his friend and courier that Louisiana, "this speck which now appears as an almost invisible point in the horizon, is the embryo of a tornado which will burst on the countries on both sides of the Atlantic and involve in it's effects their highest destinies."[2]

In a follow-up letter to Livingston, the president noted that the administration's public policy was contained in Madison's official letters, not in the president's private communications. But the president and the secretary of state were in complete agreement about the seriousness of the threat created by French possession of the mouth of the Mississippi. If it became a reality, Madison wrote, it could lead to the "worst events" since the majestic Mississippi was "the Hudson, the Delaware, the Potomac, and all the navigable rivers of the Atlantic States, formed into one stream."[3] Privately, Jefferson took an even stronger stand, telling Livingston: "There is on the globe one single spot, the possessor of which is our natural and habitual enemy. It is New Orleans, through which the produce of three-eighths of our territory must

---

1. TJ to Robert R. Livingston, Apr. 18, 1802, in Ford, VIII, pp. 143–47.
2. TJ to Pierre-Samuel du Pont de Nemours, Apr. 25, 1802, in *Correspondence of Jefferson and du Pont de Nemours, with an Introduction on Jefferson and the Physiocrats,* ed. Gilbert Chinard (Baltimore, 1931), pp. 46–49. TJ asked du Pont to show this letter to Livingston.
3. JM to Robert R. Livingston, May 1, 1802, in Malone, IV, p. 258, and JM to Charles Pinckney, Nov. 27, 1802, *ibid.,* p. 266.

pass to market, and from its fertility it will ere long yield more than half of our whole produce and contain more than half our inhabitants."

One week later, he told du Pont de Nemours that "the day that France takes possession of New Orleans fixes the sentence which is to restrain her forever within her low water mark. It seals the union of two nations who in conjunction can maintain exclusive possession of the ocean. From that moment," he warned ominously, "we must marry ourselves to the British fleet and nation."[4]

The idea of purchasing New Orleans was first set forth by Madison, who asked Livingston in May 1802 to determine the price. Although the American minister tried to explore that possibility, the imperious Napoleon frustrated every effort, as Livingston complained to the secretary of state: "There never was a Government in which less could be done by negotiation than here. There is no people, no Legislature, no counsellors. One man is everything. He seldom asks advice, and never hears it unasked."[5]

A dramatic turn of events in New Orleans riveted attention on the Mississippi once again in the fall of 1802. The Spanish intendant suspended the right of deposit without designating another depot, in violation of the Pinckney Treaty of 1795.[6] Outraged westerners joined eastern Federalists in demanding war, forcing Jefferson and Madison's hand, which relied on diplomatic negotiations.[7] After Jefferson convinced Congress that the action by the intendant was unauthorized by Spain, the House agreed on January 7, 1803, to rely on "the vigilance and wisdom of the Executive" in reestablishing American rights of navigation on the Mississippi, thus separating the immediate issue of Spanish control of New Orleans from the question of the retrocession of Louisiana to France.[8]

Then, in a spectacular bid for peace, Jefferson, on January 11, 1803, appointed James Monroe as envoy extraordinary to assist Livingston in the negotiations in France—and, if necessary, in Spain—to purchase New Orleans and the Floridas. Jefferson and Madison had some reservations about the way

---

4. TJ to Robert R. Livingston, Apr. 18, 1802, in Ford, VIII, pp. 143-47, and TJ to Pierre-Samuel du Pont de Nemours, Apr. 25, 1802, in Chinard, pp. 46-49.

5. Malone, IV, p. 258. Livingston's role is analyzed carefully in George Dangerfield, *Chancellor Robert R. Livingston of New York, 1746-1813* (New York, 1960), pp. 309-94.

6. See JM to TJ, Mar. 10, 1803, below, Mar. 14, 1803, below, and Mar. 21, 1803, below; TJ to JM, Mar. 17, 1803, below.

7. TJ to JM, Mar. 22, 1803, below. For a discussion of military preparations in the West, see Mary P. Adams, "Jefferson's Reaction to the Treaty of San Ildefonso," *J. So. Hist.* 21 (1955): 173-88, and Richard A. Erney, *The Public Life of Henry Dearborn* (New York, 1979), p. 108.

8. Navigation of the Mississippi remained open even though the right of deposit had been revoked temporarily. That meant that cargoes coming down the river had to be loaded directly onto oceangoing vessels, if any were in port, or retained on flatboats instead of being deposited in warehouses until such vessels arrived. Spain subsequently restored the right of deposit at New Orleans, informing the United States on Apr. 19, 1803; see Arthur P. Whitaker, *The Mississippi Question, 1795-1803: A Study in Trade, Politics, and Diplomacy* (New York, 1934), pp. 189-99, 230-32.

Livingston was handling the negotiations, Madison being puzzled by Livingston's putting the secretary's "letter which contains confidential things not even in cypher into the hands of a British Minister" and writing reports that were an "enigma."[9] Jefferson also raised questions about "the game Mr. Livingston says he is playing." He hoped it was a candid and honorable one since "an American contending by stratagem against those exercised in it from their cradle would undoubtedly be outwitted by them. In such a field and for such an actor nothing but plain direct honesty can be either honourable or advantageous."[10]

Monroe, a friend of the West, had just ended his term as governor of Virginia. He had visited his neighbor President Jefferson several times at Monticello during the previous summer,[11] and they had doubtless discussed "this affair of Louisiana." Monroe's mission, Jefferson wrote, would determine whether the United States would, by peaceful purchase, "insure to ourselves a course of perpetual peace and friendship with all nations" or inaugurate war with France and perhaps Spain and thus "get entangled in European politics, and . . . be much less happy and prosperous" than it now was.[12]

Congress also adopted an opaque appropriation bill for $2 million "to defray any expenses which may be incurred in relation to the intercourse between the United States and foreign nations," a diplomatic way of covering part of the purchase price for New Orleans and, if possible, the Floridas, plus spoliations claims by American citizens against France.[13] Madison's instructions to Monroe, which the president praised as "entirely right," authorized the purchase of New Orleans and as much land east of the Mississippi as could be obtained for $10 million, a huge sum that indicated that the economy-minded administration meant business.[14]

Events in the Caribbean and Europe played into the hands of Livingston and Monroe. The French campaign in Santo Domingo sputtered and died with the death of General Leclerc and Napoleon's decision to squander no more armies there. Moreover, the Peace of Amiens was beginning to unravel, and Napoleon needed money to resume war with Great Britain. After Monroe arrived in France but before he reached Paris, Napoleon renounced Louisiana and instructed his finance minister, François de Barbé-Marbois, to cede "the whole colony without any reservation." Bonaparte had read of Congress's appropriation of $2 million in the London *Times* and directed his finance

---

9. JM to TJ, Mar. 14, 1803, below.

10. TJ to JM, Mar. 19, 1803, below.

11. See TJ to JM, Sept. 10, 1802, above.

12. TJ to James Monroe, Jan. 13, 1803, in Ford, VIII, pp. 190–92.

13. Concentrating on the use of the Mississippi, the American envoys were instructed to negotiate for New Orleans and territory east of the river, although Livingston had mentioned the cession of the western portion of Louisiana north of the Arkansas River; see Malone, IV, p. 288.

14. TJ to JM, Feb. 22, 1803, below. The instructions, dated Mar. 2, 1803, are in Hunt, VII, pp. 9–30.

minister to conduct the negotiations in an effort to maximize the return. After more than two weeks of bargaining, Monroe and Livingston, going beyond their instructions, agreed to pay $15 million for New Orleans and the boundless expanse of Louisiana, with one-fourth of the money set aside to pay American citizens for spoliation claims against France.[15]

The Louisiana Purchase was, as Livingston put it, "the noblest work of our whole lives." It was the most significant achievement of the president and the secretary of state during Jefferson's presidency, Jefferson hailing it for removing "the greatest source of danger to our peace" and Madison calling it "a truly noble acquisition."[16] Credit for the acquisition, according to a curmudgeon of an historian, belongs to Napoleon, who "threw the province" at the United States, and the four Americans who caught and held it—Livingston, Monroe, Madison, and Jefferson; "they share between them—equally—whatever credit there was." There seems more than enough credit to go around, however, with Jefferson and Madison planning the instructions and Monroe and Livingston implementing their goals by going beyond the instructions.[17]

But it was the British representative in Washington, writing on July 4, 1803, the day he learned of the treaty, who gave what ultimately became the historic view: "There seems to be little which can affect the tranquillity of the United States, or shake the firm footing which the President will have obtained, in the confidence of his countrymen."[18]

France conveyed Louisiana with the same extent of territory that it had when France had earlier possessed it and that it had when it was in the hands of Spain. Although the boundaries and territorial limits were not precisely known, the acquisition more than doubled the size of the United States. While he was at Monticello during the summer of 1803, Jefferson researched the boundaries of the new acquisition,[19] hoping, as Henry Adams phrased it, that "France had actually bought West Florida without knowing it, and had sold it to the United States without being paid for it."[20] To Madison, who was

---

15. See Alexander De Conde, *This Affair of Louisiana* (New York, 1976), pp. 161–75.

16. Malone, IV, pp. 262–310, esp. 284, and Brant, IV, pp. 98–140, esp. 133.

17. See Edward Channing, *History of the United States,* 6 vols. (New York, 1905–25), IV, p. 319. On the credit due to Monroe and Livingston, TJ observed that "the truth is both have a just portion of merit and were it necessary or proper it could be shewn that each has rendered peculiar service, and of important value"; see TJ to Horatio Gates, July 11, 1803, in Ford, VIII, pp. 249–50.

18. Malone, IV, p. 301. This judgment has held true despite TJ's flip-flop on the constitutionality of the acquisition; see Everett Somerville Brown, *The Constitutional History of the Louisiana Purchase, 1803–1812* (Berkeley, 1920), and John M. Belolavek, "Politics, Principle, and Pragmatism in the Early Republic: Thomas Jefferson and the Quest for American Empire," *Diplomatic History* 15 (1991): 599–606.

19. Malone, IV, p. 309.

20. Henry Adams, *History of the United States of America during the Administrations of Thomas Jefferson and James Madison,* 9 vols. (New York, 1889–91), II, p. 68.

at nearby Montpellier, he wrote that he hoped Congress would "authorise us to send embassies to the Indian tribes of Louisiane, who may at the same time explore the country and ascertain it's geography. Those large Western rivers of the Mis[s]i[ssip]pi and Missouri whose heads form the contour of the Louisiana territory ought to be known."[21]

Even before the acquisition of Louisiana, Jefferson had persuaded Congress to fund an exploratory expedition to the western country. His private secretary and neighbor, Captain Meriwether Lewis of Albemarle County, and William Clark of Kentucky headed the commercial and scientific mission, and Jefferson referred his instructions for the expedition to Madison, who questioned whether "the laws give any authority at present beyond the limits of the U.S."[22] Since the Lewis and Clark expedition did not leave Washington until the Fourth of July 1803, the day after news arrived of the Louisiana treaty, that question instantly became irrelevant.[23]

Two other issues dominated the letters exchanged by the president and the secretary of state in 1803: the resumption of war between France and England, which again raised fundamental issues related to neutral rights; and the continuing contest between the American navy and Tripoli. The Peace of Amiens, which had made the Louisiana deal possible, ended in May 1803, less than a month after Napoleon, disposing of Louisiana to finance the sinews of war, had cleared the decks for action. Madison had already directed Rufus King, American minister in London, to resume negotiations on impressments, and the admiralty had accepted a preliminary article banning impressments from ships at sea. But final negotiations first faltered, then failed after King ended his mission in 1803, and no agreement was reached.[24]

Nevertheless, Jefferson hoped that "on the subject of our seamen as both parties were agreed against impressments at sea, and concealments in port, I suppose we may practice on those two articles as things understood, altho' no convention was signed." On the related matter of "free bottoms, free goods," he was sure that "Great Britain will never yield to it willingly and she cannot be forced."[25] But Madison reported that the British were unwilling to put any restraint on impressments, noting the seizure of four seamen from an American vessel by a British frigate just off the Virginia coast. Both vessels had sailed from Norfolk, he said, and the frigate "had no doubt made her use of that port subservient to her cruises on our own coast agst our own trade."[26]

Jefferson quickly seconded Madison's official protest against British im-

21. TJ to JM, Aug. 16, 1803, below.
22. "Notes on instructions to Capt. Meriwether Lewis," in JM to TJ, Apr. 14, 1803, below.
23. TJ's letters about the Lewis and Clark expedition are in Ford, VIII, pp. 192–202.
24. Bradford Perkins, *The First Rapprochement: England and the United States, 1795–1805* (Philadelphia, 1955), pp. 154–56.
25. TJ to JM, July 31, 1803, below.
26. JM to TJ, Aug. 13, 1803, below.

pressments, which he labeled "an afflicting subject." When he learned of impressment of American sailors by a French armed vessel, he confessed that he was glad it had happened, "as it will serve as a set-off against French complaints on the British trespasses on us." But it was the British depredations that most concerned him. "With every disposition to render them all justifiable services," he told the secretary of state, "I fear they will put our patience to the proof. Their making our ports also stations for cruising from will require regulations. It seems to me that we shall be obliged to have a battery or two in our principal seaports, and to require [foreign] armed vessels to lie under them, while they are using our ports for repairs or supplies, the only legitimate purposes of entering them."[27]

Despite Madison's warnings that the British were unlikely to agree to any limitation of impressment, Jefferson hoped to salvage something from King's earlier negotiations. "With respect to the impressment of our seamen," he wrote Madison, "I think we had better propose to Great Britain to act on the stipulations which had been agreed to between that Government and Mr. King, as if they had been signed. I think they were, that they would forbid impressments at sea, and that we should acquiesce in the search in *their* harbors necessary to prevent concealments of their citizens."

The president thought that the attempt by Edward Thornton, the British chargé d'affaires in Washington, "to justify his nation in using our ports as cruising stations on our friends and ourselves, renders the matter so serious as to call, I think, for answer." He was convinced "that we ought in courtesy and friendship to extend to them all the rights of hospitality . . . , [but] that they should not use our hospitality to injure our friends or ourselves is equally enjoined by morality and honor." Impressment and searches for contraband were evils amounting to plunder, which not only justified complaints by the French, but also rendered it "indispensable that we restrain the English from abusing the rights of hospitality to their prejudice as well as our own."[28]

Madison was more cautious about replying to the British chargé d'affaires since in some parts of Thornton's letter "his manner did not deserve it, because he speaks without the known sentiments of his gov^t and because the Minister of higher grade expected, will be likely to give a more eligible opportunity for these discussions."[29] Moreover, Madison thought that the British government "will not act with us on the subject of seamen, in the manner you hint at." He reviewed King's negotiations and observed that the English would sign no convention with him "without reserving to themselves the claim to impress seamen in the narrow seas," the waters surrounding the British Isles, which the British government had always considered to be within the domain of Great

27. TJ to JM, Aug. 16, 1803, below.
28. TJ to JM, Aug. 24, 1803, below.
29. Anthony Merry, the first British minister credited to the Jefferson government, arrived in Nov. 1803.

Britain. Madison viewed this claim as having been advanced in order "to prevent any arrangement" and to make it possible for the British "to carry on the impressments as heretofore."[30] By the end of the summer, the secretary of state was listing "the pile of wrongs to be brought into our remonstrance to the British Gov! on the subject of impressments."[31]

While trying to maintain neutrality with Great Britain and France, the Jefferson administration pressed its war against Tripoli. Both the president and the secretary of state were distressed that Commodore Richard V. Morris, who had succeeded Richard Dale in 1802, had employed his fleet to convoy American vessels in the Mediterranean instead of positioning it for "a close blockade" of Tripoli. By bottling up Tripolitanian corsairs, a blockade would have been "equivalent to universal convoy."[32] Because Morris rejected a blockade, Madison lamented, "our affairs were considered in [the] Mediterranean as tending the wrong way. All agree that peace with Tripoli was for a long time in our power and almost on our own terms, and lament that the crisis is probably past."[33] To replace Morris, Jefferson dispatched Commodore Edward Preble with "two frigates and 4. small vessels" in the hope that "something will be done this season."[34]

———————— THE LETTERS ————————

Jefferson to Madison

[Washington] Feb. 5, 1803

An hostile party intend to descend the Missippi

Jefferson to Madison

[Washington] Feb. 8, 1803

I had before heard this matter spoken of, but did not suppose it [ser]iously intended. If there be any danger of it, the Secretary at war [w]ill be

---

30. JM to TJ, Aug. 28, 1803, below. Perkins, p. 155, discusses negotiations relating to "Narrow Seas."
31. JM to TJ, Sept. 12, 1803, below.
32. TJ to JM, Mar. 22, 1803, below.
33. JM to TJ, Mar. 17, 1803, below. Morris was later tried and dismissed from the navy; see Marshall Smelser, *The Democratic Republic, 1801–1815* (New York, 1968), p. 59.
34. TJ to JM, Aug. 29, 1803, below. See also Christopher McKee, *Edward Preble: A Naval Biography, 1761–1807* (Annapolis, 1972).

desired to give orders at Màssac̀ and Fort Adams to stop them by force. [Bu]t would it not be well to write to the Govr. of Kentucky to have the person [a]rrested and bound to their good behavior or the peace?

Madison to Jefferson
[Washington Feb. 21, 1803]

The inclosed report as altered is acquiesced in by M.r L. In two instances recurred to Cong.s have already interposed, one of them the Paoli at last session. The judgm.t of the Court ag.st Capt. Maly was p.d by Congs. Several Dutch and British precedents can also be cited. The 7 Arts. of the British Treaty and 21 of the Span. go on the responsibility of their gov.ts for irregular acts[1] of the officers under their auth.y or colors relative to Spanish spoliations have the same implication. If the principle be tenable, it is evidently and greatly in favor of the U.S. in a general view. Two correct copies will be sent to the P. in the morning. The present one is sent that if approved, he may accommodate his message to it without further delay.

Madison to Jefferson
Washington Feb. 22, 1803

The Secretary of State has the honor to report to the President of the United States, upon the note of the Minister of his Danish Majesty, Dated on the 9th inst., as follows:

That it appears that the Danish Brigantine Henrich, Captain Peter Scheele, sailing from Hamburgh, loaded with an assorted Cargo, and bound to Cape Francois, was captured on the 3d of October 1799 by a French privateer, and on the 8th of the same month She was recaptured by an American public armed vessel called the Pickering, and carried to the British Island of St. Christopher, where she arrived on the 10th.

That from an authenticated transcript of the proceedings in the case of the said vessel, had before the Court of Vice Admiralty at the said Island, it

---

1. Article 7 of Jay's treaty provided that owners of American vessels that were illegally or irregularly captured under color of authority of Great Britain would receive full compensation for ship and merchandise from the British government. The United States also agreed that British vessels and merchandise captured within the jurisdiction of the United States or taken by vessels originally armed in the United States would receive compensation from the United States. The article specifically incorporated TJ's letter as secretary of state to George Hammond of Sept. 5, 1793, to that effect; see Samuel Flagg Bemis, *Jay's Treaty: A Study in Commerce and Diplomacy,* 2d ed. (New Haven, 1962), pp. 463–66, 484–87.

appears that the said Court took cognizance of the case, and awarded one half of the gross amount of the sales of the Brig and her Cargo to be paid to the recaptors, and the other half after deducting costs and expences to be restored to the owners. That the rate of Salvage appears to have been adopted from the laws of the United States, as then applicable to recaptures of American property, and of such as belonged to belligerent powers in amity with the United States; but it is believed that these laws had, according to decisions of our own Courts, no reference to recaptures of Neutral property. That admitting what has received the sanction of some recent authorities, that "in certain peculiar cases of danger of a neutral being condemned" by a belligerent, the recaptors are intitled to a proportionate Salvage, there is much reason to believe this is not such a case, as the Vessel was bound from a neutral to a French port, the whole of the property being neutral, and according to the assurance of Mr. Lindemann, the Governor of the Danish West India Islands, most of the Danish Vessels carried into Guadaloupe for a year before this capture, were released, and some of them with damages. That the Courts of the United States have in cases much more strongly marked by circumstances indicating a danger of the neutral being condemned, allowed much smaller rates of salvage.

That the laws of the United States required Vessels captured under their authority to be brought within their jurisdiction, and it is conceived that it was the duty of the American Officers in this case to repel the attempt of the foreign judicatory to take cognizance much less ought they to have directly submitted their recapture to its decision, which as it could not be revised or rectified, in case of error, by the tribunals of their own Country, might tend to involve it in Claims on its responsibility from others.

That according to the representation of the Agent for the owners of the Danish Vessel, of the sum of $44,500, the value of the vessel, freight and Cargo, there remained, after satisfying the decree for salvage and expenses no more than $8,374.41.

That as the policy and interest of the United States lead them in a special manner to respect and promote the rights and facilities of neutral commerce; as the sentence in this case was permitted, if not procured by officers of the United States, to be made in a foreign, and therefore improper, tribunal, as there remains no doubt but that a Court of the United States pronouncing thereon, would either have rejected the claim for salvage altogether, or reduced it to the most moderate scale, as the declared basis of the sentence, viz: the law of the United States was inapplicable to the case; and, as it is understood, that a remedy is now unattainable in the ordinary judicial course, it is the opinion of the Secretary of State, that under all the circumstances, the case ought to be referred to the just provisions of Congress thereon.

All which is respectfully submitted by

JAMES MADISON

Jefferson to Madison

Washington Feb. 22, 1803

TH: J. TO J.M.

I return you the report, and have prepared a message, tho' I confess myself not satisfied on the main question, the responsibility of the government in this case, and with our taking wholly on ourselves the risk of the decision. For to enable Congress to judge for themselves the record must go; and the printing that would prevent it's being taken up this session. If we do not send in the record they must decide solely on our statement and throw the whole responsibility on us. It is certainly not known to us to be an entirely clear case. Honest opinions may be given both ways, and have been given as we see by Grotius and Bynkenhook. The sum is very large. How much more clear and expedient was the case of the Berciau, and yet how much dust has it enabled the disaffected party to throw in the eyes of the nation. I acknolege that where cases are doubtful I would always decide on the liberal side. But time for full consideration and enquiry into the practice of nations it seems prudent to take in a precedent of such consequences as this may produce in future cases. How would it do for Congress to authorize the advancing a certain sum for the present relief and support of the Capt. and to refer the final decision to their next meeting, on the proferred ground of want of time? However if you are perfectly satisfied, I shall be in readiness to send in the report on recieving it.[2]

I return you Monroe's instructions which are entirely right. One circumstance only might perhaps as well be left out. I mean the mention of my letter to Dupont. As that correspondence will make no part of the public records, perhaps it is as well it should not be spoken of in them. Affectionate salutations.

Jefferson to Madison

[Washington] Mar. 1, 1803

Commissions to be issued to the following persons under the bankrupt law.

John Mussey at Portland vice Joseph Boyd who has not qualified (to be so expressed)
Simeon Thomas at New London. for Connecticut
Charles Ludlow at New York for New York.

2. On Feb. 23, 1803, TJ submitted JM's report to Congress. It involved the Danish ship *Henrick,* which had been taken by a French privateer in 1799, retaken by an armed vessel of the United States, carried into a British island, and there adjudged to be neutral. The president observed that the Danish owners had requested indemnification for their losses "occasioned by our officers" and noted that their claims were "supported by the representations of their Government . . . which has observed toward us the most friendly treatment and regard"; see Richardson, I, pp. 356-57.

"This Affair of Louisiana," 1803

John Stephen at Baltimore for Maryland.
Cowles Meade, Robert Walker, and George Watkins at Augusta for Georgia
Thomas Collins at Louisville

Madison to Jefferson

Washington Mar. 10, 1803

DEAR SIR

The answers from the Govr and Intendant at N. Orleans to the Spanish Ministers letter were rec.^d by him yesterday. The Intendant himself states that he had taken his measures, merely on his own judgment, without orders from his Gov.^t and in opposition to the judgment of the Govr. but it appears that his determination had not been changed by the first interposition of Yrujo. As his second letter written after it was known that the Intendant had proceeded without orders, might have spoken with more energy, it is possible that it may have more effect. Considering however the case in all its aspects, I have thought it proper to call on Yrujo for the peremptory injunctions which he seemed willing to undertake, and am just sending him a note for that purpose, which is approved by my several colleagues. He says he will do every thing that depends on decision, and will even, in a private letter to the Govr urge him, if the Intendant should be refractory, to ship him off to Spain, which is the ultima ratio it seems of Spanish Governors ag.st Intendants. The dispatches of the Marquis will be forwarded under my cover to Claybourne, and will go by an Express who it is hoped will overtake the Mail now on the way.[3]

It appears by a letter of Novr 24 from Obrien, thro' Calhalan, that the Dey of Algiers refused the cash payment which had arrived, and insists on the stores with much irritation at the offer substituted. Will you be pleased to say to Mr Smith whether he is to forward them as soon as possible, as seems now to be indispensable. With respectful attachment I remain Y.^{rs}

JAMES MADISON

Madison to Jefferson

Washington Mar. 14, 1803

DEAR SIR

You will find in the gazette of this morning the letter from Yrujo, which he wished to be printed, and which will I hope do good.[4] Pichon has also written a strong letter to the Govr of Louisiana, summoning him on his

---

[3]. Juan Ventura Moralès, the intendant at New Orleans, had closed the American right of deposit on Oct. 18, 1802. For a full account, see Whitaker, pp. 189–234.

[4]. The Spanish minister's letter to JM disowned the closure of the right of deposit at New Orleans as the personal act of the intendant and promised the restitution of all rights under Pinckney's treaty; see Malone, IV, p. 282.

responsibility, to see that the cession of that province to France be not affected, nor the amicable relations of the Republic to the U. States, be endangered, by a perseverance of the Intendant in his breach of the Treaty. Both these Ministers are deeply alarmed at the apparent tendency of things, and seem willing to risk themselves for the purpose of checking it.

I have just rec^d and decyphered the inclosed letters from Mr Livingston. In general they wear a better aspect than heretofore, but it is remarkable, unless some intermediate letter has not been rec^d that nothing is said of the written assurance which was to be given on the return of the chief Consul, that the Spanish Treaty would be faithfully observed by France. It is still more remarkable that he should undertake to prescribe measures, without hinting even the reasons for them. The whole of his postscript of Decr 23. is an enigma; suggesting a fear of some hazardous finesse or some unwarrantable project, rather than a hope of successful negociation.[5] What inconsistency also in waiting for safe opportunities, and at the same putting his letter which contains confidential things not even in cypher into the hands of a British Minister. Surely a letter in Cypher might well be trusted to a French post office; and then he might write as frequently and fully as he pleased, thro' England, and with a much better chance of dispatch, than by direct conveyances from Paris.

OBrien says that the Dey of Algiers threatens war if the stores be not sent, and allows three months only for their arrival. He demands, over and above the stores, 1000 barrels of gun powder. The answer to this request he says must be in a separate letter from the President. But the importance of the subject requires that you should see the letter, and I therefore inclose it. With respectful attachment I remain Yours

JAMES MADISON

Jefferson to Madison

Monticello Mar. 17, 1803

DEAR SIR

Your's of the 10th is recieved and I now inclose a letter to the Secretary of the navy, which be pleased to seal and deliver after perusal. I think not a moment should be lost in forwarding the stores to Algiers, as it is of importance to keep those powers quiet. Might it not be useful to propose to the Dey with a year's annuity in stores, to recieve another year's in money?

The answer from the Intendant of New Orleans was not unexpected to me; and I question whether any thing moves him but the shipment to Spain. Accept my affectionate salutations.

TH: JEFFERSON

5. See Brant, IV, pp. 102–3.

Madison to Jefferson

Washington Mar. 17, 1803

DEAR SIR

In the inclosed Intelligences you will find the letter from Pichon to the Govr of Louisiana. Having been written without reference to its publication, it is less carefully fitted than Yrujo's for the contemplated impression, and in connection with that presents some points for sophistical comments, which are made rather more than less salient by the reflections of the Editor. The letter will however be useful in several respects, particularly in rescuing France from the odium thrown on her suspected agency.[6]

There are voluminous communications from the Mediterranean but in general of old date. The inclosed letter from the Bey of Tunis, of which a copy was some time ago rec^d claims attention. Eaton says he dreads the consequence of a refusal, yet takes for granted that it will as it ought to take place. If an account rec^d last night from Kirkpatrick be true, which appears to be authentic, Algiers will probably become more manageable.[7] He writes from Malaga, on Feby 7. that the French Consul there, had advice from his colleague at Barcelona, that a vessel had just arrived there with dispatches for the French gov.^t informing it of a declaration of war by the Dey [of] Algiers, and that the dispatches were gone by Express to Paris. In general our affairs were considered in [the] Mediterranean as tending the wrong way. All agree that peace with Tripoli was for a long time in our power and almost on our own terms, and lament that the crisis is probably past. For the present it seems essential that the gun carriages sh^d go to Morocco; the stipulated stores to Algiers, and a complaisant refusal of the Frigate, to Tunis. With respect to Tripoli, we must wait for communications from Morris and Catheart [i.e., Cathcart]. I have written to Lear to sound him on the subject of taking Catheart's place at Algiers.

The other inclosed letter has just been put into my hands by Mr Pichon. With respectful attachments always, yours

JAMES MADISON

Jefferson to Madison

Monticello Mar. 19, 1803

DEAR SIR

I wrote you on the 17th since which yours of the 14th is recieved, and I now return the letters of Mr Livingston and O'Brien. I hope the game Mr

---

6. Pichon's letter protested in the name of France, soon to receive Louisiana from Spain, against the intendant's closing of the right of deposit; see Whitaker, pp. 312–13.

7. William Kirkpatrick was American consul at Málaga; see *ASP, M,* I, p. 307.

Livingston says he is playing is a candid and honourable one. Besides an unwillingness to accept any advantage which should have been obtained by other means, no other means can probably succeed there. An American contending by stratagem against those exercised in it from their cradle would undoubtedly be outwitted by them. In such a field and for such an actor nothing but plain direct honesty can be either honourable or advantageous.

I am in hopes the stores for Algiers will be sent off without delay, so as to stop the growling of that dog. When shall we get rid of Obrien? What says Col? Lear? As to the 10,000. barrels of powder, if he refuses money for the annuity of the present year and would take that instead of naval stores, it would be well. Certainly on so slight a *verbal* intimation no answer can be expected from the hand of the president in writing. Mr Smith having observed that it would be much cheaper to have the gun carriages for the emperor of Marocco made in his vicinity [Baltimore], and that made according to his directions, they would probably be more acceptable, than those we should send at hazard. I promised to speak to you on the subject, and thought I had done so. Will you and he be so good as to conclude and do what is best? If the money be put into Simson's hands, perhaps the emperor would prefer taking it and having the gun carriages made or not made as he would prefer. Accept my affectionate salutations.

Th: Jefferson

P.S. I send you also a letter of Col? Monroe for perusal, and have to add that Edward Turner of Kentucky is to be commissioned immediately as Register of the land office at Natchez.

Madison to Jefferson

Washington Mar. 21, 1803

Dear Sir

A letter from Hulings[8] of Feb.y 15. says that at that date the Intendant had not revoked the interruption of the deposit; but had from regard to the wants of the Colony, opened the market to flour and other provisions brought down the Mississippi; the articles being subject to a duty of 6 perC? if consumed there, and to the usual export duty, (I believe 12 perC?), if sent as an indulgence in Spanish bottoms to places within the lawful trade of the Colony. It is *possible* that this may be a retrograde step of the Intendant masked by his pride under the policy of a colonial regulation. It appears that the forbearance of that officer to conform to the presumed object of Yrujo's first letters, had

---

8. William E. Hulings was vice consul at New Orleans; see *ibid.*, p. 308, and *PJM* (SS ser.), I, p. 139.

produced a general belief at N. Orleans that orders from the Spanish Gov.^t had led to the violations of our right.⁹

Eaton writes from Tunis late in Decr that the Bey had not only renewed his demand of the Frigate, but had raked together all his old claims of oxen Cattle etc. and that his Minister insisted on the gold mounted fusil in addition to the silver one re^d. He complains of the viz inertia of our marine, anticipates evils, and decides on not passing another summer there. He signifies that he shall consult with Morris and Cathcart, in case of their appearing before Tunis, on the expediency of his giving the Bey the ship; apprehending that he may not be permitted by the Bey to leave that place. It will be necessary therefore to provide immediately a successor to him as well as O'Brien.¹⁰

In consequence of my letter to Mr Lear, he came over the day before yesterday. He is willing to take an app.^t at Algiers, with a salary of $4000, but will require 6 weeks or two months, to prepare for embarkation.¹¹ With respectful attachment always Y.^{rs}

JAMES MADISON

Jarvis has pushed with great vigor and success the admission of our flour to the Portuguese Market, and the removal of the quarantine from our vessels. The result will be found in the Nat^l intelligences of this day, and his management will appear when you see his letter just rec^d which is of Feby 9.

Jefferson to Madison

Monticello Mar. 22, 1803

DEAR SIR,

Yours of the 17th is received. I concur in your ideas that the request from the Bey of Tunis of a frigate of 36. guns should be complaisantly refused. I think the greatest dispatch should be used in sending either the gun carriages or money to Simpson for the Emperor of Marocco, and the stores to Algiers; and, if you approve it, the powder *on account:* or perhaps it would be better to authorize the purchase of it in Europe on the Dey's agreeing to receive it on account. We must keep these two powers friendly by a steady course of justice

---

9. For a discussion of the channels of trade left open to Americans despite the closing of the right of deposit, see Whitaker, pp. 195–96.

10. For Eaton's criticism of American naval commanders in the Mediterranean, see Louis B. Wright and Julia H. Macleod, *The First Americans in North Africa: William Eaton's Struggle for a Vigorous Policy against the Barbary Pirates, 1799–1805* (Princeton, 1945), pp. 108–9.

11. For Tobias Lear's appointment as consul general to Algiers, replacing Richard O'Brien, see *ibid.*, pp. 133, 136. For a biography of Lear, see Ray Brighton, *The Checkered Career of Tobias Lear* (Portsmouth, N.H., 1985).

aided occasionally with liberality. Mr. Smith has suggested the sending another frigate. But no new fact justifies a change of plan. Our misfortune has been that our vessels have been employed in particular convoys, instead of a close blockade equivalent to universal convoy. I suppose Murray may be for sending more ships there.[12] Every officer in the navy, and every merchant in the U. S. would be for that: because they see but one object, themselves.

I see the federalists find one paper in Kentucky into which they can get what they write either here or there. Bradford's Guardian of freedom of Mar. 4 has a piece recommending immediate separation. A cool calculation of interest however would show that Eastern America would not be the greatest sufferer by that folly. Accept my affectionate salutations.

Madison to Jefferson

Washington Apr. 14, 1803

Notes on instructions to Capt. Meriwether Lewis.

1. Quer. if the laws give any authority at present beyond the limits of the U.S.?
2. "This Mission having reference to the Commerce" it may repell, more than the expression used, the criterion of illicit *principal* objects of the measure.
3. "including the fish"
4. if practicable he might note occasionally the variations of the Needle.[13]

Jefferson to Madison

[Washington] May 10, 1803

Commissions to be issued to

Samuel Ward of Massachusets to be Naval officer for the district of Salem in Massachusets.
Samuel Osgood of New York to be Naval officer for the district of New York
Jeremiah Bennet Junr. of New Jersey to be Collector of customs for the district

---

12. For Captain Alexander Murray's lackluster career in the Mediterranean, see Wright and Macleod, pp. 101–16, 130–31.

13. TJ sent his cabinet members a draft of his instructions to Lewis relating to Lewis's western trip; see *Letters of the Lewis and Clark Expedition with Related Documents, 1783–1854,* ed. Donald Jackson, 2d ed., 2 vols. (Urbana, 1978), I, pp. 34, 61–66.

and Inspector of the revenue for the port of Bridgetown in New Jersey George House of Connecticut to be Master of a revenue cutter.

Th: Jefferson

Jefferson to Madison

[July 1803]

Draft of a Proposed Constitutional Amendment
on Louisiana to be added to
Art. IV, Section III.

The province of Louisiana is incorporated with the U. S. and made part thereof. The rights of occupancy in the soil, and of self-government, are confirmed to the Indian inhabitants, as they now exist. Preemption only of the portions rightfully occupied by them, and a succession to the occupancy of such as they may abandon, with the full rights of possession as well as of property and sovereignty in whatever is not rightfully occupied by them, or shall cease to be so, shall belong to the U. S.

The legislature of the Union shall have authority to exchange the right of occupancy in portions where the U. S. have full right, for lands possessed by Indians within the U. S. on the East side of the Missisipi: to exchange lands on the East side of the river for those of the White inhabitants on the West side thereof and North of the latitude of 32 degrees: to maintain in any part of the province such military posts as may be requisite for peace or safety: to exercise police over all persons therein, not being Indian inhabitants: to work salt springs, or mines of coal, metals and other minerals within the possessions of the U. S. or in any others with the consent of the possessors; to regulate trade and intercourse between the Indian inhabitants and all other persons; to explore and ascertain the geography of the province, it's productions and other interesting circumstances; to open roads and navigation therein where necessary for beneficial communication; and to establish agencies and factories therein for the cultivation of commerce, peace and good understanding with the Indians residing there.

The legislature shall have no authority to dispose of the lands of the province otherwise than as hereinbefore permitted, until a new Amendment of the constitution shall give that authority: Except, as to that portion thereof which lies South of the latitude of 32 degrees; which, whenever they deem expedient, they may erect into a territorial government, either separate or as making part with one on the Eastern side of the river, vesting the inhabitants thereof with all the rights possessed by other territorial citizens of the U. S.

Madison to Jefferson

[July 1803]

[Addition to Jefferson's Proposed Constitutional Amendment on Louisiana]

Territories Eastwd. of the Mississippi and Southward of the U. S. which may be acquired by the U. S. shall be incorporated as a part thereof; and be subject with their inhabitants including Indians, to the same authorities of the general Govt. as may now be exercised over territories and inhabitants under like circumstances now within the limits of the U. States[14]

Madison to Jefferson

[July 1803]

[Substitute for Jefferson's Proposed Constitutional Amendment on Louisiana]

Louisiana as ceded by France is made part of the United States. Congress may make part of the United States other adjacent territories which shall be justly acquired. Congress may sever from the United States territory not heretofore within the United States, with the consent of a majority of the free males above twenty-one years, inhabiting such territory.

Jefferson to Madison

Monticello Aug. 24, 1803

Revised Draft, incorporating Madison's Suggestion, of Jefferson's Proposed Constitutional Amendment on Louisiana[15]

'Louisiana, as ceded by France to the US. is made a part of the US. It's white inhabitants shall be citizens, and stand, as to their rights and obligations on the same footing with other citizens of the US. in analogous situations.

14. JM, who believed that the Constitution authorized territorial acquisition, wrote this addition in pencil on TJ's draft proposal because he thought it implied lack of power to acquire Florida; see Brant, IV, p. 142. I am indebted to Jeanne Cross for furnishing this document from the files of the Papers of James Madison.

15. TJ's revised draft is printed here out of chronological sequence in order to bring together all the versions of the proposed constitutional amendment on Louisiana; it is taken from his letter to JM, Aug. 24, 1803, below. It varies in minor details about the latitude of the Arkansas River from the version printed in Ford, VIII, pp. 241–49, who says that he prints his version from JM's letter. But as Malone, IV, p. 314, points out, Ford seems to have taken his text from TJ to Levi Lincoln, Aug. 30, 1803, in the Jefferson Papers at the Library of Congress.

Save only that, as to the portion thereof lying North of the latitude of the Arcansa river, no new state shall be established, nor any grants of land made therein, other than to Indians in exchange for equivalent portions of land occupied by them, until an amendment to the Constitution shall be made for that purpose.

Florida also, whensoever it may be rightfully obtained, shall become a part of the US. It's white inhabitants shall thereupon be citizens, and shall stand as to their rights and obligations on the same footing with other citizens of the U.S. in analogous circumstances.'

Jefferson to Madison

[Washington July 1803]

Queries about Louisiana[16]

1. What are the boundaries of Louisiana, and on what authority does each portion of them rest?

2. What is the distance from New Orleans to the nearest point of the Western boundary?

3. Into what divisions is the province laid off?

4. What officers civil and military are appointed to each division, and what to the general government, with a definition of their powers.

5. What emoluments have they, and from what source derived?

6. What are the annual expences of the province drawn from the treasury?

7. What are the nett reciepts of the treasury, and from what taxes or other resources are they drawn?

8. On what footing is the church and clergy, what lands have they, and from what other funds are they supported?

9. What is the population of the province, distinguishing between white and black but excluding Indians, on the East side of the Missisipi? Of the settlement on the West side next the mouth? Of each distinct settlement in the other parts of the province? And what the geographical position and extent of each of these settlements?

10. What are the foundations of their land titles? and what their tenure?

11. What is the quantity of granted lands as near as can be estimated?

12. What is the quantity ungranted in the island of New Orleans, and in the settlement adjacent to the West side?

13. What are the lands appropriated to public use?

14. What buildings, fortifications, or other fixed property belong to the public?

---

16. Although TJ's queries are unaddressed, I assume that they went to JM since the two collaborated closely on all matters relating to the acquisition of Louisiana.

15. What is the quantity and general limits of the lands fit for the culture of sugar? What portion is granted and what ungranted?

16. Whence is their code of laws derived? A copy of it, if in print.

17. What are the best maps, general or particular, of the whole or parts of the province? Copies of them, if to be had in print.

Jefferson to Madison

[Washington] July 12, 1803

Commissions to be made out.

Thomas Rodney of Delaware to be judge of Mississ. vice St. Lewis. Thomas Rodney of Delaware and Robert Williams of N. Carolina to be Comm'rs etc. West of Pearl River. Ephraim Kerby of Connecticut and Robert Carter Nicholas of Kentucky to be Comm'rs etc. East of Pearl river. A blank commission for the Register East of Pearl river. Tenche Coxe of Pensylvania to be Purveyor, his commission to bear date Aug. 1, 1803, on which day Mr. Wheeler has fixed his own resignation.

TH: JEFFERSON.

Jefferson to Madison

[Washington] July 17, 1803

TH. J. TO J.M.

It was agreed yesterday

1. that a copy of the proclamation[17] should be inclosed to each member in a letter from the Secy. of State, mentioning that the meeting of Congress had been necessarily anticipated three weeks, because the ratifications of the treaty and conventions for the cession of Louisiana were to be exchanged on the 30th. day of October, and suggesting the importance of a punctual attendance on the 1st. day.

2. that the Secretary of State should write to Messrs. Livingston and Monroe, expressly approving their obtaining Louisiana, and the sum agreed to be given for it.

3. that Monroe be instructed to endeavor to purchase both or either Florida at the prices before settled, or at any rate to establish a plenary right to the use of all rivers which rising within the Spanish territories, pass through

---

17. On July 16, 1803, TJ issued a special presidential proclamation calling Congress into session on Oct. 17 to discuss ratification of the Louisiana treaty; see Richardson, I, p. 357.

ours. To observe at the same time that we are not now so anxious for the purchase of the Floridas because of the large sum we hope to provide for Louisiana, and because we believe they will fall into our hands in good time. But still if to be obtained easily, we will purchase. He should know their pretensions and proofs of the boundaries of Louisiana. If not gone to Madrid, he must determine according to circumstances whether to go there, or to London, or to stay at Paris. The Secretary of State to write to our Consul at N. Orleans communicating the substance of the treaty and calling his attention to the public property transferred to us, to wit public buildings etc. archives etc. and to give assurances that the rights of the inhabitants will be liberally protected.

Jefferson to Madison and Mrs. Madison

[Washington?] Wednesday July 1803

Mr. Madison and family

Many thanks to Mrs. Madison for the trouble she has been so good as to take.

Madison to Jefferson

Washington July 26, 1803

Dear Sir

Having recieved some days ago, but not in time for the last mail, the enclosed petition, I have thought it proper to forward with it a pardon, that in case it should be extended to the party, delay might be avoided. I know nothing more of the convict or of the merits of the petition than are to be gathered from the petition itself and the letter from W. Jones. It is signed, I observe by respectable names of all parties. Mr Wagner will open your answer and make the proper communication to Mr W. Jones.

No foreign information has been rec^d since your departure, nor is any thing further known with respect to Bernadotte[18] or Merry.

I have sent for a p^r of horses, and expect them here in two or three days. I am hurrying my preparations to leave this place as soon as they arrive, but have

---

18. Napoleon had appointed General Jean Baptiste Jules Bernadotte as minister to the United States on Dec. 31, 1802, in his effort to establish French occupation of Louisiana. But negotiations for the sale of Louisiana intervened before Bernadotte could depart for America; see Brant, IV, pp. 102, 122.

found the winding up the essential business more tedious than I was fully aware. Several letters which go into cypher particularly one to M̲r̲ Monroe on the subject of Spain have run into considerable length. M̲r̲ Gallatin is still here, but considers every [day] as his last. M̲r̲ E. Livingston made a visit for two days, and returned, I believe without saying a word to any one on the subject which was supposed to cause the visit, nor do I believe that a word was said to him on it.[19] With respectful attachment I remain Y̲r̲s̲

JAMES MADISON

I got M̲r̲ Wagner to see M̲r̲ Mason on the subject of the Pardon. M̲r̲ Mason has promised to write to you. I inclose a supplemental communication from M̲r̲ King, in several views important. Also a letter resigning a Commission of Bankruptcy.

Jefferson to Madison

Monticello July 31, 1803

DEAR SIR,

I return you the petition of Samuel Miller with the pardon signed. Mr. Kelty had spoken to me on this subject and told me that he and Mr. Craunch should join in a recommendation. I wish Mr. Wagner would obtain this before he delivers the pardon. I return also Mr. King's letter which has really important matter, especially what respects the mare clausum, the abandonment of the colonial system, and emancipation of S. America. On the subject of our seamen as both parties were agreed against impressments at sea, and concealments in port, I suppose we may practice on those two articles as things understood, altho' no convention was signed. I see that the principle of free bottoms, free goods must be left to make its way by treaty with particular nations. Great Britain will never yield to it willingly and she cannot be forced.

I think I have selected a governor for Louisiana, as perfect in all points as we can expect. Sound judgment, standing in society, knolege of the world, wealth, liberality, familiarity with the French language, and having a French wife. You will perceive I am describing Sumpter. I do not know a more proper character for the place. I wish we could find a diplomatist or two equally eligible, for Europe. Accept my affectionate salutations.

TH. JEFFERSON

19. Livingston, whom TJ had appointed as district attorney for New York, visited Washington early in July to discuss a shortage of about $40,000 in the accounts of a clerk in his office. But he left town without talking to Gallatin, who convinced TJ that Livingston was accountable and should resign. Livingston did so in August; see William B. Hatcher, *Edward Livingston: Jeffersonian Republican and Jacksonian Democrat* (Baton Rouge, 1940), pp. 93–97.

Jefferson to Madison

Monticello Aug. 8, 1803

Dear Sir

If M. Dalbarton be really Jerome Bonaparte, he will have satisfied thereof the minister of his nation, thro' whom we shall be apprised of the fact, and relieved from all trouble in deciding on it. This may yet be done, perhaps just as a frigate is ready to sail, and accompanied with a request of a passage in her; when no time will be left for consultation. Our duty to our constituents would require us to lose no occasion of conferring obligation on the first Consul of France personally, and of procuring by just attentions the advantages of his good will to them. The same duties require us equally to give no just offence to the other belligerent party, and that we should not expose our flag to the humiliation of having a frigate searched by superior power, the search proved rightful by it's result, and ourselves placed in the wrong. We should therefore be prepared with an answer, yea or nay, should the application be made in proper form, for which reason I ask the favor of yourself, as well as of the other gentlemen of the administration, to advise me as to the answer to be given. I presume there is little time left for it.[20]

I return you Mr Dawson's letter of July 29. 1803. Mr Pichon's papers in the case of Cloupet await the information you expect from the Collector of Norfolk. Accept my affectionate salutations and unvarying esteem and attachment

Th: Jefferson

Madison to Jefferson

[Orange] Aug. 13, 1803

Dear Sir

My arrival here was delayed till monday evening last; first by the completion of the business depending at Washington, and then by the breaking down of my carriage just after I had set out which detained me three days. I found at the post office your letter covering the pardon for Miller, which was forwarded by the evening mail, with the intimation to Wagner which you wished. Yesterday I had your favor of the 8th with the proceedings of the   Territory under another cover. On the subject of the former I am ready to say that if application were to be made for a frigate in behalf of the brother of Jerome Bona-

---

20. TJ was temporarily relieved of the diplomatic problem of furnishing passage to Napoleon's brother when the latter married Elizabeth Patterson, niece of Robert Smith, secretary of the navy. See Brant, IV, p. 166; Malone, IV, pp. 383–84; Dangerfield, p. 426. For later complications, see TJ to JM, Sept. 6, 1804, below.

parte,[21] it ought to be at once rejected, tho' in a manner as little disagreeable as possible. There is however no danger of such an application. Just before I left Washington I had a conversation with Pichon which the receipt of the letter from Dawson led me into, in which I explained to him the inadmissibility of furnishing a passage in a public ship to a military Citizen of the French Republic. He acquiesced fully in the objections, and told me that he had, by a proper explanation to young Bonaparte stifled such an expectation. I hope therefore that we shall hear nothing more of the matter. Among the papers sent for your perusal are a letter from T. Paine, and another from Duane. I shall communicate to the former what he wishes. To the latter I shall also communicate the fact that no remonstrance such as has been reported, has been made by G.B. but on the contrary that she is satisfied with the acquisition of Louisiana by the U. States. I shall at the same time withold the copy of Lord Hawksburys answer to M.[r] King, with a glance at the reasons which make it proper to do so. I am sensible of the advantage on the side of the adversary prints which mortifies him, but general rules must be observed, and it would be moreover improper to make more than one paper the vehicle of informal or formal communications from the government. In Smith's paper, it was intimated that G. Britain was satisfied with our arrangement with France. On the whole the zeal of Duane is laudable, and the manner of his application strengthens the title to tenderness in the refusal.[22]

The day before I left the City I was obliged to write to Thornton a strong complaint ag.[st] Capt Douglas of the Boston Frigate, founded on an impressment of 4 seamen two of which had protections and were known to be native citizens. The trespass was committed on board the Charles Carter ab.[t] 18 leagues at sea. She had sailed from Norfolk, the resort of the Boston, which had no doubt made her use of that port subservient to her cruises on our own coast ag.[st] our own trade.[23] Pichon is referring for a formal protest ag.[st] a like one of our ports for seizing French vessels the moment they get beyond our jurisdiction.

Be pleased to return the inclosed papers, as I shall await it, before I give answers to such as require them. With most respectful attachment I am Dr. Sr. Y.[rs]

JAMES MADISON

---

21. JM meant Jerome, the nineteen-year-old brother of Napoleon Bonaparte.

22. The Jefferson administration used the *National Intelligencer,* edited by Samuel Harrison Smith, as the unofficial outlet for both "informal or formal communications from the government"; see Brant, IV, p. 151.

23. JM had sent the British chargé d'affaires the deposition of a native-born American seaman who swam ashore from the British frigate that had impressed him and three other Americans, making it the basis for a protest against the conversion of American ports into operational centers against American commerce; see *ibid.,* pp. 161–62.

Jefferson to Madison

Monticello Aug. 13, 1803

DEAR SIR

I recieved yesterday the inclosed letter and papers from Governor Mercer, requesting my approbation of the relinquishment of a part of their claim to bank stock in England in order to obtain the residue. This it seems is required by an act of the legislature of Maryland, but with what view, or to what end I am unapprised, never having seen the act. It cannot certainly be with a view to raise any claim against the U S. As such an act of mine would be entirely extraofficial, it could not affect the U S. We have lent the agency of our minister hitherto to obtain their right: but on his departure Mr Pinckney seems to come in as the special agent of the state, and neither deriving nor needing authority from us.[24] Perhaps you may be apprised of the act of Maryland alluded to, and may be able to inform me what sort of an approbation it is desired I should give. Accept my affectionate salutations

TH: JEFFERSON

P. S. Will you direct a Commission to Jonathan E. Robinson at Bennington as Commr. of bankruptcy for Vermont?

Jefferson to Madison

Monticello Aug. 16, 1803

DEAR SIR

Your favor of the 13th. came to hand yesterday. I now return Paine's Duane's Lear's, Simpson's and Toulman's letters, and the two protests on impressment by a British and a French armed vessel. I am glad of the latter, as it will serve as a set-off against French complaints on the British trespasses on us. But the former is an afflicting subject. With every disposition to render them all justifiable services, I fear they will put our patience to the proof. Their making our ports also stations for cruising from will require regulation. It seems to me that we shall be obliged to have a battery or two in our principal seaports, and to require armed vessels to lie under them, while they are using our ports for repairs or supplies, the only legitimate purposes of entering

---

24. As American minister to Great Britain, Rufus King had negotiated in 1803 the return to Maryland of pre-Revolutionary stock owned in the Bank of England; see Robert Ernst, *Rufus King, American Federalist* (Chapel Hill, 1968), p. 235, and Perkins, p. 153, for brief mentions. For a full discussion, see Jacob M. Price, "The Maryland Bank Stock Case: British-American Financial and Political Relations before and after the American Revolution," in *Law, Society and Politics in Early Maryland,* ed. Aubrey C. Land, Lois Green Carr, and Edward C. Papenfuse (Baltimore, 1977), pp. 3-40.

them. Toulman's application is at least premature. I presume Congress will enlarge the Indian fund and authorise us to send embassies to the Indian tribes of Louisiane, who may at the same time explore the country and ascertain it's geography. Those large Western rivers of the Misipi and Missouri whose heads form the contour of the Louisiana territory ought to be known.

I think Duane's zeal merits tenderness and satisfaction, while his precipitancy makes him improper to be considered as speaking the sense of the government. With respect to Clarke's application for a consulship at Embden, I am for holding our hand as to new Consular establishments, and letting a great proportion of those existing drop with the first occasion. Their number has obliged us to be [have] very little choice in the characters appointed, and I fear they will degrade our national character. Accept my affectionate salutations and assurances of constant esteem and respect.

TH: JEFFERSON

P. S. I inclose for your perusal a letter from Cork on the same subject of the impressment of our seamen

Jefferson to Madison

Monticello Aug. 18, 1803

DEAR SIR

I inclose you two letters from Rob. R. Livingston. That of the 2^d of June is just intelligible enough in the uncyphered parts to create anxieties which perhaps the cypher may remove. I communicate them for your information, and shall be glad to recieve them decyphered. I infer that the less we say about constitutional difficulties respecting Louisiana the better, and that what is necessary for surmounting them must be done sub silentio.[25]

I inclose you also a letter from Derieux, which will explain itself. You will probably have recieved a like one. My idea as to allowance would be between the limits of what was allowed to Dawson (6. D. a day) or the half of that allowance, as Derieux was coming on his own business. But perhaps it is already sufficiently halved, as we pay his coming only and at his going. Decide on this yourself and offer him what you think proper without delaying him for further consultation.[26]

The inclosed letter from Acton to Barnes was sent me by Mazzei. It shews the government of Naples well disposed: but it shews an impropriety also in

---

25. For a discussion of TJ's changing views on the Constitution and the expanding Union, see Malone, IV, pp. 311–32.

26. Congressman John Dawson of Virginia carried the ratification of the Convention of 1800 to France in 1801. Derieux probably carried the Louisiana Purchase treaty from France to the United States in 1803.

Barnes in exciting expectations not within our view. He wishes to become diplomatic, and Mazzei has the same longing. I shall cut up the letter.

Will you be so good as to order the following commissions.

Robert Lee at Niagara, New York, to be Collector of the District of Niagara, and Inspector of the revenue for the port of Niagara

Irvine at Buffalo New York to be Surveyor of the port of Buffalo and Inspector of the revenue for the same.

I do not know Irvine's Christian name: but it is known at the War office as he is our Indian agent at Buffalo.

Mr. King said to Mr Gallatin that the idea of selling Louisiana was, 4 weeks before the treaty, assimilated at Paris with the sale of Dunkirk by Charles the 2d and that Mr Livingston had not at that time the least expectation of success. Accept my affectionate salutations and assurances of constant esteem.

TH: JEFFERSON

Madison to Jefferson

[Orange] Aug. 18, 1803

DEAR SIR

I have duly recd yours of the 13. covering the papers from Govr Mercer. The act of Maryland is I believe in the Office of State, having been sent thither by the Govr after his return to Annapolis. The object of it in requiring the sanction of the President to the measures of the Ex. of the State, was I believe to prevent an interference with national measures, as well as to be a check in general on the local authority. The letter which I have written to Mr Pinkney, pursues the course hitherto taken as well as I recollect it, and will not probably be either applied or be applicable to any improper pretension agst the U. States. If it appear in the same light to you, you will be pleased to seal and forward to Mr. Wagner the letter enclosing it. With respectful attacht Yrs

JAMES MADISON

Madison to Jefferson

[Orange] Aug. 20, 1803

DEAR SIR

I have recd yours of the 16th with the accompanying papers. The communications etc. recd since my last are enclosed. The letters from Paris are important, but I do not see in them the wish of the Fr. Govt to retract the bargain with our Ministers, so much as an anxiety to secure its execution agst the intrusions of G. B. and to feel thro' their pulse, whether we were or were [not?] likely to be in any understanding with G. B. on the subject. Thornton's letters also are in the spirit, tho' beyond the degree to have been anticipated. I should for that reason have given him no opportunity for his very exceptionable remarks on the subject of impressments, had not his interposition been wanted immediately. I presume it will be but to give no answer, notwithstanding the allegations of some facts which might seem to require notice. Clarke's remarks are judicious, but I think he might have assumed the proper course to be pursued, takg care to foster individual expectations as little as possible. The letters from C. Pinkney will require no particular answer, till we hear from Monroe. What is to be said to Graham? Will it not be but to say nothing to him also, till we hear from the same quarter?[27] You will please to decide on the subject of the gun carriages. If good ones can be sent from the Navy in time, I think Simpson's advice ought to be followed. Should this be your opinion, Mr Smith will probably expect it to go to him immediately from yourself. Perhaps you may think it proper to inclose M^r. Gallatin the letters from Paris, which refer to arrangements which touch his Dep^t With respectful attachment Y^{rs} always

JAMES MADISON

What ought to be the decision on Dereaux's claim? With an exception of the gratification for which there is no good pretext, and for which he offers very bad ones, his charge is less objectionable in itself, than as it exceeds the idea of Monroe who could best appreciate the proper extent of it.

Madison to Jefferson

[Orange] Aug. 21, 1803

DEAR SIR

Yours of the 18. with inclosures has been rec^d I must write to Wagner for Livingston's Cypher, before I can return the letter from him. I have with me Monroe's Cypher only. The letters sent you by last mail from those Ministers probably contain the information in Cyphered passages of the letter in my hands.

The subject of Duane's letter being somewhat delicate and important, under several aspects, I have thought it not amiss that you should see the answer I propose to give it. If you think it a proper one, you will please to seal and send it to the post office. If you think it ought to be in a different shape, you will be so good as to return it, with suitable suggestions.[28]

---

27. John Graham was private secretary to Charles Pinckney, American minister to Spain; see *PJM* (SS ser.), I, p. 279.

28. William Duane, editor of the Philadelphia *Aurora*, headed the radical faction of the Republican party in Pennsylvania. He generally supported the administration, although he was a harsh

The inclosed newspaper contains what is material to a full view of the paper side of the controversy between G. B. and France. Having seen no republication of it in our Gazettes I have thought it worth sending you. Y̆ʳˢ respectfully

JAMES MADISON

Jefferson to Madison

Monticello Aug. 24, 1803[29]

DEAR SIR,

Your two favors of the 18th. and 20th. were received on the 21st. The letters of Livingston and Monroe were sent to Mr Gallatin as you proposed. That of Simpson to Mr Smith for the purpose of execution. All of them will be returned. Thornton's, Clarke's, Charles Pinckney's, Graham's, Appleton's, Davis's, Newton's, and Derieux's. letters are now enclosed. With respect to the impressment of our seamen I think we had better propose to Great Britain to act on the stipulations which had been agreed to between that Government and Mr. King, as if they had been signed. I think they were, that they would forbid impressments at sea, and that we should acquiesce in the search in *their* harbors necessary to prevent concealments of their citizens. Mr. Thornton's attempt to justify his nation in using our ports as cruising stations on our friends and ourselves, renders the matter so serious as to call, I think, for answer bien motive. That we ought in courtesy and friendship to extend to them all the rights of hospitality is certain: that they should not use our hospitality to injure our friends or ourselves is equally enjoined by morality and honor. After the rigorous exertions we made in Genet's time to prevent this abuse on his part, and the indulgencies extended by Mr. Adams to the British cruisers even after our pacification with France, and by ourselves also, from an unwillingness to change the course of things as the war was near its close, I did not expect to hear from that quarter charges of partiality. In the Mediterranean we need ask from no nation but the permission to refresh and repair in their ports. We do not wish our vessels to lounge in their ports. In the case at Gibraltar, if they had disapproved, our vessels ought to have left the port. Besides, although nations have treated with the piratical States, they have not in practice ever, been considered as entitled to all the favors of the laws of nations. Thornton says they watch our trade only to prevent contraband. We say it is to plunder under pretext of contraband for which, though

---

critic of Secretary of the Treasury Gallatin, a fellow Pennsylvanian. For the factional quarrels in Pennsylvania, see Noble E. Cunningham, Jr., *The Jeffersonian Republicans in Power: Party Operations, 1801–1809* (Chapel Hill, 1963), pp. 213–17.

29. Malone, IV, p. 314, and Ford, VIII, pp. 245–46, mistakenly date this letter Aug. 25, 1803, but the date is clearly Aug. 24; see JM's acknowledgment of it in his letter to TJ, Aug. 28, 1803, below.

so shamefully exercised, they have given us no satisfaction but by confessing the fact in new modifying their courts of admiralty. Certainly the evils we experience from it, and the just complaints which France may urge, render it indispensable that we restrain the English from abusing the rights of hospitality to their prejudice as well as our own.

Graham's letter manifests a degree of impudence which I had not expected from him. His pride has probably been hurt at some of the regulations of that court, and has had its part in inspiring the ill temper he shews. If you understand him as serious in asking leave to return, I see no great objection to it. At the date of your letter you had not received mine on the subject of Derieux's claim. I still think the limits therein stated reasonable. I think a guinea a day till he leaves Washington would be as low an allowance as we could justify, and should not be opposed to anything not exceeding the allowance to Dawson. Fix between these as you please.

I suppose Monroe will touch on the limits of Louisiana only incidentally, inasmuch as its extension to Perdido curtails Florida and renders it of less worth. I have used my spare moments to investigate, by the help of my books here, the subject of the limits of Louisiana. I am satisfied our right to the Perdido is substantial, and can be opposed by a quibble on form only; and our right Westwardly to the bay of St. Bernard, may be strongly maintained. I will use the first leisure to make a statement of the facts and principles on which this depends. Further reflection on the amendment to the constitution necessary in the case of Louisiana, satisfies me it will be better to give general powers, with specified exceptions, somewhat in the way stated below. Mrs. Madison promised us a visit about the last of this month. I wish you could have met with General Page here, whom, with his family, I expect in a day or two and will pass a week with us. But in this consult your own convenience, as that will increase the pleasure with which I shall always see you here. Accept my affectionate salutations and constant attachment.

Th Jefferson

'Louisiana, as ceded by France to the US. is made a part of the US. It's white inhabitants shall be citizens, and stand, as to their rights and obligations on the same footing with other citizens of the US. in analogous situations.

Save only that, as to the portion thereof lying North of the latitude of the Arcansa river, no new state shall be established, nor any grants of land made therein, other than to Indians in exchange for equivalent portions of land occupied by them, until an amendment to the Constitution shall be made for that purpose.

Florida also, whensoever it may be rightfully obtained, shall become a part of the US. It's white inhabitants shall thereupon be citizens, and shall stand as to their rights and obligations on the same footing with other citizens of the U.S. in analogous circumstances.'[30]

30. This postscript is TJ's revised draft, based on JM's suggested substitute of his proposed constitutional amendment on Louisiana; see Brant, IV, pp. 142–45.

Madison to Jefferson

[Orange] Sunday Aug. 28, 1803

DEAR SIR

I have rec.d your two favors, one of the 24.th instant the other covering the letters from M.r Gallatin and Barnes now returned.[31]

I had thought it might be best not to answer Thornton's letter because in some parts his manner did not deserve it, because he speaks without the known sentiments of his gov.t and because the Minister of higher grade expected, will be likely to give a more eligible opportunity for these discussions. As I promise the pleasure of being able to take your directions in person in the course of this week probably towards the last of it, I shall do nothing in the case till I can do it with that advantage. The British Gov.t I apprehend will not act with us on the subject of seamen, in the manner you hint at. They would sign no convention without reserving to themselves the claim to impress seamen in the narrow seas, and as this was evidently inadmissable, it was no doubt made a condition with a view to prevent any arrangement, and to carry on the impressments as heretofore. In consequence of your letter of [Aug. 18, 1803] I had directed Derieux to be paid his charge of $300 for actual expences, as Hughes was paid his. If any thing further should be thought just in his behalf it can be added. I inclose the communications rec.d by the last mail from Washington. Pederson I presume may be told that he will have access to the gov.t as the substitute of Olsen, who signified his wish to that effect. Will you be so obliging as to have the confidential letter from Monroe to three Senators put into the hands of M.r Nicholas. You will see by his public letter that his liberality has been very near reducing him into a very ticklish situation. I have not yet been able to decypher the letter to you from M.r Livingston, having but just rec.d the cypher. I will execute the task for the next mail. I think K's prejudice must have given a strong coloring to his remarks on L. The caution alluded to in M.r Gallatin's letter, was if I do not misrecollect observed in the instructions from the Dep.t of State. Y.rs most respectfully

JAMES MADISON

Jefferson to Madison

Monticello Aug. 29, 1803

DEAR SIR

By the last post I recieved and forwarded your letter to Duane, in which there was nothing but what was safe and proper. Duane is honest, and well intentioned, but over zealous. These qualities harmonize with him a great portion of the republican body. He deserves therefore all the just and favorable

---

31. Although TJ dated his letter Aug. 24, 1803, he noted on his file copy that it "Shd be 25th."

attention which can properly be shewn him. By the same post I recieved from the collector of Norfolk the information you desired him to give in the case of Capt Cloupet and the contraband negroes. I presume it is by mistake he says he recieved the orders from the Secretary of the Treasury. I now inclose his papers to you with those recieved from you on the same subject. If you think with me that the case is of too doubtful an aspect to justify so early an interposition, it may lie awhile, and with the less inconvenience as we cannot remit the right of the prosecutor qui tam. Should you think otherwise I shall be ready to reconsider it at any time. I return you the letter etc. of Gavino.[32] Our two frigates and 4. small vessels have all sailed for Tripoli, and as those in the Mediterranean have at length appeared there, we may hope something will be done this season. I am afraid what has been done as to the Marocco-Tripoline may give us some trouble.

Govr. Page arrived here last night and will stay a week with us. I am without hopes of seeing you in that time. Altho' the post comes from Alexandria here in a day, and every other day, yet I think your letters to me and mine to you are sometimes 5. days old before they are recieved. It is true that I sometimes write on Saturday the letter which goes on Monday and often write one day before the post. This may account for one and sometimes 2. days of the five. Accept my affectionate salutations for Mrs Madison and yourself and assurances of sincere attachment.

Madison to Jefferson

[Orange] Sept. 11, 1803

Dear Sir

I have rec^d the letters sent me by the last mail under two covers, and return those belonging to your own files. I inclose herewith also the communications last rec^d from the office of State. I cannot without losing the present opportunity make comments on any of them. A few only invite them. Yours with respectful attach^t

James Madison

Dr Wallace in whose behalf the letters from Mr Brent and Mr Thomson were written is with me, and proposes I found to wait on you with a letter from Mr Wythe, who it seems is his kinsman. I have stated to him the relation of Dr Bache to the object of his pursuit.

---

32. John Gavino was American consul at Gibralter. See *ASP, M,* I, p. 307; Wright and Macleod, pp. 90–91; William M. Fowler, Jr., *Jack Tars and Commodores: The American Navy, 1783–1815* (Boston, 1984), pp. 67, 89.

Madison to Jefferson

[Orange] Monday Sept. 12, 1803

DEAR SIR

I rec^d last night the inclosed letter from Yrujo. Mr Wagner informs me that a copy was sent directly to you by the same mail, but as a further security for your receiving the communication without delay, I take advantage of the present opp^y of forwarding the original. It is a curious circumstance that near three months after the sale of Louisiana, the French ambas^r should have given the assurance stated. Still it was not to be expected that Spain would have undertaken to enter such a caveat. If it could be supposed the result of a secret understanding with France or even with G. B. the incident would take a very serious aspect; but as a collusion on the subject with either is highly improbable, the step seems most readily explained, by supposing it the offspring of a wish in Spain to make a merit or obtain a price for her consent, and to contest with more advantage the extension of Louisīna to the limits she must be aware that we have in view.[33] As Mr Pinkney will doubtless have rec^d the notice now communicated here, and have transmitted it to Paris, we may presume that our Minister there will have called on the French Gov^t to prevent any obstruction to the fulfillment of the Treaty on its part. It will notwithstanding be proper to transmit the communication of Yrujo to both. It is to be considered also whether any and what reply to Yrujo, and what intimations to Pichon, may be proper in the mean time. Perhaps, as the return to Washington is drawing so nigh, it may be as well to wait for that opp^y. of communicating with the latter; and for the same reason as well as in expectation of soon learning more on the subject, to postpone the observations due to the note of the former. Your instructions will decide those points. Whatever may be the views of Spain, there will be no difficulty, if she stands alone, and above all if she opposes the views of France, in going thro' with our own purposes.

I inclose also a letter and papers from Forbes, increasing the pile of wrongs to be brought into our remonstrance to the British Gov^t on the subject of impressments. Y^{rs} with respectful attachment

JAMES MADISON

Jefferson to Madison

Monticello Sept. 14, 1803

DEAR SIR,

I now return you the several papers received by the last post, except those soliciting office, which as usual, are put into my bundle of like papers. I think it

---

33. Martínez d'Yrujo's letter to JM of Sept. 4, 1803 (*ASP, FR,* II, p. 569), stated that Spain regarded the sale of Louisiana by France as a violation of Napoleon's promise never to alienate Louisiana; see Brant, IV, p. 152, and Malone, IV, pp. 321–22.

possible that Spain, recollecting our former eagerness for the island of N. Orleans, may imagine she can, by a free delivery of that, redeem the residue of Louisiana: and that she may withhold the peaceable cession of it. In that case no doubt force must be used. However the importance of this measure, the time and the means, will be for discussion at our meeting on the 25h. In the meantime I think Clarke might be trusted with a general hint of the possibility of opposition from Spain, and an instruction to sound in every direction, but with so much caution as to avoid suspicion, and to inform us whether he discovers any symptoms of doubt as to the delivery, to let us know the force Spain has there, where posted, how the inhabitants are likely to act, if we march a force there, and what numbers of them could be armed and brought to act in opposition to us. We have time to receive this information before the day of ratification, and it would guide us in our provision of force for the object.[34] Accept my affectionate salutations and respects.

TH. JEFFERSON

34. For TJ's preparations to use force in taking possession of Louisiana, see Whitaker, pp. 240–43, and Malone, IV, p. 335.

"THE EMPIRE FOR LIBERTY," 1803–1804

THE LOUISIANA PURCHASE was the most significant achievement of Jefferson's presidency, for it "more than doubled the area of the U. S. and," Jefferson added expansively, "the new part is not inferior to the old in soil, climate, production and important communications."[1] It was also an incredible bargain: half a continent for approximately 3 cents per acre.[2]

"The acquisition of New Orleans would of itself [have] been a great thing," the president told a colleague from the Continental Congress of 1776, "as it would have insured to our western brethren the means of exporting their produce: but that of Louisiana is inappreciable, because, giving us the sole dominion of the Mississippi, it excludes those bickerings with foreign powers, which we know of a certainty would have put us at war with France immediately: and it secures to us the course of a peaceable nation."[3] In addition to helping assure national security by eliminating a potential enemy on its borders, the acquisition of the western territory also enlarged America's "empire of liberty":[4] "I confess," he wrote, "I look to this duplication of area for the extending a government so free and economical as ours, as a great achievement to the mass of happiness which is to ensue."[5] From Tennessee, Andrew Jack-

---

1. TJ to Horatio Gates, July 11, 1803, in Ford, VIII, p. 249.
2. Thomas A. Bailey, *A Diplomatic History of the American People* (New York, 1969), p. 112.
3. TJ to John Dickinson, Aug. 9, 1803, in Ford, VIII, p. 261. In the first news accounts, the *National Intelligencer* in Washington and the Philadelphia *Aurora* stressed national security rather than territory; see Malone, IV, p. 297.
4. "By enlarging the empire of liberty," TJ said, "we multiply its auxiliaries, and provide new sources of renovation, should its principles at any time degenerate, in those portions of our country which gave them birth"; see Peterson, p. 773. TJ also used the phrase "empire for liberty" in his letter to JM, Apr. 27, 1809, below.
5. TJ to Joseph Priestley, Jan. 29, 1804, in Ford, VIII, p. 295.

son, future president of the United States, confirmed the happiness there, writing that "every face wears a smile, and every heart leaps with joy."[6] To another westerner, Jefferson wrote that he looked forward to the day when "we may lay off a range of States on the Western bank [of the Mississippi] from the head to the mouth, and so, range after range, advancing compactly as we multiply."[7]

But the purchase of Louisiana not only represented an opportunity to expand the extensive republic created by the Constitution; it also represented a constitutional problem for the president, a longtime believer in a strict construction of the Constitution. Although he, Madison, and the cabinet had agreed as early as January 1803, when they were preparing instructions for Monroe and Livingston as negotiators, that "there is no constitutional difficulty as to the acquisition of territory," Jefferson had some lingering doubts about the constitutionality of taking the territory and its inhabitants into the Union, thinking it more expedient and "safer not to permit the enlargement of the Union but by amendment of the Constitution."[8]

Once the territory of imperial dimensions was acquired, therefore, he convened his cabinet in July to deal with the practical issues of accepting, transferring, and paying for the acquisition as well as the constitutional issues and "metaphysical subtleties" of justifying an act that he considered, on sober second thought, "beyond the Constitution." "This treaty," he wrote, "must of course be laid before both Houses, because both have important functions to exercise respecting it. They, I presume, will see their duty to their country in ratifying and paying for it, so as to secure a good which would otherwise probably be never again in their power. But I suppose they must then appeal to *the nation* for an additional article to the Constitution, approving and confirming an act which the nation had not previously authorized."[9]

Indeed, he thought that ratification and retrospective amendment, one that called for a subsequent amendment, could move along parallel tracks simultaneously. When he learned of the huge purchase early in July, Jefferson cast aside "metaphysical subtleties" and drafted a lengthy and detailed amendment in order to sanction doing for the American people "unauthorized what we know they would have done for themselves had they been in a situation to do it."[10] It justified the acquisition of territory, authorized the incorporation of Louisiana inhabitants into the Union, reserved the northern portion of the

---

6. Quoted in Malone, IV, p. 348.

7. TJ to John Breckinridge, Aug. 12, 1803, in Ford, VIII, p. 244. See Reginald Horsman, "The Dimensions of an 'Empire for Liberty': Expansion and Republicanism, 1775–1825," *JER* 9 (1989): 1–20, for an excellent summary.

8. TJ to Albert Gallatin, Jan. 13, 1803, in Albert Gallatin, *The Writings of Albert Gallatin*, ed. Henry Adams, 3 vols. (Philadelphia, 1879), I, pp. 111–15.

9. TJ to John Breckinridge, Aug. 12, 1803, in Ford, VIII, p. 244.

10. *Ibid.*

territory for the Indians, and prohibited American settlement in the Indian territory until a subsequent amendment had authorized it.[11]

Since Jefferson's phrasing restricted his proposed amendment to Louisiana, thus implying a lack of power to acquire the Floridas, Madison suggested two alterations. Assuming the power of territorial expansion, he added a proviso applicable to territories east of the Mississippi "which may be acquired by the U. S." But to simplify matters, he also submitted a substitute amendment that shortened Jefferson's proposal at the same time that it broadened it: "Louisiana as ceded by France is made part of the United States. Congress may make part of the United States other adjacent territories which shall be justly acquired."[12]

Before the president and secretary of state left for Virginia for the summer, Jefferson issued a call for Congress to convene on October 17, several weeks prior to its regular session, in order to meet the time limit imposed by the Louisiana treaty for ratification. While Jefferson was at Monticello weighing the question of an amendment, he received coded letters from Robert R. Livingston "just intelligible enough in the uncyphered parts to create anxieties." Although he had not brought his cipher from Washington, he gathered that Napoleon might "retract the bargain" if there were any delay. He, therefore, forwarded the letter to Madison at Montpellier for decoding, and, as a precaution against rousing French or, worse yet, Federalist opposition, he cautioned: "I infer that the less we say about constitutional difficulties respecting Louisiana the better, and that what is necessary for surmounting them must be done sub silentio."[13]

The president, therefore, changed his tactics, though not his objectives, shifting from simultaneous action on ratification and amendment to ratification first and amendment later. At the same time, he plunged into his library at Monticello whenever he had any "spare moments[,] to investigate, by the help of my books here, the subject of the limits of Louisiana." He also had time to revise his proposed amendment: "Further reflection on the amendment to the constitution necessary in the case of Louisiana," he confessed to Madison, "satisfies me it will be better to give general powers, with specified exceptions," thus replacing his lengthy and specific amendment of July. His opening sentence, which implied the constitutional right to acquire territory, accepted Madison's first sentence from his substitute amendment: "Louisiana, as ceded by France to the US. is made a part of the US." And the final sentence in his

---

11. See TJ's draft of a proposed constitutional amendment on Louisiana, [July 1803], above. TJ prepared this draft of his amendment between July 3, when news of the treaty arrived, and July 9, when Gallatin and Secretary of the Navy Robert Smith, who proposed an alternative amendment, commented on it; see Ford, VIII, pp. 241-42, and Malone, IV, p. 314.

12. See JM's undated proposal following TJ's proposed constitutional amendment, July 3-9, 1803, above. For discussions, see Brant, IV, pp. 142-44, and Malone, IV, pp. 314-17.

13. TJ to JM, Aug. 18, 1803, above.

new and much abbreviated draft (he cut it from 375 words to 170) also followed Madison's suggestion about Florida, whenever it might be "rightfully obtained."[14]

As for Louisiana, Jefferson said, "we must take the island of New Orleans and west side of the river . . . , containing nearly the whole inhabitants, say about 50,000, and erect it into a state, or annex it to the Mississippi territory: and shut up all the rest from settlement for a long time to come, endeavoring to exchange some of the country there unoccupied by Indians for the lands held by the Indians on this [east] side [of] the Mississippi, who will be glad to cede to us their country here for an equivalent there: and we may sell out our lands here and pay the whole debt contracted before it comes due. The impost which will be paid by the inhabitants ceded will pay half the interest of the price we give: so that we really add only half the price to our debt."[15]

Early in September, the Madisons accepted Jefferson's invitation to visit Monticello,[16] and Madison finally persuaded Jefferson to drop the idea of an amendment. Letters from Monroe and Livingston had stressed the need for speedy action, and the French had dispatched "an unusual kind of letter written by their minister to our Secretary of State, direct," warning against delay. After discussing the matter with Madison, Jefferson informed Senator Wilson Cary Nicholas of Virginia that "whatever Congress shall think it necessary to do, should be done with as little debate as possible, and particularly so far as respects the constitutional difficulty." Although he still thought an amendment desirable, thus setting "an example against broad construction," he conceded that if "our friends shall think differently, certainly I shall acquiesce with satisfaction; confiding, that the good sense of our country will correct the evil of construction when it shall produce ill effects."[17]

In his message to Congress on October 17, the president made no mention of his constitutional qualms but instead stressed "the wide-spread field for the blessings of freedom and equal laws." He, therefore, proposed prompt ratification of the treaty by the Senate and quick authorization by Congress for taking possession of Louisiana.[18] Three days later, the Senate ratified the Louisiana Purchase Treaty, taking less time, a caustic Federalist complained, "to deliberate on this important treaty, than they allowed on the most trivial Indian contract. The rules of the Senate require a treaty to be read three times,

---

14. The postscript in TJ to JM, Aug. 24, 1803, above, contains TJ's final draft of his proposed constitutional amendment. See also John M. Belolavek, "Politics, Principle, and Pragmatism in the Early Republic: Thomas Jefferson and the Quest for American Empire," *Diplomatic History* 15 (1991): 599–606.

15. TJ to John Dickinson, Aug. 9, 1803, in Ford, VIII, pp. 262–63.

16. TJ to JM, Aug. 24, 1803, above.

17. TJ to Wilson Cary Nicholas, Sept. 7, 1803, in Ford, VIII, pp. 247–48. See also Malone, IV, pp. 310–19; Brant, IV, pp. 141–45; and Ketcham, p. 421.

18. For JM's suggestions on TJ's message, see his notes of Oct. 1, 1803, below. TJ's message is in Ford, VIII, pp. 266–74.

and not more than once a day. Its probable that it is owing to this rule, that the final question was not decided the first day we met—and the first time we ever heard the Instrument read."[19] The House and Senate speedily adopted legislation to implement the treaty; and, only two weeks after sending his message to Congress, the president signed the Enabling Act, authorizing him to take possession of Louisiana and to make provisions for its government until Congress enacted appropriate legislation.

On November 30, 1803, the Spanish governor of Louisiana presented a silver platter containing the keys to the public buildings in New Orleans to French functionaries, and twenty days later the French transferred possession of the territory to the United States. Upstream in St. Louis, things moved at a more leisurely pace. Not until March 9, 1804, did the double transfer of possession get under way, with Spanish officials in Upper Louisiana surrendering the territory to Amos Stoddard, an American army captain, acting on behalf of France, who next day officially transferred it to himself, acting on behalf of the United States.[20]

Did the Louisiana acquisition include any territory *east* of the Mississippi in West Florida, the territory that Livingston and Monroe had first been instructed to buy, along with New Orleans? Both negotiators argued that Louisiana extended eastward to the Perdido River (the present-day western boundary of Florida). When Livingston asked Talleyrand about the "east bounds of the territory ceded to us," the Frenchman replied: "I can give you no direction; you have made a noble bargain for yourselves, and I suppose you will make the most of it."[21]

Jefferson and Madison agreed with the American negotiators and decided to make the most of it, pursuing a policy of trying to force concessions through diplomatic channels. Noting that the Floridas were separated from Spain's other colonies in the Western Hemisphere, Madison argued that they "must ever be a dead expense in time of peace, indefensible in time of war, and always an obstacle to peaceful relations with the United States."[22] Jefferson concluded that the disputed boundary claims would be "a subject of negociation with Spain, and if, as soon as she is at war, we push them strongly with one hand, holding out a price in the other, we shall certainly obtain the Floridas, and all in good time."[23]

Accordingly, Jefferson, Madison, and the cabinet decided to merge their claim to West Florida with an effort to purchase the rest of the Floridas, making "an acknolegment of our right to the Perdido . . . a *sine qua non,* and

19. William Plumer, *William Plumer's Memorandum of Proceedings in the United States Senate, 1803–1807,* ed. Everett Somerville Brown (New York, 1923), pp. 13–14.
20. Malone, IV, pp. 328, 333, 337, and Marshall Smelser, *The Democratic Republic, 1801–1815* (New York, 1968), p. 101.
21. Robert R. Livingston to JM, May 20, 1803, in *ASP, FR,* II, p. 561.
22. JM to James Monroe, July 29, 1803, quoted in Brant, IV, p. 150.
23. TJ to John Breckinridge, Aug. 12, 1803, in Ford, VIII, p. 243.

no price to be given for it." At the president's request, Congress passed the Mobile Act of February 24, 1804, which extended the federal revenue laws to all territory ceded by France and vested the president with discretionary power to extend them to the disputed Florida territory "whenever he shall deem it expedient."[24]

On the western side of the Mississippi, the administration claimed to the Río Bravo del Norte (the Rio Grande)[25] but was willing to prohibit further settlement within a western border zone "by either party for a given time, say twenty years." The United States agreed to offer this concession and $2 million for "all the Floridas East of the Perdido" or a proportionate payment for whatever part Spain agreed to cede. During negotiations, moreover, neither side should strengthen their situation between the Mississippi and the Perdido "nor interrupt the navigation of the rivers therein." If Spain refused this last proposition, the United States, which had forborne to exercise its rights "for peace sake only," would enter "into the exercise of our right of navigating the Mobile and protect it, and increase our force there *pari passu* with them."[26]

Spain quickly rejected the American claims. Calling the Mobile Act an "atrocious libel," the marquis de Casa Yrujo, Spanish minister to the United States, broke off personal relations with Madison after a heated confrontation at the State Department. The marquis and his wife, Madison reported to the president at Monticello, left Washington for Philadelphia "two or three days ago, without calling on me either at the office or at my House." But Yrujo had sent "an apology thro' the Marchioness," the daughter of Governor McKean of Pennsylvania, "to Mrs. M. for not taking leave of her, from which he was precluded by what had passed between him and me." To make the snub more deliberate, Madison added, "he and the Marchioness together called at the Houses of my Colleagues" in the cabinet.[27]

As Spanish-American matters festered in the United States, Charles Pinckney, American minister to Spain, compounded the diplomatic difficulties by "teazing the Spanish Gov.ᵗ" about the Floridas, Madison fumed, "the subject which was not to be touched without the presence or the advice of Mʳ Monroe." Nonetheless, "he is continually offering to accept" propositions that he was prohibited from making.[28] The conduct of Pinckney, coupled with "the passions of Yrujo," Madison told the president, "threaten some unexpected difficulties at Madrid."[29]

24. TJ to JM, July 5, 1804, below. See also Brant, IV, pp. 190–99.

25.. TJ to JM, July 5, 1804, below. This claim was subsequently modified, with the United States willing to give up its claim to Texas "as the last part of the price yielded, and only for an entire cession of the Floridas, not for a part only"; see TJ to JM, July 6, 1804, below.

26. TJ to JM, July 5, 1804, below.

27. JM to TJ, Apr. 24, 1804, below. Brant, IV, pp. 205–6, discusses the the break between Yrujo and JM.

28. JM to TJ, Apr. 9, 1804, below.

29. JM to TJ, Aug. 28, 1804, below.

In an effort to smooth diplomatic relations and yet bypass the secretary of state, Yrujo and his wife journeyed to Monticello for a personal interview with Jefferson without first stopping at Montpellier. Madison had already sent Pinckney's letters to the president "that they may be at hand, if wanted during your talk with Yrujo."[30] After the visit, Jefferson told Madison that he and Yrujo had discussed diplomatic relations, "which we have smoothed off," but he reserved details for "verbal communication."[31] Yrujo, however, again ruffled relations within a week, publishing a letter to the secretary of state before delivering it to Madison's office. This was comparable to Genet's tactic of using the press to appeal to the people over the head of the president; so Jefferson and Madison, following Washington's example, instructed Monroe to ask for Yrujo's recall.[32]

A puzzling bit of diplomatic gossip diverted the president and the secretary of state during the summer of 1804. Monroe had heard that on the outbreak of war between Great Britain and revolutionary France in 1793 the British government had agreed to restore the Bourbon monarchy if the Bourbons would help Great Britain recover the United States.[33] Monroe's source was an Englishman of high authority and good character who claimed that the idea might be revived. Madison doubted the story but found it difficult to disregard because of "the reliance which Col. Monroe seems to place on what he writes."[34]

Jefferson had no such difficulty; such a deal was "impossible." Having been on the European scene himself, he knew "the immense resources of the nations there, and the greater wickedness of their courts." Indeed, he believed that the Bourbons would agree to any terms of restitution to regain the throne. But he thought it "impossible that France and England should combine for any purpose; their mutual distrust and deadly hatred of each other admit no co-operation." Even if they overcame such obstacles, however, and joined forces, they could not restore the United States to British dominion. "If these things are not so," he was convinced, "then human reason is of no aid in conjecturing the conduct of nations."

But the president drew a moral from the story. "Still however it is our unquestionable interest and duty to conduct ourselves with such sincere friendship and impartiality towards both nations as that each may see unequivocally, what is unquestionably true, that we may be very possibly driven into her scale by unjust conduct in the other."[35]

30. JM to TJ, Sept. 22, 1804, below.
31. TJ to JM, Sept. 25, 1804, below.
32. JM to TJ, Oct. 2, 1804, below. Yrujo had earlier written antiadministration articles for anonymous publication in Federalist newspapers; see Brant, IV, pp. 208-12.
33. James Monroe to JM, May 5, 1804, cited in Brant, IV, p. 207.
34. JM to TJ, Aug. 7, 1804, below.
35. TJ to JM, Aug. 15, 1804, below.

The problems of neutrality continued to trouble the administration as the election of 1804 approached. Both the English and the French violated American neutral rights, but British impressment in American waters overshadowed French infractions. "I conceive the British insults in our harbor[s] as more threatening," the president wrote the secretary of state in August. "We cannot be respected by France as a neutral nation, nor by the world [or] ourselves as an independent one, if we do not take effectual measures to support at every risk, our authority in our own harbors."[36]

Earlier in the year, Jefferson had written in a more philosophical vein about British depredations, reflecting the afterglow of the Anglo-American reconciliation during the Louisiana Purchase negotiations with France: "Would to god that nation would so far be just in her conduct, as that we might with honor give her that friendship it is so much our interest to bear her. She is now a living example that no nation however powerful, any more than an individual, can be unjust with impunity. Sooner or later public opinion, an instrument merely moral in the beginning, will find occasion physically to inflict it's sentences on the unjust. Nothing else could have kept the other nations of Europe from relieving her under her present crisis. The lesson is useful to the weak as well as the strong."[37]

As British impressments in American harbors increased, Madison denounced the intrusions to the British minister as "the rendezvous of an armed force bidding defiance to our laws, insulting the officers in the duty of executing them, committing violence on persons within their protection . . . and . . . violating the neutral regulations of the United States."[38] When the French minister complained about the ineffectiveness of American surveillance of its jurisdictional limits, particularly of its harbors, Madison noted the impossibility of guarding every inlet from Maine to Georgia, suggesting that the exclusion of belligerent ships would be preferable to the size and expense of a naval force necessary for that purpose. Instead, he supported the administration's "policy of that degree of force which is contemplated for the defence of our ports and coasts . . . as a reasonable effort to maintain our neutral character."[39]

Since the navy's new gunboats were not yet ready, Madison continued to exchange letters with the British minister, Anthony Merry, whom he described to Jefferson as "a mere diplomatic pettifogger." "Mr. Merry's answer to my several letters, co-incides with, tho' it can not be the offspring of the spirit of Pitts administration," which had succeeded the Addington ministry and was taking an increasingly hard line on British rights.[40] "He considers a simple denial of the offenders as disproof of the most regular testimony, and main-

36. *Ibid.*
37. TJ to JM, Apr. 23, 1804, below.
38. TJ to Anthony Merry, June 25, 1804, quoted in Brant, IV, p. 254.
39. JM to TJ, Aug. 18, 1804, below.
40. Bradford Perkins, *The First Rapprochement: England and the United States, 1795–1805* (Philadelphia, 1955), p. 175, and Henry Adams, *History of the United States of America during the First Administration of Thomas Jefferson,* 9 vols. (New York, 1889–91), II, p. 396.

tains the right not only to impress from American vessels in the high seas, but from British vessels in our own harbours. And by making the detention of the Enemy ships a reason for blockading our harbours and harassing our trade, leaves the continuance of the evil at the pleasure of the British Commanders."[41]

France also violated neutral rights, and both Jefferson and Madison diligently sought evidence of the illegalities committed by French privateers in American harbors. Since Jefferson planned to lay the violations of the British vessels before Congress, he also proposed to give the facts relative to French vessels so Congress could formulate impartial "measures of coercion, peaceable and of force." A balanced presentation, he told Madison, would "make our measures less pointed, and less offensive."[42]

As the United States took a tougher stance on neutral rights, it also pressed a more vigorous campaign against Tripoli, replacing "the idle and inactive" Commodore Richard Morris with a more energetic officer, Edward Preble. Preble quickly quieted the sultan of Morocco; but before he could blockade the port of Tripoli, one of his ships, the *Philadelphia,* chased pirates too close to the shore, ran aground, and was captured along with its crew, an indignity that was blown out of proportion by American agents in Europe, according to Jefferson.[43]

"In general," he told Madison, "I am mortified at the condemnation which most of our public agents abroad have manifested at the loss of the Philadelphia. It seems as if they thought on the loss of one frigate, that every thing was lost. This must humble us in the eyes of Europe, and renders it the more indispensable to inflict on Tripoli the same chastisement of which the two most powerful nations of Europe have given the world repeated examples."

Worse yet, from Jefferson's point of view, American agents had requested aid from European powers in seeking the release of the members of the *Philadelphia'*s crew. Jefferson considered foreign intervention as interference and feared that any interposition by France, Russia, and the grand seigneur at Constantinople, friendly though it seemed, might temper "the just severities we contemplate" against Tripoli. Although the leader of any country offering help should be thanked, he concluded, "perhaps it might be well he should understand that we wish to make them feel us sensibly before we offer them our peace."[44]

41. JM to TJ, Aug. 28, 1804, below.

42. TJ to JM, Sept. 6, 1804, below.

43. In a daring raid authorized by Commodore Preble and led by Stephen Decatur in Feb. 1804, the *Philadelphia* was destroyed in a surprise move that Admiral Lord Nelson called the "most bold and daring act of the age"; see Malone, V, p. 37. See also Smelser, pp. 59–61, and William M. Fowler, Jr., *Jack Tars and Commodores: The American Navy, 1783–1815* (Boston, 1984), pp. 82–105.

44. TJ to JM, Apr. 15, 1804, below; JM to TJ, Apr. 9, 1804, below, Apr. 15, 1804, below, Apr. 19, 1804, below, and Apr. 24, 1804, below.

The more the president thought about the request for foreign intervention in the Tripolitanian war, the less he liked it. Indeed, he considered it the most serious issue "which has happened to the present administration," labeling it "this sordid disposition to throw [ourselves] upon the charity of others." He viewed it as "a national stain, which unfortunately the nature of the case does not leave us free to wipe off by a disavowal" since the unauthorized requests by American agents had been generously granted by several powers, and they deserved "our grateful acknolegements."

Reviewing American policy with the Barbary powers, the president concluded that "we were free to beg or to fight. We chose the latter and prepare[d] for it. Unauthorized agents have taken the business out of our hands, have chosen to beg, and executed what they chose. Thus two inconsistent plans are going on at the same time, and will run foul of one another in a region so distant, that we cannot decide for ourselves which shall proceed."

"My great hope," he continued, "is that Tripoli will not have been as prompt as the noble-minded Alexander" of Russia, who had requested the release of the American prisoners. "If the prisoners have neither been delivered, nor agreed to be delivered, the measures of war may be pursued without just offence to the mediating powers. If they have been delivered, or are delivered to the Commodore on a demand made, we ought then to make as liberal a peace as we would have made after an unfortunate campaign, the ultimatum of which we had before settled."[45]

Since the prisoners had not been delivered, Preble's successors pressed naval measures while Tobias Lear negotiated a peace treaty with Tripoli in 1805, then signed a treaty of amity and commerce that freed American commerce from tribute. But the United States had to pay the pasha of Tripoli a tribute of $60,000 to ransom the *Philadelphia* prisoners. Although it was not everything that the president wanted, it was the best treaty yet negotiated with Tripoli and capped Jefferson's twenty-year campaign to chastise the Barbary pirates.[46]

After Congress adjourned in March 1804, Jefferson made a hurried visit to Monticello, where his younger daughter lay near death after the birth of her second child. His letters to Madison trace Maria's sad decline in a "remarkably uncheary" spring. "I found my daughter Eppes at Monticello . . . so weak as barely to be able to stand, her stomach so disordered as to reject almost everything she took into it, a constant small fever, and an imposthume [abscess] rising in her breast." At intervals of two to four days, he reported her descent: "she rather weakens"; "she still weakens." And after more suffering, as "our hopes and fears here took their ultimate form," she died and was buried at Monticello near her mother. The father stayed on the mountaintop for the

---

45. TJ to JM, Apr. 27, 1804, below.

46. Gardner W. Allen, *Our Navy and the Barbary Corsairs* (Boston, 1905), pp. 246–66, and Fowler, pp. 106–25.

funeral and lingered a week longer from "a desire to see my family in a state of more composure before we separate."[47]

———————— The Letters ————————

Madison to Jefferson

[Washington, Oct. 1, 1803]

Notes for annual message, Oct. 17, 1803: alterations and additions, etc.[1]

(o) for "before" is suggested "without" the former seeming to imply that after the suspension, an assign^t had been made.
(1) after or for "friendly" insert "proper"
omit "without difficulty of delay." There was perhaps somewhat of both, and it may become expedient to say so to Spain.
(2) "The enlightened mind of the first Consul of France saw in its true point of view the importance of an arrangement on this subject which might contribute most towards perpetuating the peace and friendship, and promoting the interest of both nations; and the property and sovereignty of all Louisiana, as it had been ceded to France by Spain, was conveyed to the U. States by instruments bearing date on the 30th day of April last. These stipulations [instruments] will be immediately laid before the Senate, and if sanctioned by its concurrence, will without delay be communicated to the House of Rep^s for the exercise of its constitutional functions thereon."

Such a modification of the paragraph is meant to avoid the implication that the transfer made by France, was covered by the terms "territory adjacent to ours" which describe our proposition. It will also avoid, what the Theory of our constitution does not seem to admit, the influence of deliberations and anticipations of the H. of Rep^s on a Treaty depending in the Senate. It is not conceived that the course here suggested can produce much delay, since the tenor of the Treaty being sufficiently known, the mind of the House can be preparing itself for the requisite provisions. Delay would be more likely to arise from the novelty and doubtfulness of a communication in the first instance, of a Treaty negociated by the Executive, to both Houses for their respective deliberations.[2]

---

47. See TJ to JM, Apr. 9, 1804, below, Apr. 13, 1804, below, Apr. 15, 1804, below, Apr. 17, 1804, below, and Apr. 23, 1804, below. For a touching account, see Malone, IV, pp. 410-18.

1. For TJ's third annual message to Congress, Oct. 17, 1803, see Ford, VIII, pp. 266-73.

2. TJ accepted JM's suggestion and thus avoided laying the treaty simultaneously before both houses of Congress prior to its ratification by the Senate; see *ibid.*, pp. 268-69. See also Malone, IV, p. 327.

(3) after "assure"—are proposed "in due season, and under prudent arrangements, important aids to our Treasury, as well as," an ample etc.

Quere: if the two or three succeeding paragraphs be not more adapted to the separate and subsequent communication, if adopted as above suggested.

(4) For the first sentence, may be substituted "In the territory between the Mississippi and the Ohio another valuable acquisition has been made by a treaty etc."[3] As it stands, it does not sufficiently distinguish the nature of the one acquisition from that of the other, and seems to imply that the acquisition from France was wholly on the other side of the Mississippi

May it not be as well to omit the detail of the stipulated considerations, and particularly that of the Roman Catholic Pastor. The jealousy of some may see in it a principle, not according with the exemption of Religion from Civil power. In the Indian Treaty it will be less noticed than in a President's speech.[4]

"Tho' not so indispensable since the acquisition of the other bank" conveys an idea that an immediate settlement of the other bank is in view, and may thence strengthen objections in certain quarters, to the Treaty with France.

With a tacit allusion to profit, "is yet well" may be struck out and "may be the more worthy" inserted.

The last sentence in this paragraph may be omitted, if the reason applied to a former one be thought good.

(5) "must also be expected" better perhaps "are also to be apprehended" for "both"—"all" or "the" belligerent etc. Holland already makes more than two

After "cover of our flag" substitute "for vessels not entitled to it," infecting thereby with suspicion the property of the real American and committing us [to the risk of war] [with controversies] to redress wrongs not our own." Instead of "to expect from every nation" which does not follow well the antecedent "endeavor" may be inserted "to exact"—"to draw."[5]

This member of the sentence may indeed be dispensed with, being comprehended in the ensuing member—"maintain the character of an independent one etc."

"maintain" being repeated several times within a small compass—"pursue this course," may be preferrable.

(6) For this conclusion is offered for consideration, the following "for the possibility of failure in these reasonable expectations, it will rest with the wisdom of Congress to consider how far and in what form, provision may properly be made for suspensions of intercourse where it cannot be maintained on

---

3. TJ's message announced the acquisition of territory by treaty from the Kaskaskia Indians; see Ford, VIII, pp. 269–70.

4. TJ accepted JM's suggestion to omit any discussion of Indian treaty requirements to maintain a Roman Catholic priest, leaving the stipulations in the treaty to "the competence of both houses . . . as soon as the senate shall have advised its ratification"; see *ibid*.

5. TJ accepted JM's second alternative, warning against unneutral acts "committing us into controversies for the redress of wrongs not our own" rather than warning against "the risk of war"; see *ibid.*, p. 272.

principles of justice and self respect," or "and therewith prevented, the necessity of remedial provisions on the part of the U. States."⁶
(7) for "unconcerned in"—"and from"

Madison to Jefferson

[Washington Nov. 5, 1803]

The Louisiana documents did not come from Mʳ Gallatin till a day or two ago. I have this morning delivered 38 revised pages which will go to the press, a few of which have been some time in the types. There will be abᵗ ⅓ or ½ as many more. No time will be lost. The bulk of the work will apologize to the House for the delay.⁷

Jefferson to Madison

[Washington Nov. 9, 1803]

Tʜ: J ᴛᴏ Mʀ. Mᴀᴅɪsᴏɴ
I inclose you Clarke's memoranda. The following articles seem proper for Executive attention.
An instrument vesting in the Collector of Natchez the powers of the administrator, Treasurer and Contador.
Instructions to Claiborne to suppress useless offices.
      to remove any existing officers.
      to appoint others.
It would be well these could go by next post.
Would it not be well to send in what documents we have, and furnish what is not yet prepared? as well as what may come hereafter in a supplementary way from time to time as received.

---

6. TJ's draft warned of the possibility of cutting off commercial intercourse with any nation that violated American neutral rights. JM suggested that this question be submitted to Congress, but Gallatin thought it premature to raise the issue, and TJ omitted it entirely; see *ibid.*, p. 273, and Brant, IV, p. 155.

7. After the Senate ratified the acquisition of Louisiana on Oct. 21, 1803, TJ transmitted the treaty to both houses of Congress on the same day and promised to submit such additional "information relative to its government as time and distance have permitted me to obtain." He submitted the information on Nov. 14, 1803; see Richardson, I, pp. 350-52. The documents are printed in *ASP, FR*, II, pp. 506-83.

Madison to Jefferson

[Washington Nov. 11, 1803]

Appointments by the President during the recess of the Senate 1803

March 4. Hore Browse Trist of the Missipi territory Collector for the District of Mississippi

" 9. Same. Inspector of the Revenue for the port of Fort Adams, in the Mississippi District

" " Joseph Turner of Georgia. Inspector of the Revenue for the port of Brunswick, in Georgia, v. Claud Thompson become incapable

" " Same. Collector of the Customs for the District of Brunswick

" " Henry Warren of Mass. Inspector of the Revenue for the port of Plymouth, in Massachusetts v. Wm. Watson removd.

" " Same. Collector of the Customs for the District of Plymouth

" 15. Thomas Dudley of N. Carolina, now Surveyor of Swansboro to be Inspector of Revenue for the port of Swansborough, in North Carolina v. Alenr. Carmalt dead.

April 20. Isaac Ilsley of Mass. Collector for the District of Portland and Falmouth, in Massachusetts instead of David Isley, jr. which was a misnomer

May 10. Jeremiah Bennet junr. of N. J. Collector for the District of Bridge Town, in New Jersey v. Eli Elmer removd. for delinquemcy

" " Same. Inspector of the Revenue for the several ports within the District of Bridge Town

" " Samuel Osgood of N. Y. Naval officer for the District of New York v. Richard Rogers removd.

" " Samuel Ward [?] of Mass. Naval officer for the District of Salem and Beverly, in Massachusetts v. Joseph Story declined

June 16. Brian Walker of N. C. Collector for the District of Beaufort, in North Carolina.

" " Same. Inspector of the Revenue for the port of Beaufort.

" " Thomas Durfes [?] of Rhode Island. Inspector of the Revenue for the port of Tiverton, in Rhode Island. new

" " Charles Gibson of Mary. Inspector of the Revenue for the port of Easton, in Maryland. new

" " Charles Gibson. Surveyor of the port of Easton, in Maryland.

" " Thomas Durfes [?]. Surveyor of the port of Tiverton, in Rhode Island.

Augt. 24. Callender Irvine of N. Y. Inspector of the Revenue for the port of Buffalo Creek. new

" " Same. Surveyor of the port of Buffalo Creek.

"   " Robert Lee of N. Y. Collector for the District of Niagara. new?
"   " Same. Inspector of the Revenue for the port of Niagara.
Sept. 16. Abraham Bishop of Conn. Collector for the District of New Haven, in Connecticut, v. Saml. Bishop dead.
    e. Edward Turner of the Mississippi Territory Register of the Land office within the same, for the Lands lying west of Pearl River, in the County of Adams*

       Isaac Briggs of Maryland. Surveyor of the Lands of the U. S. South of the State of Tennessee

    f. Charles Jones Jenkins [?] of South Carolina. A commission of the U. S. under the act of Congress of the 9th July 1798 providing for the valuation of Lands and dwelling houses and the enumeration of slaves, for the 5th Division of said State v. Saml. Hay resigned

       Thomas Rodney of Delaware. a Judge of the Mississippi Territory

       Tench Coxe of Pennsa. Purveyor of Public Supplies of the U. S. v. Isaac Wheeler resigned

       Nathan Sanford of N. Y. Attorney of the U. S. for the District of New York v. Edward Livingston

       Jared Mansfield of Connecticut. Surveyor General of the lands of the U. S. N. W. of the Ohio v. P [?] Putnam removd. for incompetence

Consuls

    E. John Leonard of New Jersey Vice-Consul of the U. S. for the port of Barcelona v. Wm Willis resigned

    F. Isaac Cox Barnet of N. J. Commercial Agent for the port of Havre de Grace in France v. Peter Dobell resigned.

    G. Levitt Harris of Pennsa. Consul for St. Petersburg in Russia

    C. James L. Cathcart. Consul of the U. S. for the City and Kingdom of Tunis v. Wm Eaton resigned.

    D. John M. Goetschius N. Y. Consul for the port of Genoa v. Fred. H. Wolleston superceded

    B. Tobias Lear of Virginia. Consul Genl. for the City and Kingdom of Algiers; also a Commissioner to treat of peace with the Bashaw of Tripoli, v. James Leander Cathcart translated to Tunis.

---

*A similar commission was issued for the County of Washington, and since, we have not been informed with whose name it was filled. [*Editor's note:* Madison does not explain why he began lettering his entries in lowercase for this entry and the next, nor does he explain why the list of consuls following "e" and "f" are lettered in uppercase but presented out of order.]

Madison to Jefferson

Washington Dec. 2, 1803

SIR:

Agreeably to a resolution of the Senate, passed on the 22d of last month, requesting the President of the United States to cause to be laid before them such information as may have been received relative to the violation of the flag of the United States, or to the impressment of any seamen in the service of the United States, by the agents of any foreign nation, I do myself the honor to transmit to you the enclosed abstract of impressments of persons belonging to American vessels, which, with the annexed extracts from the letters of some of our agents abroad, comprises all the information on the subject that has been received by this Department since the report to Congress, at its last session, relative to seamen.[8] To the first mentioned document I have added a summary, showing the number of citizens of the United States impressed, and distinguishing those who had protections as citizens; those who are stated to be natives of the British dominions, and not stated to be naturalized as citizens; and those of all other countries, who are equally not stated to have been naturalized in the United States.

Another source of injury to our neutral navigation has taken place in the blockade of Guadaloupe and Martinique, as notified in the annexed letter from Mr. Barclay, Consul General of His Britannic Majesty for the eastern States.

Besides the above, I have received no official information of any material violations of our flag during the present European war, except in the recent aggressions of the Emperor of Morocco. With very high respect, I have the honor to be, sir, your most obedient servant,

JAMES MADISON.

Madison to Jefferson

[Washington] Dec. 4, 1803

A few alterations are suggested on the supposition that it may be best to print the transaction, as a disavowal of war and a confirmation of peace, rather than as a pacification which might involve the necessary idea of Treaty. I take for granted that Mr Smith will have an opp.^{y} of expressing his opinion as to the graduation of praise to the officers—

As so many names are mentioned, and it is known that Lear was con-

---

8. For the list of impressments, see *ibid.*, pp. 593–95.

cerned in the affair and may not be known that he was unofficially there—might it not be well to throw in a clause alluding to his presence, and the aid of his zealous and judicious councils.[9] This however for consideration.

Madison to Jefferson

Washington Apr. 5, 1804

DEAR SIR

Inclose the Commission for Ruby according to your parting request; also three others for Indian Com̄ssrs. in blank, which you will be so good as to return. The last communications from N. Orleans are also inclosed. They are in several respects interesting.

We have rec^d nothing from abroad since you left us, and every thing here remains as at that date. With respectful attachment I remain Y^{rs}

JAMES MADISON

Jefferson to Madison

Monticello Apr. 9, 1804

DEAR SIR

I wrote yesterday to Genl. Dearborne on the subject of intruders on the public lands in Louisiana, inclosing a note to each of the heads of department asking them to give me their opinion thereon separately. I did this by way of beginning the practice of separate consultations, which a host of considerations satisfy me is a very salutary and useful one to be resorted to occasionally. The enclosed letter to you presents another form, inasmuch as it requests the head of the department to which the subject relates to make up a result, either by separate or common consultation, and to act on it without recurrence to

---

9. JM referred to negotiations between Commodore Preble and the emperor of Morocco, who ratified and confirmed the treaty of 1786 made by his father, thus suppressing the incipient Moroccan war. For brief accounts, see Louis B. Wright and Julia H. Macleod, *The First Americans in North Africa: William Eaton's Struggle for a Vigorous Policy against the Barbary Pirates, 1799–1805* (Princeton, 1945), pp. 132–35, and Gardner W. Allen, *Our Navy and the Barbary Corsairs* (Boston, 1905), pp. 143–45. For fuller details, see Christopher McKee, *Edward Preble: A Naval Biography, 1761–1807* (Annapolis, 1972), pp. 139–72. Although Tobias Lear, the new consul general to Algiers, participated in the deliberations, TJ did not mention him, singling out instead James Simpson, consul at Algiers, Commodore Preble, and Captains John Rodgers, William Bainbridge, and Hugh Campbell; see Richardson, I, p. 353.

the President. All these modes of determining on measures may be useful according to the special occasion.[10]

I found my daughter Eppes at Monticello, whither she had removed on a litter by hand; so weak as barely to be able to stand, her stomach so disordered as to reject almost everything she took into it, a constant small fever, and an imposthume rising in her breast. The indulgence of her friends had permitted her to be uninformed of the importance of strict attention to the necessity of food and it's quality. I have been able to regulate this, and for some days she has taken food enough to support her, and of the kind only which her stomach bears without rejection. Her first imposthume has broken, but there is some fear of a second; if this latter cause does not more than countervail the effect of her present regimen, I am not without hopes of raising her again, as I should expect that restoring her strength by wine and digestible food, her fever would wear off. Her spirits and confidence are favorably affected by my being with her, and aid the effects of regimen.[11] Accept my affectionate salutations

P.S. Will you be so good as to endeavor, in an unsuspected way, to observe to the other gentlemen the advantages of sometimes resorting to separate consultation? To Mr Gallatin may be remarked the incipient indisposition which we noted in two of our brethern on a late consultation; and to the others may be suggested the other important considerations in it's favor.[12]

Jefferson to Madison

Monticello Apr. 9, 1804

DEAR SIR

Will you be so good as to consult with the other members of the administration on the allowance to be made to Govr Claiborne? There are several elements of consideration to be attended to, to wit, as to his character 1. as Governor of Mississippi. 2. Commissioner for the receipt of Louisiana. 3. as Governor of Louisiana: as to the funds from which his compensation is to be taken, to wit, 1. the appropriation for the expences of the Missipi territory. 2. that for taking possession of Louisiana. 3. the 20,000D. for the expences of the civil government of Louisiana: the epochs too at which these funds will respectively become chargeable or discharged of his compensation.

This will of course settle the term at which Genl Wilkinson's authority as Commissioner ceased (since both his and Claiborne's must have ceased at the same instant) and will ascertain the point of time at which the 2^d fund above

---

10. For TJ's practice of consulting with his cabinet individually and collectively, see Noble E. Cunningham, Jr., *The Process of Government under Jefferson* (Princeton, 1978), pp. 60–71.
11. For Maria's illness, see Malone, IV, pp. 414–15.
12. See Cunningham, p. 63.

mentioned became discharged of his expences. When the result of your consultation shall be settled, it will of course be necessary that Claiborne and Wilkinson should be apprised of it.[13] Accept my affectionate salutations.

TH: JEFFERSON

Madison to Jefferson

Washington Apr. 9, 1804

DEAR SIR

I rec[d] last night the inclosed letters from M[r] Livingston, which afford another proof that the French Government, however deficient it may be in other attributes is an enlightened one. It would be better no doubt if our objects could be attained by our own means only, but friendly interpositions of other Gov[ts] in such a case ought not only to be accepted but to be acknowledged with respect and sensibility. And I shall presume so far on your concurrence in this idea, as to authorise M[r] Livingston, to make such an acknowledgment.[14] I have rec[d] also by the last mail letters from M[r] Pinkney down to Jany. 24. The principal one being long and in Cypher cannot be forwarded by this opportunity. It appears from the others that he is teazing the Spanish Gov[t] on the subject which was not to be touched without the presence or the advice of M[r] Monroe.[15] Under the prohibition to make and the permission to accept offers, he is continually offering to accept. And it is pretty evident that he is spurred on from intermediate quarter from motives sufficiently obvious.[16] I hope to be able to forward the communications by the next mail.

The Annual register for 1764 contains the orders of the French Gov[t] to Abbedin to deliver Louisiana to Spain, referring to the 3 of Nov[r] as the date of the Cession by France, and to the *13* of that Month for the acceptance of Spain; and observes that these acts accompany the orders. It being probable that they remain among the archives of the Province I write this day to Claibourne, to search for and transmit copies with copies of any other documents applicable to the question. I have taken up the subject of our title to the Perdido with some particularity since your departure, and shall substitute what

13. For their exchange about compensation, see JM to William Claiborne, May 1, 1804, and William Claiborne to JM, May 30, 1804, in William Claiborne, *Official Letter Books of W. C. C. Claiborne, 1801–1816,* ed. Dunbar Rowland, 6 vols. (Jackson, Miss., 1917), II, pp. 177–82.

14. For offers by France and other powers to intercede with Tripoli on behalf of the captured crew of the *Philadelphia,* see Wright and Macleod, p. 138.

15. What Pinckney discussed was whether the Floridas were included in the Louisiana Purchase, a subject reserved for the special mission by Monroe to Madrid; see Malone, IV, pp. 343–44, and Harry Ammon, *James Monroe: The Quest for National Identity* (New York, 1971), pp. 237–42.

16. The "intermediate quarter" was Livingston, who was jealous of Monroe's role in the Louisiana Purchase; see George Dangerfield, *Chancellor Robert R. Livingston of New York, 1746–1813* (New York, 1960), p. 386, and Brant, IV, pp. 208–9.

I have written in place of the brief observations which I read you in the letter to M.͟r Livingston. I thought it proper that he should be furnished with all our ideas, considering the importance of the French Gov.͟t in the question, and it will [have?] only anticipated the task which would be incident to the instructions to M.͟r Monroe.[17]

No answer has yet been rec.͟d from Russell. With respectful attachment. Y.͟rs

JAMES MADISON

P. S. I inclose herewith an Exequatur for a French Consul whose case is explained by communications from M.͟r Pichon also inclosed. Under the circumstances of the case it appears to me expedient to grant the exequatur. It has been granted on slighter grounds. And I am assured by M.͟r P. that the app.͟t to Kentucky was made solely with a view to give him his salary as Consul which is 12,000 livres a year. M.͟r P. expects that he will be app.͟d to N. Orleans, and would have sent him thither instead of to Natches, if M.͟r Laussat had not interposed a functionary at the former port. The idea of a Consul for Kentucky was suggested it seems by an Exequatur formerly granted to a Spanish Consul whose Commission comprehended Virginia and Kentucky.

The Leyden Gazettes will be worth your reading for the sake of the comment on the Rep.͟t of the Committee of Congress touching the acquisition of N. O. and the Floridas.

Madison to Jefferson

Washington Apr. 12, 1804

DEAR SIR

Inclosed herewith are the letters last rec.͟d from M.͟r Pinkney, with some communications from the Mediterranean, and from the Comissn under the 7.͟th art: of the British Treaty. The capture by Capt. Preble was in some respects very apropos; but is there not danger that it may give umbrage to the Grand Superior? I have nothing to add but assurances of my respectful attachment.

JAMES MADISON

Not knowing the address of Derrieux, I take the liberty of inclosing it. The address can be ascertained doubtless among some of his friends about Charlottesville.

---

17. For JM to William Claiborne, Apr. 9, 1804, see Claiborne, II, 140–43, which reprints the *Annual Register* for 1765 instead of 1764. On May 20, 1804, Claiborne reported his failure to locate the treaty transferring Louisiana from France to Spain in 1762; see *ibid.*, pp. 151–52.

Jefferson to Madison

Monticello Apr. 13, 1804

DEAR SIR

I recieved by last post Mr Gallatin's observations on Dr. Stevens' case. His outworks are stronger than his main citadel: that is to say, on the 1st. and great question which involves important principle, he yields a good deal, and presents no views of the residue which are new and difficult. But on his 2d. and 3d. questions relative to evidence he is truly strong, and his preliminary observations on the 5th. 6th. and 7th. heads of account have weight. You will certainly find it necessary to give it a serious consideration. Will you favor me with the view you shall take of the subject.[18]

Our spring is remarkably uncheary. A North West wind has been blowing for three days. Our peach trees blossomed the 1st. day of this month, the poplar began to leaf, so as to be sensible at a distance, about the 7th. Asparagus shewed itself about 5. days ago; perhaps we may have a dish today or tomorrow. But my beds are in a state of total neglect, and therefore not a fair measure of the season. My daughter exhibits little change. No new imposthume has come on, but she rather weakens. Her fever is small and constant. Affectionate salutations

Jefferson to Madison

Monticello Apr. 15, 1804

DEAR SIR

Your favor of the 9th was recieved on the 13th and can only be answered by tomorrow's post, the ordinary course requiring 9. or 10. days from writing a letter to the reciept of it's answer.

I return you the exequatur unsigned, but have signed a blank paper to submit to your consideration the part which shall be inserted in it. The one filled up with Natches admits that a consulship for Kentucky cannot be established within that state, but must be in one nearer the sea. I think it a question requiring great consideration whether we ought ever to permit a foreign Consul in interior positions. The seaport towns are the only places where they are permitted in Europe. Our Consuls general at Paris and Madrid are the only exceptions I know of there, and that at Paris at least, is peculiar to us, no other nation having a Consul there. Here the only places where they have ever been permitted are Charleston, Norfolk, Baltimore etc. what may be deemed the

---

18. TJ had written to Gallatin on Feb. 19, 1804, enclosing a statement of Dr. Stevens's case claiming compensation for services as consul to Santo Domingo in 1799; see L. and B., XI, pp. 4-13. For Gallatin's responses of Feb. 21, 1804, and Apr. 5, 1804, see Gallatin, I, pp. 178-79, 183.

ports of first access in the US. Even Philadelphia, which seems to be an exception, is in substance the first port made in the Delaware, in practice. In Louisiana I would be more rigorous than any where else, and with the French and Spaniards more than any other nation. I should therefore be for denying a Consul in that river but at the single port of N. Orleans; when Pichon mentioned to me Mr. Martel's Consulship of Kentucky, I told him plainly his residence could only be permitted at New Orleans; that I thought we might give him an Exequatur for that port. He acquiesced in it, only saying it must be our act, not his, and the rather as Laussat expected that place. I told him I thought it a happy occasion of procuring an additional obstacle to Laussat's coming there, for that I really thought we must object to his residence there in any capacity.[19] He appeared sensible we had reason for this. I leave it to you on these considerations to determine whether the blank should not be made an Exequatur for New Orleans, where whether he confines himself to Kentucky cases or not, is no question of ours. I think at the same time we should instruct Mr Livingston to enter into candid explanations with Mr Taleyrand against Laussat's appointment there. But Mr Livingston, I suppose from an impression in his letter, is coming away in all haste, as he says "he does not intend staying there so long as to recieve any new power, or new instructions." This is singularly inconsistent with his late letters. On this subject however we shall be in time to consult on my return. I cannot blame him absolutely his asking the interference of France with Tripoli. And yet I am very sorry for it. I am afraid her mediation may be interposed against the just severities we contemplate. But in consideration of the readiness of the first Consul to interpose, and that he had reason to think we wished it, I cannot but approve of sincere acknolegements to him. At the same time perhaps it might be well he should understand that we wish to make them feel us sensibly before we offer them our peace. In general I am mortified at the condemnation which most of our public agents abroad have manifested at the loss of the Philadelphia. It seems as if they thought on the loss of one frigate, that every thing was lost. This must humble us in the eyes of Europe, and renders it the more indispensable to inflict on Tripoli the same chastisement of which the two most powerful nations of Europe have given the world repeated examples.

You will percieve by the inclosed letter from Joseph Barnes, that Preble had taken a Tripoline vessel with 70. men, bound to Constantinople with presents for the Grand Seignieur. As these presents, for want of condemnation, may perhaps remain untouched, I wish to reserve for decision on my return, and your consideration in the meantime, whether it does not furnish

---

19. Pierre-Clément de Laussat was the French prefect who transferred Louisiana to the United States, but Governor Claiborne wished him to depart once the transfer of title was made. See Arthur P. Whitaker, *The Mississippi Question, 1795–1803: A Study in Trade, Politics, and Diplomacy* (New York, 1934), pp. 252–53; Brant, IV, p. 191; and Pierre-Clément de Laussat, *Louisiana, Napoleon and the United States: An Autobiography of Pierre-Clément de Laussat,* ed. Maurice Lebel (Lanham, Md., 1989).

us a happy occasion of producing favorable dispositions in the Porte towards us, by sending one of our vessels to Constantinople with the presents, as an evidence of our respect for the Grand Seignieur, and with a letter to his Minister of foreign affairs, avoiding at the same time all overtones of any nature whatsoever. It might aid us, if, after bringing Tripoli to terms, we should find it expedient to get on the footing with the Porte, on which it appears lately to have placed Prussia. I inclose Barnes's letter to show the necessity of silencing the empty babbler,[20] and of making him sensible that however praiseworthy may be the volunteering zeal of an individual in cases where the government has fixed the line of action, yet that it is equally reprehensible to entangle them by officious overtures with foreign nations where the plan of the government has not been manifested nor it's views made known. His forwardness and medling disposition are by no mean justifiable on any grounds we have furnished him. To whole volumes of his letters for 7. years past, I have never written one single scrip of an answer. Will you be so good as to have Gibson's commission as Secretary of Indiana, renewed and sent to him immediately? His present one expires early in May.

I can say nothing favorable of my daughter's situation; not even that she is as well as at the date of my last, because she still weakens. Accept my affectionate salutation.

Madison to Jefferson

Washington Apr. 15, 1804

To The President of the U. States

DEAR SIR

Your favor of the 9th with its inclosures has been duly rec^d and will be duly attended to.

The inclosed communications from Mr Merry are as satisfactory as they are important. On the return of them, it will be proper I presume to acknowledge the impression made by the promptitude of the interposition, and the evidence it affords of a disposition to cherish the amicable relations etc. of the two Countries. From S. E. Nepeaus letter it seems that the decisions of the British Courts on the law of Nations are prescribed even by the Board of Admiralty.

The letter from Skipwith shews that as we always supposed that the French gov^t took no particular interest in the application of the fund of 20 mils. farther than it might affect the sum chargeable on themselves. It shews

---

20. Joseph Barnes was U.S. consul in Sicily and, later, in Naples; see Dudley W. Knox, ed., *Naval Documents Related to the United States Wars with the Barbary Powers, 1785–1807*, 7 vols. (Washington, 1935–48), IV, pp. 29, 49.

also that Mr. L. had not disclosed at that date the instruction sent him, to suspend and prepare the way for remodifying the payment under the Convention. It appears by his correspondence with the Comissrs. heretofore recd. that he had notified your sanction to his choice as early as the 23 of Dec.r and this sanction was conveyed in the same letter with that instruction.[21]

The letter from Moses Young is inclosed at his request. He has not yet decided whether he will return to Madrid. Perhaps it may depend on the event of the settlement he makes with the public. Like all other claimants, tho' represented as a moderate, as well as an honest man, he is for getting all he can within the limits at least of what he thinks not unfair.[22]

Nothing has occurred, beyond the information of the Newspapers, that deserves to be mentioned. The next mail will probably give the result of the Election in N. H. In Mass.ts the progress becomes less unfavorable to Sullivan, who will not be left so far behind as his predecessor in the competition with Strong. From N. Y. nothing is heard but general reports on which no dependence can be placed. You will see the indelicate introduction of your name into the contest. Y.rs with respectful attachment

JAMES MADISON

Jefferson to Madison

Monticello Apr. 17, 1804

DEAR SIR

I recieved yesterday your letter of the 12.th and now return the letter it covered. I recieved also thro' Mr Gallatin, Gov.r Claiborne's information to you that he had chartered a state bank at N. Orleans. As the act of Congress for a bank there, and the Charter of the Bank of the US. renders Claiborne's charter a nullity, he should revoke it on that ground, as given before information was recieved of the act of Congress. I imagine this notification to him must go officially from you.[23] The extreme situation of my daughter renders me incapable of adding more than my affectionate salutns.

TH: JEFFERSON

---

21. The Louisiana treaty was accompanied by a claims convention setting aside 20 million livres ($3,750,000) of the purchase price to settle American claims against France for spoliations. For a discussion of the complicated provisions that stymied action by the claims commissioners, see Dangerfield, pp. 374–75, 380–83. For JM's instruction to suspend payments to creditors because of difficulties concerning the interpretation of the claims convention, see *ibid.*, p. 384.

22. Moses Young was American consul to Madrid; see *ASP, M,* I, p. 307.

23. For a brief discussion of the New Orleans bank, see Raymond Walters, Jr., *Albert Gallatin: Jeffersonian Financier and Diplomat* (New York, 1957), pp. 172–73, and Henry Adams, *The Life of Albert Gallatin* (Philadelphia, 1879), pp. 321–22. For Claiborne's letters to Albert Gallatin, JM, and TJ, see Claiborne, II, pp. 160–64, 172–74, 174–76, 180–82, 187–90.

Madison to Jefferson

Washington Apr. 19, 1804

DEAR SIR

The Mail of last evening brought me your favor of the 15th. with the papers sent back with it. I shall forbear using your Blank for an exequatur till I can again confer with Mr. Pichon who is at Baltimore.

The sending on the intercepted Presents to the Porte would certainly be a handsome and politic expression of respect for the Grand Seignor, who otherwise may be thrown by his displeasure into an unreasonable patronage of Tripoli. It is even to be wished that Preble may have thought of and undertaken the measure himself.

The impression made on our public agents abroad by the loss of the Philada. and the effect they give to it are both remarkable. So extravagant a solicitude tends not only to sink us in the eyes of the European Governments, but may excite calculations in the Bashaw which will in some measure balance the advantage of the friendly interpositions with him. The communication from our Consul at St. Petersburg on this subject now inclosed, is more remarkable than any thing that has occurred, not so much for the proceeding of the Consul, as for the result of it, which is to be explained only by an uncommon character in the Emperor Alexander, and some particular interest he has been led to take in the career of the U. States. It reminds me of his education by la Harpe,[24] and of some communications thro' Dr. Priestly which you once shewed me, but which my memory does not distinctly retrace. It certainly will be proper to make the acknowledgment due thro' some more respectful channel than instructions to the Consul. Whether any thing beyond a letter from the Dept. of State here to the Russian Minister be recommended by the occasion, will depend on circumstances which you can much better appreciate.

Barnes may recieve the proper check by the opp[ortunit]y which will be afforded by the Adams. Mr. Lincoln has received a letter from Russel which he will forward to you.

The lengthy communications for Mr. L. Mr. P. and Mr. Monroe, with the measures required for them, and other business of the Office have prevented me from taking up the care of Doctr. Stephens,[25] and the intrusion

---

24. In an undated memorandum of 1806, TJ made the following "extract of a letter from emperor Alexander": "M. de la Harpe, a Swiss, the primary mover of the revolution in Switzerland, one of their Directory, afterwards retired to his Chateau 2 leagues from Paris. He had been chosen by the late Empress to educate the present Emperor and Constantine his brother, and was chosen not only as a man of talents, but, still more extraordinary, as a Republican" who gave Alexander "a thoroughly republican education"; see Presidential Papers Microfilm: Thomas Jefferson Papers, reel 37.

25. Edward Stevens had been appointed by President John Adams as consul general to Santo Domingo, then controlled by Toussaint l'Overture; see Alexander De Conde; *The Quasi-War: The Politics and Diplomacy of the Undeclared War with France, 1797–1801* (New York, 1966), pp. 136–41, and Perkins, pp. 109–111.

west of the Mississippi. With respect to the latter, it does not at first view strike me that any doubt or objection can lie agst. a military expulsion, if authorized by law, as is presumed, and in cases sufficiently clear. The only question that occurs is how far the Officer should be allowed to decide an antedate to be a forgery; unless indeed records in his possession should disclose it. With respectful attachment Yrs.,

JAMES MADISON

Madison to Jefferson
Washington Apr. 20, 1804

Report on the case of Dr. Edward Stevens,
who claims reimbursement for expenses incurred
during a mission to Santo Domingo in 1799.

Case of Doctr Stephens[26]

Dr S. went in the year 1799 to St Domingo under a Consular appointment, with additional services to be performed of a nature not consular. For expences incurred in this Mission he claims reimbursement, on the ground of a promise from the Executive, on the faith of which he undertook the Mission.

1. Is the claim legally allowable, particularly from the fund appropriated to intercourse with foreign nations?
2. Is the contract sufficiently proved?
3. Are the expenditures supported by admissable vouchers?

The first question is to be decided by the scope of the laws relating generally to intercourse with foreign nations, and of those relating particularly to intercourse with St Domingo.

The general Act of Congress in force at the time when Dr S. was sent to St Domingo, pursuing the tenor of a temporary Act which had been regularly continued from the original act passed in the year 1794. [It] appropriated 40,000 dollars annually for the support of such persons as the President should *commission* to serve in *foreign parts,* and for the expence incident to the business in which they might be employed, under certain limits, to the compensations

26. For TJ's request for JM's response to Gallatin's views on Stevens's case, see TJ to JM, Apr. 13, 1804, above. Gallatin argued that Stevens's mission to Santo Domingo, while Toussaint headed the rebellion against France, "not being to the authorized government of a foreign nation, appears to me conclusive to prove the impropriety of applying to that object the moneys appropriated for intercourse with foreign nations"; see Albert Gallatin to TJ, Apr. 5, 1804, in Adams, I, p. 183.

allowable for all personal services and expences to Ministers Plenipotentiary Chargés and Secretaries of the former; with a further appropriation of 25,650 doll.^{rs} for defraying the expences of intercourse between the U.S. and foreign nations, during the current year viz. 1798.

The act further provided that all monies issued for the purposes of intercourse or Treaty with foreign nations, in pursuance of any law, should be annually accounted for, as the President might decide, either specifically, or by a certificate of the amount of the expenditures from the President, or with his sanction from the Secretary of State.

The authority here given to the President, for maintaining intercourse with foreign nations, is conveyed to him by the appropriation of money to the support of such persons as he should *commission* to serve the U. S. in *foreign parts,* and to the expence *incident to the business* committed to them. The guards provided against the abuse of that authority consistg. of the limitation of the entire sum and of that of compensations to particular classes of agents in foreign parts, to whose support the greater part of the fund was likely to be applied, and whose measure of compensation would be a guide to that of others. The rule laid down for the settlement of the accounts, in permitting a Certificate of the President, or the Secretary of State, to take the place of a specification and verification of the expenditures was an enlargement of the Executive Authority.

If the appropriation had been made without limiting the compensations to Plenipotentiaries, Chargés, and their Secretaries, the President might have regulated them as he pleased within the general limit of the appropriation. He might consequently allow to other agents serving in foreign parts, whatever compensations he pleased within that general limit; unless it could be said that the authority to give compensations in those particular cases was derived not from the appropriation itself, but from the proviso limiting their amount; which proviso gave the authority by implication. This however can not be said 1. because the fairer implication from the proviso is that without it, Ministers Plenipotentiary, Chargés and Secretaries might have recieved higher than the limited compensation. 2. because the President could not under a construction deriving the power merely from the proviso, have ever employed any other grades of Legation; which could the less have been meant by Congress, as they are not only expressly authorized by the Constitution, but one other grade, that of Resident, was at the time serving the U. States in foreign parts, and must have been known to be so by Congress.

Nor can it be said that the appropriation is limited to Foreign Agencies specified in the Constitution or authorized by law. For under that construction, besides that it would be an assumed, not a necessary one, and that the agency of Dr. S. in his Consular capacity was known both to the Constitution and to the law, the President, whilst more money was often appropriated to foreign intercourse than was likely to be required for such agencies, would have been without authority to apply any part of it for any other purpose of foreign intercourse, and would consequently be under restrictions equally inconsistent with the public interest and the presumable intention of the Legislature. It must have been known also, that the provisions in the same words in former Acts, had in practice, been otherwise understood.

It appears to have decided by practice also, that the term "Commissioned" by the President was not to be taken in the technical sense of an appointment with the sanction of the Senate and under the seal of the U. S., but as applicable to persons authorized by the President in any form to serve the U. States in foreign parts.[27]

In the case of Dr S. then, a promise of reimbursement, whether made to him in his consular capacity or as charged with services not consular, must be consid[ered] as within the Executive authority.[28] If made to him as Consul it was made to a functionary recognized in the Constitution and the law, as well as appointed and commissioned in due form, and litterally within the Act making appropriation for the support of such persons as the President should commission [to] serve the U. S. in foreign parts. The allowance of certain fees to Consuls would not, necessarily invalidate such a promise; in as much as the law has not declared that no other allowance should be made, as is declared in the case of Plenipotentiaries, Chargés etc. and inasmuch as it has been the practice to re-imburse even to these functionaries, expences incurred in official, tho' in other than ordinary services. If the promise was made to him as charged with services not Consular, it was within the legal authority of the Executive, unless the extra services were in their nature incompatible with the Consular offices, of which there is no appearance. It has been familiar in practice, to employ regular functionaries abroad, particularly Consuls, in extra services with reasonable allowances for them. Mr. Erving and Mr. Skipwith are examples.

The authority of the President, in applying the money [appropriated] to foreign intercourse, without regard to the question whether the agent receiving it, was or was not at the time in an office with legal emoluments annexed to it, may be further illustrated by the construction given by constant practice to the appropriations to intercourse with the Barbary powers, these being made in like terms with the appropriations to intercourse with foreign nations. By an act of Congress in 1794. one million of dollars, well known to be meant for a Treaty with Algiers, was appropriated without any particular reference to Barbary, "to defray expences to be incurred in relation to the intercourse between the U. States and foreign nations," and under that general appropriation was

27. JM inserted the following marginal note: "e.g. John Q. Adams mission to London. He went under the authority only of a letter from the Secretary of State, to secure the British Ratification in exchange for that of the U. S. and was allowed his expences, in addition to his salary as Minister to the Hague."

28. Unlike Gallatin, JM clearly thought that Stevens should be paid. TJ referred JM's observations to Gallatin "in the hopes that you and he would by discussion come to a common opinion." Otherwise, the president added, "I presume that I must decide between the opinions, however reluctantly"; see TJ to Albert Gallatin, June 9, 1804, in Gallatin, I, p. 196.

applied as far as was requisite to Barbary purposes; Consuls to the Barbary powers, altho' expressly allowed salaries by law, have all of them recd. or been promised, reimbursements of expence, in some cases for extraordinary services in their Consular character in others for agencies superadded to that character. The negotiation of peace with Tripoli, committed first to Mr Cathcart, and latterly to M^r. Lear are explicit examples. The Usage of national intercourse on the Coast of Barbary may indeed be different from usage elsewhere, and may be thought to countenance a greater latitude of expenditures in the means of intercourse there than elsewhere. Still however it is certain that in carrying on intercourse among other foreign nations, agenc[i]es and services are in use, of kinds sufficiently various and informal to sanction any latitude that has been taken by the Executive in the intercourse with them.

In examining the state of the Case at the time Dr. S. went to S^t. Domingo, it may be proper to observe that in the act of Cong^s. passed Mar. 2. 1799, there is, besides an [appropriation] of 21,000 doll^{rs}. in addition to the 40,000 d^{rs} a further appropriation of 78,700, for the "*contingent* expences of intercourse with foreign nations." This is perhaps the only instance in which the term "contingent" appears in this branch of appropriations. If it was meant to give an increased latitude to the authority of the President, as the term might be construed, it wd. decide at once the question whether it was applicable to the case of D^r. S. and consequently whether a promise such as he alledges was legally valid. But it is more probable that nothing more was meant by "contingent expences," than what is called in the appropriation act of June 1. 1796, extraordinary expences, by which appears to have been meant merely expences additional to those contemplated, and for purposes not different in kind from those annually provided for, but greater in number or extent, than likely to arise within the year. In one sense all the common expences of foreign intercourse are "contingent" since they depend on the will of the President and the course of events; and are consequently uncertain or contingent.

Thus stood the law untill Mar. 10. 1800, when instead of a continuation of the last temporary act which included the annual appropriation for foreign intercourse, a permanent act was passed in a form somewhat different. It simply provided that the allowances to Plenipotentiaries and Chargés etc. the Secretaries of the former should not exceed a certain rate, and that money drawn under any law making appropriation for the "*contingent expences* of intercourse with foreign nations*"*, might be accounted for either specifically or by a certificate etc. as the President might decide; leaving the appropriations for foreign intercourse to be made separately from time to time as they have since been made. And these appropriations, which have uniformly run in the phrase of "appropriations for the expence of intercourse between the U. States and foreign nations", with the permanent act, constitute and define the authority of the Executive in applying money for that purpose.

Whatever expence then is fairly within the idea of intercourse with foreign nations, is legally allowable out of the appropriations; except so far as a limitation results from some general principle, or is specifically provided by the permanent Act.

It is a general principle that an appropriation of money to a general purpose, is applicable only to particular cases designated by the Constitution or the law; and does not of itself legalize any other application. Such a construction is founded in no apparent necessity; and would narrow the authority of the Executive more than would consist with the public interest, with the probable intention of the Legislature, or with the uniform course of practice. It would in fact exclude from the support of intercourse with foreign nations, some of the modes and expences most convenient for the purpose, and which have been found so by the experience of the present and every preceding administration.

Is it a general principle that when an allowance is expressly made by law, it is a bar to all extra allowance, or extra considerations to the same person; but notwithstanding a general authority to the Executive to make allowances on such considerations. This construction also is apparently without necessity, as it would also be highly inconvenient, and contrary to the course of practice.

Does the permanent act above cited impose any limitation on the power given by the appriation [appropriation] acts equivalent to such general principles?

The permanent Act is intitled "an act to ascertain the compensations to public ministers." The Body of the act however does not strictly correspond with this limited title. The first section provides, as already observed that no salary exceeding particular rates, should be allowed to particular grades of public Ministers and the Secretaries of one of those grades, as a compensation for all personal services and expences. As the act gives no positive authority to the President to allow salaries at all, it implies that the authority is given elsewhere; and no where else is it given, unless it results from the general appropriation of money for foreign intercourse; and if it so results, the authority must extend to all other cases of foreign intercourse.

Were it admitted that the limitation of the salaries, is, by implication, the source of the authority to allow salaries in the cases where they are limited, the construction would be subject to another implication, which can not be admitted, viz. that the fund could be applied in salaries to no other functionaries than those whose salaries are expressly limited. Or were it even admitted, that notwithstanding other functionaries particularly recognized in the Constitution or the laws, might be allowed compensations, an implication would still remain equally inconsistent with the public service and the constant practice, as well as with the intention of the Legislature to be inferred from its knowledge of both, namely that no part of the fund would be applicable to any other purpose than to compensations for all *personal* services and expences; and consequently to none of those occasional agenc[i]es or even *incidental expences* which are so often indispensable means of intercourse with foreign nations: For it is to be recollected that the permanent act omits the provision contained in the preceding temporary acts for "the expence incident to the business in which persons serving in foreign parts might be employed", authorizing only, and that by a questionable implication, compensations for *personal services and expences*," to officers named in the act itself, and at most to such as are designated in other acts, or in the Constitution.

It is proper to remark that on the supposition that the foreign fund is applicable to such offices or agencies only as are found in the Constitution or the law, no salaries could be allowed to the Secretaries of public Ministers these not being found in the Constitution, nor authorized by any law creating the office: or on the supposition that salaries might be allowed to Secretaries of *Plenipos.* as implied by the legal proviso, that Salaries to their Secretaries should not exceed a fixt rate, still no salary could be allowed to the Secretaries of any other public Ministers not even to the Secretaries of Charges d'Affaires. A construction leading to this consequence can not easily be admitted. It is certainly a much more rational construction that the law in limiting the salaries to Secretaries implies that the Salaries would be otherwise at the discretion of the Executive: and that the service and expence of a Secretary, tho' not personal to the public Minister, being within the meaning of, as being incident to, "intercourse with foreign nations," every other expence and service incident to that intercourse are equally within the appropriations to it.

The effect of the other and only other section in the permanent act, on the authority of the Executive, depends on the question whether "the Contingent expences referred to", as to be settled in the way prescribed, be included in the expenses personally appropriated of foreign intercourse, or are not included and consequently to be provided for by a distinct appropriation.

It is perhaps not very easy to say precisely what is to be understood by contingent expences of foreign intercourse as distinct from those which are not contingent. In one sense, as has been already observed, all the expences of foreign intercourse; even those incurred for the salaries of the Diplomatic functionaries, are contingent; as they are not positively acquired by law, but to be incurred or not at the pleasure of the Executive. But the object of the enquiry does not make it necessary to undertake a critical discrimination between expences contingent and not contingent. This object is satisfied by the single consideration that whatever may be the meaning of the expression "contingent expences," the most reasonable, or rather the necessary construction of the law requires that they should, the former as well as the latter, be considered as within the general appropriation for the general expences of foreign intercourse.

There has not, in a single instance since the permanent act passed, been a distinct appropriation for the contingent expences of foreign intercourse, and consequently, if they are not included in the general appropriation for the expences of foreign intercourse, no provision has been made for any part of the expences of foreign intercourse, even for those on the coast of Barbary, so far as they are to be denominated contingent. Here it is certain that taking "contingent expences" in any sense the words will bear as distinct from other foreign expences, they constitute a considerable part of the annual and necessary expences, particularly on the coast of Barbary. So that if no provision has been made for them, the Legislature have equally failed in their duty, and their object; and the Executive has been every year drawing money from the Treasury for purposes to which no money has been appropriated by law. And this has been the case not only since the date of the permanent Act but [all acts passed in?] the period prior to it; except in the instance of the appropriation in 1798 "for the contingent expences of intercourse etc." In all the other instances, the appropriation has been in terms which would not provide for contingencies, unless they be included in the general terms of appropriation for intercourse with foreign nations.

There is another construction which the 2d section may be thought to bear. The section may be considered merely as providing for the settlement in a mode to be decided on by the President, of *such* contingent expences and such only as may be provided for by laws making a distinct and express appropriation for contingent expences of foreign intercourse. As this meaning of the act would not exclude from the general appropriation for foreign intercourse, contingent as well as other expences, but only take from the President the power over the mode of accounting for contingent expences incurred under that general appropriation, it is not liable to all the objections which condemn the construction just examined. There are three objections however which require that it should be rejected. 1. No appropriation, as already observed, has ever been made since the law passed in distinct and express terms, "for the contingent expence of intercourse between the U. S. and foreign nations." The *effect* of the act therefore would be not to provide a requisite mode for settling contingent expences, but to forbid the discretionary resort to that mode. This is not to be presumed. 2. Prior to the permanent act the like discretion was given to the President by every temporary act preceeding it, with respect to monies drawn under the common appropriations for foreign intercourse, which never specified contingent expences as to be distinguished from expences not contingent. 3. The construction which has prevailed since the passage of the permanent act has been that the monies drawn under the general appropriation for foreign intercourse and used for contingent expences, might be accounted for in the manner prescribed by the permanent act, and consequently that the general appropriation comprehended the contingent as well as the other expences.[29]

From this view of the subject it appears that the authority given to the Executive by the annual appropriations for intercourse between the U. S. and foreign nations is co-extensive with the "term" intercourse, limited however by one exception provided by the permanent act viz. that salaries to Ministers

---

29. JM inserted the following marginal note: "Mr. Elliot was paid under a certificate from the President which could only be on the ground that the expence was contingent, and was comprehended by the general appropriation to foreign intercourse."

Plenipos. and their Secretaries [and] to Charges des Affaires shall not exceed certain rates; and extended in one instance by that act, viz. in providing with respect to the contingent portion of the expences in foreign intercourse that the President may dispense if he thinks proper with the ordinary mode of accounting for monies drawn from the public Treasury, and substitute a certificate of the amount of the expenditures.

With such a latitude to the authority of the President, the case of Dr. S. must be within its competency, unless it should be decided that the intercourse with St. Domingo in which the expences charged by him, were incurred, was not an intercourse between the U. States and a foreign nation.

Altho' St. Domingo is to be regarded at the time as a Dependency or colony of the French Republic, being expressly so declared by Sect. 7. of the Act of Feby. 27. 1800, as well as being such by implication from other sources; still as part of a foreign nation, the local authorities there must be regarded as authorities of the French nation, and an intercourse with them, consequently as a national intercourse. This view of the matter seems to be confirmed by the clauses, in the acts for suspending commerce with the French Dominions, which exempt from the above terms of the suspension, vessels employed by the President for the purposes of *"national intercourse."* As the acts authorise the President to take off the suspension, in reference to any of the Dependences of France, as well as to France herself; as Hispaniola is particularly noticed in one of the acts, and was well understood to be principally if not exclusively the object of the exempting discretion vested in the President, and consequently the very Dependency in relation to which the vessels permitted to be employed for purposes of national intercourse would be needed, and be actually employed, the conclusion seems not to be avoided, that the intercourse with St. Domingo, was in the contemplation of the Legislature, a national intercourse, in other words, an intercourse with a foreign nation.

On the second question whether the contract be estabd. by adequate proof, the considerations on one side are the silence of the records of the Department of State, and of the correspondence of Docr. S.—the want of recollection of the fact by the then Secy. of State—the interest which the claimant may have in his own testimony—the lapse of time previous to the presentment of the claim—the improbability of such a contract drawn from the opportunities of sufficient profit otherwise incident to the mission—and the presumption that the privileged cargo in the vessel might be viewed as recompence for extra services—finally the want of a precedent for admitting a contract on parol evidence, and the danger of establishing one.

On the other side it is alledged by the claimant that the silence of the records, if a fault is chargeable on the office of the Department, and ought not to injure the claimant whose confidence in the Department was natural and proper—that the silence of his correspondence and the delay in presenting his accounts, proceeded from his finding it not necessary to draw for his advances and from his expectation of an earlier return—that the contract is positively sworn to by a credible witness; and altho' the Head of the Department who made the contract does not positively recollect it, he not only believes it on the testimony and circumstances produced, but recollects and retains impressions which enable him to declare that he thinks it extremely presumable that such a stipulation was proposed, and certain from its reasonableness that if proposed it was agreed to; and moreover that if the claim as now presented had been made whilst those connected with the transaction were in office, there would have been no hesitation in allowing it.—that the profits to be made during his mission were precarious as proved by the failure of them; besides that the chance of them was as an appurtenance to his consular services—that the amount of his expences imply a stile of living which he can not be supposed to have assumed on his private account, that he has charged less than the real amount in order to be sure that no expence was included not fairly incident to his public character. He alledges particularly that he had no interest whatever in the privileged cargo of the vessel, which carryed him to St. Domingo.

The material questions resulting from these opposing views of the case are 1st. whether a record or some office document of such a contract be the only proof that can be admitted. 2dly. whether if parol or circumstancial proof be admissible, the proof in this case be sufficient.

1. It cannot be doubted that office documents are the most regular and satisfactory evidence of official transactions; but it would seem to be going too far to say that no other evidence whatever could under any circumstances be admitted; especially if the defect of the office Archives evidence were the fault of the office, not of the private party to the contract.

Contracts between the Govt. and individuals are of different kinds and in different forms. Some of them particularly where sureties are required are always in writings and mutually executed. Others are left to slight and less formal evidence on paper. In the Department of State, particularly the foreign branch of it formality seems to have been held least essential. A proof that written or even express contract is not absolutely essential, is, that allowances have been so frequently made on the mere ground of a quantum merit, which is at most nothing more than a contract by implication.

Admitting the fact that an individual undertakes a public service on a verbal assurance from a competent public officer, that he shall receive a recompence, that he confides in that assurance, and in the attention of the officer to every circumstance of his duty, and in that confidence performs the services undertaken; and that the fact be established agst. the public by proof sufficient in private cases: it would seem that the laches of the officer ought not to invalidate the establishment of the fact by parol evidence, in any case where no law requires written in exclusion of every other evidence.

Were the Govt. constitutionally suable like an individual, or were a form prescribed by law for giving to Courts a cognizance of such cases, it would seem that a Court would be bound to admit the ordinary proof of the bargain, especially if performed on one side and the performance accepted on the other; altho' there might not, thro' the laches of the officer making the contract, or other cause, be no written memorial of it in the Office.

If such would be the decision of a Court having cognizance, the same decision would seem to be due from the cognizance of the Executive, which in usage is less restricted in many cases than Courts, in its rules both of justice and of evidence.

2. As to the particular proof of contract offered in the case of Dr. S. it consists so essentially of the testimony of Mr. Yard that it seems not necessary to weigh and compare the several circumstances and presumptions in favor of and against the claim. If unwritten proof be admissible at all, that testimony seems to be sufficient, unless discredited by the interest of the witness himself in it. If there be just ground for presuming or supposing this, the point ought to be decided by requiring the usual oath of purgation.

As it does not appear from the accts. which have been settled in cases within the Dept. of State where no written contract or promise existed, how far they may have turned on other evidence of contract than that of official documents, or on the principle of quantum merit as implying a contract, it is not easy to trace how far precedents may or may not have existed of the admission of evidence other than that of official documents. From recollections in the Office of State it may be inferred, that precedents of that sort have not been very infrequent; and taking into view all the ingredients entering into the claim in the present case, particularly the interposition and decided opinion of the ex Secretary of State who was party to the transaction, the precedent would be marked with peculiarities rendering it less liable to be drawn into injurious consequence than many others which are in force. In general it seems certain that in the course of foreign agenc[i]es and transactions, settlements and allowances have been made on more slender grounds than those which support the claim of Dr. S.; and highly probably that the same may be found just and expedient in future practice. On this consideration and in order to avoid where it can be properly done the appearance or the imputation of partialities and prejudices, it might be advisable for the Executive to settle the claim if deemed admissible, rather than by rejecting it to turn the claimant over to the Legislature. Another consideration is that if the claim be considered as turning on the question of fact whether the alledged promise was or was not made, it seems to be a question more fit for executive than for Legislative investigation and decision.

The last question is whether the vouchers for the expenditures are such as ought to be admitted. With respect to some of the charges the usual regular vouchers may justly be required. With respect to such as the Household expences other than the rent, and the travelling expences, regular vouchers have generally not been required in settling the accounts of foreign agents. And it was judged by the Department of State, on the application of the Auditor as practised in such cases, that the proof offered being stronger in the case of Dr. S. than had been admitted in others, the reality of the expenditures appeared to be sufficiently established.

In order to explain this participation of the Department of State in the settlement of accounts, it may be proper to remark that it is the effect of an arrangement which took place soon after the commencement of the present administration. Prior to that period the accounts connected with the Department of State were liquidated under the superintendance and with the sanction of the Head of it; after which they passed thro' the forms of the Treasury Department. Since that period the accounts go on the first instance to the Treasury Department, the accounting Branch of it, referring in the progress of the settlement, to the decision of the Department of State, questions, depending on transactions, circumstances or usages, concerning which this Department might be supposed to have the better means of judging; and according to its decision, the practice has been to pass suspend or reject the articles in question.

The preceding observations have been confined to the general enquiry whether the expences charged by Docr. Stephens, so far as not specially authorized by Acts of Congress, be legally allowable and ought to be allowed. If it be decided that they are of a nature not legally allowable, it will be unnecessary to go into the particular items: it being conceived, that they must be equally disallowed; (at least out of the fund for foreign intercourse) those for the hire of vessels as well as his personal expences, and his travelling as well as his stationary expences. Should it be decided that an allowance may and ought to be made, the merits of the several items may claim a particular consideration in the progress of the settlement.

Respectfully submitted to the President

JAMES MADISON

Jefferson to Madison

Monticello Apr. 23, 1804

DEAR SIR,

I return by this mail the letters etc. received with yours of the 15th. I think with you that a cordial answer should be given to Mr. Merry on the orders he communicated, altho' they were merely the correction of an injustice. Would to god that nation would so far be just in her conduct, as that we might with honor give her that friendship it is so much our interest to bear her. She is now a living example that no nation however powerful, any more than an individual, can be unjust with impunity. Sooner or later public opinion, an instrument merely moral in the beginning, will find occasion physically to inflict it's sentences on the unjust. Nothing else could have kept the other nations of Europe from relieving her under her present crisis. The lesson is useful to the weak as well as the strong.

On the 17th instant our hopes and fears here took their ultimate form. I had originally intended to have left this towards the end of the present week. But a desire to see my family in a state of more composure before we separate, will keep me somewhat longer. Still it is not probable I shall be here to answer any letter which leaves Washington after the 26th, because those of the succeeding post (the 30th) could not be answered till the 7th of May, when I may probably be on the road. Not having occasion to write to-day to the other heads of departments, will you be so good as to mention this to them? Accept my affectionate salutations.

Madison to Jefferson

Washington Apr. 24, 1804

DEAR SIR

I rec.^d this morning your favor of the 17.th instant. Among the papers inclosed from N. Orleans is a copy of the Charter issued by Govr Claibourne. From the date it appears to be prior to the Act of Congress, and not to be nullified thereby, unless the Act of Congress have a repealing effect. How far this may be the case, how far the authority of the Govr may have been sufficient to grant such a charter, or how far it may be so to set it aside, are questions which will claim attention, but on which I am unwilling to say any thing to Govr Claibourne without knowing your decisions on them. Mr Gallatin in a private letter has expressed sentiments which I have no doubt will induce him to halt in his course if a halt can be made.[30] If I add any thing officially it must be in very general terms.

I inclose herewith besides the letters from N. Orleans a letter from Mr Livingston, one from Mr. Pinkney, one from Mr Monroe and one from a candidate for office at Baltimore, to which are added several private letters from Monroe, Mazzei, and Claibourne.

The letter from Pinkney with the Communication to him from Cevallos shews that he was kept without notice of the relinquishment by H. C. M. [His Catholic Majesty] of his opposition to the transfer of Louisiana, from the 31.st of   to the 10.th of Feby The letter from Mazzei throws light on the ready

---

30. On June 14, 1804, Claiborne told Gallatin that the Louisiana Bank "will fail without any interference of the constituted Authorities" since the requisite capital would not be subscribed in time; see Claiborne, II, pp. 204–5.

and cordial interposition of the Emperor of Russia in behalf the Frigate and Crew at Tripoli.

The Marquis d'Yrujo left Washington two or three days ago, without calling on me either at the office or at my House, and even with an apology thro' the Marchioness to Mrs M. for not taking leave of her, from which he was precluded by what had passed between him and me. He and the Marchioness together called at the Houses of my Colleagues. From hints dropt, it would seem that he expects to be sent to London, where an opening may be made by the removal of the Spanish Ambassador now there to Paris where an opening is made for him by the death of Azzara.[31]

You will learn from Mr Lincoln that Russel has returned the Commission for Tunis. The business allotted to him at Naples, must, in consequence, I suppose be committed to Dugan with a Consular Commission. With affectionate and respectful attachment Y.^{rs}

JAMES MADISON

Jefferson to Madison

Monticello Apr. 27, 1804

DEAR SIR

Your's of the 19th is recieved and the papers accompanying it are returned. I am sorry that Russell declines the Consulship of Tunis, for, as declining it, we must consider the acquiescence under our wishes on the grounds and for the short time he has expressed. Whom shall we send? It will be a pity to lose the opportunity of his passage in the frigates; and yet I fear we shall. With respect to the unwarrantable commitment of us, by our agents, at Paris and St Petersburg, on the loss of the Philadelphia it is the most serious one which has happened to the present administration. This sordid disposition to throw upon the charity of others, our losses, [when] losses of the same kind are daily happening to them, without their having ever sent a brief to us for relief, is a national stain, which unfortunately the nature of the case does not leave us free to wipe off by a disavowal: because on the part of the First Consul, the Emperor, the Grand Seigneur, the humble petitions of our functionaries are granted, the relief has probably been yielded, and carried into execution. If our prisoners are given up on the firman of the Grand Seigneur we cannot replace them in captivity. On the contrary every moral principle calls for expressions from us to those powers of our grateful acknolegements. To reject their boon after it has been yielded at the request of our own agents, would make them our enemies. Their promptitude to serve us shews they are disposed to culti-

---

31. For the break between Yrujo and JM over American claims that West Florida was included in the Louisiana Purchase, see Brant, IV, pp. 188–212.

vate particular friendship with us, and we ought not to lose the occasion of meeting it. But how to combine the sentiments of gratitude, of dignity and friendly disposition which the occasion I presume requires should be expressed to the Russian minister of foreign relations, is the great difficulty to be encountered; and I am glad it falls into so good hands, as yours. Another difficulty more embarrassing is presented. In consequence of this interposition, suppose, on the arrival of our squadron, our prisoners shall have been liberated. What is the Commodore to do? To go to beating their town about their ears immediately after their having done us voluntary justice, would be an outrage which would revolt the world against us, and especially the sovereigns at whose request it was done. They would be in honour bound to take the interests of Tripoli under their care, to demand indemnification from us, and perhaps that we should pay a ransom for the prisoners liberated. Our expedition then is disarmed, our expences sunk, and the opportunity of vindicating our honor gone. We were free to beg or to fight. We chose the latter and prepared for it. Unauthorized agents have taken the business out of our hands, have chosen to beg, and executed what they chose. Thus two inconsistent plans are going on at the same time, and will run foul of one another in a region so distant, that we cannot decide for ourselves which shall proceed. We must therefore enable the Commodore to decide, and furnish him with instructions adapted hypothetically to the different conditions in which he may find things on his arrival. My general idea is that whichever plan of action is found to be ahead of the other, should be carried into execution. If the prisoners have neither been delivered, nor agreed to be delivered, the measures of war may be pursued without just offence to the mediating powers. If they have been delivered, or are delivered to the Commodore on a demand made, we ought then to make as liberal a peace as we would have made after an unfortuante campaign, the ultimatum of which we had before settled. Should we, in negociating that peace use the mediation of the three powers? These my thoughts on the subject, are thoughts only, and not decisions. If the squadron does not sail before my return, we will then consider and decide. If it shall be ready before my return, I have written fully to Mr̄ Smith on the subject, and desired him to ask a consultation with the other gentlemen, and to frame his instructions accordingly, without waiting for a recurrence to me. My great hope is that Tripoli will not have been as prompt as the noble-minded Alexander.[32] There will be some difficulty in giving rapping of the knuckles to Mr̄ Harris, which shall be unseen by the emperor, do justice to the motives of Harris, yet make him sensible of his presumption in committing us, and the sordid taint with which he has affected the character of his country. Accept my affectionate salutations and assurances of constant attachment and respect.

TH: JEFFERSON.

32. The crew of the *Philadelphia* was not released until Lear negotiated a peace treaty with Tripoli in June 1805; see McKee, p. 334.

Jefferson to Madison

[Washington] May 29, 1804

Tomson G. Skinner of Massachusetts to be Commissioner of loans for Massachusetts
William Few of New York to be Commissioner of loans for New York
Daniel Humphreys of New Hampshire to be Atty for the US. in the district of New Hampshire
Thomas Rutter of Maryland to be Marshal for the district of Maryland.
Joshua Prentis of Massachusetts to be Surveyor of the [port] of Marblehead and Inspector of the revenue for the port of Marblehead.
William G. Garland of Louisiana to be Naval officer for the port of New Orleans
Robert Carter Nicholas of Kentucky to be Surveyor of the port of New Orleans and Inspector of the revenue for the same.
Commissions to be made out accordingly.

Madison to Jefferson

[Washington] June 14, 1804

Extract from Mr. King's explanatory remarks on the project of John Chisholm, Blount, and others, to invade the Floridas from the territory of the U. S. £50 paid Chisholm by Major Lenox for Mr. King for the disclosure of the plan.

———

£50 paid to John Chisholm
Extract from Mr. King's explanatory remarks
"It will be recollected that Chisholm was confederated with Blount and others in a project to invade the Floridas from the Territories of the United States—that he went to England with letters from the B. Minister Mr. Liston, introducing him and his project to the English Ministry. Mr. King obtained from Chisholm a full disclosure of his plan, which with the names of his Associates was reported to the Secretary of State in his Despatch No. 57 Dated Dec. 10. 1797—To this Despatch Mr. King refers for the motives which influenced him in authorizing the payment of £50 Sterling to Chisholm"

The motives appear to have been a desire to obtain the information and Chisholm's request to be supplied with the money to enable him to pay his debts and the expense of his return. A receipt exists for the money, expressing it as a loan. Major Lenox paid the money for Mr. King[33]

---

33. Major David Lenox served as an aide to Rufus King, American minister to Great Britain, after being appointed special agent for negotiating the release of 1,042 impressed American seamen; see

Jefferson to Madison

[Washington] June 15, 1804

TH. J. TO MR MADISON

Can Mr King's report in his dispatch No. 57. Dec. 10, 97. be seen? The question is whether it was worth £50. sterl. Every person who undertakes to expend money for secret service, must take on themselves the risk of being approved or not by the government, on view of the nature of the service, which can only be judged by a knolege of what it was. This kind of expenditure is susceptible of such abuse, that a strict eye should be kept on it.

A commission to be issued to Peter P. Schuyler as Collector at Fort Stoddert

Jefferson to Madison

[Washington] June 24, 1804

TH: J. TO J. M.

The inclosed case respecting the construction of a treaty merits good consideration. Can broad words in a treaty be controuled by narrower in a law? And is it certain the law here intended to controul? Reason and probability is against it.

Jefferson to Madison

[Washington] July 5, 1804

We did not collect the sense of our brethren the other day by regular questions, but as far as I could understand from what was said, it appeared to be 1. That an acknolegment of our right to the Perdido, is a sine qua non, and no price to be given for it. 2. No absolute and perpetual relinquishment of right is to made of the country East of the Rio Bravo del Norte even in exchange for Florida. [I am not quite sure that this was the opinion of all.] It would be better to lengthen the term of years to any *definite* degree than to cede in perpetuity. 3. That a country may be laid off within which no further settlement shall be made by either party for a given time, say twenty years. This country to be from the North river Eastwardly towards the Rio Colorado, or even to, but not beyond the Mexican or Sabine river. To whatever river it be

---

Robert Ernst, *Rufus King, American Federalist* (Chapel Hill, 1968), pp. 237–38. For Chisholm's role in the Blount conspiracy, see William Masterson, *William Blount* (Baton Rouge, 1954), pp. 302–23, especially p. 318 on his meeting with King.

extended, it might from it's source run N. W. as the most eligible direction; but a due north line would produce no restraint that we should feel in 20 years. This relinquishment and a millions of Dollars, to be the price of all the Floridas East of the Perdido, or to be apportioned to whatever part they will cede.

But on entering into conferences both parties should agree that, during their continuance, neither should strengthen their situation between the Iberville, Missipi and Perdido, nor interrupt the navigation of the rivers therein. If they will not give such an order instantly, they should be told that we have for peace sake only, forborne till they could have time to give such an order, but that as soon as we receive notice of their refusal to give the order we shall enter into the exercise of our right of navigating the Mobile and protect it, and increase our force there pari passu with them.

Jefferson to Madison

[Washington] July 5, 1804

TH:J. TO J. M.

The case of St. Julien ought certainly to be put on trial. The local judge must decide 1. whether crimes committed against the nation of Louisiana under it's former organisation, can be punished under it's present one? and 2. whether St. Julien is guilty? The 1st question will be forced on them by other cases, and may therefore as well be met at once. But we should leave the party at liberty but under security, as we found him.[34]

I think it was an error in our officer to shut the doors of the church, and in the Governor to refer it to the Roman catholic head. The priests must settle their differences in their own way, provided they commit no breach of the peace. If they break the peace they should be arrested. On our principles all church-discipline is voluntary; and never to be enforced by the public authority; but on the contrary to be punished when it extends to acts of force. The Govr. should restore the keys of the church to the priest who was in possession.[35]

When a belligerent privateer brings one of our own vessels within our jurisdiction, it is primâ facie a trespass, and the territorial judge should arrest the trespasser and take possession of the vessel until he has enquired into the regularity of the transaction. The original act of taking could not be punished

34. Under the Spanish government of Louisiana, Lewis St. Julien was in jail awaiting trial for the murder of his wife when the territory was transferred to France. Shortly after taking possession, Pierre-Clément de Laussat, the French prefect, released St. Julien but bound him to a security bond. The former Spanish governor protested to Governor Claiborne, who sent the letter to JM.

35. Laussat had replaced one priest with another, and the head of the Catholic church in Louisiana had declared the action null and reinstated the first priest. When the rival priests and their supporters appeared for Sunday services, the American commandant closed the church; see Claiborne, II, pp. 170–71.

by him, unless it was piratical; but the continuance of the detention within our territory is cognisable and punishable by the laws of the country.[36]

Claiborne's letter to Folch is perfectly proper.[37]

I think he should be liberally treated as to his expences as a commissioner which no previous definition could fix.[38]

On this head, considering how deficient the diplomatic salaries are become, should we not extend all reasonable indulgences to them as to expences not merely personal? Would it not be as well, on the occasion of Mr King's accounts, to revise the regulation of 1790. and extend allowance to other cases? Affectionate salutations.

Jefferson to Madison

Washington July 6, 1804

In conversation with Mr. Gallatin yesterday as to what might be deemed the result of our Tuesday's conferences, he seemed to have understood the former opinion as not changed, to wit that for the Floridas East of the Perdido might be given not only the 2. millions of dollars and a margin to remain unsettled, but an absolute relinquishment from the North river to the Bay of St. Bernard and Colorado river. This however I think should be the last part of the price yielded, and only for an entire cession of the Floridas, not for a part only.[39]

Jefferson to Madison

[Washington] July 14, 1804

The inclosed reclamations of Girod and Chote against the claims of Bapstropp to a monopoly of the Indian commerce supposed to be under the protection of the 3d article of the Louisiana Convention, as well as some other claims to abusive grants, will probably force us to meet that question.[40] The

36. For the controversy in New Orleans involving a French privateer and two prizes, one American and one English, see *ibid.*, pp. 165–71, 284–86, 290–92, 300–1.

37. Governor Folch of Pensacola had protested American claims to West Florida, but Claiborne denied the charge of usurpation; see *ibid.*, pp. 182–86.

38. For Claiborne's claim for expenses as Louisiana commissioner, see his letter to JM, May 30, 1804, *ibid.*, pp. 179–80.

39. See Isaac Joslin Cox, *The West Florida Controversy, 1798–1813* (Baltimore, 1918), pp. 100–1.

40. Claiborne refused to grant a monopoly of the Indian trade to anyone, instead opening the trade "to several respectable Citizens"; see William Claiborne to TJ, June 24, 1804, in Claiborne, II, 220–21.

article has been worded with remarkable caution on the part of our negociators. It is that the inhabitants shall be admitted as soon as possible, according to the principles of our Constn., to the enjoyment of all the rights of citizens, and, *in the mean time, en attendant,* shall be maintained in their liberty, property and religion. That is that they shall continue under the protection of the treaty, until the principles of our constitution can be extended to them, when the protection of the treaty is to cease, and that of our own principles to take it's place. But as this could not be done at once, it has been provided to be as soon as our rules will admit. Accordingly Congress has begun by extending about 20. particular laws by their titles, to Louisiana. Among these is the act concerning intercourse with the Indians, which establishes a system of commerce with them admitting no monopoly. That class of rights therefore are now taken from under the treaty and placed under the principles of our laws. I imagine it will be necessary to express an opinion to Gov.' Claiborne on this subject, after you shall have made up one. Affect.te salutations.

Jefferson to Madison

Washington July 16, 1804

OFFICE OF DISCOUNT AND DEPOSIT

Pay to James Madison, Washington, or bearer, seven hundred and fifty dollars, /100

TH. JEFFERSON

Jefferson to Madison

[Monticello] July 27, 1804

TH. J. TO J. M.

I inclose you Story's oration that you may be enabled to take his measure. Be so good as to return it. I retain the letter of E. Livingston urging the validity of Baron Bastrop's monopoly of the Indian commerce for 10. years, because I presume it may be proper to lay it before Congress. The post master at Washington writes me that during our recess the post will come 3. times a week, the 3^d being extra for this particular term, to wit

	extra	*permanent*	*permanent*	
Leave Washington	Sunday.	Tuesday.	Thursday	at 7. P.M.
arrive at Milton	Tuesday	Thursday	Saturday	6. P.M.
leave Milton	Wednesday	Friday	Sunday	4. A.M.
arrive at Washington	Thursday	Saturday	Monday	8. P.M.

Affectionate Salutations

Jefferson to Madison

Monticello Aug. 3, 1804

TH. J. TO J. M.

I inclose you the S. Carolina ratification of the amendment to the constitution, and presume it possible that in a week more you may recieve that of Tennisse, after which I suppose no time should be lost in publishing officially the final ratification.[41] Prevost accepts the office of judge of the Orleans district, and Dickerson that of Attorney but as J. T. M.[42] declines the place of A. G. US. can we find a fitter person than Dickerson for this last? Can you think of any body better? I write to Mr Gallatin also on this subject, as he made the application to Dickerson and it is necessary the decision should be made before we meet again. Will you be so good as to send a commission for Philip Greene as Collector of the district of Marietta, and another as Inspector of the revenue for the port of Marietta, in the room of Griffin Greene his father decd. Affectionate salutations.

Madison to Jefferson

[Orange] Aug. 4, 1804

DEAR SIR

I inclose such of the communications from the office of State and since my arrival at home, as are worth your perusal. The letters from Mr. Livingston with the documents attached to them, being in the press copies are scarcely legible in many passages, and in some not to be made out at all. His Secretary is not only lazy but disrespectful in not revising the copies and filling up the deficiencies.[43] His long letter of May contains toward the end something on the subject of W. Florida etc. to which you may wish to read, though you may be unwilling to wade to it thro' the tedious pages which precede on the debts and commissioners. His disputes with those seem to have reached their ne plus ultra. I do not like the final ground they have taken more than the general tone of his conduct.[44] Considered as a sort of Judiciary board, and holding their

---

41. For a discussion of the Twelfth Amendment, requiring members of the electoral college to designate one of their two votes for president and the other for vice president, see Malone, IV, pp. 393–95, 407, 433.

42. "J. T. M." was John Thomson Mason, a Maryland lawyer then serving as U.S. attorney for the District of Columbia; see *PJM* (SS ser.), I, p. 66, and Malone, IV, p. 455, V, p. 37.

43. Livingston's unofficial private secretary was his son-in-law, Robert L. Livingston; see Dangerfield, pp. 380–81.

44. Although the claims commissioners, in cases of disputed settlements, were supposed to transmit their views to Livingston, who would transmit his to the French treasury for final decision, they wrote to the minister that they considered themselves responsible "only to the Administration of the United States"; see *ibid.*, p. 383.

offices under the Treaty they may be theoretically right in making that and that alone the rule of their proceeding; but they do not manifest a spirit of accomodation required by the difficulties of their business, the ambiguity of the Treaty, and the extent of the U. States. In order to decide however precisely on their conduct it is necessary to examine critically the nature of their trust as defined in the Treaty. You will find that Mr. L. is again a volunteer in diplomatic projects. The answer from the Russian Charge involves an admonition which w^d be useful to him, if he had modesty eno' to understand it.[45] The letter from the St Domingo planter at Charleston must be answered I suppose by information that Cong^s alone can decide on his application. It produces a conflict between agricultural advantages and political considerations.

I left Washington on the Wednesday succeeding your departure. Unaccustomed fatigue with the bad management of my driver foundered my horses in getting to Dumfries. I was obliged in consequence, to leave my carriage there and proceed in a Hack brought with my baggage, to Capt. Winston's; and to send for my Carriage, the horses which met us there. Owing to these delays I did not finish my journey till Sunday evening.[46] Yrs. respectfully and affcty

JAMES MADISON

Jefferson to Madison

Monticello Aug. 7, 1804

DEAR SIR,

Yours of the 4th came to hand last night and I now return you the letters of Livingston, Bourne, Lee, Lynch, Villandry and Mr. King. Stewart's is retained for communication with the P. M. Genl. I send also for your perusal a letter of a Mr. Farquhar of Malta. Mr. Livingston's letters (two short ones excepted) being all press copies and very bad ones, I can make nothing distinct of them. When manuscript copies are received I shall be glad to read them. The conduct of the commissioners at Paris merits examination. But what Mr. Livingston means by delays on our part in the execution of the Convention is perfectly incomprehensible. I do not know that a single day was unnecessarily lost on our part. In order however to lessen the causes of appeal to the Convention, I sincerely wish that Congress at the next session may give to the Orleans territory a legislature to be chosen by the people, as this will be advancing them quite as fast as the rules of our government will admit; and the evils which may arise from the irregularities which such a legislature may run into, will not be so serious as leaving them the pretext of calling in a foreign Umpire between them and us. The answer to Mr. Villandry should certainly be what you mention, that the objects of his application are only within the

---

45. When Livingston proposed a Russo-American commercial treaty, the Russian chargé d'affaires refused to discuss a subject "absolutely foreign" to his mission; see Brant, IV, p. 227.

46. JM left Washington on July 25 and arrived home on Aug. 2.

competence of Congress, to whom they must apply by petition, if they chuse it. Perhaps it would be but kind and candid to add that as there has been no example of such measures taken by Congress as they ask, they should consider whether it would not be wise in them to act for themselves as they would do were no such measures expected. I expect daily to receive answers from the principal officers for the Orleans government. These received, I will proceed to make out the whole arrangement, and inclose it to you, asking your counsel on it without delay. It will not be practicable to submit it to the other members, but I have so often conversed with them on the subject as to possess their sentiments.[47] As we count on the favor of a family visit could you accommodate that in point of time so as that we might be together at making out the final list? Affectionate salutations and assurances of friendship.

TH. JEFFERSON

Madison to Jefferson

[Orange] Tuesday morning Aug. 7, 1804

DEAR SIR

I know not what to make of the inclosed letter. The purport of it clashes with my calculation founded in probability; and yet it is impossible to disregard altogether the reliance which Col. Monroe seems to place on what he writes. We shall be better able to judge on seeing the details and the authority for them which he promises.[48]

5 inches of rain have fallen since Sunday morning. Two of the showers, one of them yesterday at ^{t} 2 O'C. have been very injurious to the soil in our corn fields. The rain however had become essential to them. We are now promised good crops in all high situations. The crops of wheat in good land of a dry soil, and Southern exposure, will turn out at least half—and the quality pretty good. Yrs. always with respectful attachment

JAMES MADISON

Madison to Jefferson

[Orange] Aug. 13, 1804

DEAR SIR

I have now to acknowledge your two letters of the 3 and 7th instant. with their inclosures, and to forward the communications from the office of State rec^d since my last.

---

47. Claiborne acknowledged his appointment as governor of the Territory of Orleans on Oct. 3, 1804; see Claiborne, II, pp. 345–46.

48. For Monroe's letter about the rumored restoration of the Bourbon monarchy by the British in 1793 if France would assist Great Britain in recovering the United States, see Brant, IV, p. 207.

Before I left Washington a circular letter was prepared and the requisite provisional steps taken for giving effect to the proposed amendment as soon as the ratification of Tennessee should be notified. As that has come to me thro' this office I take for granted that no time was lost in issuing the documents lying ready for the event.

I shall attend to your request of the *Manuscripta* communications from Mr. Livingston as soon as they come to hand. I am at a loss to know by what authority he undertook to give a part of Skipwith's salary to an additional Secretary for a purpose not included in the business allotted to Skipwith. Not possessing here the arrangements transmitted him, I can not decide positively but I suspect that he has consulted in the measure his feelings rather than his instructions.[49] I fear he has listened also more to his curiosity than to prudence in the trip to England confirmed in Monroe's letter herewith inclosed, and so severely criticised in the English newspapers.[50]

I have signed the Blank Commission and Credance for Gen! Armstrong, sent from the office, in consequence of the suggestion rec^d there from him.[51] The lapse of time makes it improbable that they will reach N. York before he sails, and the want of official notice of the new State of the French gov^t and want of a precise knowledge of it, justifies if it does not require the form of the documents he has now with him.[52] If you think it not improper, however, the Blank forms may be forwarded with your signature to Mr. Wagner, who will either fill them up if he knows the precise States, or forward them to Gen'l. Armstrong to be filled up by him, as you may direct.

Being an entire stranger to Mr. Dickerson I can only judge of him thro' others particularly Mr. Gallatin whose opinion you possess more fully than I do. No fit person likely to accept occurs as preferable. Whether Judge Livingston of N. York would accept I know not.[53] His talents are unquestionable but local and other considerations are also to have their weight. I shall be happy to make our intended visit to Monticello coincide with the purpose you intimate, but the time of it depends on circumstances not altogether within our own regulation. With respectful attachment Y^{rs}

JAMES MADISON

---

49. For Livingston's argument with Fulwar Skipwith over diplomatic procedures and the reduction of Skipwith's salary by $1,000, see *ibid.*, pp. 219–20.

50. For Livingston's visit to England while he was minister to France, see Dangerfield, pp. 387–92.

51. General John Armstrong succeeded Livingston, his brother-in-law, as minister to France. See *ibid.*, pp. 392–93; Malone, V, p. 49; and Brant, IV, p. 260.

52. Napoleon had proclaimed himself emperor in Apr. 1804, and diplomats attached to his court were required to present new credentials; see Dangerfield, p. 392.

53. Mr. Dickerson was probably Mahlon Dickerson. Henry Brockholst Livingston was a justice on the New York Supreme Court; see *ibid.*, p. 399.

Madison to Jefferson

[Orange] Aug. 14, 1804

DEAR SIR

I submit to your perusal the inclosed letter as the most ready mode of explaining the wish of Bishop Madison with respect to Mr. Mansfield. If you can furnish us with any information proper for an answer, you will oblige me by so doing. It is not improbable that the Bishop may take Monticello in his way as he proceeds Westward. In this case you will be saved the trouble otherwise imposed. Y^{rs} always with respectful affect.

JAMES MADISON

Jefferson to Madison

Monticello Aug. 15, 1804

DEAR SIR,

Your letter dated the 7th should probably have been of the 14th, as I received it only by that day's post. I return you Monroe's letter, which is of an awful complexion; and I do not wonder the communication it contains made some impression on him. To a person placed in Europe, surrounded by the immense resources of the nations there, and the greater wickedness of their courts, even the limits which nature imposes on their enterprises are scarcely sensible. It is impossible that France and England should combine for any purpose; their mutual distrust and deadly hatred of each other admit no cooperation. It is impossible that England should be willing to see France repossess Louisiana, or get footing on our continent; and that France should willingly see the U S. re-annexed to the British dominions. That the Bourbons should be replaced on their throne, and agree to any terms of restitution, is possible: but that they and England joined could recover us to British dominion is impossible. If these things are not so, then human reason is of no aid in conjecturing the conduct of nations. Still however it is our unquestionable interest and duty to conduct ourselves with such sincere friendship and impartiality towards both nations as that each may see unequivocally, what is unquestionably true, that we may be very possibly driven into her scale by unjust conduct in the other.

I am so much impressed with the expediency of putting a termination to the right of France to patronize the rights of Louisiana, which will cease with their complete adoption as citizens of the U S. that I hope to see that take place on the meeting of Congress.

I enclosed you a paragraph from a newspaper respecting Saint Domingo, which gives me uneasiness. Still I conceive the British insults in our harbor as more threatening. We cannot be respected by France as a neutral nation, nor by the world ourselves as an independent one, if we do not take effectual measures to support at every risk, our authority in our own harbors.

I shall write to Mr. Wagner *directly* (that a post may not be lost by passing thro you) to send us blank commissions for Orleans and Louisiana, ready sealed, to be filled up, signed and forwarded by us. Affectionate salutations and constant esteem.

TH. JEFFERSON

Jefferson to Madison

Monticello Aug. 16, 1804

TH. JEFFERSON TO J. MADISON

I have this day written to Mr. Wagner to send me the commissions for the Orleans territory with blanks for names and dates. The following is the arrangement which I sketch for your consideration.

Governor	Claiborne	
Secretary	James Brown.	written to
Judges of Super court	Pinkney	
	Kirby	written to
	Prevost	accepts
District judge	Hall	written to
Attorney	Dickerson	

If Pinkney should refuse, or Dickerson be otherwise disposed of, Robert Williams

Marshall	Thos. Urqhart	a Creole native
	French	American
legislative Council	Delvahar	Morgan
	Cuisagues	D. Clarke
	Dubuys	Evan Jones
	Poydrasse—of Point Coupeé	Roman of Attacapias
	Bellachasse—of Acadian coast	Wykoff of Appoliola
	Favré or Bové	Dow. or Geo. Pollock

Judge of Washington District, of Mississippi Territory. Toulman
Gov. of Mississippi Territory. Hull, or Thos. Rodney (the latter is now a judge, and Commissioner)

Will you be so good as to meditate on this against [before] we receive the commissions, which I presume will reach me on this day sennight?[54] Affectionate salutations.

Madison to Jefferson

[Orange] Aug. 16, 1804

DEAR SIR

Inclosed is a letter of late date from Mr. Monroe and the originals of those heretofore sent from Mr. Livingston, in press copies. Mr. L. now admits that the debts will exceed 20,000,000 liv^{rs} How he calculates 2 millions of interest as the effect of the delay which is less in every view than a year, or how he can charge the delay on the U. S. when he admits that the French gov't forbears to take the steps depending on them, or how he makes out an obligation on the U.S. to enlarge the payments from the Treas^y in favor of those not embraced by the last Convention, more than of those abandoned by the preceding one, I am unable to divine.[55] The fraud practiced in the name of Preble makes a hard case. In a legal view the loss I suppose falls on the Bankers. It seems equitable at the same time, considering the circumstances and the dilemma in which they stood, that they should not suffer. Cong^s alone can decide in their favor, if the law be agst them, and equity be thought for them. The subject however lies with the Navy rather than the State Dep^t Y^{rs} with respectful attachment

JAMES MADISON

Jefferson to Madison

Monticello Aug. 18, 1804

DEAR SIR

Yours of the 13th 14th and 16th were received in the evening of the 16th I now return you the papers which accompanied them, to wit the letters of Armstrong, Merry, Monroe, Claiborne, Sevier, Rhea, Clinton, Jones, Vail, Wirth [?], Skipwith, the Paris Commissioners, Livingston, Gavino, Wickelhausen, Swan, and B^p Madison. A more disgusting correspondence between men of sense, than that of Livingston and the Commissioners, I have never

---

54. James A. Brown, Ephraim Kirby, Judge Prevost, Dominick Augustin Hall, Robert Williams, Thomas Urqhart, Julien de Lalande Poydras, J. D. Bellachasse, Simon Favre, Benjamin Morgan, Daniel Clark, Evan Jones, William Wikoff (Wykoff), Dr. Robert Dow, George Pollock, and Harry Toulmin can be traced through the index to Claiborne, VI.

55. See Dangerfield, p. 386, and Brant, IV, pp. 226-27.

read. The errors of opinion into which both have run, cannot be subjects of blame, and were of a nature to do no harm, (except the non-procedure of the Comm^rs till ratification), because the Convention had provided a corrective. But all of them deserved to be immediately superseded for having mingled their old-womanish quarrels with their official communications, and suffered them to influence their public duties. The quarrelsome disposition of Livingston is a trait in his character unknown before to me. He has quarreled with every public agent with whom he had any thing to do. Thus he quarreled with his collegue Monroe, his Secretary of legation Sumpter, our Consul at Paris, Skipwith, with the Commissioners, and his letters to the department of state have been rising in the arrogance of their style till that of May 3. is such as, had he not been coming away, would have justified our informing him that we should make no further use of his services.[56]

I have signed the blanks for the new titles of Bonaparte. The letter of Credence must of course be under a flying seal, and I think Armstrong should carry them open as he receives them, to Talleyrand, fill the blanks under his direction, and deliver them. It will be a proof of our respect to the right of every nation to adopt what form, or firm of government it pleases. Accept my affectionate salutations.

TH. JEFFERSON

Madison to Jefferson

[Orange] Aug. 18, 1804

DEAR SIR

I rec^d yesterday your two favors of the 15th and 16th. Among those now inclosed is a renewal of Pichon's Complaints which strengthens your observations in the close of yours of the last date. He is well founded in the view he takes of the abuse made by the British ships of their connection with the Harbour of N. Y. He exacts too much however in requiring our effective *"surveillance"* over the jurisdictional limit of the U. S. which in the extent from St Croix to St Mary w^d be impossible and if possible call for a force and expenses inconsistent with our whole system of policy. Such a surveillance even over the limit connected with all our numerous harbors would exceed our reasonable obligation and render our exclusion of Belligerent ships altogether the more eligible horns of the dilemma. Nor would even their course avoid all difficulty; for questions might still arise whether certain acts were committed within or within [without] the distance of a league from the shore, and without a force every where, the prohibition of our ports etc. might be insulted as is now that of the general law of Nations. These observations are not meant to

---

56. See Brant, IV, p. 227.

"THE EMPIRE FOR LIBERTY," 1803-1804

invalidate the policy of that degree of force which is contemplated for the defence of our ports and coasts. Such a provision as a reasonable effort to maintain our neutral character will be a satisfactory answer to such of the Belligerent nations as are not unreasonable in their complaints and expectations.[57]

Barney's letter with its enclosure from Paris forms another comment on the squabble between Mr. L. and the Commissioners. If Barney's claim has been rejected on the ground stated, it seems to be erroneous unless the claim arose from transactions in which he was quoad such, a foreigner tho' in general a citizen of the U. S. The Convention however having provided for its own exposition and execution the Executive can only act on it diplomatically, or thro the means of more information. This course has been taken in the case of both Barney and Swan. Documents showing that Barney had been paid, were obtained thro' Gen! Smith before I left Washington and forwarded to Paris with an intimation that it was an act of justice to fair claimants not to let in unfair ones for a share in the 20 Millions which were likely to be insufficient for the former.[58] Truly and respectfully yours

JAMES MADISON

Jefferson to Madison

Monticello Aug. 19, 1804

DEAR SIR

In a conversation with Mr Granger not long before we left Washington he mentioned that he was about to establish a post line from Natchez to New Orleans, and must place an office at Baton rouge. I told him that that should have good previous consideration in the present jealous state of the Spanish officers; that perhaps they might even stop our mail carrier. I heard no more of it till last night I received the inclosed letter from Mr Granger, informing me he should not proceed in it till further directions. I should suppose it best that he should forward the blank commissions to Gov! Claiborne, but that Claiborne should be immediately instructed to enter into explanations with the Marquis Casa Calvo for making this establishment for mutual convenience, with an express declaration, if desired, that it is by mutual consent, and is not to be construed as either strengthening or weakening the right of either nation to the country. If, on consideration, you approve of this and will either so write yourself to Mr Granger, or inform me that I may write, your letter to Claiborne will get sufficiently the start to have the matter arranged by the time

57. See *ibid.*, pp. 254-55.
58. *Ibid.*, pp. 227-28.

Granger's commissions reach New Orleans, and the delay of executing the law will thus be shortened.[59]

I inclose a letter from a Mr Damen whom I knew at Amsterdam. He was quite a republican, and I was under the impression of his being a very good man. Some personal feelings may perhaps enter into his letter. As he desires it to be secret, be so good as to return it, only retaining the papers it inclosed as they are not secret and are proper to be filed away in the office. Affectionate salutations with hopes of seeing you shortly,

TH. JEFFERSON

Madison to Jefferson

[Orange] Aug. 21, 1804

DEAR SIR

I have duly rec^d yours of the 18th with the papers to which it refers. It was neither sealed, nor enclosed in the larger packet.

The accounts from the Mediterranean, as you will find are on the whole favorable. The explanation of Lear, and the reinforcement under Baron,[60] will probably overcome the repugnance of the Bey of Tunis to transact business with the Consul General on account of his Consulship at Algiers. For I take it to be that circumstances and not any personal preferance for Davis that made the difficulty. I am glad to find nothing repeated as to the present of a frigate, or the exaction of a tribute similar to that stipulated to Algiers.

The exemplification of the ratifying Act of Tennessee had arrived at the Office of State. But unfortunately none has yet been forwarded by Georgia; unless it should be among your papers which is not probable. I have written to Govr Milledge reminding him of the omission; and lest he should not be at or near Savanna, have sent a duplicate to be forwarded from Washington, where his residence may probably be ascertained. respectfully and truly yours

JAMES MADISON

Jefferson to Madison

Monticello Aug. 23, 1804

DEAR SIR

Yours of the 18th and 21st are received, and I now return the papers of Davis, Cathalan, Mansfield, Fitzsimmons, Claiborne, Pichon, Rufini, Wig-

---

59. For postal arrangements to New Orleans, see *ibid.*, pp. 207–8.
60. Commodore Samuel Barron left the United States in July to succeed Preble as commander of the Mediterranean fleet cruising along the Barbary coast; see McKee, pp. 307–8.

ginton, Wilson, Tamson, Ridgeway, Irving, Barney, and Joy. The situation of the indemnification for the Tunisian property taken by Morris has escaped my present recollection. I take for granted we have been guilty of no unnecessary delay; as were we to go to war with the Bey tomorrow, I would previously do every act of justice due to him. I think the offence he presumes to take at our Commodore not going ashore should be the subject of information to him from Davis that after his injurious detention of Morris he must expect that mark of respect from no officer of the US. until he shall give proper assurance that he will be safe from restraint and injury.

Should we not give peremptory orders for the winding up the affairs of Spain at N. Orleans, and the departure of Casa-Calvo and Morales, or at least the latter?[61] They should be gone before the 1st. of October. Wigginton's observations as to the description of the person of the holder of a certificate of citizenship are just; and it merits reformation. A particular clerk might be charged with making out the description. The appeal made by Barney to the executive is improper, the Convention having established a different course.[62]

I never recieved the ratification of Georgia.

Some other matters in the inclosed papers will be properly subjects for conversation, and the moment I have every thing ready for the arrangements of the government of Orleans (which this day's or Saturday's posts will determine) you shall see me at your house: for when I proposed the accomodating your visit to this object I had forgotten that it was a part of Mrs Madison's plan that her visit and Mrs Pichon's should be made together. With this arrangement I did not intend nor now wish to interfere. I salute you both with affection and respect.

TH. JEFFERSON.

P. S. I desire Mr Wagner to send you a blank commission for a Commr of loans in S. C. ready sealed. Will you on reciept of it be so good as to sign and forward it to me? as I must send it on blank, and the case is urgent.

Madison to Jefferson

[Orange] Aug. 25, 1804

DEAR SIR

I recd yesterday afternoon your two favors of the 19th and 23. I will write to Claiborne and Granger on the subject of the post establt thro' the territory held by them and claimed by us. I previously however submit it to your determination whether it may not be best, based on the proposed negociation with

---

61. Claiborne was convinced that the Spanish officials who remained in New Orleans after its transfer to the United States encouraged "the Discontents which arise here." He agreed to order their speedy departure; see William Claiborne to JM, Oct. 5, 1804, in Claiborne, II, pp. 347–48.

62. For Barney's claims under the convention with France, see Brant, IV, pp. 227–28.

Casa Calvo which he may reject, to provide for a simple passage of the mail with a post office, which will probably meet with no difficulty.⁶³ This alternative seems to be the more necessary, considering the temper and threats of the Gov.ʳ at Pensacola. Mr. Granger feels an obligation to establish a post office in order to put the people of the contested district on the same footing with Citizens elsewhere. As the law gives no positive orders to that effect, his discretion may I think be fairly influenced by the peculiarity of the case. If no regard is to be had to the Spanish possession, every law in force in Louisiana ought to be extended into that district.

The instructions given to Lear provided for the case of the Tunisian property. The refusal of the Bey to have any thing to do with him may prolong the difficulty. But it will be better to wait for further information than to humour the Bey.

I shall certainly be very happy to see you at my house. But I am sensible that I ought on this as on all occasions to spare you the trouble of the ride whenever you may wish an interview and will accordingly hold myself ready to obey your instructions. We have heard nothing from Mr. and Mrs. Pichon since we left Washington. They have never withdrawn their promise of a visit, and therefore we may daily expect them. Other expectations of company will detain Mrs. M. at home for some little time. Yours with respect and attachment

JAMES MADISON

Madison to Jefferson

[Orange] Aug. 28, 1804

DEAR SIR

The inclosed communications from Pinkney threaten some unexpected difficulties at Madrid. In the conduct of the Spanish Gov.ᵗ we see pretty clearly the passions of Yrujo and the policy of reserving [?] matter for negociating restrictions of Louisiana. It may be presumed that the portent of things then will hasten the departure of Monroe from London. Pinkney had not rec.ᵈ the explanation of the Act of Congress.⁶⁴

Mr. Livingston's letter tho' of old date is new, as are some of the accompaniments.

Mr. Merry's answer to my several letters, co-incides with, tho' it can not be the offspring of the spirit of Pitts administration as indicated to Monroe. He considers a simple denial of the offenders as disproof of the most regular testimony, and maintains the right not only to impress from American vessels in the high seas, but from British vessels in our own harbours. And by making

---

63. TJ approved this suggestion; see *ibid.*, p. 208.

64. Spanish authorities learned of the Mobile Act before Pinckney did and demanded that it be altered before they would ratify the claims convention of 1802; see *ibid.*, pp. 188–89, 208–9.

the detention of the Enemy ships a reason for blockading our harbours and harassing our trade, leaves the continuance of the evil at the pleasure of the British Commanders.[65]

Altho' the remarks on the conduct of the French frigate at Baltimore seems to have been meant less as a formal complaint than as a controversial artifice, I think it will be proper to cause the facts to be enquired into. Should they even turn out as they are stated, no blame can result from the delay; no earlier notice of their having been given. The readiness of the belligerent Ministers and Consuls to do this, justified the presumption that nothing seriously amiss had taken place.

This specimen of Merry shows him to be a mere diplomatic pettifogger. Yrs. with respectful attachment

Jefferson to Madison

[Washington ca. Aug. 31, 1804]

Inclose to heads of departments for their information on which the legislative council of Orleans was composed and of the result.

To be returned

The Commissioners for the legislative council of Orleans were sent blank to Govr. Claiborne to be filled up as follows.

Americans
    Morgan.
    Clarke
    Watkins
    Jones. declines acceptance
    Romans of Atlacapis instead of him Kenner is appointed
    Wikoff of Appalousas
    George Pollock or Dr. Dow } one only of these was to be appointed: but I suspect both are.

Creoles
    Boré
    Poydrasse of Pt. Coupeé
    Bellechasse
    Dubuys
    Cantavelle. Acad vest
    Souvé
    Detrahan
    Derbigny

from these 5. Claiborne was to select 3. but he has excluded the 3. last on acct. of their absence. And to make up the number I suspect he has put in both Pollock and Dow, because he says in his letter that 'excepting Kenner, all the other Councillors are taken from my list'

---

65. For Merry's defense of the British navy's impressment tactics and JM's reaction, see *ibid.*, p. 255.

Jefferson to Madison

Monticello Sept. 6, 1804

TH. J. TO MR MADISON

Should we not write to the Governors of S. Carolina and Georgia to furnish us without delay with authentic statements of the illegalities said to have been committed in their harbours by one or more French privateers? As the proceedings of the British vessels at N. York must be laid before Congress to found measures of coercion, peaceable and of force, by giving in the facts relative to the French privateer, we may make our measures less pointed, and less offensive.[66]

I have been obliged to defer my visit to Bedford, and probably shall not go at all. We shall hope to see you next week. I salute you with affection.

Madison to Jefferson

Orange Sept. 8, 1804

DEAR SIR

I rec^d yesterday yours of the 6th with a return of the letters from Appleton and Savage. Under the same cover with this are sundry communications, some of them very interesting. They need not be returned until I can receive them at Monticello, which I expect will happen early in the coming week.

Should the inclosed letter to Mr. Pichon be such as you intirely approve, I beg the favor that it be put under cover to Mr. Wagner, to be forwarded by him, after taking an office copy. Should alterations or additions be thought proper, they can be made on my arrival at Monticello under your personal directions. I have thought it best to decline any expressions which might enter in the smallest degree into the character of the Revolution in the French Gov^t or even be personal to the Emperor; altho' something of the latter kind may very probably be looked for.[67] If any such civility, consistent with our principles and our neutrality should occur as eligible, we may find a place in the communications on the subject thro' our Minister at Paris, from whom we shall soon receive the original notification by Talleyrand.

Some of the French irregularities in S. Carolina and Georgia are I believe already in the office of State. The collectors are under standing instructions to transmit them. It may be proper to remind them of their duty to call on the Gov^{rs} also. I will take your orders, when I have the pleasure of seeing you.

Pichon signifies that the French frigates and the aversion of Mrs. P. to

---

66. In an attempt to capture Jerome Bonaparte, HMS *Cambrian* searched ships in New York harbor, a flagrant violation of American rights; see Perkins, p. 177, and Brant, IV, pp. 254–55.

67. Pichon, who had served as French chargé d'affaires, was planning to return to France as soon as the new minister, General Louis Marie Turreau, arrived; see *ibid.*, pp. 266–70.

approach yet the scene of her misfortune, render their visit more than improbable. He does not however absolutely relinquish it.[68] Yours with respectful attachment

JAMES MADISON

Madison to Jefferson

[Orange] Sept. 22, 1804

DEAR SIR

I inclose the letter alluded to in my last from Mr. Merry to Mr. Wagner; also a letter from Barney and one from L. Harris. I have authorized Mr. W. to forward any more information relating to Barney's claims to Mr. Skipwith, reminding him that no further interposition could be made, unless you should so decide. A patronage of individual claims, besides its interference with the functions of the Board of Commissioners, is the more delicate as a favorable decision in one case, might be rendered, by the limitation of the sum to be dispensed, injurious in others. As to the Citizenship of Barney, it is probably sound, and can therefore be shown by himself. How far it may have been suspended *quoad* certain purposes by his temporary relations or special transactions, is a question more proper for judicial than Executive inquiry, and therefore falls naturally within that of the Board.[69] When it appeared that the Board was leaning to an opinion that a foreign partnership in one business, disqualified a claimant on the score of another altogether distinct, the subject was with others committed to Mr. Livingston, for arrangement with the French Gov^t.[70] The letter from Harris is a further proof of the kindness of the Emperor Alexander.[71] I wish however that with this obliging temper, there may not be blended some little view of drawing the U. S. into the politics of Russia. Considering the jealousy of other powers of Russia, and the possibility that Russia may get into the war, any formal connection of the U. S. with the Ports, under the auspices too of Russia, is a step suggesting much caution. The letter written last to our Consul will I hope put an end to his enterprizing patriotism. I inclose Pinkney's last communications which you have already seen, that they may be at hand, if wanted during your talk with Yrujo.[72]

68. Mrs. Pichon, who had lost her only child, decided not to make the trip from Philadelphia to Virginia since it would take her through Washington, "the scene of her misfortune"; see *ibid.*, pp. 206-7.

69. Barney had been temporarily employed in the French navy; see *ibid.*, p. 227.

70. For Livingston's role in the claims process, see Dangerfield, pp. 380, 387, and Brant, IV, p. 213.

71. Levett Harris was U.S. consul general in St. Petersburg; see Knox, IV, p. 161.

72. Yrujo, who had broken off relations with JM, sought "a direct and personal interview" with TJ, which the president granted. Pinckney had threatened to break relations with Spain unless the government changed its attitude towards ratifying the claims convention of 1802, a move that TJ disavowed; see Brant, IV, pp. 209-10.

The diameter of the Boxes for my pipes is three inches and a half, the breadth of the ring 3 inches, admitting an entrance of 1 ½ inches into the end of the logs, where they make a good joint. I omitted to mention before I left you, that Dr. Winston on learning that you w^d want laborers promised to decide as soon as he reached Hanover whither he was bound, whether he could spare any and how many, and write to me immediately on the subject. Y^{rs} always with respectful attachment

JAMES MADISON

Jefferson to Madison

Monticello Sept. 25, 1804

I intended to have been with you tomorrow evening, but it is rendered now improbable, partly by the weather, but more by the arrival of M. and Mad^e. Yrujo last night. They are now here and go back from hence to Washington. If they leave us tomorrow I shall be with you the next day. He has opened his budget which we have smoothed off. It must be the subject of verbal communication to you. Affectionate salutations.

Madison to Jefferson

[Orange] Oct. 2, 1804

DEAR SIR

I return to the Dept. of State the inclosed papers (excepting the private letter from Mr. L.) thro' your hands that you may peruse such of them as may deserve that attention. According to my recollection, the explanation of the Act of Cong^s so offensive to Spain, was communicated to Yrujo. As it is possible that I may be mistaken, it may be worth while to inquire into the fact; and if the communication should have been transmitted to Pinkney only, and consequently not known to the Spanish Gov^t or even to its Minister here, a communication of this document to the latter may perhaps be satisfactory on that point and render any thing more on it unnecessary. Mr. Wagner can give any information you may please to call for. Jackson I find has lost no time in giving publicity to the affair between him and Yrujo.[73] What course the latter will take remains to be seen. Should circumstances of any kind be thought to urge a close of the business with him or any other arrangement with respect to

---

73. Major William Jackson, a Federalist editor, sent TJ an affidavit and later published it, stating that Yrujo had tried to bribe him to insert pro-Spanish propaganda in his paper; see *ibid*.

it, why might not one of the other Secretaries, or even Mr. Wagner, be made a channel of your sentiments and declarations. I find it will be impossible for me to be in Washington before Saturday night, and that only with all the incidents to a journey favorable. Should the door be shut agst further communication with Yrujo, and Pinkney's situation at Madrid not be contradicted, a direct communication with Cevallos appears to be the next resource.[74] With respectful attachment Y.^{rs}

JAMES MADISON

Jefferson to Madison

[Washington] Oct. 4, 1804

A pardon to be issued to George McFarland according to the papers inclosed. Commissions to David Broadie of Virginia to be Collector of Hampton
    vice Mount Edward Chisman dec^d
Edmund Key of Maryland to be Surveyor of the port of Llewellensburg in the district of Nanjemoy and Inspector of the revenue for the same vice Richard Jordan dec^d
Edward Hall of Maryland to be Comm^r of loans for Maryland v. B. Harwood resigned

TH. JEFFERSON

Jefferson to Madison

[Washington] Oct. 5, 1804

The following Commissions also to be issued

Elijah Backus of Ohio. Reciever of public monies at Kaskaskiss[75]
Frederick Bates of Indiana. Reciever at Detroit
Harry Toulman of Kentucky Reciever at Fort Stoddart
Thomas Fitzpatrick of S. Carolina to be Register at Natches v. Turner the descriptions of the offices to be made agreeable to the law

TH. JEFFERSON

---

74. Don Pedro de Cevallos was Spain's foreign secretary. After Yrujo published newspaper appeals against the president and secrtary of state, Monroe was instructed to ask Cevallos to recall him; see *ibid.*, pp. 211–12.

75. For Elijah Backus, see Alfred Byron Sears, *Thomas Worthington: Father of Ohio Statehood* (Columbus, 1958), p. 112.

Jefferson to Madison

[Washington] Oct. 12, 1804

Nathaniel Ewing of Pensylvania to be Reciever of public monies at Vincennes

Th. J.

Madison to Jefferson

[Washington] Oct. 15, 1804

Perhaps the language may be a little more effectually guarded agst the idea of making a sort of stipulation the title to the Appointment.[76] All that can be effected is to strengthen his good disposition, by his knowing that they were calculated on as a proof of his general merit, and by his committing himself for a perseverence in these dispositions, by conversations and declarations on the subject with friends whom he esteems

Madison to Jefferson

[Washington] Oct. 23, 1804

The first enacting clause will be ineffectual because vessels will clear for one place, when really bound to another.[77] A principle therefore will be conceded of which advantage may hereafter be taken, without any security that will be satisfactory to complaining nations. The only adequate [?] provision would be to take bond for delivery of the Cargo elsewhere than at the forbidden ports. But this ought to be perhaps by Treaty, and the price of some equivalent stipulation. It may be added that our Collectors would often be at a

---

76. TJ endorsed this letter as referring to "my lre of Oct. 15 to Gelston," which discussed the death of Hore Browse Trist, whom he had "known from an infant," when the boy's mother, Eliza House Trist, had helped in the boardinghouse favored by him and JM. TJ had appointed Trist to office in Louisiana, and he wrote to David Gelston about the appointment of a successor; see Drew R. McCoy, *The Last of the Fathers: James Madison and the Republican Legacy* (New York, 1989), p. 208, and TJ to David Gelston, Oct. 15, 1804, in Presidential Papers Microfilm: Thomas Jefferson Papers, reel 31.

77. After Haiti declared its independence from France on Jan. 1, 1804, armed merchantmen from the United States opened trade with the area controlled by Dessalines, Toussaint's successor. When France protested against the trade, TJ urged Congress to restrain it; see his annual message to Congress, Nov. 8, 1804, in Richardson, I. p. 370, and Brant, IV, pp. 270–75.

loss to know how far at particular times and ports, the local regulations prohibit or permit the entry of our vessels, or particular articles in their Cargoes. These considerations seem to have weight, agst extending the Act beyond the case of armed vessels.

"That no vessel armed or with the means of being armed at sea, in which or the cargo whereof, a Citizen or domiciliated alien shall be interested or embarked, shall receive at any Custom House of the U.S. any clearance, or be suffered to leave the port where she is found so armed or prepared; but on security given to the U. S. in a sum equal to one third of the value on her Cargo, and double the value of the vessels, that no assault or Trespass, during the voyage and return shall be committed by such vessel or persons on board her, against any vessels, or territory of a nation in amity with U. S., nor agst any of the Citizens or subjects of such nation, and that no resistance shall be made to any lawful search, nor any other unlawful use be made of the arms on board such vessel.["]

Madison to Jefferson

[Washington ca. Oct. 25, 1804]

Notes for Annual Message of November 8, 1804

(a) and which have been increased by peculiar circumstances in the W. Indn. seas. yet in the more distant channels at least of our trade.[78]

b. The act *authorizes* etc. provisionally at least—a port etc. without the limits of the U. S. The words in [ ] may be left out.[79]

c. [on the part of Spain][80]

d. [proper to suspend] will according better with the case—as the 6th art. is also made a ground of suspension[81]

e. may reasonably be expected to replace the Spanish Govt. in the disposition which originally concurred in the Convention[82]

---

78. TJ incorporated JM's suggestion in the first paragraph of his message, noting that the harassment of neutral commerce had been less in distant parts "than on former occasions" during the European war but that "peculiar causes" had made infringements "in the American seas" a cause for serious attention; see Richardson, I, p. 369.

79. TJ accepted JM's suggestion and left out any specific reference to the provisions of the Mobile Act, which, he said, "was misunderstood on the part of Spain"; see *ibid.*, p. 370.

80. TJ omitted these words in his discussion of that government's withdrawal of "the objections which had been urged . . . against the validity of our title to the country of Louisiana"; see *ibid.*

81. TJ used JM's words, noting that Spain "had . . . thought proper to suspend the ratification of the convention of 1802"; see *ibid.*

82. TJ incorporated JM's suggestion about American efforts to reassure Spain and "replace them in the dispositions and views of the whole subject which originally dictated the convention"; see *ibid.*

f. [manifestations]—[83]
g. [on proper]—quer if the last circumstance may not be omitted in so general a paragraph—and left either to be included in some particular message—or taken up on informal suggestion[84]
h. quer here as above[85]
i. [effectual] is it not too strong[86]

and to which peculiar causes have contributed

Jefferson to Madison

[Washington ca. Nov. 4, 1804]

TH: J. TO J. M.

With La Fayette's letter to me I send you my letters to him and to Claiborne, and Armstrong's letter, that you may be possessed of every thing which has past respecting his lands.[87]

private

Jefferson to Madison

[Washington] Nov. 18, 1804

TH: J. TO J.M.

I send you 2. sheets of my commonplace, because on the 5. last pages of them are my abridgments of certain admiralty cases interesting to us, with some observations; it will be well that we mutually understand how far we go together, and what consequently we may propose with joint satisfaction. I think the English practice of not requiring a prize to be hazarded further than to the nearest neutral port is so much for the interest of all weak nations that we ought to strengthen it by our example, and prevent that change of practice which Sr. W. Scott seems to be aiming at; evidently swayed by considerations of the interest of his nation.

83. TJ retained this word, noting that the United States continued "to receive friendly manifestations" from "the Governments of the belligerent powers"; see *ibid.*

84. TJ retained the bracketed words, predicting that the naval force in the Mediterranean would "reduce the barbarians of Tripoli to the desire of peace on proper terms"; see *ibid.*, pp. 370–71.

85. TJ retained his warning that demands made by the bey of Tunis might lead to war; see *ibid.*, p. 371.

86. TJ retained the bracketed word in his discussion of Indian affairs, recommending "a moderate enlargement of the capital employed in commerce" instead of "an augmentation of military force" as "a more effectual . . . instrument for preserving peace and good neighborhood with them"; see *ibid.*, p. 372.

87. See Kathryn T. Abbey, "The Land Ventures of General Lafayette in the Territory of Orleans and State of Louisiana," *Louisiana Historical Quarterly* 16 (1933): 359–73.

Jefferson to Madison

[Washington 1804?]

Notes on right of sheriff to use posse comitatus

I have made some small verbal changes on the following grounds
1. The law recognises the right of the sheriff to use his posse comitatus without consulting any body. It is only *on his opinion* that his posse is insufficient, that the act comes into his aid by authorising him to apply to a judge or justice for an order to an officer for a military force. The law allows him to make the application without consulting us, but then it submits him to *our direction* in the use of it: and we, taking advantage of that, say he shall not use it at all unless he has previously been advised by a governor or Mayor so to do. This is an additional precaution for preserving peace which the law permits us to prescribe when once the Govr. or Mayor has advised, the marshall is then to proceed with his armed force as the law directs, that is to say by demanding a surrender of the offender[s] etc.

Jefferson to Madison

[Washington 1804]

			$\underline{D}$
La Commerce maritime	2 v.	8 vo.	2
Correspondence de Louis XVI	2 v.	8 vo.	2.375
Rivalité de la France et de l'Angleterre		8 vo.	3.875
Atlas de Mentille fol.			54.
Statistique de l France	7 v.	8 vo. et cartes	20.
Tableu de l'Espagne de			
Burgorng	3 v.	8 vo.	7.
de l'Russia	2 v.	8 vo.	4.625
Tabl. des traités par Koch	2 v.	8 vo.	3.50
Recueil des traités par Martens	7 v.	8 vo.	15.75
			114.50